The American Presidents,
Washington to Tyler

The American Presidents, Washington to Tyler

What They Did, What They Said,
What Was Said About Them,
with Full Source Notes

ROBERT A. NOWLAN

McFarland & Company, Inc., Publishers
Jefferson, North Carolina, and London

ALSO OF INTEREST AND FROM McFARLAND:
Robert A. Nowlan, often joined by coauthor Gwendolyn W. Nowlan, has written numerous works for McFarland; his most recent is *Born This Day: A Book of Birthdays and Quotations of Prominent People Through the Centuries* (2007; paperback 2011).

LIBRARY OF CONGRESS CATALOGUING-IN-PUBLICATION DATA

Nowlan, Robert A.
The American presidents, Washington to Tyler : what they did, what they said, what was said about them, with full source notes / Robert A. Nowlan.
p.   cm.
Includes bibliographical references and index.

ISBN 978-0-7864-6336-7
softcover : acid free paper ♾

1. Presidents— United States— Biography.
2. United States— Politics and government —1789–1815.
3. United States— Politics and government —1815–1861.
I. Title.
E176.1.N79 2012   973.09'9—dc23   [B]   2011039072

BRITISH LIBRARY CATALOGUING DATA ARE AVAILABLE

On the cover: *top left to bottom right* George Washington, 1796 (Gilbert Stuart); John Adams, 1792 (John Trumbull); Thomas Jefferson, 1800 (Rembrandt Peale); James Madison, 1816 (John Vanderlyn); James Monroe, 1819 (Samuel Finley Breese Morse); John Quincy Adams, 1858 (George P. A. Healy); Andrew Jackson; Martin Van Buren, 1858 (George P. A. Healy); William Henry Harrison, 1835 (James Reid Lambdin); John Tyler, 1859 (George P. A. Healy)

Manufactured in the United States of America

McFarland & Company, Inc., Publishers
Box 611, Jefferson, North Carolina 28640
www.mcfarlandpub.com

To Wendy,
my wife and best friend
and in memory of
our dear friend Dan Ort

Table of Contents

Acknowledgments   ix

Preface   1

Introduction: The American Presidency   9

One. George Washington: The Man Who Would Not Be King   23

Two. John Adams: The Revolution Was Made in the Minds of the People   73

Three. Thomas Jefferson: The Polymath President   109

Four. James Madison: That Dear Little Jemmy   155

Five. James Monroe: The Last of the Cocked Hats   187

Six. John Quincy Adams: A Man of Principles, Not Parties   219

Seven. Andrew Jackson: A Good Friend and a Bad Enemy   254

Eight. Martin Van Buren: The Foxy First Full-Time Politician   306

Nine. William Henry Harrison: Sung into the Presidency   337

Ten. John Tyler: President or Acting President?   362

Chapter Notes   389

References and Further Readings   437

Index   453

Acknowledgments

An ounce of dialogue is worth a pound of monologue.

— Anonymous

Throughout a long life and career, I have enjoyed many conversations with a great number of family friends, teachers, colleagues, students and even strangers on the topics of American history, American government, American politics and American presidents. These discussions not only furthered my understanding, they also helped me formulate my beliefs and convictions regarding these matters. I would like to thank and acknowledge as many of these individuals as possible who in some way, large or small, helped prepare me to produce this work. They include:

Esther Anderson, Martin Anisman, Isabel Anna, Jessie Anna, Harry Ausmus, Helen Bass, Birch Bayh, Helen Becker, Paul Best, Carol Birch, Anthony Black, Richard Blumenthal, Tony Bonadies, John Brademus, Kingman Brewster, Jr., Derek and Jenny Briggs, Thomas Buckley, William Buckley, Jr., Jonathan Bush, John Campeau, Donna Carvey, Rita Cassidy, John Cavanaugh, Roland Chamblee, Robert Cipriano, Miriam P. Cooney, Jim Countryman, Bill Curry, John C. Daniels, Hugh Davis, Alan Day, Rosa DeLauro, John N. Dempsey, Lawrence Denardis, John DeStefano, Jr., Biagio DiLieto, Everett Dirksen, Christopher Dodd, Bob Dole, William Dyson, Kathy Faught, Kenneth Florey, Helen Floyd, Stacia Fonseca, Gerald Ford, Howard Fussiner, A, and Rachel Garcia, Ken Gatzke, Bart Giamatti, Martin Glassner, Robin Glassman, Barbara Golden, Al and Myrna Gordon, Howard Gralla, Kerry Grant, Ella Grasso, Louis Guillou, Bodh and Santosh Gulati, Ron Heckler, Thomas Helegeson, Cheryl Henderson, Theodore Hesburgh, Lew House, David Hughes, John Iatrides, Frank Jeglic, Milko Jeglic, Manson Jennings, Nancy Johnson, Edmund Joyce, Grace Kelly, Barbara B. Kennelly, Jonathan Key, Leo Kucyznski, Maggie Kuhn, Louis Kuslan

Rod Lane, Annabel Lee, Bill Lee, Richard C. Lee, Ira Leonard, Megan Levine, Joseph Lieberman, Frank Logue, C.E. Lowe, E.F. Lowe, Mother Mary Madeleva, Richard Maiocco, Ron Malooley, Ken and Diane Maltese, Lew and Kitty Matzkin, Eugene McCarthy, Ann McCormick, George McGovern, Christian Melz, Evan Middlebrooks, Barb and Dick Moggio, E.C. Nichols, Cheryl Norton, Jay and Heather O'Connor, Sandra Day O'Connor, William O'Neill, Rocco Orlando, Sharon Ort, Ann Osler, Michael Parent, Claude Pepper, Charles Percy, Michael Perlin, Phil Poffenberger, Tom Porter, Eleanor Potter, Diane Prunier, Kul Rai, Mike Raffone, Donald Raymond, Mary Lou Redding, Jodi Rell, Mike Riordan, Barry Rothman, Jane Ruck, Richard Russo, Michael Ryan, Pete Sakalowsky, Joyce Saltzman, Lisa Sandora, Theodore Sands, Martha Schaff, Bruno Schlesinger, Dorothy Schrader, Edgar Schoonmaker, Linda Schultz, Bruce Shattuck, Chris Shays, Michael Shea, Pete Shields, Phil Smith, Adlai E. Stevenson, Irving Stolberg, Nilza Cruz Texeira, Bob Washburn, Tom

Weakley, Lowell Weicker, Nancy Wyman, Leon Yacher, and so many others, both living and dead.

Then too, there are relatives, including my parents, Robert and Marian Nowlan, my siblings, Martha "Marty" Johnson, Mary Nowlan, Michael Nowlan, Steve Nowlan, Danny Nowlan, and their spouses, children and grandchildren. My children, Bob, Phil, Edward, Jennifer, and their mother, Marilyn Nowlan; the spouses of my children, who include Andy Swanson, Chrystal Nowlan, Peter Golanski, Evan Wright and Andrew Wright and their wives, Brenda and Melanie; my grandchildren, Ally, Tommy, John, Cate, Lawson, Pierce, Alison, Owen and Elliot. Other relatives include Mary and Bill Corcoran, John and Gay Evans, John, Terri and Tara Kennedy, Lore and Jack Brown, Sandy Kennedy, Louise Kennedy, Ray and Anne Lawson, Ray and Mollie Lawson, Joe Lawson, and Pete Lawson.

I would like to further acknowledge the many men and women whose books in this area of interest have delighted, challenged and inspired me. Among them are Charles Francis Adams, Henry Adams, Harry Ammon, Lance Banning, Margaret Bassett, Charles A. Beard, Samuel Flagg Bemis, R.B. Bernstein, Paul F. Boller, Jr., Daniel J. Boorstin, Catherine Drinker Bowen, H.W. Brands, Irving Brandt, Edward McNall Burns, James McGregor Burns, Oliver Perry Chitwood, Freeman Cleaves, Donald B. Cole, Edward P. Crapol, Noble E. Cunningham, Jr., James C. Curtis, Robert Dallek, George Dangerfield, Richard J. Ellis, John Ferling, David Thomas Flexner, Edith B Gelles, Robert G. Gunderson, Marie B. Hecht, Stefan Lorant, Dennis Tilden Lynch, Dumas Malone, Drew R. McCoy, David McCullough, Paul C. Nagel, Merrill D. Peterson, Jack N. Rakove, Robert V. Remini, Robert A. Rutland, Arthur M. Schlesinger, Jr., Robert Seager II, Jack Shepard, Mary E. Stuckey, Arthur Styron, Ted Widmer, Garry Wills, and Woodrow Wilson.

Preface

To this point only forty-three men have held the office of the president of the United States. Biographers and historians examine their every deed and attempt to explain the motivations for their actions. Polls are taken to rank the best and worst United States presidents. Much of what the average person knows about the earlier presidents comes from the history they studied in school. In many cases, what is recalled from this experience is of questionable accuracy, or at least oversimplifications and in some cases pure myth.

For many people, what they know about the founding fathers and their immediate successors is that George Washington, the first president, won the Revolutionary War and lived at Mount Vernon. Those who have seen the musical *1776* or the film version are led to believe that an annoying little man named John Adams cajoled and bullied the Continental Congress into approving the Declaration of Independence, which was written by a tall redhead, Thomas Jefferson. James Madison authored the Bill of Rights and married Dolley Madison, who saved a portrait of Washington when the British threatened what was later known as the White House during the War of 1812. James Monroe is recalled as the author of the doctrine that bears his name warning European nations to keep their hands off the Americas. John Quincy Adams was the son of a president, and because of the movie *Amistad* it is known that he defended the slaves who seized a ship. Andrew Jackson won the Battle of New Orleans and introduced the "spoils system." Martin Van Buren was Dutch. About all that is known about William Henry Harrison, if anything, is that he died shortly after his inauguration. Of John Tyler, nothing significant is remembered. Yet, each of these men contributed to the evolution of the office of the chief executive of the United States and his relationship with the other two branches of the federal government. What is known about later presidents is not much more. Somewhere along the line, many Americans developed a predisposition either in favor or against each of them, based more on hearsay than on facts.

Perhaps the most imperative task of a president is to tell forthrightly and sell the story of his policies, his expectations, his plans, and his promises. In 1991, Chatham House Publishers brought out Mary E. Stuckey's *The President as Interpreter-in-Chief.* According to Stuckey, the president tells us stories about ourselves, and in doing so, he tells us what kind of people we are and how we are constituted as a community. To understand the evolution of the presidency and how each chief executive has affected its development, it is instructive to examine what presidents have written. Individuals often discover what they believe by writing about things. The presidents' speeches, whether authored by them or a team of speech writers, reveal an enormous amount about the presidents. *The American Presidents* paints portraits of the occupants of the executive mansion through their words and the words of others speaking about them.

Who? What? When? Where? Why? How? To chronicle the American presidency, many questions of this sort must be asked and possible answers considered. How much has the evolution of the presidency shaped modern society and culture? It is good sport to debate the various merits of the administrations of presidents and to rank the members of this very exclusive club. However, informed citizens must know more than trivial facts, stereotypes and myths about their commander-in-chief. One thing is guaranteed, once an individual is elected president he (or she) will be despised by a large number of citizens who disagree with his policies. Taking issue with the course and philosophy a president follows in dealing with the issues of the day is every citizen's right and probably an obligation. However, too often citizens form their opinion of the presidents based on sound bites, spin and demography, deciding on this basis they know enough to distinguish the good from the bad. In old movie westerns, the good guys wore white hats and the bad guys wore black hats to make it easy for the audience to know who to root for. In the case of the presidents of the United States, they all have worn gray hats.

Believing that people should make up their own minds about the relative contributions of the nation's various chief executives and their interpretations of their policies for the people, *The American Presidents* presents the facts, and when relating any opinions of the author or others labels them as such. There is no intention to either sanctify any of the presidents or act as an apologist for them, nor is it an excuse to smear reputations or ridicule them. They are presented for what they are, American citizens, who by some ordinary and some extraordinary circumstances are chosen to lead the nation. In doing so they are armed with their individual strengths and constrained by their weaknesses. Readers are invited to inspect the facts provided about each president, to read what each one had to say about the issues of his day and discover what others have said about these chief executives. Hopefully in this way readers may personally assess their fellow citizens who put on the mantle of leadership.

To seek the presidency is an extraordinary ambition; it is astonishing that anyone would think that he or she has what it takes to tackle the role, especially now that the position has evolved into the most powerful in the world. Only these forty-three men can readily give evidence of what it means to take on the almost impossible job. Only these two score and three have experienced the demands of the office and what its strains and responsibilities do to a person. By considering what each has said on critical issues, to discover how they are in agreement with others of their club, and to review the warnings and predictions they made that successors may or may not have heeded, readers may find they have a far greater appreciation for these leaders of the nation.

Fair-minded readers can evaluate the presidential decisions that have benefitted the nation and where these have ill served the United States. With the advantage of hindsight, one can trace the problems of one president to origins in attempts to find solutions of other problems by earlier presidents. It is unwise to judge these men in light of what is known today. Rather, their actions should in fairness be evaluated based on the situations of the times when each was president. This work considers the circumstances that existed during presidential administrations, so that each president's performance may be seen in terms of the mood and concerns of the nation during his era.

There is no ranking the presidents from best to worst, for this is but a subjective judgment often made without agreed-upon criteria. Is a president who successfully led the nation through a war greater than one who kept the country out of war? Some presidents are criticized for not having settled the slavery question, but neither did the esteemed founding fathers. Indian removal was a terrible chapter in the nation's history. The presidents, responsible for the action, have been described, appropriately, as racists—but at the time so was the majority of the white population. Presidents who encouraged the nation's "Manifest Destiny" have been accused of fomenting unnecessary wars and all but conquering lands to the west. However, who today would seriously suggest that Texas, New Mexico, California, Oregon and other states be returned to their original owners?

Certain issues occupied the attention of a succession of presidents over many years, issues such as the powers and responsibilities of the president, the relationships between the three branches of government, the national bank, tariffs, slavery, Indian removal, expansion, treatment of the southern states, voting rights, recessions and depressions, wars and threats of wars, civil rights, women's rights, financial bailouts, and other evolving controversies. A question visited, but not easily answered in this book, is how men who spoke elegantly of freedom could justify the denial of it to so many members of the nation's population.

A recurring problem that should concern Americans is whether disagreement with a president on policy, especially foreign policy, is unpatriotic. After all, no president is infallible. Both despising a president and trying to stifle criticism are harmful to the health of the nation. The responsibility of the president, Congress and all interested in good government is to seek common ground in order to serve the needs of the nation and its people. What does the president owe the people and what do the people owe the president? To what extent is a president responsible when things go wrong, and how much credit is a president due when things go well? When it comes to knowing what it is like to be president, only forty-three men can give testimony. Who are these guys, really? What are their stories?

Presidents are neither saints nor sinners, nor are they popes or kings. They are merely citizens who have accepted the burden of one of the most challenging jobs in the world. To tell the presidents' stories adequately, it is necessary to examine each of the chief executives' virtues and faults, their influences, their quirkiness, their wit, and their passions. *The American Presidents* is meant to entertain as well as to inform. It has humor, pathos, and tragedy." The goal is to look into the hearts, souls and minds of these men. Readers are left to draw their own conclusions as to the nature and character of them based on substantial evidence. In every case and every presidential administration, a significant number of U.S. citizens and people across the world have accused occupants of the office of chief executive of being inherently evil and deliberately so. However, there are no willing villains; most people can convince themselves that they are acting from principles which others may not realize. There also have always been many among those who elected the presidents who shared beliefs in their principles and programs.

This work is more factual than analytical, more objective than judgmental. To assist the readers to a better understanding of the nature, beliefs, principles, vanities, weaknesses, and strengths of these forty-three men, there are numerous quotations by each one, which reveal as much about the presidents as several paragraphs of interpretations might reveal. Included for the readers' edification are a large number of quotations from members of the presidents' families, friends, enemies, associates, politicians, foreign commentators, historians and other scholars. For each profile, there is an extensive bibliography of books about the president and his principles and policies, provided as references and suggestions for further reading.

In their rise to the presidency, all but one president had the support of at least one wife. These ladies are all extremely interesting in their own right. Some were powerful influences on the policies of their husbands; others were content to perform (or resigned to performing) the social obligations of the "hardest unpaid job," that of first lady. Other members of presidential families are visited for their effect on the lives and careers of the chief executives. In addition, there are the presidents' political families, advisors, mentors and influential friends who helped shape the character and beliefs of the men who would become chief executives of the United States. Perhaps just as valuable are the views of the opponents and enemies of these occupants of the White House.

For each president, the profile relates information about birth, family, ancestors, appearance, personality, marriage and romances, children, religion and religious beliefs, education, home, mottos or slogans, recreational pastimes and interests, pets and animals, occupations, military service, political philosophy and political party affiliation, political offices, presidential campaigns, presidency, vice president and cabinet, Supreme Court appointments, amendments to the Constitution, states added to the Union, domestic affairs, foreign affairs, after the presidency, writings, papers, nicknames and titles, health, death, place of death, final words, cause of death, place of burial, miscellaneous, presidential trivia and firsts, anecdotes, and references and further readings. Each profile contains numerous quotations by each president on various subjects and comments made about him by others. They are provided in the conviction that in order to know a president as he really is, one should consider what he says and what others say about him. Each profile has images to illustrate the text — in a belief that the ancient Chinese cliché is correct: "A picture is worth a thousand words."

In ancient Rome, when a conquering general rode in triumph, in his chariot, through the streets and the throngs of cheering people of the Eternal City, at his side was a servant who repeatedly whispered in his ear, "Remember, thou are but a man." Presidents and aspiring presidents should embrace this advice; lest they become convinced they have some divine calling to rule and such insights that they alone can decide what the country needs. It is essential for the well-being of the nation that citizens of the United States understand their responsibility of accepting that each of these presidents "are but men," imperfect and fallible. This is the principal message of *The American Presidents*.

Book I: *Washington to Tyler* relates the story of the first ten presidents of the United States. These men made vital contributions not only in establishing the nature of the presidency, but also in the course of the fledgling nation. Later presidents frequently quoted them in their speeches and continue to do so. One observer remarked that presidents should not quote the founding fathers so often, but rather follow their example and imitate their principles.

When he was president, everything George Washington did was a precedent, and he was acutely aware of this. He was most careful in whatever he did, realizing that his actions would set directions for his successors. Perhaps his greatest achievement in the evolution of the presidency was refusing to turn the chief executive into a king and stepping aside for another at the end of two terms. Efforts by many writers after Washington's death to canonize him as a standard of moral, spiritual and political perfection only succeeded in dehumanizing the man and diminishing his accomplishments. Were he superhuman and god-like, then his accomplishments would not be remarkable. On the contrary, Washington was a man — with strengths and weaknesses, doubts, prejudices and all the other attributes common to the citizens of the nation he helped create — who achieved greatness due to his own efforts.

Like all the men who have served as the president of the United States, John Adams had a complex personality in whom there is much to admire and plenty to condemn. Adams was a man of formidable intellect, a brilliant lawyer, and an untiring advocate for the creation of a new nation. He also was a tactless man who seemingly gave offense each time he opened his mouth to speak. No one has attempted to deify the second president. Nevertheless, he played a crucial role in identifying the ideals that have become typically identified with Americans, such as the way Americans achieve on their own merit, efforts and hard work.

Thomas Jefferson was a Renaissance man, one who acted time and time again on his enormous curiosity, resulting in lasting contributions to the knowledge of the human race. In approving the Louisiana Purchase, he drifted from his strong constitutional convictions, and set further presidential precedents and ratcheted up the powers and responsibilities of the president. He struggled with the question of slavery while continuing to own slaves. This was not as hypocritical as some would make it. He believed that the abolishment of slavery was necessary but that it could not be accomplished by one planter at a time. To free slaves without making any provision for their well-being and opportunities for advancement is a cruel freedom. It would take a bloody and disastrous civil war for a president with a plan for the total abolishment of slavery and provisions for the transition from slavery to freedom. Even then it would take more than another century for African Americans to achieve the same legal rights as other citizens throughout the entire nation. No, Jefferson did not solve the slavery question and neither did others, but his achievements still are worthy of admiration.

James Madison, the smallest president in physical stature, was nevertheless a giant among giants. His contributions to the Constitutional Convention and in drafting the Federalist Papers are in themselves sufficient to applaud this always frail and sickly man, who lived more than 85 years. He was the first president of the United States to ask Congress for a declaration of war, during which the British burned and destroyed the executive mansion. His wife, Dolley, was the "hostess with the mostest" for a long period in Washington, beginning with her service for the widower Thomas Jefferson.

The presidency of James Monroe was known as the "Era of Good Feeling," so named because the nation was at peace and was maturing nicely. He is also remembered for the doctrine bearing his name. He not only warned European nations that the United States would not stand for any incursion into the Western hemisphere, but he also pledged not to become involved in European disputes. Only much later did presidents roll out the Monroe Doctrine, reminding other nations to keep their grasping hands off the territories and countries that fell under the sphere of the U.S.

John Quincy Adams may have been the most intelligent U.S. president of all time, but he was no more tactful than his illustrious father. If anyone deserved the description of "he marched to the sound of his own drummer," it was the sixth president of the United States. His most impressive contributions to the growth of this country occurred before and after his single term as president. He has often been described as the greatest diplomat in the nation's history and one of its best secretaries of state. After leaving the White House, Adams became the first — and thus far only — ex-president to be elected to the House of Representatives. He served 17 years and died in the speaker's chamber. During his tenure as a congressman, he was criticized, ostracized and censored for his myriad antislavery petitions, despite a "gag rule" passed in Congress in 1836, which tabled without any debate any petition critical of slavery.

Andrew Jackson was the first person to be elected president after the vote was extended to white males who did not own property. Thus, he became known as "the People's Presi-

dent." Jackson had a nasty disposition that turned to hatred when anyone had the audacity
to challenge his opinion on any matter. An example of this was his vow to destroy the Bank
of the United States, which despite its title was a private institution. Jackson and his western
supporters considered the bank to be an elitist institution which favored eastern manufacturing interest to the detriment of common workers. Another illustration of Jackson's fiery
temperament was in the Nullification Crisis of 1832, when the legislature of South Carolina
refused to comply with a new tariff law. Jackson threatened to lead an army into South Carolina and hang anyone he found who resisted the federal law. In the first battle, Jackson's
principal foe was Henry Clay and in the second, John C. Calhoun. Jackson went to his
maker unrepentant of his hatred of the two men, confessing his sorrow for his failure to
kill both of them.

Jackson's immediate successor, Martin Van Buren, is usually considered the first full-
time politician, and an unusually crafty one at that. His forte was in working behind the
scenes, and in this area, he was a master. Becoming president, he was out in front and
things did not go as well for him or the country. The Panic of 1837, brought on by Jackson's
fiscal practices, was blamed on Van Buren, which resulted in him having only one term.

Instead, the voters turned to elderly William Henry Harrison, a military hero who ran
on the Whig ticket. Harrison earned his reputation and a shot at the presidency while
serving as governor of the Indian Territory and in the Indian Wars of the Northwest Territory. He also served as a not particularly diplomatic diplomat as ambassador to Colombia,
where he lectured Simón Bolívar on proper leadership. Harrison gave a tremendously long
inaugural address in extremely adverse weather. This circumstance contributed to his death
after only a month in office.

Harrison was followed by Vice President John Tyler, a Democrat who had fallen out
with Andrew Jackson. Tyler's outstanding contribution as president, in his eyes, was the
annexation of Texas in 1845. However, in the evolution of the presidency, of even greater
importance was his refusal to be treated as acting president of the United States after Harrison's death. He insisted, and set the precedent that if a president dies in office his vice
president succeeds him as president. On a more personal note, he was the president who
had the most children—14 who lived to adulthood, seven by each of two wives.

These, then, are the first ten presidents of the United States and here are found the
accounts of their lives, careers, and contributions to the development and evolution of the
presidency.

A Few Views of the Presidency

[The president] resembles the commander of a ship at sea. He must have a helm to grasp, a course
to steer, a port to seek.[1]— Henry Adams

He should be a master politician who is above politics.[2]— James David Barber

The presidency is now a cross between a popularity contest and a high school debate, with an
encyclopedia of clichés the first prize.[3]— Saul Bellow

PRESIDENT, n. The leading figure in a small group of whom — and of whom only — it is positively
known that immense numbers of their countrymen did not want any of them for President.[4]—
Ambrose Bierce

People often think of leaders as the repositories of unique knowledge, who by reason of their
office can survey things that others cannot.... Mere mortals are still inspired by a certain awe—

at least for the office of the presidency, if not always for the human being that occupies it.... But the real test of leadership — amongst all the tests of policy, judgment, politics and ability — is whether, in the final analysis, you put the country first, that ultimately you are prepared to put what you perceive to be the common good of the nation before your own political self. It is the supreme test. Very few leaders pass it.[5] — Tony Blair

Presidents tend to equate loyalty to integrity.[6] — Joseph A. Califano, Jr.

The character of a President colors his entire administration.[7] — Clark M. Clifford

All presidents start out to run a crusade but after a couple of years they find they are running something less heroic and much more intractable: namely the presidency. The people are well cured by then of election fever, during which they think they are choosing Moses. In the third year, they look on the man as a sinner and a bumbler and begin to poke around for rumors of another Messiah.[8] — Alistair Cooke

The exact dimensions of executive power at any given moment [are] largely the consequence of the incumbent's character and energy combined with the overarching needs of the day, the challenges to system survival and regeneration.[9] — Thomas E. Cronin

The United States brags about its political system, but the President says one thing during the election, something else when he takes office, something else at midterm and something else when he leaves.[10] — Deng Xiaoping

If the American people want me for this high office, I shall be only too willing to serve them.... Since studying this subject I am convinced that the office of President is not a very difficult one to fill.[11] — Admiral George Dewey

The president we get is the country we get. With each new president the nation is conformed spiritually.[12] — E.L. Doctorow

The farmer imagines power and place are fine things. But the President has paid dear for his White House. It has commonly cost him all his peace and the best of his manly attributes. To preserve for a short time so conspicuous an appearance before the world, he is content to eat dust before the real masters who stand erect behind the throne.[13] — Ralph Waldo Emerson

American democracy has revived the oldest political institution of the race, the elective kingship.[14] — Henry Jones Ford

Once a president gets into the White House, the only audience that is left that really matters is history. They all start competing against Lincoln as the greatest president. And the [library] building becomes the symbol, the memorial to that dream.[15] — Doris Kearns Goodwin

A successful President must want personal power and enjoy its uses.[16] — Erwin C. Hargrove

A President is best judged by the enemies when he has really hit his stride.[17] — Max Lerner

The presidency is not an office to be either solicited or declined.[18] — William Loundes

You can only judge a president by the consequence of his decisions.[19] — Bill Moyers

In our brief national history, we have shot four of our presidents, worried five of them to death, impeached one [two now] and hounded another out of office. And when all else fails, we hold an election and assassinate their character.[20] — P.J. O'Rourke

[In response to Representative William M.K. Springer's remarks in the House quoting Henry Clay: "As for me, I would rather be right than be President."] Well, the gentleman will never be either.[21] — Representative Thomas B. Reed

The presidential burden ... does not lie in the workload. It stems from the crushing responsibility of political decisions, with life and death literally hanging in the balance for hundreds of millions of people.[22] — George E. Reedy

Most Presidents would like to satisfy the historians and offer "creative leadership," but history provides very few opportunities for this sort of work. What it provides, most of the time, is trouble to be avoided. Commanding the ship of state is largely a matter of seeing to it that it stays afloat and clear of the reefs.[23] — Richard H. Rovere

A President's authority is not as great as his responsibility.[24] — Theodore C. Sorenson

The President must be greater than anyone else, but not better than anyone else. We subject him and his family to close and constant scrutiny and denounce them for things that we ourselves do every day. A Presidential slip of the tongue, a slight error in judgment — social, political, or ethical — can raise a storm of protest. We give the President more work than a man can do, more responsibility than a man should take more pressure than a man can bear. We abuse him often and rarely praise him. We wear him out, use him up, eat him up. And with all this, Americans have a love for the President that goes beyond loyalty or party nationality; he is ours, and we exercise the right to destroy him.[25] — John Steinbeck

The President must have not only the courage of his convictions but also the courage to change his convictions.[26] — Sidney Warren

The President's decisions make the weather, and if he is great enough, change the climate, too.[27] — Theodore H. White

The President is there in the White House for you, it is not you who are here for him.[28] — Walt Whitman

Introduction

The American Presidency

Introduction: At the close of the Constitutional Convention of 1787, Dr. James McHenry, one of Maryland's delegates to the convention, queried Benjamin Franklin as he left Independence Hall on the final day of deliberation: "Well, Doctor, what have we got — a Republic or a Monarchy?" Franklin replied, "A Republic, if you can keep it."[1] The struggle to keep it continues today.

The Government of the United States: Although the Declaration of Independence, issued in 1776, mentioned the United States of America, the 13 colonies did not become states of a new nation until the adoption and ratification of the Constitution. The Continental Congress had only the limited authority the states allowed it, and the Articles of Confederation were not the binding law of the land.[2] The Constitutional Convention created the United States in Philadelphia, Pennsylvania, on September 17, 1787. The document, once ratified by nine states, replaced the Articles of Confederation and Perpetual Union.[3] Eventually the legislatures of all 13 states approved the Constitution. However, in several cases, as in Massachusetts, where the vote was 187 to 168, and in Virginia, which approved the Constitution by a margin of 89 to 79, it was a close vote. Some states made ratification contingent on the promised addition of a bill of rights. Congress proposed 12 amendments in September 1789. The states ratified ten of them; and on December 15, 1791, their adoption as part of the Constitution was certified.[4]

The Constitution formally went into effect on March 4, 1789, when George Washington was sworn in as the president of the United States (POTUS). The current United States is a federal republic comprising 50 states and the District of Columbia. The government is referred to as federal because it was formed by a compact — the Constitution — among 13 political units, the original states. In the compact, each state agreed to give up some of its sovereignty in order to establish a central authority to which it would submit.[5] The federal government initially concentrated on defense and foreign affairs, and the coordination of interstate concerns, with legislation left as a function of the states, each with its own constitution, elected legislature, governor, Supreme Court, and taxation powers.[6]

A major concern of the framers of the Constitution was to limit the power of the central government and protect the liberty of citizens. The Constitution provides for the separation of the federal government into three branches; legislative, executive, and judiciary. Each branch is intended to provide checks and balances against the others. Explicit guarantees of individual liberty were designed to strike a balance between authority and liberty.[7] "Article I vests legislative powers in the Congress— the House of Representatives and the Senate. Article II vests executive power in the president and Article III places judicial power in the hands of the courts."[8]

Presidential System: A presidential system of government, in contrast to a parliamentary system, "features a president as the nation's head of state and active chief executive authority. In a presidential system, the central principle is that the legislative and executive branches of government are separate."[9] In "parliamentary systems, government is usually carried out by a cabinet headed by a prime minister," who in many instances is a member of the parliament (legislature), directly accountable to parliament and subject to dismissal by a parliamentary vote.[10] In a presidential system, the president and the legislature are elected separately for a fixed term of office. The president is not required to choose cabinet members from a legislative majority; and he can be removed from office only for a gross misdemeanor determined by the process of impeachment and dismissal.[11] In a parliamentary system, the legislature can be dissolved at any point during its term by the head of the state, usually on the advice of the prime minister.[12] In a presidential system, the legislature exists for a set term and cannot be dissolved early. The president can veto legislation, subject to the power of the legislature by a certain majority to override the veto.[13]

Qualifications to Be President: *No person*

The Seal of the President of the United States (www.wikipedia.org).

Scene at the Signing of the Constitution of the United States, painting by Howard Chandler Christy, 1940 (Architect of the Capitol).

Political cartoon by Benjamin Franklin originally published in the *Pennsylvania Gazette*, May 9, 1754 (Library of Congress).

except a natural born citizen, or a citizen of the United States, at the time of the adoption of this Constitution, shall be eligible to the office of President; neither shall any person be eligible to that office who shall not have attained the age of thirty-five years, and been fourteen years a resident within the United States.[14]

Oath of Office: *I do solemnly swear (or affirm) that I will faithfully execute the office of the President of the United States, and will to the best of my ability, preserve, protect, and defend the Constitution of the United States.*[15]

The Presidency: There are a

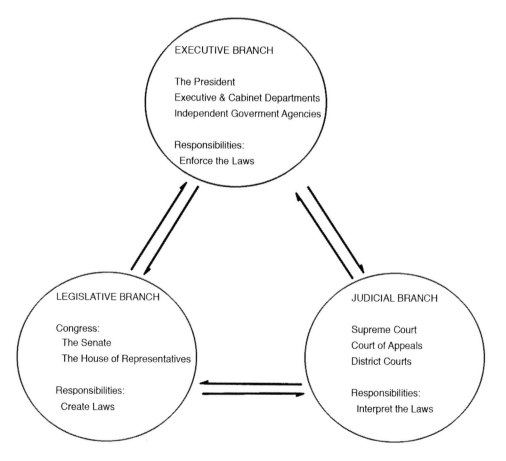

This diagram shows the separation of power by the branches of government (author's image).

number of perks in being president of the United States. As the office has become more and more imperial, the nation's chief executive knows that when he begins to sit down, someone is sure to put a chair under him. The president lives in a style of pomp and pageantry that rivals the comforts and trappings of royalty. It is difficult for people to understand how any normal person would be able to decide that they are not only worthy of the job but also greatly qualified. A president soon discovers that everything pretty much revolves around him at the White House and wherever else he may go. The deference that the office of the president is shown, if not for the one holding the office, could be heady stuff and one may come to believe that it is personally deserved. When this happens, the president may be rightly criticized for losing touch with the people he represents. When Washington assumed the post, it was not clear what were the precise authority and powers of the office.[16] The founding fathers knew they did not want an all-powerful head of state, like a king. George Washington didn't want to be a king — although he might have been one had he so desired — and he certainly didn't act like a king.[17]

The founding fathers thought of the presidency as an office of immense honor and dignity, but one with little real power.[18] The prerogatives have evolved over the years, as adventurous presidents felt it right and proper for them to expand the functions of the chief executive. The role continues to grow in complexity along paths that the founding fathers could not have imagined and perhaps would not have approved. Each president, in some little way or some considerable way, has made a mark on the office and has contributed to the enormous growth of the office's power. This was possible because Article II of the Constitution gives far more coverage to how a president is elected than it does to his responsibilities and authority. It speaks directly only of his power to make treaties, to appoint ambassadors, other public ministers and consuls, judges of the Supreme Court and all other officers of the United States, with the advice and consent of the Senate.[19]

Throughout the history of the United States, the responsibilities and prerogatives of the president have grown almost exponentially, often depending on what a president believed them to be and whether they could withstand challenges from Congress and the judiciary. The president of the United States leads the executive branch of the federal government in its broad responsibility for implementing, supporting, and enforcing the laws made by the legislative branch (Congress), as interpreted by the judicial branch (Supreme Court).[20] One of the most crucial responsibilities is to use the White House, in Theodore Roosevelt's words, as a "bully pulpit"[21] to assert and explain the administration's policies, plans and actions to the citizens of the country.

Cabinet: Among the precedents set by George Washington was the creation of a group of men to head the administrative subdivisions of the government. James Madison, then a member of the House of Representatives, was the first to refer to them as a cabinet.[22] The constant disagreements between Washington's secretary of state, Thomas Jefferson, and his secretary of the treasury, Alexander Hamilton, led to the formation of the initial two American political parties.[23]

Originally, the Cabinet was intended to meet with the president, discuss matters of state, and offer him advice. This rarely has been the case, and in modern times, Cabinet members are usually experts in a certain field. As leading the 14 government departments requires so much of their time, little is left for advising a president, even if he seeks it, which nowadays seldom happens.[24] From time to time, presidents add additional members to their cabinets and new departments for them to head. Some of these were merged, some subdivided, and one, the postmaster general, was abolished when the post office became an independent agency.[25] The president may choose to invite other members of the government to serve in the Cabinet, such as the vice president, the White House chief of staff, and the director of the Office and Management. Sometimes first ladies who had considerable influence with their husbands regularly attended cabinet meetings.[26]

Electoral College: The president (and the vice president) is selected by electors who currently comprise a 538-member electoral college. Each state has the number of electors equal to the number of its senators and representatives combined. The District of Columbia has three electors.[27] Originally, "electors were expected to exercise discretion, but they were not bound to follow the popular vote in casting their ballot. The rise of political parties led to electors' pledging to vote for the candidate of their party, and they nearly always do."[28] In 48 states and the District of Columbia, the slate of electors is decided on a winner-takes-all rule; that is, whichever candidate receives a majority of the popular vote, or a plurality (less than 50 percent but more than any other candidate) in the state, gets all the state's electoral votes. In Maine and Nebraska, two electors' votes go to the candidate with the most statewide votes. The remaining votes are awarded to the candidate who received the most popular votes in each congressional district of the state. On Election Day, the people in each state cast their ballots for slates of electors representing the political party's choice for president and vice president. On the Monday following the second Wednesday of December each state's electors meet in their respective state capitols to cast their votes—one for president and one for vice president.[29]

The candidate for president with the most electoral votes, provided that it is an absolute majority (one more than half the total of votes), is president. Similarly, the vice presidential candidate with the absolute majority of electoral votes is declared vice president.[30] Three presidents lost the popular vote but were elected by the electoral college. In 1876, Rutherford Hayes defeated Samuel Tilden by one electoral vote; Benjamin Harrison in 1888 defeated presidential incumbent Grover Cleveland 233 electoral votes to 168; and George W. Bush won the disputed 2000 election by an electoral vote of 271 to 266 for Al Gore.[31]

State	EV	State	EV	State	EV	State	EV
Alabama	9	Indiana	11	Nebraska	5**	South Carolina	8
Alaska	3	Iowa	7	Nevada	5	South Dakota	3
Arizona	10	Kansas	6	New Hampshire	4	Tennessee	11
Arkansas	6	Kentucky	8	New Jersey	15	Texas	34
California	55	Louisiana	9	New Mexico	5	Utah	5
Colorado	9	Maine	4**	New York	31	Vermont	3
Connecticut	7	Maryland	10	North Carolina	15	Virginia	13
Delaware	3	Massachusetts	12	North Dakota	3	Washington	11
Florida	27	Michigan	17	Ohio	20	West Virginia	5
Georgia	15	Minnesota	10	Oklahoma	7	Wisconsin	10
Hawaii	4	Mississippi	6	Oregon	7	Wyoming	3
Idaho	4	Missouri	11	Pennsylvania	21	Washington, D.C.*	3
Illinois	21	Montana	3	Rhode Island	4	Total electors	538

*Washington, D.C., although not a state, is granted three electoral votes by the Twenty-third Amendment.
**Maine and Nebraska electors distributed by way of the Congressional District Method.

"In the event no one obtains an absolute majority of electoral votes for president, the U.S. House of Representatives selects the president from the top three contenders, with each state casting one vote and an absolute majority of the states being required to elect. Similarly, if no one obtains an absolute majority for vice president, the U.S. Senate makes the choice from the top two contenders for the office."[32] Because no one had a majority of the electoral votes, both Thomas Jefferson in his first term, and John Quincy Adams in his only term, were chosen president by the House of Representatives.[33]

In 1800, both Jefferson and Aaron Burr had 73 electoral votes, and John Adams had 65. Throughout the election campaign, it was clear that Jefferson was the presidential candidate and Burr was his vice presidential candidate. When Burr refused to concede, the election was thrown to the House of Representatives, where it took 36 ballots for members to declare Jefferson the president.[34] The deadlock prompted the passage of the Twelfth Amendment (1804), which "required that the electors name in their ballots the person voted for as president and in distinct ballots the person voted for as vice president, and that distinct lists be made of all persons voted for president and of persons voted for as vice president and the number of votes for each."[35]

In 1824, John Quincy Adams won neither the popular vote nor the Electoral College vote. Andrew Jackson won pluralities in both but not a majority of the electoral votes. Jackson had 99 votes, Adams 84, William Crawford 41 and Henry Clay 37. In accordance with the 12th Amendment, the House of Representatives was required to choose the president from the top three vote-getters in the electoral college. Clay, who was eliminated from consideration, threw his support to Adams, who received the vote of 13 states to Jackson's seven states and Crawford's four, making Adams president.[36]

The Club: As of 2009 there have been 44 United States presidencies, although only 43 presidents, since Grover Cleveland served two nonconsecutive terms and is thus both the 22nd and 24th U.S. president.[37] Until 2009, all the presidents had been white men, with ancestries limited to some combination of seven heritages: Dutch, English, Irish, Scottish, Welsh, Swiss, and German.

Terms of Office: Fifteen presidents were elected to two terms and 21 were elected to only one term. Franklin D. Roosevelt was elected to four terms, which led to the adoption of the 22nd Amendment, limiting the presidency to two terms. It was proposed in 1947 and ratified by the states in 1951, and first affected Dwight Eisenhower.[38] Four presidents — John Tyler, Millard Fillmore, Andrew Johnson and Chester Arthur — never ran for president. Gerald Ford was not elected either vice president or president although he served in both offices. Eight vice presidents — John Tyler, Millard Fillmore, Andrew Johnson, Chester A. Arthur, Theodore Roosevelt, Calvin Coolidge, Harry Truman and Lyndon Johnson — became president because of the death of their president.[39]

Political Parties: In the beginning of the nation, there were no political parties, and if Washington could have had his way, none would have ever been formed. In his farewell address, he warned "in the most solemn manner against the baneful effects of the spirit of party."[40] The second president, John Adams, felt that parties would restrict the president's independence. Despite their protestations against political parties, both Washington and Adams are considered to be Federalists, those who advocated the ratification of the U.S. Constitution to replace the Articles of Confederation.[41] The Federalist Party grew from the mind of Washington's secretary of the treasury, Alexander Hamilton, who favored a strong central government and advocated reconciliation with Britain.[42]

Anti-Federalists soon made their opinions known. They favored state sovereignty and the diffusion of power among the people. They were suspicious of the British and held the revolutionary French in higher regard.[43] The anti–Federalist party was known as the Republican Party. Although together with James Madison, Thomas Jefferson is usually regarded as the leader of the early Republican Party, he claimed he was "capable of thinking for himself without any assistance from a political faction."[44] Jefferson's party, which believed in a "modest central government, limited commercial activity, and strong farming communities,"[45] had more in common with the present-day Democratic Party than it does with the modern Republican Party.

The first election featuring two rival political parties was in 1796, when Washington's vice president, John Adams, defeated Thomas Jefferson, who because of the rules then in effect in the electoral college, Long Tom was elected vice president. This prompted Congress in 1804 to pass the 12th Amendment to the Constitution, which was quickly ratified, preventing the election of a president and vice president from different parties.[46] The Federalists faded from the scene after Republican James Monroe was elected president in 1816 and never again fielded a candidate for the presidency.[47]

By 1828, the Republican Party had split in two. The Democratic Republican Party, led by Andrew Jackson, favored a limited national government and opposed economic aristocracy. It viewed itself as the party of the working class and finally changed its name to the Democratic Party, now the oldest political party in the United States.[48] The National Republican Party, led by John Quincy Adams, favored strong economic nationalization, much as did the previous Federalists. In 1832 the first national party conventions were held to nominate candidates, formerly selected by congressional caucuses. Anti-Jacksonians among National Republicans resented Old Hickory's membership in the Society of Freemasons and formed an Anti-Mason Party, thus becoming the first independent third party.[49]

The National Republican Party dissolved by 1834 and was replaced by the Whig Party, led by Henry Clay and Daniel Webster, who were "strongly opposed to Jackson's autocratic presidency."[50] The party's name was taken from the British Whig Party, which supported Parliament against the king. During the Revolutionary War, colonial patriots called themselves Whigs, while those loyal to the Crown were known as Tories. The Whigs "supported an expanded national government, increased commercial development and cautious western expansion."[51] The first Whig president was William Henry Harrison, and the second and last was Zachary Taylor.

Central Government vs. States' Rights: From the very beginning of the creation of the United States, there was disagreement over the powers of the president, central government versus states' rights, and whether to have a "loose" or "strict" interpretation of the Constitution.[52] These early differences, still debated, are mostly sectional. The Northeast's views were based on their desire to "encourage commerce and manufacturing, maintain close ties with Britain, and emphasize order and stability."[53] The South's and the West's vision of their new nation was one that "championed agricultural and rural life, sympathized with France, and stressed civil liberties and trust in the people."[54] Things are not quite as simple as these generalizations would make it seem. Positions on the issues often were blurred and even contradicted by proponents of one "political party" or the other.

The President and Congress: A president who neglects congressional views on major legislation invites defeat of his program. An important element of cooperation between a president and Congress is consultation. By neglecting to consult with Congress on the World War I peace treaty, Woodrow Wilson discovered to his regret that because of the snub, the legislature opposed it and refused to approve United States membership in the League of Nations.[55] One might think that it would be easier for a president to pass his agenda if his political party controlled the Congress, but that has not necessarily been the case. Presidents who are successful in getting their legislative agenda passed are those who know how to bargain privately and not get into public squabbles with Congress, no matter which party dominates. Members of Congress owe their positions to their constituents and will only pay attention to the president if he has something to trade. Presidential leadership depends upon "salesmanship, bargaining ability, and flexibility."[56] Presidents, such as Lyndon B. Johnson, who held leadership positions in Congress have been the most successful in dealing with Congress.

For most of the first 150 years of U.S. history, the president was not a major player in congressional matters. If a president did dare to assert power over Congress, he was certain to feel a backlash and hear harsh lectures from leaders in the legislative branch. Early presidents did not bring broad legislative programs to the office. They viewed their role to be mainly managing foreign affairs.[57] President Jackson, who considered himself the "Tribune of the People," did not shrink from confrontations with the legislative branch.[58] However, until the 1930s, Congress totally dominated government except for the administrations of Abraham Lincoln, James Polk and Grover Cleveland. Congress initiated programs to which the president responded, but since then, the presidency has grown more powerful, and not only during national emergencies. The president gradually supplanted Congress in establishing the nation's legislative agenda.[59]

Increasingly, Congress ceded its budget-making authority to the presidents, and the chief executives found ways to make agreements with foreign nations without congressional approval. They substituted executive agreements, which did not require the consent of Congress for treaties. Presidents took to launching military action, even though the Constitution empowers Congress as the only branch of government authorized to declare war.[60]

Article II.3 of the Constitution requires that "the President shall from time to time give to Congress Information of the State of the Union and recommend to their Consideration such measures as he shall judge necessary and expedient."[61] In modern times, the State of the Union Address serves as both a "conversation starter" between the president and Congress and an opportunity for the chief executive to sell his program to the people.

Vetoes: A veto is the power of a president to reject a bill proposed by Congress by refusing to sign it into law. The president writes the word "veto" [Latin, for "I forbid"] on the bill and returns it to Congress with a statement of his objections to it. Congress may choose to withdraw or revise the bill. Alternatively, it can override the veto and pass the law itself with a two-thirds vote in each house. The veto was "originally intended to prevent Congress from passing an unconstitutional law, but it has become a president's powerful bargaining tool, especially when his objectives are in conflict with the majority sentiment in Congress."[62] A pocket veto becomes an automatic veto of a bill if the president neither signs nor vetoes it within ten days of receiving it, and if Congress adjourns during that period. If Congress convenes during that period, the bill automatically becomes law. A pocket veto cannot be overridden by Congress, but it can be reintroduced at the next congressional session. Madison was the first president to use a pocket veto.[63]

J. Adams, Jefferson, J.Q. Adams, W.H. Harrison, Taylor, Fillmore and James Garfield never vetoed a bill. Franklin D. Roosevelt vetoed the most bills, 372 regular vetoes and 263 pocket vetoes, with only nine overridden. Of Andrew Johnson's 21 regular vetoes, 15 were overridden, the most for any president. Lyndon Johnson had the most vetoes (16 regular and 14 pocket) with none overridden. During the first 109 Congresses, presidents used 1484 regular vetoes and 1066 pocket vetoes, with 106 overridden.[64]

Impeachment: Since 1841, more than one-third of all American presidents have either died in office, become disabled, or resigned. However, no American president has ever been forced from office due to impeachment. Two presidents—Andrew Johnson and Bill Clinton—were impeached by the House of Representatives but were not convicted by the United

States Senate. Richard M. Nixon resigned on August 9, 1974, in order to escape the ignominy of a public trial in the U.S. Senate that appeared inevitable.[65]

Article I §2 of the United States Constitution gives the House of Representatives the sole power to impeach (make formal charges against) and Article I §3 assigns to the Senate the duty of trying impeachments. Article II §4 of the Constitution provides as follows: "The President, Vice President and all civil officers of the United States, shall be removed from office on impeachment for, and conviction of, treason, bribery, or other high crimes and misdemeanors."[66] There is a substantial difference of opinion over the interpretation of these words. Some legal experts believe that Congress could pass laws by declaring what constitutes "high crimes and misdemeanors," that is, a list of impeachable offenses.[67] That has never happened.

The President and the Courts: Article III of the Constitution established the judicial branch of the federal government: "The judicial power of the United States shall be vested in one Supreme Court and in such inferior courts as the Congress may from time to time ordain and establish."[68] The article leaves it to the discretion of Congress to specify the Supreme Court duties, powers and organization. It does not even mention a chief justice officer, but Congress implied that position in the impeachment section, which states, "When the President of the United States is tried, the Chief Justice shall preside."[69]

The first bill introduced in the United States Senate was the Judiciary Act of 1789.[70] It divided the country into 13 judicial districts, which were further organized into the Eastern, Middle, and Southern "circuits." The act called for a Supreme Court, consisting of a chief justice and five associate justices, which was to "sit" in the nation's capital. The Judiciary Act also created the position of the U.S. Attorney General and gave the authority to nominate Supreme Court justices to the president with the approval of the Senate. The first Supreme Court sat for the first time on February 1, 1790, in the Merchants Exchange Building in New York City, then the nation's capital.[71] For 101 years, Supreme Court justices were required to "ride circuit," which meant they were to hold court twice a year in each of the 13 districts. Since 1869, there have been nine justices of the Supreme Court, including the chief justice.[72]

Under chief justices John Jay, John Rutledge and Oliver Ellsworth, the Supreme Court lacked any real clout and little prestige. Presidents often had trouble finding willing candidates to be nominated for the bench, where there were seldom any compelling or exceptional cases to hear. This changed with the court of chief justice John Marshall (1801–1836). In 1803, in *Marbury v. Madison*, the Supreme Court unanimously declared that it has the authority to review acts of Congress and determine whether they are unconstitutional and, therefore, void.[73] This was the first time the court judged a law passed by Congress to be unconstitutional, and it firmly established "judicial review"[74] by making the court the final arbiter of the constitutionality of all laws passed by Congress. Marshall also ended the practice of each judge issuing his opinion on cases brought before them. The writing of a single opinion in each case was delivered only by Marshall, who would use the force of his intellect to stamp his Federalist views on the court.[75]

The judiciary is a separate and coequal branch of government in theory, and is assumed to be above politics. However, when presidents make a nomination to the Supreme Court or lower courts they ordinarily choose individuals who broadly share their ideological views. Of course sometimes presidents are fooled. President Eisenhower was sure that Earl Warren was a conservative when he named him chief justice, but the former governor of California was arguably the most liberal chief justice in the nation's history.[76] Any candidate the president nominates must be confirmed by the Senate. This implies that the majority of that body believes the nominee has the qualifications—whatever they may be, since the Constitution does not address the question—to sit on the highest bench.[77]

The Legislative Body: Article I of the Constitution provides for a house of representatives and a senate: "Representatives and direct taxes shall be apportioned among the several states which may be included within this Union, according to their respective numbers."[78] The first census took place in 1790 with enumerators asking for the name of the head of the family and the number of persons in each household in the categories: free white males over age sixteen, free white males under sixteen, free white females, all other free persons, and slaves.[79] The count was 3.9 million people, the English being the largest ethnic group and 20 percent slaves. Census takers did not count American Indians. In the same year, Congress passed the first Naturalization Act. It stipulated "any alien, being a free white person, may be admitted to the United States…."[80]

In the beginning of the new nation, the number of immigrants was small, due in part to the hostilities between England and France and afterwards the War of 1812. However, soon thereafter, immigration from Great Britain, Ireland, and Western Europe increased almost exponentially. With the beginning of the industrial revolution, the ending of the slave trade, and westward expansion, many jobs were created that were filled by immigrants. Ireland was decimated due to the potato famine in the 1840s and 1850s, leaving nearly 1.5 million dead and about the same number fleeing to America to prevent starvation. The Irish immigrants worked to build the nation's railroads, as did Chinese immigrants who arrived in the 1850s, entering the country at San Francisco.[81] While the economy was strong and jobs plentiful, the new immigrants were welcomed, with both the Union and Confederate armies relying on them for troops. However, with hard times, people who had been born in the United States came to resent the immigrants, accusing them of stealing jobs from "real" American workers.[82]

The Bank of the United States: Among economic issues that raised the ire of several presidents was the National Bank, which was established under the auspices of the Federalists. Alexander Hamilton proposed the bank as part of a system to establish the new government on a sound financial basis.[83] The First Bank of the United States was chartered by Congress for twenty years on February 25, 1791. It was created to handle the financial needs and requirements of the central government of the United States, which until that time had been managed by the thirteen states, each with their own banks, currencies, and financial institutions. Support for the bank came from northern merchants and New England states, but the bank was viewed with suspicion by the southern states. The difference was just a further example of the argument between those favoring a strong central government and those who championed states' rights.[84]

The bank was a "paradise for speculators who took advantage of the wildly unstable currencies issued by the states." The bank's charter expired in 1811, but President James Madison revived in it the form of the Second National Bank in 1816, once again chartered for 20 years.[85] The Bank of the United States was in no sense a national bank, but rather it was a privately held corporation, with a unique relationship with the federal government as the depository of its revenues.[86] President Jackson hated the bank because of its fraud and corruption, and he vowed to destroy it before it destroyed him.[87]

He vetoed a bill to renew the bank's charter and had his secretary of the treasury pull the government's revenues from the bank. Outraged by Jackson's actions, Henry Clay and Daniel Webster formed the Whig Party in an effort to gain enough votes in Congress in

1836 to override a second Jackson veto, but they were unsuccessful.[88] The collapse of the Bank of the United States led to the Panic of 1837, which dominated President Martin Van Buren's administration.[89]

Tariffs: Early American presidents were confronted with yet another touchy issue, the question of tariffs. A tariff is a tax on imports or exports from a country. Governments use them to protect home industries from lower-priced foreign goods and are opposed by supporters of free trade.[90] Assigning tariffs is a tricky business. To be successful tariffs must not provoke retaliatory tariffs from other countries. Once again, "a north-south, strong-central government versus states' rights fight ensued," lasting throughout the administrations of several presidents, that revolved around this issue.[91] The first complete protective tariff was adopted in the United States in 1816.[92] It was intended to foster the production of textiles, hats, leather, paper, and cabinetwork. Because it resulted in higher prices in the rural south, it was bitterly denounced by representatives of the southern states.[93]

This pattern of disagreement over tariff rates was repeated in later tariff acts, with the rates going up or going down, depending upon which president and party held sway in the government. From the 1790s until the eve of World War I, tariffs were the largest source of federal revenue, until they were surpassed by income taxes.[94] In recent times, presidents of both parties have abandoned the protectionist ideology to come out in favor of the policy of "minimal economic barriers to global trade."[95]

Recessions and Depressions: Most economists define a recession as two quarters of negative growth. The National Bureau of Economic Research (NBER) considers a recession "a significant decline in economic activity spread, across the economy, lasting more than a few months, normally visible in real Gross Domestic Product (GDP), real income, employment, industrial production, and wholesale-retail sales."[96] A depression is a recession of exceptionally low output and investment, with high unemployment. Specifically, the term describes two periods of crisis in the world economy, 1873–1896 and 1929–1939. The first of the recessions and other economic crises was the panic of 1797. It was caused by the deflation of the Bank of England and lasted three years.[97] The depression of 1807 was a direct result of the Embargo Act of that year passed by Congress and signed into law by President Jefferson.[98] It devastated shipping-related industries and lasted for seven years. The panic of 1819 was the first major financial crisis in the United States. In its five year period, there were widespread foreclosures, bank failures, unemployment and agricultural and manufacturing slumps.[99] The panic of 1837, lasting six years, was caused by bank failures, when American financial institutions ceased paying in specie (gold or silver).[100]

Foreign Affairs Issues: United States presidents have primary responsibility for foreign affairs and foreign policy. President Washington declared the U.S. was neutral in the conflict between Britain and France.[101] James Madison actively participated in the defense of Washington, D.C., during the War of 1812 with Britain.[102] His successor, James Monroe, issued the Monroe Doctrine,[103] mostly created by his secretary of state, John Quincy Adams. Presidents acted as commander-in-chief during foreign wars, and several played important roles in keeping the Cold War from becoming hot.

The White House: Leinster House, the eighteenth-century ducal palace in Dublin, served as a model for the White House.[104] The Georgian neoclassical mansion was designed by James Hoban, an Irish-American architect who won the architectural design competition in 1792. The structure was built of gray Virginia sandstone.[105] "Extra pavilions and porticos

An aerial view of the White House in Washington, D.C., 2007. Photograph by Carol M. Highsmith (Library of Congress).

(ornamental deck-like structures with columns supporting a roof) were added later," designed by architect Benjamin Latrobe, who also designed the United States capitol. Since its completion, each president had made his own additions and changes to his temporary home during his stay. President Jefferson added a colonnade to the residence, which originally concealed a stable and a laundry room.[106] The mansion was "rebuilt and restored after it was burned by the British in August 1814," its smoke-stained walls painted white.[107]

At this time, the White House has 132 rooms, 35 bathrooms and six levels in the residence. The main building is four stories high and has 55,000 square feet of floor space. The dimensions of the building are 170 feet long (not counting the porticos) and 85 feet wide. Its height is 70 feet. This does not include the east and west terraces, the executive office (West Wing), East Wing and a penthouse. The colonnade at the east side is the public entrance. The executive office is approached by an esplanade.[108]

The Oval Office in the West Wing of the White House is the "official office of the president of the United States." It has "three large south-facing windows behind the president's desk and a fireplace at the north end of the room." There are four doors in the Oval Office. The northwest door opens onto the main corridor of the West Wing. The west door leads to the president's private study and a dining room. The northeast door opens to the president's secretary's office. The east door opens to the Rose Garden. The dimensions of the Oval Office are 35 ft. 10 in. along the long axis and 29 ft. along the short axis of the oval. The height of the room is 18 ft. 6 in.[109]

Although it was President Taft who first used the Oval Office, preference for oval rooms dates at least to George Washington, who in his Philadelphia president's home had two rooms modified with a bowed-end that were used for hosting formal receptions. Washington placed himself in the center of the circle of his guests to greet them.[110] With no head or foot of the room, everyone was an equal distance from the president. The "circle became a symbol of democracy" and the Oval Office represents the modern president. Each president has found ways to put his stamp on the Oval Office. The chief executives may select art from the White House collection or private sources for the duration of their administration. Most presidents use a large partners' desk, called the "Resolute" desk, which was built from the "timbers of the British frigate HMS *Resolute.*"[111]

Presidential Salary and Perks: When George Washington was president, Congress set his salary at $25,000 a year, but since he was already a wealthy man he did not draw the money. The salary was raised to $50,000 in 1873, to $75,000 in 1909, to $100,000 in 1949, to $200,000 in 1969 and to its current rate, $400,000 in 2001.[112] The fully taxable remuneration is an extremely modest amount for the most powerful man in the world and the one with the most complex job of all. In comparison to the salaries and buyouts of the CEOs of private sector firms, it is a paltry sum. The president's salary depends upon the salary paid to all other federal employees, none of whom may earn more than the president.[113] Fortunately, those who seek the presidency are not in it for the money and many are rich to begin with, which is becoming more and more an unfortunate requirement even to be a candidate for a presidential nomination. For most occupants of the White House, the reward for obtaining the position is the power to conduct and influence the work and direction of the nation.

ONE

George Washington
The Man Who Would Not Be King

First President of the United States, 1789–1797

Abraham Lincoln liked to repeat a story attributed to Ethan Allen, a hero of the American Revolution. While he was visiting England after the war, Allen's hosts enjoyed ridiculing Americans and especially George Washington. Trying to anger Allen, they hung a picture of Washington in the outhouse (outdoor toilet). Allen's response was to say that this was a particularly appropriate place for the picture, because "there is nothing that will make an Englishman shit so quick as the sight of General Washington."[1]

Birth: George Washington was born at ten o'clock in the morning on Friday, February 11, 1732. His natal day was recorded according to the Julian calendar then in use in Great Britain and its colonies. In 1752, the more accurate Gregorian calendar was adopted, resulting in the loss of eleven days and establishing Washington's birthday as February 22, 1732, which is celebrated to this day. However, GW always observed the anniversary of his birth on February 11. He was born at his family estate, Wakefield Farm, near Pope's Creek, Westmoreland County, Virginia, situated near the Potomac and Rappahannock rivers on a peninsula known as Virginia's Northern Neck, which is located halfway between Washington, D.C., and the Chesapeake Bay.

Nicknames and Titles: George Washington's most known title, "The Father of His Country," first appeared on the cover of a circa 1778 Pennsylvania German almanac, *Nord Amerikanische Kalender*, which referred to Washington as *Der Landes Vater*, "Father of the Land."[2] He was also honored with the title "American Fabius,"[3] a reference to Quintus Fabius Maximus (c. 275 B.C.E.–203 B.C.E.), a Roman statesman and soldier noted for his superior military strategy. Another classical allusion was "The American Cincinnatus"[4] an attribution to Roman Consul Lucius Quinctius Cincinnatus (519 B.C.E.), regarded by the Romans as one of the heroes of the early empire and a model of Roman virtue and simplicity. Both Cincinnatus and Washington were farmers who were called to duty to protect their country and subsequently relinquished their power to return to farming.

Family: The Washington line was industrious and land-poor. George's father Augustine Washington (1694–1743) was born at Mattox Creek, Virginia, and by the time he was eight, both of his parents had died. Augustine's father's will[5] stipulated that upon his death, his estate should revert to and be managed by his first cousin John Washington of Chotank, Stafford County, Virginia. When Augustine came of age, he inherited 1700 acres near the Potomac River and became a leading planter in the area, also serving as a justice of the county court. On April 20, 1715, he married the 16-year-old heiress Jane Butler,[6] who died in 1729, leaving him with two sons, Lawrence and Augustine Jr., and a daughter, Jane.

Augustine remarried on March 6, 1730, to 23-year-old Mary Ball[7] (1708–1789), who was orphaned before she was thirteen. With his second wife, Augustine had six more children, of whom George was the eldest. George's siblings were Betty (1733–1797), Samuel (1734–1781), John Augustine (1736–1787), Charles (1738–1799), and Mildred (1739–1740). In the 18th century and the beginning of the 19th century, tragedy touched almost all families with early death. One quarter of the children born during that period died before they could walk and half the people in the world expired before the age of nine. A remarkable number of women died in childbirth, and there were innumerable miscarriages and stillbirths. There was no known cure or treatment for many diseases. "It was estimated that for every American soldier killed in combat during the Revolutionary War, ten others died of disease."[8] Mary Ball Washington was an assured woman, with a dynamic presence. She maintained a degree of control over her children, especially George, who, throughout her life, she treated as merely a big boy.[9] However, Mary was the source of George's admirable qualities, inheriting both her excellent health and the sturdy Spartan virtues of her mind. On one occasion, he spoke lovingly of his mother: "My mother was the most beautiful woman I ever saw. All I am I owe to my mother. I attribute all my success in life to the moral, intellectual and physical education I received from her."[10]

Mary Washington continued to live at Ferry Farm[11] and worked on the land for 45 years after the death of her husband. George tended to her wants and supplied her with what she needed, which she accepted as her due. When Mary was about 64 years old, George proposed that his mother should live with or near one of her children. However, he made it clear that the recommendation should not be construed as an invitation to live with him. GW purchased a home for Mary in Fredericksburg,

George Washington Esq., President of the United States of America. Mezzotint print by Edward Savage, June 25, 1793. George Washington is shown holding proposed plan for the new capital city of Washington (Library of Congress).

Virginia, where she lived out her life close to her daughter Betty.[12] After the Revolution, Mary suggested that she might move to Mount Vernon, prompting George to rapidly pen a letter to his mother disabusing her of the notion by asserting that she would not be comfortable in his home: "In truth it may be compared to a well restored tavern, as scarcely any strangers who are going from north to south, do not spend a day or two at it.... What with the sitting up of Company; the noise and bustle of servants, and many other things you would not be able to enjoy that calmness and serenity of mind, which ... you ought to prefer."[13]

Augustine died when the future president was eleven years old, leaving George the little Ferry Farm on the Rappahannock River where he resided with his mother and siblings. George's older half brother Lawrence inherited the larger farm at Hunting Creek and was young George's guardian.[14] Lawrence served as an agent for the extensive lands of his father-in-law, William Fairfax, proprietor

Mary Ball Washington at the Age of About Four-Score. Photo mechanical print by Robert Edge Pine, 1730?–1788, originally published c. 1916 (Library of Congress).

of the neighboring plantation of Belvoir. Lawrence served with Fairfax at Cartagena, where he made the acquaintance of Admiral Edward Vernon, for whom he later named his house and farm — Mount Vernon. Lawrence was a rising force in the House of Burgesses and one of the leaders in the Ohio Company as well as a respected role model for his half brother. but "in 1751 he was stricken with tuberculosis. In an attempt to restore his health, he and George sailed to Barbados. Lawrence continued on to Bermuda before heading back to Virginia, where he died in 1752, a deep blow to the hero-worshiping George."[15]

Ancestors: The Washington family can be traced to 1183 in the village of Wessyngton[16] in northeast England, from which the Washingtons took their name. The name of the village had various spellings before evolving into Washington. Wessyngton comes from the Anglo Saxon: "Hwaes," a Saxon chief, "Inga," meaning family of, and "Tun," an estate — the estate of Hwaes (Wassa's). The first of George Washington's ancestors to live in the village was William. Surnames were not then in fashion, so landowners and nobles took the name of the property they owned. William de Wessyngton, who descended from the younger son of an ancient noble house, was the founder of another great line, which produced the first president of the United States.

During the English civil war, the Reverend Lawrence Washington, rector of Purleigh, Essex, was accused of being a "Malignant Royalist," and expelled from his post, greatly impoverishing his family.[17] They moved into Washington Old Hall, a small English manor house, where five generations of the family lived before moving south. In 1657, the Washingtons emigrated to Virginia, the first English colony in North America. English settlers had "visions of Virginia as a source of gold, a gateway to the Orient, and a base for plundering Spanish America."[18] Instead, they became planters, with tobacco as the basis of the colony's economy. Slaves brought from Africa provided much of the labor.

Appearance: As a young adult, Washington was an imposing figure, standing more than six feet tall — rare in colonial times — and weighing 175 pounds, growing to about 220 pounds as he matured. The only time his height was accurately determined was after his death, when the measurement was needed to make his coffin.[19] In 1760, a friend, George Mercer, wrote the following:

> He may be described as being straight as an Indian, measuring 6 feet 2 inches in his stockings.... A large and straight rather than a prominent nose, blue-grey penetrating eyes.... He has a clear though rather colorless pale skin with burns from the sun ... dark brown hair which he wears in a queue.... His mouth is large and generally firmly closed, but which from time to time discloses some defective teeth.... His movements and gestures are graceful, his walk majestic, and he is a splendid horseman.[20]

George's impressive size extended to his feet; he wore size 13 boots. His face was scarred from smallpox.[21] According to William Guthrie Sayen, writing in his doctoral dissertation, "George Washington's 'Unmannerly Behavior'" (1997), when ordering clothes from London GW described himself: "[I am] a Man full 6 feet high & proportionally made; if anything rather slender than thick for a Person of that height with pretty long arms & thighs."[22]

Sayen reported that GW took pains with his clothes, a trait that was particularly important in a time when apparel still announced one's standing with the precision of a military uniform. Washington refused to adopt the fashionable habit of wearing a powdered wig. Instead, he powdered his own hair.[23] Biographer James Thomas Flexner described GW as being "very tall for his generation — over six feet — with reddish hair and gray-blue eyes, his face massive, his shoulders narrow for his height but his hands and feet tremendous, George exuded such masculine power as frightens young women just wakening to the opposite sex."[24]

Today most people can only visualize Washington as he appears in the Gilbert Stuart portrait, seen on the dollar bill, depicting him as elderly, stiff and staid. As a younger man, his imposing stature, Roman nose and stern-faced visage made him stand out among his contemporaries and inspire confidence and loyalty in his soldiers and followers.[25] James C. Rees, executive director of Mount Vernon Estate and Gardens in Virginia, observed "[he was] the most robust, the most athletic, the most outdoorsy, and the most adventurous of all the founding fathers."[26]

Recently, efforts have been made to use a combination of technology, arts and science to re-create the face of Washington at age 19, when he was a land surveyor; at 45, during the Revolutionary War; and at 57, when he became president. There are no portraits of Washington as a young man. However, in 1784, the Virginia General Assembly commissioned Jean-Antoine Houdon, the preeminent sculptor of the time, to create "a monument of affection and gratitude."[27] Houdon spent three weeks at Mount Vernon with the fifty-three-year-old, recently retired General. The sculptor modeled a clay bust of Washington and also a life mask made of plaster, which he used to cast an impression of Washington's face. In 1796, Houdon delivered the life-sized statue of Washington, now displayed in the Virginia capitol, which most of his contemporaries remarked was a "perfect likeness."[28]

Researchers at Arizona State University and the University of Pittsburgh, using anthropology, 3-D scanning and digital reconstruction, have produced life-size figures that are believed to be the most realistic images yet of Washington at the three different ages. Mount

George Washington at Mount Vernon. Plaster bust by Jean-Antoine Houdon in 1786 (Library of Congress).

Vernon historians consulted records to create a database of descriptions of Washington and his clothes.[29] Scientists used computer modeling, built on laser scans of the life mask, bust and the statue, to "reverse the aging process by filling in teeth, adding fat to GW's cheeks and smoothing wrinkles. They also aged him slightly for one image.[30] Working with Mount Vernon experts, artists decided on the models' hair color, their shading, texture, length, and style — the skin tone and texture, eye color and the size of the pupils. They painted the models' facial skin and hands and implanted the reddish-brown hair strand by strand with a needle.[31]

Personality and Character: Washington was described as "a man of dignified reserve, one who did not reveal his true feelings easily. He kept his own counsel, and few had his confidence. In his youth, he was sober, quiet, attentive and dignified. His respect for his elders won him much admiration. If GW seemed rather humorless, it was because life to him was a serious business and required a sober nature."[32] George did not care for public speaking simply because he was not particularly adept at it. He much preferred to express himself in writing. GW could be "very intimidating in dealing with people, speaking candidly and looking them directly in the eye. He set

Forensic Reconstructions of George Washington. *Left:* Depicted at ages 57, 19, and 45. *Next page:* Depicted at ages 45 (top) and 57 (bottom). Courtesy of Mount Vernon Ladies' Association and Ivan Schwartz of StudioEIS.

his own strict rules of conduct, but he also enjoyed having a good time."[33] It was recalled that he "laughed at jokes, although he seldom told any. Washington was ambitious for wealth, and although not miserly, he made sure that he received every payment to which he believed he was entitled."[34]

According to William Sayen,

[While the future president] strove to embody the manners and virtues of civility, he also pursued honor, which was the ultimate goal for ambitious gentlemen. Over the 18th century, civility began increasingly to be identified with gentility [breeding], which was more than a style and a source of pleasure; it was a badge and an instrument of authority. By the mid–18th century, genteel conduct was at least as important as clothes in announcing one's status and making one welcomed in elite circles. Washington's breeding and pleasing manners, together with his handsome looks and impressive physique helped him rise socially, economically, and politically.[35]

Washington followed certain precepts, which he referred to in one source or another of his writings, in his life, his military career, and his presidency: "[First and foremost is to] understand exactly what the primary goal is that you are seeking to accomplish. Commit all your energies to it, however long it takes. Don't allow anyone or anything to distract you from the main purpose."[36]

Washington sought out those precepts which would help him to "discipline himself, to develop his character, and to make himself more presentable to society."[37] According to his contemporaries and biographers, he valued decorous manners and meticulously refined his own type of courteousness. GW was described ordinarily as extremely self-controlled, careful of both in speech and actions. He had a temper, which, for the most part, he kept under control. However, on a few notable occasions George was unable to hide his rage. Then his displeasure, his cursing, and his withering stares were unforgettable — not something anyone wanted to experience a second time. "His temper was naturally high-toned [that is, high-strung], but reflection and resolution had obtained a firm and habitual ascendency over it,"[38] wrote Thomas Jefferson.

"If ever, however, it broke its bonds, he was most tremendous in wrath." John Adams concurred. "He had great self-command ... but to preserve so much equanimity as he did require a great capacity. Whenever he lost his temper, as he did sometimes, either love or fear in those about him induced them to conceal his weakness from the world."[39]

Gouverneur Morris agreed that Washington had, "the tumultuous passions which accompany greatness and frequently tarnish its luster. With them was his first contest, and his first victory was over himself.... Yet those who have seen him strongly moved will bear witness that his wrath was terrible. They have seen, boiling in his bosom, passion almost too mighty for man."[40] It was unwise to trifle with Washington. Fisher Ames in his Eulogy of Washington, February 8, 1800, stated, "His preeminence is not so much to be seen in the display of any one virtue as in the possession of them all, and in the practice of the most difficult. Hereafter, therefore, his character must be studied as a model, a precious one to a free republic."[41]

In *Travels in North America* Marquis de Chastellux wrote as follows: "The strongest characteristic of this respectable man is the perfect harmony which reigns between the physical and moral qualities which compose his personality.... It is not my intention to exaggerate. I wish only to express the impression George Washington has left on my mind, the idea of a perfect whole."[42] Thomas Jefferson gave his own assessment of Washington:

> He errs as other men do, but errs with integrity.... His mind was great and powerful, without being of the very first order; his penetration strong, though, not so acute as that of a Newton, Bacon or Locke; and as far as he saw, no judgment was ever sounder. He was slow in operation, being little aided by invention or imagination, but sure in conclusion.... He was incapable of fear, meeting personal dangers with the calmest unconcern. Perhaps the strongest feature in his character was prudence, never acting until every circumstance, every consideration, was maturely weighed ... a wise, a good, and a great man.[43]

Washington biographer Joseph J. Ellis wrote: "It seemed to me that Benjamin Franklin was wiser than Washington; Alexander Hamilton was more brilliant; John Adams was better read; Thomas Jefferson was more intellectually sophisticated; James Madison was more politically astute. Yet each and all of these prominent figures acknowledged that Washington was their unquestioned superior. Within the gallery of greats so often mythologized and capitalized as Founding Fathers, Washington was recognized as primus inter pares, the Foundingest Father of them all."[44]

Marriage and Romances: In 1757, Colonel George Washington returned home from duty in the frontier to regain his health. Friends introduced him to Martha Dandridge Custis, reputedly the wealthiest widow in Virginia.[45] After making two visits to her home, George and Martha became engaged. "On their wedding day, Martha gave George a miniature portrait of herself that he wore on a chain around his neck until his death 40 years later."[46] They were married on January 6, 1759, in New Kent County, Virginia, at the bride's plantation home, which was known as the White House.[47] After spending a six-week honeymoon at Martha's home, Washington took his wife and her children to Williamsburg, where he served for the first time in the colonial legislature.

Martha was born at Chestnut Grove plantation in New Kent County, Virginia on June 2, 1731, the daughter of John Dandridge and Frances Jones Dandridge. Martha's father emigrated to Virginia from England with his older brother when he was 13 or 14 years old. Martha was the eldest of three brothers and five sisters. At age 17, "[Patsy, as she was called] was what the English called, a pocket Venus, a petite, cuddlesome armful. Barely five feet tall, she had the tiny hands and feet that were considered marks of gentility. With dark brown hair and strongly marked eyebrows, smooth white shoulders sloping down to full breasts, bright hazel eyes, and a ready smile displaying beautiful white teeth (a rarity for the time) she epitomized the feminine ideal for many Virginians."[48] At the age of 18, the petite, brown haired girl with lively flirtatious eyes married Colonel Daniel, Parke Custis, a man 21 years older. Custis' father at first vehemently opposed the match, considering the Dandridge family to be socially inferior to his. The couple had four children, two who died in infancy. Martha was only 26 years old when her husband suddenly died. He left a fortune of about 18,000 acres of land and 30,000 pounds, which was divided equally among his widow and their two children.[49] "She had to be careful in her choice of a second husband. At this time, she was a feme sole in English common law, free to make her own decisions about her property. Wealthy widows were the most economically and personally independent of all American women. Once she married, however; she would become a feme covert, her legal status, wealth, children, and place and manner of her life controlled by her husband."[50]

Combined with GW's holdings, the Washington family was one of the richest in the colonies. From the moment she and George spoke their vows, Martha's "great concern was the comfort and happiness of her husband and her children." When GW's path led him to the battlefields of the Revolutionary War, she followed to be with him.[51] As Martha was not cut out for public life, it was George who established a balance of dignity during the many dinners and receptions throughout the presidential years. George described Martha as "an agreeable Consort."[52] She did not enjoy the experience as the wife of the first President of the United States: "I think I am more like a state prisoner than anything else, there are certain bounds set for me which I must not depart from...."[53]

In 1797, the Washingtons said farewell to public life and returned to Mount Vernon, surrounded by friends and family and a steady stream of guests who came to pay their respect to the celebrated couple. More comfortable at home, Martha made her guests feel welcome and put strangers at ease. One of Washington's generals observed, "Mrs. Washington is excessively fond of the General and he of her. They are very happy in each other."[54]

Martha Washington, digital file from original print, no date recorded on shelflist card (Library of Congress).

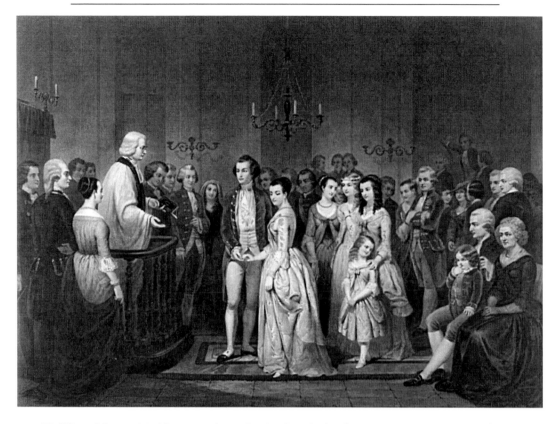

Wedding of George Washington and Martha Custis, painting by Junius Brutus Stearns. Lithograph by Régnier, imp. Lemercier, Paris, c. 1854 (Library of Congress).

Mrs. Washington survived her husband by three years. To guarantee her privacy even after her death, she burned their letters. Her death occurred on May 22, 1802, due to a "severe fever."[55] Both Washingtons are buried at Mount Vernon in an unpretentious tomb George had planned for them.

There is evidence that Martha may not have been the love of George's life. Many letters exist between Washington and Sarah Cary "Sally" Fairfax, the wife of his friend and neighbor George William Fairfax. From the time he first met 18-year-old Sally the shy 26-year-old Washington was infatuated with her. While on a military campaign against the French in 1755, Washington "initiated his flirtatious correspondence" with her. There is no evidence that their relationship ever moved beyond friendship, but "in his letters he cryptically declared his love" for her. One epistle was addressed "to one whose life is now inseparable from mine" and was signed "your ever faithful and affectionate friend."[56]

On September 12, 1758, George, by this time engaged to Martha, wrote to Sally: "You have drawn me, dear Madam; or rather I have drawn myself, into an honest confession of a simple fact. Misconstrue not my meaning; doubt it not, nor expose it. The world has no business to know the object of my Love, declared in this manner to you, when I want to conceal it."[57] Depending on how one interprets the letters between George and Sally, the relationship may be seen as a mild flirtation or something more serious and intimate. Perhaps it is well that Washington was not more successful with Sally. She and her husband were loyal to the crown and left America to spend the rest of their lives in England after the Revolutionary War. Forty years later, when Sally was a widow living in England, GW sent her a letter in which he confessed that he had "never been able to eradicate from my mind those happy moments, the happiest in my life, which I have enjoyed in your company."[58] Before his marriage to Martha, Washington also courted 16-year-old Betsy Fauntleroy, who twice turned down his marriage proposals when he was twenty.[59] Then there was 26-year-old Mary Philipse, whom he wished to make his wife when he was 24, but lacked the courage to ask her. Perhaps it was some consolation for him that, during the Revolutionary War, GW made his headquarters at the Brooklyn Heights home of Colonel Morris, a Tory who fled to England with his wife, the former Mary Philipse.[60] The discretion and innocence of Washington's affection for Sally, as well as for Betsy and Mary, are rather sweet and quaint when compared with the raunchy pursuits and captures of women by later presidents. However, scholars and others have long pounced on any hints of romances or infidelities of this man with passion and lust for life. In addition to those already mentioned, the names of Lucy Grymes, Mary Bland, Kitty Greene, Lucy Flucker Knox, Elizabeth Gates, Theodosia Prevost Burr, Kitty Duer, Phoebe Fraunces, Eliza Powell, Mrs. William Bingham, Mrs. Perez Morton and even the Marchioness de Lafayette had been rumored to have had romances of some degree or another with the general.[61]

Much used to be made of the possible double meaning of the phrase "George Washington slept here!" Kitty Greene was the beautiful wife of Nathaniel Greene, Washington's most trusted general. Allegedly, Kitty had a thing for Generals, as she is believed to have had affairs with several, including "Mad Anthony" Wayne and Lafayette.[62] Once, at a party held at Greene's home, Kitty's dance card showed that she saved every dance for the general, who wasn't her husband. Later that evening, Washington sent Greene on a mission a far distance off to meet with someone for some reason. George stayed behind with Kitty. Nathaniel accepted the errand, but no one showed up. He noted that it was a "wild-goose chase."[63]

As Jimmy Carter did much later, GW admitted to lusting after females, defending himself by saying, "Once the woman has tempted us and we have tasted the forbidden fruit, there is no such thing as checking our appetites, whatever the consequences may be."[64] On one occasion, Washington spoke of the nature of love:

> Love is said to be an involuntary passion, and it is, therefore, contended that it cannot be resisted. This is true in part only, for like all things else, when nourished and supplied plentiful with aliment, it is rapid in its progress; but let these be withdrawn and it may be stifled in its birth or much stinted in its growth…. Hence it follows, that love may and therefore ought to be under the guidance of reason, for although we cannot avoid first impressions, we may assuredly place them under guard.[65]

The General was well aware that wedded life, as marvelous as it was, was not always blissful: "I have always considered marriage as the most interesting event of one's life, the foundation of happiness or misery."[66]

Children: George and Martha had no children, but he helped raise his two stepchildren, John Parke "Jackie" Custis and Martha Parke "Patsy" Custis. Patsy expired in her stepfather's arms in 1773 — a victim of epilepsy. Jackie joined Washington during the siege of Yorktown. Two weeks after the British surrender, the young man died at age 26 of "camp fever," which was perhaps meningitis.[67] Martha and George Washington raised two of their grandchildren, Eleanor Parke Custis (Nelly) and George Washington Parke Custis (called "Wash" or "Tub"). Two of GW's nephews made names for themselves in public service. "Bushrod Washington became an Associate Justice of the Supreme Court. Burwell Basset was a longtime official in both the Virginia legislature and the U.S. Congress."[68]

Religion and Religious Beliefs: As an infant GW was baptized into the Church of England. Affiliation with this state religion was one of the requirements for office in the House of Burgesses. Washington was a lifelong member of the Anglican Church in Virginia, becoming a vestryman for Truro Parikh in Fairfax County, Virginia, in 1761.[69] According to his diaries, after the revolution Washington attended a Christian Church irregularly. Throughout his life, Washington spoke of the value of righteousness, and of seeking and offering thanks for the "blessings of Heaven."[70] While he often spoke of God and Providence, there are few existing sources in which he speaks of Jesus, Christ, or Christianity.[71] The question of the religious beliefs of the Father of His Country has engendered many investigations and publications. It is as if Washington's views on religion and God are of paramount importance in understanding the nature of the nation he helped found, and perhaps they are.

It is evident from Washington's diaries that the older he became the less use he had for attending church. His spiritual life was not marked with "enthusiasm."[72] He did not call for a minister to attend him on his deathbed. Among the comprehensive records of Washington's final hours, no reference is made to any religious words or prayers or hope of meeting again in heaven. Whether or not Washington was a Christian, he acted and spoke like a Deist.[73] Yet; the earliest biographies of Washington portrayed him as a man endowed with Christian values and something of a secular saint. Later biographers differed in their opinions of Washington's religious beliefs.

In *The Forge of Experience*, James Thomas Flexner quoted the president on religion:

> In 1793, Washington thus summarized the religious philosophy he was evoking during his Mount Vernon years. How happenings would "terminate is known only to the great ruler of events; and confiding in his wisdom and goodness, we may safely trust to him, without perplexing ourselves to seek for that which is beyond human ken, only taking care to perform the parts assigned to us in a way that reason and our own conscience approve of." George Washington was, like Benjamin Franklin and Thomas Jefferson, a deist.[74]

In *George Washington: The Making of an American Symbol*, Barry Schwartz wrote of the dichotomy of views of GW's religious faith: "George Washington's conduct convinced most Americans that he was a good Christian, but those possessing first-hand knowledge of his religious convictions had reasons to doubt."[75] Paul Boller, in *George Washington & Religion*, addresses the Issue of Washington's religious creed:

> [I]f to believe in the divinity and resurrection of Christ and his atonement for the sins of man and to participate in the sacrament of the Lord's Supper are requisites for the Christian faith, then Washington, on the evidence which we have examined, can hardly be considered a Christian, except in the most nominal sense.... Washington was no infidel, if by infidel is meant unbeliever. Washington had an unquestioning faith in Providence and, as we have seen, he voiced this faith publicly on numerous occasions. That this was no mere rhetorical flourish on his part, designed for public consumption, is apparent from his constant allusions to Providence in his personal letters. There is every reason to believe, from a careful analysis of religious references in his private correspondence, that Washington's reliance upon a Great Designer along Deist lines was as deep-seated and meaningful for his life as, say, Ralph Waldo Emerson's serene confidence in a Universal Spirit permeating the ever shifting appearances of the everyday world.[76]

In volume 12 of *The Writings of George Washington* (1834–1837), historian and clergyman Jared Sparks delved into the religious nature of Washington, and based on many letters written by friends, associates and relatives of the president, concluded the following:

To say that he was not a Christian would be to impeach his sincerity and honesty. Of all men in the world, Washington was certainly the last whom any one would charge with dissimulation or indirectedness [hypocrisies and evasiveness]; and if he was so scrupulous in avoiding even a shadow of these faults in every known act of his life, [regardless of] however unimportant, is it likely, is it credible, that in a matter of the highest and most serious importance [his religious faith, that] he should practice through a long series of years of deliberate deception upon his friends and the public? It is neither credible nor possible.[77]

Washington's most religious statement appeared in a circular letter:

I now make it my earnest prayer, that God would have you and the State over which you preside, in his holy protection, that he would incline the hearts of the Citizens to cultivate a spirit of subordination and obedience to Government, to entertain a brotherly affection and love for one another, for their fellow Citizens of the United States at large, and particularly for their brethren who have served in the Field, and finally, that he would most graciously be pleased to dispose us all, to do Justice, to love mercy, and to demean ourselves with that Charity, humility and pacific temper of mind, which were the Characteristics of the Divine Author of our blessed Religion, and without an humble imitation of whose example in these things, we can never hope to be a happy Nation.[78]

In 1831, the Rev. Dr. Wilson published a revealing episode with respect to Washington and the sacrament of the Lord's Supper. The report was based on a letter of the Rev. Dr. James Abercrombie, rector of St. Peter's Church in Philadelphia, which President and Mrs. Washington attended. "On the days when the sacrament of the Lord's Supper was administered, Washington's custom was to arise just before the ceremony commenced and leave the church. Many in the congregation felt the president was setting a bad example. Abercrombie chose to address the matter in his sermon, with a direct allusion to the president. Washington was angered by the rebuke and was heard to say that henceforth neither the doctor nor his congregation would ever again be bothered by a repeat of the incidence, and from then on Washington did not attend church on days that communion was to be distributed."[79]

During the Revolutionary War, General Washington expressed his displeasure when some of his soldiers attempted to celebrate the British holiday of Guy Fawkes Day by burning the pope in effigy.[80] Washington supported troops selecting their own chaplains, trying to avoid the spread of factions within the army. Religion offered him moral leverage to instill discipline, reduce criminal behavior, discourage desertion and minimize rambunctious behavior by the soldiers that upset local residents.[81] In a letter to the Marquis de Lafayette on August 15, 1787, Washington commented on the importance of religious tolerance: "I am not less ardent in my wish that you may succeed in your plan of toleration in religious matters. Being no bigot myself to any mode of worship, I am disposed to indulge the professors of Christianity in the church with that road to Heaven which to them shall seem the most direct, plainest and easiest, and the least liable to exception."[82]

President Washington reached out to various religious groups, assuring them that they would be allowed to practice their beliefs without any governmental interference. In 1790, he sent the following message to Catholics: "As mankind becomes more liberal, they will be more able to allow that those who conduct themselves as worthy members of the community are equally entitled to the protection of civil government. I hope ever to see America among the foremost nations in examples of justice and liberality."[83] In an address to the Jewish worshippers of Newport, Rhode Island, Washington stated: "May the children of the stock of Abraham, who dwell in this land, continue to merit and enjoy the good will of the other inhabitants; while everyone shall sit under his own wine and fig tree, and there shall be none to make him afraid."[84] And in a September 28, 1789, letter to Quakers, he said, "Government being, among other purposes, instituted to protect the consciences of men from oppression, it is certainly the duty of rulers, not only to abstain from it themselves but, according to their stations, to prevent it in others.... The liberty enjoyed by the people of these States of worshipping Almighty God, agreeably to their consciences, is not only among the choicest of their blessings, but also of their rights."[85]

GW expressed his views on the separation of church and state in a May 1789 letter to the United Baptist Chamber of Virginia: "Every man, conducting himself as a good citizen, and being accountable to God alone for his religious opinions, ought to be protected in worshiping the Deity according to the dictates of his own conscience."[86]

Education: Washington received most of his early schooling from his father and his half brother Lawrence. He attended a nearby churchyard school, after which he was sent to boarding school at a distance of some 30 miles. Undoubtedly he would have been sent to England for further education like his older half brothers had it not been for his father's untimely death.[87] GW demonstrated an exceptional interest and aptitude for mathematics, which he would later extol: "The investigation of mathematical truths accustoms the mind to method and correctedness in reasoning, and is an employment peculiarly worthy of rational beings.... From the high ground of mathematical and philosophical demonstration, we are insensibly led to far nobler and sublime meditations."[88]

Unlike many gentlemen's sons, George was not taught Latin and Greek, and he never learned a foreign language. His writing and grammar were poor. Throughout his life Washington considered his "education to be defective," but he attempted to make up for what he did not learn in school through reading and self-study. GW amassed a large and diverse library of some 900 books. He expressed how highly he valued books: "I conceive that a knowledge of books is the basis on which all other knowledge rests."[89] Washington believed strongly in the importance of a quality education and left money in his will for establishing a school in Alexandria, Virginia, as well as for a national university. Biographer Peter Lillback wrote: "Although [he] never received a college education, given his disciplined and methodical temperament, he never stopped learning. Washington's continual self-improvement by reading, experimenting, and correspondence continued his education."[90]

Washington learned social graces, including polite conversation, proper table manners, and refined entertaining, from his mother, his half brother and his sister-in-law, and their neighbors the Fairfaxes. By age sixteen, he had copied *110 Rules of Civility & Decent Behavior in Company and Conversation* from an old translation of a set of rules composed by French Jesuits in 1595.[91] These rules had a profound influence on him throughout his life. The rules he learned proclaimed that respect for others gave one dignity and heightened confidence in turn. GW acquired a strong desire always to do what was right and honorable.[92]

Home: According to Augustine Washington's will, his plantation, on the Potomac River, was to be passed on to George if his half brother Lawrence died without issue. By a 1754 agreement with Lawrence's widow, George took over the management of the estate, paying his sister-in-law annual rent until she died in 1769.[93] His marriage to Martha increased his land holdings by some 6,000 acres. The mansion at Mount Vernon was decorated with bright wall colors, art and furniture, attesting to the Washingtons' sense of fashion. The estate was divided into five farms, each being a complete unit with its own overseers, slave work force, livestock, equipment and buildings. The plantation's vast gardens included a wide variety of flowers and trees. The lower garden supplied fresh produce and herbs for the kitchen. Washington used the fruit garden and nursery to experiment with different seeds and plants before using them elsewhere on his estate.[94] Among the fruits grown were apples, pears, plums, peaches, cherries and grapes.

Family Motto: *Exitus acta probat* "Issues proveth acts" (sort of "The end justifies the means").[95] GW had sufficient family pride to have a Washington coat of arms imprinted on his bookplate and he employed a seal, using it on many of his letters. He placed a large wooden carving of the crest on a wall at Mount Vernon.

Pets and Animals: Washington bred hounds, which he treated as members of the family. Among these were Mopsey, Drunkard, Vulcan, Truman, Jupiter, Sweet Lips, True Love and Tarter. He was extremely fond of horses, maintaining a large stable, and actively participated in all facets of horsemanship, including trading, buying, selling, breeding, racing, training, hunting, carriage, and draft work. His horses included Arabian, Andalusian and Chincoteague ponies.[96] In 1788, he traded his prize Arabian, "Magnolia," to Light Horse Harry Lee for 5,000 acres of land in the Kentucky territory. GW's favorite mount was a white horse named "Nelson," which, along with "Blueskin," was his war horse.[97]

Recreational Pastimes and Interests: General Washington played the game of cricket with his troops at Valley Forge.[98] He was an accomplished dancer and loved agreeable conversation. Gambling "infatuated" him, and he attended cockfights. He enjoyed card games; his favorite was known as Loo, played for a pool made up of stakes and forfeits. Washington was extremely fond of fox hunting, and playing and collecting marbles. At the time, marbles were called "small bowls" and were equally popular with adults and children. George loved attending and helping fight fires,[99] even late into his life. His favorite foods included string

Mount Vernon, the Home of George Washington, lithograph print drawn from a sketch by Kern, executed by Middleton, Strobridge & Co., Cincinnati, Ohio, published c. 1861 (Library of Congress).

beans with mushrooms, cream of peanut soup, and mashed sweet potatoes with coconut. He was so fond of ice cream that he had "ice boxes" of the delicacy filled for his family and guests. It is estimated that they consumed thousands of gallons over the years.[100] His favorite play was *Cato* by Joseph Addison. It is the story of Cato the Younger, a foe of Julius Caesar, who loved Rome and its Republican virtues so strongly that, seeing that he could not stop the conquering Caesar, he took his own life rather than outlast liberty.[101]

Occupations

Surveyor: At age 16, George, an apprentice surveyor, "accompanied George William Fairfax and James Genn, surveyor of Prince William County, on a month-long trip west" to the Shenandoah Valley, located between the Blue Ridge and Allegheny mountains. The expedition was made on behalf of Thomas Lord Fairfax, 6th Baron Cameron and marked the "beginning of a lifelong relationship between Washington and the powerful Fairfax family."[102] The party rode on horseback for days, exploring the wilderness and sleeping in the open rolled up in blankets. At seventeen, largely through the influence of the Fairfax family, Washington secured an appointment as the surveyor of the newly created frontier county of Culpeper, which set him well on his way to a successful and profitable career. Surveying was a valuable skill in a colony where land constantly was being settled. During his three years on the frontier, GW gained a reputation for "fairness, honesty and dependability."[103]

In 1749, Washington helped lay out the Virginia town of Belhaven, now Alexandria, on the Potomac River. Three years later, he made his first land acquisition, 1,459 acres along Bullskin Creek, in Frederick County, Virginia. Over the next half century, Washington sought out, purchased and eventually settled numerous properties. In his will, he "listed 52,194 acres to be sold or distributed in Virginia, Pennsylvania, Maryland, New York, Kentucky, and the Ohio Valley." He also held the title to lots in the "Virginia cities of Winchester, Bath (now Berkeley Springs, West Virginia), and Alexandria," as well as in the newly founded city of Washington.[104] Concerned by the lack of accurate maps, as commander-in-chief of the Continental Army he created the post of Geographer of the Continental Army and appointed Scottish engineer and inventor Robert Erskine to the office.[105]

Planter and Farmer: Whatever other assignments he took, be it soldier, general or president, Washington saw himself first as a farmer and planter. He once confessed, "I had rather be on my farm than be emperor of the world."[106] GW took immense pride in this profession, writing in a letter to his manager, William Pearce: "I shall begrudge no reasonable expense that will contribute to the improvement & neatness of my Farms, for nothing pleases me better than to see them in good order, and everything trim, handsome & thriving about them; nor nothing hurts me more than to find them otherwise."[107]

From the time of his return to Mount Vernon after the Revolutionary War until his death, GW conducted an intensive scientific agriculture program for his farms. He declared in a letter to John Sinclair on July 20, 1794: "I know of no pursuit in life which more real and important services can be rendered to any country than by improving agriculture, its breed of useful animals, and other branches of a husbandman's care."[108] GW's crop rotations, use of fertilizers, experimentations with farm products, and innovative equipment made him a "pioneer of modern agriculture."[109] He realized that soil exhaustion as a consequence of one-crop agriculture was edging the Virginia farms towards disaster. He was determined to find the right items to grow for the soil, climate, and practical needs of his plantation.

George experimented with "drill culture instead of broadcasting the seed; he varied the distance between rows; he tried different rates of seeding," and he meticulously recorded everything in his diaries. Seeking to be free from single-crop farming, GW experimented with or grew "more than sixty field crops," including alfalfa, chicory, buckwheat, hemp, hop clover, Jerusalem artichoke, corn, barley, turnips, cabbage, burnet, clover, carrots, flax, millet, oats, orchard grass, peas, potatoes, pumpkins, rye, spelt, timothy and wheat.[110]

When Washington drastically reduced production of his cash crop, tobacco, he ceased being a planter and was a farmer. He tried "different kinds of plows and had a compelling interest in breeding livestock." He raised critters to provide strong work animals as well as wool, leather, meat, milk, butter, and, important to a farmer, fertilizer. GW normally raised 600 to 1000 head of sheep, chickens, ducks, geese, and an uncertain number of hogs. Cattle were raised both as oxen and for meat.[111] George took a dim view of horses on his farms, complaining that they "ate too much, worked too little, and died too young." Washington decided to breed mules, the sterile offspring of a male donkey and a female horse, because they were stronger, more sure-footed, ate less and had more endurance than horses.[112] The king of Spain provided GW with a stud donkey, which Washington named "Royal Gift."[113] The Marquis de La Fayette sent him another stud donkey, "The Knight of Malta."[114] Washington bred his "best mares to these jacks and sent them on a tour" of the south to develop a selective breeding program. He had 58 mules at Mount Vernon. Mules were soon working

George Washington standing among African American field workers harvesting grain with Mt. Vernon in background. Lithograph by Régnier, c. 1853, from a painting by Junius Brutus Stearns (Library of Congress).

on the land across the continent and served in the armed forces until the time of the Korean War.[115]

Between 1792 and 1795 Washington fully developed his plans for a barn complex at Dogue Run, one of the four working farms on his estate. His new barn, which served for grain processing and storage, consisted of a circular wooden treading floor large enough to accommodate horses and confine them from the weather. The treading floor was on the second level of the two-story, 16-sided structure, which the horses accessed via an earthen ramp. Washington "left spaces between the floorboards so that the heads of grain, once separated from the straw, could fall through to the granary below." There they were temporarily stored in a central octagonal structure, winnowed and sent to the mill.[116]

As part of Washington's vision of America as the "granary to the world,"[117] he built a water-powered grist mill. His farm manager convinced him that producing whiskey made from corn and rye grown on the plantation was a natural complement to his milling enterprise, as it was relatively easy to make. GW erected a "2,250 square foot distillery," the largest in America. In the last year of his life, the distillery "11,000 gallons of whiskey," worth at the time the substantial sum of $7,500. By the end of the Revolution, whiskey had replaced rum as the most popular alcoholic drink in America.[118]

Washington was up every morning at four to inspect his farms before sunrise, at which time "he expected all workers to be at their posts." He extolled the virtues of manure. His experiments with mulch extended to animal dung, marl, green crops plowed under, and mud from the Potomac River bottom.[119] A growing shortage of timber used for making rail fences led GW to build live hedges for barriers. "He tried honey locust, Lombardy poplar, cedar, and some of the hundreds of species of thorned trees and shrubs." However, he was forced to admit failure, convinced that no live hedge would turn back a hog.[120]

MILITARY SERVICE

Soldier: At age 20 Washington was appointed to head a Virginia expedition to deliver a letter from Colonial Governor Robert Dinwiddie challenging French claims to the Allegheny River Valley in Pennsylvania. That same year he published his diary of the adventure, *The Journal of Major George Washington*.[121] He gained additional command experience during the French and Indian War, which he put to excellent use when he became commander-in-chief of the American army.[122] At his death, Washington held the rank of major general and in ensuing years many military men outranked him. In 1976, President Gerald Ford posthumously appointed Washington General of the Armies of the United States, and specified that he would always outrank all officers of the army, past and future.[123] Washington was offered the title during his lifetime, but declined, believing in doing so he would usurp the president of the United States as commander-in-chief of the Army and Navy.

The French and Indian War: The determination of both France and Great Britain to secure and hold the supremacy of the Mississippi Valley led to a military contest between them. During his mission to the French to deliver the colonial governor's letter, Washington and his men endured extreme hardships, and endangerment of their lives. Washington completed his assignment in the middle of January 1754 when he brought Dinwiddie the French reply, along with his own report and a map of the region. In April–May 1754,[124] at age 22, with the rank of lieutenant colonel, GW led the Virginia forces to challenge the French at Fort Duquesne in the upper Ohio River Valley, where he built Fort Necessity at

Washington Appointed Commander in Chief, hand-colored lithograph published by Currier & Ives, c. 1876 (Library of Congress).

Great Meadows, Pennsylvania.[125] By mistake Washington killed a French ambassador, the first victim of what would be the Seven Years War, also known as the French and Indian War. English writer Horace Walpole said, "The volley fired by a young Virginian in the backwoods of America set the world on fire."[126]

Late in May, Washington's forces defeated a French scouting party but when he pulled his small force back to Fort Necessity, it was overwhelmed in a day-long battle fought in a drenching rain. Surrounded by superior numbers, his food supply almost exhausted and his dampened ammunition useless, Washington was forced to surrender. Under the terms of the capitulation, he was "allowed to march his troops back to Williamsburg. Discouraged by his defeat and angered by the discrimination between British and colonial officers in rank and pay,"[127] GW resigned his commission in October 1754.[128] The following year, he served as volunteer aide-de-camp to British general Edward Braddock and marched with him and British regulars against the French at Fort Duquesne.[129]

That July, the French and their Indian allies ambushed the English at the Monongahela River. Braddock was killed and Washington nearly so, having two horses shot from under him.[130] He reported in a letter to his mother: "I heard the bullets whistle and believe me, there is something charming in the sound."[131] When the British monarch read the report, he observed: "He would not say so, if he had been used to hearing many."[132]

Even in defeat, Washington "achieved recognition in official circles for bravery under fire." The governor gave Washington a "commission as colonel and commander-in-chief of all the forces raised in Virginia" for the protection of the frontier.[133] GW was frustrated by the struggle to organize forces for the defense of the region without the means with which to do so. He wrote numerous letters in an effort to convince authorities to provide him with the resources to do his job.[134]

When William Pitt became English prime minister, the tide of war in America favored the British. Sizable military forces were sent to the colonies backed by a strong naval presence, not matched by the French forces in America, who, abandoned by their Indian allies, were left to fend for themselves.[135] After the defeat of the French at Fort Duquesne (renamed Fort Pitt, the site of today's Pittsburgh), by General Forbes' troops, with Washington's command playing an active role, the border troubles ended. Washington returned to Virginia, where he left the army in 1758 to attend to his neglected estate. During this first military experience GW matured from a "brash, vain, and opinionated young officer" to a commander with a "fine grasp of administration" and the craft of "dealing effectively with civil authority."[136]

The Fairfax Resolves: Back home at Mount Vernon, Washington entered politics and was a leader in Virginia's opposition to Great Britain's colonial policies. On July 17, 1774, George Mason and Patrick Henry visited him at his home to discuss the emerging American plight. As a result, a statement was drafted, written mainly by Mason, which subsequently was adopted at a Fairfax County Convention, chaired by Washington on July 18, 1774, at Alexandria. Known as the Fairfax Resolves,[137] they were statements of fundamental constitutional rights and a revolutionary call to boycott British imports: "[We] cannot be considered as a conquered Country [because we are] Descendants not of the Conquered, but of the Conquerors."[138]

The resolves asserted American claims to equal rights under the British constitution, including representation in Parliament, control over taxation, military forces within their borders, judicial powers and commercial actions. "The citizens' protest meeting was one of many throughout the colonies called to challenge Britain's harsh retaliatory measures against Massachusetts in the aftermath of the Boston Tea Party. Washington and Mason boldly called for a general Congress, for the preservation of our Lives Liberties and Fortunes."[139] Americans came to realize that a threat against one colony, such as was occurring in Massachusetts with the imposition of the Coercive Acts as punishment for the "Boston Tea Party and other acts of defiance," was a threat to all.[140] And so the colonies formed the Continental Congress.

THE REVOLUTIONARY WAR

As a "delegate to the First and Second Continental congresses, Washington did not actively participate" in the deliberations, but his presence was a stabilizing influence. In June 1775,[141] Congress made him its "unanimous choice as commander-in-chief of the Continental forces."[142] Washington promised his wife that he would return safely to her in the fall, but except for one brief visit he did not reappear at Mount Vernon for six years.[143] GW took command of the troops surrounding British-occupied Boston on July 3, 1775. For the next several months, he trained his undisciplined 14,000-man army and scavenged for scarce gun powder, cannons and other supplies. Early in March Washington forced the British to evacuate Boston, and then he moved to defend New York City against the combined land and sea forces of Sir William Howe.[144] Washington blundered by occupying an untenable position in Brooklyn. Fortunately he saved his army by skillfully retreating from Manchester into Westchester County and across New Jersey into Pennsylvania.[145]

The general's problems multiplied as enlistments for many of his troops were almost completed and as many others were deserting. Civilian morale was as low as that of the troops.[146] Fearing an imminent British attack, Congress quit the city of Philadelphia.[147] GW commanded a ragtag army against a trained and veteran British force. He was out-gunned, out-numbered, and out-generaled. Washington protested about the lack of support for his troops: "The Army, as usual, are without pay; and a great part of the Soldiery without shirts; and tho' the patience of them is equally thread bear, the States seem perfectly indifferent to their cries."[148]

As a veteran of the French and Indian War, Washington practiced guerrilla-like operations rather than direct confrontations with the enemy on a field awaiting an order to charge. His plan was to harass, not attack, the British. Battles between the two armies saw Washington's troops slowly fall back, and then strike unexpectedly.[149] Washington knew that tactics and formations had to be adapted to terrain. He believed that an effective leader pays close attention to administrative detail, discovers how to make do with limited resources, and seeks to promote the welfare of his men. The two sides adopted different strategies. The English concentrated on occupying urban settings and sought set battles. Washington concluded that his best strategy was not to be drawn into a direct confrontation with the English troops, unless compelled to do so by a necessity. His strategy was to conduct a campaign of attrition.[150] He even formulated a set of rules by which he measured and directed the actions of his Army.

> Never attack a position in front which you can gain by turning.
> Charges of Cavalry should be made if possible on the flanks of infantry.
> The first qualification of a soldier is fortitude under fatigue and privation.
> Courage is only the second. Hardship, poverty and actual want are the soldier's best school.
> Nothing is so important in war as an undivided command.
> Never do what the enemy wishes you to do.
> A General of ordinary talent, occupying a bad position and surprised by superior force, seeks safety in retreat; but a great captain supplies all deficiencies by his courage and marches boldly to meet the attack.[151]

He emphasized preserving forces and biding his time, avoiding major defeats and acting decisively when the opportunity for surprise arose, as in the crossing of the Delaware on Christmas night in 1776. General Washington led some 2400 men in large ore-carrying Durham boats across the Delaware River at McKonkey's Ferry, Pennsylvania, and made a surprise attack, defeating the British and Hessian mercenaries at Trenton, New Jersey.[152] The success of the venture came at a time when morale was at its lowest point and it renewed hope among the army, Congress and the American people.[153] Among those accompanying Washington in the crossing were James Monroe, a future president, Aaron Burr, a future vice president, John Marshall, a future chief justice of the U.S. and Alexander Hamilton, the first U.S. secretary of the treasury.

Washington demanded that his troops treat any prisoners fairly and refrain from doing injury to them in any way. On September 14, 1775, he charged the Northern Expeditionary Force: "Should any American soldier be so base and infamous as to injure any [prisoner].... I do most earnestly enjoin you to bring him to such severe and exemplary punishment as the enormity of the crime may require. Should it extend to death itself, it will not be disproportional to its guilt at such a time and in such a cause ... for by such conduct they bring shame, disgrace and ruin to themselves and their country."[154] After the Battle of Trenton on Christmas Day, 1776, the "Continentals were preparing to run some of the British Empire's German mercenaries through what they called the 'gauntlet.' General Washington discovered this and intervened," and issued the order: "Treat them with humanity, and let them have no reason to complain of our copying the brutal example of the British Army in their treatment of our unfortunate brethren who have fallen into their hands."[155]

There were few classic victories during Washington's eight years in the field. At Long Island and Brandywine, where he did try to face the main British force, he was fortunate to escape with his army intact. Pitched battles were not the deciding factors in the victory of the new United States. It was the ability of the former colonies to outlast the British.[156] Before engaging the British in the Battle of Long Island, Washington addressed his troops on August 27, 1776:

> The time is now near at hand which must probably determine whether Americans are to be freemen or slaves; whether they are to have any property they can call their own; whether their houses and farms are to be pillaged and destroyed, and themselves consigned to a state of wretchedness from which no human efforts will deliver them. The fate of unborn millions will now depend, under God, on the courage and conduct of this army. Our cruel and unrelenting enemy leaves us only the choice of brave resistance, or the most abject submission. We have therefore, to resolve to conquer or die.[157]

John Adams, who was protective of his role in forming the new nation, was often critical of the achievements of others, even Washington: "The history of our Revolution will be one continued lie from one end to the other. The essence of the whole will be that Dr. Franklin's electrical rod smote the earth and out sprang George Washington. That Franklin electrified him with his rod and thenceforward there to conduct all the policies, negotiations, legislatures and war."[158]

Assassination Plot: As commander-in-chief Washington had to put down mutinies in his ranks as well as fighting British soldiers and Tory Loyalists. In 1776, a plot was uncovered to kidnap and murder General Washington and his chief officers and launch an insurrection against the revolutionaries. The three Tory leaders were colonial governor William Tryon, New York City mayor David Matthews, and Long Island's Richard Hewlett. They persuaded Private Thomas Hickey — newly appointed to Washington's personal guard — to deliver Washington into their hands. The plot fell apart and Matthews took refuge in a British merchant ship anchored in New York's harbor. Hewlett hid in the countryside until the British rescued him. The mayor was jailed and Hickey was found guilty of treason and publicly hanged on June 28, 1776, before nearly 20,000 Continental soldiers.[159] In a letter to Henry Laurens, president of Congress, Washington wrote: "I am hopeful this example will produce many salutary consequences, and deter others from entering into like traitorous practices."[160] Had the scheme succeeded, Washington and his officers likely would have been treated as traitors to the Crown and their fate would be hanging and their property confiscated.

The Conway Cabal: As the Revolutionary War moved into its critical phase — and General Washington's victories were few — there was a movement to replace him with General Gates, the hero of Saratoga. The matter came to a head in October 1777 when Congress considered promoting Irish soldier of fortune Brigadier General Thomas Conway, a confidant of Gates, to major-general. Learning of the proposal, Washington wrote to Congressman Richard Henry Lee warning against an appointment of an officer whose "importance in the army exists more in his own imagination than in reality."[161] He issued a veiled threat: "I have undergone more than most men are aware of, to harmonize so many discordant parts. It will be impossible for me to be of any further service, if such insuperable difficulties are thrown in my way."[162]

Informed of Washington's opposition, Conway distributed outrageous letters accusing

Washington of "recent disasters." The anti–Washington movement was known as the Conway Cabal.[163] The junta realized the effort to remove Washington would incur the wrath of his French friend the Marquis de Lafayette and jeopardize French cooperation. The conspirators invited Lafayette to dinner, where many toasts to the need for strong leadership were given. The Frenchman rose to announce, "Gentlemen, one toast, I perceive has been omitted, which I will now propose: To the commander-in-chief of the American Armies."[164] The cabal members responded coldly to the salutation but knew their schemes were unattainable.[165] Conway resigned and Gates apologized and went on to participate in the final victory at Yorktown.

Valley Forge: A valley in eastern Pennsylvania served as headquarters for the Continental Army in the winter of 1777-1778. General Washington and his troops were forced to exit Philadelphia and for six bitter months his hungry, cold, ragged, and cramped command suffered. In an April 21, 1778, letter to John Banister, GW spoke of the pitiful conditions:

> No history, now extant, can furnish an instance of the Army's suffering such uncommon hardships as ours has done and bearing them with the same patience and fortitude. To see men without clothes to cover their nakedness, without blankets to lay on, without shoes, by which their marches might be traced by the blood from their feet, and almost as often without provisions as with; marching through frost and snow, and at Christmas taking up their winter quarters within a day's march of the enemy, without a house or hut to cover them till they could be built and submitting without a murmur, is a mark of patience and obedience which in my opinion can scarce be paralleled.[166]

Though many deserted, the general managed to maintain the morale of the rest. No military battles were fought at Valley Forge, but it, nevertheless, was a great victory for Washington.

Valley Forge, 1777. General Washington and Lafayette visiting the part of the army suffering at Valley Forge, painted and lithograph drawn by A. Gilbert; published by P. Haas, 1843 (Library of Congress).

In a letter to Governor George Clinton, he proudly proclaimed: "Naked and starving as they are we cannot enough admire the incomparable patience and fidelity of the soldiery."[167]

During this period of deprivation, Baron von Steuben, a German officer on Washington's staff, trained the men in the soldiering practices of Europe. To alleviate his men's suffering, Washington organized a monumental cattle drive. Agents were sent throughout New England, Maryland and Delaware to buy herds of cattle, which were then driven to Valley Forge, some coming from as far away as 250 miles. The trickle of cattle arriving at Washington's camp grew until 1000 head were arriving each week. After three months of desperate shortages of just about everything, there followed three months of relative abundance, which led to improved morale and fighting capabilities of the troops.[168]

Surrender: Washington's main force was employed to neutralize the English army in New York while sapping the enemy's strength and resolve in other areas, principally in the south. Campaigns in Virginia and the Carolinas were carried out by other generals, including Nathaniel Greene and Daniel Morgan, but "Washington was still responsible for the overall direction of the war and in coordinating allied efforts." Washington has not been praised for being a tactical commander or even a great strategist. Rather he is renowned for holding his tiny army of volunteers together for eight desperate years, always under the harshest of conditions.[169] In the end, the British found it was too expensive and wearisome to maintain a war the way the Colonials fought it.

In 1777 "General Horatio Gates won the battle of Saratoga, and France entered the war on the American side." When the French fleet anchored off the Virginia Capes "offered the opportunity for victory, Washington struck swiftly."[170] At the siege of Yorktown in 1781, American Forces, led by Washington and French forces headed by General Comte de Rochambeau, were victorious over the British troops commanded by General Lord Cornwallis.[171] When it came time for the formal surrender, Cornwallis refused to attend, claiming illness, although he sent a message to Washington: "This is a great victory for you, but your brightest laurels will be writ upon the banks of the Delaware."[172]

According to legend, the British soldiers marched to the ceremony as the fife tune of "The World Turned Upside Down" was played. Cornwallis' deputy initially attempted to surrender his sword to Rochambeau, but his aide-de-camp, Mathieu Dumas, allegedly corrected the Englishman: "You are mistaken; the commander-in-chief of our army is to the right."[173] The officer then attempted to offer his sword to Washington, who refused it because it was not proffered by Cornwallis himself. GW "indicated that the subordinate should surrender to General Benjamin Lincoln, field commander of the American forces." When this was done, Lincoln accepted the sword and the surrender. In the custom of the time, all other British soldiers were required to surrender and trample their firearms.[174] The victory at Yorktown effectively ended the Revolutionary War but it was not clear at the time that this was the end of the war, as the "British still occupied key ports such as New York City and Charleston, South Carolina. Sporadic fighting continued after the Yorktown surrender," and Washington feared the war might drag on for another year. However, "after receiving news of the surrender at Yorktown," British Prime Minister Lord North resigned. His successors decided that it was no longer in Britain's best interest to continue the war, and peace negotiations were undertaken.[175] "All that remained was to hammer out a peace treaty" to formalize what was won on the battlefields, but this process dragged on for nearly two years. On April 18, 1783, Washington announced "cessation of Hostilities between the United States of America and the King of Great Britain." He congratulated the Continental Army for their performance of the "meanest office" in the great drama played out "on the stage of human affairs." He concluded: "Nothing now remains but the actors of this almighty Scene to preserve a perfect, unvarying, consistency of character through the very last act; to close the Drama with applause, and to retire from the Military Theatre with the same approbation of Angels and men, who have crowned all their former virtuous Actions."[176]

Newburgh Conspiracy: By early 1783, active hostilities had been over for nearly two years. However, Benjamin Franklin, John Jay and John Adams were still in Paris negotiating a final treaty with Great Britain. Congress planned to keep the Continental Army officers on duty in Newburgh, New York, as long as the British remained in northern New York. The officers were eager to go home and collect the large amounts of back pay they were owed. The restless officers conspired to stage a military coup and establish a dictatorship. General Gates became involved in the mutiny. He called a meeting to discuss the situation. Washington learned of the proposed gathering and asked permission to address the officers. Gates could not deny the request. Washington entered the room and reminisced about the many battles they had fought against great odds, of the hardships they had endured, and of the aims of freedom they sought.[177] He then said he wished to read them a letter he had recently received. After squinting at the letter for a moment, he brought out a pair of spectacles and adjusted them on his nose and ears. The officers were shocked. They had never seen him wear glasses. Washington apologized: "Gentlemen, you will permit me to put on my spectacles, for I have not only grown gray but almost blind in the service of my country."[178] The officers were moved to tears. Washington slowly folded the letter, put it in his pocket with his spectacles and left the room. The embarrassed officers immediately proposed and adopted resolutions asserting their loyalty and regrets for their mutinous behavior. Somehow Congress scared up some money to pay the officers and promise pensions.[179] However, no one ever learned what was in the letter Washington did not read to the assemblage of officers.

POLITICAL OFFICES

Political Party Affiliation and Political Philosophy: As the result of his war experiences, Washington was a nationalist rather than a states' rights advocate. He was a Federalist-leaning nonpartisan who hoped that no political parties would be formed, "never fully understanding the nature, the significance, or the inevitable necessity of party government in a republic."[180] Though GW was above political divisions, his closest advisors became divided into factions, which set the framework for the formation of parties. Secretary of the treasury Alexander Hamilton sought to establish a financially

Secretary of the Treasury Alexander Hamilton, photographic print by Daniel Huntington, 1816–1906, published c. 1903 (Library of Congress).

powerful nation and had bold plans to establish federal credit. His views formed the basis of the Federalist Party. Thomas Jefferson strenuously opposed Hamilton's plans and became the founder of the Jeffersonian Republicans, or Democratic Republican Party.[181]

However little Washington may have been disposed to ally himself with any party or subscribe to any political creed, he most often sided with Hamilton's financial agenda. The secretary of the treasury's plan insured a speedy restoration of public credit and the establishment of constitutional grounds for the new government on which to stand with respect to the states.[182] In July 1799, Washington was urged to once more stand for the presidency in 1800. He angrily remarked that the new democratic era of politics—"where parties, not great men, were important—made his candidacy irrelevant and that 'personal influence,' distinctions of character, no longer mattered."[183] Washington complained that party ruled all, and people voted only for their party's candidate. Washington said that, even if he was the Federalist candidate, he was "thoroughly convinced [he] should not draw a single vote from the anti–Federal support."[184]

First Presidential Election: In May 1787, Washington headed the Virginia delegation to the Constitutional Convention in Philadelphia and was "unanimously elected presiding officer. Dissatisfied with national progress under the Articles of Confederation," Washington advocated a stronger central government: "It is too probable that no plan we propose will be adopted. Perhaps another dreadful conflict is to be sustained. If to please the people, we offer what we ourselves disapprove, how can we afterwards defend our work? Let us raise a standard to which the wise and honest can repair; the event is in the hands of God."[185]

When a constitution was adopted, GW expressed his hopeful optimism in a letter to

The Inauguration of Washington: As First President of the United States, April 30th 1789, at the Old City Hall, New York. Original lithograph printed by Currier & Ives, c. 1876 (Library of Congress).

Patrick Henry on September 24, 1787: "I wish the Constitution, which is offered, had been made more perfect; but I sincerely believe it is the best that can be obtained at this time. And, as a constitutional door is opened for amendment thereafter, the adoption of it, under the present circumstances of the Union, is in my opinion desirable."[186] After the new Constitution was "submitted to the states for ratification and became legally operative," Washington was elected president (1789). Congress counted the ballots in March and notified Washington of the results in early April.[187] American historian and Washington biographer Stephen Ambrose reported: "Washington's character was rock solid. He came to stand for the new nation and its republican virtues, which was why he became our first President by unanimous choice."[188]

GW reluctantly accepted the position, having earlier said in a letter to Alexander Hamilton, "I should unfeignedly rejoice, in case the Electors, by giving their votes to another person would save me from the dreaded dilemma of being forced to accept or refuse."[189] Washington complained about the prospect of assuming the presidency, saying, "I call to Heaven to witness, that this very act would be the greatest sacrifice of my personal feelings & wishes that ever I have been called upon to make."[190]

HIS PRESIDENCY

It was his reluctance to fill the position as well as his many services to the new republic that he was the perfect candidate. Washington's first term passed without a major crisis, but his second featured internecine and inevitable clashes between Hamilton and Jefferson. The president continued to enjoy nearly universal admiration and support and he was reelected in 1792, winning the vote of all of the 132 electors and carrying each of the 15 states. In 1796, GW firmly rejected pleas to serve a third term.

As the first president of the United States, Washington believed it was his duty to enforce the laws and policies set by Congress. He did not exercise authority as current presidents do. "The times called for a president who would not abuse his power or allow control to slip from his grip."[191] Washington made it a point to visit each of the original thirteen states during his administrations, using his popularity to enhance the union.[192] He understood that he had to set the protocol of the presidency, and since the Constitution was rather vague about his duties, he had to tread softly in discovering what they were. GW proceeded carefully and deliberately, aware of the need to organize an executive system and establish administrative principles that would make it possible for the government to operate with energy and efficient and allow future presidents to exercise broad executive authority without corruption. In a May 15, 1789, letter to James Madison, GW mentioned this responsibility: "As the first of everything, in our situation, will serve to establish a Precedent, it is devoutly wished on my part that these precedents may be fixed on true principles."[193]

At Washington's first inauguration, he and his vice president, John Adams, were the only members of the executive branch of the federal government. GW was mindful of how careful he needed to be in making political appointments. He discussed this function in a July 27, 1789, letter to his nephew Bushrod Washington: "My political conduct in nominations, even if it was influenced by principle, must be exceedingly circumspect and proof against just criticism, for the eyes of Argus are upon me, and no slip will pass unnoticed that can be improved into a supposed partiality for friends or relatives."[194]

Washington's leadership and respect for liberty brought legitimacy to the new nation of the United States of America. He was the strong leader needed by a weak nation. He "embraced an energetic government as the only means of protecting the delicate American union from falling apart." GW "created an independent role for the president and made the chief executive the dominant figure in the government."[195] With regard to political appointments, Washington asserted, as regards to political appointments, "a due regard shall be had to the fitness of characters, the pretensions of different candidates, and, so far as is proper, to political considerations."[196] He explained this to Benjamin Harrison, who had applied for the position of naval officer of the Norfolk district, "I will therefore declare to you, that, if it should be my inevitable fate to administer the government (for Heaven knows, that no event can be less desired by me; and that no earthly consideration short of so general a call, together with a desire to reconcile contending parties as far as in me lays, could again bring me into public life) I will go to the chair under no pre-engagement of any kind or nature whatsoever. But, when in it, I will, to the best of my Judgment, discharge the duties of the office with that impartiality and zeal for the public good, which ought never to suffer connections of blood or friendship to intermingle, so as to have the least sway on decisions of a public nature. I may err, notwithstanding my most strenuous efforts to execute the difficult trust with fidelity and unexceptionably; but my errors shall be of the head, not of the heart."[197]

By declaring neutrality in disputes between Great Britain and France, without seeking approval from Congress, Washington established the precedent that the determination of foreign policy is predominately a presidential responsibility.[198] Another of his precedents that have not always been followed faithfully by some later chief executives was to refrain from taking more power than was his due. This standard of presidential integrity has rarely been met by his successors. Thomas Jefferson spoke of this admirable quality: "The moderation and virtue of a single character probably prevented this Revolution from being closed, as many others have been, by a subversion of that liberty it was intended to establish."[199]

His Vice President: John Adams, who received the second most votes in the Electoral College, both in the first two presidential elections.

His Cabinet: As with many other precedents set by the first president of the United States, Washington established a Cabinet as a privy council, constructed with an eye to sectional and ideological balance.[200] It inevitably became an arena of conflict, especially between secretary of state Thomas Jefferson and secretary of the treasury Alexander Hamilton.[201] Other members of Washington's first cabinet were Henry Knox, secretary of war; Samuel Osgood, postmaster general; and Edmund Randolph, attorney general. Jefferson was later replaced by Randolph, who in turn gave way to Timothy Pickering. Hamilton was followed by Oliver Wolcott, Jr. Knox was succeeded by Pickering followed by James McHenry. Pickering was the second postmaster general and Joseph Habersham was the third. The

"Secretary of State Thomas Jefferson," glass negative by Constantino Brumidi, 1805–1880, published c. 1904 (Library of Congress, Detroit Publishing Company).

second attorney general was William Bradford, succeeded by Charles Lee.

Supreme Court Appointments: Among the notable events during Washington's administrations was the Judiciary Act,[202] which specified the number of Federal courts and judges. With minor adjustments, it is the system in place today. The first Congress decided it should regulate the jurisdiction of all federal courts. The act they passed established a "limited jurisdiction for the district and circuit courts, gave the Supreme Court the original jurisdiction provided by the Constitution, and granted the appellate courts' jurisdiction in cases from the federal circuit courts and the state courts where these rejected federal claims."[203] To become a justice of the Supreme Court, an individual must be "nominated by the President of the United States and approved by the U.S. Senate."[204] There were no members of the Supreme Court until Washington appointed the first court, with John Jay as chief justice (1789–1795), who was left to establish court procedures. In a 1789 letter to

Vice President John Adams, engraving print after a painting by John Singleton Copley; published between 1850 and 1900 (Library of Congress).

his attorney general, Edmund Randolph, Washington expressed his desire to appoint only outstanding men to the highest court: "Impressed with a conviction that the due administration of justice is the firmest pillar of good government, I have considered the first arrangement of the judicial department as essential to the happiness of our country, and to the stability of its political system; hence the selection of the fittest characters to expound the law, and dispense justice has been an invariable object of my anxious concern."[205]

The associate justices during Washington's administrations were John Rutledge, William Cushing, James Wilson, John Blair, James Iredell, Thomas Johnson, William Paterson, Samuel Chase and Oliver Ellsworth.[206] Rutledge resigned in 1791 when he was appointed chief justice of the South Carolina Supreme Court. When Jay resigned to become governor of New York in 1795, Washington appointed Rutledge as chief justice during a recess of the Senate. Rutledge presided over one term of the court, but the Senate rejected his nomination in part due to rumors of mental illness he was said to have suffered since the death of his wife. Washington then turned to associate justice Cushing, who served as chief justice for two days before returning to his former duties. Finally, Ellsworth was confirmed by the Senate as chief justice as the third or fourth in that capacity, depending on how Cushing's short stay is regarded.[207]

States Added to the Union: During Washington's presidency five new states joined the United States: North Carolina and Rhode Island in 1789 and 1790 respectively, after ratification of the U.S. Constitution. Vermont joined the Union in 1791, Kentucky in 1792 and Tennessee in 1796.

DOMESTIC AFFAIRS — MAJOR EVENTS

The Nation's Capital: Washington was zealously involved in the creation of the District of Columbia, established by an Act of Congress in 1790. He was also instrumental in choosing the location of the president's home, now familiarly known as the White House. The federal capital was established in swamplands along the Potomac River (1791) and the city of Washington remained a marshland well into the 19th century. A "southern location for the capital was a compromise made during the writing of the Constitution as a trade-off for southern votes for important compromises."[208] Washington never lived in the nation's capital.

Amendments to the Constitution — Bill of Rights: In 1791, the first 10 amendments to the U.S. Constitution, collectively known as the Bill of Rights,[209] were adopted. The first amendment decreed freedom of religion, of speech, and of the press, the right to assemble and to petition for redress of grievances. The second deals with the right to bear arms; the third with restrictions on quartering soldiers in private homes; the fourth with freedom from unreasonable search and seizure; the fifth the ban on double jeopardy and self-incrimination; the sixth the right to a speedy and public trial; the seventh the right to trial by jury; the eighth a ban on excessive bails or fines and cruel and unusual punishment; the ninth that natural rights unspecified in the Constitution were to remain unabridged and the tenth that the individual states or people retain all powers not specifically delegated to the federal government or denied to states by the Constitution. In addition an eleventh amendment was adopted that a citizen from one state cannot sue another state.

Bank Act of 1791: The newly minted nation was broke. Washington realized that he did not know anything about commerce — neither did the other founding fathers, most of whom were lawyers and farmers.[210] He brought in Alexander Hamilton to deal with the problem. During Washington's first term, the Federal government adopted a series of measures, proposed by Hamilton, to resolve the escalating debt crisis and establish the nation's finances on a sound basis. The Bank of the United States was created to handle the financial needs and requirements of the central government with the banks of the former colonies, each with their own currencies, financial institutions and fiscal policies.[211] The bank's support came from Northern merchants and New England state governments. It was treated with suspicion in the Southern states, whose "chief industry, agriculture, did not require centrally concentrated banks." The South also saw the "creation of a national bank as a threat to states' rights."[212] The bank's charter expired in 1811, and its existence or re-chartering became

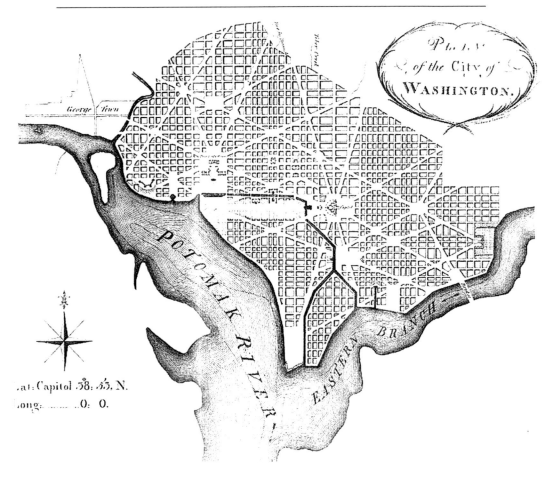

Pierre Charles L'Enfant's "Plan of the City of Washington," engraving on paper, created by the Historic American Buildings Survey, National Mall and Memorial Parks, March 1792 (Library of Congress).

a major issue of contention for many years. Hamilton, the Bank's primary author, proposed establishing the initial funding of the bank through the "sale of $10 million in stock of which the United States government would purchase the first $2 million in shares."[213]

Unconcerned that the central government did not have $2 million, the secretary of the treasury suggested the government make the "stock purchase using money loaned to it by the bank," the loan to be paid back in ten equal annual installments. Hamilton explained in a letter to Robert Morris on April 30, 1781: "A national debt, if it is not excessive, will be to us a national blessing."[214] In 1789 American obligations traded as low as 25 percent of face value in European markets. By the time Hamilton stepped down in 1795, they were trading at 110 percent of face value.[215]

Post Office and Other: Congress "established the post office as a separate entity (1792)"[216]; the New York Stock Exchange was organized (1791); and coins were minted by the government as enacted by the Coinage Act (1791).

Fugitive Slave Act: The 1793 Fugitive Slave Act was motivated by a dispute between states. Virginia claimed that Pennsylvania's recognition of the freedom of slaves directly impinged on its property rights. Slaves' status as property disqualified them from having constitutional rights, but the 1793 act denied rights to freed slaves as well.[217] The law made it a federal crime to assist an escaping slave and established a mechanism for owners to seize escaped slaves even in "free" states.

Whiskey Rebellion: At the urging of Secretary of the Treasury Hamilton, the Federal government assumed the states' debt from the American Revolutionary War. In 1791, he convinced Congress to pass taxes on distilled spirits and carriages in order to reduce the national debt. Hamilton claimed that his object was "more a measure of a social discipline than as a source of revenue."[218] Disgruntled corn farmers threatened to riot after the government imposed excise taxes on whiskey (1794). They maintained that taxing them as a minority was unconstitutional. Washington disagreed: "[If] a minority ... is to dictate to the majority, then all laws are prostrate and everyone will carve for himself."[219] The president called out the militia to suppress the armed Whiskey Rebellion in western Pennsylvania, sending a force numbering more soldiers that crossed the Delaware with him.[220]

Naturalization Act: The U.S. Naturalization Law of March 26, 1790, established the first rules to be followed by the U.S. in granting national citizenship. The law limited naturalization to aliens of "good moral character" who were "free white persons," thereby eliminating indentured servants, slaves, free African Americans, and, later, Asian-Americans.[221] The act established the citizenship of children of citizens, born aboard, without the need for naturalization. It also began an unprecedented influx of immigrants from Europe. In a letter to Francis Van der Kamp on May 28, 1788, GW mused, "I had always hoped that this land might become a safe and agreeable asylum to the virtuous and persecuted part of mankind, to whatever nation they might belong."[222]

FOREIGN AFFAIRS — MAJOR EVENTS

Washington's second term was "dominated by foreign affairs and marred by a deepening partisanship in his own administration." One of his most noteworthy accomplishments was "keeping the United States out of the war" between France and Great Britain, thus giving the new nation a "chance to grow in strength, while establishing the principle of neutrality that shaped American foreign policy for more than a century."[223]

Tariff of 1789: One of the first significant actions of the Congress was to pass the Tariff Act of 1789. The act was designed to raise revenues for the new government by placing a charge on the importation of foreign goods and encouraging domestic production in such industries as glass and pottery by taxing the importation of these products from overseas competition.[224]

Neutrality Proclamation: When Great Britain and France went to war in 1793, President Washington declared neutrality, much to the disappointment of the pro–French Secretary of State Jefferson and pro–British Secretary of the Treasury Hamilton, who reassured a British diplomat, "we think in English."[225] The Cabinet felt that neutrality was necessary because the nation was too new and its military too weak to risk any clashes with either Great Britain or France. Jefferson disagreed, asserting there was no need to make an official Proclamation of Neutrality, and probably no need to make any declaration.

The Citizen Genêt Affair: During the French Revolution, Edmond-Charles Genêt was a French ambassador to the United States. In 1793, he was sent to the U.S. to promote American support for France's war with Spain and Great Britain. He arrived in Charleston, South Carolina, but instead of going to the capitol at Philadelphia to present his credentials to President Washington, Genêt remained in Charleston, where his true purpose was to recruit and arm American privateers to join French expeditions against the British. He organized volunteers to fight Britain's Spanish allies in Florida. After commissioning four privateering ships, he finally presented himself to the president and the secretary of state. Jefferson rejected the Frenchman's request for suspension of U.S. neutrality and informed Genêt that his actions were unacceptable.[226] The ambassador continued to defy the wishes of the American government, capturing British ships and rearming them as privateers. Washington fired off an 8,000-word letter of complaint to Genêt, based on the advice of Jefferson and Hamilton, one of the rare times the two men agreed on anything. A change of the French government resulted in an arrest warrant being sent ordering Genêt back to France. Knowing this meant the guillotine, he sought asylum in the United States, which President Washington granted.[227]

Jay Treaty: The Jay Treaty signed in November 1794, averted war with Great Britain, while resolving many issues left over from the Revolutionary War. The treaty brought nearly ten years of peaceful trade between the two countries. However, Democratic-Republicans viewed the treaty as abject surrender to British demands.[228] It instantly became a dominant issue in domestic American politics, with Hamilton and chief negotiator Jay opposed by Jefferson and Madison. The latter feared that closer ties with Great Britain would strengthen the Federalists.[229]

Pinckney Treaty: The purpose of the Pinckney Treaty with Spain was to open navigation to the U.S. on the Mississippi River (1795), establish promises of friendship between the two nations, and define the boundaries of the United States with the Spanish colonies.[230]

Farewell Address: Washington issued his masterful farewell address as a public letter in 1796. It remains one of the most influential statements of American political values. Drafted primarily by Washington, with some input from Hamilton, it was intended to help form the national character of the United States based on the morals and civic virtues necessary for self-government. In the address, Washington strongly warned against permanent alliances between the United States and other countries:

> Europe has a set of primary interests which to us have none or a very remote relation. Hence she must be engaged in frequent controversies, the causes of which are essentially foreign to our concerns. Hence, therefore, it must be unwise of us to implicate ourselves by artificial ties in the ordinary vicissitudes of her politics or the ordinary contributions or collisions of her friendships or enmities.... It is folly in one nation to look for disinterested favors from another.... Why forego the advantages of so peculiar a situation? Why quit our own to stand upon foreign ground? Why, by interweaving our destiny with that of any part of Europe, entangle our peace and prosperity in the toils of European ambition, rivalship, interest, humor or caprice? The great rule of conduct for us, in regard to foreign nations, is, in extending our commercial relations, to have with them as little political connexion as possible. So far as we have already formed engagements, let them be fulfilled with perfect good faith. Here let us stop.[231]

GW warned about politicians or judges acting unconstitutionally, even if their intentions were honorable: "If in the opinion of the people the distribution or modification of the constitutional powers be in any particular wrong, let it be corrected by an amendment in the way the Constitution designates. But let there be no change by usurpation; for though this, in one instant may be the instrument of good, it is the customary weapon by which free governments are destroyed."[232] Washington restated his concern about the dangers in the formation of political factions: "One of the expedients of party to acquire influence, within particular districts, is to misrepresent the opinions and aims of other districts.... I ... intimated to you the danger of parties in the state, with particular reference to the founding of them on geographical discriminations.... The common and continual mischiefs of the spirit of party are sufficient to make it the interest and duty of a wise people to discourage and restrain it."[233]

The president touched on American patriotism: "Guard against the importance of pretended patriotism.... The name of American, which belongs to you in your national capacity, must always exalt the just pride of patriotism more than any appellation derived from local discriminations. With slight shades of difference, you have the same religion, manners, habits and political principles. You have in common a cause fought and triumphed together. The independence and liberty you possess are the work of joint councils, and joint efforts, of common dangers, sufferings, and successes."[234]

AFTER THE PRESIDENCY

Washington was eager to retire and return with Martha to his beloved Mount Vernon to spend the remainder of his life as an ordinary gentleman farmer. However, the country he magnificently served for so long made one last call on his service. When President John Adams feared a possible French invasion, he persuaded Washington to become commanding general of the provisional army that would be raised if needed to defend the country. Washington agreed on the condition that he would be allowed to work from Mount Vernon until such time that there was an actual imminent invasion — which never came.[235]

President Harry S Truman later saluted Washington: "There isn't any question about Washington's greatness. If his administration had been a failure, there would have been no United States. A lesser man couldn't have done it.... Washington was both a great administrator and a great leader, a truly great man in every way."[236]

His Papers: The Library of Congress maintains the complete collection of George Washington papers, consisting of 65,000 documents. These correspondences, letterbooks (copies of his correspondence), commonplace books, diaries, journals, financial account books, military records, reports, and notes were accumulated by Washington in the period from 1741 through 1799. During Washington's lifetime, letters served many valuable functions, being the main "means of communication between individuals at a distance from each other." Correspondents were obliged to reply to every letter received, as this was the only way a writer had of knowing that the letter had arrived.[237] Washington received letters from all over the world, each of which required a polite response. He grumbled about this chore: "Applications which oftentimes cannot be complied with. Enquiries, which would employ the pen of a historian to satisfy. Letters of compliment as unmeaning perhaps as they are troublesome, but which must be attended to."[238]

Throughout his life, George Washington wrote thousands of letters expounding on his beliefs and positions. He "kept daily diaries and journals with records of his activities, and he maintained written accounts of his expenditures." These documents provide unusual insight into his thoughts and feelings as well as offering a "unique look at life during the 18th century, the operation of a plantation, and conditions in the wars" in which he served. His own definition of a diary was "Where & How My Time Is Spent"[239] and that is about all that he recorded in them. Unfortunately, few of the diaries he kept during his presidential years survived. Many of these were casually mishandled by Jared Sparks while preparing a twelve-volume edition, *The Writings of George Washington* (1837). Sparks, one-time president of Harvard College, endeavored to make Washington a man without blemish. He corrected Washington's spelling and grammar and eliminated from the general and president's writings anything that might show the father of the country in a negative light.[240] John C. Fitzpatrick, who undertook to issue the first compilation of the Washington diaries, wrote in the 1920s: "Now that I have read every word of these Diaries, from the earliest to the last one, it is impossible to consider them in any other light than that of a most marvelous record. It is absolutely impossible for anyone to arrive at a true understanding or comprehension of George Washington without reading this Diary record."[241]

As president, Washington instituted the practice of maintaining an official journal of the daily activities of the chief executive. In the spring of 1781, with congressional approval, clerks were hired to copy Washington's letters, orders and instructions and the proceedings of his council of war, in order to preserve "valuable documents, which may be of equal public utility and private satisfaction...."[242] In August 1783, two years after the work began, twenty-eight completed volumes were delivered to Washington; six volumes of his letters to Congress; "fourteen of dispatches to his officers; four of communications to civil officials; one of letters to foreigners"; two volumes of councils of war; and one volume of his private correspondence. Most of these volumes were deposited in the Library of Congress in 1904. Scholars at the University of Virginia are currently assembling Washington's papers and before the project is completed the editors expect to issue about 90 separate volumes.

Health: Although physically strong, Washington suffered from numerous illnesses and their reoccurrences. Throughout his life, he had "repeated bouts with malaria." At about 19, he contracted a "severe case of smallpox," which apparently rendered him sterile and ruined his teeth. He developed tuberculosis, probably caught from his half brother Lawrence, and it took GW two years to recover fully. He had diphtheria and often suffered from painful fever, dysentery and pleurisy. As he grew older, GW needed reading glasses and his hearing deteriorated to the point he could not make out ordinary conversation. He almost "died of pneumonia in 1790, leaving him unable to perform his duties as President for several weeks." He had a tendency towards depression when affected by some illness.[243]

Often moody, Washington did not like to be touched. When he became president, he would not shake hands because he thought it was "beneath the dignity of his office" and practiced bowing instead.[244] Toothaches bothered Washington for years, as had the "habit of cracking nuts with his teeth, and did not practice proper dental care. He was more concerned with the health of his horses, which had their teeth brushed daily." At age 57, all of Washington's teeth were pulled and at various times he wore dentures made of "hippopotamus ivory, seahorse ivory, and lead. Other sets used the teeth of pigs, cows, elks, and humans," but not of wood as has been routinely reported over the years.[245] At his first inauguration, because of his false teeth, it took him 90 seconds to read his 183 word speech. His ill-fitting dentures distorted his lips, contributing to the dour expression seen in several of his portraits.[246]

Death: George Washington died at his home, sometime between 10 and 11 o'clock at night on December 14, 1799, at the age of 67. His final illness was a result of a throat infection — succumbing after being bled by leeches, once by his own orders, twice by his doctors. The bleedings hastened his end with approximately 35 percent of his blood being removed in 12 hours. He had contracted hoarseness and a sore throat a few days earlier after riding out to his farms in dreadful weather of rain, hail, snow and a cold wind.[247]

The president was attended by three physicians, the first of whom misdiagnosed Washington's condition as quinsy, or a peritonsillar abscess. It is likely the president had a" streptococcus infection, which resulted in asphyxia as the swelling about the glottis inhibited breathing." The youngest of the three doctors proposed a delicate operation to open the trachea below the site of the infection, enabling Washington to breathe, but he was outvoted by his colleagues, who viewed the surgery as too dangerous.[248] Washington deteriorated steadily. He sat in a chair in front of the fireplace in the morning, but then returned to bed, never to rise again. He knew he was dying, and asked the physicians to do more. At about 8:00 P.M. he whispered, "I die hard, but I am not afraid to go. I should have been glad, had

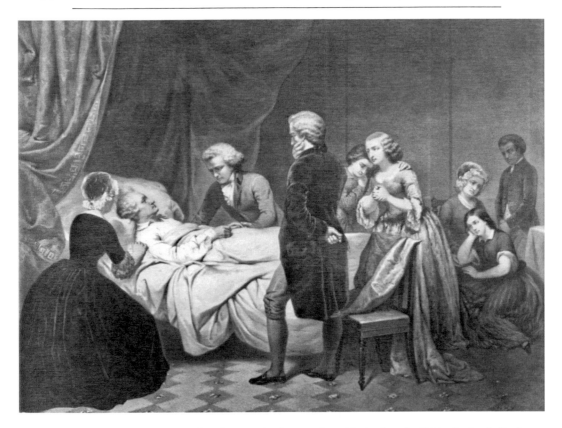

George Washington on His Death Bed, engraving by Régnier of Paris after the 1851 painting by Junius Brutus Stearns, published by Lemercier, c. 1853 (Library of Congress).

it pleased God, to die a little easier, but I doubt not it is for my good."[249] At about 11:00 P.M., he uttered his last words: "Father of mercies, take me unto thyself."[250]

Shortly before he died, Washington instructed his private secretary, Tobias Lear: "I am just going. Have me decently buried, and do not let my body be put into the Vault in less than three days after I am dead."[251] He then asked, "Do you understand me?" Tobias replied, "Yes." Washington said, "'Tis well," and died some ten minutes later after feeling his own pulse.[252] Washington feared being buried alive, so the three days' delay before putting his body in the vault was to make certain he was really deceased. The death of Washington was a subject of "popular prints that idealized the passing of a venerated hero." When Washington breathed his last, Mrs. Washington, who had been sitting at the foot of the bed, asked, "Is he gone?"[253] When her fears were confirmed, she responded, "'Tis well. All is now over I shall soon follow him! I have no more trials to pass through!"[254]

Place of Burial: The day after his death, it was arranged for a coffin to be constructed in Alexandria, while slaves opened and cleaned the modest brick family vault, located a "few hundred feet from the house." In his will Washington said that it was his "express desire that my Corpse may be interred in a private manner, without — parade or funeral Oration."[255] His wishes were overridden by officials who believed there was a strong need to grieve for the man who had given so much to his country. Congress built a vault under the capitol building to receive Washington's body. Instead his heirs honored GW's wishes that his tomb should be at his home. The vault at the capitol remains empty to this day.[256]

On December 18, 1799, Washington's open casket was placed on a wooden bier on the portico above the Potomac River, where several hundred guests paid their final respects. His body was then escorted to the vault by a large procession which included both infantry and mounted military units, a band "playing a solemn Dirge," and Washington's riderless horse bearing his pistols and holsters, led by two slaves in mourning clothes. Once the body reached the tomb, four ministers, two Anglican and two Presbyterian, officiated at the funeral rites, which were followed by a Masonic ceremony. In his will, Washington directed that a new brick tomb be built to replace the original burial vault, which was deteriorating. The new tomb was completed in 1831 and Washington's body was moved there along with the remains of his wife, Martha, and other family members."[257] On Washington's tomb at Mount Vernon the following is engraved: "I am the Resurrection and the Life; sayeth the Lord. He that believeth in Me, though he were dead yet shall he live. And whosoever liveth and believeth in Me shall never die."[258] Colonel Henry (Light Horse Harry) Lee gave the eulogy in honor of his Revolutionary War comrade in Philadelphia, Pennsylvania:

> First in war, first in peace, and first in the hearts of his countrymen, he was second to none in humble and enduring scenes of private life. Pious, just, humane, temperate, and sincere; uniform, dignified, and commanding; his example was as edifying to all around him as were the effects of that example lasting.... Correct throughout, vice shuddered in his presence and virtue always felt his fostering hand. The purity of his private character gave effulgence to his public virtues.... Such was the man for whom our nation mourns.[259]

During the Civil War, "Washington's remains were moved from Mount Vernon to Lexington," Virginia, for fear his tomb might be desecrated by Northern troops.[260] At the end of the war, his body was returned to Mount Vernon.

MISCELLANEA

Presidential Firsts and Trivia: Everything Washington did as president was a first. He was well aware that his every move was setting a precedent and he took care not to restrict his successors or to set the new nation on an undesirable course. He was also extremely sensitive to the immense power he possessed to influence public opinion and was careful to use it rarely, only when he felt that it was necessary to accomplish some exceptional good. One of the epistolary techniques he used "frequently and brilliantly was to include a paragraph saying essentially 'of course I do not mean to suggest...,' in the process saying exactly what he did mean!"[261] Washington was the only U.S. president to die in the 18th century. His farewell address used to be read aloud in the Senate every year on his birthday. He was the only president not to live in the White House. Washington, three in total, was the only president to appoint more than one chief justice of the Supreme Court. During his administration, Congress created the U.S. State Department, the War Department, the Treasury Department, and the Supreme Court, all between July and September 1789. The first Congress met at Federal Hall, New York City, on March 4, 1789. The first census was undertaken in 1790, revealing a population of just fewer than 4 million.

Mother Says No: When George was 14 years old, his half brother Lawrence decided that George should join the British Royal Navy and arranged to have him appointed a midshipman, but he needed his mother's permission. She sought the advice of her half brother, Joseph Ball. He suggested, half-jokingly, that rather than let her son go to sea it would be better to apprentice him to a tinker. From that point on, no amount of arguing or pleading from Lawrence and George moved Mary Ball Washington. She refused to give her permission and thus George had to give up hopes of becoming a sailor.[262]

Mother Knows Best: At an early point in the Revolutionary War, Washington assigned his adjunct to requisition horses from local landowners. At one county house, he was met at the door by an elderly woman. The officer informed her, "Madam, I have come to claim your horses in the name of the government." "On whose orders?" she demanded. "On the orders of General George Washington, Commander-in-Chief of the American Army," replied the officer. Smiling, the lady of the house said, "You go back and tell General George Washington that his mother says he cannot have her horses."[263]

Washington and Slavery: In the early 1790s, Washington "built a brick greenhouse at Mount Vernon with wings on the sides to house slaves," replacing a crumbling "house for Families." According to Henry Wiencek, "This new structure was meant to take slavery into the new century, woven into an architect of great beauty and permanence."[264]

By the time of his death, Washington's plantation was home to 317 slaves. He made few public statements about slavery, and many of these were contradictory. Although he did not think highly of the system, he was not entirely repelled by it and saw no way of abolishing it. He "wished from his soul" that Virginia could be persuaded to put an end to slavery as "it might prevent much further mischief." Wiencek reflected: "It's one of the mysteries of his life. You could say slavery was something he inherited, a part of the system. But he also had to learn how to be a master."[265]

During the Revolutionary War, General Washington at first was hesitant to use black soldiers, but by the end of the war, when his army marched on Yorktown, one in four soldiers in his command was black. It was the last time that black and white soldiers fought together in the U.S. military until President Truman integrated the troops during the Korean War.[266] When GW took up residence in Philadelphia as president; he was accompanied by a number of slaves from Mount Vernon. He got around the law of Pennsylvania, which required slaves who lived in the state for six months in a row to be given their freedom; by rotating the slaves back and forth from the capital to Mount Vernon.[267] Washington was only the first of several presidents who paradoxically abhorred the institution of slavery but profited from it. Even as chief executive he did not feel he had the power to abolish slavery unilaterally. In a letter to Robert Morris on April 12, 1786, he explained: "There is not a man living who wishes more sincerely than I do to see a plan adopted for the abolition of slavery. But there is only one proper way and effectual mode by which it can be accomplished, and that is by legislative authority."[268]

The next September, in a letter to John Francis Mercer, Washington expressed his hope that slavery would be legally abolished: "I never mean, unless some particular circumstances should compel me to do it, to possess another slave by purchase; it being among my first wishes to see some plan adopted by which slavery in this country may be abolished by law."[269] On one occasion Washington told a visiting Englishman that slavery was neither a crime nor an absurdity. He attempted to make a comparison by noting that the American government did not assure liberty to madmen: "Until the mind of the slave has been educated to understand freedom, the gift of freedom would only assure its abuse."[270]

Only a year after this assertion, Washington drafted his will, in which he stated he wished he could free all the slaves at Mount Vernon but could not because many belonged to his wife's heirs, and he did not wish to divide families. A provision in his will resulted in about 124 slaves, servants as he called them, to be set free at his wife's death. Washington's will required his heirs to provide "a regular and permanent fund ... for their support as long as they are subjects requiring it; not trusting to the uncertain provisions to be made by individuals."[271] The will specified that the freed children should be taught reading, writing and a trade. Washington's heirs continued to help the freed slaves until the 1830s. GW left an estate worth an estimated $500,000. Martha Washington set free both her slaves and her husband's a year after his death.

Painting George Washington: At the time of the founding of the United States and until the introduction of photography, images of individuals were either portraits or busts. Americans carry a portrait of President George Washington in their wallets on dollar bills. The image on the currency is from a portrait by the famous American artist Gilbert Stuart. He spent his youth in Newport, Rhode Island, where he studied painting before going to London in 1775. There he was "greatly influenced by the work of the English portrait painters Thomas Gainsborough and Sir Joshua Reynolds. In 1792, after establishing himself as a fashionable portrait painter in London and Dublin, Stuart returned to the United States."[272] He developed his own distinctive style, which was emulated by the next generations of paintings and led to his earning the title "Father of American Portraiture."[273] Though he had many hefty commissions, he had no business sense, drank excessively, and died broke.

With a letter of introduction from John Jay, Stuart was granted his first sitting with George Washington in Philadelphia, in March 1975. The president, who was sixty-three years old at the time, complained about the drudgery of posing. The artist observed that "an apathy seemed to seize him, and a vacuity spread over his countenance, most appalling to paint."[274] Stuart had no interest in depicting "patience on a monument,"[275] and used his considerable skills as a conversationalist to spark his subjects into animation. He remarked to the President, "Now, sir, you must let me forget that you are General Washington and that I am Stuart the painter."[276] Washington snapped, "Mr. Stuart need never feel the need of forgetting who he is, or who General Washington is."[277]

Nothing Stuart did or said interested the president. Altogether, Stuart painted Washington a total of three times and made more than a hundred copies, which he sold for substantial sums. The paintings are grouped into three categories named after the first owners of a copy of the original: the Vaughan portrait (facing to the left), the Lansdowne (full-length), and the Athenaeum (facing to the right). Samuel Vaughan was a wealthy merchant. The second portrait was purchased as a gift for the famous British Whig, Lord Lansdowne.[278] The proportions of the painting are all wrong. Washington was more than six feet tall, but "Stuart used a friend who was five foot six as a model for the body, arms and legs, and the outstretched hand belongs to Stuart himself."[279] The third picture is known as the "Athenaeum portrait, since it eventually came into the possession of the Boston Athenaeum." Stuart's daughter recalled that near the end of her father's life, he could dash off a portrait of Washington at the rate of one every two hours. The Athenaeum portrait is the one used on dollar bills and postage stamps. Stuart made many copies of the portrait, mostly vastly inferior to the original. Besides Stuart's portraits, many forgeries of his works emerged. The artist claimed the one that adorned the "White House was a forgery," but if that is so it is a good one.[280]

When Mrs. Washington wanted a picture of the president for herself, she persuaded her reluctant husband to pose again for Stuart. The artist was delighted with the result and was determined to keep it, believing he could make a fortune selling copies of it. Whenever Mrs. Washington inquired about the portrait, Stuart would apologize and claim it was not finished. In fact, it was never finished and the First Lady had to put up with a copy she said was not a good likeness.[281] Speaking of the president, Stuart observed, "There were features in his face totally different from what I have observed in any other human being."[282]

The Washington Monument: The monument is one of the most prominent attractions in Washington, D.C. The monument is shaped like an Egyptian obelisk (a four-sided shaft with a pyramid at the top) and is 555 ft., ⅝ in. high. Its width at the base of the shaft is 55 feet, 1½ inches. The weight of the monument is 90,845 tons, and it cost $1,187,710. It stands on the Washington Mall, a long rectangular stretch of parkland in the middle of the city extending from the Lincoln Memorial to the United States Capitol. "The construction of a monument to honor George Washington was first considered by the Continental Congress in 1783." By 1847, a total of $87,000 had been collected and a design by Robert Mills was selected. The cornerstone was laid on July 4, 1848, using the "same trowel that Washington used at the laying of the cornerstone of the Capitol in 1793." Work progressed until 1854 when the project was at the center of a political argument.[283]

During the Civil War, the construction was halted altogether and for nearly 25 years, the monument stood incomplete at a height of about 150 feet. In 1876, President Grant approved an act providing that the "federal government should bear the responsibility for finishing the monument." Work resumed in 1880 using the marble from the same quarry and vein of stone that went into the truncated portion. Because it was drawn from a greater depth than the original, a "ring" is visible on the shaft. The capstone was set in place on December 6, 1884, and dedicated on February 21, 1885. It was opened to the public on October 9, 1888.[284]

Mount Rushmore: George Washington is one of four sculptures of United States presidents carved on the mountain of that name in the Black Hills of South Dakota. Washington is to the far left as viewed, next to Thomas Jefferson, then Theodore Roosevelt and finally, at the far right, Abraham Lincoln. Each face is some 60 feet high, 500 feet up on the mountain. Congress authorized the memorial in 1925 and "President Coolidge insisted that along with Washington, two Republicans and a Democrat be portrayed, but the four featured were chosen by sculptor Gutzon Borglum because of their role in preserving the Republic and expanding its territory." Work was begun in 1927, employed 400 workers, and finished 14 years later at a cost of $1 million.[285] Native Americans were displeased with the project. The Lakota tribe knew the geographical formation of Mount Rushmore as Six Grandfathers. They considered it to be sacred and had been granted the Black Hills in perpetuity in the Treaty of Fort Laramie of 1868. The United States seized the area after the Black Hills War of 1876–1877. Elsewhere in the Black Hills the Crazy Horse Memorial is being constructed to commemorate the famous Native American leader. The foundation directing the project, which will be larger than the Rushmore memorial, has rejected offers of federal funds.[286]

Remuneration as General of the Continental Army: When Washington was unanimously selected as commander-in-chief of the armed forces of the United Colonies, he "reluctantly accepted the position, asking 'every gentleman in the room' to remember his declaration that he did not believe himself to be equal to the command, and that he accepted it only as a duty made imperative by the unanimity of the call."[287] He refused a salary: "I long ago despaired of any other reward for my service than the satisfaction from a consciousness of doing my duty, and from the esteem of my friends.... Sir, I beg leave to assure the Congress that as no pecuniary consideration could have tempted me to have accepted this arduous employment, I do not wish to make any profit from it. I will keep an exact account of my expenses. Those I doubt not they will discharge, and that is all I desire."[288]

Washington meticulously recorded how his money was spent, be it in running his plantation or in leading his troops against the British. He lived quite comfortably on his expense account — averaging twice his presidential salary of $25,000 per annum for each year he headed the army. Whether or not he was padding his account, it is obvious that he enjoyed wines and spirits.[289] In one period of seven months, GW spent $6000 on liquor, which bought plenty of his favorite Madeira. According to the book *George Washington's Expense Account*, by Washington and Marvin Kitman, Revolutionary era gentlemen daily consumed vast quantities of spirits: "Given cider and punch for lunch; rum and brandy before dinner; punch, Madeira, port and sherry at dinner; punch and liqueurs with the ladies; and wine, spirit and punch before bedtime, all in punchbowls big enough for a goose to swim in."[290]

Totaling everything during his eight years of service, Washington spent and was reimbursed $449,261.51 in 1780 dollars. When he offered to forego a salary as president and only collect his expenses, he was politely turned down by Congress.[291]

Profanity: Washington banned curse words from his army, although he used a lot of the banned words himself. It was said that he swore "till the leaves shook on the trees."[292] He issued the following order to his troops during the Revolutionary War:

> The General is sorry to be informed that the foolish and wicked practice of profane cursing and swearing, a vice hitherto little known in our American Army is growing into fashion. He hopes that the officers will, by example as well as influence, endeavor to check it and that both they and the men will reflect that we can little hope of the blessing of Heaven in our army if we insult it by our impiety and folly. Added to this it is a vice so mean and low without any temptation that every man of sense and character detests and despises it.[293]

The Man Who Would Not Be King: When victory in the Revolutionary War was won, Washington was the most revered man in the new nation. One less principled than Washington might have used his popularity to seize absolute power as a military dictatorship or even king. As a popular general, Washington could have imposed his will over "civilian leadership, as did Napoleon Bonaparte in France and Simón Bolívar in South America."[294] Instead, he resigned his commission and "sternly suppressed all such attempts on his behalf by his officers and continued to obey the weak and divided Continental Congress." When his officers and others suggested that he declare himself king, GW reacted strongly against the proposal: "No occurrence in the course of the War has given me more painful sensations."[295] Washington respected the republican basis of power, and believed that enduringly successful leaders depend upon the "support and trust of the people they serve." He decided that the chief executive should be called "the president," and not "the king" or "His majesty."[296] When he refused to serve a third term as president, he disappointed many followers and admirers. After two terms as president of the United States, there was considerable sentiment for him to continue in the role as long as he wished, but he stepped aside to allow John Adams to replace him. Washington was not ambitious for power and sincerely believed in the American cause and felt the need to support it openly. By his decision he established the unwritten two-term precedent that was followed until Franklin D. Roosevelt.[297]

The Medal No One Wants to Earn: The Purple Heart is the oldest military decoration still in use in the world. It was established by General George Washington in 1782 at a time when he feared losing his army to mutiny or revolt. Initially called the Badge of Merit, it was the first general decoration in the American army. GW awarded it to officers and soldiers who had performed "meritorious service."[298] For a century and a half it was almost forgotten, not being revived until the 1930s. On Washington's two-hundredth birthday, February 22, 1932, the war department issued General Order Number 3, which decreed that "the Purple Heart established by General George Washington at Newburgh, August 7, 1782, during the War of the Revolution, is hereby revived out of respect to his memory and military achievements."[299] In addition to heroism in combat army regulations "a wound which necessitates treatment by a medical officer and which is received in action with an enemy may, in the judgment of the commander authorized to make the award, be construed as resulting from a singularly meritorious act of essential service."[300] Since then, eligibility has been extended to include members of peacekeeping forces and prisoners of war, as well as victims of terrorist attacks.[301]

Hero Worship: After his death, Washington became an icon rather than a "flesh and blood" man. The story of his life was related more for moral and patriotic instruction than for accuracy. It was not until the middle of the 19th century that historians were sufficiently distant from his lifetime to consider him with scholarly detachment. However, the myths and stories of Washington's perfection survived well into the 20th century.[302] It is not surprising that the architect of the victory in the Revolutionary War and the first president of the United States would gain recognition as a man above all others. Acquiring almost godlike stature, Washington was above the interests of class and section. He delivered on his goal of establishing a strong, viable union from newly independent colonies.[303] In his farewell address, he reminded his fellow citizens that "the Unity of Government which constitutes you one people is also now dear to you. It is justly so; for it is a main pillar in the edifice of your real independence, the support of your tranquility at home; your peace abroad; of your safety; of your prosperity; of that very Liberty which you so highly prize."[304]

Washington held a worldwide larger-than-life reputation as a great patriot-hero and a man of virtue. This virtue was not innate. He had to cultivate it, and everyone who admired him sensed that. Washington realized that he was an extraordinary man and was not ashamed of being so. He enjoyed comparisons to classical heroes and closely guarded his respectable reputation. GW played the role he believed circumstances demanded of him. Through the dignity of his person, the new government found respectability and acceptance. Washington was indeed an extraordinary man, but perhaps his greatest accomplishment was to "make it possible for more ordinary people to run the country."[305]

The Cherry Tree Myth: Parson Mason Locke Weems wrote the moralistic *A History of the Life and Death, Virtues and Exploits of General George Washington* (1800) and *The Life of George Washington, with Curious Anecdotes Laudable to Himself and Exemplary to His Countrymen* (1806). The book went through more than thirty editions, including translations into German. Weems borrowed freely from other sources, collected hearsay and invented memories of people he interviewed and embellished them with stories meant to improve on history. The most famous example is his relating the tale of Washington and the cherry tree. Weems' account is as follows:

> "George," said his father, "do you know who killed that beautiful little cherry tree yonder in the garden?"... Looking at his father with the sweet face of youth brightened with the inexpressible charm of all-conquering truth, he bravely cried out, "I can't tell a lie, Pa; you know I can't tell a lie. I did cut it with my hatchet."[306]

Many American citizens if asked what they knew about George Washington, they probably would list that he was the first president of the United States, that he chopped down a cherry tree, and that he could not lie. The cherry tree story was but one of Pastor Weems' many embroideries. Perhaps he should have remembered Washington's assertion: "It is to be lamented that great characters are seldom without blot."[307]

One of the legends surrounding the life of George Washington is that he prayed for his country in the snow of Valley Forge. A number of artists have represented him kneeling in prayer. Harry Woodman in his *History of Valley Forge* (1950) reported he heard that

Father, I Can Not Tell a Lie; I Cut the Tree, engraving by John C. McRae, after a work of art by George Gorgas White, published by Joseph Laing, c. 1889. Print depicts George Washington as a young boy telling his father that he cut the cherry tree. Published in *A History of the Life and Death, Virtues and Exploits of General George Washington* by Mason Locke Weems, D.C. Lippincott, 1918 (Library of Congress).

Washington often retired to secluded places, and on one such occasion, he was observed by soldier Isaac Potts in vocal prayer.[308] Whether this actually happened or not is almost beside the point. The story of it and the representations of the act have long served as symbols of faith for many Americans.

The Myth of Washington Throwing a Silver Dollar Across the Potomac: Even a strong, athletic man like Washington could not throw a silver dollar over a river that was a mile wide. Besides, there were no silver dollars when Washington was a young man.[309] In his memoirs, Washington's step-grandson, George Washington Parke Custis, reported that Washington had once flung a piece of slate "about the size of a dollar" across the Rappahannock River, near Fredericksburg, Virginia.[310] The river at the site of the Washington family home today measures 250 feet across, still a considerable distance to throw.

Crossing the Delaware: On December 25, 1776, General Washington led some 2400 men in large ore-carrying Durham boats across the Delaware River at McKonkey's Ferry, Pennsylvania, making a surprise attack against the English and Hessian forces at Trenton, New Jersey. The success of the venture came at a time when morale was at its lowest point, and the outcome renewed hope among the army, Congress and the American people. The crossing is celebrated in a famous painting by German-born artist Emanuel Gottlieb Leutze that was completed in 1851. The 12-foot high and 21-foot long painting is a part of the permanent collection of the Metropolitan Museum of Art. A replica of the painting hangs in

Washington Crossing the Delaware print is a reproduction of Emanuel Leutze's painting used as a sheet music cover for "The Continental March." Copyright 1898 by A. W. Elson & Co., Boston (Library of Congress).

the lobby of the West Wing of the White House. Carrie Barrett, curator of art at the Met said, "[The painting] was not conceived as a monument to American patriotism. It was conceived as a work of revolutionary genius."[311] In his journal, Leutze wrote, "I think that what would make important art is art that shows the cycle of freedom, from its very beginnings to where it flowers in the United States."[312]

The painting is notable more for its composition and the artistic considerations that motivated Leutze than for its historical or physical accuracy. Among the "flaws" in the work is the inclusion of the flag ("Stars and Stripes") unfurling behind Washington's head, which did not exist at the time portrayed. The flag used would have been the Grand Union flag. The crossing took place during the middle of the night, so there would not have been any natural light to highlight Washington's face. The boat depicted is the wrong kind and it is overloaded with a cross section of American colonists, another symbolic item intended by the artist. While it is a heroic sight to see a valiant Washington standing staring to the other side of the river, it probably would have been an extremely tricky pose to maintain throughout the crossing. Standing behind Washington holding the flag is James Monroe.[313] Historical and physical flaws do not detract from the revolutionary spirit of the painting.

Washington and the Quakers: During the Revolution, many Friends suffered severely for their pacifism and testimony against the war. Fines and imprisonment were attempted to coerce them to be patriotic, but with little result. In 1777, a forged document resulted in exile to Virginia of twenty Philadelphia citizens, seventeen of whom were Friends. They remained in exile for a period of seven months and two of them died there.[314] When the others were released, they met with George Washington, to whom one of their number, Warner Mifflin, announced:

"I am opposed to the Revolution and to all changes of government which occasion war and bloodshed." Washington asked Mifflin to state the principle on which his opposition to the revolution was based. Mifflin replied, "upon the same principles that I should be opposed to a change in this government — all that was ever gained by revolutions is not an adequate compensation for the loss of life or limb." To this Washington declared: "I honor your sentiments: there is more in that than mankind have generally considered.[315]

At another time (October 1789), Washington penned a letter to the Quakers at their Yearly Meeting for Pennsylvania, New Jersey, Delaware, and the Western Part of Maryland and Virginia. He said, "Your principles and conduct are well known to me; and it is doing the people called Quakers no more than justice to say, that (except their declining to share with others the burden of the common defense) there is no denomination among us who are more exemplary and useful citizens."[316]

A Fish Story: In 1938, Harry Emerson Wildes published *Valley Forge*, in which he related quite a fish story. It seems that during the spring of 1778, the Continental Army under the command of General Washington was encamped at Valley Forge along the Schuylkill River in Pennsylvania and was extremely low on food. Wildes wrote of it:

> Then, dramatically, the famine completely ended. Countless thousands of fat shad, swimming up the Schuylkill to spawn, filled the river.... Soldiers thronged the river bank ... the cavalry was ordered into the river bed ... the horsemen rode upstream, noisily shouting and beating the water, driving the shad before them into nets spread across the Schuylkill.... So thick were the shad that, when the fish were cornered in the nets, a pole could not be thrust into the water without striking fish.... The netting was continued day after day ... until the army was thoroughly stuffed with fish and in addition hundreds of barrels of shad were salted down for future use.[317]

Regrettably, Wildes did not document the source of his story, and no known primary source material has come to light to substantiate it. However, there is information in primary sources to suggest that the British blocked the Schuylkill River, preventing shad fishing by Washington's troops. Shad have not migrated up the Schuylkill River for nearly 200 years due to the construction of dams for the Schuylkill Navigation Company beginning in 1818.[318]

Salutation: When General Howe took command of the British troops in North America, he sought to open a correspondence with General Washington but did not wish to acknowledge GW's official role as commander-in-chief of the "rebels." To that purpose he sent a letter to Washington in New York, addressed simply to "George Washington, Esquire." Now this was an appropriate salutation for a Virginia planter, but Washington refused to accept the letter, unwilling to be treated as less than an equal to his counterpart in the British army. Howe sent a second letter addressed to "George Washington, &c. &c. &c." Washington once again refused to accept the letter and was backed by Congress, which ordered that none of their officers should receive letters or messages from the British army unless they were addressed to them according to their respective ranks.[319]

Howe's Dog: Sometime later a soldier brought General Washington a dog whose collar identified him as the property of General Howe. "Writing from his headquarters at Perkiomen, Pennsylvania, two days after the battle of Germantown," Washington returned the dog by special messenger with the following note: "General Washington's compliments to General Howe. He does himself the pleasure to return him a dog, which accidentally fell into his hands, and by the inscription on the collar appears to belong to General Howe."[320]

Army Strength: During the Constitutional Convention, it was suggested that the nation's army be restricted to five thousand men at any one time. Washington did not agree, but as chairman, he was required to stay out of the debate on the subject. However, he did suggest to another delegate that a clause be added: "No foreign army should invade the United States at any time with more than three thousand troops."[321]

Movie Portrayals of George Washington: Since 1909, there have been 141 movies or TV films in which George Washington was portrayed. In most his appearance was brief and he was not one of the major characters in the film. Joseph Kilgour must have borne some resemblance to the "father of his country," as he appeared in the role on five occasions. Others who impersonated the first president more than once were Charles Ogle, George McQuarrie, George Nash, Alan Mowbray, Montagu Love, Joe Miksak, Howard St. John, Will Geer, Stephen Lang, Anthony Hopkins, Larry Nehring, and David Morse. Barry Bostwick portrayed Washington in "two miniseries, *George Washington* (1984) and *George Washington II; The Forging of a Nation* (1986)." Patty Duke appeared as Martha Washington and Jaclyn Smith as Sally Fairfax, the married woman with whom he supposedly had an affair.[322]

Overdue Books: In the spring of 2010, the New York Library reported discovering in one of its ledgers that George Washington borrowed two books in 1789 and they were never returned. One of the books was the *Law of Nations*, which deals with international relations. The other was a volume of debates from Great Britain's House of Commons. The library does not expect to collect the 220 years of late fees but would like to get the books back. The ledger lists the borrower as "president."[323]

From the Letters of George Washington[324]

I suffered every attack that was made upon my Executive conduct ... to pass unnoticed while I remained in public office, well knowing that if the general tenor of it would not stand the test of investigation, a newspaper vindication would be of little avail [Letter to W. Gordon, October 15, 1789].

The tumultuous populace of large cities are ever to be dreaded. Their indiscriminate violence prostrates for the time all public authority, and its consequences are sometimes extensive and terrible [Letter to Marquis de Lafayette, July 28, 1781].

Do not conceive that fine Clothes make fine Men, any more than fine feathers make fine Birds [Letter to Bushrod Washington, January 15, 1783].

A people ... who are possessed of the spirit of commerce, who see and who will pursue their advantages may achieve almost anything [Letter to Benjamin Harrison, October 10, 1784].

The executive branch of this government never has, nor will suffer, while I preside, any improper conduct of its officers to escape with impunity [Letter to Gouverneur Morris, December 2, 1795].

Government being, among other purposes, instituted to protect the consciences of men from oppression, it is certainly the duty of rulers, not only to abstain from it themselves but, according to their stations, to prevent it in others [Letter to Quakers, September 28, 1789].

I wish the Constitution, which is offered, had been made more perfect; but I sincerely believe it is the best that can be obtained at this time. And, as a constitutional door is opened for amendment thereafter, the adoption of it, under the present circumstances of the Union, is in my opinion desirable [Letter to Patrick Henry, September 24, 1787].

I have beheld no day since the commencement of hostilities that I have thought her liberties in such eminent danger as at present. Friends and foes seem now to combine to pull down the goodly fabric as we have hitherto been raising at the expense of so much time, blood, and treasure; and unless the bodies politick will exert themselves to bring things back to first principles, correct abuses, and punish our internal foes, inevitable ruin must follow [Letter to George Mason, March 27, 1779].

Democratical states must always feel before they can see: it is this that makes their Governments slow, but the people will be right at last [Letter to Marquis de Lafayette, July 25, 1785].

We should never despair, our Situation before has been unpromising and has changed for the better, so I trust it will again. If new difficulties arise, we must only put forth new Exertions and proportion our Efforts to the exigency of the times [Letter to Major General Philip Schuyler, July 15, 1777].

Discipline is the soul of an army. It makes small numbers formidable; procures success to the weak, and esteem to all [Letter of Instructions to the captains of the Virginia Regiments, July 29, 1759].

The consciousness of having discharged that duty which we owe to our country is superior to all other considerations [Letter to James Madison, March 2, 1788].

The best means of forming a manly, virtuous, and happy people will be found in the right education of youth. Without this foundation, every other means, in my opinion, must fail [Letter to George Chapman, December 15, 1784].

To trust altogether in the justice of our cause, without our own utmost exertions, would be tempting Providence [Letter to Governor Jonathan Trumbull, August 7, 1776].

Example, whether it be good or bad, has a powerful influence [Letter to Lord Stirling, March 5, 1780].

It is better to offer no excuse than a bad one [Letter to his niece Harriet Washington, October 30, 1791].

All see, and most admire, the glare which hovers round the external trappings of elevated office. To me there is nothing in it, beyond the luster which may be reflected from its connection with a power of promoting human felicity [Letter to Catherine Macaulay Graham, January 9, 1790].

My anxious recollections, my sympathetic feeling, and my best wishes are irresistibly excited whensoever, in any country, I see an oppressed nation unfurl the banners of freedom [Letter to Pierre Auguste Adet, January 1, 1796].

More permanent and genuine happiness is to be found in the sequestered walks of connubial life than in the giddy rounds of promiscuous pleasure [Letter to the Marquis de la Rourie, August 10, 1786].

Nothing short of independence, it appears to me, can possibly do. A peace on other terms would, if I may be allowed the expression, be a peace of war [Letter to John Banister, April 21, 1778].

Integrity and firmness are all I can promise. These, be the voyage long or short, shall never forsake me, although I may be deserted by all men; for of the consolations, which are to be derived from these, under any circumstances, the world cannot deprive me [Letter to Henry Knox, April 1, 1789].

Jealousy and local policy mix too much in all our public councils for the good government of the Union. In a word, the confederation appears to me to be little more than a shadow without the substance.... [Letter to James Warren, October 7, 1785].

Impressed with a conviction that the due administration of justice is the firmest pillar of good government, I have considered the first arrangement of the judicial department as essential to the happiness of our country, and to the stability of its political system; hence the selection of the fittest characters to expound the law, and dispense justice has been an invariable object of my anxious concern [Letter to U.S. Attorney General Edmund Randolph, 1789].

The best and only safe road to honor, glory, and true dignity is justice [Letter to Marquis de Lafayette, September 30, 1779].

Laws made by common consent must not be trampled on by individuals [Letter to Colonel Vanneter, 1781].

It is infinitely better to have a few good men than many indifferent ones [Letter to James McHenry, August 10, 1798].

My political conduct in nominations, even if it was influenced by principle, must be exceedingly circumspect and proof against just criticism, for the eyes of Argus are upon me, and no slip will pass unnoticed that can be improved into a supposed partiality for friends or relatives [Letter to Bushrod Washington, July 27, 1789].

As the first of everything, in our situation, will serve to establish a Precedent, it is devoutly wished on my part that these precedents may be fixed on true principles [Letter to James Madison, May 15, 1789].

There cannot, in my opinion, be the least danger that the President will, by any intrigue, ever be able to continue himself one moment in office, much less perpetuate himself in it. Under an extended view of this subject, I can see no propriety in precluding ourselves from the service of any man, who in some great emergency, shall be deemed universally most capable of serving the public [Letter to Marquis de Lafayette, April 28, 1788].

It is with pleasure that I receive reproof, when reproof is due, because no person can be readier to accuse me, than I am to acknowledge an error, when I am guilty of one; not more desirous of atoning for a crime, when I am sensible of having committed it [Letter to the Lieutenant Governor of Virginia, 1757].

To persevere in one's duty and to be silent is the best answer to calumny [Letter to Governor William Livingston, December 7, 1779].

When one side of a story is heard and often repeated, the human mind becomes impressed with it insensibly [Letter to Edmund Pendleton, January 22, 1795].

There is nothing that gives a man consequence, and renders him fit for command, like a support that renders him independent of everybody but the State he serves [Letter to the President of Congress, September 24, 1776].

Treaties which are not built upon reciprocal benefits are not likely to be of long duration [Letter to Comet de Moustier, March 26, 1788].

It is a maxim founded on the universal experience of mankind that no nation is to be trusted farther than it is bound by its interests [Letter to Henry Laurens, 1778].

My first wish is to see this plague of mankind, war, banished from the earth [Letter to David Humphreys, July 25, 1785].

Estimates of George Washington

BY OTHER PRESIDENTS

Washington is the mightiest name of earth — long since the mightiest in the cause of civil liberty, still mightiest in moral reformation.... On that name an eulogy is expected. To add brightness to the sun or glory to the name of Washington is alike impossible. Let none attempt it. In solemn awe pronounce the name, and in its naked deathless splendor leave it shining on.[325] — Abraham Lincoln

Eternity alone can reveal to the human race its debt of gratitude to the peerless and immortal name of Washington.[326] — James A. Garfield

BY OTHERS

[He] has so happy a faculty of appearing to accommodate and yet carrying his point, that, if he was not really one of the best-intentioned men of the world, he might be a very dangerous one.[327] — Abigail Adams

More than all and above all, Washington was master of himself.[328] — Charles Francis Adams

If I were to characterize George Washington's feelings towards his country, I should be less inclined than most people to stress what is called Washington's *love* of his country. What impresses me as far more important is what I should call Washington's *respect* for his country.[329] — Randolph G. Adams

Washington's character was rock solid. He came to stand for the new nation and its republican virtues, which was why he became our first President by unanimous choice.[330] — Stephen Ambrose

His preeminence is not so much to be seen in the display of any one virtue as in the possession of them all, and in the practice of the most difficult. Hereafter, therefore, his character must be studied as a model, a precious one to a free republic.[331]— Fisher Ames

George Washington is the only president who didn't blame the previous administration for his troubles.[332]— Anonymous

If ever a nation was debauched by a man, the American nation has been debauched by Washington. If ever a nation was deceived by a man, the American nation has been deceived by Washington. Let his conduct, then, be an example to future ages; let it serve to be a warning that no man may be an idol.[333]— Anonymous

Simple and Brave, his faith awoke / Ploughmen to struggle with their fate; / Armies won battles when he spoke, / And out of Chaos sprang the state.[334]— Robert Bridges

Washington wasn't born good. Only practice and habit make it so.[335]— William Bennet

He has become entombed in his own myth — a metaphorical Washington monument that hides from us the lineaments of the real man.[336]— Marcus Cunliffe

Washington! Here is a fine, fearless, placid man, perfectly well seated in the centre of his soul, direct and pure.... He could smile. Drink, make love.... He paraphrased Horace: "Carpe diem, carpe noctem" ... To conquer, and to make love.[337]— Joseph Delteil

Blot out from the pages of history the names of all great actors of his time in the dream of nations, and preserve the name of Washington and the century would be renowned.[338]— Chauncey M. Depew

Every hero becomes a bore at last.... They cry up the virtues of George Washington —"Damn George Washington!" Is the poor Jacobin's whole speech and confutation.[339]— Ralph Waldo Emerson

Washington was never truly a military man. He remained to the end of the war a civilian serving half-reluctantly in uniform.[340]— James Thomas Flexner

George Washington, Commander of the American armies, who like Joshua of old, commanded the sun and the moon to stand still, and they obeyed him.[341]— Benjamin Franklin

I often say of George Washington that he was one of the few in the whole history of the world who was not carried away by power.[342]— Robert Frost

It was not very long before I discovered that he was neither remarkable for delicacy nor good temper.[343]— Alexander Hamilton

Washington is now only a steel engraving. About the real man who lived and loved and hated and schemed, we know but little.[344]— Robert G. Ingersoll

General Washington seemed to arrest fortune with one glance.[345]— Marquis de Lafayette

Washington's entire honesty of mind and his fearless look into the face of the facts are qualities which can never go out of fashion and which we should all do well to imitate.[346]— Henry Cabot Lodge

Firmly erect, he towered above them all, / The incarnate discipline that was to free / With iron curb that armed democracy.[347]— J.B. Lowell

He guided passions of others, because he was master of his own.[348]— Ebenezer Grant Marsh

More than any other individual and as much as to one individual was possible, has he contributed to found this, our wide spreading empire, and to give to the Western World independence and freedom.[349]— John Marshall

Born to high destinies, he was fashioned for them by the hand of nature. His form was noble — his port majestic. On his front were enthroned the virtues which exalt, and those which adorn the human character. So dignified his deportment, no man could approach him but with respect — none was great in his presence. You have all seen him, and you all have felt the reverence he inspired.[350]— Gouverneur Morris

Washington can never be otherwise than well.... The measure of his fame is full.... Posterity will talk of him with reverence as the founder of a great empire, when my name shall be lost in the vortex of Revolutions![351]— Napoleon Bonaparte

And as to you, Sir, treacherous in private friendship (for so you have been to me, and that in the day of danger) and a hypocrite in public life, the world will be puzzled to decide whether you are an apostate or an imposter; whether you have abandoned good principles, or whether you ever had any.[352]— Thomas Paine

[Washington's] writings reveal a clear, thoughtful, and remarkably coherent vision of what he hoped an American republic would become. These notions began to emerge early in the 1770s, took on a sharper, clearer perspective during the Revolution and changed little thereafter. His words, many of them revealed only for family and friends, reveal a man with a passionate commitment to a full developed idea of a constitutional republic on a continental scale, eager to promote that plan whatever and whenever circumstance or the hand of Providence allowed.[353]— Glenn A. Phelps

Of all the founding fathers George Washington alone demonstrated fully the threefold characteristics of a visionary leader and the intellectual and moral capacity, over a long period of time and in the course of manifold difficulties, to maintain coherency between long range ideas and goals and short term actions.[354]— Richard C. Stazesky

He was ignorant of the commonest accomplishments of youth. He would not even lie.... I am different from Washington; I have a higher, grander standard of principle. Washington could not lie. I can lie, but I won't.[355]— Mark Twain (Samuel Clemens)

[The gift of silence is] a quality rare among American politicians of any era. He had learned as early as his service in command of the Virginia Regiment during the French and Indian War that it would not be necessary to retract or explain or apologize later for what he had not said in the first place. By the time he reached the presidency, it had become a habit.[356]— Dorothy Twohig

America has furnished to the world the character of Washington. And if our American institutions had done nothing else, that alone would have entitled them to the respect of the world.[357]— Daniel Webster

The crude commercialism of America, its materializing spirit ... are entirely due to the country having for its national hero a man who was incapable of telling a lie.[358]— Oscar Wilde

Two

John Adams

The Revolution Was Made in the Minds of the People

Second President of the United States of America, 1797–1801

When a monument for John Adams was suggested in 2001, Thomas Oliphant of the *Boston Globe* opposed it citing Adams' disqualifying action of signing the hated Alien and Sedition Acts. Oliphant said Adams did not deserve the honor, "the political equivalent of beatification." The publisher maintained the acts violated the Constitution that Adams had helped create.[1] Adams had no expectations of public honor, writing the following to Benjamin Rush: "Mausoleums, statues, monuments will never be erected to me. I wish them not. Panegyrical romances will never be written, nor flattering orations spoken, to transmit me to posterity in brilliant colors. No, nor in true colors. All but the last I loathe."[2]

Birth: John Adams' date of birth is October 30, 1735, by the Gregorian calendar. By the Julian calendar still in use at the time, he was born on October 19. He came to life in a small saltbox house on a farm founded by his great-grandfather about 100 years earlier, in the North Precinct of Braintree (in 1792, Braintree's North Parish was incorporated as the town of Quincy), Massachusetts, ten miles south of Boston.

Captain Wollaston founded Braintree in 1625, which was initially names Mount Wollaston.[3] The house, in which Adams lived in his youth, had three rooms and two fireplaces on the first floor and two rooms above. It still stands and is open to visitors as part of Adams National Historical Park. John's father bought the house, built in 1681, and six acres of property surrounding it in 1720.

Nicknames and Titles: Nicknames are not always meant to compliment people, but rather to belittle them. While presiding over the Senate as the nation's first vice president, Adams made such a nuisance of himself that the Senators voted to ban the vice president from participating in debate in the chamber.[4] As a result of Adams' insistence that the president should be referred to as "His Majesty" or "His Highness," Senators dubbed him, "His Rotundity,"[5] a reference to his short, stocky physique.

In this same mocking spirit, Adams earned the titles "Duke of Braintree," "Bonny Johnny," a reference to his image as a monarchist, and "His Superfluous Excellency," coined by Benjamin Franklin as a comment on the lack of responsibility of the vice president.[6] In a more flattering vein, a contemporary anointed Adams with another nickname, saying, "The man to whom the country is most indebted for the great measure of independence is Mr. John Adams.... I call him the Atlas of Independence."[7]

Family: The father of John Adams was a thrifty farmer and a shoemaker, known as

"Deacon John." He was influential in town business, serving as selectman and as an officer of the militia. The elder Adams prized godly virtues and once wrote in a letter asserting that "[without Christianity, my ancestors would have been] fops, sots, gamblers, starved with hunger, or frozen with cold, scalped by Indians ... been melted away and disappeared."[8] The younger John described his father as the "honestest man" he ever met: "In wisdom, piety, benevolence, and charity in proportion to his education and sphere of life, I have never known his superior."[9]

The elder John Adams died on May 25, 1761, during an influenza epidemic. His estate was appraised at £1,330 9s (about $15,000). John's brother Peter Boylston Adams inherited the original homestead, while John received the adjacent home and property. John eventually bought his birthplace from Peter, in 1774.[10]

Susanna Boylston Adams came from one of Massachusetts' most prominent families, mostly merchants and physicians, families referred to as the "Brahmin Class" by future generations of Bostonians. "Boston Brahmins are wealthy Yankee families characterized by a highly discreet and inconspicuous lifestyle. They are associated with the distinctive Boston Brahmin accent, and with Harvard University."[11] Susanna's parents, Peter Boylston (c. 1673–1743) and Ann White (1685–1772), married in 1704. Susanna's uncle Zabdiel Boylston, a physician, performed the first surgical operation in the colonies, the first removal of gallstones, and the first removal of a breast tumor.[12] He studied medicine with his surgeon father, Dr. Thomas Boylston, of Watertown and Dr. Cutter of Boston. During a smallpox outbreak in Boston in 1721, at the urging of Cotton Mather, Zabdiel inoculated 244 people, beginning with his son and two servants, by applying pus from a smallpox sore to a small wound on the subjects. At first, Boston religious groups reacted with hostility towards these first inoculations in what would come to be the United States. Both Mather and Boylston received death threats. Of those inoculated, "only six died of smallpox, four of whom had contracted the disease before inoculation."[13]

John Adams, Second President of the United States, lithograph print by Pendleton's Lithography, Boston, on stone by Maurin from the original portrait painted by Gilbert Stuart for Messrs. Doggett of Boston, 1828? (Library of Congress).

Devoted to her family, Susanna introduced her sons to the customs and lifestyles of the elite colonial Boston. Five years after John senior's death she married John Chenery.[14] John junior had two younger brothers, Peter Boylston (1737–1823) and Elihu (1740–1776). Peter was a farmer and militia captain of Braintree. Elihu fought as a minuteman on the

Concord Green in 1775. He died while serving as a commander in the Continental Army, reportedly from a "contagious distemper."[15] Henry Adams, the curator of American painting at the Cleveland Museum of Art and a seventh-generation descendent of John Adams, said of his family, "I suppose always part of the Adams identity is to think the world hates you for being so virtuous. The Adamses kind of felt they were less popular than they deserved to be and took a perverse pride in that."[16]

Ancestors: John Adams' parents and ancestors were honored members of the community of Braintree from its founding. He was a descendent of both Pilgrims and Puritans. His father was a fourth-generation descendent of Henry Adams, who emigrated from Devonshire, England, to Massachusetts around 1636 with his wife and eight sons. Henry received a grant of 40 acres of land at Mount Wollaston, part of North Braintree. Henry and "several of his descendants made their living as maltsters, makers of malt from barley for use of baking or brewing beer."[17] The future president was the great-great-grandson of Pilgrims John and Priscilla Alden who landed at Plymouth Rock in 1620.[18] His maternal great-great-grandfather, Thomas Boylston (1615–1653), emigrated from London to Watertown, Massachusetts around 1635.[19]

Appearance: Adams' father described his teenage son: "He was almost a man grown. He wasn't tall, not above five feet tall, but his shoulders were heavy. He was well knit, muscular, and quick and sure in his movements. His color was unusually high; just not his face was red from exertion, his blue eyes blazed."[20]

David McCullough gave a picturesque description of the second president:

[Adams] stood five feet seven or eight inches tall — about "middle size" in that day — and though verging on portly, he had a straight-up, square-shouldered stance, and was, in fact, surprisingly fit and solid. His hands were the hands of a man accustomed to pruning his own trees, cutting his own hay, and splitting his own firewood.

In such bitter cold of winter, the pink of his round, clean-shaven, very English face would all but glow, and if he were hatless or without a wig, his high forehead and thinning hairline made the whole of the face look rounder still. The hair, light brown in color, was full about the ears. The chin was firm, the nose sharp, almost birdlike. But it was the dark, perfectly arched brows and keen blue eyes that gave the face its vitality. Years later, recalling this juncture in his life, he claimed he looked rather like a short, thick Archbishop of Canterbury.[21]

Actor Simon Russell Beale said of him:

[He] had a very resonant voice, apparently. He made a very clear and bell-like sound in the court."[22] Adams enjoyed eating well, perhaps too well. A descendant reported that while living in Philadelphia "[he] throve well on turtle, jellies, varied sweetmeats, whipped syllabubs, floating islands, fruits, raisins, almonds, peaches, wines, especially Madeira."[23] Even his wife said he was fat. His "chrome-dome" baldness ran in his family.[24] By the time he became president, most of his teeth had fallen out. He refused to wear dentures, causing him to talk with a lisp.[25] At his inauguration, one newspaper referred to the president as an "old fielder." A pleased Adams explained: "[It is a] tough, hardy, laborious little horse that works very hard and lives upon very little, very useful to his master at small expense.[26]

Personality and Character: Historian Joseph J. Ellis, writing in *The Passionate Sage*, claimed that Adams had an "instinct for doing the right thing but was hopelessly inept in his dealings with people. He was a man of principle — but generally of inflexible principle."[27] "This was the established Adams pattern: to sense where history was headed, make decisions that positioned America to be carried forward on those currents, but to do so in a way that assured his own alienation from success."[28] According to David McCullough, Adams was a "great-hearted, persevering man of uncommon ability and force. He had a brilliant mind and, like many New Englanders, [was] emphatically independent by nature, hardworking and frugal. He could be high-spirited and affectionate, vain, cranky, impetuous, self-absorbed, and fiercely stubborn; passionate, quick to anger, and all-forgiving; generous and entertaining. He was blessed with great courage and good humor, yet subject to spells of despair, and especially when separated from his family or during periods of prolonged inactivity."[29]

Despite his outstanding accomplishments as a witness and performer of the American Revolution saga from beginning to end, Adams was fiercely self-sufficient. According to C. Bradley Thompson, Adams' "unyielding integrity would not allow him to compromise when he believed he was right: He was in constant battle with the accepted, the conventional, the fashionable, and the popular.... His sense of life and moral virtues were shaped early by the manners and mores of a Puritan culture that honored sobriety, industry, thrift, simplicity, and diligence."[30]

Adams was "plain-spoken, tough-minded, scrupulously honest, honorable, upright, dauntingly erudite, but also quarrelsome and stubborn."[31] In later years, in an answer to explain his "emotional outbursts that resembled tantrums, he claimed that his political enemies had exaggerated the tendency."[32] He conceded: "My temper in general has been tranquil except when any instance of Madness, Deceit, Hypocrisy, Ingratitude, Treachery, or Perfidy has suddenly struck me. Then I have always been irascible enough, and in three or four Instances, too much so."[33]

Even in his eighties, he wanted it known that the storms that once enraged him had been brought under control, and that "anger never rested in the bosom."[34] Adams always was long-winded, eager to express his opinions, which in least in his mind, were golden. His remarks to and about others often landed him into trouble due to their harsh and disapproving delivery. Even his friends warned him to be more circumspect in his speaking and writing. The Reverend Theodore Parker of Boston said of the second president: "He was terribly open, earnest, and direct, and could not keep his mouth shut."[35] For his contemporaries, John Adams' blunt persistence sometimes tried the patience even of allies. It is amazing that he had any successes as a diplomat. Paul Johnson described Adams as cantankerous, unloved, and quarrelsome.[36] Adams had little tact for avoiding disputes; but his fury, although often ferocious, was brief, and afterwards he felt no malice. He admitted that his chief shortcomings were vanity and loquacity.[37]

Presidential historian Richard Norton Smith described him: "He's short, he's fat, he's balding, he's toothless, he's the most uncharismatic of men on the surface — until you start to read his letters. Then he is engaging, riveting, entertaining, occasionally outrageous, but above all alive."[38] Benjamin Rush was quoted: "He saw the whole of a subject at a glance, and ... was equally fearless of men and of consequences of a bold assertion of his opinion.... He was a stranger to dissimulation."[39] An old friend, Jonathan Sewell, speaking in 1787, assessed Adams: "He can't dance, drink, game, flatter, promise, dress, swear with the gentlemen, and small talk and flirt with the ladies— in short, he has none of the essential arts or ornaments, which make up a courtier — there are thousands with a tenth part of his understanding, and without a spark of honesty, would distance him infinitely in any court in Europe."[40]

OTHER VIEWS OF ADAMS

This house will bear witness to his piety; this town, his birthplace, to his munificence; history to his patriotism; posterity to the depth and compass of his mind.[41] — John Quincy Adams

It has been the political career of this man to begin with hypocrisy, proceed with arrogance, and finish with contempt.[42]— Tom Paine

It's just that he wasn't very special.[43]— Harry S Truman

Adams has far less abilities that he believes he possesses.[44]— Oliver Wolcott

In a 1779 diary entry, Adams reflected:

By my physical constitution I am but an ordinary man.... Yet some great events, some cutting expressions, some mean hypocrisies, have at times thrown this assemblage of sloth, sleep, and littleness into rage like a lion.[45]

In a letter to James Madison, Thomas Jefferson analyzed Adams' character:

He is distrustful, obstinate, excessively vain, and takes no counsel from anyone.... He is vain, irritable, and a bad calculator of the force and probable effects of the motives which govern men. This all the ill which can possibly be said of him; he is profound in his views: and accurate in his judgment except when knowledge of the world is necessary to form a judgment. He is as disinterested as the Being who made him.... I like everything about Adams except his politics.... I never felt a diminution of confidence in his integrity, and retained a solid affection for him.[46]

Marriage and Romances: John was popular with girls. However, he took his father's warning that illicit sex almost always resulted in venereal disease and proudly wrote in his diary about his celibacy before marriage — "My children may be assured that no illegitimate son or daughter exists!"[47] Before meeting Abigail Smith, at age 23, Adams paid court to "handsome and brilliant" Hannah Quincy,[48] the daughter of Colonel John Quincy. Adams poetically referred to Hannah as "Orlinda," and in his diary wrote of his dream of her: "[It was] a scene which seems to be grappled to my soul with Hooks of Steal, as immoveably as I wish to grapple in my Arms the Nimph, who gives it all its ornaments. If I look upon a Law Book and labor to exert my attention, my eyes tis true are on the Book, but Imagination is at a tea table with Orlinda, seeing that Face, those Eyes, that Shape, that familiar friendly look, and hearing Sense divine come from her Tongue."[49] On one occasion, Hannah informed him that she knew some Latin and uttered *Puella amat puer*, to which John responded, "Puella what? ... The object of the verb takes the accusative, in Latin. If you are trying to say the boy loves the girl.... Or do you mean, possibly, the girl loves the boy?"[50]

Despite his pledge to himself not to marry until well-established as an attorney, he almost succumbed to Hannah's charms and nearly proposed. The moment passed and so did the possibility of a match. Adams vowed to redouble his efforts to put aside thoughts of wedded bliss, but he never forgot her. The two saw each other one more time, nearly six decades after their courtship, after both had loss their spouses, and reminisced about their romance. In his diary Josiah Quincy recalled the encounter and ensuing conversation when both were nearly 91.

JOHN: What! Madam! Shall we not go walk in Cupid's Grove together?
HANNAH: Ah, Sir! It would not be the first time.[51]

One of the happiest unions of a president of the United States and his wife was that of John Adams and Abigail Smith Adams. They wedding took place on October 25, 1764, the beginning of an eventful 54-year and three days partnership. The ceremony was celebrated by her father, William Smith, for forty-five years, pastor of the Congregational Church in Weymouth, Massachusetts.[52]

Abigail held a social position higher than that of John and, as her "demeanor demonstrated, more endowed with rare qualities of head and heart"[53] than her husband. In his diary Adams described Abigail, his third cousin: "[She is] tender, feeling, sensible, friendly. A friend. Not an imprudent, not an indelicate, not a disagreeable word or action. Prudent, soft, sensible, obliging, active."[54]

Although Abigail had little formal education; her father "encouraged her to enrich and cultivate her fine, inquisitive mind, explaining that it was priceless gift from God."[55] Her mother would not allow her to go to school, but Abigail absorbed perhaps much more in her readings at the three libraries of her family. Her education put off some possible suitors but not John, who found it delightful. Throughout their long happy marriage, they were intellectual equals.[56] Abigail was "wise, learned, strong-willed, passionate and patriotic."[57]

Abigail Adams, engraving from an original painting by Gilbert Stuart published by Johnson, Wilson & Co., New York, between 1830 and 1860 (Library of Congress).

While John served in the Continental Congress or was otherwise involved in political activities, Abigail managed the family farm and raised their five children alone. Her stewardship of the farm and other business affairs was so effective that it gave her husband time for his public service. Abigail did not seek these responsibilities. Writer Edith B. Gelles reported: "[S]he believed her performance was extraordinary, aberrant, expedient, and unnatural. She continually referred to her new situation as a patriotic sacrifice for her country."[58] She constantly encouraged her husband, once writing: "You cannot be, I know, nor do I want to see you, an inactive spectator.... We have too many high sounding words, and too few actions that correspond with them."[59]

During long separations and ever after, the Adams exchanged over a thousand letters, all extant. Their correspondence reveals the nature of their relationship. The loving couple completely committed to each other and depended on each other's advice and intelligence. In her letters to John, Abigail displayed wit and a substantial interest in public affairs. In the letters, she revealed her cares and worries, gave her frank opinions and advice to her husband, and offered "the best account that exists from the pre– to the post–Revolutionary period in America of a woman's life and world."[60] Abigail became one of the most influential women in America of her day. Throughout the years, the love letters of the couple remained playful and passionate. As was the practice at the time, they adopted pen names. She chose Diana, named for the Roman goddess of the moon, and he adopted Lysander, the Spartan war hero. John would often address his letters to "Dear Adorable" or "My dear Diana," but Abigail's salutation throughout her life was "My Dearest Friend."[61] The intimacy of their correspondence lasted throughout their marriage. In later life, Abigail ceased signing her letters Diana, replacing the name with that of Portia, the patent wife of the Roman politician Brutus.[62]

In a celebrated March 31, 1776, letter, Abigail championed women's causes, exhorting him to "remember the Ladies, and be more generous and favorable to them than your ancestors. Do not put such unlimited power into the hands of the Husbands. Remember all Men would be tyrants if they could. If particular care and attention is not paid to the Ladies we are determined to ferment a Revolution and will not hold ourselves bound by any Laws in which we have no voice or Representation."[63] In John's response to her missive, he adopted a playful tone, even perhaps flippant: "We have been told that our struggle has loosened the bonds of government everywhere ... that Indians slaughter their guardians, and Negroes grow insolent to their masters. But your letter was the first intimation that another tribe, more numerous and powerful than all the rest, was growing discontented."[64]

When John was elected President; Abigail joined him in the temporary capital of Philadelphia. She fell seriously ill during a journey home to Quincy and was near death for a time. She recovered after several months but remained weak. John returned to Philadelphia alone.[65] Early in October 1818, Abigail fell ill with typhus and died several weeks later at age 73. She managed her own death, mustering all of her strength to make it to her mother's house, so she could die among the people she loved.[66] Her final resting place is at the cemetery of First Church in Quincy.

Children: In a Letter to Abigail, May 12, 1780, John made one of the most memorable statements regarding providing a better life for children and their children:

> The science of government it is my duty to study, more than all other sciences: the arts of legislation and administration and negotiation ought to take the place of, indeed exclude, in a manner, all other arts. I must study politics and war that my sons may have liberty to study mathematics and philosophy. Our sons ought to study mathematics and philosophy, geography, natural history and naval architecture, navigation, commerce and agriculture in order to give their children a right to study painting, poetry, music, architecture, statuary, tapestry and porcelain.[67]

Abigail Adams gave birth to six children, four of whom lived to adulthood. Susanna (1768–1770) died at one year old, and Elizabeth died at birth in 1777. Abigail Amelia "Nabby" (1765–1813) was born nine months after John and Abigail Adams' wedding. Nabby was her mother's constant companion during her father's and brothers' extended absences from their farm.[68]

John missed her teen years while he was in Europe on diplomatic missions. Nabby married Colonel William Stephens Smith, who served as her father's secretary in London. They had four children, but Smith's series of get-rich-schemes, including one intended to free Venezuela from Spanish rule plagued the marriage. It cost Smith his position as a surveyor of the Port of New York, which his father-in-law had secured for him. Smith "moved his family to a farm in East Chester, New York, where Abigail was a frequent visitor. Her concern for her daughter's welfare continued; mother and daughter even discussed divorce, almost unheard at that time."[69] Nabby underwent a mastectomy for breast cancer in 1811. The rare operation, performed without anesthesia, initially appeared successful, but she died two years later at age 48.[70]

John Quincy (1767–1848) became the sixth president of the United States and more will be said of him in his own profile. Charles (1770–1812) lived a life of instability as a long-time alcoholic before dying of its effects at age 30. He read law with Alexander Hamilton and married Sally Smith, Nabby's sister-in-law, with whom he had two daughters. Like Nabby's husband, he participated in shady financial schemes and before his death, abandoned his law practice and his family.[71]

Thomas Boylston (1772–1832) passed the Philadelphia bar, but his practice failed, and in 1803 he relented to his parents' pressure to return to Quincy. He married Ann "Nancy" Harrod, with whom he had seven children. He served as caretaker for the Adams farm until drinking became a problem for him.[72]

Religion and Religious Beliefs: Adams' father-in-law, William Smith, a liberal Congregationalist, supported the doctrines of Dutch theologian Jacobus Arminius (1560–1609), which stressed man's free will in contrast to Calvinistic predestination. Smith did not preach original sin or the full divinity of Christ; instead, he emphasized the importance of reason and morality in religious life.[73] On July 26, 1796, Adams confided to his diary a reflection on Thomas Paine's *The Age of Reason*: "The Christian religion is, above all the Religions that ever prevailed or existed in ancient or modern times, the religion of Wisdom, Virtue, Equity, and Humanity. Let the Blackguard Paine say what he will; if it's Resignation to God, it is goodness itself to Man."[74]

Raised a strict Congregationalist, John ultimately rejected many fundamental doctrines of orthodox Christianity, such as the Trinity and the divinity of Jesus. He became a Unitarian, which during the Colonial times was a non–Trinitarian Protestant Christian denomination. He complained: "I have been a church going animal for seventy-six years, and this has been alleged as proof of my heresy."[75] Adams and his wife actively contributed to the United First Parish Church in Quincy, Unitarian in doctrine.

In a diary entry, on February 22, 1756, Adams imagined the lessons found in the Bible being learned worldwide: "Suppose a nation in some distant region should take the Bible for their only law book, and every member should regulate his conduct by the precepts there exhibited! Every member would be obligated in conscience, to temperance, frugality, and industry; to justice, kindness, and charity towards his fellow man; and to piety, love and reverence toward Almighty God.... What a Utopia, what Paradise would this region be."[76]

Summary of John Adams' religious views: "Adams' overall view of religion was ambivalent. He believed that religion could be a force for good in the lives of individuals and society in general, but he was aware of the abuses leading from religious beliefs. He was wary of the risks of established religions to persecute religious minorities or to wage holy wars."[77] In a letter, Adams gave an opinion on religion, which is usually incompletely quoted: "Twenty times in the course of my late reading have I been on the point of breaking out, 'This would be the best of all possible worlds, if there were no religion in it!!!' But in this exclamation I would have been as fanatical as Bryant or Cleverly. Without religion this world would be something not fit to be mentioned in polite company, I mean Hell."[78] (Lemuel Bryant was Adams' parish priest and Joseph Cleverly his Latin School master.)

Adams ardently championed the Separation of Church and State: "Nothing is more dreaded that the national government meddling with religion."[79]

In an 1813 letter, Adams wrote: "The love of God and His creation, delight, joy, triumph, exultation, in my own experience ... are my religion.... The general principles on which the fathers achieved independence were... the general principles of Christianity... I will avow that I then believed, and now believe, that those general principles of Christianity are as eternal and immutable as the existence and attributes of God."[80]

In another letter, Adams lamented what he considered the misrepresentation of original Christian doctrines: "Indeed, Mr. Jefferson, what could be invented to debase the ancient Christianism which Greeks, Romans, Hebrews and Christian factions, above all the Catholics, have no fraudulently imposed upon the public? Miracles after Miracles have rolled down in torrents."[81]

In his diary, Adams criticized Christian religious doctrine: "The Church of Rome has made it an article of faith that no man can be saved out of their church, and all other religious sects approach this dreadful opinion in proportion to their ignorance, and the influence of ignorant or wicked priests."[82]

"Old Stone Temple, United First Parish Church Quincy, Massachusetts," glass negative created c. 1904 (Library of Congress, Detroit Publishing Company Collection).

In a letter to Jefferson on December 25, 1813, Adams proclaimed, "I have examined all religions, as well as my narrow sphere, my straightened means, and my busy life, would allow; and the result is that the Bible is the Best Book in the world. It contains more philosophy than all the libraries I have seen."[83]

His biographer and grandson, Charles Francis Adams, wrote that "with the independent spirit which in early life had driven him from the ministry, he rejected the prominent doctrines of Calvinism, the trinity, the atonement and election of those to be saved."[84] John Adams professed the following: "The divinity of Jesus is made a convenient cover for absurdity. Nowhere in the Gospels do we find a precept for creeds, confessions, oaths, doc-trines, and whole carloads of other foolish trumpery that we find in Christianity."[85] In a letter to Jefferson on September 3, 1816, Adams revealed his abhorrence of the cross as a symbol of Christianity: "I almost shudder at the thought of alluding to the most fatal exam-ple of the abuses of grief which the history of mankind has preserved — the Cross. Consider what calamities that engine of grief has produced! With the rational respect that is due to it, knavish priests have added prostitution of it that fill or might fill the blackest and blood-iest pages of human history."[86]

In a letter to F.A. Van der Kamp of December 27, 1816, an aging Adams proclaimed, "As I understand the Christian religion, it was, and is, a revelation. But how has it happened that millions of fables, tales, legends, have been blended with both Jewish and Christian revelation that have made them the most bloody religion that ever existed."[87] In another letter to Van der Kamp, Adams proclaimed his admiration for the Jews:

> [T]he Hebrews have done more to civilize men than any other nation. If I were an atheist, and believed in blind eternal fate, I should still believe that fate had ordained the Jews to be the most essential instrument for civilizing the nations. If I were an atheist of the other sect, who believe or pretend to believe that all is ordered by chance, I should believe that chance had ordered the Jews to preserve and propagate to all mankind the doctrine of a supreme, intelligent, wise, almighty sovereign of the universe, which I believe to be the great essential principle of all morality, and consequently of all civilization.[88]

In an 1811 letter, Adams claimed:

> Our constitution was made only for a moral and religious people.... So great is my veneration of the Bible that the earlier my children begin to read it, the more confident will be my hope that they will prove useful citizens in their country and respectful members of society.... Statesmen, my dear sir, may plan and speculate for liberty, but it is Religion and Morality alone, which can establish the Principles upon which Freedom can securely stand. The only foundation of a free Constitution is pure Virtue, and if this cannot be inspired into our people in a greater Measure, than they have it now, they may change their Rulers and the forms of Government, but they will not obtain a lasting liberty.[89]

Education: Adams attended a public "Dame and Latin" school, with a career intention of becoming a farmer. A "Dame" school was an early form of a private elementary school. Usually taught by women, they were often located in the home of the teacher. The study of Latin served as a key part of the curriculum.[90] His schooling prepared him for college and a career in the ministry, his father's dream for his son. With some special tutoring in Latin from a local scholar, John passed the entrance examinations for Harvard College and entered it at age 16. His father sold ten acres of land to pay his son's expenses.[91]

Founded by Puritans in 1636, Harvard then was primarily an institution for the prepa-ration of clergymen and schoolmasters. Life at the college was a monastic-like experience. After morning prayers at six and a breakfast of bread and milk, classes were held from eight to noon. The midday meal of meat and vegetables, followed by outdoor activities and prayers at five. The evening consisted of study and a late supper.[92] When he returned home for a visit, his mother complained: "He was positively puny, and where were his fine red cheeks?"[93]

Like many of the founding fathers, Adams received a classical education and could read Latin and Greek. It prepared him for his role on the world stage and helped establish his conviction that he would be participating in one of the great events in history. Adams realized that he would not only be judged by his contemporaries but history as well. At Harvard, Adams was one of 100 students and a faculty of seven. Based on his family's social status, he was seated 14th among the 28 incoming students.[94] "The sole academic requirements for admission to Harvard University in the 1640s were as follows: 'When any scholar is able to read Tully [Cicero] or such like classical Latin author ex tempore and make and speak true Latin in verse and prose suo (ut aiunt) Marte [by his own power, as they say], and decline perfectly the paradigms of nouns and verbs in the Greek tongue, then may he be admitted into the college, nor shall any claim admission before such qualification.'"[95] The curriculum consisted of the great books. John brought to the birth of a new nation and government a familiarity with the writings of thinkers of the past on the structures of various forms of government. A prodigious reader, Adams devoured the writings of Cicero, Jonathan Swift, Benjamin Franklin, Machiavelli, Plato, John Milton, David Hume, Aristotle, Thucydides, Thomas Hobbes, and Jean Jacques Rousseau.[96]

Adams graduated third in his class of twenty-four at the time of the French and Indian War. Despite pressure from his father to become a clergyman, Adams found among lawyers "noble and gallant achievements" but among the clergy, the "pretended sanctity of some absolute dunces."[97] He viewed them as "effeminate and unmanly." He also concluded that he was too sarcastic, too opinionated, too impatient, and too egotistical to succeed in the ministry.[98] Adams made a conscious effort to model his public life after the glorious career of Cicero, whom he considered the greatest Roman orator, whose morals and values were unshakeable. As a politician, the Roman consistently refused to compromise. As a statesman, Cicero's ideals were more honorable and selfless than those of his contemporaries. To Adams Cicero represented patriotism, steadfastness and integrity in an unstable political environment. As a statesman, he sacrificed short-term popularity, which could only be bought through vice, for long-time fame, which only could be purchased by virtue. From Cicero, John became convinced of the importance of three branches of the government: the executive, the legislative and the judicial.[99] Adams had an enormous respect for education. In a letter to Abigail on October 29, 1776, He wrote: "Education makes a greater difference between man and man, than nature has made between man and brute."[100]

Adams believed that people could not be free without the right to learn. He pontificated:

> Liberty cannot be preserved without a general knowledge among the people, who have a right, from the frame of their nature, to knowledge, as their great Creator, who does nothing in vain, has given them understandings, and a desire to know; but besides this, they have a right, an indisputable, unalienable, indefeasible, divine right to that most dreaded and envied kind of knowledge. I mean, of the characters and conduct of their rulers.... Let us tenderly and kindly cherish therefore, the means of knowledge. Let us dare to read, think, speak and write.[101]

Home: John and Abigail purchased an estate of 40 acres of orchards and farmland in 1787. They enlarged the manor house into a rambling farmhouse with wing additions surrounded by a formal garden. John described the estate as "the farm of a patriot."[102] He spent most of his retirement at his estate in the house he called "Peacefield," but it is now referred to as "The Old House." There, he tended his fields, visited with neighbors and enjoyed his family. Abigail called the house "a wren's nest"[103] and cautioned her friends not to wear their hats or high heel shoes, because they would not be able to get into the house. Five generations of Adamses continuously occupied the dwelling from 1788 to 1927.

Motto: Adams' armorial crest featured thirteen stars representing each of the original American colonies, and the French *fleur* and two lions represent his diplomatic missions in Paris and Holland. The crest contains Adams' motto, which originates from Tacitus' *Annals* and reads, *Libertatem, Amivitiam Retinebus e Fidem* (Hold fast to liberty, amity, and faith).[104] The way Adams conducted his life, his assertion in a letter to Elbridge Gerry on

December 6, 1777, might have served as another aphorism: *Fiat Justitia ruat Coeleum* (Let justice be done though the heavens should fall).[105]

Recreational Pastimes and Interests: John Adams enjoyed a good stretch of the legs and walked every day for exercise, sometimes up to five miles. Such exercise, he believed, roused "the animal spirits" and "dispersed melancholy."[106] He was an avid collector and player of marbles, then called "little bowls." He was a dedicated reader, an interest that remained until his death, his mind remarkably sound and his curiosity unabated to the end. Adams had an extensive personal library, and his books reflect the staggering scope of his scholarly interests. He wrote constantly, noting almost everything that happened in his life. He annotated his books with intriguing comments and arguments written in the margins. Adams claimed that he had spent "an Estate on books."[107] He delighted in contemplating and exchanging ideas with his stimulating circle of friends, for whom he cared deeply. With a few exceptions, his friends were friends for life.[108]

OCCUPATION

After graduating from Harvard at age 20, Adams taught at a grammar school for boys and girls for three years in Worcester, Massachusetts. He described it as a "place of torment," where "nobody had any ideas and everybody voiced them vigorously."[109] Adams hated teaching, calling his pupils "little runtlings" who barely knew their ABCs.[110] His preoccupation was his personal study, especially Latin, history and law. After giving up the notion of becoming a clergyman, he revealed in a letter to his brother-in-law Richard Cranch that "the frightful engines of ecclesiastical councils of diabolical malice, and Calvinistical good-nature never failed to terrify me exceedingly whenever I thought of preaching."[111]

Adams read law in the office in Worcester of the distinguished attorney Rufus Putnam. John spent many days and nights in the library of Jeremy Gridley, then the attorney general of the province of Massachusetts Bay; there Adams mastered the principles and codes of civil law.[112] In his diary, He gave himself a pep talk: "Let no trifling Diversion or amuzement or Company, decoy you from your books, i.e., let no Girl, no Gun, no cards, no flutes, no Violins, no Dress, no Tobacco, no Laziness, decoy from your books."[113] In another entry he set himself tasks:

> Labour to get Ideas of Law, Right, Wrong, Justice, Equity, Search for them in your mind, in Roman, Grecian, French, English Treatises of natural, civil, common, Statute Law. Aim at an exact Knowledge of the Nature, End, and Means of Government. Compare the different forms of it with each other and each of them with their Effects on Public and private Happiness. Study Seneca, Cicero, and all the good moral Writers. Study Montesquieu, Bolingbroke [Vinnius?], &c. and all other good, civil Writers, &c.[114]

A distinguished scholar, Adams's knowledge of government and law was unexcelled in colonial America. At the time, few eminent lawyers resided in New England, nor was there much need for them; their main business derived from collecting debts. In 1758, Adams passed the bar and began his practice in Braintree writing wills and deeds. He tried his first case in November of 1759 and lost. By 1762, when he started 14 years of increasingly successful legal practice, he gained recognition as a skilled and respected lawyer, initially in Braintree and then in Boston. During this period, he also became acquainted with "many influential men who would later join with him as leaders of the Massachusetts colony," including his cousin Samuel Adams.[115] John was "well informed, ambitious and public spirited. Noted for his acquired erudition and intellectual precision, he overcame his natural timidity to become a powerful speaker and an adroit advocate."[116] As tensions mounted between the American colonies and Great Britain, Adams emerged through his writings as a revolutionary patriot.

The Braintree Instructions: Prior to the end of the Seven Years' War (known as the French and Indian War in America), American colonists were loyal subjects of Great Britain. The war — partly involved in defending American colonies from the French and their Native American allies— proved costly for Britain. Its government determined to make the "colonies bear a portion of the financial burden."[117] In the summer of 1765, Bostonians violently protested the Stamp Act, which taxed most printed material, legal documents, licenses, contracts, pamphlets and newspapers. A stamp attached to the documents signified that the tax had been paid.[118]

In his first foray into politics, Adams drafted "The Braintree Instructions," a powerful and influential document on liberty and independence, denouncing the act and asserting colonists' rights. The instructions were adopted at a Braintree town meeting on September 24, 1765.[119] Adams based his argument on English Law argument. He maintained the colonies were not bound by the act because they were not represented in Britain's Parliament and had not consented to the tax levy. Adams argued that British subjects in the colonies had the right to enjoy the same rights guaranteed to British subjects elsewhere.[120] This statement of principle became the first official formulation of American colonists' objection to "taxation without representation." The document was called "instructions" because it was designed to instruct the town's legislative representative on the tax issue. Forty other towns in Massachusetts adopted the "Braintree Instructions" for their representatives.[121]

The Boston Massacre: Great Britain repealed the Stamp Act in 1766, but in the following year, Parliament passed a new series of taxes on the colonies called the Townshend Acts.[122] Among its provisions were duties, or import taxes, on glass, lead, tea and other commodities.

The colonists responded with a boycott of British goods and violence against British Custom officials. The "stamp distributor was burned in effigy and his warehouse was put to the torch." Adams supported popular resistance to the British government but did not condone violence or mob action.[123] In 1768, the British government sent 4,000 troops (about a quarter of the city's population) to Boston to "maintain order and enforce the imposed taxes."[124] Hostility to the soldiers intensified, not merely because of their presence; due to their low wages, they took "part-time jobs in their off-duty hours that ordinarily would go to Boston workers. "The soldiers further outraged the Bostonians by "courting local women." On February 22, 1770, an eleven-year-old boy, Christopher Seider, became the "first martyr to the American cause" when a customs officer informant fired into an angry mob, killing the lad.[125]

On March 5, 1770, agitated crowds roamed the streets, leading to an argument between a local merchant and a British solider on duty at the customs house. In response to "intensive taunting, the soldier struck his tormentor with the butt of his rifle. The man screamed, and a crowd gathered."[126] When British reinforcements arrived under the command of Captain Thomas Preston, the mob jeered and taunted the eight new soldiers, hitting one with a wooden club. Someone fired a shot. Preston, "who had not given the order to fire, attempted to restore peace. However, his efforts were of no avail as more shots rang out and five new American martyrs— Crispus Attucks, Samuel Gray, Samuel Maverick, James Caldwell, and Patrick Carr — lay dead or dying in the street."[127] Adams called the incident a "slaughter."

Despite working behind the scenes against British oppression, "Adams agreed to represent the commander, Captain Preston, and eight soldiers against charges of murder."[128] His belief that everyone deserved a fair trial trumped his outrage at the killings and any

The Bostonians Paying the Excise-Man or Tarring & Feathering, lithographic print by David Clay-
poole Johnston, copied on stone by D.C. Johnston from a print published in London 1774. Published
in the ***Boston Pendleton,*** 1830, the print shows a mob pouring tea into the mouth of a Loyalist who
has been tarred and feathered (Library of Congress).

The Tea-Tax-Tempest, or Old Time with His Magick-Lanthern, cartoon etching published by W. Humphreys, March 12, 1783, based on a print attributed to Carl Guttenberg. It shows America, on the left, and Britannia treated to a glass lantern presentation on the American Revolution (Library of Congress, British Cartoon Collection).

fear he might have of how the move would affect his practice and political career. The trials were postponed for seven months until the rage had lessened. Captain Preston's trial was held first.[129] Aided by another prominent lawyer, his kinsman Josiah Quincy, Adams challenged the prosecution's assertion that Preston ordered his men to fire. In his argument, Adams gave the jury a lesson in law:

> The law no passion can disturb, 'Tis void of desire and fear, lust and anger, 'Tis *mens sine affectu*, without reason, retaining some measure of the divine perfection. It does not enjoin that which pleases a weak, frail man, but without any regard to persons, commands that which is good and punishes evil in all, whether rich or poor, high or low. 'Tis deaf, inexorable, inflexible. On the one hand it is inexorable to the cries and lamentations of the prisoners; on the other it is deaf, deaf as an adder, to the clamors of the populace.[130]

Adams's argument swayed the jury, which acquitted Preston. In his closing argument at the subsequent trial of the eight soldiers, Adams argued that they had "acted in self-defense when facing a mob." The jury acquitted six soldiers and found the two who "fired the fatal shots" guilty of manslaughter, and each had his thumb branded."[131]

Adams was criticized in the press, and the public was angered by the verdicts, but no new riots or attacks occurred, and Adams' reputation eventually was enhanced because of his principled stance. Later, reflecting on the trial, Adams said, "As the Evidence was, the verdict of the jury was exactly right."[132] For his services, Adams received a fee of nineteen guineas, but "nary a thank you from the churlish Preston."[133]

Engraving titled *The Massacre Perpetrated in King Street Boston on March 5th 1770 in Which Messrs Saml. Gray, Saml. Maverick, James Caldwell, Crispus Attucks, Patrick Carr Were Killed, Six Other Wounded, Two of Them Mortally.* Published in 1770, the print shows British troops firing on citizens in Boston. Printed by order of the town of Boston, reprinted for E. and C. Dilly, and J. Almon, 1770, frontispiece (Library of Congress).

A Dissertation on the Canon and Feudal Law (1765): In his longest political essay to then, Adams took issue with the Stamp Act. He attributed the settlement of the continent to a God-given plan for enlightment, liberty, and freedom.[134] His astute examination of the emotional and ideological demands the colonists faced was published in the *Boston Gazette* and reprinted in the *London Chronicle*, although wrongly credited to Jeremiah Gridley. The "Dissertation" contained some of Adam's strong feelings about natural rights, that is, those that are inalienable or perpetual. He asserted that it was not just to escape religious tyranny that caused Europeans to flee to the Americas, but also it was a love of general liberty.[135] He counseled: "The jaws of power are always open to devour, and her arm is always stretched out, if possible, to destroy the freedom of thinking, speaking, and writing."[136] He concluded: "No one of any feeling, born and educated in this once happy country, can consider the numerous distresses, the gross indignities, the barbarous ignorance, the haughty usurpations, that we have reason to fear are meditating for ourselves, our children, our neighbors, in short, for all our countrymen and all their posterity, without the utmost agonies of heart and many tears."[137]

Novanglus Letters: In these essays, Adams gave a point-by-point refutation of some essays by Daniel Leonard, defending Massachusetts Governor Thomas Hutchinson's arguments for the absolute authority of Parliament over the colonies.[138] Adams maintained colonial resistance to British imperial policy was justified, and to "nip the shoots of arbitrary power in the bud, is the only maxim which can preserve the liberties of any people."[139] He methodically detailed the origins, nature, and jurisdiction of the unwritten British constitution. Adams argued that the Empire was a league of nearly independent entities; in doing so, he anticipated 19th-century self-government arguments of British overseas possessions.[140] Adams insisted: "Metaphysicians and politicians may dispute forever, but they will never find any other moral principle or foundation of rule or obedience, than the consent of governors and governed."[141] He ended the essay: "[The American colonies] are a part of the British dominions, that is, of the King of Great Britain and it is our interest and duty to continue so. It is equally our interest and duty to continue subject to the authority of parliament, in the regulation of our trade, as long as she shall leave us to govern our internal policies and to give and grant our own money, and no longer."[142]

POLITICAL OFFICES

Political Philosophy and Political Party Affiliation: Adams once boasted in a letter: "I have never sacrificed my judgment to kings, ministers, nor people, and I never will, When either shall see as I do, I shall rejoice in their protection, and honor; but I see no prospect that either will ever think as I do, and therefore I shall never be a favorite with either."[143] In that same letter Adams, spoke with contempt of the French Revolution, at its commencement and predicted the slaughter of millions of people as its probable consequence. "I know that encyclopedists and economists, Diderot and D'Alembert, Voltaire and Rousseau, have contributed to this great event more than Sidney, Locke, or Hoadley, perhaps more than the American Revolution; and I own to you, I know not what to make of a republic of thirty million atheists. The Constitution is but an experiment, and must and will be altered..... If the sovereignty is to reside in one assembly, the king, princes of the blood, and principal quality, will govern it at their pleasure as long as they can agree; when they differ, they will go to war.... Too many Frenchmen, after the example of too many Americans, pant for equality of persons and property. The impracticability of this, God Almighty has decreed, and the advocates for liberty, who attempt it, will surely suffer for it."[144] Adams believed that a "stable and democratic government required the consent of the governed," separation of powers among the executive, legislature, and judicial, and a bicameral (two-body) legislature.[145] He rejected the notion of having but a single legislative body by listing the flaws of a single assembly, which he backed up with examples from Europe. He argued for the necessity of an independent judiciary, not beholden to either of the other two branches.[146] In response to a resolution of the Provincial Congress of North Carolina, which sought "Adams's suggestions on the establishment of a new government and the drafting of a constitution," he wrote "Thoughts on Government" (1776). It was in a response to Tom Paine's "overly Democratical" essay *Common Sense*. John told Abigail that in his opinion Paine was more interested in tearing down government than giving any thought to how to reconstruct it.[147] In what many considered the "most influential of all political pamphlets written during the constitution-writing period," Adams discussed the necessary existence of social estates in any political society, and the need to mirror those social estates in the political structures of the society. Adams attempted to find a balance between New England republicanism and Southern democratic skepticism.[148] His classical background prompted him to conclude that the happiness of society is the end of government, from which it follows: "[The] form of government which communicates ease, comfort, security, or, in one word, happiness to the greatness number of persons, and in the greatest degree, is the best."[149]

He contended that a form of government, whose principle and foundation is virtue, is better calculated to promote general happiness than any other form. He concluded that the only good government must be a republic — but as he observed, "[Of] republics there is an inexhaustible variety, because the possible combinations of the powers of society are capable of innumerable variations."[150] He proceeded to explore the question of how laws should be made: "[The first step is] to depute power from the many to a few of the most wise and good and decide what rules should be employed in choosing representatives of the people."[151] Adams argued that a representative assembly should be in "miniature an exact portrait of the people at large. It should think, feel, reason, and act like them."[152] He held that elections to these representative assemblies should be annual, quoting the maxim, "Where annual elections end, there slavery begins."[153]

Adams was a Federalist, who believed in a strong central government and was convinced that ordinary people were incapable of making legislative decisions. American political thinkers most resented hereditary nobility distinguished by wealth and land as in the English government. Adams believed that such people lacked the necessary virtue to balance the people in the legislature and were prone to corruption. Adams observed: "Nature has taken effectual care of her own work. She has wrought the passions into the texture and essence of the soul, and has not left it in the power of art to destroy them. To regulate and not to eradicate them is the province of policy. It is of the highest importance to education, to life, and to society, not only that they should not be destroyed, but that they should be gratified, encouraged, and arranged on the side of virtue."[154]

He did not wish to eliminate all vestiges of aristocracy. Adams was among the political philosophers who declared that "bicameralism was the best way to give representation in government to both the wealthy class of society and to the class of free men who did not have considerable wealth."[155] In his proposal for a bicameral legislature to provide checks and balances on the power of any group, Adams thought the upper house should be composed of a selected distinguished group of independent, virtuous gentlemen, who could "adequately balance the passions of the people represented in the lower house of the legislature."[156] Adams had no illusions about the relationship between the governors and the governed, no matter what form of government. As an old man, he thought of poor mankind, so often "deceived and abused" by their leaders. "But such is their love of the marvelous... that they will believe [the most] extraordinary pretensions" to selflessness and public spirit.[157]

Adams rejected abstract theories, which he dubbed "utopian ideology, which asserted that imagined ideals could be implemented in practice. In opposing popular rule, Adams' "objective was to moderate democratic government and to compensate for its leveling tendencies while preserving the principles of equal rights and the consent of the governed."[158] Federalists chiefly came from the professional classes, the men of wealth and social position, and officers of the army. They wanted a strong government, protection of infant manufactures, banks and tariffs.[159] Adams was no democrat except in recognizing popular political rights. He believed in the "rule of character as indicated by intellect and property."[160] C. Bradley Thompson asserted that the second U.S. president's political philosophical views were based on personal experience and extensive reading.[161] Among these views were that all humans need to be recognized and loved, that all governments are de-facto aristocracies, and sound governments must be constructed based on what mankind is, "rather than what one might want it to be."[162]

The Continental Congress: Adams was elected to the Massachusetts Assembly in 1770. When Britain closed the port of Boston in reprisal for the Boston Tea Party all business, including the law business, nearly came to an end.[163] Adams was selected as a delegate to the First and Second Continental Congresses (1774–1776). He confided to his diary:

> "This is the most magnificent movement of all. There is dignity, a majesty, a sublimity, in the last efforts of the patriots, that I greatly admire.... I wander alone, and ponder. I muse, I mope, I ruminate. We have not men fit for the times. We are deficient in genius, education, in travel, fortune — in everything. I feel unutterable anxiety."[164]

> "There is a new, and a grand scene open before me — a Congress. This will be an assembly of the wisest Men upon the Continent, who are Americans in principle, i.e. against the taxation of Americans in principle, by authority of Parliament.... I will keep an exact diary of my journey, as well as a journal of the Proceedings of Congress."[165]

> "The rich, the well-born, and the able acquire an influence among the people that will soon be too much for simple honesty and plain sense, in a House of Representatives. The most illustrious of them must, therefore, be separated from the mass, and placed by themselves in a Senate; this is, to all honest and useful intents, an ostracism."[166]

> "Every man in it [the Continental Congress] is a great man, an orator, a critic, a statesman, and therefore every man upon every question must show his oratory, his criticism, and his political abilities."[167]

Along with Thomas Jefferson, Benjamin Franklin, Roger Sherman and Robert R. Livingston, Adams was a member of a committee appointed to draft the Declaration of Independence. Although the declaration was written mostly by Jefferson, the fight to get it adopted was led by the unpopular and disliked Adams. He was "prominent in the debates leading to the adoption of The Articles of Confederation and Perpetual Union."[168] Adams was a delegate to the Massachusetts Constitutional Convention and principal author of that state's constitution, the world's oldest functioning constitution. It was a "government of laws, not one of men,"[169] and served as a model for the constitutions of other colonies and that of the United States. In his award-winning biography, *John Adams*, historian David McCullough praised Adams: "No one except for George Washington had more to do with our winning independence and with the establishment of the fundamental architecture or

The Declaration Committee, a lithograph print, created by Currier & Ives, 1876. Print shows members of the Declaration Committee, from left to right: Thomas Jefferson, Roger Sherman, Benjamin Franklin, Robert R. Livingston, and John Adams (Library of Congress).

structure of our government than did John Adams. This is no sunshine soldier. He never failed to answer the call of his country, never once, and it nearly always involved risk and sacrifice."[170]

Diplomatic Roles: In 1777, Adams was appointed commissioner to France. The next year, the reluctant lawyer and farmer and his son John Quincy left a resentful Abigail behind to embark from Boston across the North Atlantic. They sailed on the frigate *Boston*. The crossing was dangerous, as British warships were intent on sinking or seizing ships of the rebellious colonists. At one point, the *Boston*'s commander, Captain Samuel Tucker, saw a sail and a ship carrying the flag of Britain. He gained Adams' permission to attempt to capture the enemy ship. When the *Boston* came upon the other ship, the commander insisted that Adams not remain on deck, but go below out of gunshot range.[171] Adams was deposited with the surgeon and the captain called all hands to quarters and began the fight. In the midst of the conflict, to his surprise, the captain saw Adams on deck with a musket in hand, firing at the enemy. The captain immediately went to Adams and said, "My duty, sir, is to carry you unhurt to France, and as you are unwilling to go under hatches of your own accord, it is my duty to put you there."[172] He seized the future president, moved him to a place of safety, and took effectual measures to keep him there. The *Boston* captured the ship, the *Martha*, which was a heavily armed British merchant ship.[173]

In France, Adams found the American "delegation at loggerheads and the public accounts kept in a most lax manner. He recommended that the representation of the United States should be entrusted to a single minister instead of three commissioners." As a result,

Benjamin Franklin assumed this role, and Adams, left without any instructions, sailed for home.[174]

After a brief visit home, he once again made the long trip across the Atlantic to France as minister plenipotentiary to negotiate a peace with Great Britain. His sons John Quincy and Charles accompanied him aboard the French ship *La Sensible*. The vessel sprung leaks due to dreadful weather in the crossing and had to head for the nearest port for repairs, which was in northwest Spain. Rather than wait indefinitely while the ship was seen to, the Adams party traveled overland, "crossing the Pyrenees in winter and completing the grueling trip of 1000 miles to Paris in just less than two months."[175]

France's interest in making a peace treaty between Great Britain and the United States was not altogether altruistic. Adams and the other American negotiators were expected to play a secondary role, and their instructions from Congress were to "undertake nothing in the negotiation of a peace, or truce, without their [the French ministers'] knowledge and concurrence."[176] The French prime minister, "Count Vergennes, contrived to prevent Adams from making any official communication to Britain" of the extent of his powers. During Adams' stay in Paris, a mutual dislike and distrust grew between the two.[177]

In 1782 (1766), thanks to Adams' tireless efforts, The Netherlands recognized American independence. Two months later, Adams secured a $2 million loan from Dutch bankers. This recognition made the British more amenable to negotiations. Adams found it necessary to depart from his instructions and convince the other members of the mission to do likewise.[178] "Determined to secure the best interests of their country, regardless of the interference of the French ministers," they signed provisional articles on November 30, 1792. Then on September 3, 1783, Adams, Benjamin Franklin and John Jay signed the Treaty of Paris, ending the Revolutionary War.[179]

In January 1784, Adams returned to The Hague where he negotiated a second loan from the Dutch. On February 24, 1785, Adams was appointed U.S. minister to Great Britain. In May, his family moved to London, where they took up residence in the first American legation (embassy). Although happy to be reunited with his wife and other children, McCullough wrote that: "English attitudes towards them were generally scornful and patronizing. The press savaged them and they were socially ostracized... Much of this he and Abigail attributed to 'venom' spread by American Loyalists in London."[180] Adams certainly was not enjoying the job, complaining, "A peck of troubles in a large bundle of papers often in a handwriting almost illegible comes every day, Thousands of sea letters ... commissions and patents to sign. No company. No society, idle, unmeaning ceremony."[181] To Abigail, he lamented, "I am old, very old and never shall be very well—certainly while in this office, for the drudgery of it is too much for my years and strength."[182] To make matters worse, Adams' salary from a penniless Congress was inadequate for the expenses a minister to the Court of St. James was expected to incur in entertaining. He had just suffered a 19 percent reduction in his salary.[183] Adams journeyed to Amsterdam to obtain a third loan from the Dutch. As Adams was anxious to hold office in the new government of the United States, his request to be recalled from his minister's post was granted; but before returning home, he arranged for a fourth loan with the Dutch. Adams was "absent from his home for eight to nine years in the service of his country and separated from his wife and daughter for five of those years."[184] Finally, in 1788, his service ended, John and Abigail returned home to settle in a Braintree house formerly owned by Loyalists.[185]

His Vice Presidency: Under the "original terms of the Constitution, the members of the U.S. electoral college voted only for the office of the president. Each elector was allowed to vote for two people for president."[186] The person receiving the greatest number of votes (provided that such number was a majority of electors) would be president and the individual who received the second most votes would become the vice president. In the first presidential election in 1788, George Washington was named by every one of the sixty-nine electors, thus becoming president, while the next highest number voted by the electors went to John Adams with 34 votes, making him vice president.[187] Adams established his new residence at Richmond Hill in New York City.

When the capital was moved to Philadelphia, Adams took up residence at Bush Hill. Abigail joined John in Philadelphia, but she despised the city and after six months returned to Massachusetts, vowing never to return.[188] John spent much of his vice presidency alone while Abigail was in Braintree. As vice president, Adams had very little to do. His only real role as presiding officer of the U.S. Senate was to vote to break a tie, which he did on 20 occasions (more than any subsequent vice president), always in support of Washington's positions.[189] In his dealings with legislators, Adams acquired the image of a monarchist and earned the disrespect and ridicule of the Senators.[190] Adams did not think much of the position, which he accepted reluctantly, telling Abigail, "My country has in its wisdom contrived for me the most insignificant office that ever the invention of man contrived or the imagination conceived."[191] In 1792, Adams was again elected to be President Washington's vice president.

The Presidential Election of 1796: As George Washington rejected all suggestions that he serve a third term, Adams seemed the obvious Federalist candidate to succeed the Father of His Country. Alexander Hamilton, the ablest member of the Federalist Party, was not as well known to the public as Adams was. With Adams to head the ticket, it seemed desirous to choose a southerner as the second candidate. Thomas Pinckney of South Carolina was chosen. Hamilton schemed to get the Federalist electors, especially those from New England to cast all of their votes for both Adams and Pinckney, lest the loss of a single vote by either one should give the election to Thomas Jefferson, behind whom the anti–Federalists had united.[192] Hamilton was counting on Adams and Pinckney both receiving the same number of votes and a majority of the Electoral College. Then it would be left to a Federalist congress to decide, which one would be president, which Hamilton hoped would be the Southerner. Instead, the result in the Electoral College was 71 votes for Adams, 68 for Jefferson, 59 for Pinckney, 30 for Aaron Burr, 15 for Samuel Adams, and the rest scattered among several other names. John Adams had the majority of electoral votes, but his running mate, Pinckney, received only the third most votes, throwing the vice presidency to Thomas Jefferson. Thus, the two highest officers of the executive branch of the government were of different political parties, which did not make for a cooperative effort by the two political enemies.[193]

HIS PRESIDENCY

Adams' presidency was not a happy one. It was filled with crisis and conflict. He not only clashed with the Jeffersonian Republicans but a great deal of the time he also was at odds with his own party. He was sworn-in as the second president of the United States just after noon on March 4, 1797, in Philadelphia's House Chamber of Congress Hall. In his inaugural address, he proclaimed:

> There may be little solidity in an ancient idea that congregations of men into cities and nations are the most pleasing objects in the sight of superior intelligences, but this is very certain, that to a benevolent human mind there can be no spectacle presented by any nation more pleasing, more noble, majestic, or august, than an assembly like that which has so often been seen in this and the other chamber of Congress, of a government in which the Executive authority, as well as

that of all the branches of the Legislature, are exercised by citizens selected at regular periods by their neighbors to make and execute laws for the general good.[194]

John and Abigail rarely saw each other during his presidency. Speaking of her husband Abigail observed, "The task of the President is very arduous, very perplexing, and very hazardous, I do not wonder Washington wished to retire from it, or rejoiced in seeing an old oak [a nickname for her husband] in his place."[195]

On November 1, 1800, Adams became the first president to live in the chief executive's dwelling in Washington, D.C., although he got lost trying to find it. Both the house and the city were still under construction. Adams bestowed a benediction on the mansion, not yet referred to as the "White House": "I pray Heaven to bestow the best of blessings on this house and all that hereafter inhabit it. May none but honest and wise men ever rule under this roof."[196]

Adams participated in the first two orderly transfers of power at both the beginning and the end of his administration, a not unimportant accomplishment considering how wrenching government changes have been in other countries, not only in the past but also in the present. Adams may not have been a great president, but he was a great patriot.

His Vice President: Thomas Jefferson (1797–1801).

His Cabinet: When he assumed the presidency, Adams kept Timothy Pickering of Massachusetts as secretary of state but asked him to resign in 1800 after discovering that Pickering was "conspiring with Hamilton against administration policy."[197] John Marshall reluctantly accepted the post but resigned near the end of Adams' term when he was appointed chief justice of the Supreme Court. Oliver Wolcott of Connecticut continued as secretary of the treasury, although he criticized Adams for departing from orthodox federalism. "He resigned in 1800 due to unpopularity, and a particularly vitriolic campaign against him in the press in which, among other things, he was falsely accused of setting fire to the State Department building."[198] He was replaced by Samuel Dexter, who served from January to May in 1801. James McHenry of Maryland as secretary of war was a holdover from Washington's presidency and conspired with Hamilton against Adams. "During the election of 1800, McHenry goaded Alexander Hamilton into releasing his indictment against the President. It questioned Adams's loyalty and patriotism, sparking public quarrels over the major candidates and eventually paving the way for Thomas Jefferson to be the next President."[199] After losing re-election in 1800, Adams forced McHenry to resign and replaced him with Samuel Dexter, who served from 1800 to 1801 before becoming treasury secretary. Another Washington holdover, attorney general Charles Lee of Virginia, was loyal to Adams against the intrigues of Hamilton. Adams created a new cabinet post, in May 1798, appointing Benjamin "Stoddert, a loyal Federalist, to oversee the newly established Department of the

Chief Justice John Marshall, an engraving created by Charles Balthazar Julien Fevret de Saint-Mémin (Library of Congress).

Navy." Stoddert, who served from 1798 to 1801, established the U.S. Marine Corps as a permanent branch of the navy.[200]

Supreme Court Appointments: Adams appointed George Washington's nephew Bushrod Washington of Virginia in 1798 and Alfred Moore of North Carolina in 1799 to the bench as associate justices. John Marshall of Virginia was appointed chief justice to succeed Oliver Ellsworth in 1801.

DOMESTIC AFFAIRS — MAJOR EVENTS

Because of the narrow margin of his election, Adams promoted political harmony by seeking compromise with Jefferson while maintaining the support of the Hamiltonians who had secured his election.[201] For the most part, his style was to leave domestic matters to Congress and handle foreign affairs himself. When the Democratic-Republicans sharply criticized the president's military buildup over a conflict with the revolutionary government of France, Adams and the Federalists acted to silence their critics.[202]

The Alien and Sedition Acts: One of the most controversial issues during President Adams' administration was the enactment of laws that limited free speech and defined treasonable activities. The Federalist proponents of the laws claimed they were necessary to protect national security.[203] The Federalist-controlled Congress passed the laws to combat the threat of alien citizens of enemy powers, read "France," with whom war seemed imminent, and stop seditious attacks from weakening the government.[204] The Alien and Sedition Acts gave the president power to arrest and deport any alien suspected of having "treasonable or secret leanings."[205] This threatened many of the Jeffersonians who were not naturalized citizens.

It was made illegal to "write, print, utter, or publish"[206] anything critical of the president or Congress. Interestingly, it did not forbid criticism of the vice president and, as a result, Federalist papers continued to attack Jefferson. The first of the laws was the Naturalization Act,[207] which required aliens be residents for 14 years instead of five before becoming eligible for U.S. citizenship. The Alien Act authorized the "president to deport aliens 'dangerous to the peace and safety of the United States' during peacetime.[208] The third law, the Alien Enemies Act, allowed the wartime arrest, imprisonment and deportation of any alien subject to an enemy power."[209] The acts, which were aimed at French and Irish immigrants, who were mostly pro–French, were never enforced. Although the Federalists prepared lists of aliens for deportation and many aliens fled the country, Adams never signed a deportation order.[210]

The "Sedition Act declared that any treasonable activity, including the publication of 'any false, scandalous and malicious writing,' was a high misdemeanor, punishable by fine and imprisonment."[211] This last act allowed the president to have his "unpatriotic" opponents arrested and tried only by the Federalist judges of the Supreme Court, who would serve as "both judges and jurors."[212] Some scholars believe that this blot on Adams' administration had its origin in attacks on the president in newspapers supportive of the Democratic-Republican Party. In the eyes of John and Abigail, the worst offender in this matter was "Benjamin Franklin Bache, grandson of Benjamin Franklin and editor of the Philadelphia newspaper *Aurora*. In one op-ed piece Bache referred to the president as 'old, querulous, bald, blind, crippled, toothless Adams.'"[213] Other papers ridiculed Adams' policies and his love of formality and grandeur.

Abigail was incensed, writing to her husband that Bache was expressing the "malice" of a man possessed by Satan. She demanded that her husband and Congress act to punish the editor, whose "wicked and base, violent and calumniating abuse" against the president must be crushed.[214] Even before the laws took effect, Bache was arrested and shortly thereafter John Daly Burk, *New York Times* editor, suffered the same fate. Bache died of yellow fever while in custody awaiting trial and Burk accepted deportation to avoid imprisonment.[215] Seventeen other editors of Democratic-Republican supporting newspapers were arrested, and eleven were convicted and sentenced to prison. Bache's successor at the *Aurora*, William Duane, continued the paper's attack on Adams. Duane got evidence, which he published, that the Federalists, fearing Jefferson's challenge that surely would come in 1800, plotted to pass secret legislation that would dispute presidential elections decided "in secret" and "behind closed doors." Adams had Duane arrested, and he might have rotted in jail had not Jefferson intervened, giving Duane the opportunity to "consult his attorney." Duane went into hiding and stayed there until Adams left office.[216]

Adams and the Federalists extended the use of the Alien and Sedition Acts to ordinary citizens and even members of Congress. Late in January 1798, Vermont congressman Matthew Lyon, speaking from the floor of the House, charged that Adams and the Federalists served only the interests of the rich: "[They have] acted in opposition to the interests and opinions of nine-tenths of their constituents."[217] Two weeks later, an enraged Federalist congressman, Roger Griswold of Connecticut, attacked Lyon on the House floor with his cane. Lyon suffered repeated blows but got in a few punches to Griswold's face.[218]

Later, Lyon wrote an article outlining Adams' "continual grasp for power." The congressman claimed that the president "had an 'unbounded thirst for ridiculous pomp, foolish

"Congressional Pugilists," A satirical cartoon on the brawl between Congressmen Matthew Lyon and Roger Griswold on the floor of the House of Representatives' Chamber in 1798. Originally published in the *Hartford Echo*, 1801 (Library of Congress, American Cartoon Series).

adulation, and selfish avarice.' Federalists convened a federal grand jury and indicted Lyon for bringing 'the President and government of the United States into contempt.'"[219] Lyon had the burden of proving that he was not in violation of the Sedition Act rather than the prosecutors having to prove their case. He argued that he was merely expressing a political opinion, "which should not be subject to the truth test. The jury found Lyon guilty of expressing seditious words with 'bad intent.'" The Federalist judge sentenced him to four months in jail and fined him $1000 and court costs. Lyon was "led through the town of Vergennes, Vermont, in shackles." He ran for reelection from his tiny jail cell and easily kept his seat in Congress. When he was released he was "welcomed as a hero and was cheered along the route he took back to Congress." The Federalists tried to expel him from the House as a convicted criminal, but the effort failed.[220]

Many Americans questioned the constitutionality of these detested laws. On the day the president signed the acts, Vice President Jefferson left the capital in protest. The states of Virginia and Kentucky passed resolutions declaring the acts null and void because the government had exceeded its power. This was the first assertion of states' rights.[221] In the 1880 election Jefferson defeated Adams, with the unpopularity of the laws as the main political issue. One of Jefferson's first tasks as president was to free all the men imprisoned under the Alien and Sedition Acts and reimburse the fines they had paid, with interest. Jefferson also granted them a formal pardon and an apology.[222] The acts either expired or were repealed, hopefully never to reappear.

Jefferson's election and his party winning control of both houses of Congress were seen as signs that citizens agreed with his definition of free speech and press. Jefferson called it the right of Americans "to think freely and to speak and write what they think."[223] The puzzling and perplexing thing about the incident is that Adams, who had been such a champion of freedom, liberty and individual rights, took repressive actions that almost destroyed the United States' most precious principles. Adams was merely the first of several thin-skinned presidents who attempted to stifle criticism and restrict constitutional freedoms in the name of national security. The Alien and Sedition Acts permanently tarnished Adams' reputation.

Fries' Rebellion of 1799: In July 1798, to pay for military measures in preparation for an expected war with France, the federalist Congress approved heavy new stamp and house taxes. The tax was widely resented. German farmers in eastern Pennsylvania, led by John Fries, rioted and attacked tax collectors in an incident later known as "Fries' Rebellion."[224] The farmers "charged that the new taxes were designed to support a large standing army and navy." Adams sent federal troops to put down the uprising, and several of their leaders, including Fries, were captured, tried and sentenced to be hanged for treason. However, on the eve of the presidential election of 1800, Adams pardoned all the prisoners.[225]

FOREIGN AFFAIRS — MAJOR EVENTS

President Adams followed Washington's advice that the unstable United States should stay out of wars. The treaty with Great Britain negotiated by John Jay, the first chief justice of the United States Supreme Court, was very unpopular, not only with the American people, but also with the French. France considered the treaty to be a violation of the Treaty of Alliance of 1778, in which, in exchange for French help in the American Revolutionary War, the United States agreed not to make any treaties with Great Britain without France's consent.[226] Two years after the Jay Treaty, the outraged French revolutionary leaders seemed ready to fight a war with the United States.

The XYZ Affair: In 1789, revolution swept through France. The monarchy was overthrown and a new government was established that took a violent course, with thousands, including the king and the queen, guillotined. When some order was reestablished with the "beginning of the Directory in 1797, the French looked towards the United States for financial aid and moral support." Federalists despised the French revolution because of its mob rule and confiscation of property. In his diary, Adams declared, "Not one of the projects of the sage of La Mancha was more absurd, ridiculous or delirious than this of a Revolution in France."[227]

While Adams consistently supported Washington's policies of neutrality in wars between France and Great Britain, the Democratic-Republicans embraced the French revolution for its democratic ideals. It was increasingly difficult for Adams to follow a neutrality policy when the French attacked American shipping and seized some 300 vessels. Revolutionary France broke off relations with the United States by sending its diplomatic representative home. This period of undeclared war, waged only on the open sea, was called the "Quasi-War."[228] Many Americans, most especially the Federalists, at the urging of Hamilton, saw war with France as the lone option. Adams sought a peaceful policy and proposed that a new diplomatic mission be sent to negotiate the differences with France.

The French government refused to receive the new mission, consisting of C.C. Pinckney, John Marshall, and Elbridge Gerry. Three representatives of French foreign minister Charles Talleyrand — dubbed X, Y, and Z by Adams (later identified as Jean Conrad Hettinger, Pierre Bellamy and Lucien Hauteval) — met secretly with the U.S. diplomats and demanded $10 million in loans to the French government and a personal bribe of $250,000 for Talleyrand in order to begin negotiations. Pinckney told the French negotiator, "No! No! Not a sixpence!" "Mr. X threatened the United States with the 'power and violence of France.' News of the XYZ Affair enraged most Americans."[229] The country was on the brink of war, and a cry swept the nation: "Millions for defense, but not a penny for tribute."[230]

A famous political cartoon on the XYZ Affair shows staunch Americans resisting the threats and demands for money from Revolutionary France. Federalists called for war against France. However, a fuming President Adams merely increased military preparations and brought Washington back into duty as commander-in-chief of the army. A land tax was passed to pay for the buildup. Adams announced, "I will never send another minister to France, without assurances that he will be received, respected, and honored, as the representative of a great, powerful and independent nation."[231] Neither the United States nor France ever declared war, but the Federalists increasingly accused Jefferson and the Democratic-Republicans of being a traitorous "French Party."[232] A leading Federalist newspaper issued the warning, "He that is not for us is against us."[233]

The country having barely survived the Revolutionary War, Adams did not want to engage the United States in yet another war, fearing it might destroy the new nation. After learning of British admiral Horatio Nelson's victory against the French naval fleet off the coast of Egypt, the president felt this eliminated the danger of a French invasion. Acting without consulting his cabinet advisors, Adams informed the Senate that if France was willing, he wanted approval to send an American negotiator to "discuss and conclude all controversies between the two Republics by a new treaty."[234] His Federalist supporters, who had backed war with France, reacted with "surprise, indignation, grief, and disgust."[235] In 1800, Adams sent a mission consisting of William Vans Murray, Oliver Ellsworth and William Davie to France to work out a treaty. This time France accepted the United States as a nation, and a treaty with Napoleon Bonaparte was signed.[236] Later Adams wrote to a

PROPERTY PROTECTED. a la Françoise.

Property Protected—à la Française [*sic*], a British satire of Franco-American relations after the XYZ Affair, engraving published by S.W. Fores, June 1, 1798. Five Frenchmen plunder female "America," while five figures representing other European countries look on (Library of Congress, British Cartoons Collection).

friend: "I desire no other inscription over my gravestone than 'Here lies John Adams, who took upon himself the responsibility of peace with France in the year 1800.'"[237]

Adams averted war, and gained all the diplomatic advantages that were possible. Hamilton was so incensed that there would be no war with France; he plotted the defeat of Adams, his party's presidential candidate in 1800, even though it meant the election of the despised Jefferson.[238]

The Presidential Election of 1800: In May 1800, a Federalist caucus in Congress selected Adams and Charles Cotesworth Pinckney as the party's nominees for the presidential election.

The Democrat-Republicans nominated Thomas Jefferson and Aaron Burr. In September Adams' nemesis, fellow Federalist Alexander Hamilton, published a vitriolic attack on Adams' reelection bid, "Concerning the Public Conduct and Character of John Adams."[239] As was the custom at the time, neither candidate campaigned, leaving that issue to be fought out in partisan newspapers. The issues were mostly Adams' performance as president. Jefferson defeated Adams in the election. Hours before Jefferson was sworn in as the third president of the United States on March 4, 1801, Adams left the capital to return to Massachusetts.[240] Biographer McCullough commented: "On Inauguration Day, Wednesday, March 4, 1801, John Adams made his exit from the President's House and the capital at four in the morning.... He departed eight hours before Thomas Jefferson took the oath of office at the Capitol.... To his political rivals and enemies Adams' predawn departure was another ill-advised act of a petulant old man. But admirers, too, expressed disappointment. A correspondent for the Massachusetts Spy observed in a letter from Washington that numbers of Adams' friends wished he had not departed so abruptly. 'Sensible, moderate men of both parties would have been pleased had he tarried until after the installation of his successor. It certainly would have had good effect.'"[241] McCullough went on to say: "By his presence at the ceremony Adams could have set an example of grace in defeat, while at the same time paying homage to a system whereby power, according to a written constitution, is transferred peacefully. After so vicious a contest for the highest office, with party hatreds so near to igniting in violence, a peaceful transfer of power seemed little short of a miracle. If ever a system was proven to work under extremely adverse circumstances, it was at this inauguration of 1801, and it is regrettable that Adams was not present."[242]

AFTER HIS PRESIDENCY

Adams survived a quarter of a century after he left the presidency, writing extensively and issuing reflective and highly respected political statements. Although he never again participated in public life, he remained interested in, and informed about, the affairs of the country. The career of his son John Quincy Adams gave him pleasure, and he lived to see him elected the sixth president of the United States. Of all the founding fathers, Adams was the most vehement in his opposition to slavery. He was a farmer's son and used to working in the field himself. He never owned slaves, nor would he employ any work crews that included slaves. According to McCullough, Adams "had neither debts nor slaves and all his life abhorred the idea of either."[243]

His Papers: Adams was a prolific writer, and he saved everything he ever wrote. In November 1755, Adams began keeping a diary, which by the end of his life filled four volumes. As Beth Prindle, curator of the John Adams collection, said, "God bless the man. It seems that a thought never trickled through his mind that he didn't write down."[244]

From an early age, Adams wrote descriptions of events and his impressions of men. The earliest known example is his report of the 1761 argument of lawyer James Otis in the superior court of Massachusetts as to the legality of "Writs of Assistance."[245] British customs officials aggressively inspected ships, businesses and homes for evidence of goods smuggled into Massachusetts to avoid taxes. All the officials needed to conduct a search was to obtain a "writ of assistance," a general search warrant that allowed a search within any identified premises, with no requirement to show probable cause. "Otis' argument inspired Adams with zeal for the cause of the American colonies."[246]

John Adams, lithograph created by Albert Newsam and Peter S. Duval, 1804, published by C.S. Williams, c. 1846 (Library of Congress).

Biographer David McCullough admired Adams' musings: "His marginal notes are not the kind of notes that most of us would make.

Charles C. Pinckney, engraving after a painting by Alonzo Chappel, published c. 1862. Library of Congress).

They are conversations with the author, and there are some 50 different figures from the 18th century of huge consequence with whom he's having these conversations."[247] As an example, in 1812, Adams penned a 10,000 word analysis of Mary Wollstonecraft's *Historical and Moral View of the French Revolution* in the margins of his copy of the book. Adams strongly disputed Wollstonecraft's assertion, "The authority of the national assembly had been acknowledged nearly three months previous to this epoch, without their having taken any decided steps to secure these important ends."[248] He also penned in the margins: "Did this Lady think three months time enough to form a free Constitution for twenty five Millions of Frenchmen. 300 years would be well spent in procuring so great a Blessing but I doubt whether it will be accomplished in 3000."[249] In June and July 1763, Adams published his first newspaper pieces. Using the pseudonym "Humphrey Ploughjogger," he lampooned human nature, and as "U" he espoused balance between monarch, aristocracy, and democracy.[250] Of his numerous correspondences, Adams exchanged many letters and ideas with his old political rival Thomas Jefferson from 1812 until their deaths in 1826. In a July 13, 1813, letter to Jefferson, Adams said, "You and I ought not to die before we have explained ourselves to each other."[251]

Even in his last years, Adams' correspondence retained his sharp mind and buoyant sprits. The Massachusetts Historical Society, a major research library and manuscript depository, was established in 1791. Its holdings include the Adams family papers, including "correspondence, letterbooks, diaries, literary manuscripts, speeches, legal and business documents," and other papers, such as Adams' 1790 catalog of his Stone Library, which contains more than 14,000 historic volumes, and the books of John Quincy Adams. Included in the collection are *History of the Dispute with America*, a series of newspaper essays published in 1774 and 1775. *A Defence of the Constitutions of the United States of America* (1787–88) is a three-volume response to the British critics who questioned the political and economic promise of the United States. *Discourses on Davila: A Series of Papers on Political History*[252] (1790) is a controversial political manifesto in which Adams supports a monarchy and aristocracy in countries such as France and denounces equality based on his belief that humans naturally have "a passion for destruction."[253] The papers were first published in the *Gazette of the United States (1790–1791)*.

Adams' observations included the following:

> The great art of law-giving consists in balancing the poor against the rich in the legislature, and in constituting the legislative in a perfect balance against the executive power, at the same time then no individual or party can become its rival. The essence of a free government consists in an effectual control of rivalries.... Rivalries must be controlled, or they will throw all things into confusion; and there is nothing but despotism or a balance of power, which can control them.[254]

> The poor man's conscience is clear; yet he is ashamed.... He feels himself out of the sight of others, groping in the dark. Mankind takes no notice of him, he rambles and wanders unheeded. In the midst of a crowd, at church, in the market ... he is in as much obscurity as he would be in a garret or a cellar. He is not disapproved, censured or reproached: *he is only not seen*.... To be wholly overlooked, and to know it, is intolerable.[255]

Biographer David McCullough attempted to put the record straight about Adams' views on Democracy:

> John Adams was no monarchist. What Adams understood, and was willing to talk about, was the degree to which the structure of our government was based on the English model. He did not believe in democracy — with a lower case "d." He did not believe that all men are created equal. Essentially he said, "It's only common sense. Look around. Some people are born with more abilities than others.... We're not all equal." What he did believe passionately, and would put his life on the line for, was the notion that all men are equal in the eyes of God and before the law.[256]

Health: Adams enjoyed good health as a youth and in early adulthood. As was his practice "on or near his birthday, he recorded in his diary the events of the previous twelve months."[257] During his twenties and early thirties he made no mention of ill health, instead he reported feeling well.[258] While Adams was a student at Harvard, a smallpox epidemic broke out in Boston. He was not inoculated against the disease. At the time, inoculation — which is different from the less invasive vaccination — was followed by weeks of sickness afterwards. Not wishing to miss four weeks of classes, he braved the epidemic by returning to the campus. Soon after, he was inoculated and spent three weeks in the hospital, suffering headaches, backaches, knee aches, gagging fever, and eruption of pock marks.[259]

While studying law, Adams had recurring bouts of depression. His physician, Dr. Nahum Willard, attributed the illness to the long hours of study, which had "corrupted his whole mass of blood and juices." Willard's treatment was putting Adams on a then trendy starvation regimen of a "milk and toast diet." He abstained from meat and spirits but was allowed bread, milk, vegetables and tea. Adams improved but developed severe heartburn from drinking so much tea. On numerous occasions, Adams purged himself by ingesting a cathartic prepared from East Indian jalap. He found the benefits of the procedure mixed.[260]

Adams took up smoking at age 8 and enjoyed it so much he continued until at least 70, and probably beyond that.[261] He also chewed tobacco. Throughout his life, at times of stress — of which there were many — Adams manifested a bewildering and wide array of physical symptoms, some lasting weeks, some years. Both Adams and his mother had quick tempers and could be alternatively meek or rash, cautious or explosive. Some scholars labeled Adams' sometime irrational behavior as symptoms of being "manic-depressive," "slightly paranoid" and the actions of "a man consumed by an irrepressible urge to master the world."[262] As early as 1775, Adams developed a tremor, which he called "quiverations," in his hands, which lasted for many years. His wife Abigail suffered from rheumatoid arthritis, chronic migraine headaches, and persistent insomnia.[263]

Death: Until a few days prior to his death, Adams exhibited no indications of decline in health. However, on the morning of the July 4, 1826, he was unable to leave his bed. Neither he nor his relatives and friends who visited him thought the end was near. He was asked to suggest a toast to celebrate the fiftieth-year anniversary of the signing of the Declaration of Independence. He exclaimed, "Independence forever!"[264] At four o'clock in the afternoon, he expired.[265]

Cause of Death: According to a relative, Adams' death was "merely the cessation of the functions of a body worn out by age."[266] Some medical experts believed the true cause of death was congestive heart failure. Longevity ran in his family. His paternal grandfather lasted until he was 83. Adams' mother died at age 85, as did one of his two brothers. His father died at age 70 from an influenza epidemic.[267]

Place of Death: John Adams died at his home, Peacefield, at Braintree, Massachusetts.

Final Words: Shortly before breathing his last, Adams allegedly whispered, "Thomas Jefferson survives."[268] In this, he was wrong. Jefferson had died a few hours earlier at his home, Monticello. That two founding fathers had not only died on the dame day but on the 50th anniversary of the adoption of the Declaration of Independence seemed too much of a coincidence for some. In his two-hour eulogy of Adams at Faneuil Hall, Boston, Daniel Webster cited it as "proof" of how much God cared for the United States.[269]

Place of Burial: Adams' remains rest in a crypt beneath United First Parish Church (Unitarian) in Quincy. Income from land he donated to the town financed the current building, completed in 1828.[270] Adams stipulated that the congregation should take granite from quarries on the donated land to build a temple of worship of God. His beloved wife's remains were moved to the crypt, which also holds the bodies of John Quincy Adams and his wife. At John Adams' death, his worth was given at $100,000, a considerable fortune.[271]

A plaque in front of the church was placed by John Quincy Adams. The left side reads:

> Beneath these Walls Are deposited the Mortal Remains of JOHN ADAMS, Son of John and Susanna [Boylston] Adams, Second President of the United States. Born 30 October 1735. On the fourth of July 1776 He pledged his Life, Fortune and Sacred Honour To the Independence of His Country. On the third of September 1783 He affixed his Seal to the definitive Treaty with Great Britain Which acknowledged that Independence, And consummated the Redemption of His Pledge. On the fourth of July 1826 He was summoned To the Independence of Immortality, And to the Judgment of His God. This House will bear witness to his Piety: This Town, his Birth-Place, to his Munificence: History to his Patriotism: Posterity to the Depth and Compass of his Mind.[272]

The right side reads:

> At his Side Sleeps till the Trump shall Sound ABIGAIL, His beloved and only Wife, Daughter of William and Elizabeth [Quincy] Smith. In every Relation of Life a Pattern of Filial, Conjugal, Maternal and Social Virtue. Born November 11 1744. Deceased 28 October 1818. Aged 74. Married 25 October 1764. During an Union of more than Half a Century They survived in Harmony of Sentiment, Principle and Affection The Tempests of Civil Commotion; Meeting undaunted, and surmounting The Terrors and Trials of that Revolution Which secured the Freedom of their Country; Improved the Condition of their Times; And brightened the Prospects of Futurity To the Race of Man upon Earth.[273]

At the bottom appears the following:

> PILGRIM, From Lives thus spent thy earthly Duties learn; From Fancy's Dreams to active Virtue turn: Let Freedom, Friendship, Faith, thy Soul engage, And serve like them thy Country and thy Age.[274]

MISCELLANEA

Presidential Trivia and Firsts: John Adams and revolutionary radical Samuel Adams were second cousins. Adams referred to Benjamin Franklin as "the Old Conjuror," of whom he said his life in Paris was "a scene of continual dissipation."[275] Adams called Alexander Hamilton "a Creole bastard."[276] At his inauguration Adams wore a pearl-colored suit and a sword and a huge hat.[277] Abigail Adams was terrified by the cockroaches that infested the White House. She was appalled with the Capital's unpaved and mud rutted streets, nonexistent sewers, and the swampy surroundings infested with mosquitos.[278] While visiting William Shakespeare's home in Stratford, England, Adams carved a sliver of wood from a chair as a souvenir.[279] He felt the president should be addressed as "His Highness, the President of the United States and Protector of Their Liberties" (it was not adopted).[280] Adams was flattered that many people believed he was the author of Thomas Paine's *Common Sense*.[281]

Latin or Digging Ditches: According to Paul F. Boller, Jr., in *Presidential Anecdotes*, as a boy John Adams found the study of Latin to be boring and grew to hate it. He went to his father to see if there was not something else he could do instead. Deacon John, who had been a laborer, told his son, "You might try ditching; my meadow yonder needs a ditch."[282] So young John went about the task of digging the ditch and soon found it to be arduous work. By the end of the day, he was ready to return to the study of Latin; but being too proud to admit it, he spent one more day in digging the ditch before admitting he preferred the study of Latin. Adams said "toil conquered my pride" and ever after claimed "ditching" had played an important part in building his character.[283]

Art of Lying Together: Boller relates the story of a dinner party in Paris, where he was seated next to an elegant lady. At some point in the evening, perhaps with the intention of having fun with the American, she said to him, "Mr. Adams, by your name I conclude you are descended from the first man and woman, and probably in your family may be preserved the tradition which may resolve a difficulty which I could never explain. I never could understand how the first couple found out the art of lying together."[284] Not used to such questions in Boston, Adams blushed and, speaking through a translator (he never learned French), informed his inquisitive companion "there is a physical quality in us resembling the power of electricity or of the magnet, by which when a pair approached within a striking distance they flew together like the needle to the pole or like objects in electric experiments."[285] The French lady's response to an explanation that would do Benjamin Franklin proud was, "Well, I know not how it was, but this I know: it is a very happy shock."[286]

Mistresses: In *John Adams*, Page Smith related an amusing story that gained wide circulation. It was claimed that Adams had sent General Charles Cotesworth Pinckney to England on an American frigate to procure four pretty girls as mistresses. The general was to have two and the president two. Amused by the story, Adams wrote to William Tudor: "If this be true, General Pinckney has kept them all for himself and cheated me out of my two."[287]

Reputation: John Adams' stock as one of the important founding fathers plummeted after the appearance of his biography written by his grandson Charles Francis Adams. In it, John Adams came across as "a stuffed-shirt puritan."[288] Other historians furthered his declining importance, with Vernon L. Parrington referring to Adams in 1927 as "pragmatic, steady, solid and unimpressive."[289] Joseph Ellis wrote: "... the underlying problem for the Adams' legacy was not primarily the directness of his character so much as the character of his thought. In the search for a usable past, too much in Adams was simply not usable."[290] The 1965 publication of Irving Stone's historical novel *Those Who Love*, largely based on the release of the correspondence between John and Abigail Adams, began his return to prominence.[291] PBS put a more humane and appealing face on John Adams in its bicentennial series, *The Adams Chronicles*,[292] in which John's strong moral character and abhorrence of partisan politics came through loud and clear. Things picked up even more with the Tony Award–winning musical *1776*[293] of 1969, in which Adams was clearly the leading figure, if an unpopular one with his fellow delegates to the convention that adopted the Declaration of Independence.

In 2002, David McCullough published a Pulitzer Prize–winning biography, *John Adams*, a highly praised best seller. McCullough revealed that when John set out to attend the opening of the Continental Congress in Philadelphia, he left his home in a blizzard. It was a trip of nearly 400 miles. There were no bridges over any river he had to cross. The journey took two weeks, but Adams was on a mission to win independence from Great Britain and create a new nation. McCullough wondered what modern day politician would have done likewise.[294]

Paul Giamatti appeared as the Revolutionary War leader and president in the seven-part Tom Hanks/Playtone production, which is based closely on McCullough's biography. The HBO series shows the Revolutionary War era world as Adams lived and saw it — and in an often uncomfortably realistic way, according to McCullough, the production's consultant. "Life in the 18th century was more difficult than we have any idea," the author said. "You're going to see it with the scars a hard life left on people."[295]

Diary Entries[296]

[Benjamin Franklin] has very modest abilities. He knows nothing of philosophy, but his few experiments in electricity [Diary entry, May 10, 1779].

No man is entirely free from weakness and imperfection in this life. Men of the most exalted genius and active minds are generally most perfect slaves to the love of fame. They sometimes descend to as mean tricks and artifices in pursuit of honor or reputation as the miser descends to in pursuit of gold [Diary entry, February 19, 1756].

The longer I live and the more I see of public men, the more I wish to be a private one. Modesty is a virtue that can never thrive in public. It is now become a maxim with some, who are even men of merit that the world esteems a man in proportion as he esteems himself [Diary entry, written while living and working in Paris with Benjamin Franklin and Arthur Lee McCullough, 207].

A pen is certainly an excellent instrument to fix a man's attention and to inflame his ambition [Diary entry, November 14, 1760].

The Church of Rome has made it an article of faith that no man can be saved out of their church, and all other religious sects approach this dreadful opinion in proportion to their ignorance, and the influence of ignorant or wicked priests [Diary and Autobiography, July 26, 1796].

I am constantly forming, but never executing good resolutions [Diary entry, July 21, 1756].

The rich are seldom remarkable for modesty, ingenuity, or humanity. Their wealth has rather a tendency to make them penurious and selfish [Diary entry, March 5, 1773].

There are persons whom in my heart I despise; others I abhor. Yet I am not obliged to inform the one of my contempt, nor the other of my detestation. This kind of dissimilation, which is no more than a concealment, secrecy, and reserve, or in other words, prudence and discretion, is a necessary branch of wisdom, and so far from being immoral and unlawful, that [it] is a duty and a virtue. Yet even this must be understood with certain limitations, for there are times, when the cause of religion, of government, of liberty, the interest of the present age and of posterity, render it a necessary duty for a man to make known his sentiments and intentions boldly and publicly [Diary entry, August 20, 1770].

The manners of women are the surest criterion by which to determine whether a republican government is practicable in a nation or not [Diary entry, June 2, 1778].

I have a zeal at my heart for my country and her friends which I cannot smother or conceal. This zeal will prove fatal to the Fortune and Felicity of my Family, if it is not regulated by cooler judgment than mine has hitherto been [Diary entry and in a letter to Abigail Adams, summer 1774].

Evaluations of John Adams

It was the established Adams pattern: to sense where history was headed, make decisions that positioned America to be carried forward on those currents, but to do so in a way that assured his own alienation from success.[297]—Joseph J. Ellis

John Adams's involvement in unpopular causes extended far beyond representing the British troops in the Boston Massacre trials—his political life was a series of unpopular causes. He was a leading advocate for American independence long before others were willing to speak up. His legacy is attributable to his personal principles as much as it is to the turbulent era. Together they pre-ordained that he would play a leading role in championing the cause of independence. Adams had the clarity of vision the times needed and the ambition to welcome the responsibility. He valued personal virtue above political gain and he had the unfortunate habit of alienating others by speaking his mind too frankly and too often. Had he been less outspoken, other leaders of the revolutionary era may have succumbed to a timidity and fear that would have doomed their quest for independence. He urged, cajoled, argued, and generally made a nuisance of himself to dissuade others from seeking a middle ground with the British.[298]—Michael Foster

This scrutiny [of some of Adams' writings] enhanced my esteem in the main for his [Adams']

moral qualifications, but lessened my respect for his intellectual endowments. I then adopted an opinion, which all my subsequent experience has confirmed, that he is a man of an imagination sublimated and eccentric, propitious neither to the regular display of sound judgment nor to steady perseverance in a systematic plan of conduct.[299] — Alexander Hamilton

John Adams was also, as many could attest, a great-hearted, persevering man of uncommon ability and force. He had a brilliant mind. He was honest and everyone knew it. Emphatically independent by nature, hardworking, frugal — all traits in the New England tradition — he was anything but cold or laconic as supposedly New Englanders were. He could be high-spirited and affectionate, vain, cranky, impetuous, self-absorbed, and fiercely stubborn; passionate, quick to anger, and all-forgiving; generous and entertaining. He was blessed with great courage and good humor, yet subject to spells of despair, and especially when separated from his family or during periods of prolonged inactivity.[300] — David McCullough

John Adams was a man whose "ambition was without bounds.... He could not look with complacency upon any man who was in possession of more wealth, more honours, or more knowledge than himself," and he went over to the opposition because of a slight upon him by refusal of a place on the bench.[301] — Vernon L. Parrington

He it was who sustained the debate, and by the force of his reasoning demonstrated not only the justice but the expediency of the measure.[302] — Richard Stockton

[The] doctrine of legislative balance was one of the "core principles of political architecture that Adams found in reason and nature." These core principles "were not unlike the laws that govern the motion of the heavens and the machines that man was building in the light of a Newtonian cosmos. Adams thought government a piece of clockwork, a machine to be designed and constructed on the basis of 'principles and maxims, as fixed as any in Mechanicks.'" In fact, Adams went so far as to invoke Newton's Third Law to justify his advocacy of a bicameral legislature... Adams's attempt to use Newton's Third Law was completely muddled. Specifically, he cited the principle that to every action there is an equal and opposite reaction. But he took it to mean that a body cannot be at rest unless equal and opposite forces operate on it, which has nothing to do with Newton's Third Law and is also false. Thus, at a point where Adams was defending the core of his political science, he was demonstrably employing Enlightenment principles out of all context.[303] — C. Bradley Thompson

THREE

Thomas Jefferson

The Polymath President

Third President of the United States, 1801–1809

Thomas Jefferson was a multi-talented, ever-curious, inventive, complex and accomplished man. If any American president deserved the accolade "genius" it was the red-head from Virginia. Jefferson designed his tombstone and wrote his own epitaph, which made no mention of his presidency of the United States. He insisted that only his words be used and "not a word more" be inscribed. It reads: "Here was buried Thomas Jefferson Author of the Declaration of Independence, Author of the Statute of Virginia for Religious Freedom and the Father of the University of Virginia."[1]

Birth: Thomas Jefferson's birth happened at Shadwell in Goochland (now Albemarle) County, Virginia, on the periphery of western settlements, about four miles east of Charlottesville.[2] His birthday is April 13, 1743, by the Gregorian calendar, April 2, by the Julian, then still in effect in England and its colonies.

Nicknames and Titles: "Red Fox," "Long Tom," "Father of the Declaration of Independence," "Sage of Monticello," "Moonshine Philosopher of Monticello," and "Noble Agrarian."[3]

Family: Thomas' father, Peter Jefferson, was a third-generation colonial in the New World, the grandson of a surveyor, and the son of a "gentleman justice" Thomas Jefferson II, who lived at a place in Chesterfield called Osborne's, where he served as sheriff and captain of the militia.[4] At the time of his father's death in 1731, Peter moved to his legacy, a little undeveloped land in Goochland County. He cleared the land, built a house, and planted crops. In the mid–1730s Peter acquired a 2,000 acre tract of land on the north side of the James River in the Shadwell area, where he was one of the first justices of the peace and then sheriff of the County. He and his closest friend, William Randolph, served as magistrates and militia officers. Peter also was a member of the Virginia House of Burgesses.[5]

Although Peter Jefferson had no formal education, he read extensively, eager for knowledge and became a gifted surveyor, a lucrative occupation at the time. With mathematician Joshua Fry, Peter was chosen by the British Lords of Trade and Plantations to draw up a comprehensive map of the Virginia. Published in 1751, it showed both the "newly-settled lands of the interior and the massive unclaimed territories on the other side of the Alleghenies."[6] In 1749, with Thomas Walker, James Maury, and Thomas Meriwether, he established the Loyal Company and acquired a patent for 800,000 acres along the southern border of Virginia that is now southeastern Kentucky.[7]

At 31 Peter married William Randolph's first cousin, tall and slim 19-year-old Jane

Randolph.[8] The next year, Jane, Peter and some of his most skilled slaves moved to a basic weather-boarded house on the 400 acres he purchased on the Rivanna River. Two years later the Jefferson family moved from Goochland County to Albemarle County. Peter named his property "Shadwell" for the London parish where his wife was born and baptized in England on February 20, 1720.[9] Shadwell was the seat of a thriving tobacco and wheat planta-tion, worked by the largest slave force in the County. When Colonel Randolph died, Peter honored his promise to man-age the former's estate and serve as guardian to his son Thomas Mann Ran-dolph by moving his family to his friend's estate, Tuckahoe.[10]

Peter was a huge man with renowned strength. On one occasion, he stood between two hogsheads of tobacco that were lying on their sides. He grabbed one hogshead in his right hand and the other in his left, and stood them up properly at the same time. The standard weight for a hogshead today is around 500 pounds.[11] Peter frequently remarked that "it is the strong in body who are both the strong and free in mind."[12] Peter died suddenly at age forty-nine, when his son Tom was fourteen years old. Thomas inherited his

Thomas Jefferson, a reproduction created c. 1907 of a painting by Matthew Harris Jouet, 1788–1827, copyrighted by the W.H. Gallagher Co., N.Y. (Library of Congress).

father's desk, books, maps, surveying notes and journals, surveying instruments, and some 5,000 acres of land at Monticello. Peter left an order that Tom should attend William & Mary College, which he entered in 1760. Jane Jefferson died on March 31, 1776, at which time Thomas came into full inheritance of Shadwell. All the cherished possessions Tom inherited from his father were lost in a fire at Shadwell on February 1, 1770. Jefferson lamented the loss of "every paper I had in the world, and almost every book."[13]

Thomas had two older sisters, Jane and Mary. His other siblings were Elizabeth, Martha, Peter Field, an unnamed infant who died at birth, Lucy, Anna Scott, who died at birth, and her twin Randolph. Jefferson was very close to his sister Jane, who was three years older. She was Tom's constant companion, sharing her love of music with him. She taught Tom to read music, and when Peter learned this, he bought his son a fiddle. In the autumn of 1765 Jane suddenly died, a devastating blow to Tom.[14] His sister Martha married Tom's best friend at the College of William & Mary, Dabney Carr, who died shortly after Jane, another dreadful loss for Tom.[15]

Ancestors: For all his boundless curiosity about just about everything, Jefferson did not show much interest in investigating his ancestry. He said that family tradition thought that his paternal ancestors came from Wales at a place near the mountain of Snowden, the highest in Great Britain. Thomas was more familiar with his maternal ancestors. The pedigree of the Randolph family traces to the days of King Robert Bruce in Scotland. Among Tom's maternal ancestors was Henry de Bohun, 1st Earl of Hereford, one of the barons who forced King John of England to sign the Magna Carta at Runnymede in June 1215. The Randolph line descended from Elizabeth de Bohun, a maternal ancestor of the Randolph men who emigrated to the Colony of Virginia about the year 1660, establishing themselves at Turkey Island, some twenty miles south of Richmond.[16]

Appearance: In his prime, Thomas Jefferson stood tall, spare, and erect, but slouched in old age. His "hair, when young, was of a reddish cast; sandy as he advanced in years; his eyes hazel."[17] Contemporary William Maclay described him: "Jefferson is a slender man; has rather the air of stiffness in his manners; his clothes seem too small for him ... one shoulder elevated above the other (while sitting).... With age, he was careless in dress and slack in bearing."[18] George Fowler noted: "His dress, in color and form was quaint and old-fashioned."[19] Francis Hall observed: "I found Mr. Jefferson ... stooping and lean with old age ... exhibiting the fortunate mode of bodily decay, which strips the frame of its most cumbersome parts, leaving strength of muscle and activity of limb."[20] The following are additional descriptions of Jefferson's appearance by those who knew him:

> The stature of Jefferson was lofty and erect; his motions flexible and easy; neither remarkable for, nor deficient in grace; and such were his strength and agility....[21] — Samuel Harrison Smith, 1801–09

> Mr. Jefferson was six feet two and half inches, well-proportioned and straight as a gun barrel. He was like a fine horse; he had no surplus flesh.[22] — Edmund Bacon, overseer at Monticello, 1806–1822

> [He is] above six feet high, of an ample long frame, rather thin and spare. His head, which is not peculiar in its shape, is set rather forward on his shoulders, and his neck being long, there is, when he is walking or conversing, a habitual protrusion of it. It is still well covered with hair.... His eyes are small. His chin is rather long, but not pointed, his nose small, regular in its outline, and the nostrils a little elevated. His mouth is well formed and still filled with teeth; it is generally strongly compressed, bearing an expression of contentment and benevolence. His limbs are uncommonly long, his hands and feet very large, and his wrists of a most extraordinary size. His walk is not precise and military, but easy and swinging; he stoops a little, not so much from age, as from natural formation. When sitting he appears short partly from the disproportionate length of his limbs. His general appearance indicates an extraordinary degree of health, vivacity, and spirit.[23] — Daniel Webster, 1824

Colonel Jefferson Randolph took exception to Webster's description of his grandfather: "The general impression it was calculated to produce seemed to me an unfavorable one, that is, a person who had never seen my grandfather, would, from Mr. Webster's description, have thought him rather an ill-looking man, which he certainly never was...."[24]

Personality and Character: Jefferson detested speaking in public because he had a lisp, and was only able to mumble, being barely heard. As a result, he abandoned the custom of delivering the State of the Union in person; rather sending it as a letter to Congress, a means of communication in which he excelled. He also felt that giving the address in person was too similar to a king speaking from the throne.[25] It wasn't until Woodrow Wilson that a president once again appeared before Congress to give his State of the Union message. Jefferson gave only two public speeches during his presidency — his inauguration addresses. He explained his lack of addresses by saying: "We often repent of what we have said, but never, never, of what we have not."[26]

Although he seemed distant to strangers, visitors found him vivacious and charming. Duc de La Rochefoucauld-Liancourt, a leader of the French Revolution, wrote: "In private life Mr. Jefferson displays a mild, easy and obliging tempter, though he is somewhat cold and reserved. His conversation is of the most agreeable kind, and he possesses a stock of information not inferior to that of any other man."[27] According to Jefferson biographer Dumas Malone: "Before he became a prominent actor on the stage of public life, he had formulated for himself a stern code of personal conduct and had disciplined himself to habits of study as few of his contemporaries ever found strength to do."[28]

Biographer James Parton described Jefferson at just a year before he wrote the Declaration of Independence: "A gentleman of thirty-two who could calculate an eclipse, survey an estate, tie an artery, plan an edifice, try a cause, break a horse, dance a minuet, and play the violin."[29] Marquis de Chastellux, writing of Jefferson on December 27, 1784, said: "Let me describe to you a man, not yet forty, tall, and with a mild and pleasing countenance, but whose mind and understanding are ample substitutes for every exterior grace. An American, who without ever having quitted his own country, is at once a musician, skilled in drawing; a geometrician, an astronomer, a natural philosopher, legislator, and statesman. A senator of America, who sat for two years in that famous Congress which brought about the revolution ... a governor of Virginia, who filled this difficult station during the invasions of Arnold, of Phillips, and of Cornwallis; a philosopher, in voluntary retirement, from the world, and public business, because he loves the world, inasmuch only as he can flatter himself with being useful to mankind.... For no object had escaped Mr. Jefferson; and it seemed as if from his youth he had placed his mind, as he has done his house, on an elevated situation, from which he might contemplate the universe."[30]

Jefferson was an introvert thrust into numerous extroverted roles. Some have suggested that his curious behavioral contradictions and his depressive and manic symptoms of mood swings may have been caused by a bipolar disorder.[31] The year before he became president, he questioned his accomplishments: "I have sometimes asked myself whether my country is the better for my having lived at all. I do not know that it is. I have been the instrument of doing the following things; but they would have been done by others; some of them, perhaps, a little better."[32] Subsequent presidents frequently commented on Jefferson's impressive intelligence:

It is with much reluctance that I am obliged to look upon him as a man whose mind is warped by prejudice and so blinded by ignorance as to be unfit for the office he holds. However wise and scientific as philosopher, as a politician he is a child and a dupe of party.[33] — John Adams

It may be said of him as has been said of others that he was a "walking library" and what can be said of but a few such prodigies that Genius of Philosophy ever walked hand in hand with him.... He lives and will live in memory and gratitude of the wise and good, as a luminary of Science, as a votary of liberty, as a model of patriotism, and as a benefactor of humankind.[34] — James Madison

He was a mixture of profound and sagacious observation, with strong prejudices and irritated passions.... If not an absolute atheist, he had no belief in a future existence. All his ideas of obligation were bounded by the present life. His duties to his neighbor were under no stronger guarantee than the laws of the land and the opinions of the world. The tendency of this condition upon a mind of great compass is to produce insincerity and duplicity, which were his besetting sins through life.[35] — John Quincy Adams

The principles of Jefferson are the definitions and axioms of a free society.[36] — Abraham Lincoln

Perhaps the most incapable Executive that ever filled the presidential chair ... it would be difficult to imagine a man less fit to guide the state with honor and safety through the stormy times that marked the opening of the present country.[37] — Theodore Roosevelt

The immortality of Jefferson does not lie in any one of his achievements, but in his attitude toward mankind.[38] — Woodrow Wilson

The next great President, in my view, was Jefferson.... Jefferson was just as important [as Washington and Lincoln] because he was working continuously for the preservation of free government as established by the Constitution.[39] — Harry S Truman

I think this is the most extraordinary collection of talent, of human knowledge, that has ever been gathered together at the White House, with the possible exception of when Thomas Jefferson dined alone.[40]— John F. Kennedy

He was an idealist with sense.[41]— Richard M. Nixon

Marriage and Romance: As a college student Jefferson was not very successful with females. He fell hard for vivacious 16-year-old Rebecca Burwell. His timidity prevented him from proposing marriage. When Tom finally got up the nerve to proclaim his love and ask her to be his wife, Rebecca rejected him because she already was engaged to Jacquelin Ambler.[42] This disappointment provoked the beginning of Jefferson's recurring and often debilitating headaches. Rebecca became the mother-in-law of Chief Justice of the Supreme Court John Marshall, "who became Jefferson's mortal enemy."[43]

When Jefferson was about 25 he allegedly engaged in an adulterous affair with Betsey Moore Walker, the wife of his friend and neighbor General John Walker, who was absent due to a military campaign during the French and Indian War.[44] "Jefferson had been a bridesman, part of the groom's party, when Walker married Betsey Moore in June 1764. When Jack Walker rode north to Fort Stanwys as clerk to the Virginia delegation in July 1768, he entrusted his wife and their baby daughter, and their home at Belvoir, five miles from Shadwell, to Jefferson's particular care."[45] Walker even named Jefferson his executor when he drew up his will. Sixteen years later Betsey told her husband what had occurred that summer in 1768. Walker, who by then was a political enemy of Jefferson, wrote to Jefferson about the affair, but otherwise kept the knowledge to himself for twenty more years.[46] When Jefferson was elected president the affair became general knowledge through the labors of an unfriendly press, causing a scandal. Wesley O. Hagood revealed: "With his honor sullied, John challenged Tom to a duel.... Jefferson ... arranged a meeting with Walker at James Madison's home and narrowly escaped settling the matter with pistols...."[47]

In a letter to Light-Horse Harry Lee, Walker claimed that Jefferson had tried to seduce his wife for eleven years, but that she had always fought him off.[48] In a statement made many years later, Jefferson confessed: "When young and single, I offered love to a handsome lady. I acknowledge its incorrectedness."[49]

When Thomas Jefferson went a-courting Martha Wayles Skelton, she was already a widow and a mother at age 22. Martha was born on October 19, 1748, in Charles City County, Virginia. Her mother, Martha Eppes Wayles, died only a few weeks after giving birth to Martha. Her father, John Wayles, an enormously wealthy English-born lawyer and landowner, buried three wives and survived many years as a widower after the death of Martha's mother.[50] A month before her 18th birthday, Martha Wayles married Bathurst Skelton, four years her senior. Their son John was born on November 7, 1767, surviving but four years. Bathurst went to his grave on September 30, 1768. A widow at 19, Martha returned to her father's home.[51] Her granddaughters, Ellen Wayles Randolph Coolidge and Sarah N. Randolph, gave testimony about their grandmother (no portrait or picture of her exists): "The youngest daughter, Mrs. Skelton, left a widow when scarcely advanced beyond her girlhood, was distinguished for her beauty, her accomplishments, and her solid merit. In person, she was a little above medium height, slightly but exquisitely formed. Her complexion was brilliant — her large expressive eyes of the richest shade of hazel — her luxuriant hair of the finest tinge of auburn. She walked, rode, and danced with admirable grace and spirit — sang and played the spinet and harpsichord with uncommon skill. The more solid parts of her education had not been neglected. She was also well read and intelligent, conversed agreeably; possessed excellent sense and a lively play of fancy; and had a frank, warm-hearted and somewhat impulsive disposition. Last, not least, she had already proved herself a true daughter of the Old Dominion in the department of housewifery."[52] Grand-daughter Ellen Randolph Coolidge voiced the family's oral history by describing her grand-mother as, "... a very attractive person ... a graceful, ladylike and accomplished woman."[53] Martha's sister's husband, Robert Skipwith, assured Jefferson that she possessed "... the greatest fund of good nature ... that sprightliness and sensibility which promises to ensure you the greatest happiness mortals are capable of enjoying."[54] "She was also a graceful rider and dancer and enjoyed long walks; she was well read, preferring fiction ... she loved talking and laughter and music."[55]

Patty, as she was called by her family, had many suitors, but she and Jefferson shared a love of music. He played the violin, and when she agreed to be his wife, he ordered a harpsichord pianoforte to be installed in Monticello for his bride. Some scholars believe that among her attractions for Long Tom was that she reminded him of his sister Jane.[56] The courtship went on for two years with Martha's father standing between his beautiful daughter and her suitors. Wayles did not believe that Jefferson was wealthy enough or expe-rienced enough to manage the large estate that Martha would inherit. In a letter to a friend, Tom revealed that he feared the obstruction of "the unfeeling temper of a parent who delays, perhaps refuses to approve her daughter's choice." By November 11, 1771, he had won over Patty's father.[57] The wedding took place at her family home, "The Forest," on January 1, 1772, with the party lasting two weeks.[58] At Wayles' death, the Jeffersons inherited 135 slaves and 40,000 acres of land. Many years later Martha Randolph, Jefferson's eldest daughter, described the hazardous journey the young couple endured when they set out for Jefferson's home in a phaeton, a small four-wheeled carriage, usually drawn by one or two horses. During their trip the newlyweds ran into a furious snow storm, forcing them to spend a night at the residence of Colonel Carter, where only the overseer was present. The next morning they left the coach behind, and continued on horseback. When they reached Mon-ticello, it was surrounded by two feet of snow. As it was quite late, the servants certain that they would not arrive that night, put out the fires and went to bed. "Not wishing to rouse the house, Jefferson stabled the horses and lit a fire. There was no food in the larder, but Tom remembered that he had placed a half bottle of wine behind some books on a shelf. The happy couple toasted each other and began to sing."[59]

The susceptible young woman endured pregnancies in which her children did not sur-vive as well as several miscarriages. She was often ill and alone for long periods of time, causing her descent into states of depression. The many pregnancies sapped her strength, so Jefferson reduced his political activities to care for her.[60] In 1782, feeling her death was imminent, possibly from diabetes, Martha feared that her surviving children would be brought up by a stepmother as she had been. She extracted her husband's pledge that he would never remarry and that he would always take care of their children, a promise he kept, although he lived for another 44 years.[61] For the remainder of his life, Jefferson kept a lock of Martha's hair entwined about lines from *Tristram Shandy* by one of Jefferson's favorite authors, Laurence Sterne: "Time wastes too fast: every letter / I trace tells me with what rapidity life follows my pen. The days and hours / of it are flying over our heads like clouds of a windy day never to return/ and every time I kiss thy hand to bid adieu, every absence which / follows it, are preludes to the eternal separation which we are shortly to make!"[62]

Martha died on September 6, 1782, weakened from the birth of her seventh child only months before. Both the child and mother lingered in an enfeebled state throughout the summer months. Jefferson did not leave his wife's side during her final weeks. His daughter Martha remembered the circumstances: "He nursed my poor mother in turn with Aunt Carr and her own sister — sitting up with her and administering her medicines and drink to the last. For four months that she lingered, he was never out of calling. When not at her bedside, he was writing in a small room which opened immediately at the head of her bed."[63] In a letter to the Marquis de Chastellux, Jefferson revealed that Martha never recovered from the birth of her last child. Lucy Elizabeth was born May 8, and Martha died the following September. In this correspondence, Jefferson refers to "... the state of dreadful suspense in which I had been kept all the summer and the catastrophe which closed it." He goes on to say, "A single event wiped away all my plans and left me a blank which I had not the spirits to fill up."[64] Edmund Randolph reported to James Madison in September 1782 that "Mrs. Jefferson has at last shaken off her tormenting pains by yielding to them, and has left our friend inconsolable. I ever thought him to rank domestic happiness in the first class of the chief good; but I scarcely supposed, that his grief would be so violent, as to justify the circulating report, of his swooning away, whenever he sees his children."[65]

When Martha passed, Jefferson shut himself in his room for three weeks, marching back and forth until exhausted. Then he spent endless hours riding his horse about his plantation.[66] One may imagine that he might have felt guilt-ridden for his numerous absences when his cherished wife needed his attention. Jefferson had the following lines cut on Martha's gravestone in the family burial plot at Monticello:

To the
Memory
of
Martha Jefferson,
Daughter of John Wayles,
Born Oct. 19. 1748. O.S.
Intermarried with
Thomas Jefferson
Jan 1. 1772.
Torn from him by death
Sept. 6. 1782
This Monument of his love
Is Inscribed.
"If in the melancholy shades below,
The flames of friends and lovers cease to glow,
Yet mine shall sacred last; mine undecayed
Burn on through death and animate my shade."[67]

Gradually, Jefferson's grief lessened, and he accepted an appointment as commissioner to France. Tom was unable to bring himself to record his life with Martha, only mentioning in one memoir that they spent their ten years together "in unchecquered happiness." Jefferson burned all of their letters between them at her death.[68]

A lonely widower, 43-year-old Jefferson was serving as Minister to France, when he fell in love with 27-year-old coquettish Maria Hadfield Cosway, a golden-haired married beauty, who was an accomplished artist. Her husband was the celebrated miniature painter and art connoisseur Richard Cosway. He was probably Britain's greatest miniaturist. He had made a fortune painting pornographic miniatures on snuff boxes for noblemen, including the Prince of Wales.[69] He was shorter even than his petite wife, who was described as "a Botticelli-like beauty with blond curling hair, brilliant eyes, and exquisite skin."[70] Letters between Tom and Maria record their romance. Jefferson described her as "having qualities and accomplishments, belonging to her sex, which might form a chapter apart for her: such as music, modesty, beauty, and that softness of disposition which is the ornament of her sex and charm of ours."[71] In one correspondence Tom confessed he was "solitary and sad" without her. The letter included a conversation he said he had overheard between his head and his heart. He reported that his rational head warned his passionate heart against too much reliance on affection of objects, which he would soon lose. The heart said that knowing her, knowing the joy of their time together was worth the price of losing her.[72]

Dwindling meetings and perhaps learning of her reputation for promiscuity contributed to the cooling of Jefferson's ardor. He returned to America and after the death of Maria's husband, she moved to Lodi, Italy, where she established a convent school for girls.[73] The two former lovers corresponded sporadically over the years. At her home, Maria had a portrait of Jefferson

"Maria Louisa Catharien Cecilia Hadfield Cosway," a halftone photomechanical reproduction of rare mezzotint by Valentine Green after self-portrait by Maria Cosway, first published in 1787 (Library of Congress).

painted by John Trumbull, which is now located in the White House. For his part, Jefferson hung an engraving of the lovely Maria in Monticello's family sitting room.[74]

The claim that Thomas Jefferson fathered children with his quadroon slave Sally Hemings was apparently common knowledge in Monticello and Charlottesville. Elijah Fletcher, the headmaster of the New Glasgow Academy (Amherst County, Virginia) visited Jefferson in 1811 and reported that "The story of black Sal is no farce — That he cohabits with her and has a number of children by her is a sacred truth — and the worst of it is he keeps the same children slaves— an unnatural crime which is very common in these parts."[75] The accusation was first publicly aired during Jefferson's first presidential term by James Thomas Callender, a notorious scandalmonger, who with "fiery rhetoric was able to blow up even the minuscule rumor into a blockbuster exposé."[76] On August 28, 1802, Callender published the first account of the Jefferson–Sally Hemings affair: "It is well known that the man, *whom it delicate the people to honor*, keeps, and for many years past has kept, as his concubine, one of his own slaves. Her name is Sally. The name of her eldest son is Tom. His slaves are said to bear a striking although sable resemblance to those of the president himself. The boy is ten or twelve years of age. His mother went to France in the same vessel with Mr. Jefferson and his two daughters. The delicacy of the *arrangement must strike* every person of common sensibilities...."[77] The president did not take the bait, refusing to respond to the charge, claiming his life was the strongest proof of his character. The revelation did not damage the president's reputation, nor did it deny him from a second term. The unproven romance has persisted as a subject of argument and controversy ever since. Hemings went to Monticello as a personal servant of Martha when the latter married Tom. Martha and Sally were half sisters, since Hemings was the product of a liaison between Martha's father John Wayles and one of his slaves, Betty Hemings.[78] As a teenager Sally accompanied Jefferson's daughter Polly to France and returned with Jefferson in 1789, the year in which it is alleged they became intimate.[79] Sally was described as being "mighty near white." According to Isaac

Jefferson, "she was very handsome, with long straight hair hanging down her back."[80] Sally lived at Monticello for most of the rest of her life. According to Jefferson's records, she bore six children. Throughout most of the nineteenth and twentieth centuries, Jefferson biographers either did not bring up the charges or merely dismissed them. In 1814, Jefferson publicly specified his opposition to sexual relations between races: "The amalgamation of whites with blacks produces a degradation to which no lover of his country, no lover of excellence in the human character, can innocently consent."[81]

Hand-colored engraving with aquatint "A Philosophic Cock," 1804 political cartoon circulated by Jefferson's opponents condemning his relationship with Sally Hemings; created by James Akin, Newburyport, Massachusetts, c. 1804. Text above reads: "Tis not a set of features or complexion or tincture of a skin that I admire" (Charles Pierce Collection of Social and Political Caricatures, Courtesy American Antiquarian Society).

Privately Martha Jefferson denied the published reports, not wishing to give any weight to them by making a public denial. Jefferson freed all of Sally Hemings' children: Beverly, Harriet, Madison and Eston, as they came of age. Three of the four entered white society as adults; they were seven-eighths European in ancestry.[82] Jefferson's will made no provision for freeing Sally, perhaps because there had not been a loving relationship or possibly he felt to do so would be deserting her to a world in which her survival would be very challenging. "Following Jefferson's death, his daughter gave Sally Hemings 'her time,' by which she lived freely with her two younger sons in Charlottesville for her last nine years. She lived to see a grandchild born in the house her sons owned. After their mother's death in 1835, Eston and Madison Hemings migrated with their families to Chillicothe in the free state of Ohio."[83] In 1873, the *Pike County Republican* published a memoir by Madison Hemings, then a resident of Ross County, Ohio. He stated that his mother Sally gave birth to five children "and Jefferson was the father of them all."[84] DNA tests and investigations by specialists from the Thomas Jefferson Foundation, which owns and operates Monticello, concluded that there was a high probability that Jefferson fathered at least one of Sally's six children and perhaps all. The male descendants of her youngest son Eston Hemings were found to share Y chromosomes with the Jefferson family.[85] Scoffers claim that it is far more likely that the father was Thomas' younger brother Randolph. The *William & Mary Quarterly* published a probabilistic analysis of the timing of Jefferson's visits to Monticello and Hemings' pregnancies, concluding that it was highly likely that the two series of events were related.[86] In 2001, the *National Genealogical Society Quarterly* concluded that four children of Sally Hemings were fathered by Thomas Jefferson.[87] The debate over the alleged affair will likely continue, even if the full story may never be known.

Children (Legitimate): Martha Washington Jefferson was born on September 27, 1772, nine months after her parents' wedding. She was weak and small, but was the only offspring to live a long life. She was nicknamed "Patsy." The other Jefferson children were Jane Randolph Jefferson, infant son (perhaps named Peter), Mary Washington, and two daughters named Lucy Elizabeth Jefferson. The first Lucy died only four-and-one-half months after her birth. The second Lucy survived her mother by just two years, dying from whooping cough in October 1784.[88] Patsy, who was much like her father, married Thomas Mann Randolph. Jr., who served as governor of Virginia (1819–1822). The couple had 12 children and Jefferson became a devoted grandfather. Because Tom was a widower, Martha served as his hostess when he was president. Jefferson wrote a short verse to her from his deathbed:

> Life's visions are vanished; its dreams are no more;
> Dear friends of my bosom, why bathed in tears?
> I go to my fathers, I welcome the shore
> Which crowns all my hopes and buries my cares.
> Then farewell my dear, my lov'd daughter adieu!
> The last pang in life is in parting from you.
> Two seraphs await me long shrouded in death;
> I will bear them your love on my last parting breath.[89]

In addition to Patsy, only Mary, called "Polly," lived to adulthood. She assumed the name Maria, while with her father in France. Her niece Ellen Wayles Randolph Coolidge described her: "My aunt, Mrs. Eppes, was singularly beautiful. She was high-principled, just, and generous. Her temper, naturally mild, became, I think, saddened by ill health in the latter part of her life.... She was intellectually the somewhat superior to her sister, who was sensible of the difference, though she was of too noble a nature for her feelings ever to assume an ignoble character. There was between the sisters the strongest and warmest attachment, the most perfect confidence and affection...."[90] Polly suffered her mother's fate, dying immediately after giving birth to a third child. "It was her death that prompted Abigail Adams to send written condolences to President Jefferson, thus ending a long silence between the two families that had been brought on by political differences during the presidential campaign of 1800. Abigail wrote movingly of the immediate affection she had felt for Maria which had never altered."[91]

Religion and Religious Beliefs: Jefferson had no formal religious affiliation, leading foes in 1800 to accuse him of being an atheist and an enemy of religion. During his lifetime Jefferson believed that most of the attacks upon his religious reputation came from church leaders who wanted "'their form of Christianity established through the United States,' something he resolutely opposed."[92] However, he wrote at length on religion and many scholars concluded that he was a deist, a common position held by intellectuals in the late 18th century. Roman Catholic theologian Avery Cardinal Dulles concluded: "Jefferson was a deist because he believed in one God, in divine providence, in the divine moral law, and in rewards and punishments after death; but did not believe in supernatural revelation. He was Christian deist because he saw Christianity as the highest expression of natural religion and Jesus as an incomparably great moral teacher. He was not an orthodox Christian because he rejected, among other things, the doctrines that Jesus was the promised Messiah and the incarnate Son of God."[93]

Jefferson was raised in the Church of England at a time when it was the official religion in Virginia and the only denomination funded by tax money. During his presidency, Jefferson attended the weekly church services held in the House of Representatives but was not a member of any congregation or denomination. "Jefferson was skeptical of religious truth that depended upon 'revelation' and 'accepting by faith' beliefs which were contrary to reason.... [H]e came to a lifelong conviction that the God whom nature revealed and the religion which reason indicated were more believable than the God and doctrines of biblical revelation and dogma."[94] In a letter to Francis Hopkinson, he stated: "I never submitted the whole system of my opinions to the creed of any party of men whatever in religion, in philosophy, in politics, or in anything else where I was capable of thinking for myself. Such an addiction is the last degradation of a free and moral agent. If I could not go to heaven, but with a party, I would not go to heaven at all."[95] In another letter, he wrote: "I am of a sect by myself, as far as I know."[96] He once described himself as an Epicurean, saying: "I consider the genuine (not the imputed) doctrines of Epicurus as containing everything rational in moral philosophy which Greece and Rome have left us."[97] The Epicureanism system of philosophy maintains that soundly based human happiness is the highest good, so that its rational pursuit should be adopted.

Although Jefferson believed in a Creator, his God was not the personal god of Christianity. In his writings are found his assessments of Christianity and Christ:

> To the corruptions of Christianity I am, indeed, opposed; but not to the genuine precepts of Jesus himself. I am a Christian in the only sense in which he wished any one to be; sincerely attached to his doctrines in preference to all others; ascribing to himself every human excellence; and believing he never claimed any other.... Of all the systems of morality, ancient or modern, which have come under my observation, none appear to me so pure as that of Jesus.... In extracting the pure principles which [Jesus] taught, we should have to strip off the artificial vestments in which they have been muffled by priests, who have travestied them into various forms, as instruments of riches and power to themselves.... [T]here will be found remaining the most sublime and benevolent code of morals which has ever been offered to man.... The doctrines which flowed from the lips of Jesus himself are within the comprehension of a child; but thousands of volumes have not yet explanations the Platonisms engrafted to them.[98]

> Among the sayings and discourses imputed to him [Jesus Christ] by his biographers, I find many passages of fine imagination, correct morality, and of the most lovely benevolence; and others again of so much ignorance, so much absurdity, so much untruth, charlatanism, and imposture, as to pronounce it impossible that such contradictions should have proceeded from the same being.[99]

> Had the doctrines of Jesus been preached always as pure as they came from his lips, the whole civilized world would now have been Christian.[100]

> Paul was the great Coryphaeus, the first corrupter of the doctrines of Jesus.[101]

> Christianity neither is, nor ever was a part of the common law.[102]

For Jefferson, the separation of church and state was not an abstract right but an essential reform of the religious "tyranny" of one Christian sect over others. Until the Revolutionary War, nine of the thirteen colonies officially supported one particular religion, called an established church. But by 1787 only Massachusetts, New Hampshire, and Connecticut maintained state religions.[103] Jefferson was at the forefront of the fight for religious freedom and separation of church and state in his native Virginia, bringing him into conflict with the Anglican Church, the established church in Virginia. After a lengthy and acrimonious debate, Jefferson's statute for religious freedom was passed by the Virginia General Assembly in 1786. In Jefferson's words, there was now "freedom for the Jew and the Gentile, the Christian and the Mohammedan, the Hindu and infidel of every denomination."[104] When the First Amendment to the Constitution went into effect in 1791, Jefferson's principle of separation of church and state became part of the supreme law of the land. The statute reads: "No man shall be compelled to frequent or support any religious worship, place, or ministry whatsoever, nor shall be enforced, restrained, molested, or burdened in his body or goods, nor shall otherwise suffer, on account of his religious opinions or belief; but that all men shall be free to profess, and by argument to maintain, their opinions in matters of religion, and that the same shall in no way diminish, enlarge, or effect their civil capacities."[105] Jefferson stated:

> Believing that religion is a matter which lies solely between man and his God, that he owes account to none other for his faith or his worship, that the legislative powers of government reach action only, and not opinions, I contemplate with sovereign reverence that act of the whole American people which declared that their Legislature should "make no law respecting an establishment of religion, or prohibiting the free exercise thereof," thus building a wall of separation between Church and State.[106]

As for toleration or religious differences, in a September 26, 1814, letter to Miles King, Jefferson professed:

> We have heard it said that there is not a Quaker or a Baptist, a Presbyterian or an Episcopalian, a Catholic or a Protestant in heaven; that on entering that gate, we leave those badges of schism behind.... Let us not be uneasy about the different roads we may pursue, as believing them the shortest, to that our last abode; but following the guidance of good conscience, let us be happy in the hope that by these different paths we shall all meet in the end. And that you and I may meet and embrace is my earnest prayer."[107]

The following are further expressions of religion ascribed to the third president of the United States:

> If we do act merely from love of God and a belief that it is pleasing to Him, whence arises the morality of the Atheist? ... Their virtue then must have some other foundation than the love of God.[108]

> I have always said and always will say that the studious perusal of the Sacred Volume will make better citizens, better fathers, better husbands ... the Bible make the best people in the world.[109]

> Millions of innocent men, women, and children, since the introduction of Christianity, have been burnt, tortured, fined, and imprisoned; yet we have not advanced one inch towards uniformity.[110]

> Compulsion in religion is distinguished peculiarly from compulsion in every other thing. I may grow rich by art I am compelled to follow, I may recover health by medicines, I am compelled to take against my own judgment, but I cannot be saved by a worship I disbelieve & abhor.[111]

> For it is in our lives, and not from our words, that our religion must be read. By the same test the world must judge me. But this does not satisfy the priesthood. They must have a positive, a declared assent to all their interested absurdities. My opinion is that there would never have been an infidel, if there had never been a priest. The artificial structures they have built on the purest of all moral systems, for the purpose of deriving from it pence and power, revolts those who think for themselves, and who read in that system only what is really there....[112]

> Having banished from our land that religious intolerance under which mankind so long bled and suffered, we have yet gained little if we countenance a political intolerance as despotic, as wicked, and capable of as bitter and bloody persecutions.[113]

I never told my own religion nor scrutinized that of another. I never attempted to make a convert, nor wished to change another's creed. I have ever judged of another's religion by their lives ... for it is our lives and not from our words, that our religion must be read.[114]

If thinking men would have the courage to think for themselves, and to speak what they think, it would be found they do not differ in religious opinions as much as is supposed.[115]

Of all the systems of morality, ancient or modern, which have come under my observation, none appears to me so pure as that of Jesus. He who follows this steadily need not, I think, be uneasy, although he cannot comprehend the subtleties and mysteries erected on his doctrines by those, who calling themselves his special followers and favorites, would make him come into the world to lay snares for all understandings but theirs.[116]

In every country and in every age, the priest has been hostile to liberty. He is always in alliance with the despot, abetting his abuses in return for protection of his own.[117]

President John Quincy Adams said of Jefferson's beliefs:

He was a mixture of profound and sagacious observation, with strong prejudices and irritated passions.... If not an absolute atheist, he had no belief in a future existence. All his ideas of obligation were bounded by the present life. His duties to his neighbor were under no stronger guarantee than the laws of the land and the opinions of the world. The tendency of this condition upon a mind of great compass is to produce insincerity and duplicity, which were his besetting sins through life.[118]

Education: As a youngster, Jefferson's father taught him reading, writing, and arithmetic as well as music and the art of drafting. Later his parents hired a teacher who lived with the family and gave the children their early education.[119] Jefferson attended a preparatory school run by a Scottish minister, William Douglas, where he studied Latin and Greek, as well as French. After his father's death, he attended the school of a learned minister James Maury in Fredericksburg, 12 miles from Shadwell, boarding with the Maury family. There he received a classical education and studied history and science. According to Peter Jefferson's account books, "Douglas was paid sixteen pounds sterling per annum, for room and board. Maury received twenty pounds for the same."[120]

Jefferson entered the College of William and Mary in Williamsburg at age 16, graduating with highest honors two years later. At the college he studied mathematics, philosophy and metaphysics and read the writings of the British Empiricists, including John Locke, Francis Bacon and Sir Isaac Newton (whom he would later refer to as "the three greatest men the world had ever produced").[121] Jefferson also perfected his French, practiced the violin, and read Tacitus and Homer. His study of natural law and political thought helped form his commitment to republican government. In several letters he repeated the claim: "The *lex majoris partis* (the law of the majority) is the natural law of every assembly of men, whose numbers are not fixed by any other law."[122]

Throughout his life, Jefferson had an unlimited intellectual curiosity, which fired his interests in science and natural history, the classics, music, and the arts. He frequently said that "Nature destined him to be a scientist; but no careers to science in Virginia."[123] His devotion to science inspired numerous agricultural pursuits and his fascination with architecture was put to good use in designing his home at Monticello.[124] Jefferson felt that education of the common people was so necessary that taxes should be set aside for that purpose, asserting in a letter to George Wythe: "Preach, my dear Sir, a crusade against ignorance; establish and improve the law for educating the common people. Let our countrymen know ... that the tax which will be paid for this purpose is not more than a thousandth part of what will be paid to kings, priests, and nobles, who will rise up among us if we keep the people in ignorance."[125]

In championing the founding of the University of Virginia, Jefferson affirmed the wish to make it: "... worth patronizing with public support, and be a temptation to the youth of other states to come, and drink of the cup of knowledge & fraternize with us."[126] In a letter to James Madison, Jefferson wrote: "Educate and inform the whole mass of people. Enable them to see that it is to their interest to preserve peace and order.... They are the only sure reliance for the preservation of our liberty.[127]

Jefferson paid substantial attention to developing a theory of education, dividing it into sub-theories based on the works of Aristotle: "value, knowledge, human nature, learning, transmission, opportunity, and consensus."[128] He wrote that the universal object of his educational scheme was to provide instruction "adapted to the years, to the capacity, and the condition of everyone, and directed to their freedom and happiness."[129] Jefferson saw an individual need of education as a function of one's "conditions and pursuits of his life,"[130] but he also discriminated in education by gender. Some of his thoughts on the effect of education are found in a letter to P.S. DuPont de Nemours: "Although I do not, with some enthusiasts, believe that the human condition will ever advance to such a state of perfection as that there shall no longer be pain or vice in the world, yet I believe it susceptible of much improvement ... and that the diffusion of knowledge among the people is to be the instrument by which it is to be effected."[131]

Jefferson professed that there was a need for American education system that did not require journeying to Europe to find higher learning: "An American coming to Europe for his education loses in his knowledge, in his morals, in his health, in his habits, and in his happiness. I had entertained only doubts of this in my head before I came to Europe; what I see and hear, since I came here, proves more than I had ever suspected."[132] In a July 5, 1814, letter to John Adams, Jefferson complained: "They commit their pupils to the theatre of the world with just taste enough of learning to be alienated from industrious pursuits and not enough to do service in the ranks of science."[133] On August 1, 1816, Jefferson wrote to Adams on the subject of bigotry: "Bigotry is the disease of ignorance, or morbid minds, enthusiasm of the free and buoyant. Education & free discussion are the antidotes of both."[134] Jefferson wrote to George Ticknor on November 25, 1817: "Knowledge is power ... knowledge is safety ... knowledge is happiness."[135] In an 1820 letter to Adams, Jefferson commented on dictionaries: "Dictionaries are but the depositories of words already legitimized by usage. Society is the work-shop in which new ones are elaborated. When an individual uses a new word, if ill-formed it is rejected in society, if well-formed, adopted, and, after due time, laid up in the depository of dictionaries."[136] And in an 1826 letter to Roger C. Weightman, Long Tom spoke of the role science plays in human's freedom: "The general spread of the light of science has already laid open to every view the palpable truth that the mass of mankind has not been born with saddles on their backs nor a favored few booted and spurred, ready to ride them legitimately by the grace of God."[137]

Among other of his thoughts on education are the following:

> It is an axiom in my mind that our liberty can never be safe but in the hands of the people themselves, and that, too, often the people with a certain degree of instruction.[138]
>
> Educate and inform the whole mass of people. Enable them to see that it is to their interest to preserve peace and order.... They are the only sure reliance for the preservation of our liberty.[139]
>
> If the condition of man is to be progressively ameliorated, as we fondly hope and believe, education is to be the chief instrument in effecting it.[140]

Ten Golden Rules: Jefferson was taught the following rules by his father and the lessons stuck throughout his life.[141]

1. Never put off until tomorrow what you can do today.
2. Never trouble another for what you can do yourself.
3. Never spend your money before you have it.
4. Never buy what you do not want because it is cheap.
5. Pride costs us more than hunger, thirst, and cold.
6. We never repent for having eaten too little.
7. Nothing is troublesome that you do willingly.
8. How much pain have the evils that never happened cost us!
9. Take things always by their smooth handle.
10. When angry, count to ten before you speak; if very angry, one hundred.

OCCUPATION

Jefferson believed that a person should never be idle. He wasn't. He was a lawyer, planter, politician, diplomat, writer, architect, scientist, philosopher, and inventor.[142]

Lawyer: Jefferson worked as a surveyor before studying law with George Wythe. The latter was a delegate to the Continental Congress and a signer of the Declaration of Independence, authored by his student. Jefferson was admitted to the bar and set up a successful practice in 1767. He was a member of the colonial House of Burgesses from 1769 to 1775. He wrote an authoritative pamphlet "A Summary View of the Rights of British America" (1774)[143] as instructions for the Virginia delegates to a national congress. In it, he argued that as the sons of expatriate Englishmen, Americans possessed the same natural rights to govern themselves as their "Saxon ancestors had exercised when they migrated to England from Germany."[144] He accused the reign of King George III of violating American rights and instituting "a deliberate, systematic plan of reducing us to slavery."[145] The document made his reputation and led to his being chosen to draft the Declaration of Independence, as a member of the Continental Congress.[146]

Planter: As a plantation owner and farmer, Jefferson was a master horticulturalist. He grew tomatoes at a time when the fruit was considered dangerous. Some people of that time may have avoided eating tomatoes because of their reputation as an aphrodisiac, rather than because they feared being poisoned.[147] He grew some seventy types of vegetables. Jefferson experimented with farming, implementing innovations such as "parallel plowing and crop-rotation, and a plow of his own design."[148] While in Europe, Jefferson saw that the Dutch moldboard, which is the head of a plow that lifts up and turns over sod, was awkward and ineffective. He invented a new moldboard based on solid mathematical principles, namely, the right angle.[149]

Jefferson was a devoted wine lover and well-known gourmet. During his years in France, he frequently traveled through the wine regions and sent many vintages back to Virginia. He insisted that the United States could "make as great a variety of wines as are made in Europe, not exactly the same kinds, but doubtless as good."[150] He planted widespread vineyards at Monticello, but they did not survive the many vine diseases native to America. Jefferson was the first to introduce the olive tree to North America after returning from his diplomatic service in France.[151] Jefferson's Farm Book (1773 to 1814) documents everything that happened at his plantation. His Garden Book (1766 to 1824) chronicles his experiments with decorative planting and experimental agriculture. The books are owned and maintained by the Massachusetts Historical Society.[152] In a letter to C. W. Peale in 1811, Jefferson rhapsodized: "I have often thought that if heaven had given me a choice of my

*"**Give Me Liberty, or Give Me Death!**,"* lithograph published by Currier & Ives, c. 1876. It depicts Patrick Henry delivering his speech on the rights of the colonies during the Virginia Assembly convened at Richmond on March 23, 1775. He concluded with the quoted sentiment, which became the war cry of the Revolution. George Washington is at left forefront, and Thomas Jefferson, at right forefront, applauds (Library of Congress).

position and calling, it should have been on a rich spot of earth, well watered, and near a good market for the productions of the garden. No occupation is so delightful to me as the culture of the earth, and no culture comparable to that of the garden."[153]

Among his other comments about agriculture and farming are:

> Those who labor in the earth are the chosen people of God, if He ever had a chosen people, whose breasts He has made His peculiar deposit for substantial and genuine virtue.[154]

> Cultivators of the earth are the most valuable citizens. They are the most vigorous, the most independent, the most wedded to liberty and interests, by the most lasting bonds.[155]

> Have you become a farmer? Is it not pleasanter than to be shut up within four walls and delving eternally with the pen?[156]

Inventor: Jefferson never attempted to patent any of his inventions, even though his design of a new moldboard briefly transformed agriculture before iron came to be used in place of wooden plows. He believed that inventions should be exclusively for the good of the people and not for enriching the inventor.[157] While Secretary of State, Jefferson developed a wheel cipher to code messages for use in the struggle the new nation faced with controversial foreign policy and national security issues. The instrument consisted of twenty-six cylindrical wooden pieces, each with a hole bored in its center so that they could be threaded onto an iron spindle. All twenty-six letters of the alphabet were inscribed on the edge of each wheel. Using the cipher, it was possible to scramble and unscramble letters of a coded message.[158] Working with Benjamin H. Latrobe, Jefferson constructed a sundial in 1809, which he described it thusly:

> I had placed the Capital on a pedestal of the size proper to its diameter, and had reconciled their confluence into one another by interposing plinths successively diminishing. It looked bald for want of something to crown it. I therefore surmounted it with a globe and its neck, as is usual on gate posts. I was not satisfied; because it presented no idea of utility. It occurred then that this globe might be made to perform the functions of a dial. I ascertained on it two poles, delineated its equator and tropics, described meridians at every 15 degrees from tropic to tropic, and shorter portions of meridian intermediately for the half hours, quarter hours and every 5 minutes. I then mounted it on its neck, with its axis parallel to that of the earth by a hole bored in the Nadir of our latitude, affixed a meridian of sheet iron, moveable on its poles, and with its plane in that of a great circle, of course presenting its upper edge to the meridian of the heavens corresponding with that on the globe to which its lower edge pointed.[159]

Englishman John Hawkins invented the polygraph, a letter copying device, in 1803, which was produced in the United States by Charles Wilson Peale, but Jefferson perfected it. Hawkins described the polygraph as an "improvement in the pantograph and parallel rule."[160] It held two or more pens that were moved concurrently by the writer's hand, making a duplicate copy or copies remarkably like the original. Jefferson used the mechanical letter-copying device to produce copies for himself, as well as his correspondents. Jefferson invented a mahogany ladder that folded up into almost a pole for storage. He recommended it for pruning trees. It was the first of its kind in the United States and in the late 1880s became commonly used in libraries.[161] Jefferson also designed a unique revolving stand with five adjustable rectangular shaped rests for holding books. The rests could be folded in order to make a small smooth-surfaced box which was attached to the base.[162] Jefferson designed beds, which fit in nooks of rooms held by a web of ropes hung from the ceiling on hooks. As his bed lay in an alcove between two rooms, he installed a mechanical apparatus to raise it to the ceiling during the day to allow an opening below.[163] Jefferson introduced a new piece of furniture to the U.S. that consisted of a revolving Windsor chair combined with a writing arm and a leg rest.[164]

Home: Jefferson designed his home, Monticello, a uniquely personal creation perched on a densely wooded summit. It was his enduring passion and contained within some unique features, such as a two-faced clock that could be read from both inside and outside of the house.[165] Monticello's construction began while Jefferson was a representative to the Virginia House of Burgesses. Dissatisfied with the first version, completed in 12 years, he rebuilt it. Over a twenty-year period, Jefferson enlarged Monticello from eight rooms to twenty-one.[166] It is located in the Virginia Piedmont, two miles southeast of Charlottesville and 125 miles from Washington, D.C. Speaking of his home, Jefferson wrote: "I am happy nowhere else, and in no other society, and all my wishes end, where I hope my days will, at Monticello."[167] Monticello boasts a 1000-foot-long vegetable garden, carved into the protected south side of Monticello Mountain. The terraced beds are supported by a massive stone wall, leading one visitor to describe it as a "hanging garden." It is divided into twenty-four square plots, arranged according to which part of the plant is to be harvested. Jefferson designed the groupings, combinations, and contrasts of flowers in his flower garden.[168] Trees were an important part of Jefferson's landscape design, and he planted more than 160 species at Monticello. Because of Virginia's hot summers, Jefferson also had eighteen acres of trees pruned high, to construct "our Elysium" of shade as the branches provided an umbrella-like covering.[169] Speaking of trees, Jefferson noted: "I never before knew the full value of trees. Under them I breakfast, dine, write, read, and receive my company. What

"Monticello from the North, Charlottesville, Virginia," photograph created between 1900 and 1906 (Library of Congress, Detroit Publishing Company Photograph Collection).

would I not give that the trees planted nearest round the house at Monticello were full grown."[170]

Had he not turned to politics, Jefferson would certainly have pursued the art and science of architecture more fully. In "Notes on the State of Virginia," he proclaimed: "The genius of architecture seems to have shed its maledictions over this land."[171] And in a letter to John Rutledge, Jr., he declared: "Architecture is worth great attention. As we double our numbers every 20 years we must double our houses. Besides we build of such perishable materials that one half of our houses must be rebuilt in every space of 20 years. So that in that term, houses are to be built for three-fourths of our inhabitants. It is then among the most important arts; and it is desirable to introduce taste into an art which shows so much."[172]

Many experts in the field consider self-taught Jefferson to be America's first architect. Fascinated by octagons, he incorporated them into many of his designs. In 1806, Jefferson began construction of an eight-sided house, which was to be a retreat, where, in his own words: "[I can] detach myself from public life, which I have never loved, and retire to the bosom of my family, my friends, my farm and my books, which I have always loved."[173] The Italian-style villa, located near Lynchburg, Virginia, was not merely a place to escape the hustle and bustle of Monticello, it was a working plantation. Over the years, many modifications were made to the house and its 4,812-acre was reduced to 50 as subdivisions rose up around it.[174] The Corporation for Jefferson's Poplar Forest owns the site and house, which is opened for tours.

Eight years after Jefferson's death, Commodore Uriah Levy purchased Monticello with the intention of preserving it for the nation. He acquired 218 acres of overgrown fields surrounding a dilapidated house. He set about having both the house and Jefferson's garden restored. When it was completed Levy guided tourists through the house and grounds and finally increased the extent of the property to 2,700 acres.[175] In his will, Levy named the United States as administrator of the estate to be used as Jefferson had wished as a school for orphans of naval officers. With the coming of the Civil War, the Confederacy seized the property and sold it to another owner.[176] Following the war, there was a long period of litigation before Levy's nephew Jefferson Monroe Levy took ownership.

During the 19 years after Commodore Levy's death, the estate became a not too well kept up working farm. The younger Levy oversaw a thorough rehabilitation and restoration of the property, purchasing furniture that had been owned by Jefferson wherever he could find pieces.[177] In the depression following World War I, Jefferson Levy was forced to sell the property. The non-profit Thomas Jefferson Foundation was formed in New York to purchase Monticello. Money for the purchase was collected through a national fundraising campaign, which included an effort by schoolchildren across the nation, known as "pennies for Monticello."[178] The organization paid Levy $500,000 and the estate is now owned and operated by the Thomas Jefferson Memorial Foundation and is open to the public.[179]

Motto: "Rebellion to tyrants is obedience to God."[180]

Pets and Animals: Meriwether Lewis and William Clark brought back grizzly bear cubs as presents for Jefferson when they returned from their expedition, exploring the Louisiana Purchase.[181] Jefferson kept horses, shepherd dogs and Angora cats that he brought back from France.[182] "A widower, Jefferson lived alone in the president's house, except for his pet mockingbird, Dick, who liked to follow him around and perch on his shoulder while he was working. Jefferson taught Dick to sing along while he played the violin.[183]

Recreational Pastimes and Interests: Jefferson enjoyed solving problems and in particular devising inventions that would make things easier to do.[184] He was an enthusiastic speleologist (cave explorer). His interests included the infant discipline of archeology, and in recognition of his role in developing excavation techniques, he has at times been called the "father of archeology."[185] When exploring an Indian burial mound, rather than follow the common practice of digging downwards until something was found, Jefferson cut a wedge out of the mound. In this way, he could walk into it, look at the layers of occupation, and draw conclusions.[186]

Jefferson's favorite exercise was riding. He was a superb judge of horses and rode a particularly good one. He also was keenly fond of hunting, and he praised the virtues of walking, saying: "Walking is the best possible exercise. Habituate yourself to walk very far. The Europeans value themselves on having subdued the horse to the uses of man; but I doubt whether we have not lost more than we gained, by the use of this animal."[187]

Jefferson took special pride in his garden. He laid out a serpentine path, so as family and guests walked along among the oval beds; they could admire a vast array of flowers, particularity "handsome plants or fragrant."[188] Among these were New World curiosities, including the Jeffersonia diphylla (twinleaf), named in his honor in 1792. These delicate wildflowers bloom annually around the time of its namesake's birth.[189] Jefferson was a passionate reader, claiming he had a "canine appetite for reading."[190] He also wrote poetry. As an example, the following lines are from a poem he called "To Ellen."[191]

> 'Tis hope supports each noble flame,
> 'Tis hope inspires poetic lays,
> Our heroes fight in hopes of fame,
> And poets write in hopes of praise.

In his correspondence with John Adams on June 10, 1815, TJ announced, "I cannot live without books.... Books constitute capital. A library book lasts as long as a house, for hundreds of years. It is not, then, an article of mere consumption but fairly of capital, and often in the case of professional men, setting out in life, it is their only capital."[192]

POLITICAL OFFICES

Political Philosophy and Political Party Affiliation: Introduced to the tenets of the Enlightenment at the College of William & Mary, Jefferson projected an optimistic faith in the power of reason to monitor human rights throughout his life.[193] He believed in the natural rights of man and had faith in the people's ability to govern themselves. Jefferson believed in "the illimitable freedom of the human mind, to explore and to expose every subject susceptible of its contemplation."[194] He brought scientific reasoning to his philosophy of government. He has been called the "father of American exceptionalism, due to his firm belief in the uniqueness of America."[195] Jefferson wrote, "... wherever the people are well informed they can be trusted with their own government ..." unlike class-divided, industrialized Europe.[196]

The Democratic-Republican Party, of which Jefferson was the natural leader, opposed the views of the Federalists, in particular those of Alexander Hamilton, which they believed favored the interests of business and the upper class.[197] Like Jefferson, the Democratic-Republicans were proponents of agricultural interests and resisted the Federalist's desire to expand the power of the federal government. Jefferson summed up their positions, asserting that they should endeavor to keep "a watchful eye over the disaffection of wealth and ambition to the republican principles of our Constitution and by sacrificing all our local and personal interests in the cultivation of the Union and maintenance of the authority of the laws."[198]

Jefferson and his compatriots distrusted cities and financiers, favoring states' rights and a strictly restricted federal government.[199] They were apprehensive that unrestricted expansion of commerce and industry would populate the country with a class of wage laborers, dependent upon others for income and livelihood.[200] The Democratic-Republicans feared a reoccurrence of the calamitous social consequences of the Industrial Revolution in Britain in the second half of the 18th century. At that time, the traditional agrarian economy in Britain gave way to one dominated by machinery and manufacturing.[201] Jefferson's views on States' Rights, echoing the Democratic-Republican Party's position, are found in a series of letters written throughout his political career.[202] Biographer Dumas Malone wrote of the third president's philosophical bent:

> It is impossible to grant eternal validity to the "principles" adduced by him to support his position in particular circumstances; he was always more interested in applications than in speculation, and he was forced to modify his own philosophy in practice. But, despite unquestionable inconsistencies, the general trend of his policies and his major aims are unmistakable. A homely aristocrat in manner of life and personal tastes, he distrusted all rulers and feared the rise of an industrial proletariat, but more than any of his eminent contemporaries, he trusted the common man, if measurably enlightened and kept in rural virtue.... He is notable, not for the harmony with the life of an age, but rather for his being a step or several steps ahead of it; no other American more deserves to be termed a major prophet, a supreme pioneer. A philosophical statesman rather than a political philosopher, he contributed to democracy and liberalism a faith rather than a body of doctrine. By his works alone he must be adjudged one of the greatest of all Americans, while the influence of his energizing faith cannot be measured.[203]

Other views of Jefferson's political philosophy:

> In religion he was a freethinker; in morals, pure and unspotted; in politics, patriotic, honest, ardent and benevolent. Respecting his political character, there was (and still is) a great diversity

of opinion, and we are not yet far enough from the theatre of his acts to judge them dispassionately and justly. His life was devoted to his country; the result of his acts whatever it may be, is a legacy to mankind.[204] — B.J. Lossing

Since the days when Jefferson expounded his code of political philosophy, the whole world has become his pupil.[205] — Michael MacWhite

Americans, it has been said, venerate Washington, love Lincoln, and remember Jefferson.... It is this Jefferson who stands as the radiant center of his own history, and who makes for the present a symbol that unites the nation's birth with its inexorable ideal.[206] — Merrill Peterson

I cannot live in this miserable undone country, where, as the Turks follow their sacred standard, which is a pair of Mahomet's breeches, we are governed by the old red breeches of that prince of protectors, St. Thomas of Cantingbury; and surely Becket himself never had more pilgrims at his shrine than the Saint of Monticello.[207] — John Randolph

The ideals and values of Thomas Jefferson are at the heart of American democracy and the principal reason for the ascendancy of the United States. It is incumbent upon all of us, who cherish our freedom and strive to assure individual liberty for all peoples, to preserve Thomas Jefferson's legacy.[208] — Thomas A. Saunders III

Jefferson scarcely seems to exist as a real historical person. Almost from the beginning he has been a symbol, a touchstone, of what we as a people are — someone invented, manipulated, turned into something we Americans like or dislike, fear or yearn for, within ourselves. So it has gone for much of our history, Jefferson standing for America and carrying the moral character of our country on his back.[209] — Gordon S. Wood

The Continental Congress: As a delegate to the Second Continental Congress in 1775–1776, Jefferson "drafted the Reply to Lord North, in which Congress rejected the British prime minister's offer that Parliament would not tax the colonists if they agreed to tax themselves."[210] Jefferson wrote: "The provisions we have made [for our government] are such as please ourselves; they answer the substantial purposes of government and of justice and other purposes than these should not be answered."[211] Jefferson next entered the Virginia House of Delegates, where he initiated a comprehensive reform program for the abolition of feudal survivals. These included entail (the law limiting inheritance of real property to a specific line or class of heirs) and primogeniture (the exclusive right of the eldest son to inherit his father's property).[212] He also championed the separation of church and state.[213] As a member of the Continental Congress in 1783–1784, Jefferson helped establish the decimal system as the basis of money and drafted the first of the Northwest Ordinances for dividing and settling the Northwest Territory.[214]

Governor: Succeeding Patrick Henry as Governor of Virginia (1779–1781), Jefferson championed "religious liberty, free education, the University of Virginia and public libraries."[215] When his Statute for Religious Freedom was enacted in 1786, it disestablished the Anglican Church as the state-endorsed religion.[216] Jefferson was responsible for the abolition of property laws (relics of feudalism), but he was unable to reform Virginia's barbarous criminal code of which he said: "It is not only vain, but wicked in a legislator to frame laws in opposition to the laws of nature, and to arm them with the terrors of death. This is truly creating crimes in order to punish them."[217] Governor Jefferson proposed a "comprehensive system of public education, with elementary schools available to all," where students would be educated according to their ability. The defeat of his "Bill for the More General Diffusion of Knowledge" disgusted Jefferson.[218] He was, however, able to introduce several reforms at his alma mater, the College of William & Mary, "including an elective system of study — the first in an American university."[219] At his request, the College appointed Jefferson's mentor George Wythe the first professor of law in the United States.[220] Late in life Jefferson became the "father and founder of the University of Virginia," the first such institution at which higher education was totally separate from religious doctrine.[221]

Jefferson's tenure as governor was not very successful. Part of the problem was the constitutional limitation on the powers of the office, combined with his lack of executive experience.[222] When the British invaded Virginia in 1781, the government took flight, moving to safer quarters at Charlottesville. The redcoats followed and two days after his term ended Jefferson virtually abdicated before a successor could be chosen.[223] He retired to his home. Jefferson later recalled the political criticism of his hasty departure: "Some said in humble prose that, forgetting the noble example of the hero of La Mancha, and his windmills, I declined a combat, singly against a troop, in which victory would have been so glorious. Forgetting themselves, at the same time, that I was not provided with the enchanted arms of the knight, nor even with the helmet of Mambrino."[224]

During his period of temporary retirement from politics, Jefferson wrote the book *Notes on the State of Virginia*, a work of natural and civil history.[225] It is of great interest as a guide to Jefferson's mind and his native country. In it, he expressed opinions on a variety of subjects, from caverns to slavery, including his thoughts on agriculture: "Agriculture is the basis of the subsistence, the comforts, and the happiness of man."[226] He finally published the manuscript in a private edition in Paris (1785). In it, Jefferson lectured:

> [The purpose of written constitution is] to bind up the several branches of government by certain laws, which, when they transgress, their acts shall become nullities; to render unnecessary an appeal to the people, or in other words a rebellion, on every infraction of their rights, on the peril that their acquiescence shall be construed into an intention to surrender those rights.... An elective despotism was not the government we fought for, but one which should not only be founded on true free principles, but in which the powers of government should be so divided and balanced among general bodies of magistracy, as that one could transcend their legal limits without being effectively checked and restrained by the others.... The purpose of establishing different houses of legislation is to introduce the influence of different interests or different principles.[227]

The Declaration of Independence: Jefferson was not an orator, but he was eloquent with his pen. Known as the "silent member" of Congress, he seldom spoke in the legislature to advance the patriot cause he espoused.[228] However, as a member of a committee including John Adams of Massachusetts, Benjamin Franklin of Pennsylvania, Roger Sherman of Connecticut and Robert Livingston of New York appointed to draft a "declaration of independence," its main composition fell to the 33-year-old Virginian.[229] John Adams claimed Jefferson possessed "peculiar felicity for expression" which is unquestionably found in his draft.[230] Tom crisply set forth the bill of particular grievances against the reigning sovereign. He compressed a political philosophy and a national creed into one paragraph:

> We hold these truths to be self-evident, that all men are created equal, that they are endowed by their Creator with certain unalienable Rights, that among these are Life, Liberty, and the Pursuit of Happiness.— That to secure these rights, Governments are instituted among Men, deriving their just powers from the consent of the governed.— That whenever any Form of Government becomes destructive of these ends, it is the Right of the People to alter or to abolish it, and to institute new Government, laying its foundation on such principles and organizing its powers in such form, as to them, shall seem most likely to effect their Safety and Happiness.[231]

Adams and Franklin suggested twenty-six changes in Jefferson's draft; 23 of which were a matter of phraseology. Besides the verbal changes, three completely new paragraphs were added.[232] The revision was submitted to the Congress, which spent 2½ days debating it line by line. Though several additional changes were made, the Declaration passed by all members of the Congress on July 4, 1776, is clearly the work of Jefferson.[233] Most of the delegates signed the parchment copy on August 2, 1776. Others signed at later dates. Jefferson and John Adams were the only two future presidents to sign the document.[234] Jefferson later expounded on the right of "liberty," which he defined by saying: "Rightful liberty is unobstructed action according to our will within limits drawn around us by equal rights of others. I do not add 'within the limits of the law,' because law is often but a tyrant's will, and always so when it violates the rights of the individual."[235]

To Jefferson's way of thinking, although a government cannot create a right to liberty, it can violate the right. In his view, a proper government is one that not only prohibits individuals from "infringing on the liberty of others," but also refrains, itself, from such infringements.[236] In a letter to Roger C. Weightman, Jefferson expressed his hope for the Declaration of Independence: "May it be to the world, what I believe it will be, (to some parts sooner, to other's later, but finally to all), the signal of arousing men to burst the chains under which monkish ignorance and superstition had persuaded them to bind themselves, and to assume the blessings and security of self-government."[237]

Diplomatic Roles: Jefferson succeeded Benjamin Franklin as Minister Plenipotentiary to France (1785–1789). (TJ said he came to succeed Franklin because no one could replace him.)[238] Jefferson won valuable concessions for American commerce. Influential men in the French capitol were eager friends of the American Revolution. While in France, he frequented bookstores, for "... My greatest ... amusements, reading," patronized museums,

The Declaration Committee — Adams, Sherman, Livingston, Jefferson and Franklin — presents the draft of the Declaration of Independence to the Continental Congress, 1876 engraving by W.L. Ormsby, N.Y., of John Trumbull painting *Declaration of Independence.* The painting is found on the back of the U.S. $2 bill. The original hangs in the U.S. Capitol rotunda (Library of Congress).

concerts and theater, stating, "A mind always employed is always happy. This is the true secret, the grand recipe for felicity."[239] He toured the south of France, Italy, England, and the Rhineland, interpreting the New World for the old.

When he returned from his diplomatic missions, Jefferson did not attend the Constitutional Convention. Although he supported the new Constitution, he considered it flawed, lacking a Bill of Rights, which was later added. In a 1787 letter to James Madison, Jefferson wrote: "A bill of rights is what the people are entitled to against every government on earth, general or particular; and what no just government should refuse, or rest on inferences."[240] In a letter to David Humphreys in March 1789, TJ wrote:

> The operations which have taken place in America lately fill me with pleasure. In the first place, they realize the confidence I had that whenever our affairs go obviously wrong, the good sense of the people will interpose and set them to rights. The example of changing a constitution by assembling the wise men of the State instead of assembling armies will be worth as much to the world as the former example we had given them. The Constitution ... is unquestionably the wisest ever yet presented to men. A general concurrence of opinion seems to authorize us to say it has some defects. I am one of those who think it a defect that the important rights not placed in security by the frame of the Constitution itself were not explicitly secured by a supplementary declaration. There are rights which it is useless to surrender to the government and which governments have yet always been found to invade. These are the rights of thinking and publishing our thoughts by speaking or writing, the right of free commerce, the right of personal freedom. There are instruments for administering the government so peculiarly trustworthy that we should never leave the legislature at liberty to change them. The new Constitution has secured these in the executive and legislative department, but not in the judiciary. It should have established trials by the people themselves, that is to say, by jury. There are instruments so dangerous to the rights of the nation and which place them so totally at the mercy of their governors that those governors, whether legislative or executive, should be restrained from keeping such instruments on foot but in well-defined cases. Such an instrument is a standing army. We are now allowed to say such a declaration of rights as a supplement to the Constitution where that is silent, is wanting to secure us in these points. The general voice has legitimated this objection. It has not, however, authorized me to consider as a real defect what I thought and still think one: the perpetual re-eligibility of the President. But three States out of eleven having declared against this, we must suppose we are wrong according to the fundamental law of every society — the lex majoris partis — to which we are bound to submit. And should the majority change their opinion and become sensible that this trait in their Constitution is wrong, I would wish it to remain uncorrected as long as we can avail ourselves of the services of our great leader, whose talents and whose weight of character I consider as peculiarly necessary to get the government so under way as that it may afterwards be carried on by subordinate characters.[241]

Cabinet Member: On January 10, 1781, the Second Continental Congress "created the office of Secretary of Foreign Affairs to head a Department of Foreign Affairs."[242] In 1789, Congress passed another law giving certain additional domestic duties to the new Department and changed its name to the "Department of State, headed by the Secretary of State."[243] In the early years of the Republic, the post was considered the most powerful office after that of the President. Jefferson served as the first Secretary of State from 1790 to 1793. His negotiations with European Powers were mostly fruitless. His efforts to force the British to remove their troops from the Northwest Territory, as required by the Treaty of Paris, were failures.[244] TJ became enmeshed in an acrimonious dispute with Secretary of the Treasury Alexander Hamilton over the country's foreign policies and their conflicting interpretations of the Constitution. Jefferson described the situation: "In the discussions [on the affairs of France and England] Hamilton and myself were daily pitted in the Cabinet like two cocks. We were then but four in number, and according to the majority, which of course was three to one, the President decided. The pain was for Hamilton and myself, but the public experienced no inconvenience."[245] This divisiveness led to the establishment of the first political parties; the Federalists led by Hamilton and the Republicans (later Democratic-Republicans from which the present Democratic Party originates) with Jefferson its somewhat reluctant leader.[246] He charged that Hamilton's monetary policies were predicated on British trade, credit and power. TJ's plan turned on commercial liberation, friendship with France, and the success of the French Revolution. Jefferson charged that Hamilton's system "flowed from principles adverse to liberty, and were calculated to undermine and demolish the Republic, by creating an influence of his department over the legislature."[247] A major disagreement arose over the Bank of the United States, of which Hamilton approved and which Jefferson believed to be unconstitutional. In a letter to John Taylor, on May 28, 1816, Secretary of State Jefferson warned: "And I sincerely believe, with you, that banking establishments are more dangerous than standing armies; and that the principle of spending money to be paid by posterity, under the name of funding, is but swindling futurity on a large scale."[248]

In 1791, Jefferson sent his "Opinion of the Constitutionality of the Bill for Establishing a National Bank" to President Washington: "I consider the foundation of the Constitution as laid on this ground: That 'all powers not delegated to the United States, by the Constitution, nor prohibited by it to the States, are reserved to the states or to the people.' [10th Amendment] To make a single step beyond the boundaries thus specifically drawn around the powers of Congress is to take possession of a boundless field of power, no longer susceptible of any definition."[249] Hamilton responded that the Constitution provided implied powers to establish a Bank, but Jefferson disagreed, charging that its establishment would create conditions for the accumulation of the "power and corruption identified with the courts and monarchies of Europe." He argued that the Constitution authorizes Congress to "make all laws necessary and proper for carrying into execution the enumerated powers." TJ pointed out that these could be carried into execution without a bank and, therefore, a bank was not "necessary."[250]

Washington wrote a letter to both Jefferson and Hamilton, expressing his dismay at the political factions organizing around the two men and urging cooperation and reconciliation.[251] Jefferson equated "Hamiltonism" with "Royalism." He stated that "Hamiltonians were panting after ... and itching for crowns, coronets, and mitres.[252] He resigned when President Washington was unable to reconcile them. Later Jefferson bitterly criticized Jay's Treaty, which he claimed was too favorable to the British, who were still occupying the forts in the Northwest Territory, in violation of the Treaty of Paris.[253]

His Vice Presidency: On the eve of his inauguration as vice president in 1797, Jefferson was elected president of the American Philosophical Society, a position he retained until 1815. In accepting the office he said: "I feel no qualifications for this distinguished post, but a sincere zeal for all the objects of our institution and an ardent desire to see knowledge so disseminated through the mass of mankind, that it may, at length, reach even the extremes of society, beggars and kings."[254] Vice President Jefferson was of a different political party than that of President John Adams. He had little to do and a vast time to do it. On assuming office, Jefferson announced: "The second office of this government is honorable and easy, the first is but a splendid misery."[255]

When the Federalist Congress passed the Alien and Sedition Acts, Jefferson and James Madison, in protest, wrote the Virginia and Kentucky Resolutions, adopted by the legislatures of those states in 1798 and 1799, respectively. The statements declared that a state legislature had the authority to render a Federal law with which they did not agree to be null and void. "Where powers are assumed which have not been delegated, a nullification of the act is the rightful remedy."[256]

The philosophy of these resolutions, including the principle of nullification and states' rights, echoed down to the time of the American Civil War. In the 1798 Kentucky Resolutions, Jefferson observed: "In case of an abuse of the delegated powers, the members of the General Government, being chosen by the people, a change by the people would be the constitutional remedy."[257]

HIS PRESIDENCY

Consistent with the traditions of the times, neither Adams nor Jefferson officially campaigned for the presidency in 1800. Newspapers, supporting either candidate, took the fights publicly and their messages were virulent. Jefferson's camp accused President Adams of having a "hideous hermaphroditical character, which has neither the force and firmness of a man, nor the gentleness and sensibility of a woman." In return, Adams' men called Vice President Jefferson "a mean-spirited, low-lived fellow, the son of a half-breed Indian squaw, sired by a Virginia mulatto father." As the slurs piled on, Adams was labeled a fool, a hypocrite, a criminal, and a tyrant, while Jefferson was branded a weakling, an atheist, a libertine, and a coward.[258] Timothy Dwight, clergyman and educator, gave an election sermon in which he predicted: "If Jefferson be elected we may see our wives and daughters the victims of legal prostitution, soberly dishonored, speciously polluted the outcasts of delicacy and virtue, the loathing of God and man."[259] Jefferson went so far as to hire William Callender to dig up and spread dirt on Adams. This was the same Callender who later broke the story about Jefferson's relationship with Sally Hemings.[260] Jefferson finished tied with Aaron Burr with 73 electoral votes in the election, thus denying John Adams, who received 65 votes, a second term.

During the campaign there was no doubt that Jefferson was the presidential candidate and Burr was his vice presidential running mate. However, the ambitious Burr refused to concede the election to Jefferson. The matter fell to the House of Representatives to settle. Jefferson was eventually named president on the thirty-sixth ballot after Alexander Hamilton swung Federalist votes to Jefferson, whom he considered the lesser of two evils. Burr became Jefferson's first vice president.[261] Later Jefferson said Burr was an overrated talent, great in small matters, small in great ones, and, "No man's history proves better the value of honesty. With that, what might he not have been?"[262]

Jefferson was the first U.S. president inaugurated in Washington, D.C., which he had helped design.[263] When Jefferson became president, the population of the United States was 5.3 million, about 12 percent were slaves.[264] Through his two terms, he never used his power of veto.[265] In his First Inaugural Address, Jefferson expressed the principles of his administration:

> Equal and exact justice to all men ... freedom of religion, freedom of the press, freedom of person under the protection of the habeas corpus; and trial by juries impartially selected — these principles form the bright constellation which has gone before us.... All, too, will bear in mind this sacred principle, that though the will of the majority is in all cases to prevail, that will, to be rightful, must be reasonable....
>
> The minority possesses their equal rights, which equal laws must protect, and to violate which would be oppression.... Every man's reason is his own rightful umpire. This principle, with that of acquiescence in the will of the majority, will preserve us free and prosperous as long as they are sacredly observed.... If there be any among us who would wish to dissolve this Union or to change its republican form, let them stand undisturbed as monuments of the safety with which error of opinion may be tolerated where reason is left to combat it."[266]

Jefferson was reelected in 1804, easily defeating the Federalist Party candidate, Charles Cotesworth Pinckney of South Carolina, by an Electoral College vote of 162 to 14. By the time of this election, the method of picking a president and vice president had been amended. George Clinton of New York became vice president, replacing Burr, who had lost favor with Jefferson for refusing to concede the election in 1800 and over matters of political patronage.[267] Burr ran for governor of New York but lost, largely because of the opposition of Alexander Hamilton who declared him a dangerous man who should never be entrusted with a position in government.[268] Burr challenged Hamilton to a duel for calling his character into question and on the morning of July 11, 1804, the Federalist leader was fatally wounded. Burr was first accused of murder but he was acquitted.[269] Burr later conspired to instigate a war with Spain, with the intention of seizing the Louisiana Territory and establishing himself as the head of a new and separate government. He was arrested and tried for treason but was found not guilty and moved to England for a number of years.[270]

By the time Jefferson became president, the crisis with France had passed. He "cut Army and Navy expenditures, reduced the federal budget, eliminated the unpopular tax on whiskey, and reduced the national debt by a third."[271] Jefferson set about to establish "a 'wise and frugal Government, which shall restrain men from injuring one another' but which would otherwise leave them alone to regulate their own affairs. He wanted a government that would respect the authority of individual states, operate with a smaller bureaucracy, and cut its debts.... Most importantly, he believed that good government would promote 'the encouragement of agriculture.' Commerce, in his mind, should be the 'handmaiden' of agriculture rather than its driving force."[272] He tried to curb the authority of the judiciary, where he felt the Federalists were entrenching their philosophy.[273] In 1801 TJ composed a *Manual of Parliamentary Practice*, which is still used today.[274]

His Vice Presidents: Aaron Burr (1801–1805) and George Clinton (1805–1809).

His Cabinet: Secretary of State James

George Clinton, engraving created between 1845 and 1890 by John Chester Buttre after a painting by Ezra Ames (Library of Congress).

Vice President Aaron Burr, print created by Browne & Redmond, c. Oct. 25, 1836 (Library of Congress).

Madison (1801–1809); Secretary of the Treasury Samuel Dexter (1801); Albert Gallatin (1801–1809); Secretary of War Henry Dearborn (1801–1809); Attorney General Levi Lincoln (1801–1804) and John Breckinridge (1805–1806), Caesar A. Rodney (1807–1809); Postmaster General Joseph Habersham (1801) and Gideon Granger (1801–1809); Secretary of the Navy Benjamin Stoddert (1801) and Robert Smith (1801–1809)

Supreme Court Appointments: William Johnson (1804), Henry Brockholst Livingston (1807), Thomas Todd (1807)

States Admitted to the Union: Ohio became the seventeenth state of the union in 1803.

Constitutional Amendments: The 12th Amendment changed presidential election rules. Article Two of the United States Constitution stated that the Electoral College would elect both the president and vice president in a single election, that the individual with the majority of votes would become the president and the runner-up in votes, the vice president. When the Constitution was written political parties did not exist so the issue from rival factions being selected did not come up. Problems with this system were "demonstrated by the election of 1796 and, more spectacularly, the election of 1800." The Twelfth Amendment, proposed by Congress on December 9, 1803, and ratified by the requisite number of state legislatives on June 15, 1804, changed the system so that each elector cast a single vote for the office and another for the office of vice president, thus lessening the possibility of a tie.[275] Jefferson addressed his views on amendments to the constitution in a letter to Samuel Kercheval:

> I am not an advocate for frequent changes in laws and Constitutions. But laws and institutions must go hand in hand with the progress of the human mind. As that becomes more developed, more enlightened, as new discoveries are made, new truths discovered and manners and opinions change, with the change of circumstances, institutions must advance also to keep pace with the times. We might as well require a man to wear still the coat which fitted him when a boy as civilized society to remain ever under the regimen of their barbarous ancestors.[276]

DOMESTIC AFFAIRS — MAJOR EVENTS

In 1802, Jefferson and the U.S. Congress established the United States Military Academy at West Point, New York to educate a new cadre of officers.[277]

In the same year, Congress repealed the Naturalization Act, which extended the time for immigrants to become citizens from five to fourteen years and the Judiciary Act, which enabled President John Adams to appoint the so-called "midnight judges."[278] The Alien and Sedition Acts were allowed to expire in 1802. Congress passed an act prohibiting the importing of African slaves, effectively January 1, 1808.[279]

Marbury v. Madison: Jefferson suffered a major defeat when the Supreme Court unanimously decided in the case *Marbury v. Madison* that it had the right to review laws by Congress and declare them unconstitutional. The case, involving a man appointed justice of the peace by an outgoing administration whose appointment was not honored by the incoming administration, hinged on the authority granted by the Judiciary Act of 1789. Writing for the court, Marshall held that a section of the act contravened the Constitution and was therefore invalid, declaring that the Constitution must always take precedence in the conflict between it and a law passed by Congress, thus the court established the doctrine of "judicial review."[280]

Jefferson denounced the decision, concerned that this policy of judicial review, which was not described in the Constitution, could be used by Federalist judges to overturn Republican legislation. Further he believed that judges should be technical specialists but should not set policy. In a letter to John Hampden Pleasants, Jefferson scolded the court: "It is a misnomer to call a government republican in which a branch of the supreme power is independent of the nation."[281] However, the president did not have enough "support in Congress to propose a Constitutional Amendment to overturn the decision." Jefferson systematically identified and removed federalist office holders.[282]

Louisiana Purchase: Jefferson approved the Louisiana Purchase of 1803, an uncharted domain of some 800,000 square miles, extending from the Missouri River to the Rocky Mountains and from the Gulf of Mexico to British America (Canada). The purchase nearly doubled the size of the United States, even though such an action was nowhere expressly authorized by the Constitution.[283] In a sense the acquisition went against Jefferson's strong defense of states' rights, but he likely saw it as opening up opportunities for the expansion of the American Republic and the removal of a neighbor that might become unfriendly.[284]

Originally, Jefferson was only interested in purchasing New Orleans, "through which the produce of three-eighths of our territory must pass to market."[285] He sent James Monroe to France to assist American diplomatic representative Robert R. Livingston to negotiate the purchase. Even before Monroe reached Paris, French Minister Talleyrand made Livingston a startling offer. He said that Emperor Napoleon I was not only willing to sell New Orleans, but the whole of the Louisiana territory as well. A treaty was drawn; the purchase price was to be $15 million, which included $3.75 million to pay American claims against France, making the cost per acre three cents. Jefferson proceeded swiftly to establish United States rights in the territory, and on December 20, 1803, the United States flag was raised over New Orleans.[286] The formal ceremonies transferring the Louisiana Territory from France to the United States took place in St. Louis on March 10, 1804, attended by Meriwether Lewis and William Clark, who were prepared to explore the region.[287]

The Lewis and Clark Expedition: Even when he was secretary of state, Jefferson dreamed of exploring the West. As a scientist he wanted to learn about the land and its inhabitants.[288] Half a year before the Louisiana Purchase, Jefferson was making plans to send a team to explore the region. He appointed his private secretary, Meriwether Lewis, to lead the overland expedition, and Lewis selected William Clark, a frontiersman, as his co-leader. Lewis had seen service in the militia during the Whiskey Rebellion in western Pennsylvania and then transferred to the regular army. The two men were charged with finding a land route to the Pacific.[289] Jefferson instructed Lewis and Clark to "observe and write down the physical features, topography, soil, climate, and wildlife of the land and the language and customs of the inhabitants."[290] Clark, the brother of George Rogers Clark, the conqueror of the old Northwest during the Revolutionary War, joined the army and participated in Indian campaigns under General Anthony Wayne. A daring and resourceful leader, "Clark was credited with rescuing the exploration party from disaster on more than one occasion. He also served as mapmaker and artist, studying the natural history of the hitherto unexplored region and portraying with excellent detail animal life observed en route."[291]

The success of the Lewis and Clark Expedition was greatly due to Lewis' preparation and skill. In April and May of 1803 Lewis was in Lancaster and Philadelphia, Pennsylvania, being tutored by some of the nation's leading scientists in "map making, surveying, celestial navigation, botany, mathematics, anatomy and fossils, and medicine."[292]

With $2500 from Congress to fund the expedition, Lewis set out to recruit a team for the expedition and outfit it. At Pittsburgh, he spent over a month overseeing the construction of a 55-foot keelboat, capable of carrying 10 tons of supplies. During the expedition, the "craft was sailed, rowed, moved along by setting poles and sometimes pulled from along the bank with cordelling ropes." On a good day, the boat made 14 miles. Lewis and 11 men

Left: William Clark, a 1903 print reproduction of a watercolor facsimile of a portrait by Charles Wilson Peale, located in Independence Hall (Library of Congress). *Right:* Meriwether Lewis, a c. 1903 photographic print reproduction of a painting by C.W. Peale, located in Independence Hall, Philadelphia (Library of Congress).

headed down the Ohio River aboard it on August 31.[293] Lewis met up with Clark near present-day Louisville, Kentucky. Clark, his slave York, and nine Kentuckians joined the party. They set up winter quarters along the east bank of the Mississippi River at St. Louis. They recruited more soldiers, trained them and stocked up on supplies. The party also included Lewis' Newfoundland dog, Seaman.[294]

"The Corps of Volunteers for North West Discovery," as the Lewis & Clark Expedition was officially known, set off on May 14, 1804, and headed up the Missouri. On May 25 the party passed La Charette, a settlement of seven dwellings, the westernmost white settlement on the Missouri. On August 3, Lewis and Clark held their first council with Indians, near present-day Council Bluffs, Iowa, handing out peace medals, 15-star flags, and other gifts.[295] Sergeant Charles Floyd became the only casualty of the expedition, dying from a burst appendix on August 20 and was buried near what is now Sioux City, Iowa.[296] In September the explorers began to encounter animals unknown in the East: coyotes, antelopes, mule deer, and others. In their journals of the trip, the captains described 178 plants and 122 animals previously not recorded for science. Near the end of October the party reached the settlement of the Mandan and Hidatsa tribes, near present-day Bismarck, North Dakota. The village with 4,500 inhabitants was then larger than St. Louis.[297]

At the beginning of November, a French-Canadian trapper Toussaint Charbonneau and his Indian wife Sacagawea were hired as interpreters for the expedition.[298] On May 26, Lewis saw the Rocky Mountains for the first time and on June 13, while scouting ahead of the main party, encountered the Great Falls of the Missouri River, which the expedition

Photographic print, published c. 1912, of the Sacagawea Monument in City Park, Portland, Oregon, with a statue by Alice Cooper. On her back, Sacagawea carries her infant son. Six months pregnant when she joined the Lewis and Clark expedition, she gave birth to Jean Baptiste early in the journey (Library of Congress).

had to portage around.[299] On August 17, "Sacagawea was reunited with her brother, Cameah-wait," the Shoshone chief, and helped negotiate for horses needed to cross the Rocky Mountains. The expedition, with Shoshone guide Old Toby leading the way set off overland. By early November, they were very close to the Pacific coast and set up a winter camp south of the Columbia River.[300] On March 23, 1806, the expedition began its homeward journey. Lewis and Clark divided the men in order to explore more of the territory and to seek an easier pass over the Rockies. Lewis followed the Missouri River and Clark, the Yellowstone River. The explorers reunited on August 12 at the junction of the two rivers and arrived back in St. Louis on September 23 to great acclaim.[301] As a reward for their services, "both men received 1600 acres of land." Lewis was named governor of Louisiana Territory in 1808, but he died in 1809 under mysterious circumstances in an inn on the Natchez Trail while en route to Washington to "clear up the matter of why certain of his drafts on the government hadn't been honored." It has never been conclusively determined if his death was due to murder or suicide.[302] Clark was governor of the Missouri Territory (1813–1821) and was primarily concerned with establishing treaties with various Indian tribes.[303]

FOREIGN AFFAIRS — MAJOR EVENTS

Jefferson wrote extensively on the relationship that should exist between the United States and other countries of the world. He said: "We owe gratitude to France, justice to England, good will to all, and subservience to none."[304] Going further he wrote: "We must meet our duty and convince the world that we are just friends and brave enemies."[305] Like Washington, Jefferson was wary, lest the United States find itself involved in the conflicts of Europe, warning:

> The less we have to do with the enmities of Europe the better. Not in our day, but at no distant one, we may shake a rod over the heads of all, which may make the stoutest tremble. But I hope our wisdom will grow with our power, and teach us that the less we use our power, the greater it will be.... I have ever deemed it fundamental for the United States never to take active part in the quarrels of Europe. Their political interests are entirely distinct from ours.... They are nations of eternal war. All their energies are expanded in the destruction of the labor, property, and lives of their people.... The day is not distant when we may formally require a meridian of partition through the ocean which separates the two hemispheres, on the higher side of which no European gun shall ever be heard, nor an American on the other.[306]

Embargo Act: The turbulence of the Napoleonic Wars, with American ships and seamen ravaged in neutral trade, by France and Great Britain, led Jefferson to propose and Congress to enact, a total embargo on American's seagoing commerce, which he viewed as an alternative to war.[307] The Embargo Act, prohibiting the exportation of U.S. goods to England and France, was a test of the power of commercial coercion in international disputes. It was effectively enforced, but it failed to bring either Britain or France to justice and its injurious costs to U.S. commerce led to its repeal by Congress near the end of Jefferson's presidency.[308]

Jefferson and the Barbary Pirates: The Barbary pirates were located at the northern part of Africa in the Mediterranean. For centuries the states of modern-day Morocco, Algeria, Tunisia, and Libya controlled the shipping trade in the Mediterranean. They were not as interested in the cargo of the ships they captured as their crews, whom they enslaved. The only way these unfortunates could escape their cruel labor and starvation in workhouses was for their country to pay tribute to each of the Barbary States, and even this was not always honored. Paying tribute was a common practice for the European nations. Some countries paid sums in the millions every year.[309] Great Britain paid to protect the ships of their colonies, but after they won their independence, England no longer had any interest in paying for the safety of U.S. ships.[310] As early as 1784 Congress followed the tradition and appropriated $80,000 as a payment to the Barbary States. Ministers John Adams and Thomas Jefferson were directed to begin negotiations with them. In July 1785, the Algerians captured two American ships and held their crews of twenty-one people until a ransom of nearly $60,000 was paid. Jefferson was steadfastly "opposed to the payment of extortion, which he argued would merely lead to further demands."[311] He believed that the only way to put an end to the practice was by sending a strong navy to rout the brigands. In a letter to James Monroe, Jefferson wrote: "The states must see the rod; perhaps it must be felt by some one of them.... Every national citizen must wish to see and effective instrument of coercion, and should fear to see it on any other element than the water. A naval force can never endanger our liberties, nor occasional bloodshed; a land force would do both."[312] Jefferson's plan did not get very far as it was decided that it was cheaper to pay the tribute than fight a war. As president Jefferson "refused to accede to Tripoli's demands for an immediate payment of $225,000 and an annual payment of $25,000." The pasha of Tripoli declared war on the United States. Jefferson dispatched a squadron of naval vessels to the Mediterranean. The American show of force convinced Tunis and Algiers to break alliance with Tripoli.[313] Jefferson was criticized by his political opponents and even questioned by members of his Cabinet with the humiliating loss of the frigate *Philadelphia* and the capture of her captain, William Bainbridge, and crew by Tripoli in 1803.[314] However, Congress did not complain that Jefferson's actions were unconstitutional, thus setting a dangerous precedent that future chief executives would exploit. The "president had embroiled the nation in war without congressional assent."[315] Only after an American fleet led by Commodore John Rodgers and a land force headed by Captain William Eaton threatened to capture Tripoli and install the pasha's brother on the throne, did a treaty bring the hostilities to an end. However, the accord still required the U.S. to pay a ransom of $60,000 for each of the sailors held by the Bey of Algiers.[316] It was "not until the second war with Algiers, in 1815, that naval victories by Commodores William Bainbridge and Stephen Decatur led to treaties ending all tribute payments by the United States."[317] European nations continued to pay tribute until the 1830s.

AFTER THE PRESIDENCY

Jefferson retired to Monticello, but remained active in public affairs. He was obsessed with founding a new institution of higher learning, free from church influences, where students could specialize in many areas not offered at other universities. He planned for the University of Virginia for decades before its establishment as the nation's first comprehensive university.[318] In a letter to George Ticknor on November 25, 1817, Jefferson wrote of his efforts in behalf of education in his home state: "I am now entirely absorbed in endeavors to effect the establishment of a general system of education in my native state.... My hopes however are kept in check by the ordinary character of our state legislatures, the members of which do not generally possess information enough to perceive the important truths, that knowledge is power, that knowledge is safety, and that knowledge is happiness."[319] His dream was realized in 1819, when the university was founded. Jefferson watched its construction from his home at Monticello, using his telescope. When the University opened in 1825, it was "one of the largest construction projects to that time in North America.... It was unique in that at its center, instead of a church, was a library."[320] Jefferson proposed that well-prepared students should devote three years to general education: the first year

William Bainbridge, U.S. Navy, engraving by W. Wellstood after a painting by Chappel; copyrighted by Johnson, Fry & Co., c. 1863 (Library of Congress).

Burning of the Frigate "Philadelphia" in the Harbor of Tripoli, February 16, 1804. A photograph of the original 1805 engraving by John B. Guerrazzi shows the United States frigate *Philadelphia* aflame during the First Tripolitan War, 1803 (Library of Congress).

being the study of mathematics and languages; the second to mathematics and physics; and the third to mathematics and chemistry with the other subjects of the school. After that, Jefferson felt students should spend two or preferably three years in studies for the profession for which they were intended.[321] In a letter to Thomas Cooper, Jefferson said,

> I agree ... that a professorship of Theology should have no place in our institution. But we cannot always do what is absolutely best. Those with whom we act, entertaining different views, have the power and the right of carrying them into practice. Truth advances and error recedes step by step only; and to do to our fellow men the most good in our power, we must lead where we can, follow where we cannot, and still go with them, watching always the favorable moment for helping them to another step.[322]

The architecture of the campus buildings reflects the impact of the Classical style of architecture that Jefferson favored. In Jefferson's vision, any citizen of the commonwealth could attend school with the sole criterion for admission being ability.[323]

His Papers: During his lifetime, Jefferson wrote more than 20,000 letters and received nearly as many, including years of correspondence with his friend, rival and friend again John Adams. Jefferson's amassed papers comprise one of the largest and most significant collections of correspondence in American history. His impressive body of work replicates the drama of his era, the diversity of his interests, and the importance of his contributions. The "complete Thomas Jefferson Papers from the Manuscript Division at the Library of Congress consists of approximately 27,000 documents." Its online offering, funded by Reuters America, Inc. and The Reuters Foundation, comprise approximately 83,000 images.[324] There is also an electronic archive of Jefferson's papers, maintained by the Massachusetts Historical Society. *The Thomas Jefferson Writings*, edited by Merrill D. Peterson, was published by The Library of America in 1984.

Jefferson was an avid book collector and assembled at least three libraries during his lifetime. A fire at Shadwell destroyed Jefferson's earliest library in 1770. It was comprised of books he assembled during his education, legal training and early career. To replace the Library of Congress's collection, burned by the British in the War of 1812, some 6,000 books from Jefferson's personal library were purchased for $23,950 in 1815. Jefferson accumulated a final library after the sale.[325] He often created catalogues of his libraries, which were arranged according to a classification scheme that divided the volumes into three main categories: History, Philosophy, and Fine Arts, which were subdivided into chapters; in some cases 46 chapters.

Jefferson wrote: "I never go to bed without an hour, or half hour's previous reading of something moral, whereon to ruminate in the intervals of sleep."[326] TJ enjoyed books on mathematics and was fond of reading fiction with a moral but deplored novels, of which he said: "When the poison [a novel] infects the mind, it destroys its tone and revolts it against wholesome reading."[327]

He enjoyed the works of classic antiquity best. He could read Greek, Latin, French, Italian and Spanish. Jefferson enjoyed reading ancient history, but disliked Plato and Aristotle, rejecting their philosophical systems because of their rigidity.[328]

Jefferson read a number of newspapers with regularity, but once observed that "Advertisements contain the only truths to be relied on in a newspaper."[329] Although he often spoke of the importance of the freedom of the press, like so many presidents, he felt he frequently was misrepresented and mistreated in newspapers: "Nothing can now be believed which is seen in a newspaper. Truth itself becomes suspicious by being put into that polluted vehicle. Perhaps an editor might ... divide his paper into four chapters, heading the first, Truth; 2d. Probabilities; 3d. Possibilities; 4d. Lies."[330]

Health: From age 19, Jefferson suffered from prolonged "incapacitating headaches, which seemed to be related to periods of stress, grief or anger in his life." He slept from 5 to 8 hours a night, always rising with the Sun. Although no fan of physicians—he especially "distrusted the practice of bleeding and purging—Jefferson was not above practicing medicine on his family, friends and slaves." He treated his daughter's typhoid fever with Madeira wine, "inoculated his family against smallpox, and sutured the wound of a severely bleeding slave." Throughout his life, wherever he was, Jefferson began his day by making notes on the weather, followed by soaking his feet in cold water. He maintained the "foot bath for sixty years and attributed his excellent health in part to the habit."

"Jefferson never used tobacco in any form."[331] While stationed in Paris, he developed a fondness for fine wines, and ordered many cases of Haut-Brion, Lafite, Margaux and Château d'Yquem for the cellar of his residence at the Hôtel de Langeac on the Champs-Élysées. Back in Virginia, Jefferson planted dozens of grape varieties at Monticello and was known as a wine connoisseur.[332] His cellar contained bottles from France, Portugal, Spain, Hungary, and Italy, and he served wine after dinner daily. Jefferson believed that wine was a healthier beverage than whiskey and brandy, which were the favorite spirits of the colonies and which were consumed in huge amounts.[333] He tutored his guests about the merits of the different wines he served. His visitors were not always impressed as Americans seemed to prefer sweet wines to the "sour" French wines that Jefferson so admired. John Quincy Adams wrote in his diary of a dinner party where Jefferson lectured on wines, which Adams did not think very edifying.

In later life, TJ restricted himself to three glasses of wine a day, and "halved the effects" by drinking only the weak wines. "Malt liqueurs and cider" were his table drinks,[334] but he did not drink "ardent wines" or "ardent spirits" in any form, saying: "No nation is drunken where wine is cheap; and none sober where the dearness of wine substitutes ardent spirits as the common beverage."[335]

In June 1781, Jefferson broke one of his arms, a matter not nearly as severe as when he broke his wrist while in Paris in the summer of 1785. There are three versions of how that latter accident occurred. The most romantic, but not necessarily the most accurate, is that while attempting to impress 27-year-old Mrs. Maria Hadfield Cosway, 43-year-old Jefferson tried to "jump over a fence and did not make it."[336] More mundane explanations were that it occurred while "jumping over a kettle or falling while walking with friends." The fractured wrist was badly treated by French doctors. It remained swollen, painful and useless for weeks. This seemingly minor incident resulted in crippling rheumatism in his right hand, which troubled him for the rest of his life.[337]

Jefferson expressed the importance of one's health in a letter to Thomas Mann Jefferson: "I should have performed the office of but half a friend were I to confine myself to the improvement of the mind only. Knowledge indeed is desirable, a lovely possession, but I do not scruple to say that health is more so. It is of little consequence to store the mind of science if the body be permitted to become debilitated."[338] On another occasion, TJ observed: "Of all the faculties of the human mind that of memory is the first which suffers decay with age."[339]

At age 75, Jefferson fell from a broken step at his home, fracturing his left arm and wrist, causing him suffering in both wrists, "making it extremely difficult to write." At various times in his life, Jefferson suffered back problems, life-threatening constipation, and, late in life, extreme fatigue. He reported that his hearing had deteriorated to a degree that he lost much of the conversation in social settings when more than one voice was heard. He wrote at 75 that he had "not yet lost a tooth to age."[340]

Writer and journalist Norm Ledgin postulates that Jefferson had Asperger's Syndrome. Discovered by Hans Asperger, a Swiss scientist during World War II, the syndrome is a type of autism compatible with high achievement. It was not recognized in North America until 1994. It does not affect intelligence, language, or cognitive skills, but it does affect the way that the "sufferer interacts socially." Asperger victims are often obsessed with things. As adults, they usually stick to a single fixation. They have difficulty making friends and are "labeled as peculiar and eccentric." They often are loners, who do not like surprises and need a quiet place to retreat to when feeling overwhelmed.[341] The speculation about Jefferson and other prominent suspected Asperger sufferers is controversial, with many claiming that it is simply impossible to diagnose the dead.

Death: On July 2, 1826, Jefferson became comatose, but on the third day he awoke and asked: "This is the fourth?" Nicholas Trist was the husband of Jefferson's granddaughter, Virginia Randolph. When Jefferson asked the question on July 3, Trist at first pretended not to hear, not wishing to tell Jefferson that it was the third. But TJ repeated the question and rather than disappoint, Trist nodded yes.[342] He died 50 minutes into the next day, the 50th anniversary of the Declaration of Independence, only hours before the death of John Adams.[343] When he died, Jefferson owed more than $100,000 to creditors. His heirs were forced to auction Jefferson's slaves and the contents of Monticello and Poplar Forest. In 1831, James T. Barclay bought 552 acres of the president's land for $7,000. In his will, Jefferson "left Monticello to the United States to be used as a school for orphans of navy officers," but eventually the family was forced to sell it, with proceeds of only $4500.[344]

Place of Death: Jefferson died at his home, Monticello, near Charlottesville, Virginia.

Cause of Death: Jefferson died of old age and "debility, most likely dehydration resulting from amoebic dysentery, uremia from kidney damage and finally pneumonia." Had these not killed him, a "late diagnosed prostate cancer" probably would have.[345]

Final Words: According to B.L. Rayner his last words were: "I have done for my country, and for all mankind, all that I could do, and I now resign my soul, without fear to my God — my daughter to my country."[346] That is quite a mouthful for a dying man who had been comatose. Near the end of his life, fearing for his reputation and public legacy he begged his friend, James Madison, "To myself you have been a pillar of support thro' life, take care of me when I'm dead, and be assured that I shall leave with you my last affections."[347]

Place of Burial: Jefferson was interred in the family cemetery, which is about a quarter of a mile from his residence. His wife is buried next to him.

Jefferson Monument: In June 1934, the U.S. Congress created the Thomas Jefferson Memorial Commission to direct the construction of a memorial to Thomas Jefferson. Located at the Tidal Basin in Washington, D.C., the Memorial was modeled after the Pantheon of Rome. The original architect John Russell Pope was succeeded by Daniel P. Higgins and Otto R. Eggers after Pope's untimely death. President Franklin D. Roosevelt laid the cornerstone of the memorial on November 15, 1939. In 1941 Rudolph Evans was commissioned to sculpt Jefferson's bronze statue, which when finished was 19 feet tall and weighted five tons. Adjoining the interior of the Memorial are five quotations from the country's

Jefferson Memorial, aerial view, Washington, D.C., 2006. Photograph by Carol Highsmith of the neoclassical building designed by John Russell Pope and built by Philadelphia contractor John McShain. Construction began in 1939. The building was completed in 1943, and the bronze statue of Jefferson was added in 1947 (Library of Congress, Carol M. Highsmith Archive).

third president illustrating the principles to which he dedicated his life. The formal dedication took place in 1943, and the 200th anniversary of Jefferson's birth.[348] Jefferson is also one of the four 60-foot presidential faces on Mount Rushmore.

MISCELLANEA

Presidential Trivia and Firsts: In the treason trial of Vice President Aaron Burr, Jefferson became the first president to invoke executive privilege in rejecting Chief Justice John Marshall's subpoena to appear for questioning.[349] Jefferson and Marshall were distant cousins. Although a skeptic about the Bible, Jefferson donated money to Bible societies. In 1803, Supreme Court Justice Samuel Chase was impeached by the House of Representatives for his vicious attacks on Jefferson, but the Senate did not convict him.[350] Jefferson was the only vice president to be elected president and serve two full terms. Jefferson glued into the pages of a scrapbook an assortment of materials that captured his interests—clippings from newspapers, speeches, original poems he wrote and even a pressed oak leaf as a remembrance of a friend.[351] Jefferson was careless about his posture, whether sitting or standing.[352]

Jefferson and Slavery: Jefferson opposed slavery, calling it a disgrace that should be abolished, yet he enjoyed the life of privilege as a country squire and owned many slaves.[353] In his writings he revealed that he believed African Americans to be inferior to whites both in body and mind. James W. Loewen wrote:

> Actually, by 1820, Jefferson had become an ardent advocate of the expansion of slavery to the western territories. And he never let his ambivalence about slavery affect his private life. Jefferson was an average owner who had his slaves whipped and sold into the Deep South as examples, to induce other slaves to obey. By 1822, Jefferson owned 267 slaves. During his long life, of hundreds of different slaves he owned, he freed only three and five more at his death — all blood relatives of his.[354]

Jefferson had conflicting feelings about the institution of slavery. In "Notes on the State of Virginia," He wrote:

> The whole commerce between master and slave is perpetual exercise of the most boisterous passions, the most unremitting despotism on the one part, and degrading submissions on the others.... Nothing is more certainly written in the book of fate than that these people are to be free. [But] the two races ... cannot live in the same government. Nature, habit, opinion has drawn indelible lines of distinction between them.... Indeed, I tremble for my country when I reflect that God is just: and his justice cannot sleep forever.[355]

Historian Stephen E. Adams penned: "Jefferson, like all slaveholders and many other white members of American society, regarded Negroes as inferior, childlike, untrustworthy and, of course, as property. Jefferson, the genius of politics, could see no way for African Americans to live in society as free people. He embraced the worst forms of racism to justify slavery."[356]

On numerous occasions during his public service career, Jefferson attempted to abolish or limit the growth of slavery. He believed it was the responsibility of the state and society to free all slaves. As a member of the Virginia House of Burgess, his proposal to emancipate all slaves in Virginia was not successful.[357] In his first draft of the Declaration of Independence, he condemned the British crown for sponsoring the importation of slavery to the colonies, charging that "[The King] has waged cruel war against human nature itself, violating its most sacred rights of life and liberty in the persons of a distant people who never offended him, captivating & carrying them into slavery in another hemisphere."[358] This language was excised from the Declaration because of the objections of the delegates from

South Carolina and Georgia. Jefferson convinced the Virginia legislature to prohibit the further importation of slaves into the colony, but this did not emancipate the slaves already there. However, it at least "stopped the increase of the evil by importation, leaving to future efforts its final eradication."[359]

Jefferson's actions, inactions, words, and his alleged prolonged sexual relationship with Sally Hemings and his professed belief in human dignity seem inconsistent and perhaps hypocritical. Indeed they may be, but it is difficult to judge a person from the vantage point of some two hundred years with all that has transpired in the interval. Perhaps Jefferson should be described as being ambivalent about the question of slavery, at least with respect to his obligations to do something about it. He once explained his negligence in making a public stance on slavery, saying:

> Persuasion, perseverance, and patience are the best advocates on questions depending on the will of others. The revolution in public opinion which this cause requires is not to be expected in a day, or perhaps in an age; but time, which outlives all things, will outlive this evil also. A good cause is often injured more by ill-timed efforts of its friends than by the arguments of its enemies ... my sentiments have been made 40 years before the public. Had I repeated them 40 times, they would only have become the more stale and thread-bare.[360]

Jefferson made a distinction between the responsibilities of the state and society and his responsibilities. This was consistent with his belief in the rule of law, and that until there were laws banning slavery and freeing the slaves, there was nothing more he could or should do about the matter. He wrote: "The laws do not permit us to turn them loose, if that were for their good: and to commute them for other property is to commit them to those whose usage of them we cannot control. I hope then, my dear sir, you will reconcile yourself to your country and its unfortunate condition; that you will not lessen its stock of sound disposition by withdrawing your portion from the mass."[361] Perhaps he felt freeing his slaves was an empty gesture if there was no society to receive them as freemen. Whatever criticism he deserves for his inaction, he was not guilty of a crime, or even of a moral injustice, but of a character flaw, something common to all human beings and which are abundantly found in our forty-three U.S. presidents.

In "Notes on the State of Virginia," Jefferson disparaged African Americans:

> They are more ardent after their female; but love seems with them to be more an eager desire, than a tender delicate mixture of sentiment and sensation. Their griefs are transient. Their numberless afflictions, which render it doubtful whether heaven has given life to us in mercy or wrath, are less felt, and sooner forgotten with them. In general, their existence appears to participate more of sensation than reflection. To this must be ascribed their disposition to sleep when abstracted from their diversions, and unemployed in labor.... Comparing them by their faculties of memory, reason, and imagination, it appears to me, that in memory, they are equal to the whites; in reason much inferior, as I think one could scarcely be found capable of tracing and comprehending the investigations of Euclid; and that in imagination they are dull, tasteless, and anomalous.... Never yet could I find a black had uttered a thought above the level of plain narration, never see even an elementary trait of painting or sculpture.... Misery is often the parent of the most affecting touches of poetry—Among the blacks is misery enough, God knows, but no poetry.[362]

In a letter to Edward Coles on August 25, 1814, Jefferson expressed the hope that younger men would realize what he could not or would not do—the emancipation of the slaves: "The hour of emancipation is advancing ... this enterprise is for the young, for those who can follow it up, and bear it through to its consummation. It shall have all my prayers, and these are the only weapons of an old man."[363]

Jefferson and the Sable Genius: Among the most outstanding early American scientists was Benjamin Banneker (October 9, 1731–October 9, 1806), the son of a freed slave and a white mother. Banneker's lifetime of achievements convincingly refuted the belief held by whites that blacks were intellectually inferior, which soothed their consciences as they embraced or tolerated the degradation of other people. Banneker, called the "first African American inventor," made his mark as a farmer, a surveyor, an essayist, an astronomer, as well as a crusader for the better treatment of his brethren. One of the first African American intellectuals to achieve prominence in science, he was internationally known as the "Sable Genius."[364] From 1791 to 1802, Banneker published an annual farmer's almanac, containing his own calculations. In an era when books were scarce and expensive, found only in the houses of the wealthiest families, the few books in most homes were the Bible and almanacs. The local almanacs included such things as the planetary positions and times of sunrise, sunset, moonrise, moonset, eclipses, and tides. This was a remarkable achievement for a self-trained astronomer. The process required predicting planetary positions, sunrises, eclipses, etc., which depended upon spherical trigonometry. Banneker's almanac contained fillers he wrote on political and humanitarian issues.[365] "When Benjamin Franklin's *Poor Richard's Almanac* became famous, Banneker was called the black 'Poor Richard.'"[366]

Banneker reacted to Thomas Jefferson's assertion that blacks were void of intellectual aptitude by sending the Virginian a copy of his almanac along with a twelve-page letter in which he requested Jefferson's assistance in improving the condition of American blacks. Banneker "took Jefferson to task for not extending the right of freedom to blacks that he demanded for himself and others of the white people" in authoring the Declaration of Independence.

> This, Sir, was a time when you clearly saw into the injustice of a state of slavery, and in which you had just apprehension of the horrors of its condition. It was now that your abhorrence thereof was so excited, that you publicly held forth this true and invaluable doctrine, which is worthy to be recorded and remembered in all succeeding ages: 'We hold these truths to be self-evident, that all men are created equal that they are endowed by their Creator with certain unalienable rights, and that among these are, life, liberty, and the pursuit of happiness.' Here was a time, in which your tender feelings for yourself had engaged you thus to declare, you were then impressed with proper ideas of the great violation of liberty, and the free possession of these blessings, to which you were entitled by nature but, Sir, how pitiable is it to reflect that although you were so fully convinced of the benevolence of the Father of Mankind, and of his equal and impartial distribution of these rights and privileges, which he hath conferred upon them, that you would at the same time counteract his mercies, in detaining by fraud and violence so numerous a part of my brethren, under groaning captivity and cruel oppression, that you should at the same time be found guilty of that most criminal act, which you professedly detested in others, with respect to yourself.[367]

Jefferson's response to Banneker's letter was "typical of the mixed signals he displayed when speaking of his position on racial matters. He praised Banneker's almanac and expressed his pleasure in seeing proof that the talents of black men equaled those of other colors."[368] However, his response sounded decidedly as one would expect from a careful politician. "In 1791, Banneker was appointed astronomer to a six-member team of surveyors, headed by Major Andrew Ellicot, to make the first-ever survey of the Federal District, now Washington, D.C. After a year of work, French architect Pierre L'Enfant, hired to design the capitol, stormed off the job, fired for his awful temper, taking all the plans with him. Banneker saved the project by reproducing from memory a complete layout of the streets, parks, and principal buildings."[369]

Jefferson and Native Americans: Jefferson's views of the place of Native Americans in

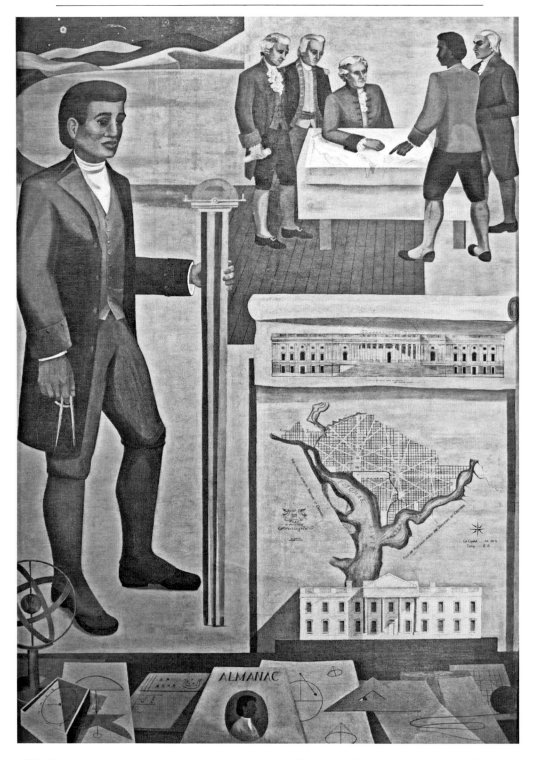

"Benjamin Banneker: Surveyor-Inventor-Astronomer." Photograph by Carol M. Highsmith of the mural by Maxime Seelbinder located at the Recorder of Deeds building, built in 1943 (Library of Congress, Carol M. Highsmith Archive).

the new nation were divided along the lines of theory and practice. While asserting, "I believe the Indian to be in body and mind equal to the white man,"[370] he professed doubt that the Native Americans and the citizens of the United States could co-exist peacefully, and that Indians should be relocated. On one occasion, Jefferson told a delegation of Cherokees: "Let me entreat you therefore, on the lands now given you to begin every man a farm. Let him enclose it, cultivate it, build a warm house on it, and when he dies let it belong to his wife and children."[371] Actually, the Cherokees already were farmers and had come to the president to request that they be assigned their lands in severalty and to make them citizens. Jefferson put them off. In a 1787 letter from Paris, Jefferson seemed to envy the "noble savage." "I am convinced that those societies (as the Indians), which live without government, enjoy in their general mass an infinitely greater degree of happiness than those who live under the European governments. Among the former, public opinion is in the place of law, and restrains morals as powerfully as laws ever did anywhere. Among the latter, under pretense of governing, they have divided their nations into two classes, wolves and sheep."[372]

In the summer/fall 2002 edition of *Early America Review*, Tom Jewett began his article by accusing the third president of the United States of beginning the sorry treatment of Native Americans that followed: "Thomas Jefferson, our icon of freedom and personal liberty, set the national policy toward Native Americans that would last for over one hundred years. He began the trail of tears, which would destroy cultures and result in the reservation system."[373]

After the Louisiana Purchase, President Jefferson developed a plan for removal of all Native Americans east of the Mississippi to ensure their lands would not fall into the hands of the British or the French. By the time of his second inauguration, he refused to guarantee that even the land to the west of the Mississippi would be available to the Native Americans. Jefferson felt the only options for the Indians were to become "civilized" or to become extinct.[374]

No Pomp and Circumstance: Jefferson was the first president to shake hands instead of bowing to people. He believed that the "Pomp and show reminded him too much of European courts."[375] He went so far in avoiding ostentation that he not merely dressed casually, but shabbily. Although his state dinners were said to have been "scrumptious and numerous," Jefferson refused to observe rules of protocol in seating his dinner guests.[376] As was his preference, as president, his honorary "first lady," Dolley Madison, and his daughters' relaxed conventions turned formal state dinners into more casual and enjoyable social events. The rule was "first come, first serve" in finding seats around the president's table. Foreign diplomats were insulted by being received by Jefferson in worn clothes and slippers and that their wives had to "scramble for seats at formal dinners in the presidential mansion."[377]

Clement Clarke Moore Lambastes Jefferson: Paul Collins related a story about Clement Clarke Moore and Thomas Jefferson.[378] Scholar and poet Moore is best known for a Christmas poem "A Visit from St. Nicholas," which many say he wrote in 1822. Some 18 years earlier Moore wrote an anonymous 32-page pamphlet, responding to Thomas Jefferson's collection of observations and musings—written while the president was a diplomat in Paris in 1785 and printed in New York in 1801. At the time, Moore was a 25-year-old theology student and staunch Federalist. He attacked Jefferson's religious observations, including his use of geological evidence to refute the biblical age of the earth. Moore was offended by Jefferson's early evolutionary ideas regarding the relationships between humans and apes. Moore accused the president of being a racist, claiming Jefferson pulled "the inoffensive Negro [down from] his rank in creation, [even as] the ape was raised above his proper sphere."[379] Warming to his criticism, Moore skewered Jefferson for his Francophilia and his rumored affair with Sally Hemings. Unlike his Christmas classic, first published anonymously in the *Troy Sentinel* on December 23, 1823, Moore's hatchet job on Thomas Jefferson has faded from memory.

Recipes: Jefferson admired the French pleasures of the table because with admirable taste they unite temperance. He acquired a collection of classic "French recipes for sauces, fruit tarts, French-fried potatoes, blood sausages, pigs' feet, rabbit, pigeons, and various other dishes," which served his guests at Monticello. Among the most popular of these recipes was "one for vanilla ice cream — written by Jefferson, with his own recipe for Savoy cookies to accompany the dessert."[380] While he was in Italy, Jefferson made drawings of a macaroni machine and collected instructions for making pasta.

The Jefferson Bible: Jefferson rejected the superstitions and mysticism of Christianity, going so far as to complete a short monograph, "The Philosophy of Jesus of Nazareth, Extracted from the account of his life and the doctrines given by Mathew, Mark, Luke, & John." In the summer of 1820, Jefferson completed a more ambitious work, "The Life and Morals of Jesus of Nazareth Extracted Textually from the Gospels in Greek, Latin, French, and English," usually is called "The Jefferson Bible."[381] In his commentary, he attempted to distinguish "ethical teachings from the religious dogma and other supernatural elements that are intermixed in the account of Jesus' life and teachings" provided by the four Gospels.

In a letter to John Adams, Jefferson maintained that much of traditional Christianity was corrupted by later followers of Jesus:

> The whole history of these books [the Gospels] is so defective and doubtful that it seems vain to attempt minute inquiry into it: and such tricks have been played with their text, and with the texts of other books relating to them, that we have a right, from that cause, to entertain much doubt what parts of them are genuine. In the New Testament there is internal evidence that parts of it have proceeded from an extraordinary man; and that other parts are of the fabric of very inferior minds. It is easy to separate those parts, as to pick out diamonds from dunghills.[382]

In a letter to Charles Thomson, Jefferson announced: "I am a real Christian, that is to say, a disciple of the doctrines of Jesus."[383]

Jefferson in Paris: The movie *Jefferson in Paris*[384] was released in 1995. One of the favorite speculations in American history is if in the years before he became president, Thomas Jefferson had a dalliance with (and fathered a child with) his 15-year-old slave Sally Hemings. The film, set against the backdrop of the beginning of the French Revolution, follows Jefferson to France (as the U.S. ambassador to the court of Louis XVI), his romance with the beautiful Maria Cosway, and his relationship with his daughters and slaves from home (especially Sally). Nick Nolte portrays Long Tom, Greta Scacchi is Maria Cosway. Jefferson's daughters Patsy and Polly are played by Gwyneth Paltrow and Estelle Eonnet, respectively. If Sally Hemings looked anything like actress Thandie Newton, Jefferson's lust for her is understandable if not defendable.

Jefferson's Maxims, Aphorisms, and Proverbs[385]

> There is no act, however virtuous, for which ingenuity may not find some bad motive [Letter to Edward Dowse, April 19, 1803].
>
> Tranquility is the summum bonum of old age [Letter to Charles Holt, November 23, 1810].
>
> All bigotries hang to one another [Letter to John Adams, 1814].

An honest heart being the first blessing, a knowing head is the second [Letter to Peter Carr, August 19, 1785].

Never fear the want of business. A man, who qualifies himself well for his calling, never fails of employment [Letter to Peter Carr, 1792].

There is no truth existing which I fear, or would wish unknown to the whole world [Letter to Henry Lee, May 15, 1826].

With the same honest views, the most honest men often form different conclusions [Letter to Robert Livingston, 1801].

Delay is preferable to error [Letter to George Washington, May 16, 1792].

It is the old practice of despots to use part of the people to keep the rest in order [Letter to John Taylor, June 1, 1798].

An injured friend is the bitterest of foes [French Treaties Opinion, April 28, 1793].

Every man has a commission to admonish, exhort, and convince another of error ["Notes on Religion," 1776].

What has no meaning admits no explanation [Letter to Alexander Smyth, 1825].

I steer my bark with hope in my heart, leaving fear astern [Letter to John Adams, April 8, 1816].

A government held together by the bands of reason only, requires much compromise of opinion [Letter to Benjamin Rush, 1824].

He is happiest of whom the world says the least, good or bad [Letter to John Adams, August 27, 1786].

History, in general, only informs us of what bad government is [Letter to John Norvell, June 14, 1807].

Nobody can acquire honor by doing what is wrong [Letter to Dr. Robert M. Patterson, 1814].

The execution of the laws is more important than the making of them [Letter to Abbé Arnond, May 27, 1789].

Lethargy is the forerunner of death to the public liberty [Letter to Colonel William S. Smith 1787].

A respectable minority is useful as censors [Letter to Joel Barlow, May 3, 1802].

A strong body makes the mind strong [Letter to Peter Carr, 1785].

Money, and not morality, is the principle of commercial nations [Letter to John Langdon, 1810].

The press is impotent when it abandons itself to falsehood [Letter to Thomas Seymour, 1807].

The good opinion of mankind, like the lever of Archimedes, with the given fulcrum, moves the world [Letter to M. Correa, 1814].

The proof of a negative can only be presumptive [Letter to John Adams, 1819].

The hole and the patch should be commensurate [Letter to James Madison, 1787].

Responsibility weighs with its heaviest force on a single head [Letter to Samuel Kercheval, 1816].

No society can make a perpetual constitution, or even a perpetual law [Letter to James Madison, 1789].

Time and truth will at length correct error [Letter to Constantin François Volney, 1805].

Traveling makes a man wiser, but less happy [Letter to J. Bannister, Jr., 1787].

Victory and defeat are each of the same price [Cited in Caroline Thomas Harnsberger, Treasury of Presidential Quotations].

The wise know too well their weakness to assume infallibility; and he who knows most, know how little he knows [Batture Case, 1812].

It is more honorable to repair a wrong than to persist in it [Address to the Cherokee Nation, 1806].

Observations About Jefferson

It may be that without a vision men shall die. It is no less true that, without hard practical sense, they shall also die. Without Jefferson the new nation might have lost its soul. Without Hamilton it would assuredly have been killed in body.[386]— James Truslow Adams

Jeffersonian Democracy simply meant the possession of the federal government by the agrarian masses led by an aristocracy of slave-owning planters.[387]— Charles A. Beard

For life was freakish / But life was fervent, / And I was always / Life's willing servant.[388]— Stephen Vincent Benét

... the first modern to state in human terms the principles of democracy.[389]— John Dewey.

[Jeffersonians are the] apostles of anarchy, bloodshed, and atheism.[390]— Chief Justice Oliver Ellsworth

Of all the Revolutionary founders, Thomas Jefferson has figured the most prominently in blacks' attempts to constitute themselves as Americans.[391]— Annette Gordon-Reed

He had a steadfast and abiding faith in justice, righteousness and liberty as the prevailing and abiding forces in the conduct of States, and that justice and righteousness were sure to prevail where any people bear rule in perfect liberty.[392]— George F. Hoar

No better minister could be sent to France. He is everything that is good, upright, enlightened and clever, and is respected and beloved by every one that knows him.[393]— Marquis de Lafayette

Though greatly impressed with French manners, he was strongly opposed to any aping of them by Americans. He was attracted by the cuisine and wines and found the French a temperate people, but thought their life lacking in domestic happiness, and on the whole rather futile. Life for him was empty when not purposeful. He thought little of French science, but was enthusiastic about their arts— architecture, painting, and most of all, music, which he valued the more perhaps because a fractured wrist had ended his days as a violinist.[394]— Dumas Malone

The patriot, fresh from freedom's councils come, / Now pleased retires to lash his slaves at home; / Or woo, perhaps, some black Aspasia's charms, / And dream of Freedom in his bondsmaid's arms.[395]— Thomas Moore

The twentieth century statesman whom the Thomas Jefferson of January 1793 would have admired most is Pol Pot.[396]— Conor Cruise O'Brien

FOUR

James Madison
That Dear Little Jemmy

Fourth President of the United States, 1809–1817

Madison was called the "Father of the American Constitution," for his key role in convincing the delegates of the virtue of a strong central government and "because in point of erudition and actual contributions to the formation of the Constitution he was preeminent."[1] Perhaps he should better be called the "Father of American Constitutionality," because of his life-long support of the principles of the Declaration of Independence.[2] In addition, he served as the recorder of the convention, making copious notes of all that transpired. "As the convention was closed to the press, Madison's notes are the only record of the deliberations that took place."[3]

Birth: James Madison, Jr., was born at Midnight on March 16, 1751 (March 5 Old Style), at Port Conway, Virginia, at the home of his maternal grandparents, who his mother was visiting at the time.[4]

Nicknames and Titles: Besides "Father of the Constitution," Madison was called the "Sage of His Time," "The Great Little Madison," "The Great Legislator," "Father of the Bill of Rights," "President Long Pants" (Madison was the first president to wear long pants instead of knee britches to his inauguration ceremony[5]), and "The Short." When one of his correspondents, Reverend William Cogswell, in 1834, addressed Madison as the Father of the Constitution, the president remarked: "Sir, you give me credit to which I have no claim.... [The Constitution] was not like the fabled Goddess of Wisdom, the offspring of a single brain. It ought to be regarded as the work of many hands and many heads."[6]

Family: James Madison, Sr. (1723–1801), was a wealthy planter who gave his namesake his estate in Orange County, Virginia. The elder Madison was the largest landowner and leading citizen of the county. In addition he served as justice of the peace and vestryman of his Anglican parish, whose duties included enforcing Sabbath observance.[7] James Jr., who was called "Jemmy" to distinguish him from the elder Madison lived in his father's home until he was fifty, the year James, Sr., who recognized and supported his son's genius, died.[8] James Sr. married eighteen-year-old Eleanor "Nelly" Rose Conway (1731–1829) on September 15, 1749. Nelly was the daughter of a prominent planter and tobacco merchant. Although she endured the effects of malaria, she lived to 98, lucid and able to read without glasses. Nelly remained very close to her famous son Jemmy, who was the eldest of seven children to live to maturity. She lived in "a semiprivate room at Montpelier and was visited each night by her son and his wife." She was said to have "fewer wrinkles than her 70-year-old son."[9] Altogether James had eleven siblings, five died in childhood. The survivors were his three brothers: Francis, Ambrose and William and three sisters: Mrs. Nelly Hite, Mrs. Sarah Macon and Mrs. Frances "Fanny" Rose.[10]

Ancestors: The first ancestor in America of the future U.S. president was ship's carpenter John Madison (sometimes spelled Maddison), who departed England for the Virginia colony in 1653. John put aside some of his wages to take advantage of the "headright" system. The English government awarded fifty acres of land to anyone who paid the passage of an immigrant to the colonies. Madison paid for himself and eleven others, earning 600 acres of land. Those whose passage was paid by John were indentured servants, who were required to work for a certain period of time, typically three to ten years in exchange for their passage fee. Madison continued to use the headright system to patent land, until his estate on the Mattapony River, at a place known as Mantapike, grew to nineteen hundred acres.[11]

After John Madison's death, his son, also called John, "continued expanding the family estate, becoming a prominent landowner, serving as sheriff and justice of the peace in King and Queen County."[12] In 1714, he and a neighbor patented two thousand acres of land, some forty miles above Mantapike. John's three sons, John, Henry, and Ambrose were given some of this land, where they established their own estates. Ambrose, the grandfather of the future president wed Frances Taylor, the daughter of a prominent landowning family that owned some 13,500 acres in Virginia. In 1723, Ambrose's father-in-law deeded some 4,675 prime acres in the Piedmont region of Virginia to his sons-in-law Ambrose and Thomas Chew. Ambrose created an estate on his land that he named Montpelier. By the time his mansion was completed in 1728, Ambrose had become the most prosperous individual in the area.[13] Ambrose and his wife had three children, one of whom, James, was the father of the future president.

The Madisons did not move to Montpelier, at the time called Mount Pleasant, until six months before Ambrose died on August 27, 1732, at the age of thirty-two. Three of his slaves, a woman and two men, were accused of conspiring to poison him. Historian Ann L. Miller wrote that the poison "did not kill him outright but rather caused sufficient damage to his system to condemn him to slow death over several months." The three slaves were all found guilty and one man, who was not owned by Augustine, was executed for the crime.[14] Frances managed the estate until her first-born son, James [Sr.], reached adulthood.

Appearance: Physically, Madison was always frail, short of stature, and slight. He was the smallest United States President, standing between 5 feet 2 inches to 5 feet 4 inches tall, and weighing no more than 100 pounds.[15] He appeared young for his age and had bright blue eyes. Margaret Byrd Bassett wrote that he "looked like a pale and sickly scholar, which in fact he was."[16] During his campaign for Congress in 1780, on the way to a debate with his opponent on a very cold and snowy night, his ears and nose froze, leaving scars that he carried for the rest of his life. In later years, he would jokingly claim it as "his scar of a wound received in defense of his country."[17] As president, "he was careful of his appearance and usually dressed in black."[18] He seldom smiled in public and a wife of one politician chided him for being "a gloomy stiff creature."[19] Another female observer claimed that in private he was entertaining and convivial, in public he was "mute, cold and repulsive."[20] In his later years, Madison's small frame shrank, leaving him little more than skin and bones. Washington Irving wrote in 1812: "Oh, poor Jemmy, he is but a withered little apple-john."[21]

Personality and Character: James Madison "labored under a serious disadvantage in the dryness of his personality, giving him the impression of being weak and nervous. In

President James Madison, engraving by David Edwin created between 1809 and 1817 based on a painting by Thomas Sully (Library of Congress Prints).

part, this was because he was modest, soft spoken, and somewhat shy."[22] He was deficient in the "politically useful art of small talk."[23] Contemporaries said Madison seemed emotionless, uncomfortable and severe in public settings, but as Augustus Foster, British minister to the United States, observed, he was "a social, jovial, and good humored companion, full of anecdote and wit."[24] His secretary, Edward Coles, who later become the second governor of Illinois, said of Madison: "No one ever had to a greater extent, firmness, mildness, and self-possession, so happily blended in his character."[25]

American historian George Tucker, who in 1825 became professor of moral philosophy and chairman of the faculty at the University of Virginia, wrote that his first impression of Madison was his "sternness rather than the mildness and suavity which I found afterwards to characterize" him. He also observed Madison's "unfailing good humor and a lively relish for the ludicrous, which imprinted everything comic on his memory and thus enabled him to vary and enliven his conversation with an exhaustless fund of anecdote."[26]

Acutely intelligent, Madison was "patient, self-restrained, and preserving." According to biographer Harold S. Schultz, he had an "'inimitable'" talent for avoiding personal attacks and for disarming his opponents with civility and calmness, but he was frequently misjudged by "those who failed to see that his modesty and reticence concealed a strong will and rare talents," including the capacity to withstand personal attacks when they did come.[27]

None of the founding fathers was more efficient in expressing and convincing others of the soundness of their ideas, especially in writing, than Madison. Patrick Henry said of him: "If convincing is eloquence, he was the most eloquent man I ever heard."[28] Madison's talents as a legislator did not serve him well as president. His unassuming personality and mild temperament, his willingness to confess the limitations of his positions, and strengths in the legislature worked against him as chief executive. Gary Wills said of him: "Though a brilliant theoretician and effective legislator and collaborator, he was not a natural leader of men, and the absence of leadership was keenly felt during wartime."[29] Some historians claimed he found it difficult to exercise leadership pressure on others to produce results. They reported that he preferred to defer decisions until all sides of an issue had been expressed and insisted on regard for popular opinion. Ralph Louis Ketcham wrote: "His manner often created the impression that he was indecisive, irresolute, ineffective and evasive — and led many people to think him unfit for executive leadership ... by scholarly and intellectual habit, he weighed matters carefully, sought subtle and sophisticated insights, and suspended judgments as long as possible; this tendency caused many to see him as a 'closer politician,' too little in touch with the practical world and too much wrapped up in his own thoughts and theories. The total effect denied him the charisma necessary for dynamic leadership."[30] To Alexander Hamilton, Madison seemed "too hopelessly idealistic, not a man familiar with the world."[31] According to Margaret Bassett: "Madison was a pacific man. He lacked the sternness to bully factions, and in relation to England and France, he trusted too much to the power of economic weapons."[32] A contrary view of Madison was given by Stanley M. Elkin and Eric McKitrick: "Madison was not a compromiser. He was a revolutionary; his ideological presuppositions, down deep, were immovable; despite all appearances to the contrary, he was one of the most stubborn and willful men of his time. In what to him was fundamental, he was quietly, implacably, determined to have his way."[33] Thomas Jefferson said of his friend and protégé: "I can say conscientiously that I do not know in the world a man of purer integrity, more dispassionate, disinterested, and devoted to genuine Republicanism; nor could I in the whole scope of America and Europe point out an abler head."[34]

Marriage and Romances: In 1780 James Madison met Catherine "Kitty" Floyd, the daughter of a New York congressman, when she was 12. When she turned 15, she was pretty and played the harpsichord, and their friendship blossomed in a romance, even though Madison was 16 years older.[35] In April 1783 she agreed to marry him, and they exchanged miniature portraits of themselves by artist Charles Wilson Peale. In July Kitty abruptly called off the wedding. Although no reason was recorded for the break-up, Kitty soon married William Clarkson, a 21-year-old medical student, who had been calling on her at the same time as had Madison.[36] As was her family's tradition, Kitty's letter of rejection was sealed with a lump of rye dough.[37] The future president was miserable and wrote of his "disappointment" to his friend Thomas Jefferson, who responded with a consoling letter, in which he reminded Madison: "The world still presents the same and many other sources of happiness."[38]

In his later years, Madison, who never saw Kitty again, inked out enciphered passages in letters sent to Jefferson in which he spoke of his engagement and pending marriage.[39] In time the ink faded, allowing scholars to decipher them. The romance was described in Irving Brant's biography of James Madison. Brandt reconstructed the inked-out 13 lines:

> At the date of my letter in April 1 I expected to have had the pleasure by this time of seeing you in Virginia. My disappointment has proceeded from several dilatory circumstances on which I had not calculated. One of these was the uncertain state into which the object, I was then pursuing has been brought by one of those incidents to which such affairs are liable. This (?) has rendered the time of my return to Virginia less material as the necessity of my visiting the state of New York [where Kitty and her family resided] no longer exists.[40]

For half a century Dolley Payne Madison was the most important woman in American social circles. She was born on May 20, 1768, in New Garden, a Quaker community located in the area now known as Guilford County, North Carolina.[41] Her father, John Payne, was a struggling businessman who freed his slaves after the Revolutionary War. Dolley "was born and raised a Quaker, and wore the religion's traditional garb through her childhood and marriage."[42] She was raised at Scotchtown near Ashland, Virginia, until her teenage years when she lived in Philadelphia with her par-

Dolley Payne Madison, engraving done in 1812 by William Chappell from an original painting by Gilbert Stuart; in possession of Richard Cutts, Esq., M.D. (Library of Congress).

ents and seven surviving siblings. By 1789, John Payne's laundry-starch business failed. He was unable to pay his debts, and his Quaker meeting expelled him.[43]

Dolley's mother, Mary, opened a boarding house to support her family. It was at this time that Dolley met lawyer John Todd, Jr., and married him in 1790. They soon had two sons, John Payne Todd and William Temple Todd.[44] In 1792, Dolley's father died, and a year later a yellow fever epidemic struck Philadelphia. In the fall of 1793, Dolley moved to the countryside outside Philadelphia, but her husband remained in the city to care for his parents and attend to his practice. First his parents died and then he too perished, followed by their infant son, William, leaving Dolley a young widow with a year-old son. The yellow fever epidemic claimed 5,000 lives in Philadelphia, nearly one-fifth of the city's population.[45]

By this time, Philadelphia had become the capital. After a few months, Dolley was feeling better, and began to appear in public. Dozens of men lined the streets of Philadelphia to get a look at the lovely widow. The charming and beautiful young woman with a sparkling personality attracted the attention of many distinguished men, including James Madison, who was 17 years her senior. They had been introduced by a mutual friend, Aaron Burr, who was Madison's classmate at college.[46] Years later, Dolley's cousin described the appearance of the attractive young widow: "She was dressed in ... satin, with a silk ... kerchief over a neck." On her head was "a cap, from which an occasional ... curl would escape."[47] Madison proposed marriage to her by letter, and she sent her acceptance by mail. Four months later Dolley and James were married and for 42 years were notably happy together.[48]

Because they were married in an Episcopal ceremony, Dolley was expelled from the Society of Friends.[49] No longer restricted by Quaker doctrine; Dolley was wed in a gown of silk and lace, with a low v-neck. On her head she wore a crown of orange blossoms and on her feet, white satin slippers, without heels, less she appear taller than her groom.[50]

Dolley served as hostess for widower President Thomas Jefferson, in which role she quickly became the "Queen of Washington City." She was "thirty-three years old and gracious, attractive, gregarious, warm and charming."[51] Her extroversion offset the austere atmosphere of the presidential mansion. But despite her graciousness, she could never satisfy the new British minister to the United States. Anthony Merry and his wife complained loudly and often to Madison of their outrage at Jefferson's indifference to protocol and his insistence on the rule of pêle-mêle, or social equality.[52]

Not only did Dolley become renowned for the fine American food served at her dinner parties, but she became a fashion icon. She liked to experiment with new styles in attire and before long women of fashion all over the nation were following her example. She took to wearing turbans adorned with feathers or jewelry and wore only the finest of fashionable garments, mostly coming from Paris. Dolley was no taller than her husband, but by wearing the turbans, she appeared so.[53] The Madisons rented a spacious three-story house in Philadelphia. Dolley's mother moved in with her sister Lucy, who wed George Steptoe Washington, a nephew of George Washington.[54] It was at this time that Dolley first experienced political society, socializing with diplomats, congressmen, and government leaders. Congressman Samuel L. Mitchell, was smitten by "her smile, her conversation, and her manners are so engaging that is no wonder that such a young widow with such blue eyes ... should indeed be a queen of hearts."[55]

When Federalist John Adams was elected president, Madison retired from Congress and moved with Dolley to their Virginia home at Montpelier. The bubbly Mrs. Madison relished holding large formal dinner parties and entertaining her guests at their manor.

Her receptions soon were the place to see and to be seen, helping to advance her husband's political career.[56] "Once described as looking like a man on his way to a funeral," he began appearing in public with his bride on his arm. At parties he became a proficient dancer and a "lively conversationalist."[57]

When Dolley became "first lady,"—a term not yet in use—she was the first to decorate the president's home, working with the famous architect Benjamin Latrobe. The two bought high-quality American goods to furnish the executive mansion. They furnished a dining room with new furniture, dishes, crystal, and serving utensils. A parlor was created where Dolley could receive visitors and the Oval room was fitted out for large state affairs.[58] If President Madison was ill at ease in social gatherings, Dolley was in her element. She advanced her husband's political agenda with a new style of entertaining—an American style. She hired the best chef in Washington and expanded the guest list beyond politicians and diplomats to include writers and artists. She mingled freely with her guests, warmly and graciously greeting all. Margaret Bayard Smith remarked that "she was all grace, dignity and affability ... such manners would disarm envy itself and conciliate even enemies. European visitors noted she looked and moved like a Queen."[59]

Dolley's weekly parties attracted so many guests, they became known as "Mrs. Madison's Crush."[60] She delighted the radical Republicans, whose support her husband needed, and the Federalists, whose hostility was part of Madison's political challenge. One young guest gushed: "her demeanor is so removed from the hauteur generally attendant on royalty that your fancy can carry the resemblance no further."[61] Dolley hosted "dove parties" for wives of politicians and government officials. She also initiated two Washington social practices: the Inaugural Ball[62] and the White House Easter Egg Roll.[63]

In 1814, while the War of 1812 raged, the British Army approached Washington. The president left the city to be at the front lines with the troops. "He ordered his wife to flee the city, but she refused to leave until she heard the advancing cannons, and even then, she kept her wits about her."[64] On August 24, 1814, the British Army advanced on Washington. Residents had been evacuating the city for days. The president "asked Dolley if she had the courage to remain at the mansion until his return. She assured him her only concern was for him."[65] The president sent two letters to Dolley from nearby Maryland. In the first he doubted the British had enough troops to threaten the capital, but admitted they might be expecting the arrival of reinforcements. As for the second dispatch, Dolley wrote to her sister Anna: "the last is the most alarming, because he desires I should be ready at a moment's warning to enter my carriage

The Dolley Madison First Spouse Coin Reverse alludes to her saving the Gilbert Stuart portrait of George Washington from the White House during in the war of 1812; released by the U.S. Mint in 2007, designed by Joel Iskowitz and sculpted by Don Everhart (United States First Spouse Gold Coin image featuring Dolley Madison, courtesy United States Mint and used with permission).

and leave the city; that the enemy seemed stronger than had been reported, and that it might happen that they would reach the city, with the intention of destroying it."[66] Dolley packed all the cabinet documents she could in one carriage, but refused to leave until the return of her husband, despite the fact that 90 percent of the city's population had already exited Washington. The mayor of the city twice pleaded with her to leave, but she resisted. Late in the afternoon with cannons booming in the distance and no sign of her husband, friends finally convinced Dolley to vacate the city.[67] Dolley described the events of her final hours in the executive mansion in a letter to her sister: "Our kind friend, Mr. Carroll [the owner of the Belle Vue House, who came for her with his carriage], has come to hasten my departure, and is in a very bad humor with me because I insist on waiting until the large picture of General Washington [painted by Gilbert Stuart] is secured, and it requires to be unscrewed from the wall. The process was found to be too tedious for these perilous moments. I have ordered the frame to be broken, and the canvas taken out."[68]

Dolley commandeered a wagon outside of the president's home and loaded it with official papers, silver and other valuables. She successfully made her escape, joining her husband at a safe distance as they sadly viewed the burning of the capital. When they could return, they found the executive mansion "an ash heap."[69] The British, hoping to capture the president and his wife to be displayed in England, forced their way into the executive mansion. Finding no one present in their search from cellar to attic, they set it ablaze. Only the bare walls survived.[70] Homeless the Madisons accepted the offer of the French Ambassador Louis Serurier to occupy his home, the Octagon House, while reconstruction was underway. They moved into it for the remainder of his presidency.[71] Dolley made the most of their temporary quarters and before long, she entertained as before. She helped a group of women to establish an orphanage in Washington, D.C.[72] Dolley's "natural charm, cultivated graciousness, and enthusiasm for public life set a standard for future First Ladies,"[73] which many were unable or unwilling to follow. After Madison's second term ended, they retired to their estate in Virginia, where she entertained guests as usual. Visitors flocked to their home, even when Madison "was confined to his bed, too ill to move about." His arthritis was so bad and his hands so swollen he could barely use them.[74] Entertaining drained the couple's finances, which had previously suffered when the economic bubble burst during the War of 1812. Cotton prices declined severely as did demand for U.S. grain and in addition there were bad seasons for tobacco and wheat.[75]

When her husband died at age 85, Dolley was forced to sell his Continental Papers and their land to pay creditors. In the fall of 1837, she left the management of the plantation to her son, Payne, and returned to Washington, where she resumed her status as an important leader of the capital's society.[76] As beloved as ever, Dolley's "friends found subtle ways to supplement her diminished income." She remained in the capital until her death in 1849, honored and cherished by all.[77] On the day of her funeral all government offices were closed. President Zachary Taylor, his cabinet members, and all other Washington dignitaries walked behind the casket. Taylor, a second cousin of James Madison, allegedly eulogized Dolley as the "First Lady,"[78] the first presidential spouse to be awarded this title, although no record of the eulogy is extant.

Children: James and Dolley Madison had no children leading to his nickname "No-Heirs Madison." He had no direct descendants but by his siblings he had more than 30 nieces and nephews who lived to maturity.[79] Dolley's son lived with them during the early years of Madison's presidency. Payne, as he was called, caused a great deal of pain for his mother and his stepfather. He was an egotistical and wearisome alcoholic. When he appeared in public with an older woman friend of his mother's, he was shipped to Saint Petersburg, Russia, as an unofficial attaché to the peace negotiations after the War of 1812. The hope that he might seek a diplomatic career and straighten out his life was dashed when he took up with a Russian princess. When she mystifyingly disappeared, Payne rambled throughout Europe, gambling and drinking, while Madison was left to bail him out—an enormous sum of $40,000 to pay for his dissolute life.[80] Dolley was aware of only $20,000 contributed by her husband. Madison kept from her knowledge of the second $20,000 until after his death "as evidence of the sacrifice he had made to insure her tranquility by concealing from her the ruinous extravagance of her son."[81] When Payne returned to America after Madison's death, he mismanaged the plantation, plunging Dolley into debt. Payne even tried to cheat his mother by selling her husband's remaining congressional papers, and even threatened to sue, when Madison's trustees blocked the sale. For the remainder of her life, he was a continuous source of concern, mortification and financial misery for his mother.[82]

Ever since she could remember, African American Massachusetts pediatrician Bettye Kearse was told by relatives, "Always remember you're a Madison. You descend from an American president."[83] She has been working with Bruce Jackson of the Roots Project, which helps African Americans trace their genetic histories. According to her family's oral history one of Madison's slaves, named Coreen, was one of the cooks at Montpelier and had a sexual relationship with Madison; the result of their relationship was a son, given the name Jim. That would make the Kearse family the only direct descendants of James Madison.

Coreen was Kearse's great-great-great-great-grandmother. The plan is to compare the Y chromosomes, which are identical across generations, of male descendants in Madison's family to the Y chromosomes of some of Kearse's male cousins.[84] However, a DNA match would show only whether Kearse's family descends from one of the four Madison brothers, but not necessarily from James. "Learning that will take detective work, Jackson said: Researchers will comb through plantation records to try to ascertain when a child was conceived, and whether James Madison or his brothers were even at Montpelier at the time. If it turns out James was the only one there, Jackson says there will be a strong case that he fathered the child."[85] Kearse and Jackson have been unable to obtain DNA samples from Madison's descendants. According to Frederick M. Smith, president of the National Society of Madison Family Descendants, "his society has received several claims of family ties to the president over the years and those wishing to test their DNA against that of a Madison family descendant can do so through an online genetic testing service ... objective and without racial bias."[86] However, Jackson called the approach "scientifically flawed." Smith disagrees.[87] If these and other claims of African Americans who believe there are his descendants can be verified, it will certainly sully Madison's legacy. "The issue of slavery haunted Madison. Liberty and justice were high on his list of concerns, so how, in a government of the people, could some people own other people? ... Madison ... owned many slaves ... and the dilemma probably tormented him. He was the Father of the Constitution—a constitution which governed a land of liberty, but he did not free the slaves he had inherited during his life or at his death."[88]

Religion and Religious Beliefs: Madison was baptized and raised in the Anglican faith, the established religion of Virginia. His family attended the nearby Brick Church where his father served as a vestryman.[89] Madison professed the tenets of the Episcopal religion, but was not especially devout and grew up to be an impassioned opponent of established religion and advocated what was then called freedom of conscience.[90] He believed in a divine creator while doubting that man could know him, probably making him a deist, like his friend Thomas Jefferson. In an October 1787 letter to Jefferson, Madison wrote about distinctions in "civilized societies." He spoke of "artificial distinctions" based "on accidental differences in political, religious or other opinions."

"However erroneous or ridiculous these grounds of dissention and faction, may appear to the enlightened Statesman, or the benevolent philosopher ... the bulk of mankind who are neither Statesmen nor Philosophers, will continue to view them in a different light."[91]

In a 1785 letter to Thomas Jefferson, Madison wrote: "The Presbyterian clergy have at length espoused the side of the opposition, being moved either by fear of their laity or a jealousy of the Episcopalians. I am far from being sorry for it as a coalition between them could alone endanger our religious rights and a tendency to such an event had been suspected."[92] Madison resolutely believed in the separation of church and state and religious freedom. He had witnessed the abuses of a state religion in Virginia, where the Church of England persecuted Baptists and other Protestant sects.[93] At college his theology and Hebrew professor, John Witherspoon, preached liberty both civil and religious: "The magistrates ought to defend the rights and consciences and tolerate all their religious sentiments that are not injurious to their neighbors."[94]

Madison vehemently opposed the Dade Code, prepared by English Anglican bishops, consisting of a list of proscriptions and punishments, up to and including execution. He wrote: "The purpose of separation of church and state is to keep forever from these shores the ceaseless strife that has soaked the soil of Europe with blood for centuries.... Religion and government will both exist in greater purity; the less they are mixed together.... In the Papal System, Government and Religion are in a manner consolidated, and that is found to be the worst of Government."[95] He wrote to William Bradford on January 24, 1774: "The diabolical, hell-conceived principle of persecution rages among some, and to their eternal infamy the clergy can furnish their quota of imps for such a business."[96] Madison's most decisive account of his feelings on religious freedom and separation of church and state are found in his Memorial and Remonstrance paper. It was written in opposition to the assessing taxes for the purposes of paying teachers of "Christian education." Madison argued that, under the Constitution:

> There is not a shadow of right in the general government to intermeddle with religion ... this subject is, for the honor of America perfectly free and unshackled. The Government has no jurisdiction over it ... that religion or the duty which we owe to our Creator and the manner of discharging it can be directed only be reason and conviction, not by force of violence.... Because Religion be exempt from the authority of the Society at large, still less can it be subject to that of the Legislative body. Whilst we assert a freedom to embrace, to profess, and to observe the Religion which we believe to be of divine origin, we cannot deny an equal freedom to choose minds who have not yet yielded to the evidence which has convinced us.... It is proper to take alarm at the first experiment on our liberties.... Who does not see that the same authority which can establish Christianity, in exclusion of all other Religions, may establish with the same ease any particular sect of Christians, in exclusion of all other sects?[97]

Madison was not anti-religion; he was only opposed to state establishment of religion. In his letter to the General Assembly of the Commonwealth of Virginia, he wrote: "It is the duty of every man to render to the Creator such homage, and such only as he believes to be acceptable to him. This duty is precedent both in order of time and degree of obligation, to the claims of Civil Society. Before any man can be considered as a member of Civil Society, he must be considered as a subject of the Governor of the Universe."[98] On another occasion, Madison penned the thought: "The belief in a God All Powerful wise and good, is so essential to the moral order of the world and to the happiness of man, that arguments which enforce it cannot be drawn from too many sources not adapted with too much solicitude to the different characters and capacities impressed with it."[99]

Education: As was the custom at the time among the landed-gentry of Virginia, Madison was home-schooled during his early childhood, under the direction of his mother and grandmother. Although his family had very few books, he was proficient in the fundamentals of reading, writing and arithmetic before attending a formal school.[100] Madison was tutored privately at boarding schools, first by a Scot, Donald Robertson, who had been educated at the University of Edinburgh. Madison later praised his teacher, saying: "All I have been in life, I owe largely to that man."[101]

Madison studied mathematics, geography and both modern and ancient languages and read Robertson's small collection of "great books." From age 16, Madison spent two years under the tutelage of the Reverend Thomas Martin, in preparation for college.[102] Unlike most Virginians of his circumstances, he did not attend the College of William and Mary, his parents fearing that the lowland climate in Williamsburg might be detrimental to his fragile health. They were also wary of exposing him to an institution which had lost its reputation for providing a fine education to one that was in a "dissolute and unenviable state."[103] Instead young Madison entered the College of New Jersey, now Princeton University, which was the alma mater of his mentor Martin. He wrote to his father describing his school: "The Rules, by which the Students & Scholars are directed, are, in my Opinion, exceedingly well formed to check & restrain the vicious, & to assist the studious, & to countenance & encourage the virtuous."[104]

Some of Madison's classmates, who remained life-long friends, were William Bradford, Jr., later U.S. Attorney General; Hugh Henry Brackenridge, jurist and novelist; and Philip Freneau, the "poet of the Revolution."[105] Madison received a remarkable liberal education, studying Latin, Greek, mathematics, rhetoric, geography and philosophy, and came under the influence of "The Old Doctor," President John Witherspoon, who constantly proclaimed his pride in "the spirit of liberty" and declared himself "an opposer of lordly domination and sacerdotal tyranny."[106] From Witherspoon, Madison learned that liberty was to be gained and preserved only at the price of eternal vigilance.[107]

Madison read "John Locke, Isaac Newton, Jonathan Swift, Joseph Addison, David Hume, Voltaire, and others whose Enlightenment world-view became his own."[108] Jemmy took their lessons to heart, and placed them at the core of the American political tradition in the Federalist Papers. Jemmy was one of the earliest members of the Whig Society, and spent a great deal of his time debating the affairs of government and society. He also wrote several comic poems that belittled, often in vulgar terms, a rival club, the Cliosophical Society.[109]

Madison graduated in two years with an A.B. degree and then spent an additional year studying theology, history and law, at the college and at his home. He was an ardent student of the scholarship of John Locke, whose thoughts became the foundation of Madison's public philosophy.[110] While at the college, Madison compiled books, collections of aphorisms, and other texts, part of which he committed to memory. One such book, apparently written by Madison, is *A Brief System of Logick*.[111] In his Second Annual Message to Congress on December 5, 1810, President Madison spoke of the importance of education in a free society: "Although all men are born free, slavery has been the general lot of the human race. Ignorant — they have been cheated; asleep — they have been surprised; divided — the yoke has been forced upon them. But what is the lesson? ... [T]he people ought to be enlightened, to be awakened, to be united, that after establishing a government they should watch over it.... It is universally admitted that a well-instructed people alone can be permanently a free people."[112]

Madison favored the education of women: "The capacity of the female mind for studies of the highest order cannot be doubted, having been sufficiently illustrated by its works of genius, of erudition, and of science."[113] The slight Virginian valued higher education. "Learned institutions ought to be favorite objects with ever free people. They throw light over the public mind which is the best security against crafty & dangerous encroachments on the public liberty.... Knowledge will forever govern ignorance; and a people who mean to be their own governors must arm themselves with the power which knowledge gives."[114]

Occupation: Madison studied law, but its practice did not appeal to him, and he was never admitted to the bar. He knew that he wished to dedicate most of his life to public service, but he needed a source of income. He felt uncomfortable depending upon the generosity of his father and younger brothers for financial support.[115] In 1774, Jemmy was appointed to the Orange County, Virginia, Committee of Safety, which oversaw local militias and carried out necessary functions of government in an event of a war for independence. A zealous patriot, Madison was profoundly involved in building up the strength of the militia.[116] After his service in the Continental Congress, Madison returned to his plantation and ventured into land speculation without much success.[117]

Military Service: During the Revolutionary War, Madison was considered too frail for regular military service. When he was twenty-four, he was a colonel of the Orange County militia of which his father was commander.[118] He never served in the field because of his poor health.

Home: Montpelier plantation, an enormous property in the middle of the Piedmont region of Virginia, was the home of three generations of the Madison family. The estate is about 30 miles (a day's travel at the time) from Thomas Jefferson's Monticello. It remained in the family until 1844 when James Madison's widow Dolley Madison sold the estate.[119] Ambrose Madison owned over 5,000 acres of land in the Tidewater region of Virginia in 1728. The land was poor, causing him to look for more promising land in Orange County. The property "consisted of red soil — a fertile clay loam, — dense forest, gently rolling hills already cultivated, deeply gullied streams, and along the eastern side of the plantation the rugged terrain of the Southwest Mountains."[120] By the time James Madison, Sr., ran the plantation it had grown to 4,000 acres, worked by about 100 slaves. The mansion's main building was built by Madison's father around 1760, the second largest brick dwelling in Orange County. It started as an eight-room house, with four rooms on the first floor, and four on the second. The home had "formal, symmetrical facades, with five vertical rows of openings on the face and three on the rear, including doors into opposite ends of the central passage."[121]

In 1797, when he retired from Congress, Madison moved to Montpelier and grafted a second residence onto the side of his parents' home. Between 1797 and 1800, with the advice of Thomas Jefferson, Jemmy added thirty feet to the northeast end of the house and a large portico with four Tuscan columns that sheltered both front doors. He turned the surrounding grounds into an English garden.[122] The older portion of the house was used by Jemmy and Dolley, with her son from her first marriage and various nieces and nephews inhabiting the addition. Interestingly, there was no internal access between the two sections of the house. To go from one to the other, it was necessary to go outside and reenter the house, described as "a fire wall between the generations."[123]

Further additions and renovations were made between 1809 and 1812, mostly in the interior and the construction of one-story wings to each end of the structure, turning "the house into a proper seat for a chief executive, his wife, and mother."[124] After Madison died, "the contents of the house were auctioned off and the estate changed hands six times until 1901 when William and Annie Rogers DuPont purchased the property. They enlarged Montpelier from thirty-six rooms above the cellar to 104. They also raised more than 100 structures on the grounds, including a general store," outbuildings, barns, storehouses, greenhouses, and even a train station. "Two of the house's first-floor spaces remained in their Madison-era form."[125] The DuPonts' daughter, Marion, and her actor husband Randolph Scott, took over the property in 1928, adding two horse racing tracks, one of which was a steeplechase. Marion Scott lived there until her death in 1983. She bequeathed the 2,750 acre property to the National Trust for Historic Preservation, expressing the wish that the property be restored to its original Madison-era form. The estate is abutted by the James Madison Landmark Forest, a 200 acre stand of old growth trees. It is one of the largest and best preserved groves of old-growth piedmont forest in the eastern United States.[126]

During Madison's lifetime, he preferred the French spelling, Montpellier, for his estate. Montpellier, a medieval term for "Mount of the Pilgrim," was a well-known university town in France, also famous as a resort. The name, Montpellier, became synonymous with pure, healthful air.[127] In October 2003, the Montpelier Foundation launched a major $30 million, four-year, restoration project, which has actually made the house smaller, as wings added by the DuPont family were removed, and the number of rooms was reduced from 55 to 22, the number in Madison's years there. Today, James Madison's Montpelier includes more than 130 buildings, a large flower garden and farmland. A new $8.8 million visitors' center opened in March 2007, featuring a theater and a gallery.[128]

Pets and Animals: James Madison had a horse named Liberty, who having "grown old in his service, was petted, fed, and stalled alone. He deserved his name; "not a gate which he could not open — nor, any outrage which cattle could commit was not, by the [slaves], ascribed to Liberty."[129] Dolley Madison had a macaw named Polly.

Recreational Pastimes and Interests: Madison enjoyed a brisk constitutional, observing nature, and horseback riding. He relaxed by playing chess.[130] He read widely and often returned to old friends, ancient Latin and Greek texts that he had read before. Throughout his life Madison kept up his interest in reading Greek and Latin. He always carried with him the booklet: *The Necessary Duty of Family Prayer, and the Deplorable Condition of Prayerless Families Considered. In a Letter from a Minister to His Parishioners. With Prayers for Their Use by Josiah Woodward.*[131]

Federalist Papers: Using the name "Publius," Alexander Hamilton, John Jay, and Madison authored *The Federalist*, a series of eighty-five essays, written in the late 1780s. It was their attempt to define the relation of the states to the nation, making the case for a central government. These articles were published in periodicals and bounded editions, with the intent of persuading the voters of the states to approve the Constitution.[132] The essays are considered "a classic defense of the American system of government as well as a practical application of political principles."[133] Madison wrote 29 of the essays, including the two most famous, Federalist 10 and 51. In the former, Madison presented a persuasive argument for a large republic and in the latter he delineated his brief for the separation of powers.

> The two great points of difference between a democracy and a republic are: first, the delegation of the government. In the latter, to a small number of citizens elected by the rest; secondly, the greater number of citizens, and greater sphere of country, over which the latter may be extended

... however small the republic may be, the representatives must be raised to a certain number, in order to guard against the cabals of a few, and that, however large it may be, they must be limited to a certain number, in order to guard against the confusion of a multitude.... [I]t clearly appears, that the same advantage which a republic has over a democracy ... is enjoyed by a large over a small republic.[134]

Liberty is to faction what air is to fire, an aliment without which it instantly expires. But it could not be less folly to abolish liberty, which is essential to political life, because it nourishes faction than it would be to wish the annihilation of air, which is essential to animal life, because it imparts to fire its destructive agency.[135]

We may define a republic ... as a government which derives all its powers directly or indirectly from the great body of the people, and is administered by persons holding their offices during pleasure, for a limited time, or during good behavior. It is essential to such a government that it be derived from the great body of society, not from an inconsiderable proportion, or a favored class of it.[136]

In order to lay a due foundation for that separate and distinct exercise of the different powers of government, which to a certain extent is admitted on all hands to be essential to the preservation of liberty, it is evident that each department should have a will of its own; and consequently should be so constituted that the members of each should have as little agency as possible in the appointment of the others. Were this principle rigorously adhered to, it would require that all the appointments be drawn from the same fountain of authority, the people, through channels having no communication whatever with one another. .. It is equally evident, that the members of each department should be as little dependent as possible on those of the others, for the emoluments annexed to their offices. Were the executive, magistrate, or the judges not independent of the legislature in this particular, their independence in every other would be merely nominal.[137]

POLITICAL OFFICES

Political Philosophy and Political Party Affiliation: Madison viewed the world as "remarkably harmonious and believed that the discovery of facts about man and society would lead to progress and enlightenment."[138] At the College of New Jersey, Madison was educated to be a statesman, seeking liberty and well-ordered government through the pursuit of virtue. Madison was a "young supporter of the world's first successful colonial revolt and of worldwide antimonarchical, antihierarchical, and anti-imperial movement of republicanism spawned by the Enlightenment and Dissenting Protestantism."[139] He differed from other revolutionaries in that he not only focused on the present vices of a government to be replaced, but also sought to "learn from the history of ancient and modern confederacies, in defining the future of American republicanism."[140]

As a member of the Virginia State Legislature after the Revolutionary War, Madison was alarmed over the "fragility of the Articles of Confederation and the divisiveness of state governments."[141] He wrote "a crisis had arrived which was to decide whether the American experiment was to be a blessing to the world, or to blast forever the hopes which the republican cause had inspired."[142] He was a solid promoter of a new constitution and his draft of the Virginia Plan in 1787, which called for the then revolutionary concept of a three-branch federal system — executive, legislative and judicial, which later became the basis of the American Constitution. Madison's most distinguishing political philosophical belief was that the republic needed checks and balances to limit the powers of special interest groups, which he called "factions." Madison sought "a republican remedy for the diseases most incident to republican government." He would not offer the remedy of banning factions, as political parties were called at the time. This he concluded would be impossible because the causes of faction were "sown in the nature of man." He noted that one could not suppress faction "without destroying liberty itself. Instead, he proposed to construct a government that would fairly represent all the various factions and interest groups in American society, in part in the hope that none would then be able to gain an undue ascendancy over the others." Madison did not believe that extending "the sphere of government," would lead to factional gridlock. He felt this could be avoided by providing the means of electing "men of discernment and reputation in public office ... and make them responsible ... for framing wise and impartial laws to safeguard the 'more perfect union' that had been established by the Federal Constitution."[143] If Madison were around today, he might question the success of his plan. "He believed very strongly that the new nation should fight against aristocracy and corruption and was deeply committed to creating mechanisms that would ensure republicanism in the United States."[144] A majority of writers attending a Madison Symposium at the University of Wisconsin at Madison, in July 2009 felt Madison's philosophy was "curiously twisted." It appeared to have been "divided in two (or sometimes three) distinctive segments, separated by a sharp, self-contradictory reversal."[145]

"Within three years, from 1789 to 1792, the scholars say, the leader of the Federalists of 1788, the 'nationalist' who hewed the path to constitutional reform and argued that extension of the sphere of the republic was essential to control majority oppressions, had transformed himself into a spokesman for states' right, joining Thomas Jefferson in an attempt to forge a party that would act, as they conceived it, as an instrument of popular opinion and of democratic choice."[146]

At the Madison Symposium, Lance Banning offers an explanation for Madison's seemingly inconsistent behavior: "Madison was not an advocate of multiplying clashing interests among the people. He believed, instead, that founders of a liberal republic, who could not eradicate the differences inseparable from freedom, ought to use the unavoidable plurality of interests in a civilized society to reduce the probability of passionate injustices and to improve the chances that the long-term public good would be preferred to the majority's immediate desires."[147]

During the Washington presidency, the political philosophies regarding the relationship between the states and the federal government diverged. Together with Thomas Jefferson, Madison was one of the founders of the Democratic-Republican Party.[148] He was "blessed with an unusual combination of statesmanlike powers. He had a penetrating intellect ... combined with a talent for political tactics and the legislative temperament suited to dealing with practical politicians."[149] However the Father of the Constitution was far less successful as a member of the executive branch, either as secretary of state or president. He was described as "naïve in foreign affairs and too trusting of incompetent subordinates in domestic issues."[150] Nor did he exhibit the governing skill so essential for presidential strength — "the ability to bargain with established powerful interests."[151] It was his nature to be more at ease and amicable in private company. According to Lee Langston-Harrison, Curator at Montpelier, George Tucker had the following to say about Madison's lighter side: "...his cheerfulness and amenity and abundant stock of racy anecdotes were the delight of every social board."[152] Senator Thomas Hart Benton recalled that "purity, modesty, decorum — a moderation, temperance, and virtue in everything — were the characteristics of Mr. Madison's life and manners."[153]

Others Comments Made on Madison's Gifts:

Madison's whole scheme essentially comes down to this. The struggle of classes to be replaced by a struggle of interests ... a safe, even energizing, struggle which is compatible with, or even promotes, the safety and stability of society.... In a large commercial society the interests of the many can be fragmented ... into relatively small groups, seeking small immediate advantages.... The mass will not unite as a mass to make extreme demands upon the few.[154]— Martin Diamond

If we really believed the pen was mightier, or even more dignified, than the sword, the nation's capital would be named not for the soldier who wielded the revolutionary sword, but the thinker who was ablest with a pen. It would be Madison, D.C. Yet until recently there was not even a government building named after him. And what has now been named for him? A library, for Pete's sake. What a put-down in a city with the world's highest ratio of action to reaction.[155]— George F. Will

Madison's claim on our admiration does not rest on a perfect consistency, any more than it rests on his presidency. He has other virtues.... As a framer and defender of the Constitution he had no peer.... The finest part of Madison's performance as president was his concern for the preserving of the Constitution.... No man could do everything for his country ... not even Washington. Madison did more than most, and did some things better than any. That was quite enough.[156]— Garry Wills

Virginia Constitutional Convention: In 1776 and 1777 Madison was elected a delegate to the Virginia Convention, where he first met Thomas Jefferson. He lost his bid for reelection over a matter of principle. "In eighteenth-century Virginia, local elections were held in public at courthouses, and the candidates traditionally treated the voters to drinks of rum or whiskey. This custom was known as swilling the planters with bumbo."[157] Madison refused to treat voters to drinks, which he considered an effort to buy the election. In 1778 and 1779 Jemmy served as a member of the Council of the State of Virginia, where he made major contributions to constitutional law in the revision of the Virginia Declaration of Rights, arguing that free exercise of religion is "a right, not a privilege."[158] In a speech at the Virginia Ratifying Convention, Jemmy said:

Is there no virtue among us? If there be not, we are in a wretched situation. No theoretical checks, no form of government, can render us secure. To suppose that any form of government will secure liberty or happiness without any virtue in the people is a chimerical idea. If there be sufficient virtue and intelligence in the community, it will be exercised in the selection of these men; so that we do not depend upon their virtue, or put confidence in our rulers, but in the people who are to choose them.[159]

The Continental Congress: In 1780, at age 29, Madison was the youngest member of the Continental Congress and served until 1783. He kept a daily journal of the proceedings of the body.[160] The confederation was merely an alliance of sovereign states who came together in a military alliance to fight the Revolutionary War. The new government's task of conducting a war with no authority to tax was compounded by the states' petty resistance to yielding power over foreign affairs to the central government.[161] Madison supported efforts to increase the power of confederation government at the expense of the state legislatures. His numerous attempts to compromise with pro-slavery delegations proved unsuccessful. As John Adams recalled, "the delegations from the free States, in their extreme anxiety to conciliate the ascendancy of the Southern slave-holder, did listen to a compromise between right and wrong— between freedom and slavery."[162]

Virginia Legislature: From 1784 to 1786 Madison served as a member of the Virginia House of Delegates. "Civil and religious liberty were intimately linked in Madison's career and thinking."[163] He blocked all efforts to establish state support for churches, culminating in ratification of the Stature for Establishing Religious Freedom.[164]

Constitutional Convention: In 1787, Madison was a delegate to the Constitutional Convention, where he presented the Virginia Plan, which championed a stronger national government operating directly for individual citizens rather than states. It became an important block of the U.S. Constitution.[165] In his speech in support of the ratification of the Constitution on June 6, 1788, Madison declared:

> Since the general civilization of mankind, I believe there are more instances of the abridgement of the freedom of the people by gradual and silent encroachments of those in power than by violent and sudden usurpations; but, on a candid examination of history, we shall find that turbulence, violence, and abuse of power, by the majority trampling on the rights of the minority, have produced factions and commotions, which, in republics, have, more frequently than any other cause, produced despotism. If we go over the whole history of ancient and modern republics, we shall find their destruction to have generally resulted from those causes. In republics, the great danger is that the majority may not sufficiently respect the rights of the minority.... In order to judge of the form to be given to the institution [the Senate], it will be proper to take a view of the ends to be served by it. These were, —first, to protect the people against their rulers, secondly, to protect the people against the transient impressions into which they themselves might be led.[166]

House of Representatives: Much of the opposition to the Constitution was that it lacked a Bill of Rights. This was not an oversight. At the convention, George Mason made a motion to have a Bill of Rights made and was voted down by a vote of ten states to none. Most of writers of the Constitution believed it was unnecessary.[167] Initially, Madison agreed, but he came to be an advocate. He earlier referred to a Bill of Rights as only a "parchment barrier" to violation of personal liberties, and would do little to guard a minority from the actions of a tyrannical majority.[168] Holding such views, he seemed an unlikely author and sponsor of amendments to the Constitution to enumerate the rights of American citizens. And yet ten of his proposed amendments to the Constitution — known as the Bill of Rights— were ratified, and are usually considered Madison's greatest service to the nation.[169]

Madison helped enact the first revenue legislation and led the opposition in Congress to Alexander Hamilton's financial proposals, in particular the establishment of the Bank of the United States. Madison felt it would disproportionately confer wealth and power upon northern financiers.[170] Madison made a further break with Hamilton and the Federalists over their support of Great Britain in its war with France. In a letter, Hamilton, referring to Jefferson and Madison, wrote: "they have a womanish attachment to France and a womanish resentment against Great Britain."[171] Madison supported the Jeffersonian view of a strict interpretation of the Constitution and argued fervently against Hamilton's notion of implied powers for the President.[172] Madison led the opposition to the Jay Treaty with Great Britain, negotiated by Chief Justice John Jay, which although widely unpopular, was ratified.[173]

First Retirement: In 1797, Madison retired from the House and returned with his family to Montpelier to take over management of the plantation. He had not actively been involved in running the estate and his brothers had been, but under primogeniture, still practiced in Virginia "as the eldest son, Madison finally was expected to take on from his 74-year-old father the burden of managing the largest estates in Orange County."[174] While in temporary retirement from politics, Madison helped Jefferson draft the Virginia and Kentucky Resolutions, intended to advise states about what they believed was the unconstitutional nature of the Alien and Sedition Acts of President John Adams' administration.[175] In 1799, Madison was elected to the Virginia Assembly and defended the Virginia Resolutions— a rallying point for fellow Republicans. He prepared the Report of 1800, which maintained that the Constitution is a compact that must be honored by the states to be effective.[176] In his "Report on the Virginia Resolutions," Madison saw an important role for the press: safeguarding liberty. "To the press alone, chequered as it is with abuses, the world is indebted for all the triumphs which have been gained by reason and humanity over error and oppression."[177]

Bill of Rights: Although it was Madison who proposed the Bill of Rights at the Constitutional Convention, he did not see it as necessary, believing that rights should be guaranteed by state governments. In a letter of 1821, he referred to "those safe, if not necessary, and those politic, if not obligatory, amendments."[178] In a speech to Congress he gave the Bill of Rights faint praise, saying that it was "neither improper nor absolutely useless."[179] But several of his fellow Virginians felt quite different. Patrick Henry attacked the proposed Constitution at the Constitutional Convention for its vagueness and lack of specific protection against tyranny. He asked, "What can avail your specious, imaginary balances, your rope-dancing, chain-rattling, ridiculous ideal checks and contrivances?"[180] Richard Henry Lee was outraged at the lack of provisions to protect "those essential rights of mankind without which liberty cannot exist."[181] Even Thomas Jefferson wrote to Madison that a Bill of Rights was "what the people are entitled to against any government on earth."[182]

Madison finally came to the conclusion that though some states had their own Bill of Rights, these varied drastically, and many states had made no such provisions. Madison's motives in proposing the Bill of Rights was a desire to control the amendment process and to block the call by several states for a new constitutional convention: "I should be unwilling to see a door opened for a reconsideration of the whole structure of the government, for a reconsideration of the principles and the substance of the powers given; because I doubt, if such a door was opened, if we should be very likely to stop at that point which would be safe to the government itself...."[183] Madison's concern was not unfounded. It wasn't easy to get the constitution ratified by the needed nine states. For instance, it was ratified in Madison's Virginia by a narrow 89 to 79 vote. The opposition was led by Patrick Henry, who with others were concerned that the strong national government proposed by the Federalists was a "threat to individual rights and that the President would become a king." They further objected to the federal court system in the proposed Constitution.[184] The Preamble to the Bill of Rights reads:

> The Conventions of a number of the States, having at the time of their adopting the Constitution expressed a desire in order to prevent misconstruction or abuse of its powers, that further declaratory and restrictive clauses should be added. And as extending the ground of public confidence in the Government will best ensure the beneficent ends of its institution. Resolved by the Senate and the House of Representatives of the United States of America in Congress assembled (March 4, 1789), two thirds of both Houses concurring that the following Articles be proposed to the Legislatures of the several states as Amendments to the Constitution of the United States, all or any of which articles, when ratified by three fourths of the said Legislatures to be valid to all intents and purposes as part of the Constitution.[185]

Historian Charles Hobson believes that Madison's sponsorship of the Bill of Rights was perhaps his most important accomplishment: "This was an achievement of incalculable importance, for it reconciled many well-meaning opponents of the Constitution, who were uneasy about the omission of a guarantee of rights. In one stroke, the Constitution itself was effectively removed from the political debate. Henceforth, debates would be about the meaning of the Constitution, not about its merits as a plan of government."[186]

Cabinet Position: Madison served as Thomas Jefferson's secretary of state (1801–1809) and strongly supported both the Louisiana Purchase and the Embargo Act. During his term, Madison attempted to maintain American neutrality in face of transgressions against U.S. trade by both France and England, who once again were at war.[187]

HIS PRESIDENCY

With the support of Thomas Jefferson, Madison was nominated the Republicans' presidential candidate on the first ballot in 1808, despite stern opposition from old-line Southern Republicans, led by John Randolph, who supported James Monroe and adherents of New York's George Clinton.[188] The latter, who openly opposed Madison, was nominated for vice president. During Madison's presidency, his opponents used the slogan "Too many Virginians spoil the broth,"[189] a reference to the fact that he was the third of four U.S. Presidents from Virginia. The Federalists chose Charles Cotesworth Pinckney of South Carolina and Rufus King of New York at its presidential and vice presidential candidates. Madison won the electoral vote with 122 votes, 47 going to Pinckney and 6 for Clinton.[190]

The war in Europe dominated Madison's presidency. Staying out of European wars was his greatest challenge. With the failure of the Embargo Act, he replaced it with what was known as the Non-Intercourse Act, which allowed trade with any country except the belligerents. When this proved unenforceable, it was replaced by the Macon Bill, which asserted that the United States would trade with any country that respected its neutrality.[191] Napoleon agreed to the proviso, but Great Britain flatly refused. The United States began again trading with France, but this only increased tensions between the U.S. and Great Britain.[192]

Madison was unanimously re-nominated in 1812 by the Democratic-Republican congressional caucus, but John Langdon of New Hampshire declined the vice presidential nomination. The New York delegation boycotted the convention and Elbridge Gerry of Massachusetts was nominated for vice president. Their rivals were DeWitt Clinton of New York, a nephew of George Clinton, for president and Jared Ingersoll of Pennsylvania, for vice president. This time Madison won with 128 electoral votes to Clinton's 89.[193]

His Vice Presidents: Both of Madison's vice presidents died while they were in office. Clinton remained aloof of the administration, with his only noteworthy act being casting the deciding vote in defiance of Madison's wishes against renewing the charter of the Bank of the United States.[194] Gerry signed the Declaration of Independence, but as a delegate to the Constitutional Convention declined to sign the document as adopted.[195] He was a member of the House of Representatives from 1789 to 1793 and served as governor of Massachusetts from 1810 to 1812. During his administration, he approved a redistricting plan that guaranteed Republican domination of the state. As one district resembled a salamander, Benjamin Russell of the Boston *Centinel* immortalized Gerry by coining the term "gerrymander," which describes a redistricting for the purpose of partisan advantage.[196]

His Cabinet: Secretary of State Robert Smith (1809–1811) and James Monroe (1811–1817); Secretary of the Treasury Albert Gallatin (1809–1814), George W. Campbell (1814), Alexander J. Dallas (1814–1816), and William H. Crawford (1816–1817); Secretary of War William Eustis (1809–1812), John Armstrong (1813–1814), James Monroe (1814–1815) and William H. Crawford (1815–1816); Attorney General Cesar A. Rodney (1809–1811), William Pinckney (1812–1814) and Richard Rush (1814–1817); Secretary of the Navy Paul Hamilton (1809–1912), William Jones (1813–1814), and Benjamin W. Crowninshield (1815–1817).

Supreme Court Appointments: Joseph Story of Massachusetts (1811–1845) and Gabriel Duval of Maryland (1812–1835).

States Admitted to the Union: Louisiana (1812) and Indiana (1816).

DOMESTIC AFFAIRS — MAJOR EVENTS:

On the domestic front, Madison proposed measures he once strongly opposed, including support for the chartering of the Second Bank of the United States and a limited protective tariff. In a letter to Jared Ingersoll on June 25, 1831, Madison eloquently defended himself against the charges of inconsistency between his objection to a National Bank in 1791 and his support in 1817.[197] In his final act as president, Madison surprised even his supporters by vetoing a bill that would approve federal funds for the construction of highways and canals. While acknowledging that such a program could prove beneficial, he felt it exceeded Congress' authority and suggested the adoption of a constitutional amendment, which would grant such authority.[198]

Nullification Acts: Some of the founders of the nation saw nullification as a remedy for the overreaching of the federal government. Nullification is the setting aside of federal laws by state governments by declaring them unconstitutional, rendering them null and void within the state's borders.[199] The right of nullification was put forth in the Virginia and Kentucky Resolutions written by Thomas Jefferson and James Madison, calling for the nullification of the Alien and Sedition Acts.

In the Virginia Resolution, Madison wrote: "In case of a deliberate, palpable and dangerous exercise of other powers, not granted by said compact [the Constitution], the states who are parties thereof, have the right, and indeed are duty bound, to interpose for arresting

The British paid a bounty to American Indians for American scalps, from "A Scene on the Frontiers as Practiced by the Humane British and Their Worthy Allies," cartoon by William Charles, 1812 (Library of Congress).

the progress of the evil...."[200] At the time of the Jefferson and Madison presidencies, states often ignored the authority of the federal government and/or of the United States Supreme Court. In retirement, Madison lent intellectual leadership and his vast prestige to fight against nullification. He wrote that it betrayed the benefits of the union for which he had fought throughout his life. He asserted that nullification could only take place when a federal act was blatantly unconstitutional, as he believed was the case of the Alien and Sedition Acts, which attacked the fundamental right of free speech.[201] Madison argued that when the individual states ratified the Constitution, they had delegated certain rights and responsibilities to the new federal government.[202]

FOREIGN AFFAIRS — MAJOR EVENTS

War of 1812: The British boarded American ships and seized sailors they considered to be English and impressed them into service in His Majesty's navy.[203] The English also incited hostile Indian nations to perform atrocities against Americans in the Northwest.[204]

War was forcefully urged by the "War Hawk" faction in Congress, largely consisting of young men from the frontier districts.[205] Unable to reach a compromise with Great Britain, President Madison asked Congress to muster forces for the defense of the country. On June 1, 1812, after four years of commercial warfare and economic depression for American merchants, Madison asked Congress for a declaration of war against the United Kingdom, launching a perilous period for the greatly under-prepared nation.

> Our commerce has been plundered in every sea, the great staples of our country have been cut off from their legitimate markets, and a destructive blow aimed at our agriculture and maritime interests.... Not content with these occasional expedients for laying waste to our neutral trade, the Cabinet of Britain resorted at length to the sweeping system of blockades, under the name of orders-in-council, which has been molded and managed as might best suit its political views, its commercial jealousies, or the avidity of British cruisers.[206]

New England was totally unsympathetic to the war. Military disasters promoted the spread of wide-ranging dissatisfaction. Large areas of the Northwest were lost to British forces from Canada. American forces launched a series of attacks on Canada, frustratingly ending in U.S. surrender of Detroit and Michigan Territory.[207] American naval forces were successful at Lake Erie, from where Master Commandant Oliver Hazard Perry sent word, "We have met the enemy and they are ours."[208] The U.S victory at the Battle of the River Thames in Canada, was more an embarrassment to the British than a major triumph for the Americans.[209] Morale and pride of the citizens were particularly lifted by the ship *The Constitution*, which earned the nickname *Old Ironsides*, when British cannon balls bounced off her sides.[210] American land forces captured and burned York (present-day Toronto).[211]

In 1814, Madison and his government were forced to abandon Washington when British forces under the command of General Cockburn overwhelmed U.S. forces in and around the city. In retaliation, perhaps for York, the Capitol building, including the Library of Congress, the White House and other public buildings were set afire by victorious English troops.[212] After the war, the presidential mansion was painted white to hide the scorch marks from its burning by the British.[213]

The following is an excerpt is from *Washington Weather — The Book*, reproduced with the permission of one of its authors, Kevin Ambrose.

> After the battle, the British Army marched quickly into Washington while American soldiers, United States government officials, and residents fled the city. There were no officials left in Wash-

Print of the Battle on Lake Erie, drawn by Sully and Kearny, engraved by Murray, Draper Fairman and Co., published by Detroit Publishing Co. between 1900 and 1920 (Library of Congress, Detroit Publishing Company Collection).

ington from whom the British could seek terms of surrender. The British admiral ate dinner in the White House, and then gave the order to set fire to Washington. Within hours, the White House, the Capitol, and many other public buildings and residences were burning....

On the morning of August 25, Washington was still burning. Throughout the morning and early afternoon, the British soldiers continued to set fires and destroy ammunition supplies and defenses around the city. As the soldiers spread fire and destruction throughout the city, the early afternoon sky began to darken and lightning and thunder signaled the approach of a thunderstorm. As the storm neared the city, the winds began to increase dramatically and then built into a "frightening roar." A severe thunderstorm was bearing down on Washington, and with it was a tornado....

The tornado tore through the center of Washington and directly into the British occupation. Buildings were lifted off of their foundations and dashed to bits. Other buildings were blown down or lost their roofs. Feather beds were sucked out of homes and scattered about. Trees were uprooted, fences were blown down, and the heavy chain bridge across the Potomac River was buckled and rendered useless. A few British cannons were picked up by the winds and thrown through the air. The collapsing buildings and flying debris killed several British soldiers. Many of the soldiers did not have time to take cover from the winds and they laid face down in the streets. One account describes how a British officer on horseback did not dismount and the winds slammed both horse and rider violently to the ground....

The winds subsided quickly, but the rain fell in torrents for two hours. (There may have been a second thunderstorm that followed quickly after the first thunderstorm.) Fortunately, the heavy rain quenched most of the flames and prevented Washington from continuing to burn. After the storm, the British Army regrouped on Capitol Hill. Hours later, the British forces left Washington and returned to their ships on the Patuxent River. The journey back was made difficult by the numerous downed trees that lay across the roads. The war ships that lay waiting for the British force had also encountered the fierce storm. Wind and waves had lashed at the ships and many had damaged riggings. Two vessels had broken free from their moorings and were blown ashore.[214]

"The Fall of Washington — or Maddy in Full Flight," cartoon, published in London by S.W. Fores, 1814, showing President James Madison and probably John Armstrong, his secretary of war, both with bundles of papers, fleeing from Washington, with burning buildings behind them (Library of Congress).

The same British force was turned back both on land and on sea at Baltimore. Francis Scott Key was inspired by the successful defense of Fort McHenry to write the words to "The Star Spangled Banner."[215] The conflict between the two nations ended with the Treaty of Ghent in December 1814.[216] The United States failed to gain any of their war aims and had to bargain from a position of weakness just to regain its territory.[217] Shortly after the war had ended, unaware of the fact, General Andrew Jackson won a popular victory over the British army at New Orleans in January 1815. Although the United States could not be considered the victor in the conflict, the war did help restore President Madison's popularity.[218] He was judged a wise leader. Marines and soldiers were acclaimed as heroes. National patriotism and pride spread across the nation.[219] Three of the great icons of the United States date from the war. Beside "The Star Spangled Banner" and *Old Ironsides*, there is the symbol of the country, "Uncle Sam."[220]

The Hartford Convention: Most Americans are aware that the secession of Southern States from the Union led to the American Civil War. However, this was not the first time that a secession movement by states sparked a crisis. In December 1814, New England Federalists met at Hartford, Connecticut, to call for states' rights. Of the 26 delegates, 12 were from Massachusetts, 7 from Connecticut, 4 from Rhode Island, 2 from New Hampshire, and 1 from Vermont. New England's opposition to the War of 1812 reached the point where secession from the Union was discussed. As the war turned against the Americans, the British blockaded the whole New England coastline. The region's uproar against the newly

The British Army invaded Washington and set fire to the city on August 24, 1814 (*Washington Weather: The Weather Sourcebook for the D.C. Area* by Kevin Ambrose, Dan Henry, Andy Weiss, Historical Enterprises, 2002. Courtesy Kevin Ambrose).

re-elected president deepened. The delegates to the Hartford Convention drafted proposals for constitutional amendments challenging what they considered to be Madison's military despotism and demanded his resignation.[221]

By the time the Hartford delegation arrived in Washington to make their recommendations to the Congress, the War of 1812 had ended and the Treaty of Ghent was signed by Madison. With Andrew Jackson's victory at New Orleans, the public convinced themselves that the U.S. was triumphant. The recommendations of the Hartford Convention were mocked and quickly withdrawn by their mortified sponsors.[222]

AFTER THE PRESIDENCY

From his home at Montpelier, Madison spoke out against the disruptive states' rights influences, which threatened to shatter the federal union. He "disavowed the right of a state to nullify a national law" and denounced "anti-union heresies" in essays published in friendly periodicals.[223] He advised his successor James Monroe on foreign policy, arranged his papers for posthumous publication, helped Thomas Jefferson design the University of Virginia, and maintained a wide correspondence. Madison was president of the Agriculture Society of Albemarle, whose goal was to save Southern agriculture through scientific farming and to sustain a rural and republican virtue in country life.[224]

Madison briefly returned to public life to attend the Virginia Constitutional Convention of 1829. There he attempted to "diminish the power of the Tidewater slave owners and extend the franchise." His efforts of compromise failed due to the pressure of proslavery forces.[225] Madison was a member of the board of visitors of the University of Virginia and the second rector (chairman of the board) after Jefferson died, serving from 1826 to 1836.[226]

"British Soldiers Sacking Washington," an illustration in *Our First Century*, by Richard Miller Devens, Springfield, MA: C.A. Nichols & Co., 1876, p. 247, an inaccurate rendering of the U.S. Capitol, as there was no center building or pediment in 1814 (Architect of the Capitol Collection).

Madison left the presidency poorer than when he entered, due to the steady financial deterioration of his tobacco plantation. Through years of bad harvests and depressed agricultural markets, he avoided bankruptcy only through his savings from the governmental offices he held and by selling off lands he owned in Kentucky.[227] Wishing to provide for his wife, he refused to allow his notes on the Constitutional Convention to be published in his lifetime. He knew their worth and expected them to provide funds for Dolley if she was forced to sell the estate after his death. More and more concerned with his legacy, Madison modified his invaluable documents, attempting to "apply an artificial consistency on them, or to tidy them up with regard to later views." He altered dates and days, added and removed sentences, and shifted about characters, thus bringing the authenticity of his papers into question. He inked out original passages and went so far as to "fake Thomas Jefferson's handwriting."[228] Madison did not consider this deception, but rather an attempt to clarify his views and to validate his actions for posterity. To him, his notes were not so much a historical document, but rather his political philosophy testament.[229]

His Papers: Madison selected and edited *The Papers of James Madison*, 3 volumes, 1840. The papers, 1781–1839, consist of correspondence, documents and the notes of the Federal Convention of 1787. Besides correspondence on subjects including the American Revolution, intelligence reports, political events, slavery, domestic issues and family affairs, there is also anonymous hate mail attacking Madison's political stances.[230] The documents in the Madison's Treasures Collection at the Library of Congress are the largest single collection of original Madison's documents in existence. His writings up to 1801 are collected in the 17-volume *Congressional Series of Papers of James Madison*, edited by William Hutchinson et al. His Secretary of States Series (1801–1809) is a 16-volume in progress from the University of Virginia, as are a 12-volume Presidential Series (1809–1817) and a Retirement Series (1817–1836).

Health: In his teens and early twenties Madison complained of a "voice impairment, a functional handicap, which prevented him from speaking in public until age 30."[231] At age 21, he pessimistically predicted a short lifetime: "As for myself, I am too dull and infirm now to look out for any extraordinary thing in this world, for I think my sensations for many months past have intimated to me not to expect a long and healthy life; though it may be better with me after some time, [but] I hardly dare expect it, and therefore have little spirit and to set about anything that is difficult in acquiring and useless in possessing after one has exchanged time for eternity."[232]

Madison was a bit of a hypochondriac, inflicted with psychosomatic seizures, which he

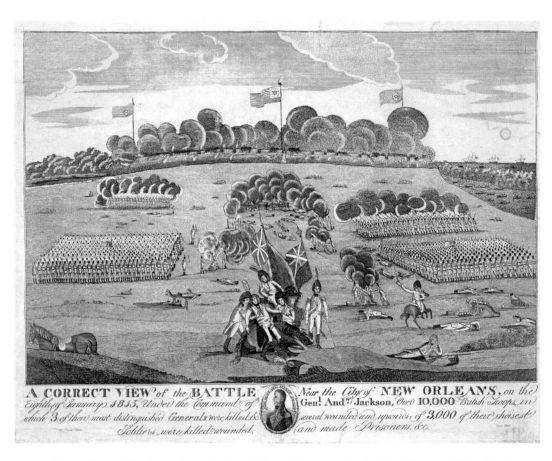

A Correct View of the Battle Near the City of New Orleans on the Eighth of January 1815. The print, created and published by Francisco Scachi between 1815 and 1829, shows British troops advancing across open ground toward the American troops behind earthworks in the background. In the foreground, critically wounded British general Edward Pakenham is held by his officers. A portrait of Andrew Jackson is below the image along with text describing the battle (Library of Congress).

termed "a constitutionally liability to sudden attacks, somewhat resembling epilepsy and suspending the intellectual functions."[233] He avoided the major maladies of his time, malaria, smallpox, tuberculosis, and yellow fever, possibly saved by his own frailty, which prevented him from exposing himself to these scourges.[234] However, he had a neurotic obsession that hidden somewhere in "his body was a horrible disease, which might strike at any time."[235] From middle age on, Madison "suffered from attacks of 'bilious fever,' a painful ailment of the bile or the liver, and he developed chronic arthritis."[236] In his late 70s, Madison's mind was still sharp, but in his early 80s, he began to fade. Both his vision and hearing deteriorated. He was weaker and thinner. In an April 21, 1831, letter to James Monroe, Madison wrote: "In explanation of my microscopic writing, I must remark that the older I grow the more my stiffening fingers make smaller letters, as my feet take shorter steps; the progress in both cases being, at the same time, more fatiguing as well as more slow."[237]

Reflecting upon his status as the last living signer of the Constitution, he wrote to Jared Sparks in 1831: "Having outlived so many of my contemporaries, I ought not to forget that I may be thought to have outlived myself."[238]

Death: As death drew near, Madison rejected medicines that might keep him alive until Independence Day, so that like Adams and Jefferson, he would die on the fourth of July. Madison died in his bedroom on June 28, 1836, "sitting in front of an untouched breakfast tray."[239] He was the last surviving founding father.

Place of Death: Montpelier, Virginia.

Cause of Death: Madison died of heart failure. It seems he did not suffer extremely from his final illness. It was a gradual weakening of his vital powers, but his mind was at times more than ordinarily clear and when stirred by the conversation of his family and friends, he was quite jovial. Dolley was with him and cheered him to the last.[240]

Final Words: According to his manservant Paul Jennings: "That morning Sukey brought him his breakfast, as usual, He could not swallow. His niece, Mrs. Willis said, 'What is the matter, Uncle James?' 'Nothing more than a change of mind my dear.'"[241] "His head instantly dropped, and he ceased breathing as quickly as the snuff of a candle goes out."[242] Madison's final message to the young nation was contained in his famous "Advice to My Country," to be opened after his death: "The advice nearest to my heart and deepest in my convictions is that the Union of the United States be cherished and perpetuated. Let the open enemy of it be regarded as a Pandora with her box opened, and the disguised one as the serpent creeping with his deadly wiles into paradise."[243]

Place of Burial: Madison's final resting place is in the family plot at Montpelier Station, Virginia, about a quarter mile from the main house. There are only a few graves in the cemetery, including those of the president's parents. Madison's grave is marked with a large obelisk.[244] Nearby is a smaller monument marking the resting place of his wife. When Dolley died in 1849, she was first interred at the Congressional Cemetery, but her remains were relocated to Montpelier in 1858.[245]

MISCELLANEA

Presidential Trivia and Firsts: Madison, Wisconsin, was created in 1836, when "former federal judge James Duane Doty purchased over a thousand acres of swamp and forest land on the isthmus between Lakes Mendota and Monona within the Four Lakes region, with the intention of building a city on the site.... Doty named the city Madison for James Madison, the 4th president of the U.S. who had died on June 28, 1836, and he named the streets for the other 38 signers of the U.S. Constitution."[246] Madison's inaugural ball was held in Long's Hotel in Washington, D.C. He and Dolley "were led into the hall to the martial air, 'Madison's March,' composed for the occasion."[247] James Madison University, "a public coeducational research university located in Harrisonburg, Virginia, was founded in 1908 as the State Normal and Industrial School for Women at Harrisonburg, the university has undergone four name changes before settling with James Madison University in 1976."[248]

Madison and Slavery: Like Jefferson, Madison found it difficult to live up to his ideals on the question of slavery. He believed that the institution was evil, but he was, nevertheless, dependent upon it. Madison referred to slavery as a "dreadful calamity" and a "sad blot on our free Country."[249] In a letter written at age 75, he asserted: "The magnitude of the evil among us is so deeply felt, and so universally acknowledged, that no merit could be greater than that of devising a satisfactory remedy for it."[250] In a speech in the House of Representatives on May 13, 1789, he stated: "It is to be hoped that by expressing a national disapprobation of this trade we may destroy it, and make ourselves free from reproaches and our posterity from the imbecility ever attendant on a country filled with slaves."[251] And in a letter to Marquis de Lafayette on February 1, 1830, Madison wrote: "Outlets for the freed blacks are alone wanted for the erasure of the blot from our Republican character."[252]

However, in another letter in 1823, containing his answers to 34 questions put to him on the question of slavery, Madison obviously feared and distrusted freed slaves. He felt slaves should not be freed, unless, "they are permanently removed beyond the region occupied by, or allotted to a white population."[253] Madison was a founding member and president of the American Colonization Society, which encouraged emigration of free blacks to Africa, after indemnifying the slave owners. In his will, Madison left $2,000 in trust to the society and the proceeds from the sale of his grist mill.[254] Madison raised the question of what to do with slaves during the drafting of the Constitution, but was persuaded to leave out measures that would have ultimately ended slavery as an institution.[255] Over the course of his lifetime, Madison owned more than 100 slaves who worked on his plantation. He told one of his overseers, "Treat the Negroes with all the humanity and kindness consistent with their necessary subordination and work."[256]

Many of his slaves were "trained in non-agricultural skills, including carpentry, smithing and brick-making." Through this work force, Madison directed the operation of a grist mill, a sawmill, a whiskey and brandy distillery, and a blacksmith shop. The enslaved also served in domestic roles as cooks, maids and gardeners. However, most were assigned to field labor or toiled around the main house.[257] Slavery remained a "moral dilemma for Madison, and he considered freeing his slaves at his death, but changed his mind in order to provide for his wife's later years."[258]

A Colored Man's Reminiscences of James Madison: Paul Jennings' pamphlet *A Colored Man's Reminiscences of James Madison* provided a "behind the scenes" portrait of the Father of the Constitution. Jennings, who was half English, one-eighth Native American and three-eighth African American, was Madison's slave and "body servant." Financially strapped, "Dolley sold Jennings to an insurance agent, who sold him to Sen. Daniel Webster for $120, who promptly set Jennings free and let him work off the debt as a servant in his home. After Jennings bought his freedom he organized an unsuccessful slave escape in 1848 in a schooner known as the *Pearl*."[259] He wrote of his association with the Madisons in a series of vignettes. Jennings denied the popular account of Dolley Madison refusing to leave the besieged presidential mansion until she had personally cut the large portrait of Washington from its frame and carried it off, barely avoiding the advancing redcoats. Jennings wrote it never happened, claiming she didn't have time and would have needed a ladder to do so. He reported that she did carry some of the silver but the portrait was rescued by the door-keeper and the gardener.[260]

Madison's Proposals for the Bill of Rights That Were Not Ratified: Several of Madison's suggestions for the Bill of Rights were not approved by Congress. When offering amendments, he proposed that the actual Constitution be revised by insertion, deletion or revision of articles and clauses. However, Congress chose to have the amendments recorded at the end of the Constitution, with footnotes signifying what portions of the body of the document had been amended.[261] Madison proposed that the amendment regarding the right to bear arms should include a clause recognizing the rights of what we would now call conscientious objectors: "No person religiously scrupulous of bearing arms should be compelled to render military service in person."[262] Although today, the rights of conscientious objectors are honored, they were not given the constitutional projection proposed by Madison.

Another of Madison's proposals not making the cut was a restriction on the states: "No state shall violate the equal rights of conscience, or the freedom of the press, or the trial by jury in criminal cases."[263] In the Bill of Rights, restrictions were only placed upon the federal government, not those of the states. Eventually they were extended to the states by the ratification of the 14th amendment and its interpretation by the Supreme Court.[264] Congress proposed twelve amendments, which they called "articles." Three-fourths of the States ratified articles three through twelve, which were renumbered from one to ten as the Bill of Rights.[265]

Not approved by Congress was Madison's proposal of Article the First, forbidding Congress to reduce the number of Representatives:

> After the first enumeration required by the first article of the Constitution, there shall be one Representative for every thirty thousand, until the number shall amount to one hundred, after which the proportion shall be so regulated by Congress, that there shall be not less than one hundred Representatives, nor less than one Representative for every forty thousand persons, until the number of Representatives shall amount to two hundred, after which the proportion shall be so regulated by Congress, that there shall not be less than two hundred Representatives, nor more than one Representative for every fifty thousand persons.[266]

Madison's other proposal that forbade an increase in Congressional pay until an election had intervened was approved by Congress but was not ratified by the states. In 1992, 160 years after the Bill of Rights, Madison's article became the 27th amendment ratified by the states; more than 200 years after Congress had approved it.[267]

Attempt to Establish a Library of Congress: On January 23, 1783, Madison chaired a committee that submitted a list of approximately 307 works, comprising 1,400 or more volumes to the Confederation Congress. The books, compiled by Madison, who was assisted by Jefferson, were described as "proper for the use of Congress."[268] Madison believed that it was essential that Congress should have a library of books on public law readily available at all times: "[Its expertise] would render ... their proceedings conformable to propriety; and it was observed that the want of this information was manifest in several important acts of Congress."[269]

The works suggested included many of the new and often radical Enlightenment writers such as Voltaire, Gibbon, Hume, Adams Smith and Priestly, as well as authorities such as Plato, Aristotle, Locke, Bacon, Montesquieu, Grotius, Coke and Blackstone. Madison's proposal was defeated because of "the inconsistency of advancing even a few hundred pounds at this crisis."[270]

An architectural drawing of the proposed plan for the facade of the Jefferson Building Library of Congress, created by architects Smithmeyer & Pelz ca. 1873 (Library of Congress).

Detached Memorandum: After he retired from public life, sometime between 1817 and 1823, Madison wrote what is known to scholars as his "Detached Memorandum," In it, he declared his opposition to the long established practice of hiring at public expense chaplains in the House of Representatives and the Senate. He argued that it violated the constitutionally mandated separation of church and state and set a dangerous precedent. Madison asked:

> Is the appointment of Chaplains to the two Houses of Congress consistent with the Constitution and with the pure principles of religious freedom? In strictness the answer to both points must be in the negative. The Constitution of the U.S. forbids everything like an establishment of a national religion. The law appointing Chaplains establishes a religious worship for the national representatives, to be performed by Ministers of religion, elected by a majority of them; and these are to be paid out of the national taxes. Does not this involve the principle of a national establishment, applicable to a provision for a religious worship for the Constituent as well as of the representative Body, approved by the majority, and conducted by Ministers of religion paid by the entire nation?[271]

Hollywood's Dolley: In 1946, Frank Borzage directed a story, which wrongly told of Dolley Payne's lack of love for her husband John Todd, and of her torn feelings about two love interests, firebrand Aaron Burr and idealistic James Madison. Burr solves the dilemma when he flees the country after killing Alexander Hamilton in a duel, leaving the field open for Madison. The film *Magnificent Doll*, based on an Irving Stone story and screenplay, bombed at the box office. Ginger Rogers was a fetching Dolley. David Niven was intense as Burr and Burgess Meredith gave a comfortable impersonation of Madison.[272]

Further Remarks by James Madison[273]

> Ambition must be made to counteract ambition [Remark on Jefferson's "Draught of a Constitution for Virginia," October 1788].
>
> I should not regret a fair and full trial of the entire abolition of capital punishment [Letter to G.F.H. Crockett, November 6, 1823].
>
> The class of citizens, who provide at once their own food and their own raiment, may be viewed as the most truly independent and happy ["Republican Distribution of Citizens," March 3, 1792].
>
> The circulation of confidence is better than the circulation of money [Speech at Virginia Convention, June 20, 1788].

Conscience is the most sacred of all property [*National Gazette*, March 29, 1792].

Whenever a youth is ascertained to possess talents meriting an education which his parents cannot afford, he should be carried forward at the public expense [*The Mind of the Founder*].

Equal laws protecting equal rights ... the best guarantee of loyalty & love of country [Letter to Jacob De La Motta, August, 1820].

I have ever regarded the freedom of religious opinions and worship as equally belonging to every sect [Letter to Mordecai Noah, May 15, 1818].

Geography is a preliminary, in all cases, to a pleasing and instructive course of historical readings [Letter to B. Chapman, January 25, 1821].

The advancement and diffusion of knowledge is the only guardian of true liberty [Letter to Samuel S. Lewis, February 16, 1829].

[I] t is proper to take alarm at the first experiment on our liberties ["Memorial and Remonstrance," 1785].

A certain degree of misery seems inseparable from a high degree of populousness [Letter to Jefferson, June 19, 1786].

Nothing is so contagious as opinion, especially on questions which, being susceptible of very different glosses, beget in the mind a distrust of itself [Letter to Benjamin Rush, March 7, 1790].

The most common and durable source of faction has been the various and unequal distribution of property ["Property," March 27, 1792].

Public opinion sets bounds to every government, and is the real sovereign in every free one [Written anonymously, December 19, 1791; *National Gazette*].

A silly reason from a wise man is never the true one [Letter to Richard Rush, June 27, 1817].

The rights of persons, and the rights of property, are the objects, for the protection of which Government was instituted [Speech at the Virginia Convention, 1829].

Religion and government will both exist in greater purity; the less they are mixed together [Letter to Edward Livingston, July 10, 1822].

Theories are the offspring of the closet; exceptions and qualifications are the lessons of experience [Letter to Charles J. Ingersoll, December 30, 1835].

A silent appeal to a cool and candid judgment of the public, may, perhaps, serve the cause of truth [Letter to Joseph C. Cabell, March 18, 1829].

Men cannot be justly bound by laws, in making which they have no share [Letter to Joseph Cabell, January 5, 1829].

Wherever there is interest and power to do wrong, wrong will generally be done [Letter to Jefferson, October 24, 1787].

Evaluations of James Madison

Pardon me if I add that I think him a little too much of a book politician, and too timid in his politics, for prudence and caution are opposites of timidity.[274]— Fisher Ames

Our President, tho a man of amiable manners and great talents, has not; I fear those outstanding talents, which are necessary to control those about him. He permits division in his cabinet.[275]— John C. Calhoun

Mr. Madison is wholly unfit for the storms of War. Nature has cast him in too benevolent a mould. Admirably adapted to the tranquil scenes of peace — blending all the mild amiable virtues, he is not fit for the rough and rude blasts which the conflicts of nations generate.[276]— Henry Clay

Mr. Madison ... rendered more important services to his country than any other man, Washington only excepted.[277]— Henry Clay

Mr. Madison is, as I always knew him, slow in taking his ground, but firm when the storm rises.[278]— Albert Gallatin

Never was a country left in a more flourishing situation than the United States at the end of your administration; and they are more united at home and respected abroad than at any period since the war of the independence.[279]— Albert Gallatin

No mind has stamped more of its impressions on American institutions.[280]— Charles Jarred Ingersoll

He always comes forward the best informed man of any point in debate. The affairs of the United States he perhaps has the most correct knowledge of any man in the Union.[281]— William Pierce

Madison's political career and influence rested, quite frankly, on the notion that a man who did his homework and thought through issues and alternatives before debate began could often lead his lazier colleagues— of whom there would always be many — along the avenues he had selected.[282]— Jack Rakove

...[S]timulating everything in the manner worthy of a little commander-in-chief, with his little round hat and huge cockade.[283]— Richard Rush

[Madison was frequently misjudged by] those who failed to see that his modesty and reticence concealed a strong will and rare talents.[284]— Harold Seessel Schultz

I do not like his looks any better than I like his Administration.[285]— Daniel Webster

He had as much as any man in framing the constitution, and as much to do as any man administering it.[286]— Daniel Webster

Madison's claim on our admiration does not rest on a perfect consistency, any more than it rests on his presidency. He has other virtues.... As a framer and defender of the Constitution he had no peer.... The finest part of Madison's performance as president was his concern for the preserving of the Constitution.... No man could do everything for his country ... not even Washington. Madison did more than most, and did some things better than any. That was quite enough.[287]— Garry Wills

FIVE

James Monroe
The Last of the Cocked Hats

Fifth President of the United States, 1817–1825

James Monroe attempted to have an administration that rose above party to unite and develop the growing nation. During the summer of his first term, as Washington had done earlier, Monroe toured New England, the region where many had opposed the War of 1812. Monroe characterized the journey as an inspection tour of naval armaments, but most knew it was a fence-mending expedition. It was so effective that the *Boston Columbian Centinel*, a Federalist newspaper, termed his reception in Massachusetts as the start of an "era of good feelings," and the appellation stuck.[1]

Birth: James Monroe's birth was on April 28, 1758, in a four room dwelling in Westmoreland County, Virginia, near the head of Monroe's Creek, which empties into the Potomac River. His birthplace, where he lived until he was sixteen, was only four miles from that of George Washington.

Nicknames and Titles: Monroe was called "The Last Cocked Hat,"[2] a reference to the fact that he was the last political figure who fought in the Revolutionary War, when some militia members wore such hats. He was also known as "Era-of-Good-Feelings President," "James the Second" and "James the Lesser." As president, Monroe preferred to be addressed as "Colonel." He was proud of his service during the War for Independence.[3]

Family: Spence Monroe (born c. 1727) was a farmer and cabinetmaker of Scottish descent. The family farm consisted of approximately 500 acres. The homestead produced cattle, tobacco, corn and barley. The family was considered moderately wealthy, enjoying standing as "landed gentry"[4] on the Northern Neck. Spence died when James was about 16. James and his brothers inherited shared ownership of the farm, which they sold in 1783. Elizabeth Jones Monroe (born c. 1729) from King County, Virginia, was of Welsh descent and because she was not referred to in Spence's will it is assumed that she predeceased her husband by a few months in 1774. Elizabeth was remembered as "a very amicable and respectful woman, possessing the best domestic qualities of a wife, and a good parent."[5]

Her father, James, was an architect and her brother Joseph was a judge and one of the most prominent leaders of the revolutionary era. The judge assumed the guardianship and advisorship of the Monroe children. Joseph Jones paid the cost of James Monroe's education at the College of William & Mary.[6] James was the second of five children to live to maturity. He had one older sister, Mrs. Elizabeth Buckner, and three younger brothers—Spence Monroe who died early, Andrew and Joseph, who served as his brother's private secretary when James was president.

James Monroe, painted by C.B. King, engraved by Goodman & Piggot, Philadelphia: W.H. Morgan, Dec. 15, 1817 (*By Popular Demand: Portraits of the Presidents and First Ladies*, Library of Congress).

Ancestors: James's branch of the Monroe family arrived in America from Scotland in the mid–17th century. "In 1650, Major Andrew Monroe, son of David Munro of Katewall, (Scotland) patented a large tract of land in Washington Parish, Westmoreland County, Virginia. He built Monrovia, also known as Monroe Hall, on Monroe Creek, a tributary of the Potomac River"[7] on the grounds of the site of the present-day University of Virginia. The plantation was cultivated by three generations of Monroes. Andrew's son William was Spence Monroe's grandfather. "Spence traced his ancestry back to King Edward III of England. James' great-grandfather Ambrose, who fought on the side of King Charles I, in the English Civil Wars, was taken prisoner and exiled to Virginia."[8]

Lieutenant Colonel James Monroe wearing a cocked hat (Painting by Chet Jezierski, National Guard Image Gallery).

Appearance: Monroe stood a bit more than 6 feet tall, with broad shoulders, a rough-hewn frame and regular features. He had "grayish-blue eyes and a lined face that conveyed an expression of kindness."[9] Historian Harry Ammon described him as president: "[He wore] the small clothes of an earlier age — usually a black coat, black knee breeches, and black silk hose. On ceremonial occasions he sometimes wore a blue coat and buff breeches, an outfit reminiscent of the Revolutionary era."[10] He completed his image with buckled shoes.

Personality and Character: Monroe was admired for his humility, decorum and what Chief Justice Joseph Story called his "plain and gentle manners."[11] James was an extremely private person. His contemporaries spoke highly of his sensible judgment, his honesty, and his kindness. Neither an intellectual nor an innovator, "his talent laid in practical implementation of ideals and policies."[12] Although not personally charismatic and devoid of the political genius of his predecessors, Monroe could "work with men of varied character and ability."[13] He was not known for his oratory nor did the importance of his writing remotely approach the brilliance of Adams, Jefferson and Madison. Colonel Monroe failed to be promoted to a field command in the Revolutionary War because, rather than being a man of action, he was described as "a deliberate, even slow, thinker. Monroe gathered ideas and advice from associates and subordinates. This practice was continued as President where he withheld his decisions until he had a chance to consider all alternatives, but nonetheless he was praised for his sound judgment."[14] A practical administrator, Monroe worked to carve out a national identity. As the nation was experiencing its first real peaceful era, Monroe assumed the presidency at a time of fiscal stability and a widespread feeling of national prosperity. "Monroe had the unique opportunity of working in a positive way to realize the long held aspirations of the nation."[15]

Marriage and Romances: There is little surviving evidence of any early romances of

James Monroe before meeting and marrying Elizabeth Kortright (1768–1830) on February 16, 1786. She was only 17 and he was 27.[16]

They honeymooned on Long Island and lived with her father in New York City. Upon Monroe's retirement from Congress in 1786, they returned to Virginia, where he practiced law, living first in Fredericksburg, and then in Charlottesville to be near his dear friend Thomas Jefferson.

When Monroe was elected to the U.S. Senate, the temporary capital of New York was moved to Philadelphia. While her husband was thus occupied, Mrs. Monroe spent most of the time in New York, visiting her sisters and their families. Elizabeth was the daughter of wealthy West Indian merchant, Lawrence Kortright, and his wife Hannah Aspinwall Kortright. Kortright made a fortune as a British privateer during the French and Indian War, but it had "largely been destroyed during the Revolution."[17] Elizabeth's paternal ancestry line traces to Bastian Van Kortryk, a Belgian, who immigrated to Holland around 1615. On her mother's side, Elizabeth was related to the Roosevelts. Elizabeth had three sisters — Hester, Mary and Sarah — and one brother John. "Much admired for her beauty, the elegance of her dress, and the refinement of her polished, if rather formal, manners, she brought to Monroe the happiness of family life so much prized by his generation. In the terms of the age, she conducted herself as an ideal wife should, devoted to her children and never obtruding in political concerns."[18]

Mrs. Monroe accompanied her husband on his mission as Minister to France and immediately fell in love with Paris and its people. Much as was the case with Jackie Kennedy

at a later time, Elizabeth was the darling of both the local and diplomatic communities. During the final days of the French Revolution, she was instrumental in saving the Marquis de Lafayette's wife, Adrienne de Noailles de Lafayette, from the guillotine. In the American Embassy's carriage, Mrs. Monroe went to the prison and asked to see Madame Lafayette. When the French authorities were made aware of the Elizabeth's "unofficial" interest in Adrienne, the prisoner was set free.[19]

Both Monroes were very popular in France, with Elizabeth being known as *la belle Americaine*.[20] "By their dignified manner, and through the relationships built by the Monroes, many foreign nations came to accept the establishment of the United States as not only a new nation, but a powerful and sophisticated one that was carrying out the principals of democracy."[21]

Elizabeth did not participate during her husband's two presidential campaigns and she was not present at either the swearing-in ceremonies nor did she hold receptions in her home. Throughout her

Elizabeth Kortright Monroe, a photographic print of an oil painting attributed to Benjamin West (illustration in Lila G.A. Woolfall, *Presiding Ladies of the White House*, 1903, published by Bureau of National Literature and Art. Library of Congress).

husband's presidency, Elizabeth suffered from poor health and as a result she limited her social activities. She suffered from what was then called "the falling sickness"[22] of epilepsy. Little was known of the causes of the illness, but it was often viewed as sign of possible demonic possession and at the very least a form of mental illness. Those suffering from the disease were usually stigmatized so Elizabeth's family hid the details of her malady.[23] As a result Mrs. Monroe was viewed as reserved and rather cold in her manner, although in private, she was a loving wife and mother. While living in France, she espoused the mannerisms of the French upper class. When she became the "first lady" of a nation that at least in theory, embraces social equality, her stately manners were not poorly received. When she did host social gatherings at the president's mansion, Mrs. Monroe sat on a raised platform to receive guests. Monroe's political enemies dubbed her "Queen Elizabeth."[24]

It could not have been easy for Elizabeth Monroe to follow the "hostess with the mostest" Dolley Madison, so perhaps she did not even try to compete for popularity. She was totally absorbed in the affairs of her family and household and isolated herself from the world of politics. Her White House dinners were served "English style,"[25] with one servant for each guest. When alone, the Monroe family spoke only French. After her husband left the presidency, Elizabeth suffered a seizure and collapsed near an open fireplace, suffering severe burns.[26] She lived only three years after the accident, dying on September 23, 1830, at their Oak Hill estate.[27] At her death James burned the letters of their life together.[28] A despondent Monroe predicted he would not live much longer — he died ten months later.

Children: The Monroes had three children: Eliza Kortright (1786–1835), James Spence (1799–1800) and Mariah Hester (1803–1850). While James was Minister to France, Eliza studied at a fashionable French school run by Madame Campan, who once had been a lady-in-waiting to the tragic Queen Marie Antoinette. Eliza married George Hay, a successful Virginia lawyer. She was described as a "haughty, pompous socialite quick to remind others of her good breeding and lofty station."[29] This worked to her detriment, when she assumed the role of substitute hostess for her father because of her mother's poor health. Eliza alienated most of Washington's society by declining to follow the expected custom of calling on the wives of congressmen and members of the diplomatic corps.[30]

However, during a fever epidemic that swept through Washington, she demonstrated her true worth by tenderly caring for its victims. After the passing of her father and her husband, Eliza returned to France, converted to Catholicism, and lived in a convent.[31] Monroe's only son James died in infancy, a crushing blow for James Sr. Maria was only fourteen when her father was elected president. She became the first presidential child to be married in the president's mansion, marrying her cousin Samuel Gouverneur in 1820. Eliza took charge of her sister's wedding, further angering Cabinet members and foreign diplomats by pronouncing that guests at the ceremony and reception would be restricted to family and a limited number of friends. After the wedding, Maria and her husband settled in New York City.[32]

Religion and Religious Beliefs: Monroe was baptized in Washington Parish in Westmoreland County and raised in the Church of England when it was the established state religion of Virginia. After winning independence from Great Britain, the denomination dropped the word "England" and adopted the term Episcopal (essentially meaning "we have bishops") and renamed their denomination the Protestant Episcopal Church in the United States of America.[33] As an adult, Monroe often attended Episcopal services, even temporarily serving as a vestryman of St. George's parish at Fredericksburg, but there is no record that he had been a communicant.[34] Monroe's public statements and speeches were curiously free of religious references. Author Bliss Isley wrote: "When it comes to Monroe's ... thoughts on religion less is known than that of any other President."[35] Historian and Monroe biographer Daniel C. Gilman stated, "He was extremely reticent in his religious sentiments, at least in all that he wrote. Allusions to his belief are rarely, if ever, to be met with in his correspondence."[36]

Surviving family letters contain no mention of his beliefs or of religion. In his inaugural addresses Monroe made references such as "the Supreme Author of All Good," "Providence," and "Almighty God."[37] It is possible that Monroe was a deist as were Washington, Jefferson, and probably Madison, his Virginian predecessors as president. "From the late 17th century on, a school of religious thought called Deism existed in England and on the Continent. It emerged from the Enlightenment, a complex movement of ideas marked by an emphasis on rationalism as well as a self-confident challenge of traditional political, religious, and social ideas. The scientific and philosophical work of three Englishmen — Francis Bacon, Isaac Newton, and John Locke — undergirded the Enlightenment."[38] In Virginia, the center of Deism was the College of William & Mary.[39] Bishop William Meade, an orthodox Virginian Episcopalian recalled: "At the end of the (18th) century, the College of William and Mary was regarded as the hotbed of infidelity and of the wild politics of France."[40]

Monroe seemed to have attended Episcopal services, not for religious uplifting, but rather because it was expected of the gentry. "The Episcopal Church ministered to the Monroe family and claimed them as its own. But the surviving evidence indicates that Monroe was not a Christian in the traditional sense. Neither his private nor his public writings suggest that he ever experienced a sense of the mystery or awe that is at the heart of orthodox Christianity. No evidence exists to show that he was an active or emotionally engaged Christian. How the Anglican interpretation of Christianity influenced his character and personality, and what depths of religious feelings he may have experienced while attending worship, scholars may never know.... James Monroe seems to have been an Episcopalian of deistic tendencies who valued civic virtues above religious doctrine. No one cared more for the identity of the new nation. His passion always seems to have been directed towards the cause of the United States."[41]

He also was a Freemason, the secret religious society that guarded the secrets of the craft of masons. "The ties between Deism and Freemasonry were close. Freemasonry ... probably originated in England in the 12th century.... Over the centuries it developed into a secret international fraternity concerned with the moral and religious improvement of its members.... In Roman Catholic countries, the Masonic lodges tended to form an underground movement antagonistic not only towards Roman Catholicism but also towards organized religion in general.... Freemasonry tended to require a belief in a monotheistic God ... and to advocate an undogmatic religion that claimed to represent the essence of all religions. [It] gave a preeminent place neither to the Bible nor to Jesus ... anyone who could accept its statements about a divine being — could belong. When the founding fathers use such terms as 'the Grand Architect' to speak of God, they are using language that comes directly from Freemasonry and not from the Bible."[42]

In his first inaugural address, Monroe extolled the idea of religious freedom, boasting that Americans are free to worship "the Divine Author" in any way they choose. In his address, he declared that "the favor of a gracious Providence"[43] guided the United States, and he concluded his speech by saying: "I enter on the trust to which I have been called by the suffrages of my fellow-citizens with my fervent prayers to the Almighty that He will be graciously pleased to continue to us that protection which He has already so conspicuously displayed in our favor."[44]

In his final message to Congress, President Monroe stated: "Deeply impressed with the blessing which we enjoy, and of which we have much manifold proofs, my mind is irresistibly drawn to that Almighty Being, the great source from whence they proceed and whom our most grateful acknowledgments are due."[45]

As further evidence of Monroe's casual religious convictions: "When his only son, James Spence Monroe, died at the age of 16 months in 1800, Monroe was clearly crushed. The funeral service and burial were at St. John's Episcopal Church, Richmond, the family church when Monroe was governor. But the letters Monroe wrote to others about his little son's death include no references to the consolation of religion. When his wife Elizabeth died in 1830, Monroe wrote to a number of their friends saying how devastating her death was, but failed to mention any religious beliefs that may have proved comforting."[46]

Education: James Monroe was tutored at home until he was twelve, at which point he attended the Academy at Kirnan run by Archibald Campbell, rector of Washington Parish, "a disciplinarian of the sternest type"[47] who taught the young Monroe a severe moral code, which he followed throughout his life. "One of his classmates was his neighbor, John Marshall, later the Chief Justice of the United States. The two boys walked the several miles to school and back each day, sometimes taking their rifles and shooting game on the way."[48] Monroe excelled in Latin and mathematics. In 1774, Monroe enrolled at the College of William & Mary, the first member of his family to attend college. At William & Mary Monroe participated in revolutionary activities. "He joined a group of students when they raided the royal governor's mansion, securing arms and munitions" consisting of 230 muskets, 301 swords and 187 pistols, "for the Virginia militia. He left William & Mary to join the Continental Army at the age of 17."[49]

Occupation: Monroe was a professional politician. From his 18th to his 73rd year, he was almost continually in public service. "He had found [the nation] built of brick," John Quincy Adams declared in his eulogy of Monroe, "and left her constructed of marble."[50]

Military: As a young man about to embark upon a hazardous frontier journey, Monroe told his friends: "It is possible I may lose my scalp from the temper of the Indians, but if either a little fighting or a great deal of running will save it, I shall escape safe."[51] Monroe did no running but fought with distinction during the Revolutionary War, first as a lieutenant and later he was promoted to captain for "conspicuous gallantry."[52] He was with Washington at Valley Forge and was appointed a lieutenant colonel by the Virginia legislature. Monroe was portrayed holding the flag in the famous Emanuel Gottlieb Leutze's painting of Washington crossing the Delaware on Christmas.[53] He had the same honor in an illustration by A.M. Turner and Harriet Kaucher for the book *George Washington*.[54]

The next day, Monroe was second in command of an advance party that crossed the Delaware ahead of the Washington's main forces. His group secured the roads to Trenton. An incidence along the Pennington road to Trenton was fortuitous for Monroe. "Lieutenant Monroe met a Jersey man who came out to see why his dogs were barking. Monroe remembered that the man thought 'we were from the British army, and ordered us off.... He was violent and determined in his manner, and very profane.' Monroe told him to go back to his home or be taken prisoner. When the man realized that he was talking to American troops, his manner suddenly changed. He brought them food and offered to join them. 'I'm a doctor,' he explained, 'and I may be of help to some poor fellow.' The offer was accepted, and Doctor John Riker joined Monroe's infantry as a surgeon-volunteer."[55] During the battle in Trenton, Monroe, at age 18, was severely wounded while attacking the Hessians. A musket ball "grazed the left side of his chest, then hit his shoulder and injured the major artery carrying blood to the arm. He was carried from the field, bleeding dangerously. His life was saved by Doctor Riker, who had joined Monroe's company as a volunteer the night before.[56] Surgeons attempted to remove the bullet, but were unable to locate it, so Monroe carried it in his shoulder for the rest of his life."[57]

For Monroe, "the Revolution was the great struggle of his age, and he consciously used it as a symbol of national unity." He used his "power and patronage of the office of president to help Revolutionary War veterans and their families."[58] As president, "Monroe viewed the future of the young republic through the lens of ... defense or national security."[59]

Lawyer: Monroe studied law with then governor Thomas Jefferson at Williamsburg, and the two became life-long friends. At the time Monroe was living at his late mother's farm, The Glebe of Handover, a 300 acre property that he would inherit.[60] Monroe practiced law in Fredericksburg, Virginia. The Monroe Law Office Museum at 908 Charles Street has been restored and is open to the public. The brick building, once believed to be his law office, is not old enough to have been in existence when James Monroe was practicing, but it stands on the actual site of Monroe's law offices and is in itself a well-preserved example of a Federal period office structure.[61]

The museum, owned by the Commonwealth is administered by Mary Washington College. The "majority of objects housed at the James Monroe Museum are part of the Laurence Gouverneur Hoes Collection, named for one of the co-founders of the museum, and its first director. The object collections include over 1,600 artifacts ranging from personal items such as jewelry and clothing, to fine arts, to decorative arts such as furniture and china (including the desk where he wrote his famous doctrine, the dress Mrs. Monroe wore at Napoleon's coronation as Emperor of France, and the china and silver the Monroes used at the White House). Most of the objects placed in the museum by Rose and Laurence Hoes in 1927 descended through James Monroe's youngest daughter, Maria Hester Monroe Gouverneur and her children."[62]

Home: In 1793 Monroe purchased Highland plantation in Albemarle County, Virginia, which originally was called Blenheim when it was owned by Champe Carter and his wife Maria.[63] "Thomas Jefferson, who lived only two and a half miles away at Monticello, selected the house's location and helped design it. In fact, an early letter written by Jefferson while in Europe to Monroe exists, in which Jefferson asks Monroe, 'What measures have you taken for establishing yourself near Monticello?' Monroe's 'cabin castle' as he called it, was once part of a 1,000-acre plantation."[64]

Because of Monroe's senatorial and diplomatic duties, the family did not occupy their new home until November 23, 1799.[65] The 3500 acre estate that Monroe operated for 24 years was his primary source of income. "The Monroe family considered Highland its home for a quarter century. Monroe intended Highland to be a working farm. To increase its productivity, he experimented with diverse crops and planting methods, becoming, like Jefferson, an early advocate of scientific agriculture. In addition to his principal crops of timber, tobacco, and grain, he, also like Jefferson, tried to cultivate Bordeaux grapes for wine, a frustrating endeavor for all farmers until modern agricultural methods were developed."[66] The property is now owned by the College of William & Mary.[67] Monroe also "purchased 50,000 acres of land in the wilderness of Kentucky," in hope of developing property west of the Appalachian Mountains.[68] He was unable to fulfill his dream to retire to Highland, as he was forced to sell it to satisfy his creditors. He described the 3,500 acres Highland as a "commodious dwelling house, buildings for servants and other domestic purposes, good stables, two barns with threshing machine, a grist and sawmill with houses for managers and laborers ... all in good repair."[69] Monroe then settled on his plantation of Oak Hill in Loudoun County, Virginia, where he lived after retirement until the year before his death.[70]

Recreational Pastimes: Monroe and his family enjoyed playing games such as draughts (checkers), chess, dominoes and various card games. He was also fond of horseback riding, but like James Madison before him he had no hobbies and played no sports while president.[71]

POLITICAL OFFICES

In 1782, Monroe was elected to the House of Burgesses from King George County. "His abilities were immediately recognized by the established leaders in the state, and the next year he was appointed a member of the Virginia delegation to the Continental Congress, serving from 1783 to 1786."[72]

Political Philosophy and Political Party Affiliation: Monroe joined the "anti–Federalists at the Virginia Convention that ratified the U.S. Constitution and in 1790." As "an advocate of Jeffersonian policies, Monroe was elected United States Senator," thus becoming a member of the Democratic-Republican Party.[73]

The Federalist Party all but vanished after the fiasco of the Hartford Convention, where the New England states threatened to secede from the Union over the War of 1812.[74] Biographer Harry Ammon described the fifth president: "[He is] a man of rather pedestrian abilities, but with a highly developed sense of republican principles and political drive who was much more instrumental in directing U.S. policy than traditionally given credit for."[75]

Monroe was neither a philosophical nor a highly intellectual individual. He was a "practical, problem-solving man, effective working on realistic matters. Monroe's style was to seek consensus, solve problems and be diplomatic. He worked to achieve the revolutionary ideal of a representative government based on free institutions."[76] He considered party divisions to be destructive to republicanism. Monroe was a "nationalist in diplomacy and defense, supported a limited executive branch of the federal government, distrusted a strong central government in domestic matters, extolled the advantages of industrious farmers and craftsmen, and advocated the republican virtue that the needs of the public should be paramount over personal greed and party ambition."[77]

In his first inaugural address, Monroe instructed the nation:

> Equally gratifying is it to witness the increased harmony of opinion which pervades our Union. Discord does not belong to our system. Union is recommended as well by the free and benign principles of our Government extending its blessings to every individual, as by the other eminent advantages attending it. The American people have encountered together great dangers and sustained severe trials with success. They constitute one great family with a common interest.... To promote this harmony in accord with the principles of our republican Government and in a manner to give them the most complete effect, and to advance in all respects the best interests of our Union, will be the object of my constant and zealous exertions.[78]

The Continental Congress: A proponent of western expansion, Monroe led the successful fight to convince Congress not to ratify the Jay-Gardoqui treaty proposals with Spain, which "took away all rights of the United States to sail the Mississippi River."[79] "During a congressional recess in 1784, Monroe journeyed through the Western territories, going up the Hudson River, passing through the Great Lakes, visiting the forts the British still held in the Northwest Territory, in violation of the Treaty of Paris, He returned by way of the Ohio River."[80] His tour made him aware of the feeling in the west that the eastern states were not just indifferent but was in fact actively hostile to the interests of the area. Monroe was convinced that Congress must promptly set up a governmental system and establish clear rules for the admission of new states. "He went back to Congress convinced from what he saw that the existing policy for the Western territory embodied in the ordinance of 1784 was impolitic due to smallness of the states projected. In effect, the first successful attempt to regulate the territory North-West of the Ohio River was the so-called Ordinance of 1784 attributed mainly to Jefferson but never actually applied. Therefore, Monroe motioned in Congress for a reduction in the number of states to be created out of the Northwest Territory."[81] Monroe's proposal was finally approved when Congress enacted the Northwest Ordinance of 1787.[82]

Monroe thought the Articles of Confederation needed a thorough overhaul. Yet, he voted against ratification of the Constitution on the grounds that it established excessive federal power and lacked a bill of rights; he also felt that the document should allow for "appointment to the Senate by population and the direct election of the president."[83] However, after the Constitution was ratified, he supported it. He referred to the Bill of Rights:

> The following appears to be the most important objects of such an instrument. It should more especially comprise a doctrine in favor of the equality of human rights; of the liberty of conscience in matters of religious faith, of speech and of the press; of the trial by jury of the vicinage in civil and criminal cases; of the benefit of the writ of habeas corpus; of the right to keep and bear arms.... [I]f these rights are well defined, and secured against encroachment, it is impossible that government should ever degenerate into tyranny.[84]

United States Senate: Monroe was elected U.S. senator from Virginia, serving from 1790 to 1794. He was the first U.S. senator to be elected to the presidency. "He was closely aligned with Jefferson and James Madison in opposition to the Federalist faction led by John Adams and Alexander Hamilton."[85]

Minister to France: Monroe resigned from the Senate to become George Washington's Minister to France (1794–1796). He opposed Jay's Treaty, which favored Great Britain and outraged France. Monroe was recalled by an angry Washington following the treaty's ratification for publicly voicing enthusiasm for the French Revolution. "Washington's advisors believed that Monroe had not tried hard enough to justify the need for Jay's Treaty to the French."[86] Monroe published a vindication of his behavior as minister, "asserting that the administration was seeking to join England in the war against France."[87] During Jefferson's presidency, Monroe returned to Europe as Minister to France and England (1803–1807). Later, with Robert R. Livingston, he negotiated the Louisiana Purchase, which "catapulted him to fame" for his role in the purchase.[88]

For the next four years Monroe's diplomatic efforts in Spain and England were far less successful. The United States and Spain argued over the exact boundaries of the Louisiana Purchase. "The Spanish controlled territory to the south and west of the Louisiana Purchase, and also controlled Florida."[89] Monroe was unable to negotiate the cession of Florida to the United States. A greater failure was the unsatisfactory treaty he and William Pinckney concluded with Great Britain. American expectations for the treaty were to improve trade and diminish maritime tensions. The United States wished for "increased commercial access to British markets in the West Indies and the revision of British policies on neutral shipping and impressment. While Britain made some concessions on trade, it refused to relinquish the right to stop foreign vessels and search their crews for deserters from the British navy."[90] President Jefferson, knowing that a treaty without a ban on impressment would never be accepted, did not even send it to the Senate for ratification.[91]

Louisiana Purchase, 1803, depicts the third signing of the Louisiana Treaty, which occurred in the New Orleans Cabildo and was the formal transfer of the purchased lands to the United States. Ever-Greene Painting Studios oil on canvas applied to the ceiling, 1993–1994 (Architect of the Capitol).

Governor of Virginia: Monroe successfully ran for governor of Virginia (1799–1802), where he demonstrated great administrative ability and won praise for his decisive action in suppressing an 1800 slave uprising, known as Gabriel's Insurrection.[92] That year, Monroe tried to defeat a yellow fever epidemic by closing all Virginia ports to Norfolk shipping, unless the vessels passed quarantine.[93] After returning to the United States from Europe in 1807, where he served as Jefferson's special envoy to France and minister to Great Britain,[94] Monroe served three additional one-year terms as governor of Virginia.[95] A split in the Virginia Republicans led to two caucuses in 1808. The Regular Republicans led by Jefferson unanimously nominated James Madison. The other caucus consisting of older Republicans and Jefferson's mortal enemy John Randolph nominated Monroe.[96] He did not seem to "cherish the illusion that he could defeat Madison."[97] He maintained his only purpose in allowing his friends to nominate him for president "was to show by attracting a sufficiently large following that he commanded the respect and loyalty of people of his state."[98] Jefferson wrote to Monroe that his refusal to disavow challenging Madison might lead to a rupture of the friendship of the two men. It did indeed. Monroe's decision did not ruin the close relationship that he had with Jefferson. The differences were eventually patched up when Madison chose Monroe to be his secretary of state in 1811.[99]

Cabinet Positions: Monroe was the only U.S. president to have served in two different cabinet posts. In 1814, as the British troops advanced on the capital, Monroe ensured that State Department papers, which included the Declaration of Independence, were taken to Virginia for safekeeping.[100] With the burning of Washington, President Madison fired Secretary of War John Armstrong, Jr., and gave Monroe the additional duties of military commander of the city and secretary of war (1814–1815).[101] Monroe left Madison's cabinet in 1815 to run for president. In his capacity as secretary of state, Monroe wrote to Henry Fox, Lord Holland, protesting Britain's "new crusade" against Napoleonic France:

> Our countries are now at peace and I am satisfied that you will unite with me, in a strong desire, that they may long remain so. I well know the interest which you take, in the preservation of free government in both countries, and indeed elsewhere, wherever it may be possible to maintain if a new storm seems to threaten Europe and perhaps this country. Why this second crusade against France? Has not that country a right to choose its own sovereign, and indeed to establish its own government?[102]

His Presidency

When Monroe was chosen as his party's nominee for the presidency, Aaron Burr lambasted Monroe's presidential candidacy in a letter to his son-in-law, the governor of South Carolina:

> The man himself is one of the most improper and incompetent that could have been selected — naturally dull and stupid — extremely illiterate — indecisive to a degree that would be incredible to one who did not know him — pusillanimous and of course hypocritical — has no opinion on any subject and will be always under the government of the worst men — pretends, as I am told, to some knowledge of military matters, but never commanded a platoon nor was ever fit to command one — "He served in the revolutionary War" — that is, he acted a short time as aide de camp to Lord Stirling who was regularly drunk from morning to morning — Monroe's whole duty was to fill his lordship's tankard and hear with indications of admiration his lordship's long stories about himself — Such is Monroe's military experience.... As a lawyer, Monroe was far below mediocrity — He never rose to the honor of trying a case of the value of an hundred pounds.[103]

The last of the founding fathers to serve as president, Monroe defeated William H. Crawford of Georgia for the presidential nomination at the Democratic-Republican convention and was elected president the first time in 1816 with 183 electoral votes to his Federalist opponent Rufus King's 34.[104]

It was the last hurrah for the Federalist Party. Monroe's inauguration was the first held outside and the first at which the U.S. Marine Band played "Yankee Doodle," beginning a tradition that survives.[105] In his inaugural speech, he viewed the United States as a self-sufficient independent state:

> Our manufacturers will ... require the systematic and fostering care of the Government. Possessing as we do all the raw materials, the fruit of our own soil and industry, we ought not to depend in the degree we have on supplies from other countries. While we are thus dependent the sudden event of war, unsought and unexpected, can not fail to plunge us into the most serious difficulties. It is important, too, that the capital which nourishes our manufacturers should be domestic, as its influence in that case instead of exhausting, as it may in foreign hands, would be felt advantageously on agriculture and every other branch of industry. Equally important is to provide a home market for our raw materials, as by expanding the competition it will enhance the price and protect the cultivator against the casualties incident to foreign markets.[106]

In his second inaugural address, President Monroe remarked as follows:

> Having no pretensions to the high and commanding claims of my predecessors, whose names are so much more conspicuously identified with our Revolution, and who contributed so preeminently

Left: John E. Howard of Maryland, c. 1834 steel engraving by E. Prud'homme after a painting by Chester Harding, copyrighted by James Herring. *Right:* Rufus King, etching by Albert Rosenthal, 1888, after a painting in the Trumbull collection (both images, Library of Congress).

to promote its success, I consider myself rather as the instrument than the cause of the union which has prevailed in the late election.... I have never dreaded, nor have I ever shunned, in any situation in which I have been placed making appeals to the virtue and patriotism of my fellow-citizens, well knowing that they could never be made in vain, especially in times of great emergency or for purposes of high national importance.[107]

The President's Home: The Presidential Mansion was still being rebuilt after being destroyed by the British during the War of 1812. In the interim, the Monroes resided at a house built in 1808 at 2017 I Street, NW. It survives and now is the home of the Arts Club of Washington, open to the public.[108] On January 1, 1818, President and Mrs. Monroe held a public reception celebrating the reopening of the chief executive's home.[109] The house was painted white, leading to its later designation as the White House. As all possessions had been lost in the blaze, the Monroes sold their own elegant furniture, purchased in France, to the government for $9,000 to furnish the president's home.[110] The charred remains of the mansion's interior were used to fill a pit on top of which Monroe planted a vegetable garden. The pit was unearthed by archaeologists at the time President Ford's swimming pool was built.[111]

Old Glory: In 1818 President Monroe signed legislation establishing the Flag of the United States. Congress fixed the number of stripes of the "Stars and Stripes" flag at 13 to honor the original colonies and a star for each state in the Union.[112]

Presidential Election of 1820: In 1820, Monroe ran unopposed and received all but one electoral vote. According to some sources one New Hampshire elector, Governor George Plummer, wishing George Washington to be the only president elected unanimously, cast his vote for John Quincy Adams. Even if the story was true, there would be no way for Plummer to know how other electors voted. According to Plummer's family sources, he didn't cast his ballot for Monroe because he didn't like Monroe.[113] Commenting on Monroe's reelection, Congressman Henry Clay observed, "Mr. Monroe has just been re-elected with apparent unanimity, but he has not the slightest influence in Congress. His career was considered closed. There was nothing further to be expected by him or from him."[114]

His Vice President: Daniel D. Tompkins was a congressman and governor of New York and the sixth vice president of the United States. A graduate of Columbia University he studied law and was admitted to the bar in 1797, practicing in New York City. He was a member to the state constitutional convention in 1801 and a member of the state assembly. Elected to the House of Representatives, he resigned to accept an appointment as an associate justice of the Supreme Court, serving from 1804 to 1807, followed by terms as governor between 1807 and 1817. He served as James Monroe's vice president for two terms.[115]

A bit of trivia about Tompkins is that in the classic 1947 movie *A Miracle on 34th Street*, trying to impress a questioner while being given a psychological evaluation, Edmund Gwenn, portraying Kris Kringle, erroneously ticked off the name of Tompkins as having served as John Quincy Adams' vice president. The screenwriter's mistake was that he apparently believed that the 6th vice president served with the 6th president, which was not the case, as Jefferson had two different vice presidents.[116]

Daniel D. Tompkins, 1774–1825, an 1892 portrait of New York's fourth governor, from a digital representation of page 19 of the 1892 *New York Red Book*, New York State Archives. Engraving by T. Woolworth after a painting by John Wesley Jarvis, in Woodrow Wilson, *History of the American People*, p. 239. Best Books, January 1918 (Library of Congress).

His Cabinet: Secretary of State John Quincy Adams (1817–1825); Secretary of War John C. Calhoun (1817–1825); Postmaster General Return J. Meigs, Jr. (1817–1823), and John McLean (1823–1825); Secretary of the Treasury William H. Crawford (1817–1825); Attorney General Richard Rush (1817) and William Wirt (1817–1825); Secretary of the Navy Benjamin W. Crowninshield (1817–1818), Smith Thompson (1819–1823), and Samuel L. Southard (1823–1825).

Supreme Court Appointments: Smith Thompson of New York (1823–1843).

States Admitted to the Union: Mississippi (1817), Illinois (1818), Alabama (1819), Maine (1820), Missouri (1821).

DOMESTIC AFFAIRS — MAJOR EVENTS

The Era of Good Feelings: Monroe's primary domestic objective was to promote national unity.[117] The War of 1812 proved divisive, as New England suffered especially because its maritime industry was destroyed by the Royal Navy. Monroe's administration was marked by the lessening of partisan political bickering, a feeling of prosperity, and a sense of national unity, although it didn't last very long.[118] Even though there was but one political party, there were sectional issues on such vital issues as the tariff, the extension of slavery and foreign affairs.[119] On the domestic front, the Missouri Compromise temporarily reduced tensions over slavery in new states, but before long they heated up again.[120] Europe was at peace with the exile of Napoleon to St. Helena. The country grew both in population and territory. It occupied all the land east of the Rocky Mountains and south of the Great Lakes except for Florida and Spanish Mexico.[121]

McCulloch v. Maryland: On March 6, 1819, the U.S. Supreme Court made a decision that affirmed the constitutional doctrine of Congress' "implied powers."[122] The case concerned the question of whether the state of Maryland had the authority to tax all the local Maryland branches of the Bank of the United States. The unanimous opinion, written by Chief Justice John Marshall and invoking the controversial principle of "federal sovereignty," established that Congress possesses not only the powers expressly conferred by the Constitution but also the "authority appropriate to the utilization of such powers," in this case the creation of a bank. Marshall wrote: "Let the end be legitimate, let it be within the scope of the constitution, and all means which are appropriate, which are plainly adapted to that end, which are not prohibited, but consist with the letter and spirit of the constitution, are constitutional."[123] This doctrine, drawn from the "elastic clause" of Article I, became a powerful force in the steady growth of federal powers.

Panic of 1819: During the "era of good feeling," the United States experienced its first "boom-bust cycle." American economist Murray N. Rothbard wrote:

> The War of 1812 and its aftermath brought many rapid dislocations to the young American economy. Before the war, America had been a large, thinly populated country of seven million, devoted almost exclusively to agriculture ... the American economy lacked large, or even moderate-scale, manufactures.... The War of 1812 and postwar developments forced the American economy to make many rapid and sudden adjustments. The Anglo-French Wars had long fostered the prosperity of American shipping and foreign trade. As the leading neutral we found our exports in great demand on both sides, and American ships took over trade denied to ships of belligerent nations.[124]

The War of 1812 made major changes in the nation's monetary system, forcing the federal government to borrow large amounts of money to finance it. In New England, where the war was opposed, banks were not a cooperative partner with the Federal treasury. The government turned to banks in other areas of the country, which were little more than note-issuing institutions, where in most cases the notes were not backed by specie. "The first war of the new nation, therefore, wrought many unsettling changes in the American economy. Trade was blocked from its former channels, the monetary system became disordered, expansion of money and a shortage of imported goods drove prices upward, and domestic manufactures—particularly textiles—developed under the spur of government demand and the closing of foreign supply sources. The advent of peace brought its own set of problems. After the wartime shortages, the scramble for foreign trade was pursued in earnest. Americans were eager to buy foreign goods, particularly British textiles, and the British exporters were anxious to unload their accumulated stocks.... The renewal of the supply of imported goods drastically lowered the prices of imports in the United States and spurred American demand. The postwar monetary situation was generally considered intolerable. Banks continued to expand in number and note issue, without the obligation of redeeming in specie, and their notes continued to depreciate and fluctuate."[125] Those who demanded a return to specie–hard money were accused of trying to turn back the clock.

Government revenues fell sharply, prompting Monroe to economize to safeguard fiscal stability. Although agreeing on the need of upgraded transportation services in the nation, he rejected appropriations for internal improvements unless there was an amendment to the Constitution permitting it. The repercussions of the Panic of 1819 were more disastrous to the South and the West than to New England. "Many were angered by Monroe's lack of response to the problems caused by the Panic, but he had little control over the nation's financial system and the problems even stretched far beyond America's borders."[126] Despite the crisis, Monroe remained the most popular president since Washington and was reelected in 1820 almost unanimously.

During his third annual address to Congress, President Monroe delivered the message:

> The great reduction in the price of the principal articles of domestic growth which has occurred during the present year, and the consequent fall in the price of labor, apparently so favorable to the success of domestic manufactures, have not yielded then against other causes adverse to their prosperity. The pecuniary embarrassments which have so deeply affected the commercial interests of the nation have been no less adverse to our manufacturing establishments in several sections of the Union.... It is deemed of great importance to give encouragement to our domestic manufacturers. In what manner the evils which have been adverted may be remedied, and how far it may be practicable in other respects to afford to them further encouragement, paying due respect to other great interests of the nation, is submitted to the wisdom of Congress.[127]

Adopting a laissez-faire position, the general concensus was that the depression had to cure itself and the government should remain aloof from the problem. The *New York Daily Advertiser* asked, "how could Congress remedy matters? It could not stop the people from exporting specie; it could not teach the people the necessary virtues of frugality and economy; it could not give credit to worthless banks or stop overtrading at home. The remedy must be slow and gradual, and stem from individuals, not governments. Any governmental interference would provide a shock to business enterprise."[128] The *New York Evening Post* echoed the theme: "Time and the laws of trade will restore things to an equilibrium, if legislatures do not rashly interfere to the natural course of events." Of the individual remedies proposed for the depression, the most popular were the twin virtues of "industry" and "economy."[129]

Missouri Compromise: In 1818, the issue of slavery threatened to destroy the Union. That year the Missouri Territory, which was acquired by United States as part of the Louisiana Purchase in 1803, petitioned Congress for admission to the Union as a state. Since the creation of the new nation, the number of states grew from 13 to 22. The balance of power was preserved with 11 free states and 11 slave states, divided along regional lines, the North and the South. Missouri's application for admission as the 12th slave state would upset the balance. The issue led to in a heated "congressional debate on the nature of slavery and the expansion of the institution into new territories."[130] Slavery had been legal when France and Spain controlled the Louisiana Territory, so the United States didn't change things when they purchased the area. New York Representative James Talmadge "offered an amendment to the Missouri Enabling Bill that would prohibit further introduction of slavery into the territory and called for the gradual emancipation of the slaves already in Missouri."[131] Both sides of the dispute made compelling arguments. Supporters of the amendment charged that if Missouri was admitted as a slave state, small farmers of the North and East could not compete with the southern plantation where the work was done by the free labor of slaves. They further argued that these small farmers had as much right to the land of Missouri as anyone else, since the purchase of the Louisiana Territory was paid for by the taxes of all Americans. As another point from those opposed to allowing Missouri to join the Union as a slave state, it would give too great a voice to slave-holding states because under the Constitution, three out of every five slaves were included in the population count to determine the number of Congressmen for each state.[132] Up to then, to maintain the balance, wherever a slave state was admitted to the union, a free state was also admitted.

Southerners countered Northern arguments in favor of the Tallmadge Amendment. While admitting that Congress had the Constitutional right to admit or reject a state, they insisted Congress did not have the right to dictate conditions for a territory to become a state. William Pinkney of Maryland argued that states already in the union had joined without any conditions. If Congress, he declared, had the right to set conditions for new states, then these new states would not be equal to the old ones. The United States no longer would be a union of equal states.[133] The amendment passed in the House of Representatives, dominated by Northerners, and sent on to the Senate, where the amendment was removed. The House would not accept its deletion and Congress adjourned, leaving the issue to be decided by the Sixteenth Congress.

By the time the New Congress convened, Maine, which was a part of Massachusetts, asked to join the Union as a free state. "The Senate debated the admission of Maine and Missouri from February 8 through February 17, 1820. On February 16, the Senate agreed to unite the Maine and Missouri bills into one bill. The following day the Senate agreed to an amendment that prohibited slavery in the Louisiana Territory north of the 36° 30' latitude line, except for Missouri, and then agreed to the final version of the bill by a vote of 24 to 20. After rejecting the Senate's version of the bill, the House of Representatives passed a bill on March 1 that admitted Missouri without slavery. On March 2, after a House-Senate conference agreed to the Senate's version, the House voted 90 to 87 to allow slavery in Missouri and then voted 134 to 42 to prohibit slavery in the Louisiana Territory north of the 36° 30' latitude line."[134] The debate was violent on both sides of the argument. The seriousness of the matter was expressed by a Georgia congressman who during the argument uttered the sentiment: "You have kindled a fire which all the waters of the ocean can't put out, which seas of blood can only extinguish."[135] The cry against the South's "peculiar institution" was echoed in the sentiments of Representative Livermore of New Hampshire: "How long will the desire for wealth render us blind to the sin of holding both the bodies and souls of our fellow men in chains?"[136] Thomas Jefferson expressed his concern over the dispute: "The Missouri question aroused and filled me with alarm.... I have been among the most sanguine in believing that our Union would be of long duration. I now doubt it much."[137]

Cooler heads prevailed, at least for the time being, when in 1820, through the efforts of Henry Clay, "the great pacificator," a compromise was reached when Maine petitioned Congress for statehood. The Missouri Compromise, proposed by Senator Jesse B. Thomas of Illinois, was enacted, forbidding slavery above 36 degrees 30 minutes latitude, thus effectively prohibiting the introduction of slavery into the remaining areas of the Louisiana Territory. Missouri was admitted as a slave state and Maine as a free state, maintaining the balance between slave and free states.[138]

On March 6, 1820, President Monroe signed the legislation, also known as the Compromise Bill of 1820, into law.[139] Missouri, named for one of the Native American groups that once lived in the territory, became the 24th and first state to lie entirely west of the Mississippi River.

The dispute over slavery was not resolved; it simmered throughout the 1840s and 1850s, as nine new states that did not allow slavery were established out of the remaining Louisiana Territory. In 1857, in the Dred Scott Decision, the Supreme Court, led by Roger B. Taney, the Chief Justice, by a vote of seven to two, declared the compromise unconstitutional.[140] In his discussion of the issue, Taney spent a considerable time justifying "the Court's momentous decision to address the Missouri Compromise issue at all, since it did not seem necessary to reach that issue in order to decide the Dred Scott case."[141] Nevertheless, the Court ruled that prohibiting slavery north of the 36°30' Parallel in the Louisiana Purchase violated the Fifth Amendment of the Constitution, which prohibits Congress from depriving persons of their property without due process of law, and slaves were considered property.[142]

The Tariff of 1824: Henry Clay of Kentucky championed a tariff passed by the House of Representatives on May 22, 1824. "In the debates upon this tariff, Henry Clay led the protectionist forces, basing his arguments upon the general distress of the country, which he explained by the loss of the foreign market for agricultural products, and which he would remedy by building up a home market by means of the support of manufacturers—the creation of an 'American system.'"[143] The tariff's protectionist measures and domestic trade initiatives were meant to break the nation's substantial dependence on foreign materials. Massachusetts Senator Daniel Webster ridiculed the legislation, dismissing it as an affront to free trade. He argued: "This favorite American policy is what America has never tried, and this odious foreign policy is what, as we are told, foreign states have never pursued."[144] The South, vigorously opposing the tariff because it hindered its trade, "argued that the power to impose taxes and duties was given for the purpose of raising revenue, not for the purpose of protection."[145] However, John Randolph, of Virginia declared, "I do not stop here, sir to argue about the constitutionality of this bill; I consider the Constitution a dead letter; I consider it to consist, at this time, of the power of the General Government and the power of the States—that is the Constitution. I have no faith in parchment, sir; ... I have faith in the power of the commonwealth of which I am an unworthy son.... If, under a power to regulate trade, you prevent exportation; if, with the most approved spring lancets, you draw the last drop of blood from our veins; if, secundum artem, you draw the last shilling from our pockets, what are the checks of the Constitution to us? A fig for the Constitution! When the scorpion's sting is probing to the quick, shall we stop to chop logic? ... There is no magic in this word union."[146] The North voted for the tariff to protect its growing industries from those of Europe. Clay, the leader of the west prevailed when his region supported the tariff because the revenue received would go to the building roads, cities, etc. in the West. "The bill passed the House of Representatives on April 16, 1824, by the close vote of 107 to 102, and subsequently passed the Senate by a small majority."[147]

FOREIGN AFFAIRS — MAJOR EVENTS

The 49th Parallel: On October 20, 1818, the Anglo-American Convention set the 49th parallel as the border with Canada and the United States from Manitoba to British Columbia on the Canadian side and from Minnesota to Washington on the U.S. side. It resolved standing boundary issues between the United States and the United Kingdom. The treaty "provided for joint control of land in the Oregon Country for ten years. It was negotiated for the U.S. by Albert Gallatin, ambassador to France, and Richard Rush, ambassador to Britain; and for Britain by Frederick John Robinson, treasurer of the Royal Navy and a member of the Privy Council, and Henry Goulburn, an undersecretary of state."[148]

The 49th parallel is a latitude coordinate—a straight line from just north of Minneapolis, Minnesota, to just past Washington State into the middle of the Strait of Juan de Fuca. Once in the strait, the boundary line loops south and then west to ensure that Vancouver Island is contained within Canadian boundaries.[149]

The First Seminole War and the Purchase of Florida: In the spring of 1818, under the command of General Andrew Jackson, American troops waged war against the Seminole Indians, who attacked settlers on the southern frontier of Georgia. Jackson pursued hostile Native Americans deep into Florida, capturing two Spanish forts. In doing so he had disobeyed President Monroe's orders.[150] Monroe's cabinet was divided; some, including John C. Calhoun and William H. Crawford, wished Monroe to condemn Jackson; John Quincy Adams urged the president to take advantage of the situation. When the public labeled Jackson a hero, Monroe felt he had no other course than to annex Florida.[151] Monroe and his "administration believed in U.S. expansion into Florida, obliterating the Seminoles, and enslaving the blacks among them."[152] However, he did so diplomatically, sending two envoys to Spain who negotiated an agreement. Florida was ceded to the United States on February 22, 1819, in exchange for the U.S. assuming $5 million in claims by American citizens against Spain and giving up any claims to Mexican territory. Formal U.S. occupation began in 1821 with Andrew Jackson appointed military governor.[153]

Monroe Doctrine: During Monroe's presidency, there were ongoing disputes between the United States and Russia over lands in the far west of North America. Other European nations had their eye on territories in the Americas. England, eager to end Spanish domination of Central and South America, sought the United States' support in issuing a joint position. Jefferson and Madison supported the British proposal but Secretary of State John Quincy Adams convinced President Monroe that the United States should make its position on the encroachments clear. "The occasion and the principles of the Monroe Doctrine ... point to the authorship of Adams. His biographer, admitting that 'as a rule, he was not very skillful with his pen...,' he probably 'had little conception of the lasting effect which his words would produce.'"[154] On December 2, 1823, in a few paragraphs of his seventh annual message to Congress, Monroe delivered the Monroe Doctrine to Congress. He stated that the "American continents were not subjects for future colonization by European powers, and since the United States stayed out of the inter–European war, the European nations should not interfere with the growth and development of other powers."[155]

Monroe announced "the determination of the United States to prevent any further colonization by European nations in either South or North America. The statement thus implied the United States would aid the South American republics, formed in the first quarter of the 19th century by revolt from Spain, in defense of their independence."[156] It was not known as the Monroe Doctrine until some 30 years after its proclamation. While it was well-received in the United States, Europe took scant notice of it. It did not become a truly effective foundation of American foreign policy until the time of the presidency of Theodore Roosevelt, who used it to assert the United States' exclusive right to intervene in the affairs of Latin American countries.[157]

The president thoroughly covered the matter of the Monroe Doctrine (a reciprocal doctrine, by the way, as the U.S. promised not to interfere with existing colonies) in his seventh annual message to Congress:

> We owe it, therefore, to candor and to the amicable relations existing between the United States and those powers to declare that we should consider any attempt on their part to extend their system to any portion of this hemisphere as dangerous to our peace and safety. With the existing colonies or dependencies of any European power we have not interfered and shall not interfere.

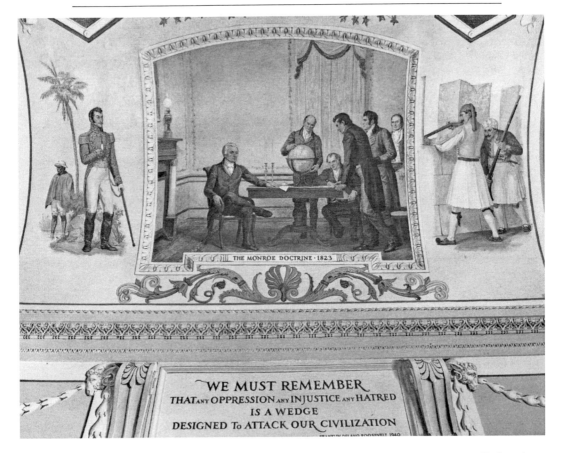

Monroe Doctrine mural in the Great Experiment Hall, by Allyn Cox; oil on canvas applied to the ceiling, 1973–1974. This mural depicts a discussion among President Monroe and his cabinet: *left to right*, President Monroe, Secretary of State John Quincy Adams, Attorney General William Wirt, Secretary of War John Calhoun, Secretary of the Navy Samuel L. Southard, and Secretary of the Treasury William H. Crawford. *Left:* Simón Bolívar, who fought for the independence of many Spanish colonies in South America, represents a commitment to liberty. *Right:* Greek freedom fighters, who were aided by Russia, Britain, and France in gaining autonomy from the Ottoman Empire, symbolize the struggle for freedom around the globe (Architect of the Capitol).

> But with the Governments who have declared their independence and maintain it, and whose independence we have, on great consideration and on just principles, acknowledged, we could not view any interposition for the purpose of oppressing them, or controlling in any other manner their destiny, by any European power in any other light than as the manifestation of an unfriendly disposition toward the United States.... The American continents, by the free and independent condition which they have assumed and maintain, are henceforth not to be considered as subjects for future colonization by any European powers.[158]

AFTER THE PRESIDENCY

During Monroe's last two years in office, the struggle over who would succeed him led to attacks on his administration by the likes of William H. Crawford, Henry Clay and Andrew Jackson. Congressional supporters of Crawford and Jackson raised questions impugning Monroe's integrity in the management of funds allotted for refurnishing the White House.

President James Monroe moved back into the house in 1817 after its restoration and redecorated the "large oval room" in the French Empire style. Monroe ordered mahogany furniture from Pierre-Antoine Bellange predominantly for formal use in the oval and state dining rooms. The president's agents, the American firm of Russell and La Farge in LeHavre, France, however, shipped 53 pieces of carved and gilded furniture with crimson silk upholstery. They informed the president that "mahogany is not generally admitted in the furniture of a Saloon, even at private gentlemen's houses."[159]

On the obverse side of the Elizabeth Kortright Monroe First Spouse $10 Gold Coin is an image of her at the reopening of the White House. "On January 1, 1818, Elizabeth and James Monroe held a grand New Year's Day reception marking the reopening of the White House, rebuilt after it was torched by the British in 1814. The Monroes brought in some of their own furniture because the White House was almost empty when they moved in. This French Empire style furniture imparted a feeling of formality that President and First Lady Monroe considered appropriate for the executive mansion. Nine pieces of it still can be found in the White House today."[160]

These harassments must have made Monroe feel a sense of relief when he relinquished the presidency to John Quincy Adams in March 1825. In a letter to General Roger Jones, Monroe asserted: "After the long and laborious service in which I have been engaged, and in the most difficult conjunctions to which our country has been exposed, it is my earnest desire to cherish tranquility in my retirement."[161]

Monroe did not immediately leave the White House at the end of his second term. His wife was too sick to travel, and so they stayed in the executive mansion a few weeks until she was well enough to make the journey.[162] Monroe was exhausted and appeared much older than his 67 years. After his presidency, he avoided partisan political involvement, but used his influence to get his son-in-law, George Hay, an appointment as a federal judge, and his other son-in-law, Samuel Gouverneur, appointed postmaster for New York.[163] As the case with several U.S. presidents, Monroe's service to his country did not provide enough money for his own needs. He asked Charles Fenton Mercer to repay him for a prior debt, as he was badly in need of cash, explaining, "My estate also having been badly managed in my absence makes the inconvenience the greater, as even my current expenses here I can derive little aid from it, at this time. I therefore hope that you will be able to reimburse me that sum without delay. I should not request it under other circumstances."[164]

More than 40 years of public service left Monroe on the brink of poverty, leaving the presidency seventy-five thousand dollars in debt. "The death of Monroe's wife early in 1830 prostrated him with grief; rarely had they ever been separated since their marriage. Monroe's health began to fail so rapidly that he moved to New York to live with his younger daughter, Mrs. Samuel L. Gouverneur. Oak Hill was put up for sale to pay the balance of his debts."[165] He only realized $20 an acre. "Monroe's efforts to obtain recompense for expenses of his past diplomatic missions (his accounts had never been settled with the State Department) were frustrated by the opposition of Jacksonians and Crawfordites."[166] In 1831 his successor as president, John Quincy Adams wrote rather unfeelingly on Monroe's misfortune: "Mr. Monroe is a very remarkable instance of a man whose life has been a continued series of the most extraordinary good fortune, who has never met with any known disaster, has gone through a splendid career of public service, has received more pecuniary reward from the public than any other man since the existence of the nation, and is now dying, at the age of seventy-two, in wretchedness and beggary."[167]

It wasn't until February 1831, after news of the former Monroe's financial predicament became public knowledge, that "Congress appropriated $30,000 in settlement of his claims. The Bank of the United States took over Highlands in lieu of a $25,000 debt."[168] In retirement Monroe served as a member of the Board of Visitors of the University of Virginia (1827–1830). His last public service was as chairman of the Virginia Continental Congress in 1829.[169]

His Papers: Monroe never wrote on nonpolitical subjects in his letters,[170] nor did he keep a diary. During the early part of his life, his correspondence was sparse, and missing from the collections of his writings are almost all the letters to and from his family. There is only one letter existing that he wrote to his wife. The correspondence he had with Thomas Jefferson and Patrick Read expresses his political views. Monroe's papers are contained in *Writings*, 7 volumes, 1898–1903, edited by S.M. Hamilton. His autobiography, published in 1959, was edited by Stuart G. Brown and Donald G. Baker. *The Papers of James Monroe*, edited by Daniel Preston, has been published by Greenwood Press (2003). Monroe's *The People, the Sovereigns: Being a Comparison of the Government of the United States and of Those of the Republics, Which Have Existed Before, with the Causes of Their Decadence and Fall*, edited by Samuel L. Gouverneur, was published by James River Press (1987). The James Monroe Museum and Memorial Library is dedicated to the president and his wife.

Health: Monroe contracted malaria while visiting a swampy area of the Mississippi River in 1785 and became very ill. He suffered several recurrences of the fever later in his life.[171] A seizure that occurred in August 1825 was so severe that he was thought to be near death. He recovered, but the cause of the ailment was never discovered.[172] Monroe developed a chronic lung illness in 1830 and, although no specific diagnosis was made, his doctor recommended that he rest at a tuberculosis hospital.[173] In April 1831, Monroe wrote: "My state of health continues, consisting of a cough which annoys me night and day accompanied by considerable expectoration."[174]

Death: On the fifth anniversary of the deaths of John Adams and Thomas Jefferson, Monroe died on July 4, 1831.

Place of Death: In the early spring of 1831, Monroe developed a persistent cough. He steadily declined and died peacefully at the home of his daughter Maria in New York City. "Thousands of mourners followed his body up Broadway to the Gouverneur family vault, in Marble Cemetery."[175] His funeral was held at Trinity Church, the principal Episcopal Church in New York City. "The Episcopal bishop of New York and the rector of Trinity Church conducted the service from the *Book of Common Prayer*."[176] Throughout the nation, his death was observed with days of mourning, memorial services and eulogies.

Cause of Death: Debility and heart failure, possibly tuberculosis caught after the onset of a cold.[177]

Final Words: When he died, Monroe left no deathbed statement. His body was deposited in a leaden coffin soon after his death and that was placed in a mahogany coffin, which bears on a plate of silver the following inscription:

JAMES MONROE
Of Virginia
Died 4th July, 1831
Aged 74 Years

Place of Burial: In 1858, on the 100th anniversary of his birth, Monroe was reinterred at Hollywood Cemetery, Richmond, Virginia, with a Presbyterian minister delivering the prayer of commitment. Monroe's body was exhumed and his casket placed on a barge located in the East River for the journey to Richmond. The trip was harrowing, beset by storms, before the barge arrived along the James River for unloading.[178] Outside his monument are

"Hollywood, Tomb of James Monroe, Richmond, Va.," glass negative photograph created c. 1905 (Library of Congress, Detroit Publishing Company Photograph Collection).

buried his wife, his daughter Maria and her husband. They were moved from Oak Hill years after the president's death. The cemetery, which was formally dedicated on June 25, 1849, is the burial place of more than 18,000 Civil War soldiers and officers. President John Tyler is also buried in Hollywood Cemetery, which remains an active cemetery.[179]

MISCELLANEA

Presidential Trivia and Firsts: Monroe was the first president to ride on a steamship. Monroe and his wife attended Napoleon Bonaparte's coronation as emperor of France. When Congress was counting the electoral votes in 1816, Representative John W. Taylor of New York objected to the counting of Indiana's votes. He argued that Congress had acknowledged the statehood of Indiana in a joint resolution on December 11, 1816, whereas the ballots of the Electoral College had been cast on December 4, 1816. He claimed that at the time of the balloting, there had been merely a territory of Indiana, not a state of Indiana. Other representatives contradicted Taylor, asserting that the joint resolution merely recognized that Indiana had already joined the Union by forming a state constitution and government on June 29, 1816. These representatives pointed out that both the House and Senate had seated members from Indiana who had been elected prior to the joint resolution, which would have been unconstitutional had Indiana not been a state at the time of their election. Representative Samuel D. Ingham then moved that the question be postponed indefinitely. The House agreed almost unanimously, and the Senate was brought back in to count the electoral votes from Indiana.[180] Although Monroe regarded his trips around the country in 1817 to be government business, he "journeyed as an independent citizen without official escort or ceremony and paid for his travel expenses out of his own pocket."[181] His only two travel companions were his secretary and the chief of the Army Corps of Engineers. He wished to be relatively inconspicuous as a "private citizen."

Speech to Massachusetts Society of the Cincinnati: In an address at Boston, Massachusetts, on July 4, 1817, President Monroe acknowledged the passing of the revolutionary generation and recalled their struggle in the "sacred cause of liberty":

> The affectionate address of my brothers of the Cincinnati awakens in my mind the most grateful emotions. No approbation can be more dear to me than that of those with whom I have had the honor to share the common toils and perils of the war for our independence. We were embarked in the same sacred cause of liberty, and we have lived to enjoy the reward of our common labors. Many of our companions in arms fell in the field before our independence was achieved, and many less fortunate than ourselves, lived not to witness the perfect fulfillment of their hopes in the prosperity & happiness of our country. You do but justice to yourself in claiming the confidence of your country, that you can never desert the standard of freedom. You fought to obtain it in times when men's hearts & principles were severely tried, and your public sacrifices and honorable actions are the best pledges of your sincere and devoted attachment to our excellent constitution.
>
> May your children never forget the sacred duties devoted on them to preserve the inheritance so gallantly acquired by their fathers. May they cultivate the same manly patriotism, the same disinterested friendship and the same political integrity, which has distinguished you, and thus unite in perpetuating that social concord and public virtue on which the future prosperity of our country must so essentially depend. I feel most deeply the truth of the melancholy suggestion that we shall probably meet no more. While however we remain in life I shall continue to hope for your countenance and support so far as my public conduct may entitle me to your confidence; and in bidding you farewell, I pray a kind providence long to preserve your valuable lives for the honor and benefit of our country.[182]

Monroe and Slavery: Monroe's relationship with his slaves demonstrated "a pattern of paternalistic racism."[183] Like his fellow Virginian presidents he detested the evil of slavery but believed it was an institution worth maintaining. His attitude toward blacks was clear in his correspondence. In a letter to Thomas Jefferson about the Gabriel Conspiracy, named after a black called Gabriel Prosser, who led an uprising of slaves that was put down by the Virginia militia, Monroe wrote:

> We have had so much trouble with the Negroes here. The plan of an insurrection was clearly proved.... We then made a display of force and out measures of defence with a view to intimidate these people. When to arrest the hand of the Executioner, is a question of great importance. It is hardly to be presumed, a rebel who avows it was his intention to assassinate his master &c. if pardoned will ever become a useful servant. Ten have been condemned and executed, and there are at least twenty, perhaps 40 more to be tried, of whose guilt no doubt is entertained.[184]

In the end, some 35 slaves were executed. In another letter, this time to the mayor of Richmond, he proclaimed, "Negroes from the country have no business in town, but to attend at market; that being ended they ought to depart."[185] The slaves who reported the conspiracy were purchased by the government and freed as a reward.[186] The Virginia legislature suggested purchasing lands outside the state to which slaves who participated in the conspiracy could be sent. "The idea of such an acquisition was suggested by motives of humanity, it being intended by means thereof to provide an alternate mode of punishment for those described by the resolution, who under the existing law might be doomed to suffer death.... We perceive an existing evil which commenced under our Colonial System, with which we are not properly chargeable, or if at all not in the present degree, and we acknowledge the extreme difficulty of remedying it."[187]

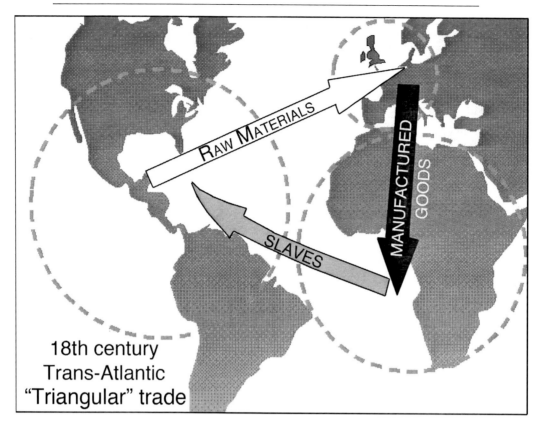

18th century trans–Atlantic triangular trade graphic showing raw materials being shipped from North America to Europe, which sends manufactured goods to Africa. From there slaves are sent to the New World (Map provided by Dr. James A. Jones, West Chester University of Pennsylvania. Used with permission).

In 1821, Monroe wrote: "[The international slave trade] is an abominable practice, against which nations are now combining, and it may be presumed that the combination will soon become universal. If it does the traffic must cease, if it does not it will be carried on, unless the nations favorable to the suppression unite to crush it, under flags whose powers tolerate it, which would in effect be to make war on those powers."[188]

Monroe signed a treaty with Great Britain that declared the African slave trade a form of piracy, thereby making it easier to fight the trade without making it easier for foreign navies to stop and search U.S. ships. He was unable to convince the Senate to ratify the treaty.[189]

The Hamilton-Reynolds Scandal: On December 15, 1792, Congressmen James Monroe and two colleagues, Frederick Muhlenberg of Pennsylvania and Abraham Venable of Virginia, arrived at the home of Secretary of the Treasury Alexander Hamilton with the distasteful assignment of confronting him with evidence that suggested he used public funds for private gain. Muhlenberg told Hamilton: "They had discovered a very improper connection" between Hamilton and a Mr. Reynolds, who claimed that the Secretary of the Treasury had given him Treasury funds to play the stock market.[190] "When they showed Hamilton his own hand-written notes to Reynolds, he instantly — and to their amazement — acknowledged their authenticity."[191] Hamilton asked the three congressmen to meet

Slave pen, Alexandria, Virginia, photographed between 1861 and 1865, printed later. Interior view of a slave pen, showing the doors of cells where the slaves were held before being sold (Library of Congress).

him at his home that evening and promised he would show them written documents that would establish his innocence. That evening, with his friend Oliver Wolcott at his side as a witness, Hamilton admitted that he had given money to Reynolds, but it was his funds. They were not given to Hamilton to play the stock market but rather were blackmail payments to keep Hamilton's affair with Reynolds' wife Maria from becoming public knowledge. After examining the documents Hamilton shared with them, the three legislators assured Hamilton they were satisfied with his version and told him it was not necessary to reveal the whole story. However, Hamilton insisted on sharing the sordid details.[192]

"Sometime in the summer of the year 1791, a young woman called at my house in Philadelphia whom Hamilton did not previously know, appeared at his home and requested to see me in private."[193] Hamilton led her to a room, where she revealed that she was Maria Reynolds of New York and that her cruel husband James had abandoned her and their daughter to take up with another woman. Maria begged Hamilton for money, so she might return to her friends in New York. For some reason, Hamilton agreed to help her, but claiming it was an inopportune time, rather than give her the sum she required and send her on

A Slave Auction at the South, wood engraving by Theodore R. Davis. African American men, women, and children being auctioned off in front of a crowd of men. Illustration in *Harper's Weekly*, 5, no. 237 (1861 July 13), 442 (Library of Congress).

Left: Am I Not a Man and a Brother? Woodcut on woven paper, published 1837. The image of a supplicant male slave in chains appears on the 1837 broadside publication of John Greenleaf Whittier's antislavery poem, "Our Countrymen in Chains." The design was originally adopted as the seal of the Society for the Abolition of Slavery in England in the 1780s and appeared on several medallions for the society made by Josiah Wedgwood as early as 1787 (Library of Congress).

her way, he asked if he might bring a "small amount of money" to her at her lodgings. Hamilton arrived that evening at 154 South 4th Street, where Mrs. Reynolds shortly led him to her bedroom. Hamilton recalled, "I took the bill (a thirty pound note) out of my pocket and gave it to her. Some conversation ensued, from which it was quickly apparent that other than pecuniary consolation would [also] be accepta-ble."[194]

The affair continued, even though Hamilton was aware or should have been aware that he was treading on a dangerous path, but his passion overruled his sensibility, and his mistress knew how to keep him on the string with her professions of love. Maria even intro-duced Alexander to her husband, at which time James Reynolds sought Hamilton's help in obtaining a government position.[195] Sometime later Reynolds "learned" of his wife's unfaith-fulness and demanded a payment of $1000, which Hamilton paid. It sounds like Hamilton was the victim of a con game, and even he speculated that Reynolds may have always been aware of the affair and even arranged it, so he could collect blackmail. Reynolds encouraged Hamilton to continue the affair with Maria, so he might receive more "loans." Whenever Hamilton's interest in the affair flagged, Maria would tell him that James was abusing her or that he threatened to go to Hamilton's wife with the news of his infidelity.[196] After this revelation, Monroe and the others declared the incident closed. According to Hamilton, they departed with "expressions of regret at the trouble and embarrassment which had been occasioned on me."[197]

Next day the three congressmen drew up and signed a report to themselves regarding their interview with Hamilton. It contained the statement, "We left him under an impres-sion our suspicions were removed."[198] Hamilton and Wolcott were convinced that the con-gressmen, as men of honor, would seal all documents of the case and show them to no one. Hamilton requested copies of the papers the congressmen had shown him, and Monroe, who was the custodian of the documents, arranged to have copies made and delivered to Hamilton by John Beckley, clerk of the House of Representatives, who made a copy for his own files. The congressmen maintained their silence, at least in public, for almost five years. However, Monroe did tell Jefferson of the affair, who spread rampant rumors about his political enemy.[199] In 1793, Maria Reynolds divorced her husband, represented in the pro-ceedings by Aaron Burr. The repentant Hamilton retired to private law practice so he could spend more time with his wife, Elizabeth, and their five children, who forgave him and stood by him.[200] Although no portraits of Maria Reynolds and her husband, James, are known to exist, in 1931 Warner Bros. Pictures, Inc., the Vitaphone Corp., released the movie *Alexander Hamilton*, which starred George Arliss—who made a good living portraying his-torical figures—as Alexander Hamilton and pretty June Collyer as the unfortunate, schem-ing Maria Reynolds.[201]

In 1797, pamphleteer James Thomas Callender obtained the secret documents of the congressmen from Beckley and published a story that implied Hamilton's guilt in a specu-lation scandal. In it Callender wrote, "we shall presently see this great master of morality, although himself the father of a family, confessing that he had an illicit correspondence with another man's wife."[202] Callender published the trove of documents Hamilton had entrusted to the three congressmen. The pamphleteer repeated the discredited charge that the secretary of the treasury had misused treasury funds. Feeling he had no choice but to respond, Hamilton published a public letter in a friendly newspaper, the *Gazette of the United States*, denying the charges and revealing that the three congressmen, with Wolcott as witness, had declared the charges false.[203] Hamilton wrote to the congressmen, saying that there had been "a dishonorable act" to what had been agreed upon; he asked that each respond immediately with a declaration that he was indeed innocent.[204]

Hamilton was informed that Beckley had supplied the documents to Callender, but he suspected that his political enemy Monroe was also somehow culpable. Hamilton learned that it was Monroe who had made the documents of their meeting available to Beckley.[205] Muhlenberg and Venable acceded to Hamilton's request, but before Monroe could do so, Hamilton demanded a meeting. The interview was witnessed by Congressman David Gelston, who kept a record of the harsh and heated exchange. Hamilton rejected Monroe's claim that he had known nothing of Callender's pamphlet before it was published. Monroe responded by calling Hamilton a "scoundrel." An angry Hamilton announced that "I will meet your lie as a gentleman" and Monroe snapped back, "I am ready. Get your pistols."[206] The two parted due to the intercession of Gelston, but after Callender's second installment of documents was printed, Hamilton fired off a letter to Monroe, the first broadside in a correspondence that almost led to a duel between the two men. The only reason the duel did not take place was because both men wished to make it seem that the other was the challenger.[207]

Meanwhile, against the advice of friends, Hamilton defended his reputation as an incorruptible public servant by publishing a pamphlet called *Observations on Certain Documents*. In it, he confessed his affair:

> [The charge against me was] a connection with one James Reynolds for purposes of improper pecuniary speculation. My real crime is an amorous connection with his wife for a considerable time, with his privity and connivance, if not originally brought on by a combination between the husband and wife to extort money from me.[208]
>
> [N]o character, however upright, is a match for constantly reiterated attacks, however false. It is well understood by its disciples, that every calumny makes some proselytes and even retains some; since justification seldom circulates as rapidly and as widely as slander. The number of those who from doubt proceed to suspicion and thence to belief of imputed guilt is continually augmenting; and the public mind fatigued at length with resistance to the calumnies which eternally assail it, is apt in the end to sit down with the opinion that a person so often accused cannot be entirely innocent.[209]

Hamilton did not spare himself for his part in the scandal and his betrayal of his trust and integrity. He published the letters he had received from both Reynolds and those he had written to them to show they pertained to blackmail and not speculation with Treasury funds. The affair severely damaged Hamilton's reputation, probably depriving him of the presidency.[210]

Tom Paine: English-born Tom Paine (1737–1809), who emigrated to America in October 1774, was known as a radical propagandist and the voice of the common man. On January 10, 1776, he published a short pamphlet, *Common Sense*, a strong defense of American independence from England. He briefly served in the Continental Army, and although he wasn't much of a soldier, his essays, published in the *Pennsylvania Journal* under the heading "Crisis," helped inspire the army. He returned to England and in 1791 and 1792 wrote *The Rights of Man* in "response to criticism of the French revolution." In it, he condemned all forms of hereditary government, including the British constitution, arguing that only a democratic republic could be trusted to protect equal political rights of all men. Labeled an outlaw, Paine was forced to leave England. In August 1792, he became a citizen of France and was elected to the National Convention.[211] Paine's association with the moderate Girondins and his refusal to endorse the execution of King Louis XVI made him suspect by the radical Jacobins. He fell a victim of the Reign of Terror and was arrested and imprisoned in December 1793 in Luxembourg prison. While incarcerated, he embarked on his third influential work, *The Age of Reason*.[212] Was it not for the intercession of the new American minister to France, James Monroe, Paine might have been executed. Monroe allowed Paine to languish in prison for nine months before writing to the imprisoned radical in 1794:

It is unnecessary for me to tell you how much all your countrymen, I speak of the great mass of the people, are Interested in your welfare. They have not forgotten the history of their own Revolution and the difficult scenes through which they passed; nor do they review its several stages without reviving in their bosoms a due sensibility of the merits of those who served them in that great and arduous conflict. The crime of ingratitude has not yet stained, and I hope never will stain, our national character. You are considered by them as not only having rendered important services in our own Revolution, but as being on a more extensive scale the friend of human rights and a distinguished and able advocate of public liberty. To the welfare of Thomas Paine we are not and cannot be indifferent.[213]

At about the same time, Monroe wrote a letter to the Committee of General Safety asking for the release of Mr. Paine, in which he said, "The services Thomas Paine rendered to his country in its struggle for freedom have implanted in the hearts of his countrymen a sense of gratitude never to be effaced as long as they shall deserve the title of a just and generous people."[214]

Paine was released and in October 1802 returned to America, where he was received by President Jefferson. Thereafter, Paine was increasingly neglected and spent his last years in poverty, poor health and alcoholism, dying a virtual outcast on June 8, 1809, in New York City.[215]

Liberia: In the early 1800s the subject of the status and rights of the black population was widely debated in the United States. Proponents of slavery defended the institution as a "necessary evil." They feared that emancipation of slaves would generate more damaging social and economic consequences than the continuance of slavery. In 1820, Thomas Jefferson wrote in a letter that with slavery "We have the wolf by the ear, and we can neither hold him, nor safely let him go. Justice is in one scale, and self-preservation in the other."[216]

Many slave-owners expected the day would soon come when there would be more and more freedmen. The question was what to do with them. One solution was to "send them back to Africa," ignoring the fact that most had been born in America and had no experience with Africa.[217] Opinion was divided even among African Americans about the idea of repatriating American blacks to Africa. Some wished to remain in America and to fight for their freedom and rights where they had been born. Others were encouraged by the promise of land. All were suspicious of the motives of the American Colonization Society (ACS), some of whose members firmly believed that the blacks would be better off in their own country. Slave owners wished to remove the possibility of free blacks organizing a slave revolution.[218]

Paul Cuffee was born on the island near New Bedford, Massachusetts, the 7th of 10 children of Kofi Slocum, a freed African slave, and Ruth Moses, a Wampanoag Indian. Paul refused to adopt his father's slave-owner's name, and chose Cuffee for his surname. Paul became a Quaker and built his own ship and despite his color and that of his crew he fruitfully traded in the ports of the South. Ultimately, he owned a small fleet of ships skippered by his relatives. "Cuffee became greatly concerned over the status of the blacks in his native state and throughout America, to the extent that he became one of the first to advocate African colonization as a solution to the incipient racial problem. In 1811, he traveled to Sierra Leone, a British colony on the west coast of Africa, where he founded the Friendly Society of Sierra Leone, for the emigration of free blacks from America. In 1815, he spent $4,000 of his own funds to transport 38 blacks to Sierra Leone. He had planned more expeditions to Africa, but his health failed and he died in 1817."[219]

In 1817, during the presidency of James Monroe, the U.S. Congress granted a charter to the American Colonization Society to repatriate slaves back to Africa. "Despite their rhetoric of sympathy for freedmen, the colonizationists' beliefs led them to oppose legislative efforts to procure civil rights for blacks and remove the barriers to work, education, and voting. Such efforts, they said, were only designed to tease an inferior people with hope of an equality that never could be real."[220] The American Colonization Society found more support from ante-bellum Northerners than did abolition societies. Its proponents included "clergy, college presidents, and politicians of all parties—among the officers of the society over the years were Daniel Webster, William H. Seward, Francis Scott Key, and Winfield Scott. It was lauded by the legislatures of 14 states."[221] Both Henry Clay and Abraham Lincoln were long-time supporters of colonization. In 1862 Abe told Congress, "I cannot make it better known than it already is that I strongly favor colonization."[222] A newspaper editorial in West Chester, Pennsylvania, in 1854 stated the case: "Abolitionists may talk twaddle till the crack of doom, but after all, Colonization is to be the great cure of Negro slavery in this country, or it remains uncured. You may free the slave in the South, but he is nevertheless a slave North or South. His shackles are only to be cast off by returning to the land of his forefathers. Here he is surrounded by a wall of prejudice as indestructible as the everlasting hills. The fires of the volcano are not more inextinguishable than this prejudice, and we would therefore remove the black man from its influence, instead of encouraging him to break it down by an insolent bearing towards those who are in ninety-nine cases out of a hundred, his intellectual superiors."[223] The federal government purchased land along the Grain Coast of Africa that became Liberia (the free land). The first group of voluntarily repatriated black American settlers arrived in 1822. At first white agents of the ACS governed Liberia, but in 1838 the Commonwealth of Liberia was established by the black American expatriates, with its capital, Monrovia, named for President Monroe. In 1847 Liberia became a republic, modeled on the government of the United States. The Liberian Declaration of Independence charged the United States with injustices that made it necessary for them to leave and make new lives for themselves in Africa. They called upon the international community to recognize the independence and sovereignty of Liberia.[224] Great Britain was one of the first to recognize the new country. The U.S. did not follow suit until the American Civil War. By 1860 more than 11,000 African Americans were transported to Liberia.[225]

The Haunting of Fort Monroe: In a section of Hampton, Virginia, there is an army base still in use, Fort Monroe, which was named for the fifth president of the United States. It was founded by Captain John Smith, who named it Old Point Comfort. From its vantage point, colonists could see who was entering the James River, giving them warning if any Spanish troops were approaching.[226] What is remarkable about the fort is that it seems to be haunted by historical ghosts. One would think that perhaps Monroe would show up, but he has never been sighted. Among the famous haunting spirits seen are Abraham Lincoln, Jefferson Davis, Ulysses S. Grant, Chief Black Hawk and Edgar Allan Poe, who as a young soldier was stationed at Fort Monroe. Among the others is a woman in white, a child, and a spirit who hates roses. Jefferson Davis, the president of the Confederacy, was imprisoned at Fort Monroe for two years after the Civil War and was mistreated severely, his wounds left unattended. The interior of Fort Monroe contains a "moat," which is said to be the home to a water monster like the one found in Loch Ness in Scotland. There have been several sightings, but no one has been able to determine what it is—perhaps nothing more than the invention of active imaginations.[227]

The Monroe Dollar: In 2005, "President George W. Bush signed the Presidential $1 Coin Act authorizing the United States Mint to strike $1 coins honoring American presidents in the order in which they served."[228] In 2008, James Monroe became the fifth U.S. president to be so honored. The coin features a likeness of Monroe on the obverse and a reverse design with a striking rendition of the Statue of Liberty. The coin features larger, more dramatic artwork, as well as edge-incised inscriptions of the mint year, "E Pluribus Unum," "In God We Trust," and the mint mark. The Monroe presidential $1 coins are circulating condition coins and can be used in daily transactions; however, since they have never before been circulated, collectors gobble them up quickly.[229]

Observations About James Monroe

By Other Presidents

If Mr. Monroe should ever fill the Chair of Government he may (and it is presumed he would be well enough disposed) let the French Minister frame his speeches.... There is abundant evidence of his being a mere tool in the hands of the French government.[230]— George Washington

He was a man whose soul might be turned wrong side outwards without discovering a blemish to the world.[231]— Thomas Jefferson

[Tranquility was] the pole-star of his policy.... There is a slowness, want of decision and a spirit of procrastination in the President, which perhaps arises from his situation rather than his personal character.[232]— John Quincy Adams

I consider Monroe a pretty minor president, in spite of the Monroe Doctrine. That's the only important thing he ever did more or less on his own, when you really get down to it.[233]— Harry S Truman

By Others

The unanimous re-election of Mr. Monroe is morally certain, as certain as almost any contingent event can be.[234]— Anonymous

I have known many much more rapid in reaching a conclusion, but few with a certainty so unerring.[235]— John C. Calhoun

His services as President might be summed up in four words— he personified an interim. The War of 1812 ... was merely the symptom of a profound change in domestic and international relations. After the shock of such a change, an interim was necessary; and if the interim was necessary, the personification was honorable.[236]— George Dangerfield

[It is difficult to make a case for considering James Monroe] a great president by the standards usually reserved for great presidents.[237]— Gary Hart

Resolved that his Excellency's wise, impartial and dignified administration of the General Government has justly entitled him to the application and affectionate regards of the good people of the Union.[238]— Maryland House of Delegates

We by no means find fault with the marks of respect paid to the chief magistrate on a tour of duty, but think there is more of pomp and parade given to it by the people than the fitness of the thing requires.[239]— Hezekiah Niles

[O]ne of those respectable mediocrities in high public station, with whom people are apt to sympathize in their troubles, when unnecessarily attacked and humiliated by persons of greatly superior ability.[240]— Carl Schurz

The old notions of republican simplicity are fast wearing away and the public taste becomes more and more gratified with public amusements and parades. Mr. Monroe, however, still retains his plain and gentle manners; and is in every respect a very estimable man.[241]— Justice Joseph Story

SIX

John Quincy Adams

A Man of Principles, Not Parties

Sixth President of the United States, 1825–1829

John Quincy Adams was a man with a complex nature which contained many contradictions. The apple did not fall too far from the tree. His career, his temperament and his viewpoints paralleled those of his famous father, John Adams. Like the elder Adams, John Quincy lacked the common touch and suffered fools badly. He described himself in a diary entry of June 4, 1819: "I am a man of reserved, cold, austere, and forbidding manners; my political adversaries say a gloomy misanthropist, and my personal enemies, an unsocial savage."[1] In the same entry, he revealed that he wasn't going to change his temperament: "With knowledge of the actual defects in my character, I have not the pliability to reform it."[2]

Birth: John Quincy Adams was born July 11, 1767, in an upstairs bedroom at 141 Franklin Street in Braintree (now Quincy), Massachusetts. It was the same home that his father, John Adams, used as a combination home and office. The younger Adams was named after his great-grandfather John Quincy, a speaker of the Massachusetts Assembly, member of the governors' council, and militia officer. The John Adams birthplace is now part of Adams National Historical Park and is open to the public. Nearby is Abigail Adams Cairn, marking the spot from where her son John and she witnessed the Battle of Bunker Hill when he was seven years old.[3]

Nicknames and Titles: "Old Man Eloquent," "King John II," "The Madman of Massachusetts," and "The Hellhound of Slavery."

Family: As a boy, John Quincy Adams was called Johnny, but as an adult John, causing some confusion with his illustrious father, so he took to using JQA in referring to himself. John Adams constantly offered his children guidance towards virtue. His letters from abroad were filled with admonitions to emulate the "piety, humility, simplicity, prudence, patience, temperance, frugality, industry and perseverance"[4] of their ancestors. In one letter, John Adams admonished JQA: "You come into life with advantages which will disgrace you if your success is mediocre. If you do not rise to the head not only of your profession, but of your country, it will be owing to your own Laziness, Slovenliness, and Obstinacy."[5]

Abigail Smith Adams vowed that her children would come to maturity, rigorously disciplined and constantly prodded along the path of righteousness. Her sternness caused Johnny to consider his maternal grandparents as surrogate parents, and to treat their parsonage in Weymouth, Massachusetts, as his second home.[6] JQA had two brothers: Charles Adams (1770–1800) and Thomas Boylston Adams (1772–1832), and two sisters: Abigail Amelia Adams (1765–1813) and Susanna Adams (1768–1770).

John Quincy Adams, 1826 engraving by Asher B. Durand of a painting by Thomas Sully, printed by B. Rogers, Philadelphia (Library of Congress).

Ancestors: John Quincy Adams was a second cousin once removed of Samuel Adams and a third cousin once removed to his own mother. JQA was the product of a consanguineous union as his parents were third cousins.[7] Through his mother he could trace several lines of descent from King Edward I of England. On his father's side, Henry Adams came from England to Massachusetts Bay in 1632 accompanied by a wife, eight sons ranging in age from six to twenty-five, and one daughter. The Adams family believed that Henry Adams came from Braintree in Essex County, embarking for the colonies from Ipswich with the Reverend Thomas Hooker's party. Adams settled in the new Braintree, a long walk from Boston, while Hooker went on to found Connecticut.[8] From Henry's arrival until 1735 when his great-great-grandson John Adams, the future second president of the United States, was born, Adams' family members made their existence as farmers and brewers.[9]

Appearance: As an adult, Adams stood 5 feet 7 inches tall and weighed roughly 175 pounds.[10] By the time he was president, he was almost totally bald. He had dark, penetrating eyes, which he injured by viewing an eclipse of the sun after forgetting to bring his smoked glasses to protect them.[11] He was not very interested in clothes. At his inauguration, he wore a black "homespun" suit, featuring long trousers, rather than knee breeches.[12] He couldn't seem to keep his cravat or his hair, what remained of it, in place. He wore the same hat for 10 years.[13] His right thumb carried a permanent ink stain from all his writing.[14]

Personality and Character: John Quincy Adams was one of the most brilliant, learned, and able men who ever held high office in the United States. JQA had a strong character, high principles, unswerving integrity, an iron constitution, and was a master of hard work.[15] He was well-read, amazingly articulate and had the brilliance of a master fencer in defending his opinions or demolishing the positions of opponents.[16]

He had a high, shrill voice, a gruff exterior, and was cool and aloof. Despite being considered one of America's greatest diplomats, "his manners were stiff and disagreeable."[17] He could be offensively blunt in telling the truth, sarcastic and openly intolerant. He never took pains to conciliate anyone and outside a very small number of warm friends, he seemed best at making enemies.[18] His son Charles said of his father that his feelings seemed "impenetrable," as if he were hiding behind an "iron mask." Because of his recurring depression John Quincy often appeared dour or angry.[19] A contemporary said of Adams: "[He had] an instinct for the jugular and the carotid arteries as unerring as that of any carnivorous animal."[20]

George Waterton described Adams: "Sedate, circumspect and cautious; reserved, but not distant; grave but not repulsive. He receives but seldom communicates, and discerns with great quickness motives, however latent, and intentions, however concealed.... Mr. Adams has more capacity than genius; he can comprehend better than he can invent; and execute nearly as rapidly as he can design."[21] John Randolph compared JQA to his illustrious father: "The cub is a greater bear than the old one."[22] Adams' outgoing, social and even joyful side was seen only infrequently. He was a man of letters with a passion for science and technology. "Few men in American history have, during their lifetime, been regarded with so much hostility and attacked so vehemently by their political enemies."[23]

Marriage and Romances: From his childhood John Quincy Adams loved the theater. While in Paris, at age 14, a theater outing led to what he later would half seriously describe as his first romance: "The first woman I ever loved was an actress."[24] The girl was a member of a company of children performers. She was about the same age as Johnny. Although he never actually met the young lady, he later admitted: "She remains upon my memory as the most lovely and delightful actress that I ever saw."[25]

JQA wished he could have told her "how much he adored her."[26] He later confessed to his wife that before leaving Europe, he had learned of the loose morals of actresses. He thanked "my stars and my stupidity" for not approaching his beloved.[27] As to his morals, Johnny was constantly bombarded in letters from his mother warning him of worldly temptations that lured young men into sinful ways. As one of her brothers had lived a dissolute life, she sternly told her son that he must "never disgrace his mother," and he must "behave worthy of his father."[28] At one time she lectured her son: "For dear as you are to me, I had much rather you should have found your grave in the ocean you have crossed, rather than see you an immoral profligate or a graceless child. You must keep a strict guard upon yourself, or the odious monster will soon lose its terror by becoming familiar to you."[29]

At age 22, JQA fell deeply in love with Mary Frazier, but was dissuaded from marrying her by his mother, arguing that he could not support a wife. As a result of the breakup, he sank into a deep depression.[30] JQA and Louisa Catherine Johnson first met when she was four, and he was eight, during his travels through France with his father. Louisa was born in London on February 12, 1775, the second oldest of three lovely daughters of Joshua Johnson, an American merchant, born in Maryland, and Englishwoman Catherine Nuth Johnson. Shortly after Louisa's birth, the Johnsons took refuge in Nantes, France, because of the American Revolution, but moved back to London once peace was restored.[31] JQA met Louisa again in London when he was a career diplomat of age 27 and she was 19.[32]

In contrast to the stiff and dominant Adams, Louisa was intelligent, assertive, light-hearted and something of a tease. She had delicate features, reddish blond hair and brown eyes.[33] The two shared a love of books, plays and music.[34] Their personalities, however,

Left: A young John Quincy Adams, photograph between 1900 and 1912 of a painting by John Singleton Copley, 1738–1815, located at the Museum of Fine Arts, Boston (Library of Congress, Detroit Publishing Company Photograph Collection). *Right:* John Quincy Adams print, associated name on shelflist card: Andrews, no date of creation or publishing recorded on shelflist card (Library of Congress).

were very different. She was sensitive, gentle, graceful, impulsive, forgiving and outgoing. He had a quick temper, was stern, duty-driven, dogmatic, had no use for small talk and did not enjoy social events.[35] For months Adams visited the Johnson home nightly, but always left when the daughters sat down to play music and sing, as he hated the sound of the female voice in song.[36] When Louisa dared to compliment his looks at a get-together after annoying him, by asking him to "dress himself handsomely and look as dashing as possible," Adams exploded. He told her that the woman he married must "never take the liberty" of telling him what to wear. Louise replied that he had better "choose a Lady who would be more discreet" and threatened to break up with him.[37]

Adams was initially reluctant to marry, not wishing to yield his independence to a woman and besides, he was not sure to which of the three Johnson daughters to declare his love. He finally settled on Louisa and three years later they were married in London at the All Hallows Barking Church, making her the only U.S. first lady not born in America.[38] The couple immediately left for Berlin where JQA was minister. At the Prussian court, the charming young lady displayed all the style and grace of a diplomat's lady. However, the couple had an intense argument over Louisa's use of rouge, given to her by the Prussian queen. At first, the gift was declined by Mrs. Adams, on orders by Mr. Adams. When she applied rouge to her face to attend the opera, her enraged husband grabbed a towel and wiped it off. But as she prepared to attend a court function, she applied rouge again. JQA demanded that she wipe it off. She refused defiantly. At that John went to his carriage and went to court without her.[39]

Four years after their marriage, a citizen by birth, Louisa made her first trip to the United States, and found the ways of the Yankee farming community of Braintree to be particularly strange. She was startled to discover that women there were expected to devote themselves completely to their husbands and their children, without any thought for themselves.[40] The couple divided their time at the Adams family home, their house in Boston, and a political home on F. Street in Washington, D.C., the former home of James and Dolley Madison. She resided there at the time of her death. Louisa's fragile health was evidenced by her migraine headaches and fainting spells. In spite of this, she proved to be a gracious hostess and her preferred designation for both spouses, "helpmate."[41]

Louisa Catherine Johnson Adams, engraving by G.F. Storm, from a C.R. Leslie portrait. Created between 1834 and 1860 (Library of Congress).

Louisa left her two oldest sons in Massachusetts for education in 1809 when she and her two-year-old son Charles Francis accompanied JQA to his post as Minister to Russia.[42] The years in Russia were a struggle for her, what with cold winters, strange customs, limited funds, and poor health. While there, she gave birth to a daughter who died the following year.[43] When JQA was called to Ghent in 1814 and then onto London to engage in peace negotiations, Louisa braved a forty-day journey across war-torn Europe by coach in winter to join him. Roving bands of stragglers and highwaymen filled her with "unspeakable terrors" for her son.[44] JQA and Louisa were away from the United States for eight years. Later she blamed this long absence from her two sons left in Massachusetts for their untimely deaths.[45]

When Adams was secretary of state, Louisa was a well-known Washington hostess. But during his presidency, suffering from poor health and depression, she rarely entertained. Although she continued her weekly "drawing rooms," she preferred quite evenings—reading, composing music and verse and playing her harp.[46] The marriage had its stormy moments. Adams was cold and often depressed, admitting to the faults his political opponents laid on him as a "gloomy misanthropist" and an "unsocial savage."[47] He was too occupied with politics to have much time for his family. Adams did not value women's intelligence and was not a very considerate husband.[48] They quarreled incessantly, mostly about the education of their children, but the effects were not lasting. Biographer Margaret Bassett reported: "It was her misfortune that her health was at its lowest ebb in the White House, and the demands of that position, plus a season of family anxieties, bore too heavily upon her, so that her depression, fits of hysteria, and fainting spells kept the household constantly hopping to her side in alarm, an attention she relished exceedingly."[49]

Theirs was not a great romance, yet they lived to see their fiftieth wedding anniversary before his death.[50] Louise wrote her life story for her children. The first portion of the autobiography, "Record of a Life, or My Story" described her life up to her 26th birthday, the time when she arrived in the United States.[51] She found that her husband's family, especially Abigail, did not consider her good enough for Johnny and as she was a foreigner, she was made to feel like an intruder. Louisa wrote that "to a woman like Mrs. (Abigail) Adams, equal to every occasion in life, I appeared like a maudlin hysterical fine Lady...." Abigail felt her European daughter-in-law lacked the sturdiness of American women and that her thinness and poor health indicated a short life.[52] Louisa concluded that the only reasons JQA wed her was because he lost his true love Mary Frazier, and because he mistakenly thought the Johnson family to be wealthy. Try as she would, she could never be Bostonian. She could never feel that she belonged in the Adams' compound. She later wrote: "Had I stepped into Noah's Ark, I do not think I could have been more utterly astonished."[53] Her second account was self-deprecatingly labeled as "Adventures of a Nobody" and brought her story to 1812, ending in Russia, where her infant daughter died.[54]

After her husband's death, Louisa remained in Washington until her demise on May 14, 1852. To honor her, both houses of Congress adjourned for the day of her funeral, the first woman so honored.[55] Her grandchildren, who called her "the Madam," brought her some happiness. One, Henry Adams, the historian author of the marvelous *The Education of Henry Adams*, wrote a memoir about his grandparent, in which he detailed how hard it was for Louisa to be married into the Adams family. Henry's sympathy for his grandmother was matched for his bitterness toward his grandfather for the indignities he inflicted on his wife.[56] Henry's younger brother Brooks arranged to have Louisa's "Narrative of a Journey from Russia to France, 1815" published in *Scribner's* magazine in 1903.[57]

Children: Louisa Adams was sickly and suffered through fourteen pregnancies, nine miscarriages, four live births, and one still-born.[58] Their surviving children were George Washington Adams (1801–1829), John Adams II (1803–1834), Charles Francis Adams (1807–1886), and Louisa Catherine Adams (1811–1812). George Washington Adams, a lawyer, born in Berlin, was brilliant but unstable. He lived a dissipated life, neglected his practice, ran up large debts that his father was forced to pay and got a girl pregnant. He became paranoid and died at age 28, when he jumped or accidentally fell overboard from a steamer. His body was discovered along the New York coast.[59] John II was expelled from Harvard for participating in a riot. He studied law with his father and served as his private secretary when JQA was president. John II also was an alcoholic and died suddenly in 1834.[60]

Charles Francis Adams was born in Boston but from age two grew up in St. Petersburg, Russia. He was educated in England and at Harvard. He studied law, but decided instead on a literary career. He was an accomplished editor and published numerous volumes based on his family's papers, including *Letters of Mrs. Adams*; *Works of John Adams: Second President of the United States* and *Memoirs of John Quincy Adams, Comprising Portions of His Diary from 1795 to 1848*. Charles served in the Massachusetts legislature and in 1848 was Martin Van Buren's running mate on the Free Soil Ticket in an unsuccessful bid by Van Buren to regain the presidency. Charles served a single term in the House of Representatives, before being appointed by President Lincoln to the post held by both his father and grandfather, Minister to Great Britain.[61]

Religion and Religious Beliefs: JQA was nominally a Unitarian, even though he did not agree with all its doctrines. The Unitarian church in Quincy was the only congregation he ever joined.[62] Originally the Adamses were members of Congregational churches. By 1800, most Congregationalist churches in New England were ministered by Unitarian preachers, who taught the strict unity of God, the secondary nature of Christ, and salvation by character.[63] John Quincy Adams preferred Unitarian preachers, but predictably, Adams found much in Unitarian teachings to disagree with and to criticize. He forcefully rejected Joseph Priestley's materialism and ultra-rationalism and later opposed the Transcendentalist philosophy of Ralph Waldo Emerson and Orestes Brownson, whom he described as "vipers" and "enemies of public virtue." JQA labeled Emerson's "Divinity School Address" as "crazy" and claimed that Brownson was an advocate of "self-delusive atheism." Adams felt it was "everyman's duty [to] take the field" against these foes of public virtue. Following his obligation in the matter, he prepared and delivered a lecture on "Faith," theorizing that religious and moral faith is dependent on will.[64]

Adams frequently worshiped at All Souls Unitarian Church in the nation's capital, which he helped found.[65] As an interested spectator, he attended services of numerous denominations, including Catholic and Orthodox churches, while stationed in Russia and appreciated many theological perspectives.[66] He insisted that Christians of various denominations were traveling by different routes to the same destination. In a letter to Richard Anderson, JQA insisted: "Civil liberty can be established on no foundation of human reason which will not at the same time demonstrate the right to religious freedom."[67]

Adams was devout, reading three chapters of the Bible in Greek, German, French and English daily on arising, finishing the entire book each year.[68] Beginning in 1819, he attended services twice every Sunday. He tried to limit his activities on Sundays, believing the Lord's Day should be devoted to religious activities and attendance at church services. He wrote: "I can frequent without scruple the church of any other sect of Christians, and join with cheerfulness the social worship of all without subscribing implicitly to the doctrines of any

(Denomination)...."[69] A Quaker meeting was an exception: "We sat nearly two hours in perfect silence — no moving of the spirit; and I seldom, in the course of my life, passed two hours more wearily.... I felt, on coming from this meeting, as if I had wasted precious time."[70]

JQA preferred preachers to speak of the fruits of religion rather than to linger over dogma. He approved of sermons based on "sound morals without doctrinal speculation and without enthusiasm [excessive fervor]."[71] He found sermons on subjects such as human depravity, predestination, and vicarious atonement were absurd and aggravated him. On hearing a hymn by Isaac Watts "which declared that we were more base and brutish than the beasts," he asked, "What is the meaning of this? If Watts had said this on a weekday to any one of his parishioners, would he not have knocked him down?"[72] Adams was particularly fond of the sermons of John Tillotson, Archbishop of Canterbury from 1691 to 1694. Adams read Tillotson's homilies (compiled in ten volumes) throughout his life.[73]

When he was sworn in as president, not wishing to involve the Bible in politics, Adams took the oath of office on a book of laws, the Constitution and American laws. He was swearing allegiance, not to God, but to the Constitution.[74] Desiring to make the Bible widely available and to encourage people to read it, he agreed to serve as one of the vice presidents of the American Bible Association (1824–1848).[75] In debates, he often quoted Scripture to support his arguments. In 1811, he wrote from St. Petersburg to his sons at Harvard:

> The first and almost the only Book deserving of universal attention is the Bible.... In what light soever we regard the Bible, whether with reference to revelation, to history, or to morality, it is an invaluable and inexhaustible mine of knowledge and virtue.... So great is my veneration for the Bible, that the earlier my children begin to read it the more confident will be my hopes that they will prove useful citizens to their country and respectable members of society.[76]

In another letter to his boys, JQA addressed the Ten Commandments: "The law given from Sinai was a civil and municipal as well as a moral and religious code ... laws essential to the existence of men in society and most of which have been enacted by every nation which ever possessed any code of laws."[77] Adams prayed constantly about all aspects of his life and often asked others to pray for him in his discharge of his public duties and at those times when he was afflicted with grief at the death of his sons.[78] Near the end of his life, he confided to his diary: "For I believe there is a god who heareth prayer, and that honest prayers to him will not be in vain."[79]

He wrote religious verse and composed numerous hymns. Adams claimed the "three fundamental pillars" of the Bible were "the unity and omnipotence of God"; "the immortality of the human soul, and its responsibility" to the "Creator in a future world for all the deeds done in the present"; and "a system of morals based on the commandments to love God with all one's heart, mind, and strength and one's neighbor as oneself."[80] He had complete faith in the existence of a personal God and of His role in guiding men, but he had more difficulty with the tenets of various religions and religious denominations, summing up his doubts with: "How can I believe what I can not understand?"[81]

He rejected what he considered the more extreme doctrines of the Unitarians and the Trinitarians, who debated the doctrine of the Trinity, announcing he was neither. He asserted: "I believe in one God, but His nature is incomprehensible to me."[82] Adams considered Jesus to be the greatest human being and the consummate role model. Summarizing his beliefs, Adams wrote: "I reverence God as my creator. As the creator of the world, I reverence Him with holy fear. I venerate Jesus Christ as my redeemer; and as far as I can understand, the redeemer of the world. But this belief is dark and dubious."[83] Adams believed in life after death, saying: "If the existence of man were limited to this life, it would be impossible for me to believe the universe made any moral sense."[84]

Adams agreed with German philosopher Immanuel Kant that as virtue is not always rewarded or vice punished in life, there must be an afterlife where accounts are balanced. Speaking of the Christian system of morals, Adams wrote: "Man is an immortal spirit, confined for a short space of time, in an earthly tabernacle. Kindness to his fellow mortals embraces the whole compass of his duties upon earth, and the whole promise of happiness to his spirit hereafter. The essence of this doctrine is, to exalt the spiritual over the brutal part of his nature."[85]

Education: JQA was educated at home by his parents. His father taught him mathematics, languages and classics. The elder Adams encouraged Johnny to revere scholarship as his "preeminent entertainment."[86] While in Europe with his father, the younger Adams attended schools in France and Holland. After Johnny and his family settled in Passy, he was placed in a weekday boarding school run by Monsieur Le Coeur that catered to American boys. The curriculum emphasized Latin and French and included training in fencing, dancing, drawing and music.[87] In France, Johnny experienced boundless cultural riches, but his favorite entertainment was the theater, particularly French comedy and the tragedies of Corneille, Racine and Voltaire. He contended that for the best of "the language, the wit, the passions, the oratory, the poetry, the manners, and morals" one must attend French Comedy.[88] During his second stay in France, Johnny entered a pension academy operated by the Pechigy family, where many Americans in Paris sent their children. Besides the essential studies of Latin and Greek, Johnny studied geography, mathematics, and writing. He was proficient in seven languages, which proved invaluable to him in his diplomatic career.[89] Thirteen-year-old Johnny was an independent student at Leyden University, taking lessons privately and attending lectures at what was then one of the world's finest centers of learning.[90]

After two years in Russia accompanying Francis Dana on a diplomatic mission, Johnny returned to Massachusetts and entered Harvard College, where, among other things, he mastered the flute, demonstrated his abilities in what later would be known as differential calculus, conic sections, and astronomy.[91] At a public exhibition in his senior year, he delivered an oration on the topic "Whether the Introduction of Christianity has been serviceable to the temporal interests of man." In it, he declared:

> Christianity, it is true, has been the immediate object of many contests: But when mankind has no inclination to quarrel with one another, a motive is easily found; the causes of dispute are innumerable, and had Christianity never appeared, the power of Discord would probably have been much greater than it has been. Every candid reader of history will acknowledge that the Christian institution has gradually inspired into the hearts of men, sentiments of compassion, benevolence, and humanity even towards their enemies, which were entirely unknown to the savage barbarians of antiquity.[92]

After graduating second in his class in 1787, JQA studied law at Newburyport with Theophilus Parsons. He was admitted to the bar in 1790 and began practicing law in Boston, but he found it boring. He was more than willing to satisfy his parents' desires that he dedicated his life to public service.[93] He was an accomplished linguist and an assiduous diarist. He faithfully kept a diary from the time he was twelve. In a letter to his mother, he explained: "My Pappa enjoins it upon me to keep a Journal, or Diary of the Events that happen to me, and of objects that I see, and of Characters that I converse with from day to day; and although I am convinced of the utility, importance, and necessity of this Exercise, yet I have not patience and perseverance enough to do it so constantly as I ought."[94] His perseverance in the task suggested by his father continued nearly 70 years. His diaries form a conspicuous account of his doings and those of his contemporaries for the next 60 years of American history. JQA once immodestly but sincerely said that "[It might have become] next to the Holy Scriptures, the most precious and valuable book ever written by human hands."[95]

Like his father before him, John Quincy considered it his duty to instruct his children on many subjects, and particularly in history and the Bible. In the case of history, in a letter to his sons in Massachusetts, while he was Ambassador to Russia, he encouraged the study of history by quoting Cicero, speaking of the history of one's country: "It is not so much praiseworthy to be acquainted with it as it is shameful to be ignorant of it."[96]

Occupation: Adams briefly practiced law after being admitted to the Suffolk, Massachusetts bar. To escape the tedium of his profession, he wrote occasional articles for the *Columbian Centinel* under the signature "Publicola" (Latin for "friend of the people").[97] In 1791 he attacked some positions taken by Thomas Paine in his *Rights of Man* and criticized Thomas Jefferson for his support of Paine. When these pieces were republished in England, they were generally believed to have been written by his father, causing a breach between the two founding fathers.[98] In December 1792, the younger Adams protested Boston's anti-theater ordinances in articles signed "Menander."[99] JQA wrote another series of articles for the *Columbian Centinel*, signed "Marcellus," in which he defended Washington's policy of neutrality, concluding with the statement: "It is our duty to remain, the peaceful and silent, though sorrowful spectators of the sanguinary scene."[100]

Adams published a third series, signed "Columbus," in which he denounced the "political villainy" of France's Genêt mission.[101] His dream of an independent life, free of his parents' domination was not to be. Washington appreciated the support of the younger Adams and appointed him Minister to Holland, a position he accepted only after much inner turmoil and parental prodding. He complained, "I wish I could have been consulted before it was irrevocably made." Adams proved to be much more skilled as a diplomat and statesman than a lawyer, if less so as a politician.[102]

Home: The primary home for both John and John Quincy Adams was called "Peacefield" or "Old House." Built in 1731, it was the residence of four generations of Adams.[103] The elder Adams was born in the saltbox house only 75 feet from the birthplace of his son. Nearly identical, the brick birthplaces of the first father and his son were covered with clapboard siding, framed with huge beams, and enlarged with rear lean-to additions. Multiple fireplaces fed into central chimneys and small windows protected the inhabitants from New England winters.

From his grandparents, the Smiths, John Quincy Adams inherited the ancient Quincy estate on the seashore in Braintree. The first English settlement in the area was led by a Captain Wollaston in 1625. Thirty or forty colonists cleared the land and built log huts, calling the settlement Mount Wollaston. Wollaston remained in the area for a year before moving on to Virginia.[104] He was replaced as leader by free-thinking adventurer Thomas Morton, who named the place Mare Mount (also known as Merry Mount or Merrymount).

It wasn't long before Morton and his followers' behavior outraged their neighbors, the Pilgrims. Just how is best stated in Morton's own words in his book *The New England Canaan*:

> The inhabitants of ... Mare Mount ... did devise amongst themselves ... Revels and merriment after the old English custome; (they) prepared to sett up a Maypole upon the festival day ... and

therefore brewed a barrell of excellent beare ... to be spent, with other good cheare, for all comers of that day. And ... they had prepared a song fitting to the time and present occasion. And upon May Day they brought the Maypole to the place appointed, with drums, gunnes, pistols and other fitting instruments, for the purpose, and there erected it with the help of Savages, that came there to see the manner of our Revels. A goodly pine tree of 80 foot longe was reared up, with a peare of buckshorns nailed one somewhere neare upon the top of it: where it stood, as a faire sea mark for directions how to finde out the way to mine Hoste of Mare Mount.[105]

Nathaniel Hawthorne wrote a fictionalized account of the revels in his story "The Maypole of Merrymount." The author claimed, although providing no evidence, that Morton sold liquor, guns and ammunition to the Indians, thereby threatening the security of Plymouth colony. In 1628 the Puritans dispatched Miles Standish to put an end to the disorder. He promptly cut down the maypole and took Morton into custody. Morton's associates were too drunk to resist. They were all exiled to a small nearby island to await transportation back to England. With the assistance of his Native American friends, Morton escaped and returned to England on his own. He returned to Massachusetts in 1642, was imprisoned in Boston, and when he was released, he was exiled to Maine, where he lived out his life. Morton always maintained that the real reason for his expulsion was that he and his men were better at trapping and trading with the Indians and were thus posed an economic threat to the Puritans.[106]

Mount Wollaston became the home of William and Anne Hutchinson in 1636. Anne, the mother of twelve, began a career as a pioneering female preacher in New England but was excommunicated for her liberal religious views. "Hutchinson interpreted the doctrine of the Perseverance of the saints according to the Free Grace model, which taught that the saved could sin freely without endangering their salvation, instead of the Lordship salvation model prevalent at that time, which noted that those who were truly saved would demonstrate by seeking to follow the ways of their Saviour. She also claimed that she could identify 'the elect' among the colonists."[107] These positions caused John Cotton, John Winthrop, and other former friends to condemn her as an antinomian heretic. She moved to Rhode Island to establish a colony based on religious freedom. She was killed by Indians in New York in 1643.

In 1635, the magistrates of Boston granted about 400 acres to Edmund Quincy who renamed the farm Mount Wollaston. In 1640 the inhabitants of Mount Wollaston were granted the right to establish a town separate from Boston, which was renamed Braintree. William Smith, the grandfather of John Quincy Adams, the father of Abigail Smith Adams, owned the Mt. Wollaston farm in the early 1700s.[108]

Motto: "Watch and Pray" was the title of a sonnet that he wrote and sent to his son George.[109]

Pets and Animals: In 1826, the Marquis de Lafayette gave JQA an alligator, which lived in the East Room of the White House for several months. Louisa raised silkworms at the White House and used the silk in making her gowns.[110]

Recreational Pastimes and Interests: One of John Quincy Adams' intellectual passions was the art of translation. He rendered the *Fables choisies, mises en vers* (12 volumes, 1668–1694) of Jean de La Fontaine into English.[111] Adams enjoyed billiards, going to the theater, reading, horseback riding, walking and swimming. He maintained a life-long interest in natural history and one of his hobbies was the domestication of wild plants. Despite the history of alcohol abuse in the Adams family, JQA was a connoisseur of good wine. He lauded the temperance movement, but never pledged to abstain from alcohol, arguing that wine consumed in moderation was a gift from God and that there was no place in the Bible that called for abstinence totally from liquor.[112] Adams did call intoxication "a heinous crime" and cited efforts to reduce drunkenness "a holy work."[113]

Political Philosophy and Political Party Affiliation: Adams believed that government was an instrument the Creator employed to glorify Him and benefit humanity. He argued that as God was the supreme sovereign, the authority of nations was delegated and derivative. Political officials could not merely do what the majority of people wanted; they were obligated to do what was morally right. JQA was convinced that his ultimate responsibility was to the Creator and moral principle, not to a political party or its constituents. This explained why Adams would do what he considered to be morally correct, even if it was unpopular.[114]

Adams considered the United States a Christian nation with a God-given mission to redeem the world and this meant expansion across the entire continent. In his first annual address to Congress, JQA stated "liberty is power ... the nation blessed with the largest portion of liberty must in proportion to its numbers be the most powerful nation upon earth, and that the tenure of power by man is, in the moral purposes of his Creator."[115] To Adams' thinking, God had chosen America to serve as exemplars of liberty, to spread democracy in the world, and to eradicate all forms of European colonialism. He envisioned the creation of a model republic, which by example would shine liberty and virtue throughout the world. In an 1830 letter to the American Bible Society, Adams wrote: "Whoever believes in the divine inspiration of the Holy Scriptures must hope that the religion of Jesus shall prevail throughout the earth."[116]

John Quincy Adams was elected to the U.S. Senate as a Federalist, but broke with the party of his father and became a supporter of Democratic-Republican policies. In reality, he was not a member of any party, in that he didn't support the notion of political parties. He was intent on voting his conscience based on what it told him was right. He was confounded that anyone should put party above conscience. His affiliation rested on his actions, not his endorsement of a particular political party.[117]

DIPLOMATIC ROLES

Secretary to the U.S. Minister: At age 14, Adams served as private secretary and French interpreter to Francis Dana, the U.S. Envoy to Russia in 1781. They lingered for more than a year at St. Petersburg but were not received by the Russian government.[118] JQA returned to Paris by way of Scandinavia, Hanover, and the Netherlands. In France, he acted as an additional informal secretary to the American commissioners in the negotiation of the Peace of Paris that concluded the American Revolutionary War.[119]

Minister to The Netherlands: George Washington appointed Adams minister to The Netherlands (1794) and Portugal (1796). He had little to do at The Hague, so he made good use of his free time to further his studies.[120]

Minister to Prussia: In 1797 JQA was promoted to minister to Prussia by his father, serving until 1801, when his father recalled him from the post after the election of Thomas Jefferson. While in Berlin, Johnny negotiated a treaty of amity and commerce with Prussia.[121] The post gave Adams a chance to study German. He translated poems of Friedrich Schuller and Christoph Martin Wieland's heroic poem, "Oberon," into English.[122]

Minister to Russia: President Madison appointed JQA the United States first Minister to Russia (1809–1811). His mission was to urge freedom of the seas, to seek favorable treat-

Peace of Ghent 1814 and Triumph of America, engraving by Mme. Plantou, citizen of the United States pinxit; Chataigner, sculptor. Published in Philadelphia by P. Price, Jr., ca. 1820. The print is an allegorical reference to the Treaty of Ghent, which ended the War of 1812 (Library of Congress).

ment for American shipping in Russian waters, and to reaffirm the desire of the United States to avoid entanglements in continental policies.[123] He persuaded Czar Alexander I to intercede when fifty-two U.S. ships were seized by Danish privateers, having the ships released.[124] In 1812, Adams wrote to his mother about the unsuccessful invasion of Russia by Emperor Napoleon I, saying: "The two Russian generals who have conquered Napoleon and all his Marshals are General *Famine* and General *Frost*."[125]

While in Russia, Adams declined an appointment to the U.S. Supreme Court.[126] His salary was insufficient for the expenses required to live as part of the diplomatic delegations in St. Petersburg. The extreme cold of Russia contributed to Louisa's poor health, making her stay in the country very difficult.[127]

Treaty of Ghent: JQA was the chief negotiator of the U.S. Commission for the Treaty of Ghent in 1814. Because of American defeats and New England Federalists' threats of secession, the American position at the conference table was weakened. However, by the end of 1814, the war had become a stalemate and England, more concerned with European affairs, offered peace. On Christmas Eve, the treaty returning to the status quo before the war was signed.[128] Signatories for Britain included diplomats William Adams, James Lord Gambier and Henry Goulburn, who took orders from London. The Peace Commission representing the U.S. consisted of JQA, James A. Bayard, Sr., Henry Clay, Jonathan Russell, and Albert Gallatin. Adams referred to the treaty as "a truce rather than a peace."[129] Fighting immediately stopped when news of the treaty reached the battlefronts, but not before the Americans won a decisive victory at the Battle of New Orleans in January 1815.

Minister to Great Britain: From 1815 to 1817, Adams was minister to the Court of St.

James in England. He spent two years, with little success, trying to resolve differences between Britain and the U.S. He laid the groundwork for the Rush-Bagot Convention of 1817 that provided disarmament along the U.S.-Canadian border. JQA also helped fix the boundary between the U.S. and Canada.[130]

POLITICAL OFFICES

United States Senator: Adams returned to Quincy, and in 1802 was elected to the Massachusetts Senate. That same year he was an unsuccessful Federalist candidate for the House of Representatives.[131] Adams was elected to the United States Senate as a Federalist, serving from 1803 to 1808. In 1804, JQA confided to his diary:

> I have already had occasion to experience, what I had before the fullest reason to expect, the danger of adhering to my own principles. The country is so totally given up to the spirit of party, that not to follow blindfold the one or the other is an inexpiable offense.... Between both, I see the impossibility of pursuing the dictates of my own conscience without sacrificing every prospect, not merely of advancement, but even of retaining that character and reputation I have enjoyed.[132]

The Federalist Party was deeply divided by a feud between partisans of John Adams and those of Alexander Hamilton. Unlike the other senator from Massachusetts, Timothy Pickering, JQA wished to serve the whole country, not just a region of it or a political party. He spoke of trying to serve as a man above the "baneful weed of party strife."[133] As a result, Pickering barely spoke to him, he was repeatedly insulted, and any motion he made was rejected by the combined votes of the Republicans and Hamilton's Federalists.[134] Frequently, Adams was not informed of the time or place of the meeting of committees to which he belonged. His treatment was due not merely because he was the son of a president but because of his stubborn independence, a family trait.[135] He endorsed Democratic-Republican President Jefferson's then controversial purchase of the Louisiana Territory from France, which the Federalists bitterly opposed and fiercely censured. Adams was the only New England Federalist to vote in favor of it.[136]

JQA's problems with his party only worsened when both Great Britain and France plundered American commercial ships. Although there was little to choose from in the harm the two countries were inflicting on American commerce, one incident turned most Americans against England rather than France. In the summer of 1807, in full sight of the American coast, the British ship *Leopard* fired upon the *Chesapeake*,[137] killing and wounding several of its crew. This was not enough to turn the Federalists from their hatred of France. One prominent Federalist, John Lowell of Boston, was overheard defending the action of the *Leopard*. Later, Adams said: "This was the cause which alienated me from that day and forever from the councils of the Federalist Party."[138]

When Adams was put on a committee by the Republicans to draft resolutions condemning Britain, Federalists clamored that he should "have his head taken off for apostasy."[139] Adams supported Jefferson's Embargo Act which did not achieve its avowed purpose of forcing Britain and France to respect U.S. rights on the high seas. Instead, it dealt a blow to U.S. commerce and Massachusetts shipbuilders, especially.[140] The final straw occurred in 1808, when the Massachusetts legislature elected a senator to replace him, several months before his term was up. Five days later JQA resigned, thumbing his nose in a letter to the Massachusetts Legislature, informing them: "I now restore to you the trust committed to my charge." That same year, he attended the Democratic-Republican congressional caucus that nominated James Madison, thus joining the party of Jefferson.[141]

During his Senate tenure, JQA was an adjunct Boylston Professor of Rhetoric and Oratory at Harvard College. In his Inaugural Oration, Adams stated:

> The peculiar and highest characteristic, which distinguishes man from the rest of the animal creation, is reason. It is by this attribute that our species is constituted the great link between the physical and intellectual world. By our passions and appetites, we are placed on a level with the herds of the forest; by our reason we participate of the divine nature itself.... The only birth place of eloquence ... must be a free state. Under arbitrary governments ... where the despot, like the Roman centurion, has only to say to one man, go, and he goeth, and to another, come, and he cometh; persuasion is of no avail....
>
>   Eloquence is the child of liberty, ... she will find her most instructive school ... in a country, where the same spirit of liberty, which marks the relations between the individuals of the same community, is diffused over those more complicated and important relations between different communities ... where the independence of the man is corroborated and invigorated by the independence of the state ... where the same power of persuasion, which influences the will of the citizen at home, has the means of opening upon the will and the conduct of sovereign societies.... [There,] eloquence will spring to light; will flourish; will rise to the highest perfection of which human art or science is susceptible.[142]

He wrote his brother that he could be content spending the remainder of his life as a college professor "if he who rules the destinies of men had so decreed."[143] According to Denise M. Henderson:

> Adams viewed his responsibility to the students at Harvard, of whom he had been one, in the most far-ranging way possible. He appealed to their souls more than to their speaking abilities.... Adams provoked his students to examine the purpose of their future lives, and their principles. Unless his students were to take up the challenge of the ancient Greek sage Socrates, to "know thyself," they would fall short of the qualities of leadership needed to defend the endangered young republic.[144]

Some members of Harvard's faculty criticized John Quincy's orations because they were delivered in English, instead of the traditional Latin. He answered by saying that since his remarks were intended to sketch the nature, history, and practice of oratory, he felt they ought to be understood by his entire audience. Of course, at the time, an audience at Harvard would understand a lecture given in Latin.[145]

Cabinet Position: Adams was President Monroe's secretary of state (1817–1825), and was considered by many scholars as possibly the greatest of all time.[146] He was instrumental in Spain ceding East and West Florida to the U.S and keeping the U.S. from becoming dependent on the United Kingdom. The Adams-Onís Treaty with Spain established the boundary between Louisiana and Mexico as running along the Sabine and Red rivers, the upper Arkansas, the crest of the Rocky Mountains and the 49th parallel.[147] JQA supported the policy of recognizing the independence of colonies that revolted in Spanish America. Adams not only convinced Monroe to issue the Monroe Doctrine, he was the primary author of its decisive enunciation. Adams told Monroe: "It would be more candid, as well as more dignified, to avow our principles explicitly to Russia and France, than to come in as a cock-boat in the wake of the British man-of-war."[148]

After the Missouri Compromise was passed by the Congress and sent to the president for his signature, Monroe put two questions to his Cabinet. The first was: did Congress have a constitutional right to prohibit slavery in a territory. Secondly, in prohibiting slavery "forever" in the territory north of the Mason and Dixon line, did the bill refer to this district only so long as it remained under territorial government, or did it apply to such states as might in the future be formed from it. The Cabinet was unanimous in the affirmative to the first question, but only Adams replied that "forever" meant forever.[149] This was Adams' initial stand against slavery, a position which thereafter made him famous. JQA was sometimes referred to as the "Lone Wolf" for his positions, as he so often went against the majority opinion of Monroe's Cabinet. However, being in the minority didn't prevent Monroe from going along with his secretary of state's positions and recommendations.[150]

HIS PRESIDENCY

As was customary at the time, as secretary of state, Adams was considered the political heir to the president. Although only one political party existed, the Democratic-Republican, there were factions and sectionalism. Adams desired the presidency; however, true to his nature he did nothing to promote his election, insisting that it should come as unsolicited popular trust in him. When Edward Everett asked him if he was "determined to do nothing with a view to promote his future election to the presidency as the successor of Mr. Monroe," he replied that he "should do absolutely nothing."[151] In 1824, Adams received only 84 votes in the Electoral College, with 99 going to Andrew Jackson, the hero of the Battle of New Orleans, 37 to Henry Clay and 41 to William H. Crawford.

With no one having a clear majority, the election was thrown into the House of Representatives to decide among the top three vote getters, thus eliminating Clay. Crawford had been President Monroe's secretary of war and secretary of the treasury. His explosive temper alienated a number of political leaders, including Monroe. The two men almost came to blows in a cabinet meeting before Crawford came to his senses and apologized. The two men seldom spoke to each other from that time on. Crawford suffered several paralyzing strokes during the campaign, bringing the choice down to Jackson or Adams.[152]

Clay favored a program similar to that of Adams: internal improvements, the national bank, and a high tariff on importation, and felt Jackson was not fit for the presidency. He threw his support to Adams, whom the House elected president. Later, when JQA appointed Clay secretary of state, Jackson and his followers were livid, charging that a "corrupt deal" had been brokered. They accused Clay of soliciting the Cabinet position that traditionally was held by the next in the succession to become president first from Jackson, and when he angrily refused, Clay made the deal with Adams.[153]

John Quincy Adams was not a political president. His presidency was a political failure due to the powerful opposition forces in Congress. Jackson immediately resigned from the Senate and his followers began their campaign to deny Adams a second term.[154] The general planned a "spoils system," which would reward supporters with governmental positions. Adams would never consider loyalty to him as a test for holding a governmental office. JQA was concerned with a man's competence, not his political affiliation.[155] According to journalist Joseph Wheelan: "Rather than build a political apparatus through the wholesale replacement of civil servants with his supporters, as his predecessors had, Adams insisted on only filling vacancies when they occurred — and in keeping employees if they were competent, even if they were political enemies."[156] Adams' refusal to dispense patronage to make influential friends, along with his personality and political philosophy, alienated the party that helped elect him. He maintained that the president should be a "remote, powerful personage." JQA was often depressed, aloof and angry.[157] Each day he conferred with a steady procession of congressmen and department heads, which he described in his diary: "I can scarcely conceive a more harassing, wearying, teasing condition of existence."[158]

Whether the Jacksonians fully believed the charge of a corrupt bargain, they derived great political capital out of the charge. With the appointment of Clay, supporters of Jackson,

Calhoun, and Crawford had a perfect pretext for mounting four years of never-ending opposition to the Adams administration and all its proposals. John Quincy Adams' idealistic and uncompromising notions of political leadership were out of touch in an increasingly democratic and materialistic republic. Still it is doubtful that he would have had success or re-elected no matter how admirable his political program or if he had more consummate political skills. His enemies conducting opposition to his programs with the sole aim of guaranteeing he would be a one-term president. His detractors were able to muster broad geographical and financial support to their cause. Westerners demanded free or very cheap land and Southerners called for increased states' rights.[159] Opposition newspapers lampooned JQA's schemes. Edward Pessen said of JQA: "Son, like father, lacked the common touch, appeared to suffer fools badly, and had neither zest for nor skill in playing the political games that evidently had to be played if a chief executive hoped to achieve success, whether in securing the enactment of a program or in assuring his continuation in the nation's highest political office."[160]

Adams asked no favors and granted none. He was the most independent president since Washington. On the other hand, Jackson promised his supporters a share of government offices that would come available when he made a "clean sweep" of turning out incumbents.[161] In the 1828 election in which 56 percent of the eligible voters cast their ballots, Jackson defeated Adams in both popular vote and in the electoral college, 178 votes to 83. The campaign was very much a personal one. While neither candidate actively campaigned, their political followers and supporting newspapers attacked the candidates. The lowest point in the mudslinging was when Jackson's wife Rachel was accused of bigamy. She died a few weeks after the elections, and Jackson never forgave Adams for the smear.[162] Like his father, JQA did not attend the inauguration of his successor, because the two men were bitter enemies.[163]

His Vice President: John C. Calhoun (1782–1850) of South Carolina held many high government posts in the years before the Civil War. He represented his home state both in the U.S. House of Representatives and the Senate. He was President Monroe's secretary of war and President John Tyler's secretary of state. He was vice president under both John Quincy Adams (1825–1829) and Andrew Jackson (1825–1832). When he first entered Congress in 1811, he joined the "War Hawks," who helped bring about the war with Great Britain. Early in his congressional career he supported a strong national government but later argued that the states did not have to obey federal laws they considered unconstitutional.[164]

His Cabinet: Secretary of State Henry Clay (1825–1829); Secretary of the Treasury Richard Rush (1825–1829); Secretary of War James Barbour (1825–1828) and Peter B. Porter (1828); Attorney General William Wirt (1825–1829); Secretary of the Navy Samuel L. Southard (1825–1829).

Supreme Court Appointments: Robert Trimble of Kentucky served as an associate justice 1826–1828.

Domestic Affairs — Major Events:

Not faced with any great foreign problems, Adams argued that the federal government should use its resources to improve the new republic's transportation system as well as its political, social, intellectual, and moral life. JQA was convinced that government must be an agent of social progress. His proposals for the creation of a Department of the Interior were rebuffed.[165]

Internal Improvements: Despite no electoral mandate to do so, Adams proposed a bold program of domestic reform. In his "Lighthouses of the Skies"[166] message to Congress on December 5, 1825, to spur commerce he urged the use of Federal funds to build a comprehensive system of roads and canals. To stimulate manufacturing, he recommended a high protective tariff. In his ambitious program, he stressed the need for government encouragement of the arts and sciences, including establishment of a national university, erection of an observatory, and financing of scientific expeditions.[167] Not only was his plan criticized and opposed by constitutionalists and states' righters, his proposals failed to stir public support.[168] Even many of his supporters in Congress had trouble with his proposals. Critics claimed it was arrogant for a president, elected by only one vote in the House, to believe he was entitled to act as though he had received a national mandate for action. Others protested that these internal improvements would benefit specific parts of the nation over others and involve the federal government into regional affairs.[169]

Adams was ahead of his time, as many of his ideas found favor in later years. He was confident that establishing a first-rate educational, physical and social environment where reason was allowed to flourish would also enhance moral behavior. John Quincy Adams envisioned education as the natural complement to religion. "He believed that God's laws could be discerned by scientific investigation, and that, once learned, these laws could be used for improvement of humanity."[170] In May 1829, Adams won congressional approval for a program of internal improvements that included the construction of the Chesapeake and Ohio Canal.[171] The rejection of his plan to unify the nation and to propagate republican government across the continent was a severe blow to Adams. His objective was to use the proceeds from the sale of land acquired between 1803 and 1819 and those gathered from the tariff to build roads and canals.[172] As a result, he was confident that the Union would be integrated both politically and commercially. He also wished to dedicate a portion of these revenues to advance the arts and sciences, which in turn he believed would advance the progress of the nation. It was his fervent opinion that the program would make all sections of the country so dependent upon each other, that sectionalism would all but disappear.[173] Adams had long been a proponent of internal improvements. In 1807, he made the first motion in the Senate concerning establishing a program of internal improvements, but it failed to be acted upon. In his final year as President Monroe's secretary of state, he reflected on the importance of such a system:

> The question of the Power of Congress to authorize the making of internal improvements, is, in other words, a question, whether the People of this Union, in forming their common social compact, avowedly for the purpose of promoting their general welfare, have performed their work in a manner so ineffably stupid, as to deny themselves the means of bettering their own condition. I have too much respect for the intellect of my country to believe it. The first object of human association is the improvement of the condition of the associates — Roads and canals are among the most essential means of improving the condition of Nations, and a People which should deliberately by the organization of its authorized power, deprive itself of the faculty of multiplying its own blessings, would be as wise as a Creator, who should undertake to constitute a human being without a Heart.[174]

JQA was convinced that the internal improvements he sought would "afford high wages and constant employment of hundreds of thousands laborers."[175] He reasoned that as a result the Southern economy would be modernized and would lead gradually to the end of slavery. Southerners recognized this portion of Adams' program and wanted nothing to do with it. They argued that in opposing the president's plan, they were defending American liberty against a tyrannical government dictating to the people about how they should live. Adams was disgusted with what he viewed as the immoral and paradoxical arguments of Southerners to complain about infringement on their liberties, when they denied liberty to slaves. White Southerner politicians took the questionable position that black slavery was indispensable to white liberty.[176] JQA told a friend that all of his problems as president could be traced to the maneuvers of Andrew Jackson and a small, but purposeful proslavery cabal: "When I came to the presidency, the principle of internal improvements was swelling the tide of public prosperity, till the Sable Genius of the South saw the signs of his own inevitable downfall in the unparalleled progress of the general welfare of the North, and fell to cursing the tariff and internal improvement by natural means and national energies."[177] Adams reflected upon his plight and that of the nation:

> The great object of my life therefore as applied to the administration of the Government of the United States has failed — The American Union as a moral person in the family of Nations, is to live from hand to mouth, to cast away, instead of using for the improvement of its own condition the bounties of Providence to rivet into perpetuity the clanking chain of the slave, and to waste in boundless bribery to the west the invaluable inheritance of the Public Lands.[178]

In a diary entry late in his life, JQA foresaw a war between the North and the South over the question of slavery: "It seems to me that its result might be the extirpation of slavery from this whole continent; and, calamitous and desolating as this course of events in its progress must be, so glorious would be the final issue, that, as God shall judge me, I dare not say that it is not to be desired."[179]

The Erie Canal: On October 26, 1825, the 425-mile Erie Canal opened, connecting the Great Lakes with the Atlantic Ocean by way of the Hudson River. Settlers poured into western New York, Ohio, Michigan, Illinois, and Wisconsin. Goods were moved at one-tenth the previous cost in less than the previous time. Barges filled with manufacturing goods and supplies flowed west while others filled with farm produce and raw materials moved east. In nine years, tolls paid the cost of the construction, once referred to as "Clinton's Ditch," named for DeWitt Clinton, the politician who oversaw the project from 1816 until its completion.[180]

Tariff of 1828: New Englanders proposed a protective tariff with very high rates. The South, which opposed the measure, was too smart for its own good. Southern congressmen amended the motion to include higher protective rates not only for the goods but also for raw materials. Their thinking was that, if passed, it would leave manufacturers with little profit, and so they would vote against the tariff. However, what became known in the South as the Tariff of Abominations passed in the Senate by a vote of 26 to 21 and in the House by 105 to 94.[181]

Adams was maneuvered into signing the bill, which incensed the South. His opponents had intended the bill to be an embarrassment to the president. JQA disliked the act but as was customary to that time, presidents did not use their veto power, unless they believed a bill was unconstitutional.[182] In protest, flags were flown at half-mast in the Carolinas. Southern leaders and Vice President Calhoun wrote his "South Carolina Exposition and Protest" in which he argued that nullification was constitutional and tariffs were not.[183] The South vowed to boycott New England goods and nullify the tariff.[184] The split between the North and the South was deepening.

FOREIGN AFFAIRS — MAJOR EVENTS

Not much happened on the international front during JQA's presidency, and he paid little attention to foreign affairs. The world was peaceful with the monarchy returned in France, which was not threatening or being threatened by Great Britain. The U.S. signed a reciprocal trade agreement with the Federation of Central America, made up of Guatemala,

San Salvador, Honduras, Nicaragua and Costa Rica. Favorable trade agreements were concluded with Sweden, Denmark, Norway, and the Hanseatic cities. The newly independent states of Central America convened the Panama Congress in 1826. Adams wanted to send two U.S. delegates to the conference, but Southerners objected, fearing that the Central American nations would ask the U.S. to join them in banning slavery. By the time Congress approved sending delegates, the Congress had adjourned.[185] Great Britain and the United States reached an agreement in 1826 for restitution of property damages incurred by the U.S. during the War of 1812. The following year, they agreed to the joint occupation of the Oregon Territory.[186]

AFTER THE PRESIDENCY

On January 1, 1829, Adams confided to his diary: "The year begins in gloom. My wife had a sleepless and painful night. The dawn was overcast and as I began to write my shaded lamp went out, self-extinguished. It was only for lack of oil, and the notice of so trivial an incident may serve but to mark the present temper of my mind."[187] He continued to express his depression, adding:

> Three days more and I shall be restored to private life, and left to an old age of retirement though certainly not of repose. I go into it with a combination of parties and public men against my character and reputation, such as I believe never before was exhibited against any man since the Union existed. Posterity will scarcely believe it, but so it is, that this combination against me has been formed and is now exulting in triumph over me, for the devotion of my life and of all my faculties of my soul to the Union, and to the improvement, physical, moral, and intellectual of my country.... No one knows and few conceive the agony of mind that I have suffered from the time that I was made by circumstances, and not by my own volition, a candidate for the Presidency till I was dismissed from that station by the failure of my reelection. They were feelings to be suppressed; and they were suppressed.[188]

JQA resolved "to go into the deepest retirement and withdraw from all connection with public affairs,"[189] but comforted himself with the hope that he would be provided "with useful and profitable occupation, engaging so much of his thoughts and feelings that his mind may not be left to corrode itself."[190] While waiting for fulfillment of this wish, Adams wrote unsigned essays dealing with the Russo-Turkish War and on Greece, in which he compared Christianity and Islam. His observations included:

> And he [Jesus] declared that the enjoyment of felicity in the world hereafter would be reward of the practice of benevolence here. His whole law was resolvable into the precept of love; peace on earth — good will toward man, was the early object of his mission; and the authoritative demonstration of the immortality of man, was that, which constituted the more than earthly tribute of glory to God in the highest.... The first conquest of the religion of Jesus, was over the unsocial passions of his disciples. It elevated the standard of the human character in the scale of existence.... On the Christian system of morals, man is an immortal spirit, confined for a short space of time, in an earthly tabernacle. Kindness to his fellow mortals embraces the whole compass of his duties upon earth, and the whole promise of happiness to his spirit hereafter. The essence of this doctrine is to exalt the spiritual over the brutal part of his nature.... The philosophical spirit of the last century, under the fair and virtuous visor of religious toleration, harbored a deadly hatred to Christianity, and a secret devotion to the absurdist of all dogmas, the superstition of atheism.[191]

Turning to Islam, JQA warned:

> [Muhammad] ... declared undistinguishing and exterminating war, as part of his religion, against all the rest of mankind.... The precept of the Koran is, perpetual war against all who deny, that Mahomet is the prophet of God.... Adopting from the sublime conception of the Mosaic Law, the doctrine of one omnipotent God, he [Muhammad] connected indissolubly with it, the audacious

falsehood, that he was himself his prophet and apostle. Adopting from the new Revelation of Jesus, the faith and hope of immortal life, and of future retribution, he humbled it to the dust by adapting all the rewards and sanctions of his religion to the gratification of the sexual passion. He poisoned the sources of human felicity at the fountain, by degrading the condition of the female sex, and the allowance of polygamy; and he declared undistinguishing and exterminating war, as part of his religion, against all the rest of mankind. The essence of his doctrine was violence and lust: to exalt the brutal over the spiritual part of human nature.[192]

Adams concluded:

Between these two religions, this contrasted in their characters, a war of more than twelve hundred years has already raged. That war is yet flagrant; nor can it cease but by the extincture of that imposture, which has been permitted by Providence to prolong the degeneracy of man. While the merciless and dissolute are encouraged to furnish motives to human action, there never can be peace on earth and good will toward men. The hand of Ishmael will be against every man, and every man's hand against him.[193]

House of Representatives: JQA found the greatness that escaped him as president when he became the first and thus far only ex-president to be elected to the House of Representatives, serving from 1831 to 1848. He wrote in his diary: "My election as President of the United States was not half as gratifying."[194]

As congressman, Adams advocated large scale public improvements and repeatedly acted to enhance America's stature in business, industry, and science. He fought against "circumscription of civil liberties."[195] JQA was an unsuccessful candidate for governor of Massachusetts in 1834. In various Congresses, he was chairman of the Committee on Manufactures, the Committee for Indian Affairs and the Committee on Foreign Affairs. He was against the annexation of Texas by the United States because it would upset the balance between slave and free states, further extending the power of slave owners.[196] In a diary entry, "I have been for some time occupied day and night, when at home, in assorting and recording petitions and remonstrances against the annexation of Texas, and other anti-slavery petitions, which flow upon me in torments."[197] In a speech in the House, Adams argued against the annexation of Texas: "Have you not enough Indians to expel from the land of their fathers? Are you not large and unwieldy enough already?"[198]

Adams' influence in the House of Representatives, as it was when a diplomat, did not depend upon his manner or presence of pleasing voice, but rather that he had something worth saying and worthy of being heard. He even championed women's rights in a February 1838 speech in the House of Representatives: "Why does it follow that women are fitted for nothing but the cares of domestic life, for bearing children and cooking the food of a family? ... I say women exhibit the most exalted virtue when they depart from the domestic circle and enter on the concerns of their country, of humanity, and of their God!"[199] Despite this, Adams did not believe that women were equal to men. In addressing a delegation of women who had gathered at his home to honor him and his wife: "Adams made it clear that while he thought it appropriate for women to concern themselves with humanitarian matters like slavery, no one could expect them to have opinions on presumably more complex questions like banking, currency, or internal improvements. He remained opposed to women's suffrage."[200]

Joshua R. Giddings said of JQA: "Mr. Adams belongs to no local district, to no political party, but to the Nation and to the people; he is elected by his district in Massachusetts, comes here with his family during the sessions of Congress, and keeps house by himself, while in the House of Representatives he consults with no one, takes the advice of no one, and holds himself accountable to no one but the Nation."[201]

The Gag Rule: Adams abhorred slavery and wished to see it eradicated, but more importantly, as he saw it, he was a nationalist. As such, his priority was to secure national unity rather than risk sectionalism by forcing debate on slavery's abolition. As a spokesman for the antislavery forces in Congress, JQA limited his efforts to constitutional means. He was willing to fit the slave question into the national agenda but would not alter the national agenda to fit in the liberty of slaves' agenda. He was a "better nationalist than an abolitionist."[202] He noted in his diary: "He [Benjamin Lundy, a Quaker abolitionist] and the abolitionists generally are constantly urging me to indiscreet movements, which would ruin me, and weaken and not strengthen their cause."[203] The Constitution guarantees citizens the right "to petition the government for a redress of grievances." In 1834 the American Anti-Slavery Society began an antislavery petition drive. Over the next few years the number of petitions sent to Congress asking for the abolition of slavery in Washington, D.C., increased sharply, with more than 130,000 in 1837–38. Adams introduced many of these petitions, memorials, and resolutions.[204] At 70 years of age, JQA became the champion of the right of U.S. citizens to free speech and the right to petition. His nine year campaign to make the debate on slavery official and respectable has been called "the Pearl Harbor of the Slavery Controversy."[205]

Angered by the petitions and Adams for introducing them, proslavery congressmen passed a series of resolutions called "Gag Rules." Slave owner Henry L. Pinckney of South Carolina proposed three resolutions meant to stifle Adams and the petitions. Pinckney declared that Congress had no authority to interfere with slavery in the states, that it ought not to oppose it in the District, and that all slavery petitions, memorials, and related materials should be immediately tabled without discussion. Adams tried to be recognized and allowed to speak against the resolutions, but Speaker of the House James K. Polk, a supporter of slavery, instead recognized George W. Owens of Georgia, who immediately called for a vote. The proposal was adopted 95 to 82 on May 26, 1836.[206] Adams got his chance to make his statement at the time the third resolution was proposed, crying-out: "I hold this resolution to be a violation of the Constitution, of the right of petition of my constituent and of the people of the United States, and of my right to freedom of speech as member of this House."[207]

Considering the resolutions to be a violation of the right to free speech, JQA continued to introduce petitions, often when recognized on completely unrelated questions. Once, during a debate on a resolution about the distribution of rations to refugees from Indian hostilities, Adams gained recognition. Under the assumption that the United States was at war with the Indian nations, he turned the question into what wartime powers Congress had to preserve the general welfare of all the people of the United States. In the case of a "servile war," into which he felt slaveholders were leading the country, he contended Congress would extend its powers to interfere with slavery anywhere.[208]

In April 1844, John Quincy Adams received an ivory cane "made from a single tooth" from Julius Pratt & Company of Meriden, Connecticut. It was given to him for his efforts to end the gag rule, which prevented discussions in the House of Representatives about the abolition of slavery. Adams noted in his diary: "There is in the top of the cane a golden eagle inlaid, bearing a scroll, with the motto 'Right of Petition Triumphant' engraved upon it. The donors requested of me that when the gag-rule should be rescinded I would cause the date to be added to the motto."[209] When the gag rule was repealed on December 3, 1844, Adams had that date engraved on the top of the cane. Adams willed the cane to the American people, and it is presently at the Smithsonian Institution.

Accusations of treason, assassination threats, and introduction of censure motions by

ABOLITION FROWNED DOWN.

Abolition Frowned Down, lithograph by Henry Dacre, b. ca. 1820, published by Henry R Robinson, 1839. It is a satire on enforcement of the "gag-rule" in the House of Representatives prohibiting discussion of the question of slavery. John Quincy Adams cowers prostrate on a pile composed of petitions, a copy of the abolitionist newspaper the *Emancipator*, and a resolution to recognize Haiti. He says, "I cannot stand Thomson's [sic] frown." South Carolina representative Waddy Thompson, Jr., a Whig defender of slavery, glowers at him from behind a sack and two casks, saying, "Sir the South loses caste whenever she suffers this subject to be discussed here; it must be indignantly frowned down" (Library of Congress, American Cartoon Print Series).

House members did not deter Adams. He defended himself with remarkable skill. He wrote in his diary: "One hundred members of the House represent slaves; four-fifths of whom would crucify me if their votes could erect the cross; 40 members, representatives of the free, in the league of slavery and mock Democracy, would break me on the wheel, if their votes or wishes could turn it round...."[210] Adams was defiant: "If they say they will try me, they must try me. If they say they will punish me, they must punish me. But if they say that in peace and mercy they will spare me expulsion, I disdain and cast away their mercy; and I ask them if they will come to such a trial and expel me, I defy them. I have constituents to go to who will have something to say if this House expels me. Nor will it be long before the gentlemen will see me here again."[211]

At each session of Congress, the majority against Adams decreased until finally on December 3, 1844, his motion to repeal the gag rule carried by a vote of 108 to 80, giving him his last great triumph. Once again, the freedom of petition and debate on them were allowed in Congress. Adams struggle was not so much a call for the abolition of slavery as a defense of free speech.[212] He was of the opinion that the Constitution did not give the federal government the power to abolish slavery, saying: "The abolition of slavery where it is established must be left entirely to the people of the state itself."[213]

In his diary about the time of the Missouri Compromise, which Adams supported, he recorded thoughts on black bondage in a letter to Richard C. Anderson:

[Slavery promotes] perverted sentiment — mistaking labor for slavery and dominion for freedom. The discussion of this Missouri question has betrayed the secret of [slave-holder's] souls. In the abstract they admit that slavery is an evil, they disclaim all participation in the introduction of it, and cast it all upon the shoulders of our old Grandam Britain. But when probed to the quick upon it, they show at the bottom of their souls pride and vainglory in their condition of master-dom. They fancy themselves more generous and noble-hearted than the plain freeman who labor for subsistence. They look down upon the simplicity of a Yankee's manners, because he has no habits of overbearing like theirs and cannot treat Negroes like dogs. It is among the evils of slavery that it taints the very sources of moral principle. It establishes false estimates of virtue and vice; for what can be more false and heartless than this doctrine which makes the first and holiest rights of humanity to depend upon the color of the skin? It perverts human reason and reduces man endowed with logical powers to maintain that slavery is sanctioned by the Christian religion, that slaves are happy and contented in their condition, that between master and slave there are ties of mutual attachment and affection, that the virtues of the master are refined and exalted by the degradation of the slave; while at the same time they vent expectations upon the slave trade, curse Britain for having given them slaves, burn at the stake Negroes convicted of crimes for the terror of the example, and writhe in agonies of fear at the very mention of human rights applicable to men of color.... If the Union must be dissolved, slavery is precisely the question upon which it ought to break. For the present, however, this contest is laid asleep.[214]

Despite Adams championing the abolitionist cause, he held racist views, as in the case of his essay "The Character of Desdemona" from his "Personifications of the Characters of Shakespeare." He was shocked and appalled about the interracial union of Othello and Desdemona. "No! Unnatural passion! It cannot be named with delicacy. Her passion for him

Aerial view of the Smithsonian Castle, located on the National Mall in Washington, D.C. The building is constructed of red Seneca sandstone in the faux Norman style (a 12th-century combination of late Romanesque and early Gothic motifs) and is commonly referred to as the Castle. Photograph by Carol M. Highsmith, September 20, 2006 (Library of Congress, Carol M. Highsmith Archive).

is unnatural; and why is it unnatural but because of his color? Desdemona's perversity drove her to elope in the dead of the night to marry a thick-lipped, wool-headed Moor."[215]

Smithsonian, Adams and Delambre — The Smithsonian Institution: In December 1835, JQA was appointed chairman of a House special advisory committee regarding the $500,000 bequest of James Smithson to establish the Smithsonian Institution in Washington. Smithson was born Jacques Louis Macie in Paris around 1764 to Elizabeth Macie, mistress to Hugh Smithson, the first Duke of Northumberland. When his mother died, he changed his name to James Smithson, although he never met his father. Smithson had a passion for science, and by age 22 was a fellow of the Royal Society of London. It's not quite clear how he came by his fortune, but it was sufficient for him to view life as an extended grand tour throughout Europe, although he never visited the United States or as far as has been determined ever had any contact with anyone in the former British colony.[216]

Smithson bequeathed his property to his nephew Henry Hungerford, a dandy who went by the name Baron Eunice La Batur. Smithson's will contained the proviso that, in case the former died without issue, which he did in his late twenties, the estate would go to the United States of America to found "an establishment for the increase and diffusion of knowledge among men."[217] The estate amounted to about a half a million dollars, ($5,470,000,000.00 in 2011, using the relative share of GDP). President Jackson notified the Congress of the bequest in December 1835. Senator John Calhoun of South Carolina led the fight against accepting the money because of his concern about the expansion of federal power.[218] Adams saw the money as an opportunity to create an American scientific community. JQA recommended the approval of the Smithsonian Institution, by Congress: "Whoever increases his knowledge, multiples the uses to which he is enabled to turn the gift of his Creator."[219] Adams fought, wrote, and lectured for ten years for a bill creating the institution, with success finally in 1846, at which time he reported to the House: "To furnish the means of acquiring knowledge is ... the greatest benefit that can be conferred upon mankind. It prolongs life itself and enlarges the sphere of existence."[220]

Jean Baptiste Joseph Delambre (1749–1822), an eminent French mathematician and astronomer, may have been responsible for the existence of one of the most remarkable institutions in Washington, D.C. In 1809 while serving as *secrétaire perpétuel* (perpetual secretary) for the mathematical sciences of the Institut de France, Delambre received a letter from Sir Joseph Banks, the president of the Royal Society of London. Banks requested that Delambre intercede on behalf of a naturalized British chemist and mineralogist, born in France as Louis Macie, who was being held as a political prisoner of war by the French military. Delambre wrote a letter to the French minister of war that resulted in the scientist's release. If Delambre had not honored Banks' request and contributed to the release of Macie-Smithsonian, leaving him to die in prison, and Adams had not fought so long and hard, the United States would have been denied the gift that started its national museum.[221]

His Papers: JQA kept a diary from 1779 to 1848, a period of more than sixty-eight years, including an unbroken daily record for more than twenty-five years. The fifty-one manuscript volumes are comprised of 14,291 manuscript pages. His other papers include *Memoirs* (12 volumes, 1874–1877) and *Writings of John Quincy Adams* (7 volumes, 1913– 1917). *The Adams Papers* were published by the Massachusetts Historical Society and Harvard University. Books by Adams include *Dermot MacMorrogh, or The Conquest of Ireland: An Historical Tale of the Twelfth Century* (book of poetry, 1832) and *The Lives of James Madison and James Monroe* (1850). Russell Kirk praised Adams' journal: "His immense Diary is the best window upon the thought of his age in America, his scientific diligence advanced

American learning, and his aspirations for developing national character were eloquently noble.... He sensed that his duty was the conservation of America's moral worth; he knew his age for a time of transition."[222]

Health: John Quincy Adams suffered from depression throughout his life. He was plagued with digestive problems and his physician prescribed a drink of three drops of sulfuric acid in a glass of water daily. Adams assumed if three drops were good, more would better, and took to dissolving five drops in his water, which resulted in massive blisters on his tongue and a nasty sore throat.[223] He suffered a paralytic stroke in 1846. By the following year, he recovered full use of his body and returned to Congress, where he finally was accorded the respect and honor he had always deserved from his colleagues.[224] According to Congressman Josiah Quincy III, at the beginning of Adams' last term in Congress in 1848: "The House rose as one man, business was at once suspended, his usual seat surrendered to him by the gentleman to whom it had been assigned, and he was formally conducted to it by two members."[225]

As early as 1839, JQA described his aging: "My eyes are threatening to fail me. My hands tremble like an aspen leaf. My memory daily deserts me. My imagination is fallen into the sear and yellow leaf and my judgment sinking into dotage."[226] Ralph Waldo Emerson commented on the aging Adams: "When they talk about his old age and venerableness and nearness to the grave, he knows better. He is like one of those old cardinals, who as quick as he is chosen Pope throws away his crutches and his crookedness, and is as straight as a boy. He is an old roué, who cannot live on slops, but must have sulphuric acid with his tea."[227]

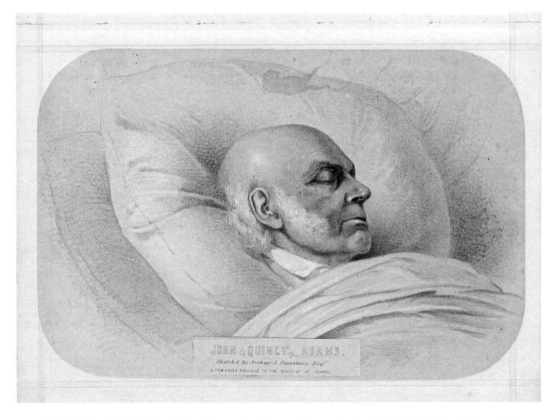

Original sketch by Arthur J. Stansbury a few hours prior to the death of John Quincy Adams, lithograph by Sarony & Major (Library of Congress).

Death: JQA wrote in his diary in 1840: "More than sixty years of active intercourse with the world has made political movement to me as much a necessity of life as the atmospheric air."[228] He told his wife: "I will die the moment I give up public life."[229] He passed over on February 23, 1848, still in service.

Place of Death: Adams died in the Speaker of the House of Representatives' room at the U.S. Capitol in Washington, D.C.

Cause of Death: Adams suffered a cerebral hemorrhage at his desk in the House of Representatives, shortly after rising and loudly exclaiming his "No!" vote to a resolution to present swords to veterans of the Mexican War (a conflict Adams had strongly opposed, labeling it an unjust war). Adams became flushed and unable to speak, clutched his chair and fell into the arms of fellow House members.[230] He was attended by five physicians in the Speaker's office but nothing could be done to save him. He died two days later, surrounded by his wife and family members.

Thomas Hart Benton, not a great friend of Adams, nevertheless eulogized him thusly: "Punctual to every duty, death found him at the post of duty; and where else would it have found him, at any stage of his career, for the fifty years of his illustrious life."[231]

Final Words: "This is the last of earth. I am content (or he may have said 'I am composed')."[232]

Place of Burial: At his funeral and the period of public mourning that preceded it, it was said of him: "A Patriarch has gone to his rest — a link between the past and the present is broken — a sage has fallen at his post."[233] Thousands filed past his bier in the Capitol. Funeral ceremonies were held in House of Representatives, after which his body was carried to Boston where a memorial service was held in Faneuil Hall. At the service in Quincy, the Reverend William Lund, Adam's pastor and friend preached on the text, "Be thou faithful unto death, and I will give thee a crown of life."[234] Adams was buried in the family tomb in Quincy, Massachusetts. At the death of his wife in 1852, the two were buried with his parents John and Abigail Adams, beneath the Congregational Church in Quincy.

Miscellanea

Presidential Trivia and Firsts: Mathew Brady created a daguerreotype of Adams, making him the first U.S. president to be photographed, although not until many years after his term of office.[235] John Quincy composed an original poem to celebrate his father's eighty-eighth birthday. JQA witnessed Napoleon's invasion of Russia while he was secretary and interpreter to Francis Dana, ambassador to Russia. Adams correctly predicted that slavery would break up the Union.[236] Each night before he went to sleep, Adams recited the childhood prayer, "Now I lay me down to sleep."[237] Adams wrote the long narrative poem "Dermot MacMorrogh," as therapy for losing the presidential election to Andrew Jackson in 1828.[238] His usual night's sleep was three or four hours. In the Adams mansion, the only way to exit John Quincy's bedroom was to go through the guest room. Because he was such an early riser, he woke up many of his guests. The problem was solved when a corridor was built from his bedroom to the main hallway. JQA had one of the tiles in his library reversed in response to a statement made that the Adams family was perfect.[239]

He was the first of 15 presidents who were elected without receiving the majority of the popular vote. JQA was the first U.S. president to be involved in a railroad accident. He was a passenger on a Camden & Amboy train that derailed near Highstown, New Jersey, on November 11, 1833; his coach was the one ahead of the first to derail. He was unhurt and continued his journey to Washington, D.C.[240] "When a newfangled indoor toilet was installed in the White House during John Quincy Adams's presidency, Quincy enjoyed a brief vogue in America as a euphemism for this convenience. ('If you'll excuse me, I need to go visit Quincy')."[241]

Skinny Dipping: As president, John Quincy Adams, weather permitting, regularly swam nude in the Potomac River. On one occasion, he and his assistant Antoine Guista decided to row an old boat across the wide river and swim back. Halfway across the wind picked up and the boat began taking water. The two were forced to jump over and swim for the nearest shore; but Adams, still dressed in a long-sleeved shirt and pantaloons, gasped for breath and struggled to stay afloat as the clothes took on weight from the water. After moments of terror the 57-year-old president made it to shore. Guista put on Adams' outer clothes and set off for Washington to find a vehicle to bring the president to the mansion. It took over an hour before he found help. In the meantime, a passerby, who had witnessed some of the episode, brought a garbled version of it to town, spreading the rumor that Adams had drowned, which was printed in some newspapers. Adams swore never to swim to show off again and henceforth limited himself to healthy exercise near the shore. Adams took his last nude swim in the Potomac when he was 79.[242] This was not the only notable incident related to Adams' nude swims. Anne Newport Royall was the first professional woman journalist in the United States. She married American Revolution major William Royall. After his death, she went to Washington in 1824 to petition for a federal pension as the widow of a veteran, which according to the law then in effect, must be pled before Congress. Royall sought an interview with President Adams to gain his support for her case. He repeatedly refused to see her. Learning of Adams' morning swims, she followed him to the Potomac, and once he entered the water, she stationed herself near his clothes. When he finished his swim and found Royall sitting on his clothes, he pleaded with her to leave the scene and allow him to get dressed. He promised that he would grant her the interview if she would only go away. The determined woman and reporter refused, insisting she would not leave until she got her interview. She threatened to scream loud enough to be heard by nearby fishermen. Adams finally agreed and answered all her questions while remaining submerged in the Potomac. Adams supported Royall's petition for a pension and invited her to visit his wife at their home, which she did.[243]

Hymn Text Writer: John Quincy Adams may have secretly desired a literary career. Even in his busy diplomatic and political life, he found time to write poetry and compose numerous hymn texts. After his death, a collection of his poems was published as *Poems of Religion and Society*. One hymnal used in the 1840s contained 22 of Adams' compositions, though none are found in recent ones. Probably his most well-known poem is "The Wants of Man,"[244] which includes the stanzas:

> I want the genius to conceive, the talents to unfold
> Designs, the vicious to retrieve, the virtuous to uphold.
> Inventive power, combining skill; a persevering soul,
> Of human hearts to mold the will, and reach from Pole to Pole.
> ...
> These are the Wants of mortal Man, — I cannot want them long,
> For life itself is but a span, And earthly bliss — a song.
> My last great Want — absorbing all — Is, when beneath the sod,
> And summoned to my final call, The Mercy of my God.

Amistad: In 1839 two planters, José Ruiz and Pedro Montez, in the Spanish colony of Cuba purchased a group of about 50 Africans of the Mendi tribe in present day Nigeria, who had been transported there in violation of bans on international slave trading. The planters obtained false identification papers in which the Africans were given Spanish names and designated as "black Ladinos." This was meant to establish their status as long-term legal slaves in Cuba. The slaves were placed on the schooner *Amistad* ("Friendship") and set sail across the Caribbean, with plans of selling them to owners of sugar planta-tions.[245]

After several days at sea the Africans, led by Cinque (Sengbe Pieh), broke their chains and attacked their captors, killing the captain of the ship and one crewman. They ordered the planters to sail to Africa, but instead the former masters secretly navigated the ship towards the U.S. The Coast Guard seized the ship off Long Island and the Africans were taken to New London, Connecticut. Ruiz and Montez denounced the Mendians as revolted slaves, pirates and mutineers, and claimed them as their property. The Mendians, who spoke neither English nor Spanish, were not able to tell their side of the case when they were brought before a federal judge. Meanwhile the Spanish ambassador demanded that President Van Buren return the ship and the slaves to Ruiz and Montez, and allow the matter to be handled under Spanish law. Not wishing to offend his Southern supporters, Van Buren agreed, but the matter had already been put under court jurisdiction.[246]

Three prominent abolitionists, Lewis Tappan, the Reverend Joshua Leavitt and Simeon S. Jocelyn, intervened and raised funds for the defense and care of the Mendians. The abo-litionist movement formed the "Amistad Committee," headed by New York City merchant Lewis Tappan, and collected money to mount a defense of the Africans. Initially, commu-nication with the Africans was difficult, since they spoke neither English nor Spanish. Yale Professor of Linguistics, J. Willard Gibbs, Sr., learned to count to ten in their native Mendi language, went to the harbor of New York City, and counted aloud in front of sailors until he located a person able to understand and translate. That was James Covey, a twenty-year-old sailor of the British man-of-war HMS *Buzzard.* Covey was himself a former slave from West Africa. Through Covey, the abolitionists learned that the Africans had been kidnapped, having been in Cuba only a few days, and were not Ladinos.[247]

Their trial commenced on January 7, 1840, in the District Court of Hartford, Con-necticut. When the judge heard the Medians' testimony and showed the documents estab-lishing them as Ladinos were forged, he was persuaded that even under Spanish law, they were free men. The judge ordered President Van Buren to have them transported back to Africa. Furious, Van Buren ordered the government's lawyers to appeal the case to the Supreme Court.[248]

Tappan convinced 73-year-old JQA to argue in behalf of the Mendians before the high court. Evidence in his diaries revealed that Adams was aware of the danger he faced as a politician and an individual by accepting a role in the case in the midst of a deeply divided and emotional nation. Allegedly Adams told Tappan: "Well when I was an attorney, a long time ago, young man, I err ... I realized after much trial and error, that in the courtroom, whoever tells the best story wins. In unlawyer-like fashion, I give you that scrap of wisdom free of charge."[249] On February 23, 1841, Attorney General Henry D. Gilpin began the oral argument phase before the Supreme Court. Gilpin first entered into evidence the papers of *Amistad* which stated that the Africans were Spanish property. The documents being in order, Gilpin argued that the Court had no authority to rule against their validity. Gilpin contended that if the Africans were slaves (as evidenced by the documents), then they must

Sengbe Pieh Statue, New Haven, Connecticut. Sculpted by Ed Hamilton in 1992, this monument of Sengbe Pieh, known as Joseph Cinqué, stands on the former site of the New Haven Jail, where the Africans from the *Amistad* were imprisoned in 1839 while awaiting trial. The work is a 14-foot relief sculpture cast in bronze distinguished by its three-sided form. On the base are Cinqué's words, "Make us free." The ten-foot three-panel bronze top of the memorial deals with the three phases of the *Amistad* incident. The first depicts Sengbe Pieh in Africa before he and the other Africans were kidnapped. The back side is a scene of the courtroom trial. The third shows Cinqué ready to board a ship back to his homeland. The Amistad Memorial was cast and finished in Louisville, Kentucky, at Bright Foundry. The architects for the project were Herbert S. Newman & Associates of New Haven, CT (courtesy David B. Flapan, ChiGuy.net).

be returned to their rightful owner, in this case, the Spanish government. Gilpin's argument lasted two hours.[250]

While writing his brief for the "Amistad" case before the Supreme Court, he reflected in his diary:

> The world, the flesh, and all the devils in hell are arrayed against any man who now in this North American Union shall dare to join the standard of Almighty God to put down the African slave-trade; and what can I, upon the verge of my seventy-fourth birthday, with a shaking hand, a darkening eye, a drowsy brain, and with all my faculties dropping from me one by one, do for the cause of God and man, for the progress of human emancipation, for the suppression of African slave trade? Yet my conscience presses me on; let me die upon the breach.[251]

Adams made extensive preparations, poring over hundreds of documents in forming his argument. His appearance before the court extended over two days, lasting seven hours. Early in his statement he said:

> I derive, in the distress I feel both for myself and my clients, consolation from two sources—first, that the rights of my clients to their lives and liberties have already been defended by my learned

friend and colleague in so able and complete a manner as leaves me scarcely anything to say, and I feel that such full justice has been done to their interests that any fault or imperfection of mine [if he exhibited the infinities of age] will merely be attributed to its true cause; and secondly, I derive consolation from the thought that this Court is a Court of JUSTICE. And in saying so very trivial a thing I should not on any other occasion, perhaps, be warranted in asking the Court to consider what justice is. Justice, as defined in the Institutes of Justinian, nearly 2000 years ago, and as it is felt and understood by all who understand human relations and human rights is— "*Constants et perpetue vouluntas, jus suum cuique tribuendi,*" "The constant and perpetual will to secure to every one HIS OWN right."[252]

Adams' argument was based on the principle of habeas corpus, which he considered to be the cornerstone of Anglo-American rights and liberties. Adams said that even by Spanish law, the Mendians were illegally enslaved. He argued if the president could hand over free men on the demand of a foreign government, how could any man, woman or child in the U.S. be sure of their "blessing of freedom."[253] In his argument before the Supreme Court, Adams stressed that the Constitution nowhere recognizes slaves as property, but only as persons— even if three-fifths of a person: "The words slave and slavery are studiously excluded from the Constitution. Circumlocutions are the fig-leaves under which these parts of the body politic are decently concealed. Slaves, therefore, in the Constitution of the United States are recognized only as persons, enjoying rights and held to the performance of duties."[254]

In his diary, Adams recorded the court's decision, delivered by Justice Joseph Story: "It affirms the decision of the District and Circuit Courts, exception with regard to the Negroes.... It reverses the decision below placing them at the disposal of the President of the United States to be sent to Africa; declares them to be free and directs the Circuit Court to order them to be discharged from the custody of the Marshal."[255] The vote in favor of the Mendians was made with but one dissent. Tappan and other abolitionists provided a ship and missionaries to accompany the Africans home. Cinque returned to become chief of his people.[256]

Adams and Freemasonry: From the earliest days of the American republic, the purposes and meaning of the Masonic Lodge were disputed and debated. For John Quincy Adams, there was no doubt; he asserted that the teachings and practices of Freemasonry were detrimental, noxious, and unfortunate. He wrote that Freemasonry was tainted by its oaths, penalties, ritual and the actions of its leaders and members. He believed that the secrets of Freemasonry could easily undermine and impartial judicial process, with police, lawyers, statesmen and judges who were Masons holding secret allegiances, beyond the constitution, thus undermining the due process of law.[257] Adams was incensed by the evidence that "Masons had kidnapped Captain William Morgan in New York State in 1826 and ritually murdered him in a particularly gruesome manner. His crime as an ex–Mason was in revealing the oaths, handshakes and ritual trappings of the organization." When evidence that the Masonic Society has assisted the culprit's responsible for the murder escape justice, it caused a national scandal.[258]

Adams was instrumental in forming the Anti-Mason Party to elect candidates and enact legislation to overturn what many, including Adams, suspected to be the Lodge's undue influence on government and society. Adams hoped Freemasonry would disappear from America. It didn't and so far fourteen U.S. presidents, including Washington, Monroe, Jackson, Garfield, McKinley, both Roosevelts, Truman and Ford were Freemasons. Truman appears to have been the most active president in Freemasonry, having been Grand Master of Masons in Missouri.[259]

Dear Diary

The following are additional excerpts from the diaries of John Quincy Adams[260]:

We cross'd the Rhine again, when we got opposite Cologne, where there is a village, inhabited by Jews: a nasty, dirty, place indeed, and fit only for Jews to live in [July 12, 1781].

I began this day to translate the Eclogues of Virgil. What a difference between this study, and that of a dry barren Greek Grammar. But without sowing the grain there certainly can be no harvest, and there is no Rose, without a thorn [October 4, 1785].

The laws of man may bind him in chains or may put him to death, but they never can make him wise, virtuous, or happy [1810, while at St. Petersburg, Russia].

It is the law of nature between master and servant that the servant shall spoil or plunder his master [December 17, 1810].

The only temper that honors a nation is that which rises in proportion to the pressure upon it [September 14, 1814].

The extremes of opulence and of wants are more remarkable, and more constantly obvious, in this country (Great Britain) than in any other that I ever saw [November 8, 1816].

All the public business in Congress now connects itself with intrigues, and there is great danger that the whole government will degenerate into a struggle of cabals [January 1819].

Slavery is the great and foul stain upon the North American Union [January 10, 1820].

It is, in truth, all perverted sentiment — mistaking labor for slavery and dominion for freedom [March 3, 1820].

I take it for granted that the present question is a mere preamble — a title page to a great tragic volume [March 1820, concerning the first congressional debate on the morality of slavery].

They [journalists] are a sort of assassins with loaded blunderbusses at the corner of streets and fire them off for hire or for sport at any passenger they select [September 7, 1820].

The object is vast in its compass, awful in its prospects, sublime and beautiful in its issue. A life devoted to it [Emancipation] would be nobly spent or sacrificed [1820].

I would take no one step to advance or promote pretensions to the Presidency. If that office was to be the prize of cabal and intrigue, of purchasing newspapers, bribing by appointments, or bargaining for foreign missions, I had no ticket in that lottery [February 25, 1821].

The nation blessed with the largest portion of liberty must in proportion to its numbers be the most powerful nation upon earth [1821].

There is nothing so deep and nothing so shallow which public enmity will not turn to account [August 19, 1822].

The public history of all countries, and all ages, is but a sort of mask, richly colored. The interior working of the machinery must be foul [November 9, 1822].

Were we to slumber in indolence or fold up our arms and proclaim to the world that we are palsied by the will of our constituents, would it not be to cast away the bounties of Providence and doom ourselves to perpetual inferiority? (Journal entry of notes for his First Annual Message to Congress, December 6, 1825].

No one knows and few conceive the agony of mind that I have suffered from the time that I was made by circumstances, and not by my own volition, a candidate for the presidency till I was dismissed from that station by the failure of my reelection. They were feelings to be suppressed, and they were suppressed [1829].

Duty is ours; results are God's [1830].

My whole life has been a succession of disappointments. I can scarcely recollect a single instance of success to anything that I every undertook. Yet, with fervent gratitude toward God, I confess that my life has been equally marked by great and signal success which I neither aimed at nor anticipated [August 9, 1833].

My public life will terminate by the alienation from me of all mankind.... It is the experience of all ages that people grow weary of old men. I cannot flatter myself that I shall escape the common law of our nature [December 14, 1833].

The prosperity of the country, independent of all agency of the Government, is so great that the people have nothing to disturb them but their own waywardness and corruption [October 9, 1834].

All rising to great place is by a winding stair [Diary entry, quoting Francis Bacon].

The public history of all countries, and all ages, is but a sort of mask, richly colored. The interior working of the machinery must be foul [November 9, 1832].

The prosperity of the country, independent of all agency of the Government, is so great that the people have nothing to disturb them but their own waywardness and corruption [October 9, 1834].

The most insignificant error of conduct in me at this time would be my irredeemable ruin in this world; and both the ruling political parties are watching with intense anxiety for some overt act by me to set the whole pack of their hireling presses upon me [April, 1837].

Such is the condition of things in these shambles of human flesh that I cannot now expose the whole horrible transaction but at the hazard of my life [1837, on threats to his life for his antislavery position].

The neglect of public worship in this city is an increasing evil, and the indifference to all religion throughout the whole country portends no good. There is in the clergy of all the Christian denominations a time-serving, cringing, subservient morality, as wide from the spirit of the Gospel as it is from the intrepid assertion and vindication of truth. The counterfeit character of a very large portion of the Christian ministry in this country is disclosed in the dissensions growing up in all Protestant churches on the subject of slavery [May 27, 1838].

More than sixty years of active intercourse with the world has made political movement to me as much a necessity of life as the atmospheric air [1840].

Providence has showered blessings upon me profusely. But they have been blessings unforeseen and unsought. Non nobis, Domine, non nobis, sed nomini to do gloriam ("Not to us Lord, not to us, but to your name be the glory") [near the end of his life, February 21, 1848].

If your actions inspire others to dream more, learn more, do more and become more, you are a leader [1821].

The manners of women are the surest criterion by which to determine whether a republican government is practicable in a nation or not [1820].

Patience and perseverance have a magical effect before which difficulties disappear and obstacles vanish [1823].

Always vote for principle, though you may vote alone, and you may cherish the sweetest reflection that your vote is never lost [1844].

Evaluations of John Quincy Adams

BY OTHER PRESIDENTS

I shall be much mistaken if, in as short a period as can well be expected, he is not found at the head of the diplomatic corps; let the government be administered by whomsoever the people may choose.[261]— George Washington

From his proceedings in Congress, he appears demented, and his actings and doings inspire my pity more than anger.[262]— Andrew Jackson

Mr. [John Quincy] Adams' general personal demeanor was not prepossessing. He was on the contrary quite awkward, but ... he was a small and agreeable party, one of the most entertaining table companions of his day.... He loved his country, desired to serve it, and was properly conscious of the honor of doing so.[263]— Martin Van Buren

It is said he is a disgusting man to do business with. Coarse, dirty, clownish in his address and stiff and abstracted in his opinions, which are drawn from books exclusively.[264]— William Henry Harrison

His disposition is as perverse and mulish as that of his father.[265]— James Buchanan

He was a conscientious and well-meaning man, and I wish I could say more about his achievements.... I just don't think there were any events in Adams' administration that were very interesting.[266]— Harry S Truman

BY OTHERS

Quiet is not his sphere. And when a legitimate scene of action does not present itself, it is much to be feared that he will embrace an illegitimate one.[267]— Charles Francis Adams

Well has he been called "The Massachusetts Madman." He boasts that he places all his glory in independence. If independence is synonymous with obstinacy, he is the most independent statesman living.[268]— Anonymous

Like George Washington he did not believe in parties or in sections, the essential realities of American politics— and they did not believe in him.[269]— Samuel Flagg Bemis

Adams grasped the essentials of American policy and the position of the United States in the world more surely than any other man of his time. He availed himself of matchless opportunities to advance the continental future of his country and the fundamental principles for which it stood in the world.[270]— Samuel Flagg Bemis

I have found in him since I have been associated with him in the executive government as little to censure and condemn as I should have suspected in any man.[271]— Henry Clay

In politics he was an apostate, and in private life a pedagogue, and in everything but amiable and honest.[272]— De Witt Clinton

Few men in American public life have possessed more intrinsic worth, more independence, more public spirit and more ability than Adams, but throughout his political career he was handicapped by a certain reserve, a certain austerity and coolness of manner, and by his consequent inability to appeal to the imaginations and affections of the people as a whole.[273]— *Encyclopædia Britannica* article

Between 1803 and 1809, John Quincy Adams became the conscience of New England. Not only did he provide leadership so the troubled young nation, he sought to reproduce it in the next generation of Americans.[274]— Denise M. Henderson

Like a kite without a tail he will be violent and constant in his attempts to rise ... and will pitch on one side and the other, as the popular currents may happen to strike without soaring to his intended point.[275]— Stephen Higginson

[He was] in many respects the most wonderful man of the age, certainly the greatest in the United States— perfect in knowledge but deficient in practical results. As a statesman he was pure and incorruptible, but too irascible to lead men's judgment.[276]— Philip Hone

He was educated as a monarchist, has always been hostile to popular government and particularly to its great bulwark the right to suffrage ... he affected to become a Republican only to pervert and degrade the Democratic party, and to pave the way for such a change in the Constitution as would establish the United States an aristocratically and hereditary government.[277]— Samuel D. Ingram of Pennsylvania

Of all the men, whom it was ever my lot to accost and to waste civilities upon, [he] was the most doggedly and systematically repulsive. With a vinegar aspect, cotton in his leathern ears, and hatred of England in his heart, he sat in the frivolous assemblies of Petersburg like a bull-dog among spaniels; and many were the times that I drew monosyllables and grim smiles from him and tried in vain to mitigate his venom.[278]— W.H. Lyttleton

You are perfectly insane and should apply for admission to the Lunatic Asylum. You have cost the government more than half your state is worth. You are a curse to the Whig Party and to the nation.[279] — Isaac Milne of Ohio

The slave has lost a champion who gained new ardor and new strength the longer he fought; America has lost a man who loved her with his heart; religion has lost a supporter; Freedom an unfailing friend, and mankind a noble vindicator of our inalienable rights.[280] — Theodore Parker of Massachusetts

This is the first Administration that has openly run the principle of patronage against that of patriotism that has unblushingly avowed, aye and executed the purpose of buying us up with our own money.[281] — John Randolph

John Quincy Adams was a short, stout, bald, brilliant and puritanical twig off a short, stout, bald, brilliant and puritanical tree. Little wonder, then, that he took the same view of the office of President as had his father.[282] — Alfred Steinberg

SEVEN

Andrew Jackson
A Good Friend and a Bad Enemy

Seventh President of the United States, 1829–1837

Andrew Jackson despised Henry Clay and John Calhoun for their actions against him, telling Martin Van Buren, "[Henry Clay is] certainly the basest, meanest scoundrel that ever disgraced the image of God, nothing is too mean or low for him to condescend to.... [He is] reckless and as full of fury as a drunken man in a brothel...."[1] "I will hang [John Calhoun] higher than Haman!"[2] "When Andrew Jackson hated, it often became grand passion. He could hate with Biblical fury and would resort to petty and vindictive acts to nurture his hatred and keep it bright and strong and ferocious."[3] Even on his death bed Jackson could not find it in his heart to forgive and forget, saying the only two great regrets of his life were that he "did not hang Calhoun and shoot Clay."[4]

Birth: Andrew Jackson was born on March 15, 1767, in the backwoods settlement of Waxhaw on the border of the Carolinas. Historians cannot agree as to whether he was born in North Carolina or South Carolina.[5] It depends upon which of her sisters' homes his mother delivered her baby. On a stretch of road that is the north-south boundary of the Carolinas are two signs only miles apart. A North Carolina historical marker announces that: "ANDREW JACKSON. Seventh President of the United States was born a few miles southwest of this spot."[6]

The sign refers to the George McCamie cabin in North Carolina. The other marker proudly proclaims that Andy Jackson was born less than three miles from the McCamie cabin, on the James Crawford plantation, which is in South Carolina. Although Jackson was in no position to tell by personal experience where he was born, he held no firmly fixed position on the matter. At the time of his birth the boundary line was not precisely known and wasn't set until 1813, when this section of the Waxhaws was surveyed. Jackson was the only first generation American to become president and the first born in a log cabin.[7]

Nicknames and Titles: During the War of 1812, Jackson was conspicuous for his bravery and success. A strict officer, he was very popular with his troops, who claimed he was as "tough as old hickory," resulting in the nickname: "Old Hickory." A Captain William Allen related how Jackson got the nickname: during the Creek War, Jackson caught a severe cold during the advance against the Indians. There were no tents, but Allen had his brother cut down a stout hickory tree, peeled off the bark and persuaded Jackson to use if for a covering. A drunken citizen stumbled over the general the next morning and as Jackson crawled out of the bark, greeted him with, "Hello, Old Hickory! Come out of your bark and join us for a drink."[8]

President Andrew Jackson, engraving by A.H. Ritchie c. 1860 from a painting by D.M. Carter (Library of Congress).

Left: John C. Calhoun, print by C.G. Crehen, no date recorded on shelflist card. *Right:* Henry Clay, an original drawing by D. Dickinson c. 1844, from a painting by P.S. Duval (both images, Library of Congress).

Make of this story what you will. For those who doubt the accuracy of this source of Jackson's nickname, there are others. General Jackson emerged a national hero from the War of 1812, primarily because of his decisive defeat of the British at the Battle of New Orleans. "Jackson had been ordered to march his Tennessee troops to Natchez, Mississippi.

When he got there he was told to disband his men because they were unneeded. General Jackson refused and marched them back to Tennessee. Because of his strict discipline on that march his men began to say he was as tough as hickory."[9] The nickname "Hero of New Orleans"[10] praised his victory over the British at New Orleans after the War of 1812 was officially over. "King Andrew the First"[11] was a derogatory nickname given by his opponents who accused him of behaving like a despotic king. "Sharp Knife"[12] was pinned

Bust portrait in uniform with epaulets of Major General Andrew Jackson at the time he was military governor of Florida, lithograph by Edwin after a painting by Nathan Wheeler, no date recorded on shelflist card (Library of Congress).

on him by the Indians during the war with the Creek tribes of Georgia. During the 1828 election, his opponents referred to him simply as "Jackass."[13]

Family: Elizabeth "Betty" Hutchinson Jackson (c. 1740–1781) married Andrew Jackson, Sr. (c. 1730–1767), in Carrickfergus, a seaport on Belfast Lough, County Antrim.[14] In 1765 they moved to America, accompanied to their new home by their two sons, Hugh and Robert, and their neighbors James and Isabella Crawford. Isabella was Elizabeth's sister. They were welcomed to Waxhaws by the George McCamie family. Mrs. McCamie was another sister of Elizabeth. Several other of her sisters also lived there, as two of Elizabeth's sisters married brothers by the name of Leslie. Andrew Jackson, Sr., took up farming in the backwoods settlement in the Waxhaws area. Jackson's father died in a logging accident while clearing land in February 1767, at the age of 29, three weeks before his son Andrew was born.[15] The widow Jackson moved with her three sons into the home of the Crawfords.[16] Andy spent his early life growing up with a large extended family — aunts, uncles, and cousins.

The American Revolution, begun in 1775, did not reach the Carolinas until 1778. Andy's brother Hugh died of heat stroke following the Battle of Stone Ferry in 1779.[17] The next year 13-year-old Andrew was an orderly and messenger in the mounted militia of South Carolina. He took part in the Battle of Hanging Rock against the British and in a few skirmishes with British Loyalists. When British troops raided Waxhaw, Robert and Andrew were taken prisoner.[18] When they refused to polish the boots of a British officer, the brothers were struck across their arms and faces with a saber. Andrew's wrist and forehead were cut to the bone and he carried the scar on his face for the rest of his life.[19]

The Brave Boy of the Waxhaws, Currier & Ives lithograph, 1876 (Library of Congress).

During their imprisonment in Camden, South Carolina, both boys contracted smallpox during an epidemic of the disease in the region. Their mother, who was described "as gentle as a dove and as brave as a lioness" came to their rescue and managed to gain the boys' release in a prisoner exchange.[20] Andy's mother and critically ill brother rode on horseback, while he walked barefoot and without a jacket in the pouring rain during the 40-mile trek to their home. Robert was so far gone that he died two days later and Andrew was soon wild in delirium. After a long struggle with the loathsome disease, he recovered, but he "was a mere skelton."[21] With her son seemingly out of danger Betty sent him to stay with a brother-in-law and set off for Charleston to carry food and medicine to the injured and sick Continental soldiers aboard a British prison ship.[22] She contracted cholera, "died and was buried near Charleston; but her dust lies in a grave that cannot be found."[23] At age fourteen, Andrew Jackson's childhood was over. "Jackson spent most of the next year and a half living with relatives and for six of those months was apprenticed to a saddle maker."[24] Jackson blamed the death of his family upon the British. "This anglophobia would help to inspire a distrust and dislike of Eastern 'aristocrats,' whom Jackson felt were too inclined to favor and emulate their former colonial 'masters.'"[25]

Ancestors: The Jackson and Hutchinson families were both from the north coast of Ireland. Andrew's grandfather, Hugh Jackson, was a linen draper. His mother's family were linen weavers.[26] "Nothing is known of Andrew Jackson's direct paternal line beyond his great-grandfather Thomas Jackson, a resident of Ballyregan, Dundonald Parish, County Down, Ireland."[27] In a biography of "Stonewall" Jackson, Harry L. Jackson asserts that Andrew Jackson and the Confederate general are related. He further asserted that "[Old Hickory's mother, Elizabeth] was one of the six noted and popular daughters of Cyrus Hutchinson, a soldier who fought in the battle of Carrickfergus in Ireland."[28] In Ronald Vern Jackson's *Andrew Jackson and Rachel Donelson Ancestry*, Elizabeth is listed as the "daughter of Robert William Hutchinson and Margaret Lisle, both of Antrim, Ireland." As this is based in part on family traditions and some old books in the National Archives, it has not been verified.[29]

Appearance: In his youth Jackson was tall, skinny, lithe, rough-hewn, and freckle-faced. Mrs. Anne Rutherford, who knew him well, gave a long and thorough description of the young man: "he had his abundant suit of dark-red hair, combed back carefully from his forehead and temples.... He was a full six feet tall and very slender ... in feature he was by no means good-looking ... his face was long and narrow, his features sharp and angular, and his complexion yellow and freckled ... his eyes were very handsome; they were very large, a kind of steel blue and when he talked to you he always looked you straight in your own eyes ... as much as to say 'I have nothing to be ashamed of and I hope you haven't'.... There was always something about him, something I can't describe, except to say it was a *presence*, or a kind of majesty I never saw in any other young man."[30] Andy had a habit of slobbering, which he was unable to control until almost a grown man.[31] His biographer Robert Remini offered a colorful and complete description of Andy's physical features. "Part of Andrew's charisma was his appearance. Erect in posture and slight of build — indeed cadaverously thin — he exuded toughness and strength. A ramrod, he stood six feet one inch in height and had a long, thin face accentuated by a strong shaft of jaw. His nose was slender and flared a little at the tip. At twenty Jackson was a fair, clear-complexioned young man, despite having a bout of smallpox. His high, rather narrow and sloping forehead was topped by a shock of long, sandy, almost reddish hair. As he grew older his hair became very dry and bristling, standing nearly as straight as he did and adding to his height ... it was a powerful appearance ... his presence signaled authority."[32] "It was said that if Andrew Jackson joined a party of travelers and they were attacked by Indians, he would instinctively take command and the party would just as instinctively look to him for leadership."[33] A British visitor to America wrote that "He has (not to speak disrespectfully) a game-cock look all over him. His face is unlike any other; its prevailing expression is energy; but there is, so to speak, a lofty honorableness in its thin worn lines, combining with a penetrating and sage look of talent that would single him out, even among extraordinary men, as a person of more than usually superior cast."[34] An enemy observed that "his conduct puts us in mind of the exasperated rhinoceros, wreaking his fury on every object that presents itself."[35] After the victory at the battle of New Orleans, his wife Rachel, at this time a rather heavyset woman, joined the general just in time for a series of victory balls. One merchant described the couple: "The General, a long haggard man, with limbs like a skeleton, and Madame *la Generale*, a short, fat dumpling, bobbing opposite each other on the dance floor."[36]

As a result of the death of his beloved wife, Jackson "entered the White House as a bereaved widower and continued to grieve for Rachel throughout the remainder of his life."[37] At his inauguration he "wore a suit of plain black cloth, manufactured in Baltimore,"[38] which was his usual attire throughout his eight years as president. He suffered so severely from so many different ailments, it was doubted he would survive his first term, let alone two, but somehow, perhaps due to his iron will, he made it through, but was barely alive at the end. His eyesight deteriorated and he needed a cane to get around, not just for fending off an attempted assassination. "Jackson had been wounded so many times in fights that he joked that he 'rattled like a bag of marbles.'"[39] He made a pitiful appearance as he departed the White House for a trip home to the Hermitage despite doctors' advice to postpone his return until he had gained some strength. His look was in sharp contrast to his attire in the defense of New Orleans. General Jackson's uniform consisted of a "blue wool uniform coat, gold colored buttons on jacket front and sleeves, gold trim at neck and cuffs with epaulets. This coat adheres to the 1813 uniform regulations; single breasted, of dark blue wool; four buttons placed lengthwise on the sleeves and skirts. A gold star is embroidered on each turnback; gold embroidery adorns the collar and cuffs. Epaulets are bullion and gold lace with cloth strap and gold lace, mounted on board."[40]

Personality and Character: It is not easy to pin down Jackson's complex personality. His intelligence and political sagacity still challenge historians and biographers. "There was in Jackson's personality a paradoxical combination: imperiousness (unassailable opinions) and identification with the democratic (folk) temper. Whatever made him ambitious and at times ruthless also made him desirous of giving generously.... He was not given to reflection, but he maintained sturdy principles of conduct that, in his mind, never steered him wrong.... He was blunt. He was opinionated.... When power was put into his hands, there were no half measures—he understood friendship on terms he dictated, and that generally demanded subordination."[41] He was the "nation's most enigmatic hero, a man who was revered and reviled and little understood."[42] "Andrew Jackson's youth was like the Carolina frontier where he grew up—wild, unpredictable, and continually changing. He could be hot-tempered, brash, and violent but had a solid work ethic and was able to apply himself when it counted. He made, and fought, a lot of enemies, but he also made life-long friends."[43] Andy was uniquely American, educated in the militant ethic of the frontier. He said of himself" "I was born for a storm and a calm does not suit me."[44] As a young man he developed a reputation "as a gambler, drinker, partyer, brawler and prankster. He went in for cockfights, horse races and maybe even women of ill repute. In Salisbury, he faced lawsuits and left unpaid bills in his wake."[45] He was a violent and dangerous man. But this didn't much distinguish him from others of his age. As an old man Jackson's thoughts strayed back to his Salisbury days. "Ah, I was a raw lad then," he said, "but I did my best."[46] An acquaintance of the time announced: "Andrew Jackson was the most roaring, rollicking, game-cocking, horse-racing, card-playing, mischievous fellow, who ever lived in Salisbury ... the head of the rowdies hereabouts ... more in the stable than in the office."[47] He was a notorious brawler who would fight at even the slightest provocation, no matter how great the odds against him. "The rough people among whom he lived were afraid of him. One day he was eating at a long table which the keeper of the tavern had set out of doors for the crowd that had come to see a horse race. A fight was going on at the other end of the table; but fights were so common in this new country that Jackson did not stop eating to find out what it was about. Presently he heard that a friend of his, one Patten Anderson, was likely to be killed. Jackson could not easily get to his friend for the crowd, but he jumped up on the table and ran along on it, putting his hand into his pocket as though to draw a pistol. He cried out at the same time, 'I'm coming, Patten!' and he opened and shut the tobacco box in his pocket with a sound like the cocking of a pistol. The crowd was so afraid of him that they scattered at once, crying 'Don't fire!'"[48] Jackson adopted a manly code of behavior, which was influenced by the western expansion of the nation. His convictions about honor sometimes exploded in violence. "Jackson was hot-tempered, arrogant, violent and a ferocious partisan."[49] His favorite expletive was "By the Eternal."[50]

Jackson was known to have an iron will and reputedly could accept only one solution to any problem — his solution. Compromise, even discussion, was foreign to his nature. In his eulogy of Jackson, Levi Woodbury, who had served in Andy's cabinet, referred to this iron will not as a fault but as a virtue. "His iron will was mere firmness or inflexibility in the cause he deemed right. It was an indomitable resolution to carry out what conscience dictated.... He may well had been called a man of iron — a man of destiny — or the hero of the iron will."[51] His character polarized contemporaries. He was loved or hated with equal depth of passion. "Jackson's appeal to the American people was the appeal of the chieftain to the tribe. They loved him because he was their protector, their hero. But they also loved him because he embodied their hopes and fears, their passions and prejudices, their insight and their ignorance, better than anyone before him."[52]

"Jackson was a symbol of the new age of democracy — the 'age of the common man' — both an average and ideal American who was able to draw support from every section and social class. Jackson could be charming, and he was basically honest; there was never any doubt about his courage, either physical or moral. But he was anything but a thoughtful subtle intellectual ... Jackson was a charismatic but not intellectual leader; highly intelligent, shrewd and practical. A true westerner at heart, and a slave holder, Jackson resented the North and East.... He had reputation as a hotheaded brawler who never forgave enemies. He was not above using that reputation to make an impression on people. (In a famous incident in the White House, he apparently lost his temper and fumed at some unwelcome guests, who fled in horror. When they had gone, he turned to an aide, grinned and said, 'They thought I was mad, didn't they?')"[53] He was hailed as a hero by the people everywhere he went. When Jackson died, an observer said, "If Andy Jackson decides on heaven, that's where he'll go."[54]

Presidential biographer Margaret Bassett assessed Jackson:

Andrew Jackson was purely a man of the people, with most of the prejudices and many of the antique beliefs of simple folk. His extreme sense of personal honor, enough to kill a man in a duel for an insult; his knightly feeling for womanhood, his highly colored language and emotions, all related him to the unschooled but highly moral frontier society from which he sprang.... It was a liberal frontier society, where rough justice, bad grammar, personal quarrels, and robust pastimes such as gambling, cockfighting, and running fine horses were accepted. Jackson had all these inclinations.[55]

H.W. Brands, in *Andrew Jackson, His Life and Times*, wrote the following: "Jackson could be a hard man, as the many who ran afoul of him during his life discovered. Yet toward Rachel he was tender to a fault, as he was toward children and horses. His feelings toward slaves fell between his feelings for children and for horses."[56] An earlier biographer of Jackson, William Garrott Brown had similar comments: "In Lafayette Square, which fronts the White House at Washington, there is an equestrian statue of a very thin, long-headed old man whose most striking physical characteristics are the firm chin and lips and the bristling, upright hair. The piece is not a great work of art, but it gives one a strong impression of determination, if not of pugnacity. Sculptors have not the means to represent the human eye; else this impression might have been made stronger; for the old gentleman whose warlike aspect is here reproduced had a glance like a hawk's. He had, moreover, a habit of gazing fixedly at any one who attracted his attention. When he was angry, as he was quite frequently, few men could meet his look with composure. When he was in good humor, however, as he usually was when he dealt with his friends, or with women or children, his eyes could be very kindly, and his grim lips could part in a smile that was extremely attractive."[57] In 1837 William Cullen Bryant reported in an editorial: "Faults he had, undoubtedly; such faults as often belong to an ardent, generous, sincere nature — the weeds that grow in rich soil. Notwithstanding this, he was precisely the man for the period in which he well and nobly discharged the duties demanded of him by the times. If he was brought into collision with the mercantile classes, it was more their fault than his own."[58] In *Jackson and the Quest for Empire*, David and Jeanne Heidler maintained "Jackson was an angry young man who became an angry old man."[59] Despite his backwoods upbringing Jackson fit quite comfortably in social settings. He maintained that he enjoyed surprising those who felt he would arrive brandishing "a tomahawk in one hand and a scalping knife in the other."[60]

Marriage and Romances: When Jackson was seventeen years old, he arrived in Nashville, Tennessee, to practice law. He acquired an 18-year-old black female slave named Nancy, as compensation for legal services from a cash-strapped client.[61] "Owning a slave ... said something about one's drive, character, and ability. Nancy surely did Jackson's housekeeping. She may also have been his sex partner ... as chattel — property ... by law, slaves did not own their bodies."[62] It was not unusual in the 17th and 18th centuries for men to take Indians and slaves as their concubines and even as wives due to the scarcity of white women. "Colonial laws regarding statutory rape were not applied to Blacks and Indians. Indians and Blacks, as well as their children, were prohibited by law from defending themselves against abuse, sexual and otherwise, at the hands of Whites. A slave who defended herself against the attack of a White person was subject to cruel beatings by either the master or mistress. Liaisons between Whites and Blacks or Indians were illegal. The females of color received the harshest punishment if discovered in a liaison with a White male. Females of color, regardless of their young age, were viewed as seducers of White men. Pregnancy became the evidence of the illegal liaison and a mulatto baby the indicator of the race of the father — White male. The child, by statute took the status of the mother and was thus born into slavery. The full benefit of the relationship and the off-spring enured to the White male. Under English precedent, the status of children was determined by the father.

The colonists changed the law to increase the wealth and domination of the White master who had eliminated certain costs of purchasing human labor by becoming 'a breeder of slaves.' The Black female, woman or child, was forced into sexual relationships for the White slave master's pleasure and profit."[63] White southerners like Jackson did not consider their actions of taking a black woman as rape. She was the property of her master, "their bodies were for their masters to do use as they pleased."[64] Saying this was the common belief and practice is not meant to be a defense of the behavior, which certainly was worse than rape, but to offer an explanation as to why at the time it was considered acceptable. "Enslaved Africans were debased for the benefit of certain Whites. Their plight as accepted 'as natural' by the majority of American society. Not all Whites owned slaves. But, the American socio-political and economic structure was formed with Blacks as a disenfranchised group. The life of sexual debasement and cruelty which was the reality of female slaves was largely ignored by white Christian society in America."[65]

Rachel Donelson Robards was born in July 1767, the ninth of eleven children of Colonel John and Rachel Stockley Donelson, from Virginia. Donelson, an "educated surveyor, planter, and land speculator ... acquired an iron foundry and a plantation worked by some thirty slaves" in what is present-day Accomac County, Virginia.[66] In 1779–80, Donelson led a contingent of more than 100 family members, slaves and friends, including 12-year-old Rachel, west over a distance of more than a thousand miles on some 30 flatboats, dugouts, and canoes, to reach the last outpost of the American frontier — Fort Nashborough, today Nashville, Tennessee. After less than a year in Tennessee, frequent Indian attacks caused the large Donelson clan to saddle up and head north to a more civilized area at Harrodsburg, Kentucky.[67]

Sometime, possibly as early as 1782, Lewis Robards met Rachel. He was a captain of the militia and a merchant. When she was 18, Rachel married 27-year-old Robards on October 1, 1785, at Harrodsburg.[68] The couple moved in with his widowed mother, along with several other Robards siblings and their young children, boarders, and a large slave community. Rachel's family moved to Nashville that summer after her father, John Donelson, was killed.[69] The Robards marriage apparently was an unhappy one. Robards, an "intensive jealous and possessive man,"[70] was driven mad by the qualities which had first attracted him to Rachel. "Her beauty, sociability and warmth became triggers for anger, reproach and scenes."[71] She was very comfortable in the company of men and they reciprocated. Robards accused her of being unfaithful with boarder Peyton Short, who had indiscreetly proposed that they elope in a letter, intercepted by Robards.[72] Rachel contended that she had done nothing to encourage Short's attention or to give him any hope that they could become lovers.

In her young days Rachel was described as "a black eyed, black-haired brunette, as gay, bold, and handsome a lass that ever danced on a flatboat or took the helm while her father took a shot at the Indians"; as a woman she was "gay and lively, ... the best story-teller, the best dancer, the sprightliest companion, the most daring horsewoman in the county."[73] Biographer John Spencer Bassett wrote that the young wife "is described as a woman of a lively disposition, by which is meant that she was not that obedient, demure, and silent wife which some husbands of the day thought desirable."[74] If so, the personalities of Rachel and Robards were bound to conflict. Depending upon whose side of the story one believes, either Robards lost his temper when he came across Rachel talking to Peyton Short and "sent her back to Tennessee, where her mother, the widow Donelson, ran a boarding house near Nashville," or, by Robards family accounts, she simply went to visit her family.[75] About this time, Andrew Jackson, a 21-year-old attorney for the state of North Carolina, resided at Rachel's mother's home.[76] In July 1788, Robards bought some 1,700 acres in the Cumberland area including a 640-acre plantation near the widow Donelson, indicating an intention of satisfying his wife's desire to be close to her mother. Rachel and Robards reconciled and moved into the Donelson home.[77] Jackson's chivalrous respect for women and courtly manners were interpreted by Robards as something sinister, leading to words between the two men. The jealous husband claimed that he thought Jackson was "too intimate with his wife."[78] Jackson told Robards if he ever connected his name "in that way" with Rachel again, "he would cut his ears out of his head, and that he was tempted to do so any how."[79] Jackson immediately sought other lodgings.

According to the Jackson and Donelson families Robards was physically abusive to Rachel. If so, this would not have been sufficient grounds for her to divorce him. "Southern legislators saw nothing amiss with a man chastising his wife, even hitting her now and then when provoked, in order to maintain proper

Rachel Donelson Robards Jackson, c. 1883 engraving by John Chester Butte after a painting by Ralph E. W. Earl (Library of Congress).

masculine order and authority in his household."[80] Soon thereafter, Robards abandoned Rachel, returning to Kentucky and threatening to "haunt her."[81] Rumors of his possible return in 1790 to "retrieve his wife, by force, if necessary," prompted Mrs. Donelson, fearing for her daughter's life, to send her to seek refuge with relatives at Natchez, which was in Spanish territory. Jackson accompanied the group as an armed escort but returned to Nashville once Rachel and the others were safely at their destination.[82] In 1791 Kentucky was still a part of Virginia, and if a husband wished to divorce his wife on the charge of unfaithfulness, he had to petition the legislature to allow him to bring the case before a jury. Robards obtained the preliminary act from the legislature, maintaining that the trip to Natchez was an illegal elopement and that one of the travelers with them gave evidence of their "bedding together."[83] However, Robards deferred going to a jury to make the divorce final. This may have been because he knew that Rachel wished to be free of him in order to marry Jackson, and he had no desire to oblige them. Then too, there was the matter of the will of Rachel's father, which had not yet been settled. Robards would be entitled to any bequest intended for Rachel as long as she was still his wife.[84]

By Jackson's account, acting upon a mistaken report that Robards had obtained the divorce, his regard for Rachel blossomed into love. He went to Natchez, where the couple was married and then returned to Nashville and settled down on a farm that he had purchased.[85] Robards reappeared two years later and now with undeniable evidence of his wife's adultery, "was granted the divorce on the grounds that his wife had deserted him and 'hath and doth still live in adultery with another man.'"[86] Friends urged the couple to have a second wedding ceremony. At first Jackson refused, feeling it would be seen as an admission that they were not already married and were guilty of adultery and bigamy. But finally, Jackson gave in and he and Rachel were legally wed in a ceremony on January 17, 1794.[87]

The Robards' perspective of the marriage and divorce of Rachel and Lewis Robards is related in the family's self-published book, *History and Genealogy of the Robards Family*.[88] The Jackson version is found in Judge John Overton's narrative, written in response to accusations made by the general's political rivals. Overton was a boarder in the residence of both Mrs. Robards and Mrs. Donelson at the time of Rachel's marriage to Robards, and he depicted Andy and Rachel in the most favorable moral light.[89]

Years later Jackson's biographer Robert Remini discovered evidence that contradicted Overton's story. Others in the area of Nashville said the couple had eloped or merely lived together as early as 1790, and no documentation of their 1791 marriage ever was found.[90] "Although Rachel Donelson and Andrew Jackson did in truth flaunt the moral and legal codes of their times, today they are legendary lovers. If Andrew Jackson is admired for anything, even by his most determined critics, it is for his devoted marriage to Rachel and his vigorous defense of her reputation. She is now a stick figure in the story; a passive belle tossed away by one man and swept up by another. Lewis Robards is hardly more than a name, although in 1790 he was the frontier nabob and Jackson little more than a knave. By an effective campaign strategy, the 'American Jezebel' and the 'Great Western Bluebeard' have come down to us as the most romantic pair in presidential history."[91] Attacks on Rachel's character and honor led to numerous fistfights and duels for Andy.[92]

At the moment of his greatest triumph, Jackson experienced the most crushing blow of his life. As they were preparing to move to Washington in 1828, only a month after the election, Rachel suddenly fell ill. A physician was called to treat her for pain in the chest and irregularity in her heartbeat. She was bled and felt well enough three days later to sit up and receive visitors. However, she caught a cold and was diagnosed as having a slight case of pleurisy. On the twenty-second, Rachel collapsed while sitting in a chair in her bedroom. She died almost immediately, leaving Andy broken-hearted. The exact cause of her death is not known, although it has been listed as a heart attack. Over 10,000 people attended her funeral. She was buried in the gown she bought to wear to her husband's inauguration.[93]

Jackson's reaction to his loss was one of shock, devastation and perpetual mourning. He believed that her death was the result of the attacks on her character by his political enemies. During the 1828 election John Quincy Adams' supporters had circulated a pamphlet that asked, "Ought a convicted adulteress and her paramour husband to be placed in the highest offices of this free and Christian land?"[94] At Rachel's funeral President-elect Jackson promised he would take vengeance upon those who had spread lies about her: "In the presence of this dear saint, I can and do forgive all my enemies. But those vile wretches who have slandered her must look to God for mercy."[95]

Rachel reportedly dreaded enduring four years of insults and innuendo. She stated that she would "rather be a doorkeeper in the house of God than live in that palace in Washington."[96] Andrew built a shrine to Rachel at the Hermitage, designed by architect David Marison, who completed the tomb in 1832. It is set in her beloved garden, with weeping willows around her burial place. In his declining years, Jackson nightly visited her grave.[97] As a widower, Jackson invited Rachel's niece, 21-year-old Emily Donelson, to act as his

White House hostess and unofficial First Lady. Later he asked Sarah Yorke Jackson, wife of his adopted son, Andrew Jackson, Jr., to become his hostess at official events.[98]

Inscription on Rachel's Tomb: Jackson built a permanent temple made of limestone resembling a Greek styled gazebo to replace Rachel's temporary grave site. He had the following tribute inscribed on her tombstone:

> Here lies the remains of Mrs. Rachel Jackson, wife of President Jackson, who died the 22d of December, 1828, aged 61. Her face was fair, her person pleasing, her temper amiable, and her heart kind; she was delighted in relieving the wants of her fellow creatures, and cultivated that divine pleasure by the most liberal and unpretending methods; to the poor she was a benefactor, to the rich an example; to the wretched a comforter; to the prosperous an ornament; her piety went hand in hand with her benevolence, and she thanked her Creator for being permitted to do good. A being so gentle and yet so virtuous, slander might wound but could not dishonor. Even death, when he tore her from The arms of her husband could but transport her to the bosom of her God.[99]

Children: The Jacksons had no children of their own. They adopted one of Rachel's nephews, one of the twin sons born to her brother Sevren and his wife, Elizabeth Rucker Donelson. They renamed the boy Andrew Jackson, Jr. Andrew Jr. and his wife Sarah had four sons and one daughter. Two of the sons died as infants and a third died during the Civil War. Andrew Jr. had eleven grandchildren, two by his son Andrew III and nine by his daughter Rachel.[100] The General adopted a Creek Indian orphan named Lyncoya, whose parents were killed during the Creek war. The youngster died at age 16, probably of pneumonia or tuberculosis.[101] Another child, Andrew Jackson Hutchins, the orphaned grandnephew of Rachel, was raised by the Jacksons from age five. Jackson and his wife acted as guardians of eight other children, mostly cousins, nieces and nephews. President Jackson loved children and the executive mansion was always filled with them.[102]

Religion and Religious Beliefs: Jackson was born into a Presbyterian family; although he did not officially join the church until about a year after retiring from the presidency.[103] He believed that the Constitution demanded a strict separation of church and state. In a letter to Ellen Hanson, he commented on religious faiths:

> I was brought up a rigid Presbyterian, to which I have always adhered. Our excellent Constitution guarantees to everyone freedom of religion, and charity tells us—and you know charity is the real basis of all true religion—and charity says "judge the tree by its fruit." All who profess Christianity believe in a Savior and that by and through him we must be saved. We ought therefore to consider all good Christians whose walks correspond with their professions, be they Presbyterian, Episcopalian, Baptist, Methodist, or Roman Catholic. Let it be always remembered ... that no established religion can exist under [our] glorious Constitution.[104]

Jackson had only to look to England to find support for the separation of church and state: "The alliance between church and state and the vast power they have again acquired [in England], with the national debt and pauperism which they have produced, shews that corrupt influence is as potent in suppressing the rights of human nature and rendering the great majority of the people miserable as the most unlimited sovereignty concerted in a single individual."[105]

In 1832, with cholera causing high mortality in the American cities, Jackson was urged by both lay officials and clergymen to declare a national day of prayer and repentance in hopes of stemming the epidemic. Jackson refused on constitutional grounds. "I could not do otherwise without transcending the limits prescribed by the Constitution for the President and without feeling that I might in some degree disturb the security which religion nowadays enjoys in this country in its complete separation from the political concerns of the General Government."[106] In 1787 the Presbyterians were first among the national churches to adopt an official position aimed at abolishing slavery. "Jackson found no conflict between his religious views and his strong support for the institution of slavery, nor with his support for the forcible relocation of Native Americans."[107] In a letter, Jackson expressed his belief concerning religious tolerance: "[J]udge the tree by its fruit. All who profess Christianity believe in a Savior and that by and through Him we must be saved. We ought, therefore, to consider all good Christians whose walks correspond with their professions, be they Presbyterian, Episcopalian, Baptist, Methodist or Roman Catholic."[108]

In his will, written just a few weeks before his death, Jackson intoned:

> Sir, I am in the hands of a merciful God. I have full confidence in his goodness and mercy.... The Bible is true. I have tried to conform to its spirit as near as possible. Upon that Sacred Volume I rest my hope for eternal salvation, through the merits and blood of our blessed Lord and Savior, Jesus Christ.... First, I bequeath my body to the dust whence it comes, and my soul to God who gave it, hoping for a happy immortality through the atoning merits of our Lord Jesus Christ, the Savior of the world.[109]

Education: Jackson received sporadic schooling as a lad, little more than learning the "three R's" and even there his mastery was limited. He never learned to write English correctly. John Quincy Adams boycotted Harvard University's awarding of a doctorate of laws degree to Jackson in 1833, declaring "I would not be present to witness her [Harvard's] disgrace in conferring her highest literary honors on a barbarian who could not write a sentence of grammar and could hardly spell his own name."[110] Jackson retorted, "It's a damn poor mind indeed which can't think of at least two ways to spell any word."[111]

The fact that he learned to read at all was a rarity in rural America at the time. His mother taught him reading and sent him to James Stephenson's school, thinking that classical instruction might prepare him for the Presbyterian ministry.[112] At age nine, he had the important job of reading newspapers aloud to his illiterate neighbors.[113] His schooling ended at age 13 when he joined the militia to fight in the Revolutionary War. Despite his disdain for studying, he even worked for a time as a schoolteacher.[114] With a $300 inheritance from his grandfather, Andy went to Charleston, South Carolina, where he made a dashing figure in the local society until the money ran out.[115] At seventeen, he decided to become an attorney. He moved to Salisbury, North Carolina, where he read law in the offices of prominent local lawyers. After three years, he received a license to practice law.[116]

Dueling: Andrew Jackson was involved in 13 duels, killing one person.[117] The unfortunate victim was a brave, reckless Nashville lawyer and plantation owner, Charles Dickinson. He was a nationally famous duelist and expert marksman whose "kills" numbered 24.[118] Most accounts claim the duel was the result of a nasty argument over a horse race between Jackson's "Truxton" and "Ploughboy," owned by Dickinson's father-in-law. There was "considerable betting on the outcome. 'Truxton' won. Dickinson, flushed with liquor and exasperated by his losses, was bitterly prejudiced against Jackson, they being rival lawyers, and continued to talk about the General and Mrs. Jackson. Jackson denounced him as a 'base poltroon and cowardly talebearer.' Dickinson replied that Jackson himself was 'a worthless scoundrel, a base poltroon, and a coward,'"[119] which led to blows between the two men. It might have ended there, but Jackson's political rivals goaded Dickinson to say something derogatory about Rachel. Dickinson published a statement in the *Nashville Review* in May 1806, calling Rachel "a bigamist."[120]

Finally, in 1806, Jackson challenged Dickinson to a duel, and Dickinson quickly accepted. It was decided that they should meet on Friday, May 30, 1806, at Harrison's Mills on Red River, in Logan County, less than two miles west of Adairville, Kentucky.[121] The two adversaries met to settle the score. Dickinson was favored to win, as he was known far and wife for his keen marksmanship. Jackson was aware of this and decided his course of action would be to hold his fire, and then take careful aim.[122] At the appointed time, the two stood eight paces apart. At the word, they were to turn towards each other and fire as they chose. At the command, Dickinson fired and Jackson pressed his hand over his chest as dust flew from his loose-fitting clothes, which masked the outline of his lean figure. Dickinson, obviously shocked exclaimed, 'Great God! Have I missed him?'"[123] By the code of dueling etiquette, Dickson was required to stand on his spot and receive his opponent's shot. ""Jackson took aim and steadily pulled his trigger. His gun did not fire; his pistol had locked at half cock. According to the code duello, this was not a fire, and Jackson still had his shot. He took aim a second time and this time the weapon fired. Dickinson fell backward and his surgeon quickly agreed the wound was fatal."[124]

"Only later as his boot filled with blood after he had left the dueling ground, did the extent of Jackson's wound become clear."[125] Dickinson's shot had broken a rib or two and scraped Jackson's breastbone. The wound never healed properly and many attributed his death to it many years later. "'If he had shot me through the brain, sir,' he told a friend, 'I would have still killed him.'"[126]

More than a month passed before Jackson could move around without difficulty. The wound caused him considerable discomfort over the remaining 40 years of his life.[127] Friends of Dickinson and Jackson's enemies circulated charges of unfairness in the fight, but witnesses agreed that the duel went according to agreements arrived at beforehand by the combatants.[128] "Though acceptable by the code of the times, many people considered it a cold-blooded killing ... the rules of engagement were for each man to draw and fire at the same time, upon hearing the signal, but if one fired, there was no second round until the other man fired. The implication is that magnanimity would have required Jackson to fire into the air rather than taking a slow deliberate aim at 24 feet."[129]

Jackson experienced another bullet wound in September 1813 in a tavern gunfight in downtown Nashville with brothers Jesse and Thomas Hart Benton.[130] Jackson was shot by a slug and a ball. The slug shattered his left shoulder and the ball embedded itself against his left humerus. Jackson bled profusely and it was believed that the arm would have to be amputated. He refused, announcing, just before losing consciousness because of the loss of so much blood, "I'll keep my arm."[131]

Andy needed to keep to his bed for three weeks, but five weeks after the shooting, he was commanding troops in the field. Jackson and Thomas Hart Benton later reconciled.[132] By 1831 the "bullet had migrated in Jackson's body, causing him immense pain."[133] In January 1832, the "president summoned the chief of the navy's Bureau of Medicine to remove the bullet. No anesthesia was available so Jackson merely stretched out his bare arm and told the physician, 'Go ahead.'" The surgeon made an incision, squeezed Jackson's arm and the bullet popped out. Jackson's health improved immediately." Jackson offered the ball to Benton as a souvenir but he declinded.[134]

Home: The Hermitage in Nashville, Tennessee, was Jackson's plantation for over 40 years. "When Andrew Jackson bought the Hermitage in 1804, he owned nine enslaved African Americans. By 1829, that number had increased through purchase and reproduction to over 100 African American men, women, and children. At the time of his death in 1845, Jackson owned approximately 150 human beings who lived and worked on this property."[135] A two-story log farmhouse stood at the site when Jackson purchased from Nathaniel Hays in 1804. Before moving in, "Jackson hired a local French-speaking craftsman to dress up the interior with painted trim and French wallpaper. Jackson also hired local men to clear fields, build fences, and construct new outbuildings, including a 30' × 18' log kitchen, which doubled as the cookhouse and as slave quarters for Betty the cook and her family."[136] The Jackson "family lived in the farmhouse until 1821, when they moved to the newly completed mansion."[137] Jackson had an adjoining kitchen/slave quarters built. There once was a complex of cabins for family, guests, kitchens and storerooms. "The enslaved lived in 'family units,' which often included extended kin and persons not related by blood. They lived in groups of five to ten individuals in 20-foot-square cabins with one floor, one door, one window, a fireplace, and a small loft."[138] During Jackson's lifetime there were at least one hundred buildings and structures on the Hermitage property.[139] The current Greek revival home was begun in 1819 and completed in 1821. After the Jacksons moved, the "original Hermitage farmhouse [was] converted into a single-story slave cabin, where perhaps dozens of enslaved African Americans lived for the next thirty years."[140] The Hermitage mansion "was remodeled in 1831 and a Palladian façade was added. The current structure was completed in 1836."[141] Much of the mansion's furniture was purchased in Philadelphia in the newly popular classical styles. The building was partially destroyed by fire in June 1845.

The original farm consisted of 425 acres and grew to about 1000 acres at the time of Jackson's death. The main crop was always cotton, but sheep, cattle and dairy cows also were raised. The Hermitage contained a nationally renowned racing and breeding stable.

The Hermitage, 4580 Rachel's Lane, Nashville, Tennessee, chromolithograph, by Samuel B. Jones, of Andrew Jackson's Tennessee estate and his tomb, March 29, 1856 (Library of Congress).

Jackson typically grew two hundred acres of cotton as his cash crop with the remainder of the farm dedicated to producing foodstuffs for the inhabitants of the plantation.[142] Rachel's garden, covering more than an acre, was designed by English gardener William Frost and was completed in 1819, "as a typical four-square English garden common in Europe since the Middle Ages, consisting of four quadrants and circular center beds."[143] It contained varieties of shrubs and flowering plants of the time. In 1823, when the church of the area burned down, Jackson took the lead in erecting a new church building, providing three acres of the Hermitage grounds for its location and assisting in gathering funds to pay for its construction. "The church's original nine members named their new house of worship Ephesus Church. Originally non-denominational, the congregation soon affiliated with the Presbyterian Church."[144] Today it is known as the Old Hermitage Presbyterian Church. Opened as a museum in 1889, it has been preserved to look much as it did during Jackson's lifetime.[145]

The state of Tennessee purchased the Hermitage property from the Jackson family in 1855. Since 1889 the Ladies' Hermitage Association has cared for the property as a historic site museum. The first project of the LHA took was to repair and restore the plantation's buildings. Repairs continued throughout the 20th century and professional documentation began as part of the Bicentennial in 1976.[146] The first Hermitage farmhouse and kitchen were restored to their slave quarters appearance during a multi-year $2.5 million restoration project completed in 2005. Today the Hermitage is a 1,120-acre National Historic Landmark property with museum, recreational, and farming activities ... "almost all of the mansion's contents are original ... making this dwelling one of the most accurately preserved early president homes in the country."[147]

Pets and Animals: Andrew Jackson's white wartime mount was named Sam Patch.[148] An exceptional horseman, Jackson owned a number of horses and ponies. He bred and raced some of the finest racehorses in the state. "In 1804, the first official horse race in Tennessee was held in Gallatin, in which Jackson's horse Indian Queen lost to Polly Medley. Soon after, Jackson purchased a famous Virginia thoroughbred, Truxton; a white racehorse foaled in 1800" as well as "Greyhound, a horse that had beaten both Indian Queen and Truxton."[149] Another of his prized thoroughbred racers was Pacolet, foaled in 1808. "After becoming president, Jackson took three horses to Washington to race them there. He was the last president to race horses in the nation's capital."[150] Jackson's other horses were the fillies: Bolivia, Emily, and Lady Nashville.[151] Andy had "a pet parrot, Poll, which he taught to speak in both English and Spanish. At Jackson's funeral, Poll had to be removed because it was swearing in both languages," probably picked up from its master.[152]

Recreational Pastimes and Interests: Jackson enjoyed billiards, swimming and walking. His passion was breeding racehorses and attending horse races. "At age 16, Jackson was ... a recognized appraiser of horseflesh, as a 1783 document with his signature appraising a bay horse attested.... After the (Revolutionary) war, Jackson gambled an inheritance away partly on horse racing."[153] His racehorse Truxton made him many thousands of dollars but was also prominent in the dispute that led to Jackson's duel with Charles Dickinson. The General was also fond of cock-fighting, wrestling and boxing. "He owned a bird named Bernadotte." He would challenge: "Twenty dollars on my Bernadotte! Who'll take me up?"[154]

Occupation: Jackson was admitted to the North Carolina bar in 1787 and began his legal career in McLeansville, located in Guilford County. "Finding no immediate law practice, he accepted an appointment as constable and special deputy sheriff."[155] To further supplement his income, he worked in small-town general stores.[156] Shortly after his 21st birthday, the North Carolina legislature elected John McNairy, with whom Jackson had studied law, as Superior Court judge of its Western District, which stretched from the Appalachian Mountains to the Mississippi River. McNairy appointed Jackson public prosecutor, and the two men followed the Wilderness Road across the rugged Cumberland Mountains, settling in the frontier village of Nashville, which was then in the Western District of North Carolina.[157] Jackson practiced law in Jonesborough and Greenville, where he became very successful, even serving as solicitor general for the region.[158]

In one case as solicitor, Jackson faced the more experienced and better educated defense attorney, Colonel Waigthstill Avery. In frontier courts it was a tactic of lawyers to use sarcasm and insults of one's opponent as much for the entertainment of the spectators as for making a point of law.[159] Of this tactic, Avery was a master. He constantly referred to Jackson's ignorance of the law and ridiculed his young adversary with zingers such as: "It would pay the Territory to employ competent counsel to conduct its solicitor' cases." "My young friend on the other side seems to think he can make up in noise what he lacks in knowledge!"[160] An angry Jackson addressed the judge in the case, "I thought until now that I was dealing with a lawyer and a gentleman!"[161] To which Avery retorted: "I never suspected the young man of being a lawyer. As for the gentleman, I am willing to leave that question for his own decision in a more sober moment!"[162] Afterwards, Jackson challenged Avery, who promptly accepted. At the dueling site each participant fired one shot and missed. No one called for a second shot. The participants shook hands and journeyed back to town together. It was the first-known occasion of Jackson in a duel.[163] It's true Jackson didn't know much law, but in a frontier society a little legal knowledge went a long way. He was a counselor in a great number of cases that didn't require much more than good sense, settling disputed landowner claims and cases of assault and battery.[164] In December 1780, the legislature elected him to a judgeship. In this capacity, he earned a reputation as "a fearless, fair, and swift dispenser of justice, running his court with complete authority, and with no tolerance for any disrespect of the law or of himself."[165] Life on the frontier was rough and, "as one writer put it, often the settlers would rather have 'an ounce of justice than a pound of law.' Jackson fit the bill. He practiced his profession with the same righteous intensity he brought to all of his endeavors."[166] When court was in session in Tennessee towns it was a "great occasion in that wild community, bringing crowds of men into the county town to exchange gossip, discuss politics, drink whiskey, and break heads. Probably each court day produced as many new cases as it settled. Jackson proved up to the task of maintaining law and order in the chaotic setting."[167] Besides the white population, Jackson also had to contend with the Indians, who lived in the "immediate neighborhood of Nashville and on average murdered one person every ten days."[168]

MILITARY SERVICE

Although he had no formal military training, in 1803 Jackson was elected major general of the Tennessee militia — but not without a struggle with former Tennessee governor John Sevier, a Revolutionary War hero who sought the command. Jackson and Sevier represented the two political factions in the state. The vote in the legislature was a tie, but the sitting governor cast the tie-breaking vote for his friend Jackson. Sevier and Jackson were ever after fierce enemies.[169] A few years later, the two met on a street, and much name-calling ensued. Finally Sevier snarled at Jackson, "I know of no great service you have rendered the country, except taking a trip to Natchez with another man's wife."[170] Outraged, Jackson shouted, "Great God. Did you mention her sacred name?"[171] As Jackson was carrying only a cane, while Sevier had a sword, the conflict ended before anyone was seriously wounded. The next day, Jackson wrote to Sevier demanding an "interview" with him that is, he challenged Sevier, who was once again governor of Tennessee, to a duel. Sevier's reply "matched Jackson's insult for insult, in some cases word for word."[172] In a further exchange of notes, the two would-be combatants could not agree on a time or a place for the duel. They even took their feud to the newspapers, each calling the other "poltroon and coward."[173] When they finally agreed on a place and time for the "interview," there was great deal of name-calling, but not a shot was fired, each leaving the field of honor, feeling vindicated.[174]

During the War of 1812, Britain allied itself with a number of American tribes hostile to the United States. "In 1813, the Creek Indian tribes of Georgia and Alabama split over supporting the British during the war. The Lower Creek group continued their support of U.S. forces,"[175] while the Upper Creeks also "known as the Red Stick Creeks for their red-painted wooden war clubs as well as supposed magical red sticks used by their shamans,"[176] opposed American expansion and sided with the British. On August 30, 1813, a force of seven hundred Red Stick warriors stormed Fort Mims, located at Tensaw in Baldwin County, Alabama. "The attack was both a preemptory strike and retaliation for being ambushed at Burnt Corn Creek a month earlier. Nearly 250 of the settlers, allied Creeks, and members of the Mississippi Territorial and local militias living in the one-acre facility at the time were killed in the day-long struggle. The news of the disaster jolted the nation, and galvanized Americans, especially those living in states bordering the Mississippi Territory, in support of measures to put down the rebellion."[177] Jackson's militia, now in the service of the United States, was joined by "the 39th United States Infantry and about 600 Cherokee, Choctaw and Lower Creeks caught up a tribe of Red Stick Creeks,"[178] led by Chief Menawa, who had been pushed the into a defensive position in Horseshoe Bend in the Tallapoosa River in central Alabama. "On March 27 at 10:30 A.M., Jackson began an artillery barrage which consisted of 2 cannons firing for about two hours. Little damage was caused to the Red Sticks or their fortifications. General John Coffee's Cherokees and cavalry began crossing the river and fought the Red Sticks on their rear. Jackson then ordered a bayonet charge. The infantry charged the breastworks surrounding the camp and caught the Red Sticks in a cross fire."[179] Speculation is that there would have been no need for bloodshed if Jackson had chosen to wait and surround the approximately 100 acres of the Creek compound. His troops numbered 5,000, whereas the Creeks had but 900 braves, and were encumbered by the presence of their wives and children. They "had no supplies and no way to get any" and would have been forced to surrender. However, Jackson was in no mood to wait.[180] "In the early stages of the battle the allied Native Americans crossed the river upstream in stolen canoes and attacked the Muskogee village, taking the women and children prisoner, and then proceeded to attack the barricade from the rear. Jackson commenced a frontal assault on the barricade and succeeded in taking it after fierce fighting," in which more than 800 warriors were killed.[181]

Twenty-one-year-old ensign Sam Houston, later governor of Tennessee and president of the Republic of Texas, was a member of the militia. Many years later he recalled the battle: "The sun was going down, and it set on the ruin of the Creek nation. Where, but a few hours before a thousand brave ... [warriors] had scowled on death and their assailants, there was nothing to be seen but volumes of dense smoke, rising heavily over the corpses of painted warriors, and the burning ruins of their fortifications."[182] Without authorization from Congress, Jackson forced the warring Creeks into signing a treaty that "ceded to the United States 23 million acres of land owned by Creeks and other tribes, including some land belonging to tribes allied with the U.S. government. This victory opened much of the lower South to settlement by European Americans, and the white population of Alabama boomed from 9,000 in 1810 to 310,000 in 1830."[183] No other Indian-fighter had so many Indians under his command. The Cherokees allied themselves with Jackson and helped him defeat the Creeks at the Battle of Horseshoe Bend. Jackson reportedly told Cherokee chief Junaluska, "As long as the sun shines and the grass grows, there shall be friendship between us, and the feet of the Cherokee shall be toward the east."[184]

In a few years, Junaluska recalled Jackson's words with bitterness, at the time of great removal of Cherokees from their lands, saying, "If I had known that Jackson would drive us from our homes, I would have killed him that day at the Horseshoe."[185]

Battle of New Orleans: In 1814, President Madison appointed Jackson a major general and assigned him to the defense of New Orleans. "Jackson arrived in New Orleans on December 2, 1814. News of a possible British attack had been circulating for weeks, which created panic among some inhabitants and inert resignation in others. Though he was in poor health, Jackson set about reconnoitering all access points to the city, mediating between the bickering factions of the city's civil authorities, and attempting to calm the situation."[186] Territorial Governor Claiborne, who earlier had been "elected to Jackson's vacant seat in the United States House of Representatives,"[187] resented Jackson, who he considered a social inferior. The French Creoles class resented the Americans who had been flocking to the city since the Louisiana Purchase. The Creoles "found the Americans grasping and lacking in proper manners."[188] On the other hand the newly arrived Americans viewed the Creoles as

Battle of New Orleans, lithograph by Kurz & Allison, c. 1890, shows General Andrew Jackson on horseback in foreground commanding troops in battle against British troops commanded by General Pakenham, January 8, 1815 (Library of Congress).

morally corrupt, "reveling in the 'delights of the table, the boudoir, and the gaming boards.'"[189] What Jackson found was a city "unprepared to defend itself due to petty disputes between two committees formed to come up with a plan"[190] to save the Crescent City. In preparation for the expected battle with the British, Jackson recruited frontiersmen, pirates led by a famous local buccaneer, Jean Lafitte, and some 600 free blacks, Frenchmen, and anyone else he could find. "After his habit of giving his personal attention to every detail. General Jackson ... visited Fort St. Philip, ordered the wooden barracks removed, and had additional heavy artillery mounted. He caused two more batteries to be constructed, one on the opposite bank of the Mississippi, and the other half a mile above, with twenty-four pounders in position, thus fully guarding the approach by the mouth of the river. He then proceeded to Chef Menteur, as far as Bayou Sauvage, and ordered a battery erected at that point. He continued to fortify or obstruct the larger bayous whose waters gave convenient access to the city between the Mississippi and the Gulf."[191] On Sunday January 8, 1815, Jackson's 3,500 to 5,000 militiamen took their positions behind barricades of cotton bales on the Chalmette plantation, just below the city. "The parapet was about five feet in height, and from ten to twenty feet thick at the base, extending inland from the river one thousand yards."[192] Some 12,000 of Britain's finest troops, drawn from Europe and the West Indies, marched in columns across an open field towards the American position. "It was not yet daybreak on the morning of the eighth of January when an American outpost came hastily in, with the intelligence that the enemy was in motion and advancing in great force ... as the day began to dawn, the light discovered ... what seemed the entire British army in moving columns, occupying two thirds of the space from the wood to the river.... Suddenly a Congreve rocket, set off at a point nearest the wood, blazed its way across the British front in the direction of the river. This was the signal for attack.... [The British] quickly formed in close column of more than two hundred men in front and many lines deep. These advanced in good order in the direction of Batteries 7 and 8, and to the left of these. It was now evident that the main assault would be made upon that part of the breastwork occupied by the Tennesseans, with the intent to break the line here and flank Jackson's army on the right. These were quickly joined by the Kentucky troops, forming ranks of five or six men for several hundred yards."[193] The battle was an American rout. The British attack began under a heavy fog, but as the redcoats neared the American line, the fog suddenly lifted, exposing the soldiers to withering gunfire of "the musketry and rifles of the Tennessee and Kentucky militia, joining with the fire of the artillery."[194] The British troops retreated but were rallied together by their officers and joined by additional soldiers to make a second and equally disastrous attack on Jackson's line. "Nearly one hundred of the enemy reached the ditch in front of the American breastwork, half of whom were killed and the other half captured."[195] "Many passed the ditch and scaled the parapet only to be shot down in the redoubt by the unerring riflemen behind the entrenched line."[196] "The dead and wounded lay thick along the road, the levee, and the river bank, as far out as the range of our guns. A flanking fire from the battery across the river harassed the troops in this column both in the advance and retreat, as they passed in plain view, from which fire they sustained severe losses."[197] In a letter to a friend, Jackson stated, "It appears that the unerring hand of Providence shielded my men from the shower of balls, bombs, and rockets, when every ball and bomb from our guns carried with them a mission of death."[198] Jackson informed Secretary of State James Monroe: "Heaven, to be sure, has interposed most wonderfully in our behalf, and I am filled with gratitude, when I look back to what we have escaped."[199] General Jackson later credited God for giving him a sign. "I was sure of success, for I knew that God would not give me previsions of disaster, but signs of victory. He said this ditch can never be passed. It cannot be done."[200]

According to British estimates, the troops led by General Edward Pakenham suffered 2,000 casualties, including Pakenham. "General Jackson was not far wrong in estimating the entire losses of the British, during the two weeks of invasion, at more than four thousand men. If the large number who deserted from their ranks after the battles of the eighth of January be included, the excess would doubtless swell the numbers much above four thousand. Their killed, wounded, and missing on the eighth approximated three thousand. So decimated and broken up were their columns that they dared not risk another battle."[201] Jackson estimated the number his force lost — only 8 killed and 58 wounded or missing. These numbers do not include the vast numbers of Red Coats who deserted. The surviving British troops returned to their ships and sailed away, never to return. The Treaty of Ghent had been signed on December 24, 1814, but news of the peace would not reach the combatants until February. The battle is widely regarded as the greatest American land victory of the war.[202] After the humiliation of the burning of the president's mansion, the battle proved to be a major morale boost to the nation and "was a major factor in Jackson's election to the presidency 14 years later."[203] In the meantime, back in New Orleans, "Louisianans gave Andrew Jackson mixed reviews. Some hailed him as a 'conquering hero' and honored him with parades, balls, and parties. Others scorned him as the 'butcher of New Orleans' and master of 'bloody deeds,' blaming him for what few casualties there were from the campaign"[204] and placing the city under martial law. Numerous citizens were detained without being charged and local militiamen who wished to go home to sow their cotton were arrested and tried for desertion. "After Jackson's victory over the British, the citizens of New Orleans expected him to rescind the order for martial law. However, Jackson continued to wait until he received word that peace negotiations underway at Ghent were complete."[205]

In September 1814, the general sent a proclamation to the people of Louisiana from Mobile: "The individual who refuses to defend his rights when called by his government, deserves to be a slave, and must be punished as an enemy of his country and friend to her foe."[206] Jackson's defense of his refusal to comply with a habeas corpus order in New Orleans was, "Is it wise to sacrifice the spirit of the laws to the letter, and be adhering too strictly to the letter, lose the substance forever, in order that we may, for an instant, preserve the shadow?"[207]

"The General" did not endear himself to local plantation owners with his 1815 address to his officers defending New Orleans against the British: "Private property is held sacred in all good governments and particularly in our own. Yet shall the fear of invading it prevent a general from marching his army over a cornfield or burning a house which protects the enemy? A thousand other instances might be cited to show that laws must be silent when necessity speaks."[208]

Seminole War: "Seminoles were a confederacy of multiple clans that had splintered from various southwestern tribes ... and drifted into southern Georgia and northern Florida in the early 1700s. These disparate bands, without much in common but geography, began to hunt, fish, farm, and herd livestock in the area. By 1750 clans had built towns along the Suwannee River, linked to other Native American and maroon (runaway slave) villages through infrastructure (roads, shared outbuildings) and intermarriage."[209] The Spanish at St. Augustine referred collectively to the Indians as *Cimarrones*, the likely source of the word Seminole, which roughly translates to "wild ones" or "runaways."[210] Escaped slaves also entered Florida, "trying to reach a place where their U.S. masters had no authority over them" and were integrated into the tribes.[211] "Floridian territory was nominally under Spanish sway; the Spanish permitted the Seminole to settle there in order to create a buffer zone between their sphere of influence and that of the British."[212] When the British controlled Florida during the Revolutionary War, they "incited Indians and escaped slaves against American settlers."[213] "After the American Revolution (1776–1783), Spain regained control of Florida from Britain as part of the Treaty of Paris."[214] Spanish colonists as well as settlers from the newly formed United States came pouring in. "Many of these new residents were lured by favorable Spanish terms for acquiring property called land grants."[215] Florida was divided into East Florida and West Florida, extending from the Apalachicola River to the Mississippi River. When the U.S. made the Louisiana Purchase, they claimed that it "included West Florida west of the Perdido River."[216] "A force of volunteers (who were promised free land) was raised in Georgia. In March 1812 this force of 'Patriots', with the aid of some United States Navy gunboats, seized Fernandina. The 'Patriots' were unable to take the Castillo de San Marcos in St. Augustine, however, and the approach of war with Britain led to an end of the American incursion into East Florida."[217] "Before the 'Patriot' army withdrew from Florida, Seminoles, as allies of the Spanish, began to attack them. These attacks reinforced the American view that the Seminoles were enemies. The presence of black Seminoles in the fighting also raised the old fear of a slave rebellion among the Georgians of the 'Patriot' army."[218]

By 1817, there was trouble again with the Seminoles, who had been allies of Great Britain during the War of 1812. When the war ended, the British exited Florida, except for Major Edward Nicholls of the Royal Marines. He directed the provisioning of a fort at Prospect Bluff on the Apalachicola River with cannon, muskets and ammunition. Before he left in 1815, "Nicholls invited the runaway slaves to take possession of the fort, which came to be known by white southerners as the 'Negro Fort.'"[219] "By June of 1815, approximately 330 black warriors and 30 Seminole Indians were stationed on the banks of the Apalachicola at Prospect Bluff, protecting the region with four pieces of artillery, six light cannon, and a large stock of British ammunition and arms."[220] An American officer, Colonel Patterson, wrote: "The force of the negroes was daily increasing; and they felt themselves so strong and secure that they had commenced several plantations on the fertile banks of the Apalachicola, which would have yielded them every article of sustenance, and which would, consequently, in a short time have rendered their establishment quite formidable and highly injurious to the neighboring States."[221]

Col. Patterson commended its elimination: "The service rendered by the destruction of the fort, and the band of negroes who held it, and the country in its vicinity, is of great and manifest importance to the United States, and particularly those States bordering on the Creek nation, as it had become the general rendezvous for runaway slaves and disaffected Indians; and asylum where they were assured of being received; a stronghold where they found arms and ammunition to protect themselves against their owners and the Government."[222] The fort was considered a menace to all slaveholders in the vicinity and on March 15, 1816, William Harris Crawford, the secretary of war, "ordered General Andrew Jackson to call attention to the governor of Pensacola to the fort. If the Spanish governor refused to 'put an end to an evil of so serious nature,' the U.S. government would promptly take measures to reduce it. If the Spanish government was too weak to destroy it, then the U.S. was more than willing to take it into its own hands. On April 23, Jackson transmitted the demands of Secretary Crawford, ordering the Spanish governor to 'destroy or remove from out frontier this banditti, put an end to an evil of so serious a nature, and return to our citizens and friendly Indians inhabiting our territory those negroes now in said fort, and which have been stolen and enticed from them.' The blacks at the Apalachicola Fort were supposedly 'enticed from the service of their masters.'"[223] Since Spain was too weak either to help or hinder Jackson, the general gathered forces for an invasion. He dispatched a company of 100 American soldiers and some 150 Creek allies and two gunboats across the river from the fort on a slave-catching expedition.[224]

As Jackson had hoped, the former slaves hoisted the Union Jack and fired on the gunboats, giving him the excuse for destroying the fort. This came about when a "cannonball heated to a red glow and shot from a gunboat landed in the fort's powder magazine, resulting in an explosion that immediately killed more than 250 of the citadel's 320 residents, with many others dying thereafter."[225] Jackson recalled his troops, but American squatters and outlaws made raids against the Seminoles, killing many and stealing their slaves and cattle. The Seminoles retaliated by raiding American settlements across the border of the U.S. Late in 1817, an American boat carrying supplies was attacked by the Seminoles on the Apalachicola River, "killing most of the vessel's forty to fifty passengers, including twenty-six soldiers, seven wives of soldiers, and possibly some children."[226]

On March 13, with a force of "800 U.S. Army regulars, 1,000 Tennessee volunteers, 1,000 Georgia militiamen and some 1,400 friendly Creek warriors, Jackson entered Florida."[227] His goal was to destroy the Seminole havens for fugitive slaves while establishing American military dominance over Florida. "The Indian town of Tallahassee was burned on March 31, and the town of Miccosukee was taken the next day. More than 300 Indian homes were destroyed. Jackson then turned south, reaching St. Marks on April 6,"[228] where he believed escaping Seminoles and blacks had taken refuge. The general sent a letter to the Spanish Governor, explaining his objects and purposes. He had come, he said, "to chastise a savage foe, who, combined with a lawless band of negro brigands, had been for some time past carrying on a cruel and unprovoked war against the citizens of the United States.... To prevent the recurrence of so gross a violation of neutrality, and to exclude our savage enemies from so strong a hold as St. Marks, I deem it expedient to garrison that fortress with American troops until the close of the present war. This measure is justifiable on the immutable principle of self-defense, and cannot but be satisfactory, under existing circumstances, to his Catholic Majesty the King of Spain."[229] At St. Marks, two Indian leaders, Josiah Francis, a Red Stick Creek, and Homathlemico, were captured and promptly hanged.[230] Jackson took prisoner Alexander George Arbuthnot, "a Scottish trader working out of the Bahamas. He traded with the Indians in Florida, and had written letters to British and American officials on behalf of the Indians. He was rumored to be selling guns to the Indians, and to be preparing them for war. He probably was selling guns, as the main trade item of the Indians was deer skins, and they needed guns to hunt the deer."[231] "About this time, Robert Ambrister, a former Royal Marine and self-appointed British 'agent,' was captured by Jackson's army."[232] Having destroyed the major Seminole and black villages a military tribunal at St. Marks was convened, and "Ambrister and Arbuthnot were charged with aiding the Seminoles, inciting them to war and leading them against the United States. Ambrister threw himself on the mercy of the court, while Arbuthnot maintained his innocence, saying that he had only been engaged in legal trade. The tribunal sentenced both men to death, but then relented and changed Ambrister's sentence to fifty lashes and a year at hard labor. Jackson, however, reinstated Ambrister's death penalty. Ambrister was executed by a firing squad on April 29, 1818. Arbuthnot was hanged from the yardarm of his own ship."[233] The fact that the trial and the executions were not legal didn't faze Jackson. He justified his actions by saying, "The laws of war did not apply to conflicts with savages.... I hope the execution of these two unprincipled villains will prove an awful example to the world."[234]

Jackson's actions led to international repercussions. Spain protested the invasion and seizure of its territory just as Secretary of State John Quincy Adams was in negotiations to purchase Florida. The Spanish suspended the negotiations until Adams apologized for the seizure of West Florida and offered back St. Marks and Pensacola to Spain. Spain accepted and the negotiations resumed.[235] Britain protested the execution of two of its citizens who had not even been on American territory and threatened reprisals, which never took place.[236] Jackson traveled to Washington to defend his actions. Except for Adams, Monroe's Cabinet members wanted to put Jackson in prison. Congressional committees held hearings into the irregularities of the trials of Ambrister and Arbuthnot. Resolutions were introduced to condemn Jackson's actions, but he was too popular a hero and they failed.[237]

POLITICAL OFFICES

Political Philosophy and Political Party Affiliation: Jackson's new Democratic Party became a coalition of farmers, city-dwelling laborers, and Irish Catholics.[238] "It was weakest in New England, but strong everywhere else and won most national elections thanks to strength in New York, Pennsylvania, Virginia ... and the frontier. Democrats opposed elites and aristocrats, the Bank of the United States, and the whiggish modernizing programs that would build up industry at the expense of the yeoman or independent small farmer.[239] The key issues it promoted were opposition to elites and aristocrats, popular democracy (in terms of voting rights and access to government patronage jobs) and opposition to the Bank of the United States.[240] Thus Jacksonian Democracy was born. "To the average voter in 1828, Jackson was a great popular leader, because they held him also to be a typical democrat."[241] In contrast to Jeffersonian democracy, Jacksonian democracy was built on the following general principles. Expanded Suffrage: "The Jacksonians believed that voting rights should be extended to all white men."[242] Manifest Destiny: "This was the belief that white Americans had a destiny to settle the American West and to expand control from the Atlantic Ocean to the Pacific."[243] Patronage: This "was the policy of placing political supporters into appointed offices. Many Jacksonians held the view that rotating political appointees in and out of office was not only the right but also the duty of winners in political contests."[244] Strict Constructionism: "Jacksonians initially favored a federal government of limited powers. Jackson said that he would guard against 'all encroachments upon the legitimate sphere of State sovereignty'.... As the Jacksonians consolidated power, they more often advocated expanding federal power and presidential power in particular."[245] Laissez-faire Economics: "Jacksonians generally favored a hands-off approach to the economy."[246] Banking: "Jacksonians opposed government-granted monopolies to banks, especially the national bank."[247]

As president, Jackson believed that he was the lone guardian of the people against special interests and their cohorts in Congress. Unlike most southerners and slaveholders, Jackson did not prize states' rights over the union, asserting that the national union was indivisible and perpetual: "When a faction in a state attempts to nullify a constitutional law of congress, or to destroy the union, the balance of the people composing the union have a perfect right to coerce them to obedience. This is my creed!"[248]

As national politics polarized around Jackson and his opposition, two parties grew out of the old Republican Party. The Democratic Republicans, or simply Democrats, supported Jackson. "On April 14th 1834 [Henry] Clay made a speech and reminded his listeners that during the American Revolution the Tories were loyal to the King, but the Whigs 'stood foursquare for freedom and independence.' He referred to those who opposed the growing executive powers of President Jackson as, 'The Whigs of the present day.' The name probably originated in New York City, or possibly the *Salem Gazette* in Massachusetts. It soon became the new name for the party that would oppose Jackson in 1836."[249] For the first time since the death of the Federalist Party in the early 1800s there was a political party robust enough to contest Democratic authority. "Henry Clay and others had called themselves National Republicans—based on their vision of the United States as a nation while others saw it as a confederation of states—taking strong national measures like building inter-state roads. When a number of southern Democrats like John C. Calhoun, threw their lot in with the National Republicans, they were united only by their opposition to the growing 'kinglike' strength of the president. Thus they came to be called Whigs, implying that the Jacksonians were Tories, in favor of 'King' Andrew.'"[250] The Whigs were conservative on social issues but progressive with respect to the economy.

U.S. Congress: Jackson was the first U.S. representative from Tennessee (1796–1797) after it became a state in June 1796.[251] He soon allied with the Jeffersonian Party criticizing Washington and his administration. Jackson disliked the Jay Treaty with Great Britain and believed that the federal government had not acted to defend the frontier from Indians. After one year in the House, he moved to the Senate. He served in the Senate from September 1797 to April 1798 and then retired to private life.[252] He was appointed to the United States Senate a second time, in 1823, serving until 1825, when he resigned once again, noting in a letter to John Coffee, "I am a Senator against my wishes and feelings, which I regret more than any other of my life."[253]

Justice on the Tennessee Supreme Court: Jackson returned to Tennessee and served as a state Supreme Court judge from 1798 to 1804.[254] Once, an accused man stormed out of Jackson's courtroom cursing the judge and jury and brandishing weapons. When no one dared arrest the man, Jackson adjourned the court for ten minutes, approached the man with two loaded pistols and roared, "Surrender you infernal villain, this very instant, or I will blow you through."[255] The man meekly put down his weapons and the court continued. Jackson's decisions were said to be "short, untechnical, unlearned, sometimes ungrammatical, and generally right."[256] In 1801, "Jackson helped organize the Order of Freemasons in Tennessee, aware that the Masons were a useful friend to an ambitious man."[257] In March 1804, Orleans Territory was created and Jackson unsuccessfully sought the governorship.[258] After retiring from the court, he devoted his time to the development of his plantation.

Governor of the Florida Territory: After acquiring Florida from Spain, President Monroe appointed Jackson territorial governor of Florida (1821). Jackson wasn't happy in the post and resigned after only four months, returning home to Tennessee.[259]

Presidential Campaign of 1824: Four Democratic Republicans—John Quincy Adams of Massachusetts, Andrew Jackson of Tennessee, William Harris Crawford of Georgia, and Henry Clay of Kentucky—vied for the presidency in 1824.[260] Adams served as a minister to several countries, in the U.S. Senate, and as President Monroe's secretary of state. Jackson was seen as a down-to-earth man of the people, a complete opposite of the aristocrats who had been president up to that time. Crawford was the chosen candidate of the last of the unpopular congressional caucuses, which most people viewed as undemocratic. Before the election, Crawford suffered a paralytic stroke that weakened him throughout the campaign. Clay was a popular legislator who earned the title "The Great Compromiser," for his efforts to prevent what would become the Civil War.[261]

The campaign was more about the candidates' personalities and regional rivalries than about partisan politics. "Andrew Jackson's emphasis on the will of the people and the virtue of the majority was the actualization of the upper-class' greatest fears. A true democracy, with power in the hands of the common man, was not desired by the elite class that occupied most government positions. An ideal existed that the educated and cultured minority should make the decisions for the uncouth, incompetent majority. Jackson's appeal in the South and West was particularly frightening to these Northeastern elites, as the frontiersmen represented the worst of the under classes—violent, rowdy and uneducated men who might somehow gain a voice in the government of the country."[262] Adams attacked Jackson on many fronts, making his perceived lack of control central to the argument that he would ruin the integrity of the republic and its institutions. Rachel Jackson's possible bigamy was used mostly in a "whispering campaign" and both the notion of the "sanctity of marriage and the chaos of adultery became questions debated in newspapers. This was the first time that a deeply personal event would be used against the candidate. At this time, they also took into consideration what kind of a personal background a First Lady should have."[263]

"Old Hickory" lost the presidential election of 1824 to Adams, despite receiving the majority of the popular vote in the states that had a popular vote. But at that time, in 6 of the 24 states, the legislature picked the electors. The election was unlike those of today. The campaign was for Electoral College votes, not popular votes. Jackson had the most Electoral College votes, but as none of the four candidates had the necessary majority of the votes, the election was thrown to the U.S. House of Representatives, where Adams was chosen. Thirteen House state delegations voted for Adams, 7 for Jackson and 4 for Crawford. Jackson believed the results were due to a deal made by Henry Clay to receive appointment as secretary of state for throwing his support to Adams. As a result, Jackson resigned from the Senate in 1825 to prepare for the election of 1828.[264] In a February 10, 1825, letter to John Coffee, Jackson lamented, "I weep for the liberty of my country when I see at this early day of its 'successful experiment' that corruption has been imputed to many members of the House of Representatives, and the rights of the people have been bartered for promises of office."[265]

Presidential Campaign of 1828: In the late 1820s, Andrew led a splintered group of Democratic-Republicans to form the Democratic Party. Opponents called Jackson a "jackass" during the campaign, and Jacksonians adopted the donkey as a political symbol for a while, but it died out. However, it later became the symbol for the Democratic Party when cartoonist Thomas Nast popularized it.[266] Thomas Jefferson assailed Jackson's candidacy:

> I feel much alarm at the prospect of seeing General Jackson President. He is the most unfit man I know for such a place. He has had very little respect for laws and constitutions, and is, in fact, an able military chief. His passions are terrible. When I was President of the Senate, he was a Senator, and he could never speak on account of the rashness of his feelings. I have seen him attempt it repeatedly, and as often choke with rage. His passions are, no doubt, cooler now; he has been much tried since I knew him, but he is a dangerous man.[267]

Adams' and Jackson's political agendas were not much different on the major issues of the day. It was clear that the election would be a "personality contest." Besides the attacks on the reputation of Jackson's wife and the circumstances of their marriage, "slander and mud-slinging became the "issues" of the campaign. Adams' supporters were concerned with keeping Jackson, the so-called "representative of mob-rule," out of the White House." The "Coffin Hand Bill" was a pamphlet printed by John Binns and depicted the "six coffins of the militiamen executed for robbery, arson, and mutiny while serving under Jackson in the

War of 1812."[268] "Jackson was characterized as a rowdy, drunken murderer, while Adams was pictured as a man extravagant with the people's money and stingy with his own."[269] Opposition newspapers pilloried Rachel with some of the most savage cartoons ever seen in American political history.

In an editorial, the *Massachusetts Journal* blustered:

> [If] "The Great Western Bluebeard," [persisted in placing his wife] among modest women, he shall meet a firmer resistance before he fights her and his own way into the presidential mansion.... Who is there in all this land that has a wife, a sister, or a daughter that could be pleased to see Mrs. Jackson presiding in the drawing room at Washington? There is pollution in the touch; there is perdition in the example of a profligate woman and shall we standing in a watch-tower to warn our countrymen of approaching danger seal our lips in silence to this personage and her paramour, great and powerful as he is and captivating as he renders himself with his "bandana handkerchief," "his frock coat," his amiable condescensions, and the fascination of his barroom and public table talk.[270]

Even Jackson's dead mother was a target. A pro–Adams newspaper charged, "General Jackson's mother was a common prostitute brought to this country by British soldiers! She afterward married a mulatto man, with whom she had several children, of which number General Jackson is one."[271]

Democrats recalled the "corrupt bargain" of 1824 and denounced Adams for owning a billiard table and an ivory chess set. They also accused him of traveling on Sunday and having premarital relations with his wife and claimed she was an illegitimate child. They savaged Adams for allegedly arranging for an American girl to satisfy the lust of Czar Alexander I during his service as minister to Russia, dubbing JQA "The Pimp."[272] "In the words of one historian, the election of 1828 boiled down to: do you want to vote for someone whose wife is a whore or do you want to vote for someone who pimped for the czar of Russia?"[273] "Jackson was the first U.S. president that was not from an aristocratic Massachusetts or Virginia family, and the first from the West. For this reason, Jackson was considered ... 'the people's president.' Jackson's victory was considered a triumph for the common man."[274] At the time, states changed eligibility for voting, allowing those who did not own land the right to vote. The "common folk" were given the ballot, and they cast it for Jackson. He won the popular vote, with 56 percent to 44 percent for Adams, and the electoral vote by a margin of 178 to 83.[275] Adams' reaction to his loss to Jackson was this: "[He is] incompetent both by his ignorance and by the fury of his passions. He will be surrounded and governed by incompetent men, whose ascendancy over him will be secured by their servility and who will bring to the Government of the nation nothing by their talent for intrigue."[276]

Motto: "Let the people rule."[277]

HIS PRESIDENCY

Throughout his presidency, Jackson was a populist. He had no stated program and dealt with issues as they arose. "Jackson adopted the view that this was going to be a government not simply of the people, but by the people ... that there was nothing so difficult about running the country that ordinary people couldn't figure out and do it. It was a rather unusual notion, but it was the path the U.S. took and the path that we've followed until now."[278] The victory in 1828 was declared a triumph of democracy over aristocracy by the Democrats. Jackson resolutely held that it was his charge to liberate the American government from the wealthy and the elite and make it responsive to the will of the majority. Jackson was responsible for molding the modern presidency and the conviction that the chief executive is the only official who represents all of the American people. "Jackson's appeal

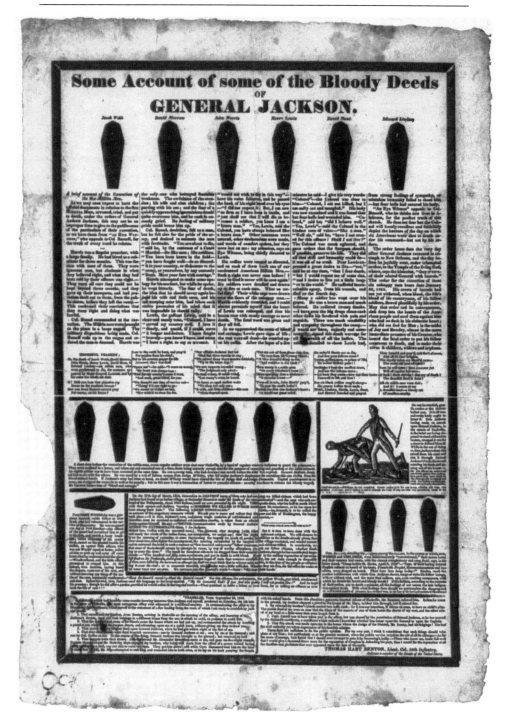

Coffin handbill, woodcut printed by John Binns, a Republican newspaper editor. During the 1828 presidential campaign, Andrew Jackson was condemned for being a bloodthirsty disciplinarian because he ordered the execution of six mutinous militiamen during the Creek War in 1813. Other coffins represent soldiers and Indians allegedly condemned and executed by Jackson (Library of Congress).

to the American people was the appeal of the chieftain to the tribe. They loved him because he was their protector, their hero. But they also loved him because he embodied their hopes and fears, their passions and prejudices, their insight and their ignorance, better than anyone before him."[279]

"He frustrated the professional politicians of Congress with his insistence that any man should be able to hold elected office and by his forceful and effective use of the presidential veto and bully pulpit."[280] In his first annual message to Congress, Jackson recommended eliminating the electoral college: "To the people belongs the right of electing their Chief Magistrate; it was never designed that their choice should in any case be defeated, either by the intervention of electoral colleges or by the agency confided, under certain contingencies, to the House of Representatives.... I would therefore recommend such an amendment of the Constitution as may remove all intermediate agency in the election of the President and Vice President."[281]

His Vice President: John C. Calhoun (1829–1832) resigned when he was elected to the U.S. Senate. "Although anti-tariff southern Democrats had serious reservations about [Martin] Van Buren, Jackson's sentiments prevailed. By an overwhelming margin, the convention chose Van Buren on the first ballot"[282] and he served in the office from 1833 to 1837.

His Cabinet: Secretary of State Martin Van Buren (1829–1831), Edward Livingston (1831–1833), Louis McLane (1833–1834), and John Forsyth (1834–1837); Secretary of the Treasury Samuel D. Ingham (1829–1831), William J. Duane (1833), Roger B. Taney (1833–1834), and Levi Woodbury (1834–1837); Secretary of War John H. Eaton (1829–1831) and Lewis Cass (1831–1836); Attorney General John M. Berrien (1829–1831), Roger B. Taney (1831–1833), and Benjamin F. Butler (1833–1837); Postmaster General William T. Barry (1829–1831) and Amos Kendall (1835–1837); Secretary of the Navy John Branch (1829–1831), Levi Woodbury (1831–1834), and Mahlon Dickerson (1834–1837).

Supreme Court Appointments: John McLean (1830), Henry Baldwin (1830), James Moore Wayne (1835), Roger Brooke Taney, chief justice (1836), Philip Pendleton Barbour (1836).

States Admitted to the Union: Arkansas (1836) and Michigan (1837).

The People's Inauguration: When Andrew Jackson was inaugurated on March 4, 1829, Washington, D.C., was filled with people who had come to see their hero take the oath of office. "Jackson was America's first "Frontier President"—the first president who did not come from the nation's east-coast elite. His victory was seen as a triumph for the common man and for democracy. The celebration of his inauguration was an opportunity for America's ordinary citizen to rejoice."[283] Jackson's investiture was an opportunity for America's ordinary citizens to celebrate, and celebrate they did. Jackson threw open the doors to the White House to all comers. Throngs of people in buckskin clothes and muddy boots descended upon the presidential mansion. Those more accustomed to dignified receptions at the president's home were aghast at the "rabble" that converged in a crush to get refreshments.[284] Margaret Bayard Smith, a long-time member of Washington Society, commented on the scene in a March 11, 1829, letter to a Mrs. Kirkpatrick:

> Thousands and thousands of people, without distinction of rank, collected in an immense mass round the Capitol, silent, orderly and tranquil, with their eyes fixed on the front of that edifice, waiting the appearance of the President in the portico.... The south side of the Capitol was literally alive with the multitude, which stood ready to receive the hero and the multitude who attended him.... When the speech was over, and the President made his parting bow, the barrier that had separated the people from him was broken down and they rushed up the steps all eager to shake hands with him.... But what a scene did we witness! The Majesty of the People had disappeared,

and a rabble, a mob, of boys, negros [sic], women, children, scrambling fighting, romping. What a pity what a pity! No arrangements had been made, no police officers placed on duty and the whole house had been inundated by the rabble mob.... The President, after having been literally nearly pressed to death and almost suffocated and torn to pieces by the people in their eagerness to shake hands with Old Hickory, had retreated through the back way or south front and had escaped to his lodgings at Gadsby's.

Cut glass and china to the amount of several thousand dollars had been broken in the struggle to get the refreshments, punch and other articles had been carried out in tubs and buckets, but had it been in hogsheads it would have been insufficient, ice-creams, and cake and lemonade, for 20,000 people, for it is said that number were there, tho' I think the number exaggerated.

Ladies fainted, men were seen with bloody noses and such a scene of confusion took place as is impossible to describe, — those who got in could not get out by the door again, but had to scramble out of windows. At one time, the President who had retreated and retreated until he was pressed against the wall, could only be secured by a number of gentleman forming around him and making a kind of barrier of their own bodies, and the pressure was so great that Col. Bomford who was one said that at one time he was afraid they should have been pushed down, or on the President. It was then the windows were thrown open, and the torrent found an outlet, which otherwise might have proved fatal. This concourse had not been anticipated and therefore not provided against. Ladies and gentlemen, only had been expected at this Levee, not the people en masse. But it was the People's day, and the People's President and the People would rule.[285]

One observer of the crowd of Jackson's "people," lamented, "The Reign of King 'Mob'

Andrew Jackson is sworn in by chief justice John Marshall. Photograph by Allyn Cox of ceiling mural, east central portico, U.S. Capitol (Architect of the Capitol).

seemed to be triumphant."[286] Although Jackson was hailed as a man of the people, he was, in fact, at this time a wealthy, slave-owning, plantation aristocrat.[287]

First Term: Daniel Feller wrote in "King Andrew and the Bank": "Jackson came to the presidency with a deep sense of grievance against his enemies, real and imagined, in the existing political establishment and with a conviction that the government had fallen from Jefferson austerity into profligacy and corruption. This he was determined to reverse."[288]

DOMESTIC AFFAIRS — MAJOR EVENTS

The Spoils System: Jackson introduced the "spoils system" to American politics. State machines were formed on patronage, and New York senator William L. Marcy, a Jackson ally, openly proclaimed that "to the victors belong the spoils."[289] Jackson didn't quite echo that belief but he "decried officeholders who seemed to enjoy life tenure, he believed Government duties should be 'so plain and simple' that offices should rotate among deserving applicants."[290] A sizable number of people holding government positions in Washington were suddenly replaced by supporters of Jackson. In his journal he expressed that "every man who has been in office a few years believes he has a life estate in it, a vested right. This is not the principle of our government. It is a rotation in office that will perpetuate our liberty.... In the performance of a task thus generally delineated I shall endeavor to select men whose diligence and talents will insure in their respective stations able and faithful cooperation."[291]

The practice has endured in political circles in the United States in one form or another ever since. On one occasion Jackson reportedly commented to Secretary of War John Eaton, "If you have a job in your department that can't be done by a Democrat, then abolish the job."[292] "Jackson saw this system as promoting the growth of democracy, as more people were involved in politics.... Additionally, Jackson pressured states to lower voting requirements to further the expansion of democracy."[293] Jackson maintained that the governmental system had been corrupted by "abuses," brought on by personal ambition, office seeking, favoritism, and special interests. At the core of the corruption was Congress. Although for many the "spoils system" is negatively associated with the administration of Andrew Jackson, Harold C. Syrett offers the view that Jackson had of it:

> Although Jackson dismissed far fewer government employees than most of his contemporaries imagined and although he did not originate the spoils system, he made more sweeping changes in the Federal bureaucracy than any of his predecessors. What is even more significant is that he defended these changes as a positive good. At present when the use of political patronage is generally considered an obstacle to good government; it is worth remembering that Jackson and his followers invariably described rotation in public office as a "reform." In this sense the spoils system was more than a way to reward Jackson's friends and punish his enemies; it was also a device for removing from public office the representative of minority political groups that Jackson insisted had been made corrupt by their long tenure.[294]

Kitchen Cabinet: Early in his administration, Jackson was displeased with his official Cabinet and abandoned its meetings, leaving the official duties to department heads. He was "thought to have relied more on informal advisors.... Most of these advisors, whom critics dubbed a 'Kitchen Cabinet,' were either newspaper editors or personal friends of Jackson from Tennessee."[295] This was hardly the case, as Jackson seldom depended upon any one man or group of men in order to make up his mind. But he did listen to the advice of this unofficial cabinet. The primary members of the original Kitchen Cabinet were long-time Jackson confidant William B. Lewis; journalist Amos Kendall: editor of the *Washington Globe* Francis P. Blair; the president's nephew and private secretary, Andrew Jackson Donelson; and *United States Telegraph* editor Duff Green. Other members were regular Cabinet members John Eaton, Roger Taney and Martin Van Buren, who was surely the most influential member. After most of Jackson's Cabinet resigned, the role of the Kitchen Cabinet was greatly diminished.[296]

Peggy Eaton Affair: Jackson's choice of his close friend Major/Senator John Eaton of Tennessee as secretary of war was not popular in Washington society. Peggy O'Neal was a barkeep at a commodious Washington, D.C., boardinghouse and tavern, owned by her father, the Franklin House on I Street. One admirer described her as "having a 'well-rounded, voluptuous figure, peach-pink complexion large, active dark eyes, [and] full sensuous lips, ready to break into an engaging smile.'"[297] Margaret grew up in an unconventional atmosphere, an undisciplined girlhood, high-spirited, with a magnetism that drew the interest of many of the opposite sex. "She did not conduct herself within the expected limits of feminine behavior of the time, but spoke her mind freely."[298] The tavern was especially popular with congressmen, senators, and politicians from all over the growing United States. Margaret, the name she preferred to Peggy, "observed the nation's lawmakers at their best and at their worst, and the experience taught her that politicians were as flawed and fallible as anybody else. Far from home and family, these gents were easily charmed by the precocious and beautiful girl and did their best to spoil her rotten. 'I was always a pet,' she later remarked."[299] Reports of the time say that "while still in her teens, (she) had reportedly caused one suicide, one duel, one nearly ruined military career, and one aborted elopement."[300] "Clearly, everyone was attracted to the 'dark-haired vamp' and Senator Eaton was downright infatuated."[301] Only one problem; she was married to a navy purser named John B. Timberlake, but the marriage was not a happy one.

"Due to her most unsavory reputation at the tavern, Peggy was thought to be sleeping with the boarders, principally Eaton. Senator Eaton used his influence to get Timberlake transferred to the Mediterranean squadron, where he died of asthma, 'although proper Washingtonians preferred to believe that Timberlake had cut his throat because of his wife's unfaithfulness.'"[302] Scandalmongers spread the news that Peggy's two daughters, whom she had while married to Timberlake, were actually fathered by Eaton. However, Eaton reportedly was a friend of John Timberlake, and "tried to help him with his petition for a pension from the Navy.... Timberlake had left a letter stating that if anything happened to him, he wanted Eaton to take care of Margaret and their two daughters."[303] Jackson planned on "naming Eaton his secretary of war, but he insisted that the Senator first marry Peggy in order to shut up Washington's scandalmongers, saying "If you love the woman, and she will have you, marry her ... and restore Peggy's good name."[304] Margaret Eaton was not welcomed by Washington society and even was socially boycotted by the president's niece, his hostess at official functions. Led by Vice President Calhoun's wife, the spouses of other cabinet members snubbed Mrs. Eaton. They "were outraged that someone with Peggy Eaton's reputation was in such an important position. They refused to associate with her, basing their stand on woman's duty to protect society from immorality."[305] "President Jackson was known for his gallantry towards women. He considered them the weaker sex that needed to be protected at all costs."[306] He regarded the treatment of Margaret as unjustified and unfair. In it he saw reflections of the malicious treatment of his own late beloved wife. Consistent with his conviction that a gentleman must defend the name and honor of a gentlewoman, the president came to Peggy's defense, naming her his "unofficial niece."[307] At a Cabinet meeting he declared, "She is as chaste as a virgin.... Female virtue is like a tender flower; let but the breath of suspicion rest upon it, and it withers and perhaps vanishes forever."[308]

Reportedly Jackson said of the treatment of Margaret Eaton, "I had rather have live vermin on my back than the tongue of one of these Washington women on my reputation."[309] Daniel Webster quipped about the matter: "Age cannot wither her nor custom stale her infinite virginity."[310] Margaret said of herself, "When I was still in pantalets and rolling hoops with other girls, I had the attention of men, young and old."[311]

Secretary of State Van Buren, a widower, included both the Eatons when he entertained. Things were not resolved until Van Buren formulated a plan that would require all Cabinet members to resign, to be replaced as the president saw fit, thus putting an end to what had become known as "The Eaton Malaria."[312] Even in her later years, Peggy still scandalized, when after Eaton died she married her daughter's dancing teacher.[313]

Indian Removal: Jackson believed that the white people of the United States—and the white people only—should become citizens, and that they had a sacred duty to claim new lands and expand the frontiers of the nation. "Jackson's attitude toward Native Americans was paternalistic and patronizing—he described them as children in need of guidance and believed the removal policy was beneficial to the Indians. Most white Americans thought that the United States would never extend beyond the Mississippi. Removal would save Indian people from the depredations of whites, and would resettle them in an area where they could govern themselves in peace. But some Americans saw this as an excuse for a brutal and inhumane course of action, and protested loudly against removal."[314] Jackson believed that Indians and whites could not live together peacefully. He also believed that freed blacks should be banned forever from white society and returned to Africa. He even served as vice president of the American Colonization Society, an organization dedicated to precisely that purpose. "The goal of the long-running American colonization movement was to encourage planters to free their slaves, then return them along with their free black comrades to their African homeland. Colonization supporters also sought to provide Africa with a group of black missionaries who would 'civilize' and 'Christianize' the 'Dark Continent.' Their objective was inherently racist, for they sought to remove all black people from American society. From hindsight, they were correct in their belief that white prejudice was so deeply engrained in America that blacks and whites would not be able to peacefully or successfully coexist as equals for some time, if ever. Through their actions, however, they may have helped to make this a self-fulfilling prophecy."[315]

In each of his addresses to the U.S. Congress, Jackson addressed the "Indian problem." His solution was to remove the Native Americans from the United States and send them to the Indian Territory (now Oklahoma) as their permanent homeland. The plan was portrayed as merely a trade of one area of land (which was good producing land) for other land (which was poor producing land). Southern states eagerly supported the Indian Removal Act of 1830. "Land greed was a big reason for the federal government's position on Indian removal. This desire for Indian lands was also abetted by the Indian hating mentality that was peculiar to some American frontiersman."[316] Most white Americans favored its adoption, although it passed only after bitter debate in Congress. The act's strongest opponent was Tennessee congressman Davy Crockett, the celebrated 19th century American folk hero, frontiersman and soldier, usually referred to by the popular title "King of the Wild Frontier." As a consequence of his opposition to President Jackson, Crockett was defeated for reelection in 1831. He said of his loss: "I would rather be beaten and be a man than to be elected and be a little puppy dog. I have always supported measures and principles and not men. I have acted fearless[ly] and independent and I never will regret my course. I would rather be politically buried than to be hypocritically immortalized."[317] Crockett was returned to Congress in 1833.

The Celeste-Al Cabinet, lithograph by Albert Hoffay, published by H.R. Robinson, 1836. A mild satire on Jackson and his Cabinet, portraying in imaginative terms a White House reception of popular French dancer and actress Madame Celeste. President Jackson is seated behind the table while Jimmy O'Neal (standing) presents Madame Celeste. Seated in chairs in a White House parlor are six cabinet members: (left to right) secretary of the navy Mahlon Dickerson, attorney general Benjamin F. Butler, secretary of war Lewis Cass, postmaster general Amos Kendall, treasury secretary Levi Woodbury, and Vice President Martin Van Buren (Library of Congress).

The Removal Act pledged to enact its policy on a strictly voluntary basis, although this does not appear in the statement of the bill. "Those wishing to remain in the east would become citizens of their home state.... The removal was supposed to be voluntary and peaceful, and it was that way for the tribes that agreed to the conditions. But the southeastern nations resisted, and Jackson forced them to leave."[318] By the end of Jackson's second administration the U.S. Army had moved most of the eastern tribes, known as the five civilized tribes (Cherokee, Seminole, Choctaw, Creek and Chickasaw), to their new "home." "Although the five Indian nations had made earlier attempts at resistance, many of their strategies were non-violent. One method was to adopt Anglo-American practices such as large-scale farming, Western education, and slave-holding.... They adopted this policy of assimilation in an attempt to coexist with settlers and ward off hostility. But it only made whites jealous and resentful."[319] The great Cherokee nation had heeded the advice of the U.S. government to accept the ways of the whites. In 1827 the Cherokee adopted a written constitution based on United States policy, declaring themselves to be a sovereign nation. In former treaties, Indian nations were declared sovereign so they would be legally capable of ceding their lands, publishing newspapers, starting schools and churches, and becoming farmers and planters.[320] President Jackson met with the Choctaw chiefs to break the news that they were moving: "His [the President's] earnest desire is, that you may be perpetuated and preserved as a nation; and this he believes can only be done and secured by your consent to remove to a country beyond the Mississippi.... Where you are, it is not possible you can live contented and happy."[321]

In his annual message to Congress, President Jackson addressed the matter and made his case for the passage of the Indian Removal Act. Among his remarks was his reference to states' rights in the matter:

> Towards the aborigines of the country no one can indulge a more friendly feeling than myself, or would go further in attempting to reclaim them from their wandering habits and make them a happy prosperous people. I have endeavored to impress upon them my own solemn conviction of the duties and powers of the Central Government in relation to the State authorities. For the justice of the laws passed by the States within the scope of their reserved powers they are not responsible to this Government. As individuals we may entertain and express our opinions of their acts, but as a Government we have as little right to control them as we have to prescribe laws for other nations.[322]

In an address to Seminole chiefs, President Jackson offered them a Hobson's choice:

> The tract you have ceded will soon be surveyed and sold, and immediately afterwards will be occupied by a white population. You will soon be in a state of starvation. You will commit depredations upon the property of our citizens. You will be resisted, punished, perhaps killed. Now, is it not better peaceably to remove to a fine, fertile country, occupied by your own kindred, and where you can raise all the necessaries of life, and where game is yet abundant? ... You have no right to stay, and you must go.[323]

Jackson made a similar statement to a delegation of Cherokees: "I have no motives, Brothers, to deceive you, I am sincerely desirous to promote your welfare. Listen to me, therefore, while I tell you that you cannot remain where you are now. Circumstances that cannot be controlled, which are beyond the reach of human laws, render it impossible that you can flourish in the midst of a civilized community."[324]

Jackson supported the state of Georgia in its efforts to deprive the Cherokee nation of its land. He decided the Indians had no right to change their customs and ordered their eviction. In his address Jackson offered a justification and desirability of leaving one's home for a new place:

> Doubtless it will be painful to leave the graves of their fathers; but what do they more than our ancestors did or than our children are now doing? To better their condition in an unknown land our forefathers left all that was dear in earthly objects. Our children by thousands yearly leave the land of their birth to seek new homes in distant regions. Does Humanity weep at these painful separations from everything, animate and inanimate, with which the young heart has become entwined? Far from it. It is rather a source of joy that our country affords scope where our young population may range unconstrained in body or in mind, developing the power and faculties of man in their highest perfection.... And is it supposed that the wandering savage has a stronger attachment to his home than the settled, civilized Christian? Is it more afflicting of him to leave the graves of his fathers than it is to our brothers and children? Rightly considered, the policy of the General Government toward the red man is not only liberal, but generous. He is unwilling to submit to the laws of the States and mingle with their population. To save him from this alternative, or perhaps utter annihilation, the General Government kindly offers him a new home, and proposes to pay the whole expense of his removal and settlement.[325]

Samuel Worcester, a native of Vermont, was a minister sent to join a Cherokee mission in Brainerd, Tennessee. Two years later he was ordered to the Cherokee national capital of New Echota, in Georgia. Worcester became a close friend of the Cherokee leaders and often advised them on their legal rights. The state of Georgia would have none of that and the legislature passed laws that whites were not allowed to live in Indian territory without state approval. Worcester and other ministers challenged the law and were arrested on several occasions. They were tried, convicted, and sentenced to four years at hard labor.[326] The ministers, represented by lawyers hired by the Cherokees, appealed to the U.S. Supreme Court. In the case of *Worcester vs. Georgia* (1832), the Court "struck down Georgia's extension laws. In the majority opinion Marshall wrote that the Indian nations were 'distinct, independent political communities retaining their original natural rights' and that the United States had acknowledged as much in several treaties with the Cherokees. Although it had surrendered sovereign powers in those treaties with the United States, he wrote, the Cherokee Nation remained a separate, sovereign nation with a legitimate title to its national territory. Marshall harshly rebuked Georgia for its actions and declared that the Cherokees possessed the right to live free from the state's trespasses."[327] Incensed, President Jackson got around the inconvenience of the Supreme Court decision by entering into a treaty with a small faction of the Cherokees. "The Treaty of New Echota was a Cherokee Indian removal treaty signed in New Echota, Georgia, by officials of the United States government and several members of the so-called Ridge faction within the Cherokee Nation on December 29, 1835. The Ridge faction, aka Ridge Party, which represented a minority faction of the Cherokee, believed that the Cherokee would eventually lose their eastern lands and that removal to the west was the only way to preserve the Nation. The Ross Party, which represented the Cherokee majority argued that the Cherokee Nation should remain in its current homeland and that the recent U.S. Supreme Court decision in *Worcester vs. Georgia* (1832) secured that right. John Ross, then principal chief of the Cherokee, gathered 16,000 signatures of Cherokees who opposed removal. However, the U.S, Senate ratified the Treaty of New Echota by a single vote, making removal of the Cherokee possible. The Cherokee leaders who had agreed to the treaty faced a punishment of death according to Cherokee law, and all were assassinated."[328]

Jackson continued to demand the removal of Native Americans from their lands in each annual message to Congress. In 1833 he said, "That those tribes [the Sac and Fox Indians] cannot exist surrounded by our settlements and in continual contact with our citizens is certain. They have neither the intelligence, the industry, the moral habits, nor the desire of improvement, which are essential to any favorable change in their condition."[329]

"Ordered to move on the Cherokee, General John Wool resigned his command in protest, delaying the action. His replacement, General Winfield Scott, arrived at New Echota on May 17, 1838, with 7,000 American soldiers, evicted the Cherokee from their land, and forced them to march west."[330] They were required to leave all their possessions behind. Hundreds drowned as they were sent across the Mississippi in rotting boats. Thousands more died of starvation, disease and exposure. "About 4,000 Cherokee died before they reached the lands of Oklahoma. The route they traversed and the journey itself became known as 'The Trail of Tears' or, as a direct translation from Cherokee, 'The Trail Where They Cried' ('Nunna daul Tsuny')."[331] Even though it took place after Jackson's presidency, the roots of the march can be found in his failure to enforce the Supreme Court's ruling in *Worcester vs. Georgia* in which the court found that the state of Georgia had no jurisdiction over the Cherokee. President Van Buren, Jackson's hand-picked successor, enforced the Indian removal. In all, some 15,000 Cherokee marched from their Georgia homeland to what is now Oklahoma. Without adequate food and supplies, the trek took 116 days, "escorted by federal troops who did not allow them to rest or tend to the ill."[332]

Black Hawk War: Born in 1767 in the Sauk village on the Rock River near present-day Rock Island, Illinois, Native American leader Black Hawk resented the Americans as dispossessors of the Spanish, with whom his people had traded for many years. "He had fought with the British in the War of 1812 and maintained relations with officials in Canada in later years."[333] His hatred grew when members of the Sauk and Fox tribes, headed by his young rival Keokuk, were persuaded by U.S. Army officers to sign a treaty in 1804, ceding all of their land east of the Mississippi River to the U.S. In 1832, Black Hawk led his tribe to resettle their disputed homeland in Illinois. Federal troops under the command of General Henry Atkinson arrived at the Rock River in May. When two Indian envoys, under a white flag of truce, were dispatched to confer with Atkinson, they were shot by Illinois volunteers, sparking what is known as the Black Hawk War. "In retaliation, Black Hawk and his warriors surprised a militia encampment with a nighttime attack.... The natives under Black Hawk's command retreated northward ahead of the combined militia and regular forces, moving from northern Illinois into present-day southwestern Wisconsin ... on July 21 at Wisconsin Heights.... Black Hawk demonstrated great skill in avoiding a crushing defeat, but paid a heavy price in the lives of his dwindling number of warriors. The climax came in early August where the Bad Axe River flows into the Mississippi. On August 1, Black Hawk, under a white flag, attempted to surrender to forces aboard the steamboat Warrior, but the vessel's suspicious captain opened fire, killing and wounding a number of Black Hawk's followers. That evening, Black Hawk decided to continue the northward retreat, but the bulk of the native force chose to remain and make a stand. On the 2nd, the Sauk and Fox were decisively defeated on the banks of the Bad Axe. Over an eight-hour period, soldiers slaughtered fleeing Indians indiscriminately."[334] Black Hawk was captured and imprisoned in the East. In a letter to Black Hawk, President Jackson wrote the following: "We do not wish to injure you.... But if you again plunge your knives into the breasts of our people, I shall send a force which will severely punish you for your cruelties."[335]

Ma-Ka-Tai-Me-She-Kia-Kiah, Black Hawk, a Saukie Brave, lithograph drawn, printed and colored by McKenney & Hall at I.T. Bowen's Lithographic Establishment, published by F.W. Greenough, c. 1838 (Library of Congress).

Black Hawk was taken to meet President Jackson in 1833, the same year the chief dictated an autobiography that is considered a classic statement of Native American resentment against white interlopers.[336]

FOREIGN AFFAIRS — MAJOR EVENTS

In general, foreign affairs were not a great concern during Jackson's two terms. He made it known at the outset of his administration that he intended to take no aggressive action against any foreign nation with a simple principle: "The foreign policy adopted by our government is to do justice to all, and to submit to wrong by none ... to ask nothing that is not clearly right, and to submit to nothing that is wrong."[337] Jackson tried repeatedly to purchase Texas from Mexico with no success.

SECOND TERM

Presidential Campaign of 1832: For the first time presidential candidates were nominated by national party conventions. The Democrats met in Baltimore and overwhelmingly renominated Andrew Jackson with reliable Martin Van Buren as his chosen running mate. Jackson's previous vice president, John C. Calhoun, was in disfavor and had resigned. Henry Clay was nominated by the National Republicans at their convention, also held in Baltimore. Clay's support was largely confined to New England, his home state of Kentucky and some areas in the mid–Atlantic states. He tried to strengthen his appeal by selecting John Sergeant of Pennsylvania, an official of the Bank of the United States, as his running mate. There were two other candidates. John Floyd of Virginia was nominated by the Independent Democrats, running with Henry Lee. The Anti-Mason Party chose a team of William Wirt of Maryland and Amos Ellmaker.[338] "The major issue in the campaign was Jackson's determination to eliminate the Bank of the United States. Jackson had vetoed the bill reauthorizing the bank shortly before being renominated. Henry Clay decided to make the veto the major issue in the campaign. Clay's campaign headquarters were in Pennsylvania where the bank was headquartered and was thus very popular. The issue backfired since the bank was considered a tool of the rich and was extremely unpopular. Jackson won by an overwhelming margin."[339] Jackson defeated Clay with 55 percent of the popular vote and won the electoral vote with 219 votes to 49 for Clay, 11 for Floyd and 7 for Wirt. Jackson carried 16 states, Clay 6 and Floyd and Wirt each one state, South Carolina and Vermont, respectively.[340]

DOMESTIC AFFAIRS — MAJOR EVENTS

Second Bank of the United States: The greatest party battle in Jackson's administration centered on the Second Bank of the United States. Although three-quarters privately owned and managed by a private corporation, it was virtually a government-sponsored monopoly. "This function brought it into frequent conflict with state and local banks, particularly in the South and West. Those other institutions often issued large amounts of paper money and followed liberal loan policies; such practices were frowned upon by the conservative directors of the Second Bank of the United States."[341] The bank was introduced originally by the first secretary of the treasury, Alexander Hamilton, as, as a means of providing a national debt and in creating the power of the federal government. Credit was vital for the new nation, but it was often uncertain. The "country's only legal money, gold and silver coin," was chronically in short supply and never sufficient for everyday exchange. Many people "resorted to barter in their exchange of good and services."[342] States' rights advocates such as Thomas Jefferson and James Madison "believed this centralization of power away from local banks was dangerous to a sound monetary system and was mostly to the benefit of business interests in the commercial north, not southern agricultural interests-arguing that the right to own property would be infringed by these proposals."[343] State and federal governments incorporated banks, authorizing them to lend their own credit in the form of banknotes, ostensibly redeemable in specie. These banknotes were used in lieu of coins in everyday commerce. They served in practice, if not in law, as money.[344]

Jackson's reasons for wishing to dismantle the bank were based on several points. In his opinion, it was unconstitutional; an excessive amount of the nation's financial strength was concentrated in the bank; the bank exercised too must influence and control of members of Congress; and the bank favored the northeastern United States over the southern and western regions.[345] He insisted: "I have been opposed always to the Bank of the United States as well as all state Banks of paper issues, upon constitutional ground,"[346] Jackson complained that the Bank's president, Nicholas Biddle, was unaccountable to Congress.

While it was instrumental in the growth of the U.S. economy, Jackson supported an "agricultural republic" and felt the Bank improved the fortunes of an "elite circle" of commercial and industrial entrepreneurs at the expense of farmers and laborers.[347] When the president demonstrated hostility to it, the bank threw its power against him. Henry Clay and Daniel Webster, who had been attorneys for the bank, led the fight for its recharter in Congress. Nicholas Biddle implicitly threatened retribution if Jackson refused to go along with the recharter, saying, "[I]f he means to wage war on the Bank, he may perhaps awaken a spirit which has hitherto been checked & reined in — and which it is wisest not to force into offensive defence.... The worthy President thinks that because he has scalped Indians and imprisoned judges, he is to have his way with the Bank. He is mistaken."[348]

On one occasion, President Jackson forcibly evicted a delegation of international bankers from the Oval Office, shouting, "You are a den of vipers and thieves. I intend to rout you out, and by the eternal God, I will rout you out."[349]

In his second State of the Union message in 1830, Jackson raged:

Nothing has occurred to lessen in any degree the dangers which many of our citizens apprehend from that institution as at present organized.... [The Bank of the United States should] be shorn of the influence [that allowed it to operate] on the hopes, fears, or interests of large masses of the community. [Its continuation would only lead to] occasional collisions with the local authorities and perpetual apprehension and discontent on the part of the States and the people.[350]

Angrily, Jackson told Martin Van Buren, "The bank is trying to kill me, but I will kill it."[351] Jackson's unflinching determination prevailed against Biddle and the bank. The president called the bank a monster and stated that he was "ready with the screws to draw every tooth and the stumps."[352] Jackson insisted the U.S. must have a real currency consisting of gold and silver coins, calling paper money, "rag money," saying "The paper-money system and its natural associations — monopoly and exclusive privileges — have already struck their roots too deep in the soil, and it will require all your efforts to check its further growth and to eradicate the evil."[353]

In 1832, Congress passed a slightly modified bill to extend the bank's charter. Biddle and Clay dared Jackson to veto the bill, and he did. In his veto message, he charged the bank with undue economic privilege:

Distinctions in society will always exist under every just government. Equality of talents, of education, or of wealth cannot be produced by human institutions.... Mere precedent is a dangerous source of authority, and should not be regarded as deciding questions of constitutional power except where the acquiescence of the people of the States can be considered as well settled.... Every monopoly and all exclusive privileges are granted at the expense of the public, which ought to receive a fair equivalent. It is to be regretted that the right and powerful too often bend the acts of government to their selfish purposes.... In the full enjoyment of the gifts of Heaven and the fruits of superior industry, economy and virtue, every man is equally entitled to protection by law.... In the full enjoyment of the gifts of Heaven, and the fruits of superior industry, economy, and virtue, every man is entitled to protection by law; but when the laws undertake to add to these natural and just advantages artificial distinctions, to grant titles, gratuities, and exclusive privileges, to make the rich richer and the potent more powerful, the humble members of society — the farmers, mechanics, and laborers — who have neither the time nor the means of securing like favors to themselves, have a right to complain of the injustice of their government.... There are no necessary evils in government. Its evil exists only, in its abuses. If it would confine itself to equal protection, and, as Heaven does its rains, shower its favors alike on the high and the low, the rich and the poor, it would be an unqualified blessing.[354]

On July 10, 1832, President Andrew Jackson sent a message to the United States Senate. He returned unsigned, with his objections, a bill that extended the charter of the Second Bank of the United States, due to expire in 1836, for another fifteen years. This was the first time a president had justified a veto on policy grounds, rather than on constitutionality. During his second term, when the Bank of the United States still had three years to run by its original charter, Jackson removed federal deposits from it and placed them in state banks, or so-called pet banks. Daniel Webster charged that Jackson's veto of the bank bill "manifestly seeks to influence the poor against the rich. It wantonly attacks whole classes of the people, for the purpose of turning them against the prejudices and resentments of other classes."[355] In a letter to Martin Van Buren, Jackson wrote, "Were all the worshippers of the gold calf to memorialize me and request a restoration of the deposits I would cut my right hand from my body before I would do such an act. The gold calf may be worshipped by others but as for myself I serve the Lord."[356]

On March 27, 1834, the Senate passed a resolution against Jackson by a vote of 26 to 20 for assuming power not conferred by the Constitution in his actions in defunding the bank. "The Senate did not actually censure Jackson. The resolution did describe the events in controversy and conclude that Jackson's act was improper, but it did not inflict any punishment. It did not remove him from office. It did not disqualify him from seeking future office. It did not fine him. And it did not condemn him with words of censure."[357] Jackson responded with a lengthy protest denying the validity of the Senate's action:

> The ambition which leads me on is an anxious desire and a fixed determination to return to the people unimpaired the sacred trust they have confided to my charge; to heal the wounds of the Constitution and preserve it from further violation; to persuade my countrymen, so far as I may, that it is not in a splendid government supported by powerful monopolies and aristocratical establishments that they will find happiness or their liberties protected, but in a plain system, void of pomp, protecting all and granting favors to none, dispensing its blessings, like the dews of Heaven, unseen and unfelt save in the freshness and beauty they will contribute to produce. It is such a government that the genius of the people requires; such one only under which our states may regain for ages to come united, prosperous, and free.... Public money is but a species of public property. It cannot be raised by taxation or customs, nor brought into the Treasury in any other way except by law, but whenever or however obtained, its custody always has been and always must be, unless the Constitution be changed, entrusted to the executive department.... Congress cannot ... take out of the hands of the executive department the custody of the public property or money without an assumption of executive power and a subversion of the first principles of the Constitution.[358]

In an unprecedented move, the Senate voted to refuse to print the president's message in its journal. "For nearly three years, Missouri Democrat Thomas Hart Benton campaigned to expunge Jackson's censure resolution from the Senate Journal. By January 1837, having regained the majority, Senate Democrats voted to remove this stain from the record of an old and sick president just weeks from his retirement. With boisterous ceremony, the handwritten 1834 Journal was borne into the mobbed chamber and placed on the secretary's table. The secretary took up his pen, drew black lines around the censure text, and wrote 'Expunged by the order of the Senate.' The chamber erupted in Democratic jubilation and a messenger was dispatched to deliver the expunging pen to Jackson. Dressed in the deep black of a mourner, Henry Clay lamented: 'The Senate is no longer a place for any decent man.'"[359]

Nullification Crisis: Many people in southern states viewed high tariffs on import of common goods as unfairly benefiting northern merchants and industrialists at the expense of those who had to buy the goods subject to tariffs. Jackson met a head-on challenge by his vice president, John C. Calhoun, who "supported the claim of his home state of South Carolina that it had the right to 'nullify'— declare illegal — the tariff, and more generally the right of a state to nullify federal laws that went against its interests."[360] Jackson sympathized with the Southern interpretation of the tariff debate, but he was a strong supporter of federalism, believing in a strong Union with considerable powers vested in the central government.[361] Things came to a head between the two when Jackson attempted to face Calhoun down over the issue. At a Jefferson Day dinner on April 13, 1829, Jackson was in a dark mood. His quarrel with Vice President Calhoun over the tariff and the right of states to nullify federal laws had turned ugly. He made his toast as a virtual command: "Our federal Union: it must be preserved."[362] As it was meant as a clear challenge to his vice president, Calhoun responded with his own toast: "The Union: next to our liberty, most dear! May we always remember that it can only be preserved by distributing equally the benefits and the burdens of the Union."[363]

In 1832, with Calhoun's support, South Carolina nullified the tariffs of 1828 and 1832. Jackson immediately and vehemently denounced the move. In a letter to Joel Poinsett, Jackson maintained "nullification ... means insurrection and war; and the other states have a right to put it down."[364]

In March 1832 the president ordered armed federal forces to Charleston to insure the state's compliance with federal law and privately threatened to hang Calhoun. In a

King Andrew the First, lithograph caricature of Andrew Jackson as a despotic monarch, probably issued during the fall of 1833 in response to the president's September order to remove federal deposits from the Bank of the United States. Jackson, in regal costume, stands before a throne in a frontal pose, holding a "veto" in his left hand and a scepter in his right. The federal Constitution and the arms of Pennsylvania (the United States Bank was located in Philadelphia) lie in tatters under his feet. A book, *Judiciary of the U[nited] States,* lies nearby (Library of Congress).

proclamation of December 10, 1832, the president raged: "I consider, then, the power to annul a law of the United States, assumed by one state, incompatible with the existence of the Union, contradicted expressly by the letter of the Constitution, unauthorized by its spirit, inconsistent with every principle on which it was founded, and destructive of the great object for which it was formed."[365] In a December 19, 1832, proclamation, President Jackson threatened the people of South Carolina:

> The Constitution of the United States ... forms a government, not a league.... It is a government in which all the people are represented, which operates directly on the people individually, not upon the States.... The laws of the United States must be executed. I have no discretionary power on the subject.... Secession, like any other evolutionary act, may be morally justified by the extremity of oppression; but to call it a constitutional right is confounding the meaning of the term.... Each State, having expressly parted with so many powers as to constitute, jointly with the other States, a single nation, cannot, from that period, possess any right to secede, because such secession does not break a league, but destroys the unity of a nation.... Their [South Carolinian political leaders] object is disunion. But be not deceived by names. Disunion by armed force is treason. Are you really ready to incur its guilt?[366]

President Jackson instructed a South Carolina congressman to relay his threat to his constituents: "Say to them that if a single drop of blood shall be shed there in opposition to the laws of the United States, I will hang the first man I can lay my hands on engaged in such treasonable conduct upon the first tree I can reach."[367] When the South Carolina senator doubted that Jackson would actually hang anyone, Senator Thomas Hart Benton responded: "...when Jackson begins to talk about hanging, they can begin to look for ropes."[368]

A convention of delegates met in Charleston, South Carolina, where they adopted an ordinance entitled "An ordinance to dissolve the union between the State of South Carolina and other States united with her, under the compact, entitled the Constitution of the United States of America," whereby it is declared that the said Union is dissolved.[369] The Pennsylvania Legislature adopted joint resolutions relative to the maintenance of the Constitution and Union, based on Jackson's words in a special message to Congress on January 16, 1833, "The right of the people of a single State to absolve themselves at will and without the consent of the other States from their most solemn obligations, and hazard the liberties and happiness of the millions composing this Union, cannot be acknowledged."[370] In a February 23, 1833, letter to James Hamilton, Andy asserted, "Nullification cannot be recognized as a peaceful & constitutional measure, and the American system of M. Clay being on the wane, a union between these two extremes [Clay and Calhoun] are formed, and I have no doubt the people will duly appreciate the motives which have led to it."[371] In 1840, Hamilton abandoned the Democratic Party and supported the Whig Presidential candidate, William Henry Harrison. During the Civil War, Hamilton was an early proponent of slave emancipation as war measure. In a letter to Andrew I. Crawford, the president once again asserted that hanging of traitors was called for: "Human gallows ought to be the fate of all such ambitious men who would involve their country in civil wars, and all the evils in its train that they might reign & ride on its whirlwinds & direct the Storm — The free people of these United States have spoken, and consigned these wicked demagogues to their proper doom."[372]

Violence was avoided when Senator Henry Clay mediated a compromise between South Carolina and the federal government in 1833 but the crisis deepened the divide between the north and the south and planted the seeds for the Civil War.

Assassination Attempt: Jackson was the first president to face an assassination attempt. A mentally ill, English-born house painter, Richard Lawrence, imagined that the American government owed him a large sum of money. He blamed the president for preventing him from receiving the payment. He said that when he received the money, he could take up his rightful place as King of England. Lawrence also blamed Jackson for killing his father.[373] On January 30, 1835, as Jackson exited the funeral service of South Carolina congressman Warren S. Davis, "Lawrence had found a space near a pillar on the East Portico where Jackson would pass. As Jackson walked, Lawrence stepped out and fired his first pistol at Jackson's back; it misfired. Lawrence quickly made another attempt with his second pistol but that also misfired. It was later determined that the weapons he had chosen were noted for being vulnerable to moisture and the weather on that date was extremely humid and damp."[374] "Lawrence's unsuccessful attempts had drawn the attention of the crowd and he was quickly wrestled into submission by those present (including Congressman Davy Crockett). It is reported that Jackson assisted in subduing his attempted assassin, striking him several times with his cane."[375] The weapons employed in the assassination attempt were derringers. They were tested and both discharged on the first try. It was calculated that the odds of both derringers misfiring was one in 125,000.[376]

Lawrence was brought to trial on April 11, 1835. The prosecuting attorney was Francis Scott Key. The jury took only five minutes to decide that Lawrence was "not guilty by reason of insanity. He spent the remainder of his life, which ended in 1861, in various institutions and hospitals."[377] As in later assassinations, several conspiracy theories were advanced, and even Jackson suspected that the attempt was "abetted by his political oppo-

The Attempted Assassination of the President of United States, etching, c. March 21, 1835. This print of the assassination attempt against Jackson by Richard Lawrence, created twenty years after the incident, was made from a sketch by an eyewitness (Library of Congress).

nent, Whig senator George Poindexter."[378] Jackson appointed a special commission to investigate the possible connection. It quickly found Poindexter had no connection with the attack and that all evidence pointed to the deranged Lawrence acting alone. Lawrence wasn't the first person to attempt to do the president bodily harm.[379] On May 6, 1833, in Alexandria, Virginia, "Robert B. Randolph," recently dismissed from the navy for embezzlement upon Jackson's orders, "struck the president. Before he could do any real harm, he was chased from the scene by several members of Jackson's party. Jackson declined to press charges."[380]

Specie Circular of 1836: Jackson was a staunch believer in a specie basis for currency. In a letter to Captain John Donelson III, he made himself clear on the matter: "I am fearful that the paper system [of money] ... will ruin the state. Its demoralizing effects are already seen and spoken of everywhere.... I therefore protest against receiving any of that trash."[381] The Specie Circular (Coinage Act) of 1836 was "an executive order issued by U.S. President Andrew Jackson in 1836 and carried out by President Martin Van Buren. It required that all public lands be paid for in gold or silver. It broke the speculation boom in western lands, cast suspicion on many of the bank notes in circulation, and hastened the Panic of 1837."[382] Congress passed a law distributing to the states some $35,000,000 belonging to the United States, which till then had been deposited in some eighty banks that had looked upon the money as something of a permanent loan and had inflated credit based on it. To meet the drafts in favor of the states, the banks called in their loans. "The panic, which had some of its roots in earlier crop failures and in overextended speculation, was a factor in the administration of Martin Van Buren, who was Jackson's choice and a successful candidate for the presidency in 1836."[383]

FOREIGN AFFAIRS — MAJOR EVENTS

Jackson was the only president to pay off the national debt. He succeeded in collecting old claims against various European nations for spoliations inflicted under Napoleon's continental system. "In an 1831 treaty, France agreed to pay claims for Napoleonic depredations on American shipping. However, by 1834, the French Chamber of Deputies had not appropriated the necessary funds for the first two installment payments. Jackson's patience was severely tried and in his sixth annual message to Congress, on December 1, 1834, he asked for the authorization of reprisals if the money was not forthcoming."[384] "It is a well-settled principle of the international code that where one nation owes another a liquidated debt which it refuses or neglects to pay, the aggrieved party may seize on the property belonging to the other, its citizens or subjects, sufficient to pay the debt without giving just cause of war."[385]

The French government demanded a retraction of what they considered an insult as a condition of payment. Jackson responded in not very diplomatic terms that what he said to Congress was none of a foreign government's business. The impasse deepened through 1834; ministers were recalled and military preparations begun. Finally, in 1836, at the urging of the British, the French agreed to "construe a conciliatory passage in a later message of Jackson as sufficient apology."[386] France paid four overdue installments, diplomatic relations between the two countries were reestablished and the crisis passed. In other matters, Jackson obtained favorable treaties with Turkey and Cochinchina and recognized the independence of Texas in 1837, although he resisted attempts at annexation to avoid splitting the Democratic Party on the slavery question.

AFTER THE PRESIDENCY

In his farewell address, Jackson warned of what would happen if the Union was dissolved:

> If the Union is once severed, the line of separation will grow wider and wider, and the controversies which are now debated and settled in the halls of legislation will then be tried in fields of battle and determined by the sword.... No free government can stand without virtue in the people and a lofty spirit of patriotism, and if the sordid feelings of mere selfishness should usurp the place which ought to be filled by public spirit, the legislation of Congress will soon be converted into a scramble for personal and sectional advantages.[387]

He concluded his address with the following words. "My own race is nearly run; advanced age and failing health warn me that before long I must pass beyond the reach of human events and cease to feel the vicissitudes of human affairs. I thank God that my life has been spent in a land of liberty and that He has given me a heart to love my country with the affection of a son. And filled with gratitude for your constant and unwavering kindness, I bid you a last and affectionate farewell."[388]

The General's health declined, leaving him progressively weaker. "In his last year as President, Jackson suffered from an unusually severe attack of coughing, leading to another profuse pulmonary hemorrhage. It is reported that his doctors treated Jackson by bleeding him of two additional quarts of blood. The indestructible patient survived even this murderous therapy."[389]

On the day of his successor's inauguration, Old Hickory was the main attraction, prompting Senator Thomas Hart Benton to say, "For once, the rising was eclipsed by the setting sun."[390] "To the surprise of all, the President, who had been considered physically unable to outlast his first term, survived his second term in March 1837; though in such poor shape the doctors thought he could not stand the three-week trip back to the Hermitage. Against their advice the patient insisted on departing immediately, and at President Van Buren's request, the surgeon general and a relay of other army doctors accompanied him all the way."[391] Three days after the inauguration, as Jackson left the White House, thousands of people turned up at the railroad station for one last look at their hero. Jackson left the office more popular than when he entered it. Jackson gave careful attention to his plantation, which had been poorly managed by Andrew Jr. in his absence. Junior "had a reputation of being a poor businessman and farm manager."[392] In retirement Jackson continued to be active in Democratic politics after leaving office. He was particularly strong in his support of Martin Van Buren and later James K. Polk.[393]

His Papers: Andrew Jackson's letters and papers are not at The Hermitage. The original documents are in hundreds of libraries, museums, and private collections. The Library of Congress owns the largest collection, with over 20,000 items. Since 1971, the Andrew Jackson Papers Project at the University of Tennessee has been gathering copies of Jackson's papers from all sources: *The Papers of Andrew Jackson*, Daniel Feller, ed., University of Tennessee; *Correspondence of Andrew Jackson*, 7 volumes, 1926–1935, J.S. Bassett and J.F. Jameson, eds.; *Papers of Andrew Jackson*, Sam B. Smith, ed., University of Tennessee Press, 1980.[394]

Health: In addition to the saber wound and smallpox that he contracted during the Revolutionary War, Jackson experienced great pain and hardship. His medical history has been described as "encyclopedic." The loss of his brother Robert to smallpox and his brother Hugh to a heat stroke after the Battle of Stone Ferry burdened him with great sorrow and a deep-seated depression.[395] Old Hickory developed diarrhea during the War of 1812, a condition that afflicted him for the rest of his life. He contracted malaria and dysentery in the swamps of Florida during the Seminole campaigns of 1818–1821.[396] Andy suffered from chronic abdominal pains for many years, which may have been caused by lead poisoning as the result of two bullets he took in his arm in Nashville in 1813 during his campaign against the Creeks. Doctors advised him to have the affected limb amputated, but he refused, announcing to his troops, "The health of your general is restored [and] he will command in person."[397] Jackson once told his physician, "Now, Doctor, I can do anything you think proper, except give up coffee and tobacco."[398]

Jackson suffered from chronic headaches from his use of tobacco. Jackson's favorite home remedy was called "Matchless Sedative." Taken with a glass of wine, it allegedly calmed the mind from perplexing thoughts. Jackson believed it also cured headaches, earaches, and pulmonary symptoms. He purchased the "medicine" from a traveling salesman for $2.50 a bottle.[399] Historians suggest that Jackson experienced lead and mercury poisoning following his therapeutic use of calomel (mercurous chloride) and sugar of lead (lead acetate). Examination of specimens of Jackson's hair obtained in 1815 and 1839 confirmed that he had mercury and lead exposure, but also indicated that his death was probably not due to heavy metal poisoning.[400] In a letter to Amos Kendall in April 1844, Jackson prophesies his death: "My health is very bad, my affliction & debility increasing & unless a change soon for the better, I cannot hope to live long."[401]

Death: At the beginning of 1845, Jackson began experiencing suffocating shortness of breath. Early in April, his feet and legs swelled, then his hands and abdomen. He was unable to lie flat and required propping up with pillows in both his bed at night and his chair during the day.[402] During the period of his final illness, Jackson suffered greatly from a pulmonary hemorrhage. He reacted bravely, saying, "When I have suffered sufficiently, the Lord will take me to himself — but what are all my sufferings compared to those of the blessed Savior, who died upon that cursed tree for me, mine are nothing."[403]

By late spring his face was edematous as well. Late in the evening of Saturday, June 7, his physician, John N. Esselman, was called to the Hermitage, but there was nothing the doctor could do for the dying man. Jackson and his physician discussed religion for about thirty minutes, during which time, Jackson confessed, "I'm ready to forgive the whole crews of them [his enemies] collectively, but not as individuals."[404]

Place of Death: As he desired, Jackson passed away at the Hermitage in Nashville, Tennessee.

Cause of Death: Jackson's death was the result of consumption, dropsy (an early name for edema, an abnormal accumulation of fluid in cells, tissues or cavities of the body, resulting in swelling), and tubercular hemorrhaging, and the immediate cause of death was congestive heart failure.[405] He wrote about his final illness: "It may be that my life ends in dropsy, all means hitherto used to stay the swelling has now failed to check it."[406] A bit later Jackson complained, "I am blubber of water."[407]

Final Words: Just before giving up the ghost, Jackson heard the grieved moaning of the servants and said, "What is the matter, my dear children, have I alarmed you? Oh, do not cry. Be good children, and we shall all meet in heaven."[408] Shortly thereafter the weary warrior fainted and Esselman pronounced him dead at 6:00 P.M. on June 8, 1845. One of his servants, Nicholson, remembered the final death-bed words of Jackson to be "God will take care of you for me, I am my God's. I belong to him, I go a short time before you, and I want to meet all in heaven, both white and black."[409]

Place of Burial: Jackson is buried next to his beloved Rachel in the garden of their

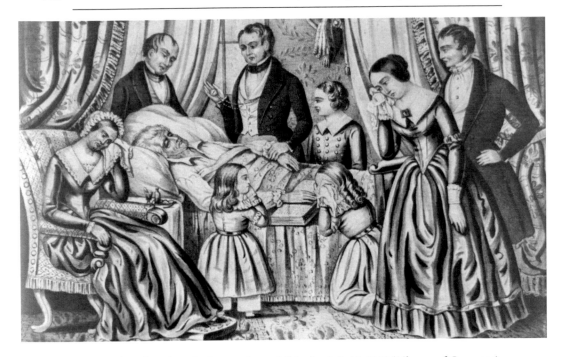

Death of Gen'l Andrew Jackson, print published c. July 15, 1845 (Library of Congress).

home at the Hermitage. The tomb is on the side of the house that faced Jackson's bedroom, from which he could see the grave when he got up in the morning and before going to bed at night.[410] Compared to the lengthy inscription he had carved on his wife's tomb, his is graced simply with the words: *General Andrew Jackson, Born March 15, 1767, died June 8, 1845.* In his will, Jackson left his entire estate to his adopted son, Andrew Jackson, Jr., and several slaves to his daughter-in-law and grandchildren.[411] Jackson had been offered a sarcophagus from Palestine, believed to have been made for the Roman emperor Servus. In a letter to James Duncan Elliott, Jackson explained why he refused the gift: "I cannot consent that my mortal body shall be laid in a repository prepared for an Emperor or a King — my republican feelings and principles forbid it — the simplicity of our system government forbids it."[412]

MISCELLANEA

Presidential Trivia and Firsts: Jackson was the only president to serve in both the Revolutionary War and the War of 1812. He was the only president to have been a prisoner of war. He was the first president to ride in a railroad train. Jackson believed the world was flat. Old Hickory was the first presidential candidate to personally campaign for the position and was the first president to be offered a baby to kiss. He declined and turned the task over to his secretary of war, John Eaton, who did the honors. Both Andy and Rachel smoked corncob pipes.[413] When he was shown a photograph taken of him when he was a very old man, the General denounced the photographer, saying the photograph made him "look like a monkey."[414]

Memorials to Andrew Jackson include a set of three identical equestrian statues located in different parts of the country. One is in Jackson Square in New Orleans. Another is in

Nashville on the grounds of the Tennessee state capitol. The third is a bronze statue in Washington, D.C., in Lafayette Park, near the White House. It was cast from a bronze cannon captured at Pensacola during Jackson's last campaign in 1818.[415] Jackson still appears on the $20 bill, but he once also appeared on $5, $10, $50, and $10,000 bills, as well as on a Confederate $1,000 bill.[416]

The story of Andrew and Rachel Jackson was effectively told in Irving Stone's best-selling 1951 novel, *The President's Lady*, which was made into a 1953 movie of the same name, starring Charlton Heston and Susan Hayward. Jackson was portrayed again by Heston in the 1958 film *The Buccaneer*, which told of the role of the pirate Jean Lafitte, played by Yul Brynner with hair, in the Battle of New Orleans. It was a remake of a 1938 film starring Fredric March as Lafitte and Hugh Sothern as Jackson.[417] Jackson once held an open house party at the White House, where a 1,400-pound wheel of cheddar cheese was served as refreshment and consumed in two hours. The White House smelled of cheese for several weeks.[418]

Jackson and Slavery: The momentous question of slavery became a hot political issue during Jackson's administration. Northern abolitionists organized and bombarded the nation and Congress with pleas and petitions to rid the nation of this great wrong. Defenders of the practice of slavery responded with denunciations and violence. They demanded that in the interest of public safety criticism of slavery should be silenced. Congress adopted "gag rules" to keep discussion of abolition petitions from the floors of the two houses of Congress. There seems no evidence that Jackson ever considered slavery a moral question. He grew up with it and accepted it uncritically. Like his neighbors, he bought and sold slaves and used them to work at his plantation and serve his needs.[419]

"The Hermitage was a 1,050 acre self-sufficient plantation that raised cotton as its sole cash crop and relied on the labor of African American men, women, and children. The enslaved performed the hard labor that allowed for the Jackson Family survival and profit on this land.... When Andrew Jackson bought The Hermitage in 1804, he owned nine enslaved African Americans. By 1829, that number had increased through purchase and reproduction to over 100 African American men, women, and children."[420] Although Jackson cared for his slaves, as evidenced by adequate food, housing, and the ability of slave women to reproduce, slavery was a brutal and cruel system. "The most well-known story about Jackson's treatment of slaves is his promise in 1804 to pay for someone to give one of his runaway slaves 300 lashes upon capture."[421] Concerned that the abolitionist controversy was a threat to sectional harmony and his own political party; he rejected it on purely political terms. Abolitionists organized a postal campaign in 1835, sending massive amounts of antislavery literature through the mails. Southerners and most Northerners branded this literature as dangerous, and the Democratic administration could not avoid the issue... (Jackson noted the 'painful excitement' caused by the abolitionist tracts and recommended that Congress prohibit their circulation in the South) rather than formally censor the mail, (Jackson) simply allowed local postmasters to destroy mail that they considered dangerous."[422] His proposal prompted a heated debate in the Senate when Calhoun objected to giving Congress power to exclude material.

The Worst President Ever? Among the questions that is visited from time to time in this work, but not answered, is the interesting and debatable "who was the best president?" For that matter, the answer to the question "who was the worst president?" won't be found here either. Although there are a number of candidates nominated by one group or another for these distinctions, deciding the best and the worst seems impossible, or at least to be a completely subjective activity. Presidents cannot even be easily compared or contrasted without identifying all of the criteria to be used in the comparison. Debate over the best and worst presidents brings to mind a version of a riddle: "What do they call the person who finished last in his medical school class?" The answer is "Doctor!" Likewise, "what do they call the worst chief executive of the United States?" brings the answer "Mr. President."

That being said, at least one group would argue that Andrew Jackson was the worst president ever. Native American Cherokees once were allies with General Jackson in his battle against the Creek Indians. According to the Cherokees, he repaid them with enforcement of the Indian Removal Act, which forced them off their land, despite the existence of treaties guaranteeing their rights to their property. They were forced to march to the "Indian Territory," resulting in the death of about 4,000 men, women and children. Jackson and those who approved of the removal of the Cherokees from their homes tried to put a humanitarian spin on it, claiming that it would separate them from white encroachment and allow them to live their lives according to their own traditions and customs. In a meeting with a large delegation of Cherokee chiefs, he explained his concern for their well-being. "You are now placed in the midst of a white population.... You are now subject to the same laws which govern the citizens of Georgia and Alabama. You are liable to prosecutions for offenses, and to civil actions for a breach of any of your contracts. Most of your people are uneducated, and are liable to be brought into collision at all times with your white neighbors. Your young men are acquiring habits of intoxication. With strong passions ... they are frequently driven to excesses which must eventually terminate in their ruin. The game has disappeared among you, and you must depend upon agriculture and the mechanic arts for support. And yet, a large portion of your people have acquired little or no property in the soil itself.... How, under these circumstances, can you live in the country you now occupy? Your condition must become worse and worse, and you will ultimately disappear, as so many tribes have done before you."[423] He scolded the Cherokees for not following his "advice," concluding "I am sincerely desirous to promote your welfare. Listen to me, therefore, while I tell you that you cannot remain where you are now.... It [is] impossible that you can flourish in the midst of a civilized community. You have but one remedy within your reach. And that is to remove to the West and join your countrymen, who are already established there. The choice is yours. May the great spirit teach you how to choose."[424] To critics of Indian removal, "Jackson painted a picture of the Cherokees as illiterate, uncivilized, savage hunters, when, in fact, 90 percent of that Indian nation could read and write, a large number also reading and writing English, and most were farmers."[425]

Private John G. Burnett, a member of Captain Abraham McClellan's company of mounted infantry, sadly commented on the Cherokee Indian Removal:

> I saw the helpless Cherokees arrested and dragged from their homes, and driven at the bayonet point into the stockades. And in the chill of a drizzling rain on an October morning I saw them loaded like cattle or sheep into six hundred and forty-five wagons and started toward the west.... On the morning of November the 17th we encountered a terrific sleet and snow storm with freezing temperatures and from that day until we reached the end of the fateful journey on March 26, 1839, the sufferings of the Cherokees were awful. The trail of the exiles was a trail of death. They had to sleep in the wagons and on the ground without fire. And I have known as many as twenty-two of them to die in one night of pneumonia due to ill treatment, cold and exposure.[426]

Is it any wonder that today many Cherokees would prefer to carry two ten-dollar bills or four fives, or twenty ones rather than a single twenty dollar bill, which features the image of Andrew Jackson? However, biographer Robert V. Remini in *The Legacy of Andrew Jackson* contends that Americans blame Jackson for the removal of the Native Americans from their lands so that the nation doesn't have to take any responsibility for the deed. He says most whites in the 1830s were racists: "Americans need to realize that it wasn't just Jackson who removed the Indians; it was the American people who did it. And not only that, we've kept on doing similar things. We 'removed' Japanese Americans during World War II, and the Congress and the Supreme Court and the vast majority of Americans approved of it. And we, as a nation and as a people, continue to do morally questionable things today."[427] Remini points out that American leaders, including Thomas Jefferson, had been moving toward a policy of Indian removal for decades. Remini claims that Jackson acted to protect the security of white settlers and their young nation: "[Native Americans and whites] despised and feared each other and this prejudice and mistrust saturated both their cultures."[428]

Scholar Daniel Feller, director of the *Papers of Andrew Jackson*, University of Tennessee, reports that many young people who experienced, or have studied, the civil rights movement consider Jackson's role in the subjugation of the slaves and Indian removal reminiscent of Adolph Hitler and the Jews. Feller said, "If you're talking about Hitler, you don't say, 'Well, he built roads and put the German people to work,' because it simply doesn't matter, given the horror of the other things he did. And that's how some people today view Jackson."[429]

Evaluations of Andrew Jackson

BY OTHER PRESIDENTS

Incompetent both by his ignorance and by the fury of his passions. He will be surrounded and governed by incompetent men, whose ascendancy over him will be secured by their servility and who will bring to the Government of the nation nothing by their talent for intrigue.[430] — John Quincy Adams

I never knew a man more free from conceit, or one to whom it was a greater pleasure, as well as a recognized duty, to listen patiently to what might be said to him upon any subject under consideration.... Neither, I need scarcely say, was he in the habit of talking, much less boasting, of his achievements.[431] — Martin Van Buren

An overwhelming proportion of the material power of the Nation was against him. The great media for the dissemination of information and the molding of public opinion fought him. Musty reaction disapproved him. Hollow and outworn traditionalism shook a trembling finger at him — all but the people of the United States.[432] — Franklin D. Roosevelt

Jackson is my next choice as a great president after Jefferson, the next president who really did things.[433] — Harry S Truman

BY OTHERS

Not only was Jackson not a consistent politician, he was not even a real leader of democracy.... [H]e always believed in making the public serve the ends of the politicians. Democracy was good talk with which to win the favor of the people and thereby accomplish ulterior motives. Jackson never really championed the cause of the people.[434] — T.P. Abernethy

Let it be remembered that every military chieftain, Sylla, Caesar, Cromwell, all have obtained unlimited and despotic power by pretending to be the sole friends of the People and often by denouncing the rich, and by cajoling the poor with prospects, which they never intended to be realized, or only realized with chains and slavery, and dungeons, or enrollment in the legions assembled to add to the power of the tyrant.[435] — Anonymous

Where is there a chief magistrate of whom so much evil has been predicted, and from whom so much good has come?[436] — Thomas H. Benton

A man of intelligence, and one of those prompt, frank, ardent souls whom I love to meet.[437] — Aaron Burr

He did not accept the rule of law, unless he made it.[438] — Andrew Burstein

[Jackson was a] Shakespearean tragic hero [whose tragic flaw was] his incessant pursuit of virtue in the political realm.[439] — Andrew Burstein

With money and corrupt partisans, a great effort is now making to choke and stifle the voice of American liberty. When the deed will be done — the revolution is completed.... [A]ll the powers of our Republic, in like manner [will] be consolidated in the President, and perpetuated by his dictation.[440] — John C. Calhoun

He is ignorant, passionate, hypocritical, corrupt and easily swayed by the base men who surround him.[441] — Henry Clay

It was expected of me that I was to bow to the name of Andrew Jackson ... even at the expense of my conscience and judgment, such a thing was new to me, and a total stranger to my principles.[442] — Davy Crockett

The sagacity of General Jackson was the admiration of the sophist and the wonder of the savage; it unraveled the meshes of both, without the slightest seeming effort.[443] — George M. Dallas

His stern, inflexible adherence to Democratic principles, his unwavering devotion to his country, and his intrepid opposition to her enemies, have so long thwarted their unhallowed schemes of ambition and power, that they fear the potency of his name on earth, even after his spirit shall have ascended to heaven.[444] — Stephen A. Douglas

[He is] an honest man and the idol of the worshippers of military glory, but from incapacity, military habits, and habitual disregard of laws and constitutional provisions, altogether unfit for office.[445] — Albert Gallatin

He was a simple, emotional, and unreflective man with a strong sense of loyalty to personal friends and political supporters; he swung to the democratic camp when the democratic camp swung to him.[446] — Richard Hofstadter

This feeling has been impressed on my heart by the instruction and the example of the great man, whom when I was a boy, I followed as a soldier.[447] — Sam Houston

Andrew Jackson was eight feet tall / His arm was a hickory limb and a maul. / His sword is so long he dragged it on the ground. / Every friend was an equal. Every foe was a hound.[448] — Vachel Lindsay

The wild asses of the west, led by Andy Jackson, will ruin the government.[449] — John Marshall

Run the eye across the history of the world. You observe that there are certain cycles, or ages, or periods of time, which have their peculiar spirit, their ruling passion, their great, characterizing, distinctive movements. He, who embodies in its greatest fullness, the spirit of such an age, and enters with most earnestness into its movements, received the admiration of his contemporaries.... And why? because they see in him their own image. Because, in him is concentrated the spirit that has burned in their own bosom. Because in him exists, in bodily form, in living flesh and blood, the spirit that gives them life and motion. The spirit of God descended upon the Saviour of the world in the form of a dove. The spirit of an age sometimes descends to future generations in the form of a man ... in proportion as an individual concentrates within himself, the spirit which works through masses of men, and which moves, and should move them through the greatest cycles of time, in that proportion, he becomes entitled to their admiration and praise.... Because his countrymen saw their image and spirit in Andrew Jackson they bestowed their honor and admiration upon him. The spirit of an age sometimes descends to future generations in the form of a man ... in proportion as an individual concentrates within himself, the spirit which works through masses of men, and which moves, and should move them through the greatest cycles of time, in that proportion, he becomes entitled to their admiration and praise.... Because his countrymen saw their image and spirit in Andrew Jackson, they bestowed their honor and admiration upon him.[450] — Washington McCartney

Little advanced in civilization over the Indians with whom he made war.[451] — Elijah Hunt Mills

He was too generous to be frugal, too kindhearted to be thrifty, too honest to live above his means.[452]— Vernon Parrington

His instinctive love of justice ... gave a high tone to his government and exalted the honor of his country. His hatred of corruption rendered his administration pure.... I will content myself with expressing my belief that in future time the impartial historian will justify both his motives and his conduct on this trying occasion.[453]— J.R. Poinsett

[T]he chief, who violated the Constitution, proscribed public virtue and patriotism and introduced high handed corruption into public affairs and debauchery into private circles was the first President who received insult in his person and was the object of assassination.[454]— William Henry Seward

The inflation and crises of the 1830's [sic] had their origin in events largely based beyond Jackson's control and probably would have taken place whether or not he had acted as he did.[455]— Peter Temin

General Jackson is the majority's slave; he yields to its intentions, desires, and half-revealed instincts, or rather he anticipates and forestalls them.[456]— Alexis de Tocqueville

EIGHT

Martin Van Buren

The Foxy First Full-Time Politician

Eighth President of the United States, 1837–1841

Congressman Davy Crockett of Tennessee, no friend of Andrew Jackson, apparently thought even less of Martin Van Buren, saying:

Van Buren is as opposite to General Jackson as dung is to diamond.... He is what the English call a dandy. When he enters the senate-chamber in the morning, he struts and swaggers like a crow in the gutter. He is laced up in corsets, such as women in town wear, and, if possible, tighter than the best of them. It would be difficult to say, from his personal appearance, whether he was a man or woman, but for his large ... whiskers.[1]

On another occasion Crockett penned a little ditty about the eighth president of the United States:

Good Lord! What is VAN!—for though simple he looks,
Tis a task to unravel his looks and crooks;
Tis a task to unravel his looks and crooks;
All in all, he's a RIDDLE must puzzle the devil.[2]

Birth: Martin Van Buren was born in a long one-and-a-half-story clapboard farmhouse located at 36 Hudson Street in the small village of Kinderhook on December 5, 1782. Kinderhook is located in the Hudson Valley in southern Columbia County, New York, about 20 miles south of Albany. It was settled by Dutch immigrants in the 1600s, shortly after Hendrick Hudson sailed up the river which bears his name today. The Englishman's journey under the Dutch flag — Hudson's 58-foot (17.4-meter) ship left Amsterdam on the morning tide of April 4, 1609, and headed west — was yet another attempt by Europeans to find a "northwest passage" to Asia. Hudson and his 20 crewmen got only as far as modern-day Albany.[3] It is believed that it was in Kinderhook waters that were too shallow for Hudson to continue, he turned his ship, the *Half Moon*, around and headed for home. "Early inhabitants settled in what is now known as Stuyvesant Landing and gradually moved inland. The town originally stretched from the river to the present site of Chatham. 'Kinderhook' means 'Children's Corner' and still retains its Dutch atmosphere."[4]

Nicknames and Titles: Van Buren had several nicknames, including "Old Kinderhook," "Red Fox of Kinderhook," "Little Magician," "Martin Van Ruin," "Mistletoe Politician," and "Machiavellian Belshazzar." In his youth he had a reputation for being able to consume large quantities of alcohol without appearing drunk, earning him the appellation "Blue Whiskey Van."[5]

Family: Martin's father, Abraham Van Buren (1737–1817), who "served as Captain in the Seventh Regiment, Kinderhook District, New York Levies and Militia"[6] in the war for Independence was a tavern-keeper and a farmer with slaves. A historical marker stands where the tavern (which no longer exists) was located. The Van Buren family was never wealthy, but neither was it poor. Abraham was active in the Democratic-Republican Party. Abraham's hostelry was frequented by government workers traveling between Albany and New York City. "He held the post of town clerk for extra money, and the tavern hosted political meetings or elections. Guests at the tavern, such as Alexander Hamilton and Aaron Burr, offered young Martin his first glimpses of American politics."[7] He died when his famous son was a state senator. Young "Matty," as the future president was called, worked in the tavern and on the farm.[8] Maria Hoes (originally spelled Goes) Van Alen Van Buren (1747–1817) had been married to Johannes Van Alen, with whom she had three children. After Van Alen's death, she married Abraham Van Buren in 1776. Maria was very fond of politics. A neighbor recalled her as "distinguished for her amiable disposition, her exemplary piety, and more than ordinary sagacity." She died less than a year after the death of her second husband.[9] Van Buren had two older sisters, Dirckie, also known as Derike, and Jannetje, also known as Hannah, and two younger brothers, Lawrence and Abraham. By his mother's first marriage, he had a half sister, Marytje Van Alen, and two half brothers, Johannes Van Alen and Jacobus Van Alen.[10]

Ancestors: Martin Van Buren's large family, like their Dutch immigrant predecessors of 150 years, made a moderate living farming in the Hudson. "Almost everyone in Kinderhook was related. Most spoke Dutch with their fellow townspeople and English to outsiders."[11] The Dutch "Van" means "of" or "from" and denotes the place of birth or residence, or the place from which the person came, and, in some cases, the name of the person whom he served. The future president's earliest ancestor in America, "Cornelis Maessen Van Buren was born in Burmalsen, Provence of Guelderland, Holland, [c. 1610] and died in Papsknee, New York, in 1648. His name was variously spelled Bruyen, Burjmalsen, Buurmalsen, or

Martin Van Buren, print created c. 1839. Associated name on shelflist card, Fenderich (Library of Congress).

Burren. Catalyntje Martensen was born in Guelderland, Holland, and died in 1648. Both Cornelis and Catalyntje were buried on the same day on their farm. They were married in Holland in 1635–1636. She took the name Catalyntje Van Buren. They had five children."[12] In the books of the ship on which he sailed his name is given as "Cornelis Maessen Van Buren." Even so, he did not at that time bear the van Buren name. It was not the custom at the time he came to America for Dutchmen to have a family name. Surnames as family names were rare prior to the middle of the 11th century. It was not until about the third generation in America that "Van Buren" was adopted as the family name.[13]

Van Buren is a Dutch origin surname meaning "of Buren," which means a neighbor-hood and as such was the name of a county in the Dutch province of Gelderland. "The name has a certain prominence in Holland because Anna van Egmond en Buren was the first wife of William of Orange, the founder of the Dutch royal family. The Dutch royals have been known to use the name van Buren in situations that require anonymity."[14] No mention of the lords of Buren is made before 1145 CE when Alard Van Buren married Ida, the daughter of Roelof, the lord of Beusichen. When Van Buren was visiting The Nether-lands, he was received by Queen Adelaide, who inquired of the Dutch American how far back he could trace his ancestry. His self-effacing response was "As far back as Kinderhook, your Majesty."[15]

Appearance: As an adult Van Buren stood only about five feet six inches tall, making him the shortest leader since James Madison. Some Whig opponents passed around the rumor that as he got older and heavier, he wore corsets to maintain his trim appearance.[16] He had a fair complexion, deeply set calculating blue eyes, a large head with a prominent brow and a classic Roman nose. He grew large mutton-chop red sideburns. Detractors referred to him as "Sweet Sandy Whiskers" for his habit of scenting his reddish whiskers.[17] By the time he was inaugurated president, Matty was mostly bald, with a crown of unruly white hair. He was always impeccably dressed, although he wore loud prints and bright colors, often a source of scorn by the press.[18] According to Louis W. Koenig in "The Rise of the Little Magician," which appeared in the *American Heritage* magazine in June 1982, Van Buren's interest in fine clothes was a result of his clerkship with Francis Sylvester, the first lawyer of Kinderhook. Matty arrived in the law office dressed in the coarse homespun linens and woolens made by his mother. Sylvester took the lad aside and lectured him on the importance of proper dress. Matty was duly impressed and the next day he surprised Sylvester by showing up wearing "a complete gentleman's outfit, consisting of a black broad-brimmed cocked hat, a waistcoat with layers of frilly lace, velvet breeches, silken hose, and huge flash-ing silver buckles."[19]

Former President Martin Van Buren, photographed between 1840 and 1862, printed later (Library of Congress).

Matty "spoke rapidly with crisp enunciation, but when he became excited, it is said, a touch of Dutch accent crept into his speech."[20] Dur-ing the 1840 presidential campaign against William Henry Harrison, known as "Old Tippecanoe," Van Buren's opponents came up with a lit-tle ditty that proved popular:

> Old Tip he wears a homespun suit,
> He has no ruffled shirt — wirt, wirt;
> But Mat he has the golden pate,
> And he's a little squirt — wirt, wirt.[21]

Personality and Character: Van Buren had a good nature and a kindly manner that won him many friends. He "always maintained a perfect composure, frustrating anyone who tried to upset him or disparage him."[22] He did not let anger distort his judgment or warp his manner. He was an even-tempered but resourceful and eloquent politician. He led by persuasion, often by careful scheming. "He learned to hold his counsel as others debated the hotly contested issues of the day, carefully observing the course of a debate and weighing all of the issues before staking out a position of his own."[23] He preferred to discover the opinions of others while keeping his own closely guarded. "Even after Matty decided upon his position, he spoke cautiously in an air of evasive circumspection that left others still in the dark as to his real feelings."[24]

Van Buren's "please everyone" attitude brought him as many critics as supporters. His opponents "denounced him during his life for subtle intrigue, scheming pragmatism, and indecisive 'non-commitalism.'"[25] "They coined the adjective, 'vanburnish' to mean a person who is evasive on noncommittal in politics."[26] Davy Crockett echoed these sentiments: "It is said at a year old, he could laugh on one side of his face and cry on the other, at one and the same time."[27] In social situations, which he enjoyed, his charm, cheerfulness, courtesy, wit and fine manners made him a much sought after party guest. From an early age he was an engaging conversationalist. "Charmingly witty and imperturbably amiable, Van Buren never let political differences master his emotions or cloud his social relations."[28] His agreeable disposition helped establish him as an effective politician. Mayor George Opdyke of New York City expressed his admiration of Matty: "His purity of character, his marked ability as a statesman, his exalted patriotism, and his distinguished public service, which extended over nearly half a century, have given his name deserved prominence in the history of our country."[29] Andrew Jackson biographer Glyndon G. Van Deusen said of Van Buren: "[W]ith all his weaknesses, the fact remains that Van Buren was honest; that he knew the value of and habitually sought counsel; that he deliberated before making decisions; and that his four years in the White House, demonstrated, for better or worse, a perfectly logical development of the left-wing tendencies of Jacksonian Democracy, a development which it took courage to foster in the face of a catastrophic depression."[30]

Marriage and Romances: Hannah Hoes Van Buren, Martin's childhood sweetheart, was born in Kinderhook in 1783. The blonde-haired, blue-eyed daughter of Johannes Dircksen and Maria Quakenbush Hoes was distantly related to her husband through his mother. They were married February 21, 1807, at Catskill, New York. He called her Jannetje, Dutch for Hannah. In 1808, "the newlyweds moved to Hudson, the county seat and a somewhat larger town than Kinderhook."[31] A niece remembered Hannah as having a "loving and gentle disposition" and emphasized "her modest, even timid manner."[32] From church records, Hannah appears to have considered formal church affiliation a matter of importance.[33]

After about ten years of marriage Mrs. Van Buren contracted tuberculosis and died on February 5, 1819, at age 35. The local newspaper called her "an ornament of the Christian faith."[34] At her request, the "custom of providing scarves for the pallbearers to wear at the funeral was abandoned. The money set aside to pay for them was used to feed the poor."[35]

Her obituary, probably written by her pastor, appeared in the *Albany Argus*: "As a

Hannah Van Buren, original engraving by John Chester Buttre published in *The Ladies of the White House, or, In the Home of the Presidents* by Laura Carter Holloway Langford, Funk & Wagnalls, 1886 (Library of Congress).

daughter and a sister, wife and a mother, her loss is deeply deplored, for in all these varied relations, she was affectionate, tender and truly estimable. But the tear of sorrow is almost dried by the reflection that she lived the life and died the death of the righteous. Modest and unassuming, possessing the most engaging simplicity of manners, her heart was the residence of every kind affection, and glowed with sympathy for the wants and sufferings of others. Her temper was uncommonly mild and sweet, her bosom was filled with benevolence and content. No love of show, no ambitious desires, no pride of ostentation ever disturbed its peace.... Humility was her crowning grace; she possessed it in rare degree; it took root and flourished full and fair, shedding over every act of her life its general influence. She was an ornament of the Christian faith.... Doubtless, twas gain for her to die. Doubtless, she is now enjoying that rest which remaineth for the people of God. Precious shall be the memory of her virtues, sweet the savor of her name, and soft her sleeping bed."[36] Van Buren never remarried and although he referred to her as the guiding force in his life, he never mentioned her even once in his autobiography because a gentleman of his day would not "shame" a lady by public references.[37] When Van Buren moved into the White House with four bachelor sons, Dolley Madison, still the matriarch of Washington society, brought Angelica Singleton, her cousin from South Carolina, to the White House, where she met Van Buren's eldest son, Abraham. A year later they were married.[38] During his presidency, Angelica served as Van Buren's hostess at the White House. One newspaper described her: "[She is a] lady of rare accomplishments, very modest yet perfectly easy

Angelica Singleton Van Buren, a 1913 copy of an engraving from an 1842 portrait by Henry Inman that hangs in the Red Room of the White House (Library of Congress).

and graceful in her manners and free and vivacious in her conversation ... universally admired."[39]

Although not much is known about any later romances, there were rumors of flirtations and a proposal of marriage to Ellen Randolph, a granddaughter of Thomas Jefferson in her mid–20s, shortly before she married Joseph Coolidge.[40] On retirement to Lindenwald at Kinderhook, Van Buren courted Margaret Sylvester, a daughter of one of the men under whom he had studied law in his youth. A spinster of forty she declined his proposal of marriage, indicating it was her desire to remain single. Their friendship survived the rejection.[41]

Children: Van Buren had four sons survive to maturity. Abraham, who attended the U.S. Military Academy, served as an officer in the West and later was his father's personal secretary. John, who attended Yale, was a lawyer and was elected to the U.S. House of Representatives in 1841. Martin, "Mat," a student of political science, died suddenly while visiting Europe with his father. Smith Thompson drafted many of his father's speeches and became his literary executor. Winfield Scott died in infancy.[42]

Religion and Religious Beliefs: Van Buren's religion is usually listed as Dutch Reformed or no affiliation. He is not known to have joined any church while in the nation's capital, nor in his hometown of Kinderhook. He did attend an Episcopal church while in Washington. Franklin Steiner, in his book *The Religious Beliefs of Our Presidents*, categorized Van Buren among "Presidents Whose Religious Views Are Doubtful."[43] He rarely made biblical references in his speeches. However, in his inaugural address, he stated that "I only look to the gracious protection of the Divine Being whose strengthening support I humbly solicit, and whom I fervently pray to look down upon us all. May it be among the dispensations of His providence to bless our beloved country with honors and with length of days."[44] In his second annual message to Congress he asserted, "All forms of religion have united for the first time to diffuse charity and piety, because for the first time in the history of nations all have been totally untrammeled and absolutely free."[45]

Education: At the time, most students of Van Buren's social and economic class dropped out of school after a few of years to help their parents. At an early age Matty exhibited indications of a superior intellect. "Young Martin inherited his ambition from his mother, who insisted that her sons receive the best education possible, given their limited resources."[46] He attended a small village school, acquiring the barebones of an English education and Kinderhook Academy where he made sizable headway in the study of English literature and obtained a basic knowledge of Latin. He desperately wished to attend Columbia College, like his wealthier classmates, but his father, a man of modest means, was able to provide him with only a rudimentary education, so the lad was forced to leave school and find work to help his family. "One of Van Buren's better-educated associates observed that his 'knowledge of books outside of his profession was more limited than that of any other public man' he had ever known and that Van Buren never prepared a state paper without asking a friend to 'revise and correct that document.'"[47] Van Buren is a good example of a man who became an eminent success both in public speaking and composition despite a lack of a classical education. Van Buren was the first president of the United States elected without the benefit of a university degree or a military commission. The only other president with this distinction was Grover Cleveland.[48] In his autobiography, Van Buren appears to place the blame for his lack of higher education on the failures of his father, who he said was "an unassuming amicable man ... utterly devoid of the spirit of accumulation ... his property, originally moderate, was gradually reduced until he could but ill afford to bestow the necessary means upon the education of his children."[49] Denial of a chance at higher education had a profound and life-long effect on Van Buren. He came to venerate the learning that had been denied him. Because of his lack of formal education, he developed a conspicuous sense of intellectual inferiority.[50] When he left school at 14, he was apprenticed to lawyer Francis Sylvester. His duties included sweeping out the office, lighting the log fire, and running errands, but he advanced to serving as a law clerk and copyist of pleas.[51]

Occupation: In 1796 Van Buren took up the study of law, quickly absorbing ideas and concepts from the legal field. For those without a college education the period of time in preparation to pass the bar was seven years. Greatly ambitious and conscious of his talents, Mat "pursued his studies with indefatigable industry."[52] He read all the law books he could get his hands on and eagerly pored over every journal he found on Jeffersonian politics. "The Federalist Party enjoyed dominance in the Hudson Valley region but Van Buren joined the Democratic-Republicans, largely, it seems, because his father and his family's friends were Jeffersonians. Van Buren's political party affiliation alienated many friends and colleagues, and he often had to tangle with Federalist judges and lawyers. But he more than held his own, and his party's leaders quickly tagged him as one to watch. Most important, his decision to join the Jeffersonians marked the beginning of a commitment to Jeffersonian principles of limited federal government, defense of individual liberties, and the protection of local and state prerogatives in American politics."[53] At age 15 he presented his first legal argument to a local court. Early Van Buren biographers related a story that the youngster was in courtroom during the trying of a trifling case. "The judge suddenly turned to him and invited him to sum up the arguments for the jury. Because he was rather short, he was told to stand on a bench so he could be seen. 'There, Mat, beat your master,' was what the judge supposedly said as he instructed Van Buren to begin the summation."[54] Whether this actually occurred on not, it is true that Van Buren's skill was recognized from the start of his career. "Combining with ... a fondness for extemporaneous debate, he was early noted for his intelligent observation of public events and for his interest in politics. He was chosen to participate in a nominating convention when he was only eighteen years old."[55] Mat completed his preparation in 1802 in New York City. He studied under eminent lawyer William Peter Van Ness, who later acted as Aaron Burr's second in the duel in which Alexander Hamilton was killed.[56] Van Buren was admitted to the bar in 1803 and maintained an active and successful practice in Kinderhook for twenty-five years in partnership with his stepbrother James Van Alen, becoming financially independent.[57]

Home: After serving as president, Van Buren returned to Kinderhook and purchased a mansion on the Hudson River known as Lindenwald, named for the linden trees on the estate. Van Buren lived there for 21 years, until his death at age 79.[58] The house was built in the 18th century. At one time the property was owned by Van Buren's paternal grandmother's family, the Van Alstynes. They sold it in 1787 to Peter Van Ness, one of the wealthiest men in Columbia County. Van Ness, who was a boyhood friend of Van Buren, built a Federalist style manor on the property.[59] "The estate moved through a number of hands before Van Buren bought the house and 130 acres of land. In the next six years, he purchased more land bringing his holdings to 220 acres."[60] He added rooms, kitchen ranges and a furnace to his home. Among the more unique features for the time, the house had inside running water and a flush toilet. Van Buren created large rooms on the first and second floor of his mansion by "removing the central stairway in the entrance hall. The stair was relocated to an enclosure in the den, with the resulting alcove, formed off the south parlor, in the Gothic style in contrast to the classic Federal woodwork of the room."[61]

In Van Buren's day, the grounds had a formal flower garden with ornamental fish ponds. Van Buren grew crops, including turnips, beans, peas, peppers, grapes, cherries, apples, plums, pears, rye, corn, oats, potatoes and wheat. In 1849 he "added a four-story brick tower in the Italianate style, a central gable, attic dormers and a heavily Victorian veranda," which Van Buren called "as beautiful a porch as you ever laid eyes upon."[62] The manor was transformed from the 18th to the mid–19th century, when fashionable builders modeled their works after the grand villas of northern Italy. After 1849, the "house consisted of thirty-six rooms and passageways." In the 20th century, owners of the estate transformed it by replacing Van Buren's Victorian entrance to the house with a "Southern Colonial portico extending across the front" of the building. This and other changes to the appearance of the house when Van Buren resided there "were removed when the property was acquired by the National Park Service in 1976."[63] While living at Lindenwald, Van Buren enjoyed the pleasure of having his sons and their families' company. In his office, Van Buren hung some of the unflattering political cartoons from the time of his service in national office.[64] Washington Irving wrote his classic story "The Legend of Sleepy Hollow" while a guest at Lindenwald.[65] The Van Alen house, built in 1737, is just north of Lindenwald. It is now a museum, along with the original Ichabod Crane Schoolhouse adjoining the property.[66]

Pets and Animals: Van Buren kept two tiger cubs as pets, given to him by the Sultan of Oman.[67]

Recreational Pastimes and Interests: Van Buren enjoyed the theatre and opera. He took several glasses of wine with his meals, and his favorite foods were oysters, doughnuts, raisins, figs and apples.[68] His favorite sport was horseback riding, and he often fished.[69]

POLITICAL OFFICES

Political Philosophy and Political Party Affiliation: Van Buren was an adherent of the Jeffersonian ideals of limited federal power, civil liberties, and a strict interpretation of the Constitution. As a U.S. senator, he was an outspoken critic of the Supreme Court, especially in relation to its practice of judicial review.[70] Van Buren was "among the first American politicians to understand the role of political parties in a democracy. Before him, parties were viewed disdainfully as dangerous factions threatening the unity of society.... Van Buren saw parties as salutary institutions within a working democracy, and as a New York state politician, he built the first real political party apparatus in the United States."[71] Mat was "one of the most consummate backroom strategists in helping to mastermind a reemergence of ideologically distinct political organizations out of the corrupt and faction-ridden interlude of single party rule that had followed the War of 1812."[72] Van Buren represented "a new breed of professional politicians."[73] Foes condemned him for subtle plotting, devious pragmatism, and fickle commitment. "A discreet, guarded man, Van Buren worked best behind the scenes."[74]

Van Buren, called the first national politician, was one of the founders of the Democrat Party, "resuscitating the old Jeffersonian alliance between planters of the South and plain Republicans of the North, united behind the charismatic hero of the West, General Andrew Jackson."[75] Among his other political accomplishments were founding "the party caucus, the nominating convention, the patronage system,"[76] and a process for successfully marketing a candidate for a political position.[77]

Van Buren was always regarded as more a politician than a statesman. "He habitually thought in terms of political forces and was fertile in conceiving, and able in executing, plans to weaken the opposition and advance his own party."[78] He created the first political machine and is considered the first of the "Party Bosses." He said: "Without strong national political organizations, there would be nothing to moderate the prejudices between free and slaveholding states."[79]

In 1840, "Martin Van Buren charged that the nation's incorporated voluntary associations, like so many of its business corporations, were agents of aristocracy."[80] By some mysterious "law of their nature," these organizations seemed always to "resist the will of the people. Van Buren's tone reflected some befuddlement," but this "mastermind of democratic party organization did not slow down to consider the reasons why literary and benevolent societies were so dominated by Whigs, 'federalists,' and other contemnors of democracy."[81] Van Buren said this of political parties:

> [The] American people [hold dear] the republican principle for which their fathers fought....
> [But the division] of the people of the United States between two parties [was] undeniably
> [grounded] in ... principles & objects, which are ... identical with those for which the Revolution
> itself was waged.... Federalist to 1798 [had been almost universally] Tories of the Revolution, [but
> their policies of the 1790s] excesses and apostasies from the principles of the Revolution [had
> raised up the] Old Republican Party of the United States [which had been drawn from] the
> Whigs of the Revolution [who] brought into the political field an enthusiastic devotion to its
> principles.[82]

Surrogate of Columbia County: At Hudson, Van Buren became involved in politics. He was skilled in settling differences in the local Democratic caucus. "He supported Morgan Lewis for governor of New York against Aaron Burr in 1803, but in 1807 he supported Democratic-Republican candidate Daniel D. Tompkins against Lewis. For his efforts, he was elected to a county post, surrogate of Columbia County (1808–1813), a local judicial officer, displacing his half brother and partner, a supporter of the losing faction."[83]

State Senate: In 1812 Van Buren was elected to the state Senate (1812–1815) and gained a reputation as a "War Hawk." These were a "group of young politicians, mostly from southern and western states, who called for war against Great Britain."[84] In 1814, Van Buren sponsored an effective war measure known as "the classification bill" that provided "for the levy of 12,000 men, to be placed at the disposal of the government for two years."[85] His position was extremely unpopular in New England, whose primary trading partner was Great Britain. Resentment of Van Buren's position only deepened early in the War of 1812, when the victories of the British piled up. "When the Battle of Lake Champlain ended in American victory, however, Van Buren's stance became the popular one, and his fame spread to the national level."[86] He became New York attorney general. In 1816, Van Buren advocated the surveys preliminary to the plan for uniting the waters of the Great Lakes with the Hudson River. Governor DeWitt Clinton fired Van Buren when a riff developed between the two politicians. Van Buren was very popular, more popular than Clinton, and the firing outraged Matty's supporters, causing a split in the Democratic-Republican Party. Van Buren organized his own circle of politicians, known as the Albany Regency or "Bucktails," which is regarded as the first "political machine" in American politics.[87] The Bucktails, opponents of De Witt Clinton, "took their name from the distinctive plumes they affixed to their hats, rapidly gained in influence under Van Buren's tutelage."[88] "At a Bucktail-controlled convention, major changes were made to New York's constitution in 1821–1822, expanding the suffrage and curbing upper-class influence, reforms that broke De Witt Clinton's grip on the state."[89]

United States Senate: So many opposing factions existed in New York that none could find votes enough in the legislature of 1818–1819 to elect its candidate for the U.S. Senate.

"Yet out of this medley of factions and muddle of opinions Van Buren, by his moderation and his genius for political organization, evolved order and harmony at the election for senator in the following year. Under his lead all parties united on Rufus King, a Federalist of the old school."[90] "In December 1919, a pamphlet entitled 'Considerations in favor of the appointment of Rufus King, to the Senate of the United States' was addressed to the republican members of the Legislature of New York, by one of their colleagues,"[91] who of course was Martin Van Buren. At the New York State Constitutional Convention, Van Buren told the delegates, "I believe ... that constitutions are the work of time and not the invention of ingenuity; and that to frame a complete system of government, depending on the habits of reverence and experience, was an attempt as absurd as to build a tree or manufacture an opinion."[92]

On February 6, 1821, Van Buren was easily elected to the U.S. Senate, receiving a clear majority in both houses of the New York legislature. He took his seat on December 3, 1821, and served until 1828. His formidable political organization, the "Albany Regency," managed the New York Republican party while he was in Washington. "The name 'Albany Regency' was a disparaging description used by Thurlow Weed to describe the Democratic political machine created in New York State by Martin Van Buren in the 1820s. The machine continued to operate while Van Buren was out of the state serving in the Senate, hence the allusion to a regency, which is government by designated people who rule during a time when the king is not available."[93] Weed also wrote that he "had never known a body of men who possessed so much power and used it so well."[94] The organization maintained rigid discipline, rewarding loyalty with patronage appointments and disciplining errant members. "Delegates to [nominating] conventions who were ambitious of office were controlled by the knowledge that the regency never forgot or forgave insubordination or rebellion, and never forgot or abandoned a friend who had suffered in its service."[95] Although centered in Albany, the organization's control also extended to local political organizations and clubs. The success of Van Buren's apparatus, according to a scholar of the day, "was not so much the rewarding of partisans and the mass lopping off of rebellious heads that explained the Regency success as it was the skillful, highly judicious manner in which the power was exercised."[96]

In Washington, the Little Magician continued his wheeling-and-dealing brand of politics. He succeeded in removing the Speaker of the House, John Taylor of New York, who was firmly in the camp of Clinton, Van Buren's foe. The master of behind-the-scenes politics was able to have Philip Barbour of Virginia elected to the leadership role, solidifying Van Buren's ties to Virginian Republicans.[97] The little politician from Kinderhook proposed no significant legislation and seldom spoke on the floor or in the Senate, because this was not his forte, being a mediocre orator. He advocated moderate reforms in extending democracy, including the virtual elimination of the property qualification for white manhood suffrage. On all questions, he was a strenuous champion of a "strict construction of the constitution." Van Buren was convinced that Republicans had strayed from the Jeffersonian creed, and he intended to restore the party to its "first principles."[98]

Initially Van Buren and other Jeffersonians opposed the building of the Erie Canal, arguing it was an improper use of public funds and would lead to higher taxes. "Later Van Buren supported it when the Bucktails were able to gain a majority in the Erie Canal Commission, and backed a bill that raised money for the canal through state bonds."[99] He was opposed the Canal for political reasons as well, "fearing that the project would be a career boon to Clinton, then his archrival. It took many years for Clinton to get the legislature to approve funding for the Canal. Once Van Buren realized his opposition was a lost cause, he changed sides. It's one of the reasons why he could never escape the charges of being a slippery politician: he sometimes was one. So Martin Van Buren tried to stop a project that would prove to be of enormous economic benefit to his state and to an entire region for misguided ideological reasons and pure political calculation."[100] It was a serious blunder on the part of Van Buren, but changing his position enhanced his political standing. His opponents proclaimed it was a further example of his lack of consistent principles. "The Erie Canal was officially opened on October 25, 1825. It linked Lake Erie and all the Great Lakes to the Hudson River and New York. Construction on the canal began in 1816. The canal spanned 363 miles, and its completion helped to speed up the development of the West.... No one building the canal had any previous experience constructing locks. The U.S. did not have any Engineering schools at that time. The builders needed to learn as they worked."[101] The original canal was 40 feet wide and 4 feet deep, with a towpath built along the side. When the canal exceeded its capacity in was enlarged in 1862. The 9000 workers who were awarded jobs on the engineering marvel were expected to show their indebtedness by doing favors for the Bucktails.

In 1824 Van Buren opposed the nomination of Andrew Jackson as his party's presidential candidate. Instead he backed the Republican caucus nominee, treasury secretary William H. Crawford. "The two had a great deal in common: Crawford was a states' rights advocate, a strict constructionist, and—a consideration of overriding importance to Van Buren—a dedicated party man."[102] Mat's first venture in the "art and business of President-making" as he called it, turned out badly, when Crawford was felled by a paralytic stroke and permanently lost the use of his lower limbs and temporarily his sight. Nevertheless, Crawford stayed in the race. His political handlers had quite a task to prevent the public from learning of his infirmity.[103] Van Buren was bitterly disappointed when the House of Representatives elected John Quincy Adams president.

By 1827, Van Buren had become Andrew Jackson's "campaign manager" in the northeast part of the nation, while Old Hickory stayed in the background. After the misadventure of backing the unfortunate Crawford, the masterful politician wanted to find a man who would restore the party to Jeffersonian purity. Van Buren intoned: "If Gen Jackson ... will put his election on old party grounds, preserve the old systems, avoid if not condemn the practices of the last campaign, we can by adding his personal popularity to the yet remaining force of old party feeling, not only succeed in electing him but our success when achieved will be worth something."[104] As the leader of the opposition to John Quincy Adams' administration in the Senate, Van Buren played a major role in ensuring that Andrew Jackson was elected president. The Little Magician "plunged wholeheartedly into the contest, serving as fund-raiser, strategist, publicist and counselor. Several states liberalized their election laws, expanding the franchise to those without land. Matty wooed these first-time voters with parades, rallies, speeches, and calls for 'reform.'"[105]

Governor: Van Buren ran for and was elected governor of New York in 1828, but he served only four months before resigning to become Jackson's secretary of state. As governor he "sponsored the Safety Fund Plan, which required banks to contribute a fixed percentage of their capital to a reserve fund that would be used to redeem the outstanding paper currency of any bank that collapsed."[106]

His Cabinet Role: As secretary of state, Van Buren joined a cabinet packed with an assortment of second-rank appointees chosen to achieve sectional and ideological balance. Most were the "minions of Vice President John C. Calhoun, who proposed to dominate the administration and ruthlessly advance his long-cherished goal of the presidency."[107] Martin was the leader of Jackson's "Kitchen Cabinet," an unofficial but influential group of presidential advisors. He was the president's sounding board and friend, offering well-timed and perceptive counsel to the lonely old hero. "He encouraged Jackson to use the spoils system,"[108] which was used so effectively in New York State. In 1830 Van Buren negotiated a treaty with Turkey that granted the U.S. navigational rights to the Black Sea. The same year, he concluded a treaty with Great Britain, renewing trade with the West Indies.[109]

Maysville Veto: Van Buren's strict constitutionalism is apparent in President Jackson's veto of the Maysville Road Bill, a veto Van Buren drafted. The bill would have provided federal funds to build a highway from Maysville to Lexington, completely in the state of Kentucky. "Van Buren argued against the bill on constitutional grounds, insisting that the road was of concern only to Kentucky. He went on to challenge a basic premise of Henry Clay's American System — that a state's internal improvements were a federal concern. The effect of the veto was the transfer of the building of roads and canals to the states, a policy that Van Buren, as a Jeffersonian, had long advocated."[110]

The Fox at Work: Van Buren's enemy John C. Calhoun gave him a nickname that stuck: "He is not ... of the race of the lion or the tiger; he belonged to a lower order — the fox."[111] Van Buren plotted to discredit Calhoun and ruin his chances to succeed Jackson as president. The Foxy Van Buren planned a roundabout route to seal Jackson's growing distrust of his vice president. During the Seminole War of 1812, General Jackson overextended his authority and without consulting President Monroe seized Spanish forts in Florida. "Jackson wrote to President Monroe: 'Let it be signified to me through any channel (say Mr. John Rhea) that the possession of the Floridas would be desirable to the United States, and in sixty days it will be accomplished.' Mr. Rhea was a representative from Tennessee, a confidential friend of both Jackson and Monroe. The president was ill when Jackson's letter reached him, and does not seem to have given it due consideration. On referring to it a year later he could not remember that he had ever seen it before. Rhea, however, seems to have written a letter to Jackson, telling him that the president approved of his suggestion ... whatever the president's intention may have been, or how far it may have been correctly interpreted by Rhea, the general honestly considered himself authorized to take possession of Florida.... Jackson acted upon this belief with his accustomed promptness."[112] Although the citizenry praised Jackson as a hero, the president felt that the general had gone too far, considered the general insubordinate and, as was his practice, sought advice from his cabinet. Calhoun, then secretary of war, was outraged at what he considered disregard of his direct orders and recommended that General Jackson be arrested and punished. "With one exception, all his cabinet agreed with him that it would be best to disavow Jackson's acts and make reparation for them. But John Quincy Adams, secretary of state, felt equal to the task of dealing with the two foreign powers, and upon his advice the administration decided to assume the responsibility for what Jackson had done. Secretary of State John Quincy Adams' arguments against censuring the General finally prevailed."[113] "The Cabinet pledged itself to secrecy in regard to all that was proposed on the subject and that for ten years Jackson supposed that Calhoun was the friend in the Cabinet who had successfully defended him against the other members under the lead of secretary of the treasury William H. Crawford."[114] Crawford recorded the Cabinet's discussion in a letter. Van Buren learned of the letter and its contents when he visited Crawford in April 1827. Through an intermediary, James A. Hamilton, Van Buren got his hands on the minutes of the cabinet meeting, which were found in an old trunk in Crawford's Georgia home. Confederates of the Fox made certain that the president became acquainted with the particulars of the contents. Still seething over the upstaging toast offered by Calhoun at the Jefferson Day dinner, supporting nullification, Jackson demanded Calhoun's explanation of his conduct in the Monroe Cabinet.[115]

In a painstaking answer, running to fifty-two pages, Calhoun freely admitted the charges, defended his own conduct, and condemned Crawford for betraying the secrets of the Cabinet. The vice president responded that he did not "recognize the right on your part to call in question my conduct."[116] Calhoun insisted that "when orders were transcended, investigation, as a matter of course, ought to follow."[117] Fully cognizant that his political opponents were using the incident to discredit him with Jackson, the vice president warned. "I should be blind not to see, that this whole affair is a political manoeuvre."[118] Jackson informed Calhoun that his reply was unsatisfactory. "Anxious to contradict inaccurate press accounts of his quarrel with the president, Calhoun published the correspondence in the *United States' Telegraph* of February 17 and 25, 1831, prefaced with a lengthy explanation addressed 'To the People of the United States.'"[119] Knowing of Jackson's unhappiness of the treatment of Peggy Eaton, the wife of his secretary of war, John Eaton, Van Buren deftly handled the Eaton malaise by offering a strategy to allow Jackson "to clear his cabinet of John C. Calhoun and other divisive forces."[120] Van Buren and Eaton resigned in 1831, and as he expected, the rest of the Cabinet did likewise. Members of the new cabinet were mostly men loyal to Van Buren, so he knew he was not at risk by being out of the White House.[121]

Minister to England: Jackson rewarded his crafty friend with a recess appointment of Van Buren minister to the Court of St. James's (ambassador to Great Britain). When the little New Yorker arrived in London in September, he was cordially received, where he worked to expand the U.S. consular presence in British manufacturing centers. In February, he was shocked to learn that his nomination had been rejected by the Senate on January 25, 1832. The rejection was the work of Vice President Calhoun. The vote was staged to be a tie when enough of the majority refrained from voting give Calhoun his "vengeance" by voting nay. The Senate's rejection backfired, creating sympathy for Van Buren.[122] "Jackson was deeply angered by the rejection, and Calhoun's chances of remaining as vice president were over. Jackson selected Van Buren to be his running mate in the election of 1832."[123] Calhoun resigned on December 28, 1832, before the end of his term — the first vice president to do so — to take a seat in the Senate. Calhoun was the first vice president in U.S. history to resign from office (Spiro Agnew did so in 1973).[124] Van Buren's campaign to oust Calhoun as Jackson's heir apparent and substitute himself was complete. "Van Buren found every reason imaginable to remain abroad after learning of his rejection by the Senate. He could not break his lease or abruptly discharge his servants, he protested, nor could he pack up his household on such short notice. But his biographer suggests that he delayed his departure because he believed that the 'opposition would splinter ... if left alone; it stood a good chance of coalescing if he returned with undue haste for vindication.'"[125] The cunning Van Buren was still in Europe when Democratic delegates gathered at Baltimore on May 21, 1832, and by an overwhelming margin, chose him as Jackson's running mate on the first ballot.[126]

His Vice Presidency: While vice president (1833–1837), Van Buren publicly supported Jackson on all issues except the withdrawing of funds from the Bank of the United States, though he supported the move after it was made. "He feared that Jackson's removal of the government's deposits from the Bank before the expiration of its charter might produce a major schism in the party."[127] In the nullification crisis over the hated tariff, led by Calhoun, now back in the Senate, Van Buren moved the Jacksonians into the nationalist camp of Daniel Webster. President Jackson proclaimed that both nullification and secession were unconstitutional. Van Buren moved to avoid a direct collision between state and federal governments and to remove a festering grievance. "In order to avert civil war, Calhoun reluctantly collaborated with his political opponent Henry Clay" and Vice President Van Buren "to craft the Compromise Tariff of 1833."[128] Presiding over the Senate was among Van Buren's most challenging and frustrating tasks. It required all of his legendary tact and good humor. Things were so contentious in the U.S. Senate that Van Buren presided over it with "loaded pistols."[129] "During one particularly heated March session, Clay addressed him directly, pleading with him to tell Jackson 'in the language of truth and sincerity, the actual condition of his bleeding country.' Van Buren listened politely as Clay, obviously playing to the galleries, reminded him of his 'well-known influence' in the administration. At the conclusion of Clay's remarks, Van Buren handed the gavel to Hugh Lawson White and stepped down from the dais. Clay rose to his feet as the vice president deliberately approached his desk, and the crowds in the galleries fell silent. Then, with a deep bow, and a voice dripping with sarcasm, Van Buren returned fire: 'Mr. Senator, allow me to be indebted to you for another pinch of your aromatic Maccoboy.' The galleries erupted in a wave of laughter as Clay, speechless and humiliated, gestured helplessly at the snuff on his desk. Van Buren helped himself and returned to the chair, all the while maintaining his studied composure."[130]

Campaign of 1836: Van Buren was unanimously nominated for president by the Democrats in 1836. The newly formed Whig Party developed a scheme to get the election thrown into the House of Representatives, where they believed they had a better chance of winning. They chose four candidates, William Henry Harrison of Ohio representing the West, Daniel Webster of Massachusetts representing the Northeast, and Hugh Lawson White of Tennessee and Willie Pearson Magnum of North Carolina representing the South.[131]

Before the election Van Buren made clear his opposition to rechartering the Bank of the United States:

> To these sentiments I have now only to add the expression of an increased conviction that the reestablishment of such a bank in any form, whilst it would not accomplish the beneficial purpose promised by its advocates, would impair the rightful supremacy of the popular will, injure the character and diminish the influence of our political system, and bring once more into existence a concentrated moneyed power, hostile to the spirit and threatening the permanency of our republican institutions.[132]

Van Buren was elected president with 51 percent of the popular vote and 170 electoral votes. Harrison came in second with 36 percent of the popular vote and 73 electoral votes. White's totals were 10 percent and 26 electoral votes, while Webster brought up the rear with 3 percent and 14 electoral votes. Willie P. Magnum, who wasn't a declared candidate, received the 11 electoral votes of South Carolina.[133] In his inaugural address on March 4, 1837, Van Buren acknowledged Andrew Jackson and others who had served as president of the United States:

> I tread in the footsteps of illustrious men ... in receiving from the people the sacred trust confided to my illustrious predecessor.... Unlike all who have preceded me, the Revolution that gave us existence as one people was achieved at the period of my birth, and whilst I contemplate with reverence that memorable event, I feel that I belong to a later age and that I may not expect my countrymen to weigh my actions in the same kind and partial hand.... How imperious, then, is the obligation imposed upon every citizen, in his own sphere of action, whether limited or extended, to exert himself in perpetuating a condition of things so singularly happy! All the lessons

of history and experience must be lost upon us if we are content to trust alone to the peculiar advantages we happen to possess.... I desire to declare that the principle that will govern me in the high duty to which my country calls me is a strict adherence to the letter and spirit of the Constitution as it was designed by those who framed it.[134]

His Presidency

Van Buren "announced his intention 'to follow in the footsteps of his illustrious predecessor,' and retained all but one of Jackson's cabinet."[135] but he was unable to promote his own agenda as well as he had done that of Jackson. The contrast between the two men was as day to night. Jackson was a celebrated, charismatic hero. Van Buren operated most effectively behind the scenes, away from public scrutiny, an advantage he would not have as president. "In his later years Van Buren realized sadly that the wizardry had failed, that the political system he had helped to create would not prevent civil war."[136] "If Andrew Jackson was the symbol of a political renaissance in the United States, Martin Van Buren was its chief architect and prime beneficiary."[137] Van Buren successfully manufactured the popular image of Jackson as the simple backwoods representative of the common people. However, "in Tennessee he was allied by marriage, business, and political ties to the state's elite. As a land speculator, cotton planter, and attorney, he accumulated a large personal fortune and acquired more than 100 slaves. His candidacy for the presidency was initially promoted by speculators, creditors, and elite leaders in Tennessee who hoped to exploit Jackson's popularity in order to combat anti-banking sentiment and fend off challenges to their dominance of state politics."[138] Jackson's electoral victories were as due to the organizational skills of Martin Van Buren skills as Jackson's magnetism.[139] "Van Buren was also better attuned to Old Republican antistatism than the irascible, impulsive, and militaristic Old Hickory."[140] Jackson's reputation didn't help and probably actually hurt Van Buren. "Plagued from the start of his presidency with the knowledge that he would not be able to match the record and success of his predecessor, it seemed that Van Buren just decided to follow in Jackson's wake. Although Van Buren was both elegant and sophisticated, he was misunderstood, and it didn't matter how much he played into the fact that he was Jackson's 'hand-picked successor'; the U.S. public still appeared to miss their 'Old Hickory.'"[141]

Van Buren's administration was ravaged by an economic depression of titanic proportions, in great part due to the economic policies of Jackson's presidency. "Whigs were quick to blame the nation's economic woes on Jackson and, by extension, on Van Buren, sometimes dubbed 'Martin Van Ruin' during this period. He had inherited a situation that one scholar has characterized as a 'potentially devastating emergency.'"[142] Van Buren, who so masterfully brokered compromises during his predecessor's administration was put to the test during his own and found wanting. "Van Buren's solution was to 'divorce' the government from the banking sector by establishing a treasury independent of the state bank-based system that, contrary to Jackson's expectations, had fuelled the speculative frenzy of the mid–1830s. Whigs succeeded in blocking this initiative until 1840, when Congress finally passed an independent treasury bill. In the meantime, the panic gave way to a depression of unprecedented severity. Up to one third of the factory workers in some northeastern towns were thrown out of work; in the South, vast expanses of once productive farmland went untilled. Prices of food and other necessities skyrocketed, with soup kitchens the only source of sustenance for many destitute residents of Washington, D.C., and other cities."[143] On another front, Van Buren's "failure to find a middle ground on the most pressing issues of his day — such as the growing regional conflict over slavery — eroded his effectiveness."[144] Van Buren restored the Cabinet's traditional role, discontinuing Jackson's practice of turning to an informal group of advisors. Van Buren sought advice from his Cabinet members, especially during times of domestic and foreign turmoil, when they met daily. At their first meeting, he proposed calling on each member of the Cabinet to give their views on issues before them.[145] "When it was suggested that Van Buren, as chairman of the Cabinet, should give his views first, Van Buren declined. He encouraged open exchanges between his counselors, preserving for himself the role of "a mediator, and to some extent an umpire between the conflicting opinions." In this way, the president could reserve judgment and maintain his prerogative for making final decisions.[146] In an effort to restore party harmony, the president sought out the aid of key Democrats in Congress, where discord and rancor had festered during the nullification crisis.[147]

His Vice President: Richard M. Johnson, the former Kentucky Democrat and military hero, was the only vice president selected by the U.S. Senate. No one received a majority of electoral votes for the vice presidency since Virginia electors cast its votes for William Smith because slave owners objected that Johnson, who never married, had two daughters with his slave mistress Julia Chinn. As a result, Johnson failed by one vote of the number needed to be declared elected. The election went to the Senate, which overwhelmingly chose Johnson.[148]

His Cabinet: Secretary of State John Forsyth (1837–1841); Secretary of the Treasury Levi Woodbury (1837–1841); Secretary of War Joel R. Poinsett (1837–1841); Attorney General Benjamin F. Butler (1837–1838), Felix Grundy (1838–1839) and Henry D. Gilpin (1840–1841); Postmaster General Amos Kendall (1837–1840) and John M. Niles (1840–1841); Secretary of the Navy Mahlon Dickerson (1837–1838) and James K. Paulding (1838–1841).

Richard Mentor Johnson, photograph, created between 1900 and 1912 by Detroit Publishing, of a painting by artist John Neagle (Library of Congress, Detroit Publishing Company Photograph Collection).

Supreme Court Appointments: John Catron (1837), John McKinley (1838), Peter Vivian Daniel (1842).

DOMESTIC AFFAIRS — MAJOR EVENTS

Panic of 1837: Warnings of a major economic crisis spread from the beginning of the campaign of 1836. During the first week in office, President Van Buren was warned by both Democrats and Whigs of an impending crisis. "Whig leaders saw Van Buren as a 'wiser and better man than Jackson' even if he was a Democrat. They hoped they could convince him to act immediately to avert an economic disaster."[149] The signs were there: inflation soared, fed by a huge increase in cotton prices. There were extensive reports of potential bank closings, and workers in New York City rioted to protest food prices. A prominent New York Democrat businessman warned Van Buren that Jackson's policies had "brought this flourishing country to the eve of a fiscal revolution."[150] President Jackson left office having paid off the national debt for the first and only time. Not a penny was owed to anyone, foreign or domestic. In 1824, Jackson had written that "a national debt is a national curse."[151] "Income to the federal government from tariffs and the sale of public land in the West soon created a surplus in the U.S. Treasury."[152] As it turned out this was not to be such a good thing. Huge sums of money that should have been in circulation and returned to the states were idly held in the treasury. "Banks began to overextend credit by issuing notes far in excess of the gold and silver, or specie, that they actually had in their vaults ... so-called wildcat (financially unsound) banks, especially in the West, issued notes of their own that were backed by insufficient specie reserves. Soon the ratio of paper notes to gold or silver was 12 to 1: $12 of paper money was in circulation for every $1 of gold or silver in the nation's banks. The result was runaway inflation: people had little confidence in the money, so they spent it faster and prices went higher. Since the federal government accepted paper money for the Western land it was selling, the Treasury was filled with bank notes of doubtful value."[153]

"Members of Congress responded to pressures from home and passed a measure distributing the surplus to the states. The windfall was quickly invested in further internal improvement projects— more railroads and canals."[154] Speculation went wild, "western swamps and woods and rock and prairie sold for the value of improved land"[155] in the East and South. Most state governments, as well as individuals, preferred to hoard gold and silver, and to discharge debts with paper money. "Strengthened with federal deposits and with no central bank to control the bank note issuing, state banks went on a lending spree, leading to high inflation. Fearful of paper currency's decreased value, Andrew Jackson issued the 'Specie Circular' executive order in 1836, which required the purchase of all government lands had to be done exclusively by gold and silver. The rush to redeem paper money with hard currency from banks with insufficient reserves led to the economic crash known as the 'Panic of 1837.'"[156]

Van Buren's administration inherited a "superheated economy that was completely unregulated in some ways, and draconically controlled in others."[157] On the day of Van Buren's inauguration, J.L. & S. Joseph & Co., one of the nation's most prominent trading houses suspended payments. "In May 1837 New York banks ceased specie payments to investors, leading other banks across the nation to do the same. With no coin to back it paper currency lost its value. During a brief ensuing time span many companies crashed and fortunes were lost. Unemployment skyrocketed, especially in the West and South with a loss of agricultural exports and crop failures. Public calls for banking reform increased as a six-year depression followed."[158] Jackson's "hard money" fiscal policies were only partly to blame for the panic. "An unfavorable balance of trade with England deepened instability" and a sharp decline in the price of American cotton also contributed to the crisis, which was international in scope.[159] In his biography of Martin Van Buren, historian Edward M. Shepherd described the situation: "Fancied wealth sank out of sight. Paper symbols of new cities and towns, canals and roads were not only without value, but they were now plainly seen to be so. Rich men became poor men. The prices of articles in which there had been speculation sank in the reaction far below their true value."[160]

Another contributing factor was Jackson's opposition to the national bank. "In his crusade against the bankers and moving the Fed's reserves to state banks, Jackson created the conditions that the state banks could cause this credit bubble."[161] Paper money was utterly discredited and specie almost completely disappeared. "Banks suspended payment on specie, and for the next three years, the country was beset by unemployment and extreme financial difficulties."[162] An accompanying crop failure added to the problem. As construction companies were unable to meet their obligations, many railroad and canal projects failed, leading to the ruin of thousands of land speculators. "Prices of many commodities had ... been enhanced by speculation beyond all proper relation to other commodities, measured by the ultimate standard of the quantity and quality of labor."[163]

"It was generally held that the government should abstain from interfering with the country's general economic life, so Van Buren did nothing to alleviate the effects of the depression."[164] He "was inundated with urgent requests that he act to halt the inflationary spiral. Most correspondents urged the new president to reconsider the Specie Circular of 1836."[165]

"The desperate New York commercial community genuinely sought economic relief from the president, but they did not actually expect Van Buren to find an immediate solution to the crisis. Rather, their appeal to Van Buren should be understood as a gesture designed to reaffirm their status in the eyes of the public. By implying that the Federal government could provide an economic panacea, the New Yorkers laid a publicity trap for the President. If Van Buren offered assistance after the New Yorkers' appeal, Whigs could claim political victory over Democrats. If Van Buren failed to help, Whigs could blame the turmoil of the panic and horrors of the coming depression on the paralysis of Democratic leadership."[166] It was a win-win situation for the merchants and bankers. Bankers accused the Jackson "substitution of metallic for paper currency"[167] meant that both Whig and Democrat constituencies would suffer, and implied what turned out to be so, that "Van Buren would bear the burden of the erosion of credit."[168] In their shrewdly written entreaty, penned by Isaac Hone, the privileged elites of New York City represented themselves as concerned national commercial leaders. They entreated Van Buren to act in behalf of families and democracy by interposing "the paternal authority of the Government, and abandon the policy, which is beggaring the People."[169] On May 4, 1837, unmoved by the appeal, Van Buren penned his response in which he refused to act, saying he found it "inconsistent with the public good and with my official duty to take either of the steps proposed."[170] "He blamed the merchants in New York and the rest of the nation for the panic ... and refused to accept the commercial crisis as his problem."[171] He insisted that government manipulation would only further weaken the economic structure. "True to Jacksonian laissez-faire philosophy, Van Buren called for the creation of an independent treasury system that would separate the federal government from the banking system. The Independent Treasury Bill, passed in 1840, had no real impact on the economy, however. Furthermore, it alienated many of Van Buren's fellow Democrats."[172] In making this recommendation, the president told a special session of Congress on September 4, 1837, "All communities are apt to look to government for too much. If therefore, I refrain from suggesting to Congress any specific plan for regulating the exchanges of the country, relieving mercantile embarrassments, or interfering with the ordinary operations of foreign or domestic commerce, it is from a conviction that such measures are not within the constitutional province of the general Government."[173]

"In recommending an independent treasury to the new Congress, he abandoned the conciliatory language of the past. He blamed renewed financial failures on foreign investors and state banks, urging Congress to adopt measures to safeguard the country from further speculative crazes. For the first time, he urged that all government revenue be collected and disbursed in gold and silver. This provision, coupled with the proposed subtreasury system, would have 'a salutary influence on the system of paper credit with which all banks are connected.' Although careful to recognize that some banks were already 'sound and well managed,' Van Buren advocated the subtreasury system as a mechanism for reform and regulation of the nation's economy. He told supporters that he had taken 'strong ground' that he hoped would break the congressional deadlock."[174]

In a message to a special session of the Senate and House of Representatives on September 4, 1837, Van Buren announced the following:

> There can be no doubt that those who framed and adopted the Constitution, having in immediate view the depreciated paper of the Confederacy — of which $500 in paper were at times only equal to $1 in coin — intended to prevent the recurrence of similar evils, so far at least as related to the transactions of the new Government. They gave to Congress express powers to coin money and to regulate the value thereof and of foreign coin; they refused to give it power to establish corporations— the agents then as now chiefly employed to create a paper currency; they prohibited the States from making anything but gold and silver a legal tender in payment of debts, and the first Congress directed by positive law that the revenue should be received in nothing but gold or silver.... It is our duty to provide all the remedies against a depreciated paper currency which the Constitution enables us to afford.[175]

In his third annual message to Congress, President Van Buren spoke of his belief in the country's recovery from its financial difficulties:

> By ceasing to run in debt and applying the surplus of our crops and incomes to the discharge of existing obligations ... we shall see our country soon recover from a temporary depression.... Fortunately for us at this moment, when the balance of trade is greatly against us and the difficulty of meeting it enhanced by the disturbed state of our money affairs, the bounties of Providence have come to relieve us from the consequences of past errors.... Our surplus profits, the energy and industry of our population, and the wonderful advantages which Providence has bestowed upon our country ... will in due time afford abundant means.[176]

Jeffrey Rogers Hummel relates in "Martin Van Buren: The American Gladstone" that "Van Buren's closest political advisors privately urged him to start a foreign war in order to distract public attention from the administration's domestic difficulties."[177]

The Independent Treasury Bill passed in 1840 by a vote of 24 to 18 in the Senate and 124 to 117 in the House. It ushered in "an era of financial deregulation at the national level. Although repealed in 1841, after the Whigs captured the White House, they could not agree among themselves about an alternative."[178] Despite being disapproved by Congress, "the independent treasury existed. By the conditions of the circular on bank suspensions, the collection, keeping and paying of federal monies continued to be done by federal officers."[179] The economic depression was due to the policies of Jackson, but "Van Buren got the blame for it, even though it occurred only two months after he took office, and effectively killed any chances of his ever achieving popularity."[180] Further damaging to his presidency, Van Buren was criticized for his enjoyment of the finer things of life, accused of being a dandy who did not understand the problems of the average American. It's true that Van Buren's "Manhattan tailor dressed him in latest styles. A fine horseman, he rode spirited mounts, and his carriage with its soft satin lining, 'V.B.' imperiously engraved on its silver buckles, was positively regal."[181] Whig Congressman Landaff Watson Andrews, from Kentucky, attended one of Van Buren's White House dinners. He picked up a "golden spoon" from the table and said, "Mr. Van Buren, if you will let me take this spoon to Kentucky and show it to my constituents, I will promise not to make use of any other argument against you: this will be enough."[182] Andrews later denied that he had ever said such a thing to the president. But the story was too good not to use by a little-known Whig from Pennsylvania named Charles Ogle, who delivered a filibuster in which he lambasted the president for spending $4,675 in improvements to the White House. Ogle then accused Van Buren of eating with golden spoons. The attack gained the name "The Golden Spoon Oration."[183] It went to press immediately and was distributed as a string-bound pamphlet in tens of thousands. It found its way to the newspaper offices across the nation. Many have claimed that it was one of the most amusing speeches made at the time, and rivaled in humor, the works of Mark Twain.[184] Van Buren was unable to ignore being "the butt of popular merriment." He sought some authority that would help redeem him. This was accomplished in the statement: "I, William Noland, Commissioner of Public Buildings, do certify that no gold knives or forks or spoons of any description have been purchased for the President's house since Mr. Van Buren became the Chief Magistrate of the Nation."[185] Van Buren never understood why he was being attacked so by his critics, saying, "Why the deuce is it that they have such an itching for abusing me. I try to be harmless and positively good natured & a most decided friend of peace."[186]

Second Seminole War: Van Buren continued President Jackson's policies towards the Seminole Indians. Because the latter harbored fugitive slaves, the war in Florida was intertwined with concessions made to slaveholders.[187] In 1842, the Second Seminole War ended with the Native Americans' defeat. "Van Buren had 3500 of the 4000 Seminole Indians removed from the State of Florida ... in a war which had caused 1500 casualties to U.S. forces."[188] The conflict, which began in 1835 prior to Van Buren's inauguration, degenerated into a vicious and expensive struggle that wasn't concluded until 1842, when then President John Tyler finally ended it.[189] "The conflict cost the government between 40 and 60 million dollars."[190]

Trail of Tears: The forced removal of some 18,000 Cherokees, most of them from Georgia, to the Indian Territory west of the Mississippi, was ordered by President Jackson but executed during Van Buren's administration. "Van Buren's relations with Native American nations were not much more than an extension of the policies of his predecessor. Enforcing the Indian Removal Act of 1830, Van Buren's administration removed Cherokee and other native peoples from their homes to be relocated west of the Mississippi, an event known as the 'Trail of Tears' that resulted in the death of one quarter of the Cherokee nation."[191] The removal was widely denounced by humanists and constitutional experts. The Supreme Court ruled that the Indians had the legal right to their ancestral homes. Nevertheless, Jackson ordered the army, under the leadership of General Winfield Scott, to move the Indians out of Georgia. Van Buren did not interfere with the policy, despite the frequent criticism.[192]

In his first State of the Union Message in 1837, Van Buren reported:

Stipulations have been made with all Indian tribes to remove them beyond the Mississippi.... The resistance which has been opposed to their removal by some of the tribes even after treaties had been made with them, to that effect, has arisen from various causes, operating differently on each of them. In most instances, they have been instigated to resistance by persons to whom the trade with them and the acquisition of their annuities were important, and in some by the personal influence of interested chiefs. These obstacles must be overcome, for the Government cannot relinquish the execution of this policy without sacrificing important interests and abandoning the tribes remaining east of the Mississippi to certain destruction.... If they be removed, they can be protected from those associations and evil practices which exert so pernicious and destructive an influence over their destinies. They can be induced to labor and to acquire property, and in its acquisition will inspire them with a feeling of independence. Their minds can be cultivated, and they can be taught the value of salutary and uniform laws and be made sensible of the blessings of free government and capable of enjoying its advantages.[193]

In his second State of the Union message, Van Buren claimed "the United States have fulfilled in good faith all their treaty stipulations with the Indian tribes, and have in every other instance insisted upon a like performance of their obligations."[194]

Slavery: As a young man Mat owned a slave, but the man ran away and Van Buren made no great effort to bring him back. "But ten years later, in 1824, the escapee was discovered living in Worcester, Massachusetts, and at that point Van Buren agreed to sell him to another man if he could be captured 'without violence.'"[195] Van Buren came to oppose slavery in principle. "But as a matter of public policy, he adhered closely to his sense of the compromises that the Constitution and Congress had set up to preserve both slavery and the union. And as a politician trying to build a national party, he found himself obliged to accommodate growing southern anxieties about northern abolitionism over the 1830s. He was a northerner, a Yankee, of course, and that was enough to make him suspect in southern eyes. So in 1835, preparing to run for president, he had to assure southern politicians and editors that he did not oppose slavery in those states where it already existed, that he opposed abolitionism, and specifically that he opposed the campaign to abolish slavery in the District of Columbia."[196]

As president, he attempted to steer a middle course, avoiding the "taint of abolitionism on the one hand and utter capitulation to radical southern pro-slavery demands on the other."[197]

The *Amistad* Affair: A group of Africans from Sierra Leone, purchased as slaves by two Spanish planters, seized the Cuban ship *Amistad*, killing two of its crew. It was captured off Long Island by the U.S. brig *Washington*. "The planters were freed and the Africans were imprisoned in Connecticut on charges of murder. Although these charges were dropped, the Africans became the center of a case of salvage and property rights."[198] Newspaper editorials throughout the East explored the legal questions presented by the slaves' mutiny and their capture. Even editors unsympathetic to the abolitionist cause hesitated over pronouncing the Africans guilty. "We despise the humbug doctrines of the abolitionists and the miserable fanatics who propagate them; but if men will traffic in human flesh, steal men from their homes on the coast of Africa, and sell them like cattle at Cuba, they must not murmur if some of the men stealers get murdered by the unfortunate wretches whom they have wronged and stole. It is certain that the Spanish Government, at Havana, recognizing the right to steal, buy and sell blacks, will, instantly demand the slaves of this government; it is also possible that this government will give up the men, and sell the vessel and cargo for salvage; in that case it is also certain that every one of the male blacks, who rose on the captain will be executed."[199]

"Van Buren was not in Washington when the affair broke; he was campaigning in upstate New York. His cabinet therefore formulated the administration's initial response: meeting in mid–September, they took [Secretary of State] Forsyth's lead and arranged for federal authorities to support Spanish demands that the slaves be returned to Cuba to face trial as murderers and pirates. Van Buren soon returned to the capital, but he seems to have paid little attention to the matter, letting Forsyth continue to handle the situation. The president did not replace any judges in the case. But he did put federal attorneys on the case and he did sign off on an effort to have the Africans shipped immediately to Cuba if the court found for the administration, before any appeals could be filed. In sum, Van Buren wanted this problem to go away, cleanly and quietly. From his point of view, this was not only a potential diplomatic crisis with Spain, but more fundamentally a slave revolt — a dangerous provocation to southerners already unsettled by the rise of northern abolitionism."[200] Van Buren signed the orders for the transport of the *Amistad* captives, prepared by Forsyth: "The Marshal of the United States for the District of Connecticut will deliver over to Lieutenant John S. Paine, of the United States Navy, and aid in conveying on board the schooner *Grampus*, under his command all the negroes late of the Spanish schooner *Amistad*, in the custody under process now pending before the District Court of the United States for the District of Connecticut. For so doing this order will be his warrant."[201]

Northern abolitionists raised funds to defend the Africans. At a trial in the federal district court in Connecticut, Judge Andrew Judson ruled that the Africans "were born free and ever since have been and still of right are free and not slaves."[202] That should have been the end of the matter, but the government appealed Judson's decision, which was upheld by Circuit Judge Thomson. Van Buren, still fearful of the consequences of the verdict to his re-election, ordered federal prosecutors to appeal the verdict to the U.S. Supreme Court. Former president John Quincy Adams defended the accused and argued for their rights to regain their freedom. The court decided in favor of the Africans, and the survivors were returned to their homeland in Africa.[203]

Later Van Buren became an uncompromising force against the expansion of slavery and remained so until his death after the Civil War began. "After working behind the scenes among the anti-slavery Democrats, Van Buren joined in the movement that led to the Free-Soil Party, which 'sought to stem the extension of slavery' and became its candidate for president in 1848. He subsequently returned to the Democratic Party while continuing to object to its pro–Southern policy."[204]

Texas: The northern states opposed granting statehood to the newly independent Texas, as it would enter the Union as another slave state. "Van Buren refused to support expansionist Democrats, fearing further damage to the North-South axis of the party."[205] Another reason for his opposition to the annexation was to "avert a war with Mexico, which had not recognized the independence of its lost province."[206] His decision was unpopular and cost him the Democratic nomination for president in 1844. In 1838, the Texan emissary Memuscan Hunt wrote of it: "Many of our friends as well as enemies in Congress dread the coming of the question at this time on account of the desperate death-struggle, which they foresee, will inevitably ensue between the North and the South, a struggle involving the probability of dissolution of this Union."[207]

FOREIGN AFFAIRS — MAJOR EVENTS

In his inaugural address, President Van Buren spoke of his administration's foreign policies:

> We sedulously cultivate the friendship of all nations as the conditions most compatible with our welfare and the principles of our Government. We decline alliances as adverse to our peace. We desire commercial relations on equal terms, being ever willing to give a fair equivalent for advantages received. We endeavor to conduct our intercourse with openness, and sincerity, promptly avowing our objects and seeking to establish that mutual frankness which is beneficial in the dealings of the nations of men.[208]

Van Buren acted swiftly and surely in times of international tension. His handling of crises on the northern and southern borders of the nation revealed his sincere and consistent commitment to neutrality and peaceful settlement of disputes. While presidents who have led the United States into wars get most of the glory, there is much to be said for those who

Destruction of the *Caroline* steamboat, photograph created between 1900 and 1920 of a print of the steamer *Caroline*, which was burned by the British in December 1837 for supplying the Canadian rebellion and drifted over Niagara Falls (Library of Congress, Detroit Publishing Company Photograph Collection).

prevented conflicts. In his fourth annual message to Congress on December 5, 1840, Van Buren explained: "A faithful observance in the management of our foreign relations of the practice of speaking plainly, dealing justly, and requiring truth and justice in return [are] the best conservatives of the peace of nations."[209]

Caroline Affair: In an effort to help Canada in its rebellion against British rule in 1837, a revolutionary group led by William Lyon Mackenzie attacked Navy Island, which was a short distance above Niagara Falls on the Canadian-American border. "Many in the United States were sympathetic to the rebels, seeing them as successors to the American independence movement."[210] Americans leased the U.S. paddle-wheel steamship *Caroline*, a forty-six ton vessel, to run supplies to Navy Island for the support of Canadian revolutionaries. "Late in December, Canadian loyalists crossed into American territory, cut the Caroline loose and allowed it to drift over Niagara Falls. One U.S. citizen was killed in the incident and American outrage quickly followed."[211] The ship sank before it reached the falls, but rumors of the raid quickly spread and exaggerated the outcome. It was claimed that forty unarmed Americans were butchered in cold blood while sleeping, by a party of British assassins who then sent the living and the dead in the ship hurling over the falls. "In retaliation, the British steamship Robert Peel was attacked and burned and several small raiding parties went into Canada."[212]

Van Buren was upset with both the British and the Americans involved in the affair.

In a message to Congress, he announced, "I regret ... to inform you that an outrage of the most aggravated character has been committed, accompanied by a hostile though temporary invasion of our territory, producing the strongest feelings of resentment on the part of our citizens in the neighborhood and on the whole border line, and that the excitement previously existing has been alarmingly increased."[213] The president sent a force commanded by General Winfield Scott to call out the militia, but he was to employ it only as a last resort and avoid putting arms into the hands of border residents, who might join the rebellion. Van Buren then issued a "neutrality proclamation calling for strict adherence to the law."[214] These combined actions defused the border crisis.

Aroostook War: Another issue between the United States and British-held Canada was the so-called, nonviolent, Aroostook War, a border dispute over a thousand miles along the Maine/Canadian border on the Aroostook River. The Treaty of Paris in 1783, between the United States and Great Britain, specified the location of the border between New Brunswick and the Maine territory: "From the northwest angle of Nova Scotia, to wit, that angle which is formed by a line drawn due north from the source of the St. Croix river to the highlands, along the said highlands which divide those rivers that empty themselves into the St. Lawrence, and those which fall into the Atlantic ocean, to the northwestern most head of the Connecticut river."[215] This inexact sketch was interpreted quite differently by the neighboring countries. The immense region had not been explored or mapped, and at the time the description of the border was composed, the actual geography of the area was unknown.

Lumberjacks from the two countries disputed the ownership of the area's more than seven million acres of virgin timber. "In January 1839, Canadian authorities arrested a Maine land agent and took him to a New Brunswick jail. New Brunswick's lieutenant governor, Sir John Harvey, justified the arrest and issued a proclamation calling for withdrawal of all American forces from the disputed region. Maine's governor, John Fairfield, assembled nearly a thousand men and asked the state legislature for money and authority to call out another ten thousand."[216] When Van Buren learned of the local combustible situation, he feared it could lead to another war with Great Britain. The president appealed to the British minister, Henry Fox, and together they "drew up a memorandum calling for all parties to withdraw from the Aroostook Valley."[217] Governor Fairfield angrily denounced the president's call for peace. "Should you go against us on this occasion, or not espouse our cause with warmth and earnestness and with true American feeling, God only knows what the result would be politically."[218] Van Buren took little note of this empty threat. Once again the president sent General Scott to maintain the peace. He arranged a truce, and both parties agreed to refer the dispute to a boundary commission. The issue was settled in 1842 by the Webster-Ashburton Treaty. The compromise awarded 7,015 acres to the United States and 5,102 to Great Britain.[219]

AFTER THE PRESIDENCY

Campaign of 1840: Van Buren was denied reelection in 1840 by William Henry Harrison, who received 53 percent of the popular vote and 234 electoral votes. Van Buren received 47 percent of the popular vote and 60 electoral votes. The Whigs unfairly painted Van Buren as a wealthy man, one ignorant of and disdainful toward the common people, who suffered because of "his" economic depression.[220] Van Buren labeled the results of the election a "catastrophe," due more to Whig fraud than Democratic collapse. "Time will unravel the means by which these results have been produced," he wrote to Andrew Jackson, "and then the people will do justice to all."[221]

In his farewell address, Van Buren warned one final time about a national bank: "A concentrated money power, wielding so vast a capital and combining such incalculable means of influence would inevitably prove an overmatch of the political power of the people themselves."[222]

Van Buren tried for the Democratic nomination in 1844, but was unable to win support from the South due to his opposition to the annexation of Texas. The convention chose James K. Polk.[223] In 1848 Van Buren headed the Free Soil Party ticket, which opposed extension of slavery, but he knew he had no chance of returning to the White House. In his acceptance letter, Van Buren laid it on the line regarding slavery and the working class:

> The future condition of the respective States in regard to the probable continuance or abolition of slavery was correctly foreseen at the formation of the Government. Those of the Old Thirteen which are now exempt from it, acted under a confident anticipation that they would soon become so; while those of the number where slavery still exists, could not look forward to an equally favorable result in regard to themselves.... From the first institution of government to the present time there has been a struggle going on between capital and labor for a fair distribution of profits resulting from their joint capacities.[224]

His running mate was Charles Francis Adams, son of President John Quincy Adams and grandson of President John Adams. Their slogan was "free soil, free speech, free labor, and free men."[225] They siphoned off enough votes from the Democratic candidate, Lewis Cass of Michigan, to ensure the election of Zachary Taylor, the Whig candidate. However, they didn't receive any electoral votes.[226]

Retirement: Van Buren was ever "a prudent man, of frugal habits, living within his means, and in his declining years enjoyed his estate as a wealthy and cultured man of leisure."[227] He was "pampered by his daughters-in-law, honored by his neighbors and had many famous visitors."[228] During a European trip of two years' duration, he wrote his memoirs.[229] President Harry Truman, always handy with an opinion of others who held the office, said this of Van Buren:

> I've got to say our country would have done just as well as not to have Van Buren as president.... My particular reason for not thinking much of him is that he was just too timid and indecisive. I don't know whether or not he even had any personal philosophy on the role of government. I think he was a man who was always worrying about what might have happened if he did this or that, and always keeping his ear to the ground to the point where he couldn't act as the chief executive, and for that reason he was just a politician and nothing more, a politician who was out of his depth.[230]

His Books: *Inquiry into the Origin and Course of Political Parties in the United States*, 1867; *The Autobiography of Martin Van Buren*, John C. Fitzpatrick, editor, 1920.

His Papers: Martin Van Buren's papers are contained on 55 microfilm reels, a collection produced by Chadwyck-Healey in 1989. Not as comprehensive is the Library of Congress' 35-reel microfilm collection of Van Buren's papers.

Health: At various periods in his life Van Buren suffered from dyspepsia associated with stress. He treated the affliction with water, soot, and powered charcoal.[231] During his 50s, he developed gout caused in part from his diet and heavy wine consumption. During the summer of 1840 he gained temporary relief from this ailment with a stay at a spa in White Sulfur Springs, New York.[232] When he was 71, Van Buren was treated for the ailment at Aix-les-Bains in France.[233] In his final illness, he declared, "The atonement of Jesus Christ is the only remedy and rest for my soul."[234]

Death: In early 1862, Van Buren was attended by Dr. Alonzo Clark of New York City

Marching banner for Van Buren on the Free Soil Ticket in the presidential race of 1848: Martin Van Buren and Charles Francis Adams lithograph published by Nathaniel Currier, c. 1848, from daguerreotypes by John Plumbe (Library of Congress).

The Buffalo Hunt, lithograph published by H.R. Robinson, 1848. An optimistic view of the presidential prospects of Martin Van Buren in 1848. Van Buren rides a buffalo and thumbs his nose as he sends Democratic candidate Lewis Cass and Whig Zachary Taylor flying (Library of Congress, American Cartoon Print Series).

for an asthma-like condition. The ex-president returned to his upstate home in May. He was very weak and became largely bed bound. In mid–July, he developed signs of circulatory failure. On July 21 he became comatose and died three days later.[235] He had lived long enough to see the southern states secede from the Union. Van Buren's last public statement before his death was a declaration: "[I offer my] earnest and vigorous support to the Lincoln administration for ... the maintenance of the Union and the Constitution."[236]

 Place of Death: Van Buren died at his estate, Lindenwald, at Kinderhook.

 Cause of Death: His cause of death has been given as heart failure, a complication of his "old enemy," bronchial asthma.[237]

 Final Words: "There is but one reliance, and that is upon Christ, the mediator of us all."[238] In his will, he asserted, "I, Martin Van Buren ... heretofore Governor of the State and more recently President of the United States, but for the last and happiest years of my life, a farmer in my native town...."[239]

 Place of Burial: After Van Buren's funeral, 81 carriages, including that of the governor of New York, followed his hearse to the cemetery. He is buried in the family plot at the Kinderhook Reformed Cemetery, which dates from 1817. Near him are buried his wife, his parents, and his son Martin Jr. Over Van Buren's grave is a "plain granite shaft," fifteen feet high, bearing a simple inscription about halfway up on one face, which the passing of the years has faded away. The lot is unfenced, unbordered and unbounded by any shrubs or flowers. A memorial ceremony is held annually on the president's birthday.[240] At the time of his death the trustees of the village of Kinderhook passed the resolution: "That in Mr.

Van Buren we recognize the profound jurist and statesman, who without the aid of adventitious circumstances, by the force of native talent, severe study and untiring industry attained successively and by quick gradation distinguished posts of honor and trust in the State and Nation."[241]

MISCELLANEA

Presidential Trivia and First: Van Buren was the first president born after the signing of the Declaration of Independence, making him the first president born a citizen of the United States.[242] In 1692 one of his earlier cousins was hanged in Salem, Massachusetts, as a witch. On May 10, 1692, George Jacobs, Sr., and his granddaughter Margaret were examined before magistrates John Hathorne and Jonathan Corwin. Margaret confessed and testified that her grandfather and George Burroughs were both witches. Margaret said: "They told me if I would not confess I should be put down into the dungeon and would be hanged, but if I would confess I should save my life."[243] On August 19, George Jacobs, Sr., Martha Carrier, George Burroughs, John Proctor and John Willard were hanged on Gallows Hill. Jacobs' last words were: "Because I am falsely accused. I never did it."[244]

Van Buren was the only incumbent president to run for reelection without a vice presidential running mate. He made three unsuccessful tries for reelection. Van Buren took his entire presidential salary for his four years in office, $100,000, as a lump sum at the end of his term.[245]

O.K.: The term "O.K." allegedly comes from Van Buren, who grew up in Kinderhook, New York, and was known popularly as Old Kinderhook, or O.K. There were many apple orchards in Van Buren's home county. Back in the 1700s, apples from the area were packed in crates marked "Old Kinderhook." Apparently people started referring to them as "O.K." apples. Gradually, the term was taken to mean a description of apples of "good quality" rather than their origin. After he went into politics, people asked "Is it OK?" referring to Van Buren.[246]

Was Martin Van Buren Aaron Burr's Illegitimate Son? A vicious rumor, whispered in Van Buren's campaign for president, survived into the 20th century that Burr was Van Buren's illegitimate father. In his novel *Burr*, Gore Vidal repeated the rumor that Aaron Burr had fathered the 8th president of the United States as a plot device. The narrator of the fictional piece is a fictional character Charles ("Charlie") Schuyler, a young man of Dutch descent working as an apprentice in Burr's New York law office some 30 years after the treason trial. Charlie is enlisted by Martin Van Buren to write a pamphlet proving that Van Buren is Burr's bastard son, which would ruin the future president's political career.[247] There is no evidence of this relationship, "except that Burr sometimes stopped overnight at the tavern in Kinderhook which was kept by Van Buren's putative father, and that Van Buren in later life showed an astuteness equal to that of Aaron Burr himself.... But, as Van Buren was born in December of the same year (1782) in which Burr was married to Theodosia Prevost, the story is utterly improbable when we remember, as we must, the ardent affection which Burr showed his wife, not only before their marriage, but afterward until her death."[248]

Loco-Foco Party: In the 1830s and 1840s, the Democratic Party was split into warring factions. In 1835, New York pro–Jackson Democrats organized the Equal Rights Party. Equal Righters were "primarily working men and reformers, who were opposed to state banks, monopolies, paper money, tariffs, and generally any financial policies that seemed to them antidemocratic and conducive to special privilege."[249] They won the nickname of Loco-

Foco when party regulars in New York turned off the gas lights to oust the radicals from a Tammany Hall nominating meeting. The radicals responded by lighting candles with the new self-igniting friction matches known by the brand name, loco-foco, and proceeded to nominate their own slate. When newspapers learned of the episode, they began calling the Equal Rights Party, the Loco-Focus Party. The Whig Party began applying the term loco-foco as a derogative label for all Democrats, implying the party members were loco, that is, "Crazy." "Foco" is probably derived from "fuego," Spanish for "fire."[250]

Fire at the White House: Once during a White House dinner party, a servant rushed into the dining room and whispered to the president, "The house is on fire!" Van Buren excused himself and followed the servant to the kitchen, where he helped put out the blaze. Returning to the table, he explained what has just transpired. Among the guests was his political opponent Henry Clay, who remarked as he put his hand to his heart, "I am doing all I can to get you out of this house, but believe me, I do not want to burn you out."[251]

Sunrise: Fellow politicians claimed that Van Buren was evasive and noncommittal, an equivocator. John Randolph of Virginia put it this way: "He rowed to his objective with muffled oars."[252] Most biographers tell the story of a friend who asked jokingly if Van Buren thought the sun rose in the east. His careful reply was, "I have heard that that is the common belief, however, I do not arise before dawn, so I could not say with any certainty."[253]

Van Buren and the Mormons: In 1838, Joseph Smith, the founder of the Mormon Church, visited Van Buren, pleading for the president to aid the 40,000 Mormon settlers of Independence, Missouri, who had been attacked, killed, raped, and forced off their lands. Lilburn Boggs, governor of Missouri, issued an executive order on October 27, 1838, known as the "Extermination Order." In it he authorized Missourians to "exterminate" Mormons and encouraged them to do so. Reportedly, the president's response to Smith was this: "Your cause is just, but I can do nothing for you. If I take up for you, I shall lose the vote of Missouri."[254] Smith has been quoted as saying of Van Buren, "His Majesty... to come directly to the point he is so much a fop or a fool ... we could find no place to put truth in him.... [M]ay he never be elected again to any office or trust or power."[255]

Edgar Allan Poe: "The Devil in the Belfry" is a short satirical comedy first published by Edgar Allan Poe in 1839. In the story, the little town of Vondervotteimittis is said to never have changed as long as anyone can remember. All the homes look the same, both inside and out, and everyone dresses exactly the same, with the exception that the more respect a person has in the town the longer are his coat-tails and the bigger his pipe and shoe buckles. The only things the inhabitants care about are cabbages and clocks. Everyone has a watch and all watches are synchronized. There is one very large town clock with seven faces that can be seen from every part of the town. At noon each day, the citizens pause long enough to count the 12 strokes of the clock. This perfectly set little town is thrown into an uproar when a devilish stranger arrives playing a large fiddle and goes directly into the belltower and kills the belfry-man. With the story, Poe is making fun of Martin Van Buren and his election methods. It can be seen as a satire of New York City, originally settled by the Dutch as New Amsterdam. The Devil represents the new immigrants—the Irish—as he plays a tune called "Judy O'Flannagan and Paddy O'Rafferty," which were stock names for Irish newcomers.[256]

Pithy Comments by Martin Van Buren

"Youth at the prow, and pleasure at the helm."[257]

"It is easier to do a job right than to explain why you didn't."[258]

"Most men are not scolded out of their opinion."[259]

"The second, sober thought of the people is seldom wrong, and always efficient."[260]

"The presidency in our system, like the king in a monarchy, never dies."[261]

"I hope, Judge, you are now satisfied that there is such a thing in politics as killing a man too dead."[262]

"Is it possible to be anything in this country without being a politician?"[263]

"Ignorance and vice bred poverty which was as immutable as the seasons."[264]

"The less government interferes with private pursuits, the better for general prosperity."[265]

Observations About Martin Van Buren

BY OTHER PRESIDENTS

[Van Buren was a] serious dough-face.... The most disgusting part of his character, his fawning servility, belonged neither to Jefferson or Madison. Van Buren is, like the Sosie of Molière's *Amphitryon*, "*l'ami de tout le monde.*" This is perhaps the great secret of his success in public life and especially against the competitors with whom he is now struggling for the last step on the ladder of his ambition.... Van Buren's principle is the talisman of democracy, which, so long as this Union lasts, can never fail.... His principles are all subordinate to his ambitions.[266]— John Quincy Adams

It is said that he is a great magician. I believe it, but his only wand is good common sense which he uses for the benefit of the country.[267]— Andrew Jackson

[I] believe him not only deserving of my confidence, but the confidence of the Nation.... He ... is not only well qualified, but desires to fill the highest office in the gift of the people, who in him will find a true friend and safe repository of their rights and liberty.[268]— Andrew Jackson

Mr. Van Buren became offended with me at the beginning of my administration because I chose to exercise my own judgment in the selection of my own Cabinet, and would not be controlled by him and suffer him to select it for me. Mr. Van Buren is the most fallen man I have ever known.[269]— James K. Polk

The grief of his patriotic friends, will measurably be assuaged by the consciousness that while ... seeing his end approaching, his prayers were for the restoration of the authority of the government of which he had been head, and for peace and good will among his fellow citizens.[270]— Abraham Lincoln

BY OTHERS

The masterpiece of his magic wand cast a spell over the heterogeneous mass, and the wolves and kids mingled together in peace and love.[271]— Anonymous

Even his best friends were apprehensive that he was overcautious and lacked the moral or political courage ... to meet those exigencies which might require bold and decisive action.[272]— Anonymous

[He is like] the fox prowling near the barn; the mole burrowing near the ground; the pilot fish who plunges deep in the ocean in one spot and comes up in another to breathe the air.[273]— Anonymous

We have heard it said of Mr. Van Buren with striking frequency and earnestness, among those friends who, from nearest and longest personal intercourse know him best, that as a man and statesman, he is "too good and pure for the times." No President has ever filled that office more upright in integrity, more true patriotism, more sincere philanthropic sympathy with the rights and interests of the masses, more devoted in duty, comprehensively wise in judgment. He is the furthest in the world removed from the negativeness of character.[274]— Anonymous

He stood on the dividing-line between the mere politician and the statesman — perfect in the arts of the one, possessing largely the comprehensive powers of the other.[275] — James G. Blaine

[At six, he] could actually tell when his book was wrong end upwards; and at twelve, he could read it just as well upside-down as right-side up, and ... practiced in both ways to acquire a shifting knack for business, and a ready turn for doing things more ways than one.[276] — Davy Crockett

[H]is outward appearance [is] like the unruffled surface of a majestic river, which covers rocks and whirlpools, but shows no mark.[277] — Philip Hone

Although the Little Magician's Faustian bargain to hold together the sectional wings of a national party dedicated to frugal government was more pronounced during his presidency than either before or after, its extent should not be exaggerated.[278] — Jeffrey Rogers Hummel

The more I see of Mr. V.B., the more I feel confirmed in a strong personal regard for him. He is one of the gentlest and most amicable men I have ever met with.[279] — Washington Irving

Martin Van Buren, Andrew Jackson's right-hand man, was a master of political intrigue who let nothing block his one unwavering ambition — the Presidency. But sometimes he was too smart for his own good.[280] — Louis W. Koenig

Above all, the practical way Van Buren implemented classical republicanism and liberal republicanism through the law forged the basis for party principles and programs, many of which anticipated Jacksonianism. In short, whatever Van Buren archived in politics was impossible without his life in the law.[281] — Jerome Mushkat

Van Buren [as president] was weak in the very respect in which he might have been expected to excel — as a politician.[282] — Arthur M. Schlesinger, Jr.

NINE

William Henry Harrison

Sung into the Presidency

Ninth President of the United States, March 4, 1841–April 4, 1841

In the presidential campaign of 1840, Whigs flooded the nation with so many satirizing songs that one Democratic editor commented, "I shall never forget. They rang in my ears wherever I went, morning, noon, and night.... Men, women and children did nothing but sing. It worried, annoyed, dumfounded, crushed the Democrats, but there was no use trying to escape. It was a ceaseless torrent of music.... If a Democrat tried to speak, argue, or answer anything that was said or done, he was only saluted with a fresh deluge of music."[1]

Among the many ditties composed in support of William Henry Harrison's candidacy was this one:

> Let Van from his coolers of silver drink wine
> And lounge on his cushioned settee,
> Our man on a buckeye bench can recline,
> Content with hard cider is he.[2]

Birth: William Henry Harrison entered life on February 9, 1773, the youngest child and third son born into a distinguished and wealthy Virginia family at Berkeley Plantation, Charles County, Virginia, located between Williamsburg and Richmond. The early 1726 Georgian mansion is said to be the oldest three-story brick house in Virginia.[3] Built of brick fired on the plantation, the original mansion occupies a beautifully landscaped hilltop overlooking the historic James River. Berkeley's ten acres of formal terraced boxwood gardens and lawns extend a quarter mile from the front door to the river.[4]

Eleven years after the first British settlement of Jamestown, William Throckmorton, Richard Berkeley, George Thorpe and John Smyth met in London to form a company that would establish a new settlement in Virginia, which would be called "Berkeley Hundred, Virginia ... similar to Berkeley Hundred in England. Their motive was strictly profit making."[5] King James I granted over 8,000 acres with three miles of waterfront in Virginia to the four.[6] The company commissioned Captain John Woodlief to lead the expedition to the colony. He and 38 other men on the ship *Margaret* arrived at Chesapeake Bay after a hazardous two-and-a-half months at sea. The expedition continued on up the St. James River, finally arriving at the Berkeley site on December 4, 1619.[7] When on shore, the company fell on their knees and were led in prayer by Woodlief, who declared, "We ordain that this day of our ships arrival, at the place assigned for plantacon, [meaning plantation] in the land of Virginia, shall be yearly and perpetually kept holy as a day of Thanksgiving to Almighty

William Henry Harrison, hand-colored lithograph published by N. Currier between 1835 and 1856 (Library of Congress).

God"[8] Thus the first official Thanksgiving was held at Berkeley Plantation, more than a year before the Puritans landed at Plymouth Rock. "The celebration was strictly a religious experience, focused entirely on prayer. It was a solemn affair, not a festival of food"[9] as was the case in Massachusetts.

Starting with George Washington, each of the first nine presidents of the United States enjoyed the hospitality of this stately home.[10] The first bourbon-style whiskey made in America was distilled at Berkeley in 1661 by George Thorpe, an Episcopal priest.[11] "Taps" was composed at Berkeley in 1862 by General Daniel Butterfield at the headquarters and supply base for General George B. McClellan's Union army.[12] John Jameson, who had been a drummer boy at Berkeley in 1862, purchased the property in 1907, beginning a new era of its restoration and rebirth. Jameson's son Malcolm inherited the deteriorating property and with his wife Grace brought it back to its former splendor. Today, Berkeley remains a working plantation, with 450 of its 1000 acres farmed.[13]

Nicknames and Titles: "Old Tippecanoe," "Old Tip," and "Washington of the West." In the presidential election campaign of 1840 the Democrats attempted to ridicule Harrison by labeling him "Granny Harrison, the petticoat general."[14] The unflattering sobriquet was inspired by a leave Harrison took from the army before the War of 1812 ended. He "undertook a tour of New York, Philadelphia, and Washington, soaking up the adulation offered by each city. He stayed in the East for months, choosing celebrity over duty, enjoying parties and banquets in his honor. In May of 1814, with the war still raging, William Henry Harrison resigned from the Army once again and settled into life on his farm in North Bend, near Cincinnati. He was forty-one years old."[15]

Family: Beginning in the seventeenth century, five Benjamin Harrisons contributed greatly to Colonial Virginia. The fifth Benjamin, born in 1726, was William Henry's father. He was an intimate friend of George Washington. As a Virginia delegate to the First Continental Congress Benjamin Harrison was a signer of the Declaration of Independence. "Because of his rotundity, joviality, love of good foods and wines, and fondness for luxury, he acquired the nickname 'Falstaff of Congress.'"[16] "He was the Speaker of the Lower House of the Virginia state legislature from 1777 to 1781 and served three terms as governor of Virginia from 1781 to 1783. He was originally in opposition of the new Federal Constitution, but later favored it when it was decided to add a bill of rights."[17] He died on April 24, 1791, when his son William Henry was 18 years old.[18] Elizabeth Bassett Harrison, a member of one of the "first families" of Virginia, was born on December 13, 1730, at Eltham Estate, New Kent County.[19] She was "remarkable in her youth for her beauty and still more eminent for her piety."[20] William's parents married in 1748. Elizabeth died about a year after Benjamin. William Henry had seven sisters— Judith, Tabitha, Elizabeth, Anna, Lucy, Sarah and Eleanor — and four brothers— Benjamin, Carter Bassett, Nathaniel and a second Benjamin.[21]

Ancestors: On December 4, 1619, early settlers from England came ashore at the location of Berkeley. After receiving a grant of twenty-two thousand acres, Benjamin Harrison IV built the impressive Berkeley mansion in 1726.[22] His name and that of his wife, Anne Carter Harrison, daughter of the wealthiest man in the colony, appear in a datestone over a side door.[23] William Henry Harrison described himself as "a child of the Revolution."[24] He was about nine years old when the British landed and marched triumphantly through the Berkeley Plantation on the way to seize Richmond. "The British troops under Benedict Arnold raided Berkeley Hundred, killed the livestock, stole a number of the slaves, and burned the Harrison's personal belongings, family portraits, and the mansion's damask draperies and other furnishings in a spectacular bonfire."[25] Young Harrison recalled the British streaming back from defeats at nearby Yorktown, with French and American troops moving to surround them. During the siege, Washington and the Marquis de Lafayette dined at Berkeley.[26]

Appearance: "Harrison was slim, of average height, with thin brown hair that had grayed by the time he became president and that he combed rather carelessly straight down over his forehead or sloping slightly to the right. He had a long, thin, angular face, of fair complexion, distinguished by a long sharp-bridged nose, closely set eyes, thin lips, and a strong jaw. A female observer once described his expression as 'serene and engaging.'"[27] In a campaign biography, he was described as "tall and slender; his features are irregular, but bold and strongly marked; his eyes are dark, keen, and penetrating, his forehead is high and expansive, his mouth peculiarly denotes firmness and genius, and the expression of his countenance is highly indicative of intelligence and benevolence of character."[28] His narrow face was long and angular, sporting a long nose and closely set eyes. His lips were thin but his jaw was strong. He had bushy eyebrows and tufts of hair that reached his ears. While serving in the military and as territorial governor he made a handsome appearance.[29]

Personality and Character: Harrison's campaign biographer described Harrison thusly: "His manners are plain, frank and unassuming, and his disposition is cheerful, kind, and generous, almost to a fault."[30] He was described as confident but modest, a gentleman in manners, and incorruptibly honest. In a letter to James Heaton, he insisted "there is no one I believe who knows me that can for a moment entertain the opinion that I would change my political principles for personal advantage."[31]

Marriage and Romances: As a young officer, Harrison paid court to a young woman, referred to only as Miss M. of Philadelphia.[32] He confided to his brother in a letter that he intended to pursue his suit, even though he acknowledged she probably wouldn't have a poor military man, suggesting that she might have come from a prominent or well-off family.[33] He confessed that "I love her so ardently; I would forego my happiness forever to contribute to hers."[34] Apparently, he did. William Henry Harrison married Anna Tuthill Symmes (1775–1864) on November 25, 1795.[35] She was the only first lady born in the state of New Jersey. Small in height, with dark brown hair and eyes, she completed her education at a boarding school in New York City.[36] At age 19, she accompanied her father, Judge John Cleves Symmes, to a settlement on the "north bend" of the Ohio River where he held a patent for a vast acreage of Ohio land.[37] Initially, Symmes opposed the marriage, not wishing his daughter to face the hardship of living in frontier forts. He asked Harrison how he intended to support a wife. The future president replied, "By my sword, and my own right arm, sir."[38]

When Symmes was away on business the couple eloped and was married in a clandestine wedding performed by a justice of the peace.[39] Seeing his daughter's happiness, Symmes relented and accepted his new son-in-law into the family. However, in a letter to a friend in 1798, Symmes said this of Harrison: "He can neither bleed, plead, nor preach, and if he could plow, I should be satisfied."[40]

For Harrison the marriage was politically astute. The Symmes family had connections with the local land speculators, something he exploited.[41] Anna Harrison had no ambitions either socially or politically. She derived her satisfaction solely from her role as wife and mother and as a devoted member of her Presbyterian Church community. She was in the habit of "inviting the whole congregation of her beloved church ... to dinner on Sundays after the morning service and serving food raised on the Harrison farm."[42] She moved with her children to the former French trading post of Vincennes, Indiana, when her husband was named territorial governor of Indiana.[43] During the War of 1812, Mrs. Harrison took her family back to North Bend, Ohio, where they would be safer. When her father died in 1814, Anna inherited his substantial land holdings but also his great debts. The Harrisons expanded their log home built on 169 acres in North Bend into a 22-room house. "Despite Harrison's subsequent election to the U.S. House and Senate and his term as minister to Columbia, Anna remained in Ohio."[44]

Mrs. Harrison was too ill to travel with her husband as he set out in 1841 for his inauguration as president. It was a long trip and difficult even by steamboat and railroad in February.[45] When Anna decided not to make the trip, the president-elect asked his daughter-in-law Jane Irwin Harrison, the widow of his namesake son, to accompany him and act as hostess until his wife's planned arrival in April.[46]

Anna Tuthill Symmes Harrison, photographic print of a portrait by Jane Johnson Lewis. Illustration in Lila G.A. Woolfall, *Presiding Ladies of the White House*, 1903 (Library of Congress).

As Harrison died on April 4, Anna never made the trip to Washington, being the only incumbent first lady who never entered the White House.[47] Anna Harrison was the first presidential widow to be awarded a pension by Congress, a lump sum of $25,000.[48] Within four years of her husband's death, she lost her three remaining daughters. She outlived all but one of her ten children. She moved in with her last surviving son, John Scott Harrison, until her death at age 88 in February 1864.[49] In a letter to her son William in 1819 when he was away at college, Anna wrote: "I hope my dear, you will always bear upon your mind that you are born to die [as] we know not how soon death may overtake us, it will be of little consequence if we are rightly prepared for the event."[50]

Children: "Anna Harrison bore the largest number of children by a First Lady, and she outlived all but one."[51] The Harrisons had six sons and four daughters: Elizabeth Bassett, called Betsey, who died a few years after her father, wed John Cleves Short. John Cleves Symmes, usually called Symmes, married Clarissa Pike, daughter of General Zebulon Pike, for whom Pike's Peak is named. His father helped secure him a position with the government land office, but he was fired after being accused of embezzlement by a political foe. Hurt by the false accusation, he died several years before his father became president.[52] Lucy Singleton married a judge of Ohio's Superior Court, Davis Este, and gave birth to four children before her early death at age 26.[53] William Henry, Jr., was a lawyer in Cincinnati married to Janet Findlay. He turned to drink, which affected his health.

John Scott was the only one of the Harrison children to live to an advanced age. He was twice elected to Congress, but he was primarily concerned with the family farm at North Bend, Ohio. Married twice, he had nine children in all, including Benjamin, who became the 23rd president of the United States, making his father the only person whose father and son were U.S. presidents.[54] Benjamin VI fought in the Texas War and was captured by the Mexicans. He became a doctor and had five children with his two wives.[55] Mary Symmes married a doctor and died one year after her father's death. Carter Basset, a lawyer, married Mary Anne Sutherland. He died before his father became president.[56] Anna Tuthill married a cousin, William Henry Harrison, who was named for her father.[57] James Findlay was the only one of the Harrison children not to survive childhood.[58]

Religion and Religious Beliefs: Some sources state that Harrison was an Episcopalian and devout in his religious beliefs throughout his life. "Harrison was a vestryman of Christ Episcopal Church in Cincinnati, Ohio after resigning his military commission in 1814."[59] Others list him among the U.S. presidents with no religious affiliation. "Franklin Steiner lists four presidents as 'not affiliated' and six others as 'religious views doubtful.'"[60] Harrison is on his list as doubtful. His funeral service was "conducted by Rev. Hawley of Washington's St. John's Episcopal Church. At the service, Hawley asserted that Harrison began each day by reading from the Bible and that he had informed the minister that he intended to join the church."[61] In 1840, during his campaign for the presidency, Harrison commented to the pastor of a Methodist Church in Cincinnati: "I know there are some of my political opponents who will be ready to impugn my motives in attending this revival-meeting at this peculiar time; but I care not for the smiles or frowns of my fellow-countrymen. God knows my heart and understands my motives. A deep and an abiding sense of my inward spiritual necessities brings me to this hallowed place night after night."[62]

In his inaugural address, Harrison seemed to view God as a champion of American values: "We admit of no government by divine right, believing that so far as power is concerned the Beneficent Creator has made no distinction amongst men; that all are upon an equality, and that the only legitimate right to govern is an express grant of power from the governed."[63] Later in the same address, the president remarked:

> I deem the present occasion sufficiently important and solemn to justify me in expressing to my fellow-citizens a profound reverence for the Christian religion and a thorough conviction with all true and lasting happiness; and to the good Being who has blessed us by the gifts of civil and religious freedom, who watched over and prospered the labors of our fathers and has hitherto preserved to us institutions for exceeding in excellence those of any other people, let us unite in fervently commending every interest of our beloved country in all future time.[64]

Education: Harrison received private tutoring at home until age 14 before attending Hampden-Sydney College (1787–1790), where he studied classics and history but apparently didn't graduate.[65] Fulfilling the wish of his father, he took up the study of medicine in Richmond, Virginia, and at the University of Pennsylvania in Philadelphia from 1790 to 1791 with Dr. Benjamin Rush, a founding father of the United States, a signatory of the Declaration of Independence and a member of the Continental Congress. When his father died, Harrison inherited no money, only land. Unable to continue his education, he gave up the study of medicine to join the U.S. Army.[66]

Home: Harrison was appointed governor of the Indiana Territory in 1800. Vincennes, which was centrally located and the most populated area was made the capital.[67] When Harrison arrived in Vincennes, he built a home, which he called Grouseland, that could also serve as a fortress for protection. Inspired by his family's home at Berkeley in Virginia, Harrison began construction of a Georgian style plantation in 1803.[68] The blended plantation mansion and fortress is located along the Wabash River. The building is a 2½-story brick house containing 26 rooms and 13 fireplaces. "Because of the threat of Indian raids, the exterior walls were 18 inches thick with portholes for sharpshooters."[69] During Harrison's governorship Grouseland was the focal point of the social and official life of the territory. It was here that Harrison negotiated the Treaty of Grouseland with a number of important Indian leaders and where he had two confrontations with Tecumseh.[70]

With the outbreak of the War of 1812, Harrison moved his large family to a farm inherited by his wife at North Bend, Ohio, and took up the life of a planter. He kept servants, dispensed generous hospitality, and soon was in debt. Harrison had little income except from the farm, whose crop yields were small, and from a minor political job as a county recorder.[71] Looking for a way to augment his finances, he cultivated large quantities of corn and established a distillery to produce whiskey. Before long, he became disturbed by the effects of his product on its consumers and ceased producing the liquor.[72] "He later addressed the Hamilton County Agricultural Board in 1831, claiming that he had sinned in making whiskey, and hoped that others would learn from his mistake by stopping the production of liquors."[73] The house at North Bend caught fire one night in 1858 and burned to the ground. Although nobody was injured, all the contents of the house, including Harrison's papers, were destroyed.[74]

Motto: "To be eminently great, it is necessary to be eminently good."[75]

Pets and Animals: At the White House he had a pet goat named "His Whiskers."[76] The general had two horses. The one he usually rode was white. It was kept saddled and bridled the night before the Battle of Tippecanoe. The stake to which the horse was hitched pulled up, so a servant tied the animal to a wheel of a wagon. When the attack began the servant didn't remember where he had left the horse. Another officer loaned Harrison his steed. Early in the battle one of the general's aides, riding a white horse was shot.[77] "The Indians thought the horse carried Harrison and they believed that if they killed the leader the American troops would become confused and lose their courage to continue the fight."[78]

Recreational Pastimes and Interests: Harrison enjoyed hunting grouse, thus the name of his home in Indiana, which abounded with these game birds.[79]

Occupation: William Henry Harrison was the first professional soldier to become president of the United States. Washington, Monroe, and Jackson fought as soldiers, but the military was not their primary occupation.[80]

MILITARY SERVICE

In 1791, at the age of 18, through the influence of Senator Richard Henry Lee of Virginia, Harrison was commissioned as an ensign in the Tenth Regiment of the United States Army. He was sent to Fort Washington (near present-day Cincinnati) in the Northwest Territory (present-day Ohio, Indiana and Illinois) where he spent much of his life. His commission was personally approved by President Washington.[81] Harrison had a modest military career highlighted by two significant triumphs. At the Battle of Tippecanoe in 1811, he put down a Shawnee uprising. Following the outbreak of the War of 1812, Harrison's victory near Canada's Thames River in the province of Ontario ensured that the United States continued to control its western territory.[82] Major Richard M. Johnson is quoted, referring to his commander: "He has the confidence of the forces without a parallel in our history except in the case of General Washington in the revolution."[83] Henry Clay said of Harrison, "No military man in the U.S. combines more general confidence in the West."[84]

Indian Wars: Harrison served in the Northwest Territories as aide-de-camp to General

"Mad Anthony" Wayne at the Battle of Fallen Timbers (near present-day Toledo, Ohio), which opened much of the area of Ohio to settlement. He was promoted to captain and then commander of Fort Washington, the main American stronghold.[85] By the late 1790s, Harrison had gained a reputation among white settlers as a great Indian fighter. He was present at the negotiation and signing of the Treaty of Greenville. In 1809, the threat from Native Americans to white settlers was serious.[86]

The eloquent and energetic Shawnee leader Tecumseh and his religious brother Tenskwatawa, known as the Prophet, formed a confederacy of all tribes west of the Appalachian Mountains to resist further expansion of white settlers.[87] Tecumseh explained his position to Harrison in a speech in 1807:

> You try to force the red people to do some injury. It is you that is pushing them on to do mischief. You endeavor to make distinctions, you wish to prevent the Indians to do as we wish them to unite and let them consider their land as common property of the whole. You take tribes aside and advise them not to come into this measure and until our design is accomplished we do not wish to accept of your invitation to go and visit the President.... The reason I tell you this is— you want by your distinctions of Indian tribes in allotting to each a particular tract of land to make them to war with each other. You never see an Indian come and endeavor to make the white people do so. You are continually driving the red people when at last you will drive them into the Great Lake, where they can't either stand or work.[88]

War of 1812: When the War of 1812 erupted between the U.S. and Great Britain, President Madison appointed Harrison commander of the army in the Northwest, with the rank of brigadier general. His duty was to protect American settlements in the West from English and Indian attacks. Fearing the continuing influx of American settlers, most Native Americans sided with the British.[89] Once Commander Oliver Hazard Perry defeated the English fleet on Lake Erie, severing England's prime supply line, Harrison's forces retook Detroit and ferried across the lake into Canada. At the October 5, 1913,

Top: An 1842 engraving of Tecumseh, based on a pencil sketch by Pierre le Dru. Tecumseh's native costume was replaced with a British uniform. No fully authenticated picture of Tecumseh exists. *Bottom: Ten-Squat-A-Way, the Open Door, Known as the Prophet, Brother of Tecumseh*, an engraving on wood 1830 (both from Lossing's *Field Book of the War of 1812*, Harper & Brothers, 1868).

Death of Tecumseh at the Battle of the Thames, Oct. 5th, 1813, lithograph by John Dorival published c. 1833. Print shows American forces fighting Tecumseh's Indian confederation. In the center Col. R.M. Johnson shoots Tecumseh, who has raised his tomahawk (Library of Congress).

Battle of Thames—a river in what is now Kent County in the province of Ontario north of Lake Erie—Harrison's army engaged and defeated the combined British and Indian forces. The English ran from the battlefield, leaving the Indians to fight on alone. The Americans crushed the Native Americans, killing Tecumseh, whose body was then mutilated and torn apart.[90] The Indian tribes never again posed serious resistance in the Northwest Territory. Harrison resigned from the army in 1814, but from then on, because of his victories at Tippecanoe and the Thames, he always was thought of popularly as a military hero.[91]

Harrison respected Tecumseh's military and leadership abilities, saying:

> The implicit obedience and respect which the followers of Tecumseh pay him is really astonishing and more than any other circumstances bespeaks him as one of those uncommon geniuses, which spring up occasionally to produce revolutions and overturn the established order of things. If it were not for the vicinity of the United States, he would perhaps be the founder of an Empire that would rival in glory that of Mexico or Peru. No difficulties deter him. His activity and industry supply the want of letters. For four years he has been in constant motion. You see him today on the Wabash and in a short time you hear of him on the shores of Lake Erie or Michigan, or on the banks of the Mississippi and wherever he goes he makes an impression favorable to his purpose.[92]

POLITICAL OFFICES

Political Philosophy and Political Party Affiliation: Prior to his election as president, Harrison did not make known his political views. The only time his positions were revealed was in his inauguration address, in which he confirmed his belief in a limited role for the

U.S. president.[93] He announced he would serve only one term, limit his use of the veto, and leave revenue schemes to Congress.[94] In a letter to John Brown Dillon, who published a pamphlet on slavery, Harrison declared, "The slave holding states ... retained the complete control of slavery within their boundaries.... [The citizens of free states] have the right as individuals to give their opinion to their brethren in the Slave States upon the subject of Slavery ... but they have no power whatever to control them upon any of these subjects."[95]

Harrison steadfastly believed in states' rights, opposed patronage and similar use of federal powers, and championed the Manifest Destiny of western expansion.[96] "Harrison's views on slavery were moderate, and he was not considered wholly reliable on this issue by the South. As was usual at the time, he regarded it as a states' rights issue, which, of course, meant that he was not going to make enemies over it. He brought a slave with him from Virginia to Ohio, and later to Vincennes, as a personal servant, but did not use slaves for farming or business.... He freed his own servant, and successfully fought for the admission of Indiana as a free state (that is, one in which the slave trade was illegal). In Virginia, he had joined an emancipation society that supported emancipation by emigration. He often rescued slaves by buying them in Kentucky, bringing them to Ohio and Indiana, and indenturing them for a period of years, after which they would have earned their freedom. He looked forward to a time when there would be no more slavery, but thought it could only be brought about gradually, any more rapid movement being dangerous to the white south."[97] Ralph Waldo Emerson saw Harrison as basically as belonging to no political party: "General Harrison was neither Whig nor Tory, but the 'Indignation President' and, what was not at all surprising in this puny generation, he could not stand the excitement of seventeen million people but died of the presidency in one month."[98]

Northwest Delegate to the U.S. House of Representatives: After Harrison resigned from his commission in 1798, viewing the army as a career dead end, his father-in-law arranged to have him appointed secretary of the Northwest Territory (1798–1799) by President John Adams.[99] At the age of 27, Harrison served as the Northwest Territory's first delegate to Congress (1799–1800). Although he did not have a vote, he was "instrumental in the establishment of the Harrison Land Act of 1800. It favored individual settlers over wealthy land speculators; assisting working-class Americans acquire government land in the Northwest Territory."[100] They were allowed to purchase cheaply—"a minimum of 320 acres of land for a minimum of two dollars per acre—with an initial payment of at least 330 dollars for one-half the cost plus administrative costs. The remainder was to be paid in four equal installments over the next four years. Squatters, people who already lived on the land but who had not purchased it legally, were evicted by the government if any new people wished to purchase the property."[101] Harrison also helped obtain legislation dividing the territory into the Northwest and Indian territories.[102]

Governor of Indiana Territory: In 1800, President John Adams appointed Harrison governor of the Indiana Territory—then consisting of present-day Indiana, Illinois, Wisconsin and Michigan. Harrison served four terms in this capacity, ruling with an iron fist. Coming from a prominent slave-owning family, he allowed slavery to exist in the territory.[103] "Harrison did permit the formation of a territorial legislature in 1805, but he was not receptive to many of its requests."[104] He ignored it when it suited his purposes to do so. "His authority remained virtually unchallenged until 1809, when the United States government separated modern-day Indiana from the other lands originally included in the Indiana Territory. Because he was a strong leader, Harrison was a man with firm friends and equally firm antagonists."[105] Many of the residents remaining under Harrison's command despised him. "In 1810, the legislature outlawed slavery and ended land ownership as a requirement for adult white men to be allowed to vote."[106] During Harrison's 12 years in the post, his "main accomplishments were the establishment of a legal system, the settlement of land disputes, and the management of Indian affairs."[107]

While he was governor, Harrison served also as superintendent of Indian Affairs. His primary responsibility "was to obtain title to Indian lands so that white settlement could expand into the area."[108] To many Native Americans, the idea of owning land was a totally alien concept. Harrison took advantage of the Indians' communal approach to territory. "He convinced many Native Americans to relinquish millions of acres of land in the northwestern part of the United States,"[109] even though the U.S. government had guaranteed the Native Americans this land in the Treaty of Greenville. Native Americans, not willing to cede their land to the whites, sometimes attacked during the encroachment of white settlers. Harrison acted to improve the conditions of the Native Americans by banning sale of intoxicating liquor to them and introducing inoculation for smallpox.[110] He frequently held councils with the Indians, and although on occasion his life was endangered, he succeeded by his calmness and courage to avert many outbreaks.[111]

On September 30, 1809, Governor Harrison "concluded a treaty with several tribes by which they sold to the United States about 3,000,000 acres of land on Wabash and White rivers. This, and the former treaties of cession that had been made, were condemned by Tecumseh and other chiefs on the ground that the consent of all the tribes was necessary to a legal sale. The discontent was increased by the action of speculators in ejecting Indians from the lands ... and it was evident that an outbreak was at hand."[112] In June 1810, pursuing a conciliatory course, Harrison invited Tecumseh and the Prophet to a "council at Vincennes requesting them to bring with them not more than thirty men. In response, the chief, accompanied by 400 fully armed warriors, arrived at Vincennes on the twelfth of August."[113] Harrison ordered a chair to be brought for Tecumseh. When it was procured, the servant who brought it bowed and said, "Warrior, your father, General Harrison, offers you a seat."[114] Tecumseh, lifting his arms to the sky, exclaimed, "My father! The sun is my father, and the earth is my mother, and on her bosom will I recline."[115] With that Tecumseh stretched out on the ground. The Indians insisted on the return of all the lands that had recently been acquired by treaty. "On the day after the council Harrison visited Tecumseh at his camp, accompanied only by an interpreter, but without success. In the following spring depredations by the savages were frequent, and the governor sent word to Tecumseh that, unless they should cease, the Indians would be punished. The chief promised another interview, and appeared at Vincennes on 27 July, 1811, with 300 followers, but, awed probably by the presence of 750 militia, professed to be friendly."[116] Convinced of the chief's insincerity, Governor Harrison was authorized to attack the confederacy.

In November, while Tecumseh was away, Harrison's force of 1000 men marched on the Prophet's town (near present-day Lafayette, Indiana).The Americans camped near the Tippecanoe River and Harrison met with Indian messengers seeking a parley. A council was agreed to for the next day, but at four o'clock in the morning, the Indians attacked the camp. Fierce fighting continued until daylight, when the Indians were driven from the field by a cavalry charge. The battle earned Harrison his nickname Tippecanoe. His troops suffered 190 dead and wounded. The general buried his dead and burned logs over their graves to conceal the spot of interment. However, the Indians found the place and dug up the

Battle of Tippecanoe, chromolithograph by Kurz & Allison, published c. October 15, 1889. The print shows American troops under the leadership of General William Henry Harrison fighting Tecumseh's Indian confederation in a forest (Library of Congress).

bodies and scattered their remains. The battle merely hardened the Indians' resolve not only to recover their land but also to avenge their losses.[117]

U.S. Representative: Harrison was elected to the Fourteenth Congress to fill a vacancy caused by the resignation of John McLean.[118] Harrison was reelected to the next Congress and served from 1816 to 1819. "He supported Henry Clay's so-called American System, which favored internal improvements funded by the federal government."[119] Harrison served as chairman of the Militia Committee, "worked in behalf of more liberal pension laws and a better militia organization, including a system of general military education, of improvements in the navigation of the Ohio, and of relief for purchasers of public lands, and for the strict construction of the power of Congress over the Territories, particularly in regard to slavery."[120] He opposed laws that would restrict slavery. He voted against New York Congressman General James Tallmadge's proposed amendment, limiting the extension of slavery in the Louisiana Territory as a condition for admitting Missouri to the Union of states.[121]

Harrison joined with other congressmen in an attempt to censure General Andrew Jackson for his invasion of Florida without specific orders. This "caused great animosity between the two war heroes."[122] While in Congress, Harrison was referred to as a "Buckeye," as were other pioneers of the Ohio frontier, a term of endearment derived from the buckeye chestnut tree. He made the tree the symbol of his campaign.[123] Harrison unsuccessfully maneuvered to be named secretary of war by the new president, James Monroe, who chose John C. Calhoun instead.[124]

Ohio State Senator: Harrison served in the Ohio state senate from 1819 to 1821 and the next year he was a presidential elector in Ohio. He was an unsuccessful candidate for the U.S. House of Representatives in 1822.[125]

U.S. Senator: Harrison was elected to the United States Senate, serving from 1825 to 1828, where he focused on military issues and used his influence as chairman of the Committee on Military Affairs to lobby for increases in army pay and an expansion of the navy.[126] In 1828, Harrison failed to secure the post of commander of the army after the death of Major-General Jacob Brown. He also was denied the nomination for the vice president on the ticket headed by John Quincy Adams.[127]

U.S. Minister to Colombia: President John Quincy Adams named Harrison U.S. minister to Colombia (1828–1829). When Harrison arrived at Bogotá, the capital of Colombia, early in 1829, that country had been involved in two recent revolutions and Peru had just declared war on it. Harrison disregarded Clay's instructions not to become involved in Colombian factional politics. Believing that President Simón Bolívar planned to make himself emperor, Harrison cooperated with Bolívar's rival, General José María Córdoba. This aroused the

Colombian government's resentment. Harrison was saved from expulsion by the Bolívar regime only because the new U.S. president, Andrew Jackson, recalled him to give the position to one of his party supporters. Before leaving, Harrison compounded his diplomatic errors by sending a strongly worded letter to Bolívar on September 27, 1829, advising him to "uphold the republic."[128] In the communication, Harrison employed no diplomatic language in lecturing Bolívar on the behavior of tyrants. His words almost seemed to be saying, "Does this remind you of anyone?":

There is nothing more corrupting, nothing more destructive of the noblest and finest feelings of our nature, than the exercise of unlimited power. The man who, in the beginning of such a career might shudder at the idea of taking away the life of a fellow-being, might soon have his conscience so scarred by the repetition of crime, that the agonies of his murdered victims might become music to his soul, and the drippings in his scaffold afford "blood enough to swim in." History is full of such examples.... The successful warrior is no longer regarded as entitled to the first place in the temple of fame.... The pleas of necessity, that eternal argument of all conspirators.[129]

Simón Bolívar, photomechanical print made between 1890 and 1940. Reproduction of artwork with quotation (not shown) from Bolívar to Sir Robert Wilson commenting on the exactness of his portrait (Library of Congress).

The Presidential Campaign of 1836: In 1836, the National Republicans joined disgruntled Democrats angered by President Jackson's opposition to states' rights to form the Whig Party.[130] Unable to decide on a single candidate, they ran three different candidates in each section of the country, hoping to deny Van Buren a majority and to throw the election to the House of Representatives, where it was expected one of the Whig candidates would be chosen.[131] Hugh Lawson White of Tennessee was chosen as the Whig candidate from the South and Daniel Webster of Massachusetts was chosen from the North. Selected as the Western Whig and Anti-Masonic candidate, Harrison faired the best of the three Whigs but was defeated by Martin Van Buren. He received 73 electoral votes to Van Buren's 170.[132] As he polled such a large number of votes in the West, he appeared as a promising candidate for the next presidential election.[133] In a letter to Stephen Van Rennesselar, he made light of the notion of his becoming president of the United States: "Some folks are silly enough as to have formed a plan to make a President of the United States out of this Clerk and Clodhopper."[134]

The Presidential Campaign of 1840: "In 1840 the Whigs saw an opportunity to win the White House. The nation was suffering a catastrophic financial collapse: inflation and unemployment soared, businesses were lost and crop prices plummeted. President Van Buren blamed the crisis on unscrupulous bankers and greedy Americans, and maintained that the government should not interfere with private business."[135] Harrison's candidacy appealed to the leaders of the Whig party because his views on the controversial issues of the day were unknown and for this reason he hadn't offended any groups of voters.[136] The Whig managers had no intention of publicizing the general's positions. Instead they planned a personality driven campaign. Henry Clay, the acknowledged leader of the Whigs, was passed over because he was an advocate of a protective tariff which would repel many southerners. The other well-known Whig, Daniel Webster, was just that too well-known to rally around. New York Whigs, headed by Thurlow Weed, had wrestled the leadership of the party from the "Great Compromiser."[137] "While Clay led after the first canvassing, he fell short of the needed majority. By the time of the first ballot, Whig delegates had turned to Harrison."[138] The Whigs adopted no platform and made no declaration of principles, not wishing to offer voters who opposed Van Buren's programs the opportunity to discover proposals that they liked even less. In their acceptance speeches, Harrison and Tyler refrained from political discussions.[139]

The Whigs wanted a candidate who would not interfere with their plan of making President Van Buren the major issue of the race. Harrison was just the man, a military hero who would avoid discussion of national issues. At their Convention the Democrats issued a lengthy statement defending Van Buren and the party's record and principles. They also accused Harrison of being a Federalist and questioned his military achievements.[140] The contest between Martin Van Buren and William Henry Harrison marked the first truly modern multimedia presidential campaign — and the most expensive up to that time.[141] Harrison's supporters "created an image of him as a war hero, and touted his experience at the Battle of Tippecanoe, 28 years earlier. While it's true that Harrison had been the commander at that battle against the Indians, he had actually been criticized for his actions at the time. The Shawnee warriors had surprised his troops, and casualties had been high for the soldiers under Harrison's command."[142]

Harrison's campaign managers stirred up the emotional state of so many of the poor farmers and frontier dwellers that it didn't occur to them to ask what the issues in the election were. "Telling the electorate that they must choose between Harrison and Prosperity

THE POLITICAL DANCING JACK:
A Holiday Gift for Sucking Whigs!!.
Sold at No. 104 Nassau, and No. 18 Division Streets, New-York.

The Political Dancing Jack: A Holiday Gift for Sucking Whigs!!, woodcut and letterpress print issued anonymously by Robert N. Elton, Huestis & Co., 1840. A rare anti–Whig satire, giving a cynical view of the party's image-building and manipulation of candidate William Henry Harrison. Two influential Whigs, Senator Henry Clay and Congressman Henry A. Wise, operate the strings of a "dancing-jack" toy figure of Harrison in military uniform (Library of Congress).

or Van Buren and Ruin, the Whigs gave the voters an easy decision to make."[143] The Whigs called their fight "Hurrah and Hallelujah" campaign, Harrison was the first presidential candidate to go on the stump, and gave speeches at Fort Meigs, Columbus, Cleveland, and elsewhere. Harrison's campaign trips in June and September 1840 were to show he was healthy. In these trips he made no political statements, only recounting military anecdotes. His victory was due to his reputation as an Indian fighter. His managers used political songs, partisan slogans, and symbols to capture the public's imagination, not their intellects.[144]

The Whig party leadership worried about a possible rift in the Whig voters. "However, after privately proclaiming, 'My friends are not worth the powder and shot it would take to kill them,' Clay gave his full public endorsement of the Whig candidate. Clay's support ensured the vote of the party in the South and announced the advent of the frightening unity that would mark Harrison's campaign. Whig supporters, such as Thurlow Weed from New York, realized that the nation was aching for a change. All they needed now was an

General Harrison's Log Cabin March & Quick Step, lithograph published by Samuel Carusi, Edward Weber & Co., 1840. An illustrated Whig campaign music sheet. Before a log cabin in the wilderness Harrison greets a crippled veteran (Library of Congress).

identity to sell to a hungry electorate."[145] On February 7, 1839, three months after the Whig Convention Henry Clay gave his famous Senate speech, "I had rather be right than president."[146] At a rally for Harrison, Daniel Webster shouted, "The time has come when the cry is change. Every breeze says change; every interest of the country demands it."[147]

The old general was chosen for his popularity, not for his political expertise. His running mate, John Tyler of Virginia, was chosen to help ensure the southern vote. In his acceptance speech at the Dayton Convention, September 18, 1840, Harrison made a promise: "I pledge myself before Heaven and earth, if elected President of these United States, to lay down at the end of the term faithfully that high trust at the feet of the people."[148] In one of the few speeches made during his presidential campaign, Harrison spoke of the misuse of power: "Power is insinuating. Few men are satisfied with less power than they are able to procure.... No lover is ever satisfied with the first smile of his mistress."[149]

Harrison was presented to the citizens as a military leader, a man of the people — born in a log cabin — who loved to partake of hard cider. This image was a gift from the Democrats, which the Whigs exploited. In a dismissive editorial, the *Baltimore Republican,* a Democratic supporter, commented about how easy it would be to be rid of Harrison: "Give him a barrel of hard cider and settle a pension of two thousand a year on him, and take my word for it, he will sit the remainder of his days in his log cabin by the side of a sea coast fire, and study moral philosophy."[150]

Harrison's managers seized on these remarks to create the highly popular and successful "Log Cabin and Hard Cider" campaign, which portrayed Harrison as a man of the people. "The log cabin became a commonplace symbol of Harrison's candidacy. In its collection of materials related to the 1840 Harrison campaign, the Smithsonian Institution has a wooden model of a log cabin that was carried in torchlight parades."[151] Their claims about Harrison, other than his military experience, were misleading at best. "Although Harrison had come from a wealthy, slaveholding Virginia family, in this campaign he was promoted as a humble frontiersman in the style of the popular Andrew Jackson."[152] While part of his home at North Bend, Ohio, had originally been a log cabin, it had long since been covered with clapboards. The campaign slogans of "Log Cabins and Hard Cider" and "Tippecanoe and Tyler Too" are among the most famous in American political history.[153] "Horace Greeley, a Weed protégé and future newspaper editor, seized upon the symbolism and begin a campaign paper entitled 'Log Cabin.' On the back page were lyrics, often penned by Greeley, to be sung to the tunes of popular melodies. The 'Log Cabin' sold some 80,000 copies each week, and the *New York Times* called it 'the most effective campaign paper ever printed.' 'Our songs are doing more good than anything else,' Greeley wrote Weed."[154] Comparing Harrison to the Roman hero Cincinnatus, log-cabin campaign artifacts read, "He leaves the plow to save the country."[155]

The odds against Harrison were formidable. He was running against an incumbent and one who had already beaten him once. Harrison, at 68, was "criticized as too old and feeble to be president."[156] His campaign managers successfully contrasted Harrison with Van Buren. The latter was unpopular because of the great depression in the country and because he was considered an "aristocratic champagne-sipping dandy," too well off to understand the plight of the general public.[157] "In their image remaking of Harrison, the Whigs misrepresented him to the electorate. Harrison was a learned student of classics," given to quoting Roman historian Tacitus and famed orator Cicero, and a man "who enjoyed luxurious living to the point that he was continually in debt."[158] Van Buren was a self-made man who spoke with a Dutch accent. He tried to run an issue-driven campaign, but the "voters wanted to identify with a war hero who shared their down-to-earth values."[159]

The mudslinging during the campaign was of two kinds. The Whigs attacked Van Buren's foibles, while the Democrats attacked Harrison the man. The Democrats questioned whether Harrison should be elected and noted that his name spelled backwards was, "No Sirrah."[160] The Democrats also took to song to belittle Harrison: "Rockabye, baby, Daddy's a Whig /When he comes home, hard cider he'll swig/ When he has swug / He'll fall in a stu/ And down will come Tyler and Tippecanoe./ Rockabye, baby, when you awake / You will discover Tip is a fake./ Far from the battle, war cry and drum / He sits in his cabin a'drinking bad rum./ Rockabye, baby, never you cry/ You need not fear OF Tip and his Ty. /What they would ruin, Van Buren will fix./ Van's a magician, they are but tricks."[161] Harrison was called senile and accused him of being mentally and physically impaired. The Democrats said he was an "imbecile" and that the Whigs had to keep him caged, lest he would be seen and disgrace himself. "General Mum ... whose fame is like his fav'rite drum; which when most empty makes most noise."[162] They charged him with shocking profanity and of cohabitation with Indian squaws during his days on the frontier. Harrison replied to the personal attacks on the stump: "I am the most persecuted and calumniated individual now living."[163] At a Chillicothe, Ohio rally, he responded to Democratic mockery: "I am not with you today, Fellow Citizens, in accordance with my own sense of propriety. Much more consonant would it be with my feelings to remain at the domestic fireside.... Indeed I sometimes fear that upon me will fall the responsibility of establishing a dangerous precedent.... You must have already perceived, that I am not CAGED, and that I am not the old man on crutches ... they accuse me of being."[164] "I suffer from the numerous (and as to the larger portion) most rediculous [sic] applications for opinions on almost every subject."[165]

Van Buren wasn't spared imaginative smearing. Horace Greeley in the *New York Tribune* thundered: "Wherever you find a bitter, blasphemous atheist, there you may be certain of one vote for Van Buren."[166] Oversimplification was in order. The *Political Tornado* advised, "Take Harrison and good, or reject him for Van Buren and evil."[167] Former president John Quincy Adams observed: "The whole country is in a state of agitation upon the approaching Presidential election such as was never before witnessed.... Not a week has passed within the last few months without convocation of thousands of people to hear inflammatory harangues against Martin Van Buren and his Administration! Here is a revolution in the habits and manners of the people. Where will it end? These are party movements, and must in the natural progress of things become antagonistical.... Their manifest tendency is to civil war."[168] Among the accusations made against Van Buren were that he was "a graceless aristocrat and a dandy, but a cunning conspirator, seeking the overthrow of his country's liberties by uniting the sword and the purse in his own clutches."[169] In his famous "Gold Spoon Oration" given by Congressman Charles Ogle, a Harrison supporter, he denounced him for the "regal splendor of the President's Palace." "Quite memorably, Ogle charged Van Buren with having the White House landscaper build rounded mounds on the grounds with little gazebos on top, which at a distance supposedly resembled a woman's erect nipple."[170] Van Buren remained in the White House, trying to "appear aloof from all the mudslinging," but Harrison appeared on the campaign trail, "entertaining the public with his impressions of Native American war whoops (loud yells)."[171] He studiously refrained from making any statements on the issues of the day, other than maintaining that the poor would be taken care of and inflation would be contained, although offering no details of how this was to be accomplished. Because of his lack of comments on the issues, the Democrats labeled Harrison "General Mum."[172] A frustrated Democrat complained: "In what grave and important discussion are the Whig journals engaged? ... We speak of the divorce of bank and state; and the Whigs reply with a dissertation on the merits of hard cider. We defend the policy of the Administration; and the Whigs answer 'log cabin,' 'big canoes,' 'go it Tip, Come it Ty.' We urge re-election of Van Buren because of his honesty, sagacity, statesmanship ... and the Whigs answer that Harrison is a poor man and lives in a log cabin."[173]

Hard times crippled Van Buren's cause, making Harrison's victory relatively easy. Harrison received 234 electoral votes and 53 percent of the popular vote to 60 and 47 percent for Van Buren, although the popular vote was considerably closer: 1,275,017 votes to 1,128,702. The voter turnout was a remarkable (by today's standards at least) 80.2 percent of eligible voters.[174] Democrats complained that the voters had been fooled by Whig songs, parades and avoidance of the issues. On the other hand, the Whigs were delighted, and they declared that Harrison's victory had "redeemed" the country. New York Whig leader Philip Hone wrote in his diary: "General Harrison was sung into the Presidency."[175] William Cullen Bryant agreed: "We could meet the Whigs on the field of argument and beat them without effort.... But when they lay down the weapons of argument and attack us with musical notes, what can we do?"[176]

Writing more than forty years later, George W. Julian summed up the campaign of 1840. "No one will now seriously pretend that this was a campaign of ideas, or a struggle for political reform in any sense. It was a grand national frolic, in which the imprisoned mirth and fun of the people found such jubilant and uproarious expression that anything like calmness of judgment or real seriousness of purpose was out of the question in the Whig camp."[177] John C. Calhoun described Harrison's delight with his election: "As unconscious as a child of his difficulties and those of his country, he seems to enjoy his election as a mere affair for personal vanity. It is really depressing to see it."[178]

HIS PRESIDENCY

In a letter to his wife, General Harrison wrote: "I retired into the presence of my Maker, and implored his gracious guidance in the faithful discharge of the duties of my high station."[179] As for Mrs. Harrison, she complained: "I wish that my husband's friends had left him where he is, happy and contented in retirement."[180] Martin Van Buren said of his successor, "The President is the most extraordinary man I ever saw. He does not seem to realize the vast importance of his elevation.... He is as tickled with the Presidency as a young woman with a new bonnet."[181]

On March 4, 1841, a crowd of fifty thousand people waited at the Capitol's east portico to witness the president's oath-taking. At nearly two hours, Harrison gave the longest inaugural address on record (an hour and 45 minutes— 8441 words). Although long orations were common at the time, because of the cold, drizzly conditions, his must have seemed to some present longer than his time in office.[182] He allowed his friend Daniel Webster to edit the speech — ornate with classical allusions— which resulted in some deletions. Webster boasted in jolly fashion, "I have killed seventeen Roman proconsul as dead as smelts, every one of them."[183]

Harrison wanted to shed the image created for him as a simple frontiersman and show that he was a cultured and educated man, every bit as presidential as Virginians such as Washington, Jefferson and Madison. Harrison's address was nationalistic in outlook but emphasized his pledge to follow the will of the people as expressed through their representatives in Congress. In his lengthy inaugural address, the short-termed president intoned:

> Our citizens must be content with the exercise of the powers with which the Constitution clothes them. The attempt of those of one State to control the domestic institutions of another can only result in feelings of distrust and jealousy, the certain harbingers of disunion, violence, and civil war, and the ultimate destruction of our free institutions.... The people are the best guardians of their own rights and it is the duty of their executive to abstain from interfering in or thwarting the sacred exercise of the lawmaking functions of their government.... It may be observed ... as a general remark, that republics can commit no greater error than to adopt or continue any feature in their systems of government which may be calculated to create or increase the lover of power in the bosoms of those to whom necessity obliges them to commit the management of their affairs; and surely nothing is more likely to produce such a state of mind than the long continuance of an office of high trust.[184]

It was a cold, wet and blustery day when Harrison came to Washington for his inauguration. He wanted to show that he was still the steadfast hero of Tippecanoe. He took the oath of office on March 4, 1841, wearing neither an overcoat nor hat. Then, dressed in his military uniform, he rode through the streets in the inaugural parade. The White House was poorly heated and Harrison couldn't find a quiet room in which to rest because of the multitudes of office seekers.[185] Harrison's biographer, Freeman Cleaves, said that the president died not due to a sickness contracted during his inaugural address but as a consequence of walks taken some three weeks later in the cold and slush to do some household shopping, which made his cold even worse.[186] By March 27 he was extremely ill with right lower pneumonia and "congestion of the liver."[187]

William Henry Harrison's inauguration on the 4th of March 1841, Charles Fenderich, lithographer, published 1841 (Library of Congress).

His Vice President: John Tyler of Virginia. When "Old Tippecanoe" died on April 4, the country was thrown into a constitutional crisis, that of the presidential succession. The Constitution wasn't clear as to whether on the death of a serving president his vice president would become acting president or the legitimate president. Tyler assumed the office and began to function as president, not acting president.[188] The issue was not finally resolved until the passing of the 25th Amendment to the Constitution clarifying the ambiguous provision regarding the succession to the presidency. Passed by Congress July 6, 1965, and ratified February 10, 1967, it replaced part of Article II, section 1 of the Constitution, originally written in 1783. In the interim, other vice presidents who succeeded a president who died in office followed Tyler's lead and considered themselves truly the president, as did almost everyone else.[189]

His Cabinet: Secretary of State Daniel Webster (1841); Secretary of the Treasury Thomas Ewing (1841); Secretary of War John Bell (1841); Attorney General John J. Crittenden (1841); Postmaster General Francis Granger (1841); Secretary of the Navy George E. Badger (1841).

Harrison's Only Official Act as President: "Harrison's only official act of consequence was to call Congress into a special session. He and Henry Clay had disagreed over the necessity of such a session, and when on March 11 Harrison's cabinet proved evenly divided, the president vetoed the idea. A few days later, however, Treasury Secretary Thomas Ewing reported to Harrison that federal funds were in such trouble that the government could not continue to operate until Congress' regularly scheduled session in December; Harrison thus relented, and on March 17 proclaimed the special session in the interests of 'the condition of the revenue and finance of the country.' The session was scheduled to begin on May 31."[190] Other than that, Harrison spent his brief time as president dealing with the scores of people showing up at the White House seeking governmental appointment. "General Harrison was ... smothered by the most shameless swarm of fortune hunters the capital had seen since the coming of another Hero twelve years before [Jackson, 1829].... They filled every room [of the lower level of the White House] and defied eviction. The President opened a door, expecting to meet his Cabinet. The spoilsmen crushed about him. Soon the Executive's pockets were filled with their petitions, then his hat, then his arms; and thus he staggered upstairs to revive himself with 'stimulants.'"[191] The stress of these interviews further weakened the ailing president.

His Papers: Harrison was the author of *A Discourse in the Aborigines of the Valley of the Ohio* (1838). In a report to the secretary of war, William Eustis, on August 28, 1810, Governor Harrison wrote: "The mind of the savage is so constructed that he cannot be at rest, he cannot be happy unless it is acted upon by some strong stimulus that which is produced by war is the only one that is sufficiently powerful to fill up the intervals of the chase if he hunts in the winter he must go to war in the summer, and you may rest assured ... that the establishment of tranquility between the neighboring tribes will always be a sure indication of war against us."[192] Douglas E. Clanin edited *The Papers of William Henry Harrison, 1800–1815*. The majority of Harrison's papers were destroyed in a fire in 1858. The best source of his papers is found in three reels of microfilm at the Library of Congress.

Health: Generally Harrison enjoyed good health, "but he suffered from what was called ague and fever, which was actually malaria, from time to time. The general unhealthiness of the American west is not appreciated. Sanitation was poor, so typhoid fever and cholera were scourges.... Malaria was so prevalent that the shakes were felt to be a normal part of life. The cows ate a poisonous weed that made their milk dangerous; the resulting milk fever was very prevalent, especially among children, and its cause was unknown. To be safe, people drank a lot of whiskey. The state of medicine at the time was such that the sufferer was safer in the absence of medical attention than with it, as Harrison himself later found. Diet was appalling, consisting mainly of fried fat salt pork, potatoes, and whiskey. Fruit and vegetables were scarce and very inferior, where they existed, and little effort was spent in cultivating proper species. Johnny Appleseed tried to overcome this lack. Most of the land was occupied by dark, gloomy forest that was generally hated, though the prairie lands beginning in Illinois were also considered useless and unhealthy."[193] Harrison could eat only certain foods, such as cheese and milk products, which were the only things that would ease his gnawing pains. He may have suffered from ulcers.[194]

Death: Harrison's death occurred on April 4, 1841. At that time the germ theory of disease had not yet been established. Medical science believed that disease was caused by the accumulation of harmful substances in the body, and to cure the illness these had to be removed.[195] Harrison's physicians tried just about everything to save him, including "bleeding" to rid the body of illness and "cupping," which involved applying heated cups to the skin to create suction and "cleanse" the body of impurities.[196] In addition he was dosed with opium, castor oil, hot whiskey, and Virginia snakeweed, a Seneca Indian remedy using live snakes, but the treatments only made matters worse, and he went into delirium.[197] Some historical records indicate that doctor-prescribed remedies for the pneumonia also gave Harrison a deadly case of hepatitis.[198]

Place of Death: Harrison died at the White House in Washington, D.C. It was said of

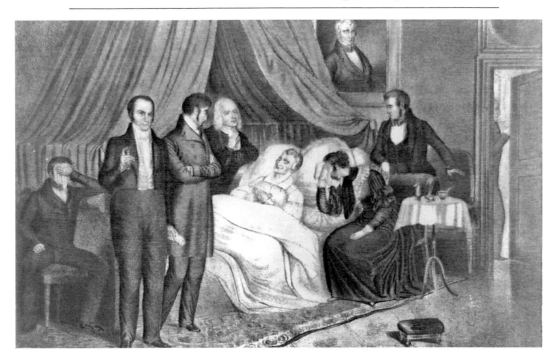

William Henry Harrison on his deathbed, with the Rev. Hawley, a physician, a niece, and a nephew in attendance, as well as Thomas Ewing, secretary of treasury, Daniel Webster, secretary of state, and Francis Granger (waiting at the door), postmaster general. An 1841 lithograph by Nathaniel Currier (Library of Congress).

him that "he was not a great man, but he had lived in a great time, and he had been a leader in great things."[199]

Cause of Death: Harrison died of right lower lobe pneumonia, jaundice and overwhelming septicemia.[200]

Final Words: During his final days, the president said, "This may be the last time I have the pleasure of speaking to you on earth. I bid you farewell; if forever, fare thee well."[201] Different sources provide alternate final words. Some sources give this quote: "I cannot bear this. Don't trouble me."[202] However, most claim that in his delirium, believing he was speaking to his vice president, he said, "Sir, I wish you to understand the true principles of government, I wish them carried out. I ask nothing more."[203]

Place of Burial: Harrison was the first U.S. president to be given a state funeral. As there were no established ceremonies for an official state mourning, a prominent Washington merchant, Alexander Hunter, was asked to handle the arrangements. He borrowed from the rituals of royal funerals, setting a basic model and precedent for all future presidential funerals. Harrison lay in state in the East Room of the White House where his funeral was held. "Hunter draped the White House in black. Official buildings and many private households followed suit, starting a now-lost tradition that was repeated at Lincoln's funeral 25 years later. For Harrison, Hunter ordered a curtained and upholstered black and white carriage, which was drawn by black-clad horses, each accompanied by a black groom dressed and turbaned entirely in white. Along the side marched white pallbearers, dressed in black. Before Harrison, the funerals of former presidents saw little pomp in the capital."[204] After the funeral, Harrison's body was held in a receiving vault of the Congressional Cemetery in Washington. D.C., until arrangements were made to transfer it to its final resting place.[205] He is buried in the William Henry Harrison Memorial State Park, on Mt. Nebo in North Bend. An obelisk of Bedford limestone, with marble entranceway, rises 60 feet above his tomb.[206] Cut into the limestone, in 6-inch letters, are all of Harrison's military and political achievements. His wife is buried next to him.[207]

MISCELLANEA

Teetotaler: Harrison saw the evil effects of liquor while in the army. He was a man of strict temperate habits and set an example of total abstinence before his comrades and soldiers. Harrison always drank moderately, and less and less in his later years.[208] "Every farm had a distillery to make whiskey ... but he closed his and altered it to parch corn. Kiln-dried corn could be stored, and was a useful commodity, if not as profitable as whiskey."[209] At the Cabin, Harrison only served and drank sweet cider. "The Cabin and the cider played a large role in the election of 1840. On political flyers, the cabin was a single-room log cabin, with the hard cider in a barrel beside it. Neither presumption was true, but Harrison was indeed a liberal host whose hospitality was always freely given."[210] Its not known if Harrison used tobacco. "Cigars and chewing were both popular at the time and spitting made all horizontal surfaces in the reach of American men slippery, and occasionally, their ladies' dresses as well. Carpet was used to absorb the juice and give better footing."[211]

Tecumseh's Curse: According to legend, with his dying breath Shawnee leader Tecumseh placed a curse on Harrison, claiming that he would die in office. "Whether it was truly an 'Indian curse' placed on Harrison and his successors by Tecumseh (sometimes attributed to his brother, Tenskwatawa) or simply a superstition that was somehow realized, the 'curse' lasted for 140 years and, even then, almost claimed another victim, which makes it an extraordinarily odd historical coincidence."[212] Perhaps the curse came to currency when it was noticed beginning with Harrison's election in 1840, every president for more than a hundred years elected in a year ending in "0" died in office. This prophecy continued to come to fruition every 20 years: Lincoln elected 1860, Garfield elected 1880, McKinley elected 1900, Harding elected 1920, Roosevelt elected 1940 and Kennedy elected 1960. Reagan elected in 1980 broke the curse, although there was an assassination attempt on his life in 1981. George W. Bush was elected in 2000.[213] We will have to wait until 2020 to see if the curse strikes again.

Keep the Ball Rolling and Booze: During the campaign of 1840, a group of Whig Party members pushed a ten-foot paper and tin ball emblazoned with pro–Harrison slogans for hundreds of miles. Others handed out whiskey in log cabin–shaped bottles supplied by the E.C. Booz distillery. As a result, "keep the ball rolling" and "booze" were added to the American idiom.[214]

Abolitionist Liberty Party Candidate: James G. Birney of Kentucky was the leader of the conservative abolitionists in the United States from about 1835 to 1845. "In the general assembly of Kentucky in 1816, and in that of Alabama in 1819, he opposed inter-state rendition of fugitive slaves and championed liberal slave-laws."[215] Around 1826 he became active in the American Colonization Society, serving as its agent in the Southwest in 1832–33. In 1833 he returned to Danville, Kentucky and "devoted himself wholly to the antislavery cause. He freed his own slaves in 1834. Convinced that gradual emancipation would merely stimulate the inter-state slave trade, and that the dangers of a mixed labor system were greater than those of emancipation en mass, he formally repudiated colonization in 1834; moreover, gradualism had become for him an unjustifiable compromise in a matter of religion and justice."[216] "He favored immediatism, but he differed sharply from the Garrisonian (William Lloyd Garrison) abolitionists, who abhorred the federal Constitution and favored secession. Birney always wrote, spoke and labored for the permanent safety of the Union. The assaults of the South in defense of slavery upon free speech, free press, the right of petition and trial by jury, he pronounced 'exorbitant claims ... on the liberties of the free states'; the contest had become, he said, 'one not alone of freedom for the blacks but of freedom for the whites.'"[217] Birney proclaimed: "There will be no cessation of conflict until slavery shall be exterminated or liberty destroyed"—"liberty and slavery cannot both live in juxtaposition."[218] He advocated the formation of an independent anti-slavery party. "In 1840 the new party was formed, and in 1840, and again in 1844, as the Liberty Party, it made Birney its candidate for the presidency. In 1840 he received 7069 votes; in 1844, 62,263."[219] In 1840 his vice presidential running mate was Thomas Earle of Pennsylvania and in 1844, Thomas Morris of Ohio.

Observations About William Henry Harrison

BY OTHER PRESIDENTS

[An] active but shallow mind, a political adventurer not without talents but self-sufficient, vain, and indiscreet.[220]— John Quincy Adams

The greatest beggar and the most troublesome of all the office seekers during my Administration was General Harrison.[221]— John Quincy Adams

Harrison comes in upon a hurricane; God grant he may not go out upon a wreck.[222]— John Quincy Adams

The Republic ... may suffer under the present imbecile chief, but the sober second thought of the people will restore it at our next Presidential election.[223]— Andrew Jackson

It is true, the victory of 1840 did not produce the happy results anticipated; but it is equally true, as we believe that the unfortunate death of General Harrison was the cause of failure. It was not the election of General Harrison that was expected to produce happy effects, but the measures to be adopted by his administration.[224]— Abraham Lincoln

Harrison didn't accomplish a thing during the month he was in office. He made no contribution whatsoever. He had no policy. He didn't know what the government was about, to tell the truth. About the only thing he did during that brief period was see friends and friends of friends, because he was such an easy mark that he couldn't say no to anybody, and everybody and his brother were beseeching him for jobs.[225]— Harry S Truman

BY OTHERS

When Martin was housed like a chattel, / Opposed to the war as you know, / Our hero was foremost in battle, / And conquered at Tippecanoe.[226]— Anonymous

Harrison ... resorted to new modes of electioneering in order to broadcast a very old-fashioned message.[227]— M.J. Heale

The American eagle has taken his flight which is supplied by the cider barrell.... Hurrah for Tippecanoe is heard more frequently than Hurrah for the Constitution, and whatever may be the result of the election, the Hurrah is heard and felt in every part of the United States.[228]— Philip Hone

I believe him to be one of the first military characters I ever knew; and, in addition to this, he is capable of making greater personal exertions than any officer with whom I have ever served.[229]— Governor Isaac Shelby of Kentucky

My faithful and gallant aide-de-camp, Lieutenant Harrison, rendered the most essential service, by communicating my orders in every direction, and by his conduct and bravery exciting the troops to press for victory.[230]— General Anthony Wayne

TEN

John Tyler

President or Acting President?

Tenth President of the United States, 1841–1845

As a boy, John Tyler attended a small school kept by Mr. McMurdo, who diligently disciplined his charges with a birch switch. Tyler later would recall, "It was a wonder he did not whip all the sense out of his scholars."[1] At the age of eleven, Tyler was one of the leaders in a rebellion against their savage teacher. The pedagogue was overwhelmed by their sheer numbers, tied hand and foot, and left locked in his own schoolhouse. Late at night he was discovered by a passing traveler. When McMurdo complained to Judge Tyler about the actions of his son, the elder Tyler responded, "*Sic semper tyrannis*" (Thus always to tyrants), which is the motto of the state of Virginia."[2]

Birth: The future president was born on March 29, 1790, in a "setting of landed gentry, genteelism, slaves, in essence a typical Virginia Tidewater planter with a developed aristocracy."[3] The site was the twelve-hundred acre Tyler family plantation of Greenway on the James River in Charles City County (10 miles from Berkeley plantation where William Henry Harrison was born), located between Richmond and Williamsburg, Virginia.

Nicknames and Titles: "His Ascendancy," "His Accidency," "Executive Ass," and "President Without a Party"[4] were derisive nicknames laid on him by his political opponents. Of a more flattering nature, he was called "Honest John," as he was truthful and kind to people.[5]

Family: John Tyler was the sixth child and second son of John Tyler, Sr., and Mary Armistead Tyler. His father was 43 and his mother was 29 at the time of John Jr.'s birth, an age discrepancy that the future president would replicate and some with his second wife.[6] John Sr. (1747–1813), was a prosperous Virginia tobacco planter and slave owner. He owned 1,900 acres in Charles City County, James City County plus a property investment in Kentucky. He was a roommate of Thomas Jefferson at the College of William and Mary. Father Tyler served in the Virginia House of Burgesses from 1778 to 1786. He was speaker of the house for four years.... His friends included Patrick Henry and James Monroe and he played the violin as his son would eventually do.[7] The elder Tyler served in the Continental Army in 1775, and after the Declaration of Independence, he was a member of the Virginia House of Delegates for several years, beginning in 1777. He was Speaker from 1781 to 1784. He was a member of the Virginia Council of State from 1780 to 1781, and was vice president of the Virginia Convention to ratify the United States Constitution in 1788.[8] "A fervent advocate of states' rights, which would preserve his power, he vigorously opposed the Constitution and the rights it might give to commoners."[9] He served as the governor of Virginia from 1809 to 1811. President Madison nominated Tyler to be a judge of the U.S. District Court, District of Virginia circuit court for Tyler County, which was formed in 1815 from the southern part of Ohio County and is named for John Tyler, Sr. He was confirmed by the Senate on January 3, 1811, and received commission on January 7, 1811.[10] He died when his son John Jr. was a member of the Virginia house of delegates.[11] One of the biographers of John Tyler, Jr., noted "the most important single fact is that he absorbed *in toto* the political, social, and economic views of his distinguished father."[12]

Mary Marot Armistead Tyler (1761–1797) married John Tyler in Weyanoke on the outskirts of Alexandria, Virginia, in 1776 and died when John the younger was seven years old.[13] According to family tradition, one evening, as his mother sat at the window of Greenway, while the rays of the moon's silver light chased one another into the room through the giant branches of a grand old willow, John, then an infant, happened to catch a glimpse of the moon, eagerly stretched out his hands and cried bitterly for it. This prompted Mary to prophesy, "This child is destined to be president of the United States, his wishes to fly so high."[14] John Jr.'s siblings were Anne Contesse, Elizabeth Armistead, Martha Jefferson, Maria Henry, Wat Henry, William, and Christiana Booth.[15]

Ancestors: The ancestors of John Tyler were among the earliest English settlers of Virginia. His first American ancestor, Henry Tyler, lived on the outskirts of what now is the city of Williamsburg.[16] Although it hasn't been verified the Tyler family believe they trace their lineage back Walter Hilliard, usually called Wat Tyler, a man of obscure origin who led an English peasants' revolt in 1381 in the reign of the second Richard, headed the insurrection in England known by his name.[17] The Dukes of Lancaster, York and Gloucester, regents of the child king Edward III, made several unsuccessful expeditions against France and to pay for the excursions they burdened the working class with more and more taxes.[18] Wat Tyler was a heroic soldier in a number of battles with the French and some naval battles as well. After returning to his home in Broxley, he married and worked as the village smith.[19] In 1381 the effort to strictly enforce the collection of taxes created discontent throughout England. "Wat Tyler's rebellion was ignited when a tax collector tried to make a determination that Wat Tyler's daughter was of taxable age (15) by stripping her naked and assaulting her. Tyler, who was working close by, heard the screams

John Tyler, photographic print, created between 1860 and 1865 (Library of Congress, Brady-Handy Collection).

of his wife and daughter, came running and smashed in the tax collector's skull with a hammer. He was cheered by his neighbors and the commoners of the western division of Kent were brought together by his courage. Wat Tyler was elected their leader."[20] "Wat Tyler's group joined another group led by two itinerant priests named John Ball and Jack Straw, and rose 100,000 strong to invade London. The enraged mob broke open every prison and beheaded every judge and lawyer they could capture."[21] They stormed the Tower of London, where the Lord Chancellor and Archbishop of Canterbury Simon Sudbury and Sir Robert Hales had taken refuge. Sudbury was hated due to his leadership of what was seen as a corrupt church. Even more hated was Hales, Lord Treasurer and the man responsible for bringing in the hated poll tax. These men were viewed by many as corrupt officials who ruthlessly exploited the weaknesses of the young King for their own ends. The pair were seized by the mob and dragged outside to Tower Hill where they were both beheaded.[22] While trying to "present the peasants' grievances to sixteen-year-old King Richard II, the mayor of London, Sir William Walworth, slashed the unarmed Tyler, who was then immediately stabbed by John Standwick, one of the king's squires."[23] "Watching from a distance the peasants instantly arranged themselves in order of battle with their longbows. Richard II rode up to them and said, 'Wat Tyler was a traitor. I'll be your leader.' Confused, the peasants followed the king until his soldiers met him and dispersed the crowd. Minus their leader, the peasants went home. Richard reneged on his promises and hanged 1500 of the rebels after 'jury trials.' Those trials were presided over by Judge John Tresilian, who told the jurors in each case that he would hang them if they didn't convict. Tresilian was hanged himself seven years later. Richard II was forced to abdicate in 1399."[24] He is thought to have starved to death in captivity at Pomfret Castle. The rebellion came to an end soon after Tyler's death. "Although the Peasants' Revolt ended in ultimate failure it has remained one of the most significant domestic events in English history and did much to bring attention to bear on the suffering and hardship of the English lower-class.[25]

Appearance: Tyler's appearance was impressive. According to his biographer and son by his second wife: "His hair was silky brown wavy," curling around and framing his face; "his eyes blue" and deeply set; "his nose large, and after the Roman order," long with a sharp ridge, featured a bump; his mouth firm set; and his brow lofty and expanded. "He was thin and tall, — six feet in height, and capable of enduring great labor and fatigue despite his rather uncertain health and."[26] He was considered handsome, with all the "features of the best Grecian model."[27] Some said he looked like busts of the Roman orator Cicero. Tyler wasn't sensitive about the size of his nose, and he often joked about it. On one occasion, he was riding a stagecoach with a destination of Washington. One of his fellow passengers was a little, short and dumpy man, with a small, stumpy and turned-up nose. Within a few miles of their destination, someone remarked that they must be near the capital, to which the little man, sniffing facetiously at the air, announced, "Yes, I smell it." Tyler, speaking with solemnity, responded, "Why sir, if you can smell Washington with your nose, my nose must be there already."[28]

Personality and Character: John Tyler, Sr.'s, personality was characterized by rugged individuality. Tyler Jr. "embodied more of the gentle virtues of his mother than the stern qualities of his father."[29] He possessed a smoothness and gentleness of character that enabled him to "make contacts with others with as little friction as possible."[30] Gracious, mild-mannered, and charming, Tyler "always comported himself with the proper decorum and dignity."[31] It was said of him that "one of his fortunate traits was the ability to conciliate opponents and inspire them with a feeling of sympathetic friendship."[32] Henry S. Foote, senator from Mississippi recalled: "He was one of the most genial and captivating men I ever encountered; there was not a particle of hauteur or assumption in his aspect or demeanor; he seemed to be eminently frank and unconstrained in his conversation; had a clear and ringing voice; possessed a ready and insinuating smile, and, in fact, few could hold converse with him for ten or fifteen minutes even without feeling strongly impressed with his many high qualities, nor without feeling more or less inclined to sympathize with his fortunes."[33] However, Tyler was stubborn and didn't believe in compromise. This alienated not only his opponents, but his supporters as well. He was a political independent, acting on what he believed to be right, rather than following the dictates of politicians or even constituents. In accessing Tyler's personality, his biographer Oliver Chitwood observed: "If we should accept the answers of his opponents ... we would conclude that an emissary of Satan had once again slipped into a place of undue prominence."[34]

Tyler was a man of principle and integrity, even if his principles in hindsight do not appear to be in line with what the American Constitution promised. Tyler was the last of the Virginia aristocrats in the White House, and had a deep and abiding allegiance to the South. In 1834, he said, "The Southern States are in constant apprehension lest the national government should be converted in a mere majority machine."[35] Confederate general Henry A. Wise is quoted in Robert Seager II's *And Tyler Too: A Biography of John and Julia Gardiner Tyler*: "[Tyler was] an honest, affectionate, benevolent, loving man, who had fought the battles of his life bravely and truly, doing his whole great duty without fear, though not without much unjust reproach."[36]

Marriage and Romances: Soon after his graduation from William and Mary, Tyler met beautiful Letitia Christian (1790–1842) at a private party on a plantation near her home and a romance blossomed. Tyler's wedding to the lovely young woman with dark brown hair and dark brown eyes took place following a five-year engagement. The attractive young couple married on March 29, 1813, Tyler's birthday, at her parents' home, Cedar Grove, in New Kent County, Virginia.[37] Tyler revealed that until merely three weeks from their marriage that he had not dared to kiss her hand, "so perfectly reserved and modest had she always been."[38] However, he did compose sonnets dedicated to Letitia. Although their courtship does not appear to be very thrilling by later standards, it was a love match, which proved to be an extremely happy marriage. A short time after the wedding, Letitia's parents— planter Robert Christian and his wife, Mary Eaton Browne Christian — died.[39] Letitia's substantial inheritance permitted her husband to pursue a career in public service and move into a succession of larger homes: Mons-Sacer, Woodburn, and finally Greenway, the Tyler family home.[40] The management of a large plantation placed a heavy burden on the mistress of the house, who handled the family assets. "The lady of the 'big house' could make ends meet in the farm economy, only if she was an efficient entrepreneur."[41] These were stressful periods for Mrs. Tyler, whose health was always fragile. She preferred domestic pursuits and took little active interest in her husband's political career.[42] It was said of her: "She was perfectly content to be seen only as a part of the existence of her beloved husband; to entertain her neighbors; to sit gently by her child's cradle, reading, knitting, or sewing."[43] While her husband was in the U.S. Congress, Mrs. Tyler enjoyed the social affairs, but she refused to allow her daughters to attend the fashionable Georgetown Academy for Girls because it was a Catholic institution and she was strong in her Episcopal faith. Instead the girls were sent to a school in Williamsburg.[44]

"In 1839 Letitia Tyler suffered a stroke that left her partially paralyzed. When Tyler was elected vice president, he intended to conduct his duties from his home so he could stay close to his wife."[45] The Tylers were at their home when news came of President Harrison's death. Tyler immediately set out for Washington, where he took the oath of office. Letitia was unable to be at the ceremony, and it wasn't until late May that she joined him at the White House. She was an invalid for the entire time she lived in the White House.[46] She presided as White House hostess only in a very limited way. During the year-and-a-half Letitia lived at the White House her only public appearance was at her daughter Elizabeth's 1842 wedding.[47] She worried about the continuous drain on the family finances, since Congress made no provision for paying the president's expenses.[48] Early in 1842, Mrs. Tyler suffered a second stroke and died at age 52, clasping her favorite flower, a damask rose, surrounded by her family. "Her end was quiet and tranquil, like one falling from weariness into profound slumber, exhibiting a mind at rest with itself, and a heart of virtue."[49] *The National Intelligencer,* no supporter of President Tyler, eulogized Letitia Tyler: She was "in life, a wife, a mother, a Christian, loving and confiding to her husband, gentle and affectionate to her children; kindly and charitable to the needy and affected; and in death she sleeps the sleep of the righteous and the beloved of Heaven!"[50] As the first incumbent presidential wife to die, her coffin lay in state in the East Room of the White House. An "official committee of the citizens of Washington" accompanied her casket from the White House to her final resting place at Cedar Grove Cemetery.[51]

After Letitia died, Tyler's daughter-in-law Priscilla Cooper Tyler, wife of his oldest son, Robert, acted as presidential hostess at state functions. Priscilla was a former actress who went on the stage at age 17. She was the daughter of the famous actor and tragedian Thomas Apthorpe Cooper and New York socialite Mary Fairlee.[52]

Priscilla captivated citizens and politicians alike with her dark hair, dark eyes, great wit, and sparkling conversations. She held two formal dinners a week when Congress was in session and biweekly open houses for the public.[53] "During the summer of 1843, Priscilla accompanied her father-in-law on an official presidential tour, the first time any president traveled across the United States with a female member of his family. At Baltimore the president, his son Robert, and Priscilla were feted at a public banquet and reception. In New York, they were treated to the sight of a flotilla of seventy-four ships, many booming their cannons. An estimated 40,000 citizens turned out to cheer them as their carriage passed by on streets strewn with flowers."[54] When Robert moved to Philadelphia to practice law, his sister Letitia "Letty" Tyler Semple briefly assumed the duties as the president's hostess.[55]

In 1842, President Tyler, still mourning Letitia, met Julia Gardiner (1820–1889) at a White House reception and immediately was smitten, attracted to her "raven tresses." She was the beautiful daughter of prominent landowner and New York state senator David Gardiner and his wife, Juliana McLachlan Gardiner. Julia was born on May 4, 1820, at Gardiner's Island off the eastern tip of Long Island, New York.[56] "She was 5 feet 3 inches tall, with dark black hair, usually worn parted in the middle; gray eyes, beautiful shoulders and a good figure. She was flirtatious, prone to be indiscreet, and very daring for her day. Impulsive and reckless at times, the young Julia Gardiner was one who loved being center stage."[57]

Brought up in a world of wealth and position, she and her equally beautiful younger sister Margaret were educated at Madame N.D. Chagaray's Institute for young ladies in New York City. Julia studied French, arithmetic, literature, history and composition.[58] By fifteen, she was already seeking an advantageous marriage and was something of a trial to her staid parents. In 1839, at age nineteen, she allowed her image to be used for an advertisement for a dry goods store, under the title "The Rose of Long Island."[59] "A young, unmarried woman's public exposure, especially in a commercial venture, was considered humiliating within the mores of her parents' socially elite class."[60] Extremely upset they took Julia and her sister Margaret first to Washington, D.C., and then to Europe. "Julia Gardiner was presented to the Roman Catholic Pope Leo, and kissed his ring in the traditional ceremony.... She also carried on brief romances with a German baron and a Belgian count.... The American Ambassador to France, Lewis Cass arranged for the Gardiners' presentation at the royal court of King Louis Philippe and Queen Marie Amelia."[61] All the images of royalty that she saw gave the young Julia Gardiner a severe case of "Queen fever" that would be reflected during her time in the White House.[62] Back in Washington, D.C., the Gardiner girls entertained so many gentlemen callers the senator was forced to take a few extra rooms in their boardinghouse to accommodate them.[63] "Sometimes Julia entertained her guests by playing the guitar and singing."[64] She was much sought after. According to writer

Julia Gardiner Tyler, glass negative created in 1913 (Library of Congress, Harris and Ewing Collection).

Elizabeth Ellett, "Sparkling and attractive, without affectation, she had a high and daring spirit."[65] Julia received numerous proposals of marriage, including two from congressmen, a Supreme Court justice, John McLean, and President Tyler, who was thirty years her senior. He proposed marriage at the 1843 George Washington's Ball, but she declined.[66]

Senator Gardiner and his daughters Julia and Margaret spent Christmas Eve 1843 with President Tyler at the White House. By February 1844, gossips were talking about the apparent relationship between Tyler and Julia. He sent her flowery love letters, which she read aloud to her family,[67] Dolley Madison arranged a trip up the Potomac on the gunboat USS *Princeton*, on February 28, 1844. Among the guests were the president, most of his Cabinet and the Gardiners. About 4:30, the ship's captain, R.P. Stockton, obliged Secretary of the Navy Thomas Gilmer by firing the ship's "peacemaker," a large gun station at the bow of the ship. Meant as a salute as the vessel passed Mount Vernon, the gun exploded, killing the secretary of state, Abel P. Upshur, Gilmer and Senator Gardiner, among others. Julia fainted into the arms of Tyler.[68]

Julia, who was extremely close to her illustrious father, later said that after his death, Tyler seemed to fill the void that no younger man ever could.[69] Amidst great secrecy, John married Julia on June 26, 1844, at the Church of the Ascension, New York City. Only the president's son John was in attendance, as the other children were not informed of the nuptials. Julia was twenty-four at the time of the ceremony; her groom was fifty-seven.[70]

Awful Explosion of the "Peace-Maker" on Board the U.S. Steam Frigate, Princeton, *on Wednesday, 28th Feb. 1844,* lithograph by N. Currier, 1844 (Library of Congress).

Although some have claimed she was more intrigued with being the president's wife than being Tyler's wife, she came to adore him and admired everything he did. His causes became her causes. In this she was a brilliant ally. She ensured the 1844–1845 social season was the grandest and most dazzling since Dolley Madison was mistress of the White House. Julia sought and received advice from Dolley on how to entertain the assortment of guests among friends and foes that must be invited to her parties.[71] Though stunned by the suddenness of the wedding, Tyler's sons were quite taken by the lovely and vivacious Julie. His daughters were less so and Letty Tyler Semple, named for her mother Letitia, always remained hostile to her father's new wife.[72] As for the president, he told his young wife that the honeymoon would likely go on eternally, because he fell in love with her again each day.[73] Although Julia did not live long at the White House, she made the most of her time. She wrote, "I have commenced my auspicious reign and am in quiet possession of the Presidential Mansion.... This winter I intend to do something in the way of entertaining that shall be the admiration and talk of all Washington world."[74]

The new first lady was "able to bring a certain style and opulence to a rather dull and staid White House,"[75] Still in mourning for her father, Julia "wore either white, black lace or royal purple (also a mourning color), and in her hair, ending on her forehead, a headpiece made of black jet beads, later changed to diamonds. She often appeared in public with the greyhound given to her by her husband."[76] She gave offense by appearing "too royal" or "queen like" and was frequently referred to as "Lady Presidentress" and "Her Loveliness."[77] She enjoyed dancing and introduced both the polka and the waltz to Washington society.[78] She so charmed the *New York Herald*'s Washington correspondent, F.W. Thomas, that he gladly published favorable press notices for her parties and acted almost like a press agent for the first lady.[79] When Tyler's presidential term ended the couple returned to their Virginia plantation. Living up to her motto, "the full extent or nothing,"[80] she redid the plantation home with her own money, making it a showplace. In February 1853, Julia wrote a letter to the *Southern Literary Messenger* rejecting the pleas by "the Duchess of Sutherland and Ladies of England" to southern women to help end slavery. Julia praised slavery as a civilizing influence and noted that the slaves at the Tyler plantation were far better off than the poor in London and those starving in Ireland, which she had observed first hand when she and her family made their visits to the British Isles. She warned that "governments and countries which are now looked upon as stars of the first magnitude, will ere long, if the United States roll on their present orbit, be secondary and tertiary in the political hemisphere."[81] She wrote that if the noble ladies wished to fulfill their philanthropic efforts, they should apply them to the needy of their own country.[82]

Mrs. Tyler chided the English ladies for being meddlers and assured them that all right thinking women in the United States would never consider scandalizing their husbands by engaging in politics.[83] Julia's defense of the institution of slavery was based on the belief that the "South's labor system was more benign and much less harsh than that of industrial capitalism."[84] When Virginia seceded from the Union in 1861, Julia eagerly supported the Confederacy and encouraged her sons who were old enough to join the Southern army. When her husband died in 1862, the young widow fled Virginia when her plantation was occupied and plundered by Union forces.[85] A Union office reported his findings of the result of the sacking of the mansion by the black troops under General Wild: "all of the furnishings of Sherwood Forest had been broken and smashed to pieces — mirrors, furniture, china, and beds. John Tyler's valuable and extensive library was vandalized, with the 'books and papers mutilated — simply for mischief.'"[86] Julia Tyler took several of her children to her family home in New York. Julia spent the remainder of her life defending her husband and the Confederacy as well as trying to keep their Virginia home in the family.[87] She settled in Richmond, and in 1872 she and her youngest daughter, Pearl, converted to Roman Catholicism.[88] In 1881, Julia won her battle to receive a pension as a president's widow. She was awarded $1,200 a year, later increased to $5,000 a year.[89] Mrs. Tyler died in 1889 at sixty-nine years of age in a room of the hotel only doors away from where her husband had died, and was buried in Hollywood Cemetery, next to him.[90]

Children: Tyler had more children than any other U.S. president. He had eight with his first wife — Mary, Robert, John Jr., Letitia Christian, Elizabeth, Anne Contesse, Alice and Tazewell — and seven with his second wife — David Gardiner, John Alexander, Julia Gardiner, Lachlan, Lyon Gardiner, Robert Fitzwalter, and Pearl. All but Anne Contesse, who died at birth, survived to maturity.[91] Letty Tyler Semple, the beautiful daughter of John Tyler, was still grieving her mother when the president married Julia Gardiner. All Julia's efforts to befriend Letty were rebuffed. Two decades later, Letty accused Julia of seducing her own husband, James A. Semple. When she discovered he was spending time at Julia's New York apartment, Letty became furious and ended her troubled marriage.[92]

As of 2007, one of Tyler's grandchildren, 78-year-old Harrison Tyler, enjoyed telling people "if my grandfather were here to talk with you, he would be more than 225 years old."[93]

Born a slave, John William Dunjee (or John Dungy or John Dugee), a prominent African American missionary, educator, and founder of many Baptist churches across the country, claimed to be the illegitimate child of John Tyler and one of his female slaves. Some sources allege that Tyler had a number of other children by his slaves.[94]

Religion and Religious Beliefs: Tyler was classified an Episcopalian, but according to his biographer Robert Seager, he was not one to take "a denominational approach to God."[95]

His views of religious doctrines were similar to his hero Thomas Jefferson. Some sources classify him as a deist in belief and practice. Following his death a friend said, "He was a firm believer in the atonement of the son of God, and in the efficacy of his blood to wash away every stain of mortal sin. ... He was by faith and heirship a member of the Episcopal Church and never doubted divine revelation." However, no pastor came to his home to administer the last sacrament, and in her account of his last illness, Tyler's wife wrote nothing of faith, hope, Christ or eternity.[96] Tyler was a strong supporter of religious tolerance and separation of church and state. He adamantly believed that political issues had no business being preached from the pulpit; including such sensitive issues as slavery. In a letter of July 10, 1843, to Joseph Simpson, he made the following statement:

> The United States have adventured upon a great and noble experiment, which is believed to have been hazarded in the absence of all previous precedent — that of total separation of Church and State. No religious establishment by law exists among us. The conscience is left free from all restraint and each is permitted to worship his Maker after his own judgment. The offices of the Government are open alike to all. No tithes are levied to support an established Hierarchy, nor is the fallible judgment of man set up as the sure and infallible creed of faith. The Mohammedan, if he will come among us would have the privilege guaranteed to him by the constitution to worship according to the Koran; and the East Indian might erect a shrine to Brahma if it so pleased him. Such is the spirit of toleration inculcated by our political institutions.... The Hebrew persecuted and down trodden in other regions takes up his abode among us with none to make him afraid.... And the Aegis of the Government is over him to defend and protect him. Such is the great experiment which we have tried, and such are the happy fruits which have resulted from it; our system of free government would be imperfect without it.[97]

In a May 19, 1856, letter to his son Robert, Tyler lectured: "The intolerant spirit manifested against Catholics, as exhibited in the burning of their churches, etc., will so soon as the thing becomes fairly considered, arouse a strong feeling of dissatisfaction on the part of a large majority of the American people; for if there is one principle of higher import with them than any other, it is the principle of religious freedom."[98]

Education: Tyler was educated as befitting a scion of the tidewater plantation gentry. His father and mother supervised his early education, grooming him from an early age for playing a prominent role in serving his state and the nation as would be expected of a member of Virginia's most distinguished family. Early in his life he was taught at home by his father and mother, so when he started school he could already read and write. John Jr. soon showed to be a lad of more than ordinary ability. He had a quick mind, an excellent memory, and was a great reader.[99] "At the age of twelve, he entered the preparatory branch of the elite College of William and Mary, continuing the Tyler family's tradition of attending the college. Tyler graduated from the school's collegiate branch in 1807, at age seventeen. Among the books that informed his economic views was Adam Smith's *The Wealth of Nations*. His political views were deeply shaped by Bishop James Madison, the college's president, who served as a second father and mentor to him."[100] At his graduation from the college, Tyler delivered an address on the subject of female education. He favored it. While it was hailed by many as the best commencement speech ever, Bishop Madison was outraged that his favorite student would speak such heresy and tried to silence Tyler to no avail.[101] The honorary degree of doctor of laws was conferred on him by his alma mater in 1854. Until 1776, the Chancellor of the College of William and Mary, which had been "chartered in 1693 by King William III and Queen Mary II," was an English subject — "usually the Archbishop of Canterbury or the Bishop of London — who served as the College's advocate to the crown, while a colonial president oversaw the day-to-day activities of the Williamsburg campus."[102]

Following the Revolutionary War, George Washington was appointed as the first American chancellor of the college, serving until his death in 1799.[103] "The office remained vacant until another United States president, John Tyler, was appointed as chancellor, serving from 1859 until 1862."[104] With the commencement of the Civil War, all of the staff and students of William and Mary joined the Confederate army. The college was closed May 1861 through the fall of 1865. The Battle of Williamsburg took place on May 5, 1862. Federal troops occupied the city for the remainder of the Civil War and the Wren Building was used as a hospital during the Union occupation of the area.[105] "On September 9, 1862, the Wren Building was almost totally consumed by a fire set by members of the 5th Pennsylvania Cavalry Regiment. Some other buildings and enclosures belonging to the college were also destroyed."[106] The college was revived in 1888 under President Lyon G. Tyler, thirteenth child of United States president John Tyler. In 1893, Congress appropriated $64,000 to the college for "the destruction of its buildings and other property without authority by soldiers of the United States during the late war."[107]

Pets and Animals: Tyler had a horse named "General," a pet canary named "Johnny Ty," and an Italian greyhound called "Le Beau," a gift from the consul of Naples "to grace the White House lawn."[108] On a grave in Virginia, Tyler had the following engraved: "Here lies the body of my good horse, The General. For 20 years he bore me around the circuit of my practice, and in all that time he never made a blunder. Would that his master could say the same!"[109]

Home: Tyler bought the Virginia plantation "Walnut Grove" near his birthplace in 1842 for his retirement. "The plantation, first recorded in a 1616 land grant, was originally known as Smith's Hundred. It had several owners before Tyler purchased the home and its surrounding 1,600 acres in 1842. He bought the plantation from his cousin, Collier Minge, while he was still in the White House."[110] Having supported James Knox Polk instead of Henry Clay for president, Tyler was accused by Clay of being an outlaw who was retiring to his Sherwood Forest — a reference to the legendary outlaw Robin Hood. So Tyler renamed his home "Sherwood Forest."[111] Known as the longest frame house in America, its façade stretched over 300 feet long by 1845. Tyler expanded the manor house by connecting his separate law office to the main house with a 68-foot-long ballroom designed for dancing the Virginia Reel.[112]

Completed in 1844, the home is three stories tall but only one room deep. This unique mansion has 24 rooms, seven sets of stairs, and 18 fireplaces. The house, circa 1720, is a classic example of Virginia Tidewater design: big house, little house, colonnade and kitchen. Sherwood Forest remained unique because of its mirror-image symmetry.[113] During the years of his retirement Tyler owned between sixty and ninety slaves, of which 13 were house slaves and resided in the mansion. The others lived in some twenty cabins of the grounds and worked the corn and wheat fields. Tyler was reputed to be a benign master who treated his slaves humanely.[114] The Tylers were often cash poor and, due to Julia's extravagance, more money was spent than the plantation brought in. Tyler frequently borrowed from bank to pay off loans from other banks. Speculation in timber and mining didn't bring him the expected fortune. Although he sold off some land, he had to turn to the Gardiner family for financial assistance. Tyler's descendants still live at Sherwood Forest, although the home is open to public tours.[115]

Recreational Pastimes and Interests: Tyler played the violin and loved to dance, but that was after he married Julia. While married to Letitia, he disapproved of dancing, telling his daughter Mary that he considered the waltz to be rather vulgar. Even after leaving the

White House Tyler received letters from ministers complaining of Julia's dances.[116] He was fond of poetry, especially the works of Shakespeare, and frequently composed long poems of his own.[117] "While Tyler's poetry went unseen and unheard among most outsiders, it featured regularly in his private life as a source of consolation, reflection, and delight." On his sixtieth birthday Julia Tyler wrote a poem to her husband, saying, "What e'er changes time may bring, I'll love thee as thou art!"[118]

On January 1, 1855, sixty-five-year-old Tyler composed a love poem for her:

> The seamen on the wave, love,
> When storm and tempest rave, love,
> Look to one star to save love,
> Thou are that star to me![119]

Tyler was often inspired to write poetry when faced with a difficult or transitional moment in his life. He wrote the ballad "Sweet Lady, Awake! A Serenade" in 1843 when he was courting his wife-to-be, Julie Gardiner, who later set it to music. Among its lines are these:

> Sweet lady awake, from your slumbers awake
> Weird beings we come o'er hill and through brake
> To sing you a song in the stillness of night
> Oh, read you our riddle fair lady aright?
> We are sent by the one whose found heart is your own,
> Who mourns in thy absence and sighs all alone.
> Alas, he is distant — but tho' far, far away,
> He thinks of you, Lady, by night and by day.
> Sweet lady awake, sweet lady awake![120]

When his three-month-old daughter, Anne, died in July 1825, Tyler composed an elegy, which included the following stanza:

> Oh child of my love as a beautiful flower;
> Thy blossom expanded a short fleeing hour.
> The winter of death hath blighted thy bloom
> And thou lyest alone in the cold dead tomb.[121]

Occupation: Tyler studied law with his father, then with a cousin and finally with Edmund Randolph, the nation's first attorney general. Young Tyler was appalled by Randolph's advocacy of a "supreme central government." After being admitted to the bar in 1809, Tyler practiced law, developing a reputation as an eloquent and effective advocate in criminal defense cases.[122]

Military Service: In the summer of 1813, word reached Tyler that a British raiding party had plundered Hampton, Virginia, and appeared to be planning a march on Richmond. Tyler immediately joined the Charles City Rifles, a local militia company formed to defend the city. Most of the force consisted of farmers unacquainted with military discipline. Tyler was commissioned a captain and drilled the men. The company was attached to the Fifty-Second Regiment of the Virginia militia and ordered to report to Williamsburg to resist a British offensive. Tyler and his men did not see any action because the British withdrew from Hampton. The Charles City Rifles returned home triumphantly.[123]

POLITICAL OFFICES

Political Philosophy and Political Party Affiliation: Tyler was an advocate of states' rights and believed the Constitution should be strictly construed, and he never wavered from that conviction. However, as president, Tyler "trampled on States' rights" on several occasions by exercising executive privilege, which were not quite the acts of a strict constructionist.[124] Like all southern aristocrats, he believed in low tariffs and thought only educated white men who owned property should have the vote.[125] Tyler distrusted Andrew Jackson, fearing a military man might bypass the Constitution to establish a dictatorship.[126] Tyler believed that the question of a state's "free" or "slave" status ought to be decided by the state itself and not by the federal government. A slave owner, he accepted slavery as a fact of life. "If his son Lyon Tyler is to be believed, John Tyler had troubling doubts about slavery, deploring it as an evil, and never rationalizing the South's 'peculiar institution' as a blessing or positive good."[127] He believed that to abolish it quickly would create more problems for southern whites than it would solve problems of the slaves. He favored gradual abolition, but in the meantime felt it should be extended to regions where it would be economically advantageous. In 1835 Tyler described an Abolitionist publication to a gathering of Virginians "Here ... is a picture upon the external covering, designed to represent each of you, gentlemen. A scourge is in your hand, and three victims bound and kneeling at your feet. You are represented as demons in the shape of men; and by way of contrast, here stands (Abolitionist) Arthur Tappan, Mr. Somebody Garrison, or Mr. Foreigner Thompson, patting the greasy little fellows on their cheeks and giving them most lovely kisses."[128]

Tyler's proposal is found in *The Letters and Times of the Tylers*, edited by his son Lyon Gardiner Tyler:

> Slavery has been represented on all hands as a dark cloud, and the candor of the gentleman from Massachusetts [Mr. Whitman] drove him to the admission that it would be well to disperse this cloud. In this sentiment, I entirely concur with him. How can you otherwise disarm it? Will you suffer it to increase in its darkness over one particular portion of this land till its horrors shall burst upon it? Will you permit the lightnings of its wrath to break upon the South, when by the interposition of a wise system of legislation you may reduce it to a summer's cloud?[129]

In opposing the Missouri Compromise Tyler argued that New York and Pennsylvania had been able to emancipate their slaves only by reducing their number by deportation. He challenged the argument that the slave population would keep up with the nation's territorial expansion. Tyler insisted that any restriction on a new state in regard to keeping slaves was unconstitutional. If Missouri, when it became a state, was forbidden to have slaves, while an old state, such as Virginia, could, then Missouri and Virginia were placed on a different footing in the Union. "Tyler concluded: '[Y]ou ameliorate the condition of the slave [and] you add much to the prospects of emancipation, and the total extinction of slavery." Those who rejected the proposed bill would receive the 'blessings of their countrymen.' Those who did not would earn 'the deepest curses of prosperity.'"[130] "Years later, as the Civil War approached, he looked back on the Compromise of 1820 and recalled: 'I believed it to be unconstitutional. I believed it to be ... the opening of Pandora's Box, which would let out upon us all the present evils which have gathered over the land. I never would have yielded to the Missouri Compromise. I would have died in my shoes, suffered any sort of punishment you could have inflicted upon me, before I would have [supported] it.'"[131] Tyler grew increasingly alienated from the Jacksonian Democrats, especially after Jackson's aggressive actions during the South Carolina nullification crisis. In a speech at Gloucester Court House, Virginia, in 1833, Tyler stated, "Let the government be just and nullification has no food on which to exist. Injustice alone begets resistance, and that is not all. In order to rouse a whole community to resistance, the sense of oppression must be greater than under which they labor."[132]

Virginia House of Delegates: From 1811 to 1816 Tyler served as a Jeffersonian Republican (Democratic Republican) in the state legislature. After a recovery from a mysterious illness, Tyler returned to the Virginia legislature, serving from 1823 to 1825. In 1838 he was back in the state legislature and was unanimously chosen speaker.[133]

U.S. House of Representatives: While serving in the House of Representatives (1816–1821), Tyler voted against most nationalist legislation and opposed the Missouri Compromise on constitutional grounds. "Like his father, Tyler firmly supported states' rights. He let it be known that he would work to stop any politician who was trying to make the federal government more powerful."[134] Tyler was forced to resign from the House due to poor health. In his farewell to his constituents he urged them to look to a future that promised "the march of this favored land in the road of power and glory [and] the high destinies that await us."[135]

Governor of Virginia: At age 35 Tyler was elected governor of Virginia; just 14 years after his father had held the same office. John Jr. served two terms as governor of Virginia, from 1825 to 1827, resigning when elected to the U.S. Senate.[136] As governor, Tyler was called upon to deliver a eulogy at the time of Thomas Jefferson's death. Tyler predicted that "when the happy era shall arrive for the emancipation of nations, hastened on as it will be by the example of America, shall they not resort to the Declaration of our Independence as the charter of their rights, and will not its author be hailed as the benefactor of the redeemed?"[137]

U.S. Senate: As a member of the Senate (1827–1836), Tyler based his votes on his beliefs, ignoring his political constituency. He reluctantly supported Andrew Jackson over John Quincy Adams for president because, like Jackson, Tyler hated the national bank.[138] In a letter to former U.S. senator and governor of Virginia L.W. Tazewell in 1834, Tyler made in quite clear where his sentiments lay: "I believe the Bank to be the original sin against the Constitution, which, in the progress of our history, has called into existence a numerous progeny of usurpations. Shall I permit this serpent? However, bright its scales ... to exist by and through my vote?"[139] It was upon his initiative that the Compromise Tariff of 1833 was negotiated and a crisis ended. Tyler's succinct objection to a protectionist tariff was, "We sell cheap and are made to buy dear."[140] On February 9, 1832, during the congressional debate on the tariff, Tyler addressed the Senate:

> I have been reared in a reverential affection for the Union. My imagination has led me to look into the distant future, and there to contemplate the greatness of free America. I have beheld her walking on the waves of the mighty deep, carrying along with her tidings of great joy to distant nations. I have seen her overturning the strong places of despotism, and restoring to man his long-lost rights. Woe, woe betide that man who shall now sow the seeds of disunion among us. Better for him if he had never been born. If he calls on the mountains to hide him — nay, if he bury himself at the very center of the earth, the indignation of mankind will find him out and blast him with its lightnings.[141]

After his reelection in 1833, Tyler was drawn into the newly formed Whig Party, in which the principal glue holding together disparate groups was hatred of Andrew Jackson. States' rights southerners in Congress banded with Henry Clay and Daniel Webster to censure Jackson for his removal of federal deposits from the national bank. Tyler rose in the Senate, expressing outrage at Jackson's action: "Is the presidential power only to be considered dangerous when he is the head of an army? Patronage is the sword and cannon by which war may be made on the liberty of the human race.... Give the president control over the purse — the power to place immense revenues of the country into the hands he may please, and I care not what you call him, he is 'every inch a king.'"[142]

When the Virginia legislature instructed Tyler to support Senator Thomas Hart Benton's resolution to expunge the censure of Jackson, Tyler refused and resigned. In his "these are sacrifices that give me pain to make"[143] letter of resignation to the Virginia legislature, he spoke with indignant eloquence:

> I should be afraid, after performing such a deed, if Virginia is as she once was ... to return within her limits. The execrations of her people would be thundered in my ears; the soil which had been trod by her heroes and statesmen would furnish me no resting-place. I should feel myself guilty, most guilty; and however I might succeed in concealing myself from the sight of men, I could not, in my view of the subject, save myself from the upbraidings of my own perjured conscience. How could I return to mix among her people, to share their hospitality and kindness, with the declaration on my lips, "I have violated my oath of office, and, sooner than surrender my place in the Senate, have struck down the Constitution."[144] That same day the president of the Senate, Martin Van Buren laid before the Senate, Tyler's announcement his resignation. In his statement, he declared: "In taking leave of the body..., I should be faithless to the feelings of my heart if I did not frankly confess that I do so with no ordinary emotion."[145]

Oliver P. Chitwood praised Tyler for his stand on the censure issue:

> In taking this aggressive stand against the country's idol [refusing to change his vote censuring Andrew Jackson]; Tyler was exhibiting a courage and disinterestedness that have been only too rare in the history of American statesmanship. Nor can we explain his action on any other ground than that of patriotism and loyalty to principle. It is hardly believable that he was prompted by partisanship in his opposition to Jackson. This young doctrinaire, who was trying to carry the ideals of youth into politics, was too guileless to be motivated by anything less noble than loyalty to conviction.[146]

Vice President of the United States: In 1836 the Whig party adopted a strategy of encouraging several sectional leaders to run for president and vice president, They anticipated that no one would have enough electoral votes and the election would be thrown into the House of Representatives to elect a president and the Senate to elect a vice president, where the Whigs had a better chance of winning. Hugh L. White of Tennessee was the "state-rights Whig" presidential nominee and Tyler his running mate. Tyler carried only four states, but not his own. Martin Van Buren was easily elected president.[147] By 1839, the Whigs were strong enough to hold a national nominating convention, where they chose former general William Henry Harrison of Ohio to head their ticket and Tyler as something of an afterthought to balance it as his running mate. Tyler switched to the Whig Party because of his disagreement with the policies of Andrew Jackson, but he was still a Democrat, in principle, an advocate of states' rights and a strict constitutionalist. He opposed many of the issues the Whigs favored, which became clear to all once he assumed the presidency.[148] Tyler, who preferred to return to the U.S. Senate, made no effort to win the vice presidential nomination, saying, "I do declare, in the presence of my Heavenly Judge, that the nomination given to me was neither solicited nor expected."[149]

HIS PRESIDENCY

Tyler was vice president for only thirty-three days, and he presided over the Senate for less than two hours.[150] He was home in Virginia playing marbles when word reached him that President Harrison had died. U.S. circuit court judge William Cranch administered the oath of office to Tyler at his residence in the Indian Queen hotel on April 6, 1841.[151] At 51, Tyler was the youngest president inaugurated up to that time. In his address, as he assumed the presidency, Tyler asserted as follows:

> For the first time in our history the person elected to the Vice Presidency ... has had devolved upon him the Presidential office.... My earnest prayer shall be constantly addressed to the all-wise

and all-powerful Being who made me, and by whose dispensation I am called to the high office of President.... Confiding in the protecting care of an ever watchful and overruling Providence, it shall be my first and highest duty to preserve unimpaired the free institutions under which we live and transmit them to those who shall succeed me in their full force and vigor.[152]

Tyler was aware of the precedent he was making in insisting he was not the acting president, but the actual president of the United States. In his letters, he described the reaction to his position on the matter: "From the moment of my assuming the helm my ship was tempest tossed. A Vice President who succeeds the presidency in this way has no party to sustain his nature.... If the tide of defamation and abuse shall turn and my administration come to be praised, future vice presidents who may succeed to the presidency may feel some slight encouragement to pursue an independent course."[153]

The Whigs expected Tyler to adhere closely to their policies and work closely with the party's leaders, in particular Henry Clay. At his first meeting with his inherited Cabinet Tyler was informed that he should obtain their consensus before acting and that in the Cabinet he had only one vote, as did the others.[154] Tyler responded: "I am very glad to have in my Cabinet such able statesmen as you. But I can never consent to being dictated to as to what I shall or shall not do.... I am the President.... When you think otherwise your resignations will be accepted."[155] Clay raged: "Tyler dares not resist. I'll drive him before me."[156] Equal to the challenge, the new president shot back: "I pray you to believe that my back is to the wall, and that while I shall deplore the assaults, I shall, if practicable, beat back the assailants."[157]

In his first message to Congress, President Tyler recounted the recent history of the U.S. Bank and ended the address with a warning: "I shall be ready to concur with you in the adoption of such system as you may propose, reserving to myself the ultimate power of rejecting any measure which may, in my view of it, conflict with the constitution or otherwise jeopardize prosperity of the country, a power which I could not part with, even if I would, but which I will not believe any act of yours will call into requisition."[158] Stubborn, proud and unpredictable, Tyler shocked congressional Whigs by vetoing nearly their entire agenda. Twice he vetoed Clay's legislation for a national bank act on states' rights grounds. Tyler was willing to compromise on the establishment of the bank, but Clay wouldn't budge, refusing to accept Tyler's "exchequer system," thus throwing the government into a virtual deadlock.[159] In retaliation the Whigs expelled the maverick from the party in 1841, only a few months after he assumed office. Thus, at least technically, Tyler was a "president without a party."[160] Tyler wrote to Former Virginia Governor L.W. Tazewell:

> I am in the condition of Macbeth, without either his ambition or his vices, or other care than to acquit myself with some little honor from my remaining brief career of public life; but I would feign consult the weird sisters or their interpreters, and I know of no one more fully possessed of their counsels as to political events than yourself. If storms are to continue to assail, I would seek to reef my sails and adopt other preparations in order to live out the gale.[161]

Clay did everything he could to force Tyler to resign from the presidency. Once, Tyler had to remind him that he, not Clay was the president and on another occasion he told the senator, "Go you now then, Mr. Clay, to your end of the avenue, where stands the Capitol, and there perform your duty to the country as you shall think proper. So help me God, I shall do mine at this end as I shall think proper."[162]

A year later after Tyler vetoed a tariff bill, "Congress received the veto message with great indignation. On the motion of ex–President John Q. Adams it was referred to a committee,"[163] which accused Tyler of misusing his veto power and condemned it as an unwar-

"The United States Senate, A.D. 1850," published by John M. Butler and Alfred Long, c. 1855. Henry Clay addressing the Senate, engraving by Robert Whitechurch after a painting by Peter Rothermel, 1855. Daniel Webster is seated to the left of Clay and John C. Calhoun is to the left of Speaker Millard Fillmore's chair (Library of Congress).

rantable assumption of power. "After a caustic summary of Mr. Tyler's acts since his accession to office, the committee concluded with an allusion to impeachment,"[164] but the resolution failed. In a letter Robert McCandlish, Tyler confessed to his "crimes": "The high crime of sustaining the Constitution of the country I have committed and to this I plead guilty. The high crime of arresting the lavish donation of a source of revenue; and the high crime of daring to have an opinion of my own, Congress to the contrary notwithstanding, I plead guilty also of that; but be assured that this is the full extent of my offending."[165]

Although Tyler is considered to be one of the forgotten presidents, as his accomplishments were modest, there are some notable achievements to mention. The navy was reorganized and steps were taken to establish the nucleus of the present Naval Observatory and to promote a national telegraph system, which became the center of the Weather Bureau.[166] The costly Seminole War and Dorr's Rebellion were ended.[167] A trade agreement with China was reached[168] and Texas was annexed on his last day in office.[169]

His Vice President: None, but two individuals, Samuel Southard from 1841 to 1842 and Willie P. Mangum from 1842 to 1845, served as president pro tempore of the Senate and stood next in line to the presidency, after the speaker of the house. Clay crusaded to force Tyler to resign, to be replaced by Southard, who would do as he was told.[170]

His Cabinet: Secretary of State Daniel Webster (1841–1843), Abel P. Upshur (1843–1844) and John C. Calhoun (1844–1845); Secretary of the Treasury Thomas Ewing (1841), Walter Forward (1841–1843), John C. Spencer (1844–1844) and George M. Bibb (1844–1845); Secretary of War John Bell (1841), John C. Spencer (1841–1843), James M. Porter (1843–1844), and William Wilkins (1844–1845); Attorney General John J. Crittenden (1841), Hugh S. Legare (1841–1843) and John Nelson (1843–1845); Postmaster General Francis Granger (1841) and Charles A. Wickliffe (1841–1845); Secretary of the Navy George E. Badger (1841), Abel P. Upshur (1841–1843), David Henshaw (1843–1844), Thomas W. Gilmer (1844) and John Y. Mason (1844–1845). President Tyler has the dubious distinction of having four of his proposed cabinet members rejected by the Senate, the most by any president. "These were Caleb Cushing (Treasury), David Henshaw (Navy) James Porter (War), and James S. Green (Treasury). Henshaw and Porter served as recess appointees before their rejections. Tyler aggravated this problem when he repeatedly renominated Cushing. As a result, Cushing was rejected three times in one day, March 4, 1843, the last day of the 27th Congress."[171]

Supreme Court Appointments: Samuel Nelson (1845).

States Admitted to the Union: Florida.

Domestic Affairs — Major Events

Right of Succession: As the matter had never come up, the question of what succession at the death of a sitting president meant had never been decided. The debate was between those who believed that the vice president was merely an acting president and those who believed that he was the president just as if he had been elected to the post. The Constitution was not too explicit on the matter of succession (until the ratification of the 25th Amendment to the Constitution in 1967). The Constitution stated only that: "In Case of the Removal of the President from Office, or of his Death, Resignation, or Inability to discharge the Powers and Duties of the said Office, the same shall devolve on the Vice President."[172] Tyler's biographers recognized the magnitude of his insistence that he was the legitimate president, and that he would not relinquish the office or accept limitations of his powers. In doing so the government's checks and balances were maintained and a precedent was established that future vice presidents called upon by the death of a president followed to make an orderly transfer of power. "By claiming the right to a fully functioning and empowered presidency instead of relinquishing the office or accepting limits on his powers, Tyler set a hugely important precedent. [...] Unfortunately, Tyler proved much better at taking over the presidency than at actually being President."[173] Congress agreed with Tyler that he was president and not merely acting president. Tyler went so far as to return mail addressed to him as "acting president."[174]

Fiscal Bank Bill: On July 28, 1841, the U.S. Senate narrowly passed the Fiscal Bank Bill, which called for the creation of a federal financial institution to be located in the District of Columbia. The Whigs who sponsored the bill wanted nothing less than the establishment of the Second Bank of the United States. Former Whig ally Tyler vetoed the bill on August 16, 1841. In his message, he explained his veto of the bill:

> I can not conscientiously give it my approval.... Under an impressive dispensation of Providence I succeeded to the Presidential office. Before entering upon the duties of that office I took an oath.... I could not give my sanction to a measure of the character described without surrendering

all claim to the respect of honorable men, all confidence on the part of the people, all self-respect, all regard for moral and religious obligations, without an observance of which no government can be prosperous and no person can be happy.[175]

The legislation was bounced back to the Senate, but the Whigs did not have the votes to override the president's veto. It "sparked a riot outside the White House, as incensed — and drunk — members of the Whig party bombarded the White House with stones, fired their guns in the air and burned Tyler in effigy — the most violent demonstration ever held outside the White House. In response the government formed the District of Columbia's police force."[176]

Preemption Act: In 1841, Congress passed the Preemption Act, which provided that settlers on land that had not been surveyed would have the first right to preempt the land before it was offered for public sale. "Specifically, it permitted 'squatters' on government land who were heads of households, widows, or single men over 21; who were citizens of the United States, or intended to become naturalized; and who had lived there for at least 14 months to purchase up to 160 acres at a price no lower than $1.25 per acre."[177] Opposition to preemption came from eastern states, which saw any encouragement of western migration as a threat to their labor supply. "After the passage in 1862 of the Homestead Act, the value of preemption for legitimate settlers declined, and the practice more and more became a tool for speculators."[178] Congress repealed the Preemption Act in 1891.

The Dorr Rebellion: Thomas William Dorr was an agitator against the electoral system of the state of Rhode Island, which maintained the rule of its original charter in 1663 that only landowners could vote. With the industrial revolution, the population ceased to be mostly farmers as large numbers moved into the cities. By 1829, a total of 60 percent of the state's free white males, including many recent Irish immigrants, were ineligible to vote.[179] Several attempts were made to have the charter revised and extend the vote, but the state's legislature consistently failed to liberalize the constitution. By 1840, Rhode Island was the only state in the Union without universal suffrage for white males.[180]

"In 1841, suffrage supporters, led by Dorr, gave up on attempts to change the system from within. In October, they held an extralegal People's Convention and drafted a new constitution that granted the vote to all white males with one year's residence."[181] The People's Convention constitution was overwhelmingly supported in a referendum in December. Governor Samuel Ward King made no efforts to introduce the new constitution, and "when matter came to a head he declared martial law. On May 4 the state legislature requested federal government troops to suppress the 'lawless assemblages.'"[182]

Tyler sent an observer, but decided not to send soldiers because "the danger of domestic violence is hourly diminishing."[183] He recommended that the franchise be enlarged to let most men vote. In his letter to King, the president reviewed the pertinent sections of the Constitution that authorized him to call forth the militia of a state in the case of an insurrection. He concluded: "No power is vested in the Executive of the United States to anticipate insurrectionary movements against the Government of Rhode Island, so as to sanction the interposition of the military authority, but that there must be an actual insurrection manifested by lawless assemblages of the people or otherwise, to whom a proclamation may be addressed, and who may be required to betake themselves to their respective abodes."[184]

Tyler did promise that in case an actual insurrection broke out in Rhode Island, federal assistance would be given to assist the regular, or charter, government. Dorr's short-lived armed insurrection soon fell apart and the governor issued a warrant for Dorr's arrest. Dorr fled the state, but returned in 1843 when he was found guilty of treason against the state and sentenced to solitary confinement and hard labor for life. By 1845, his health broken, he was released from prison. He was restored his civil rights in 1851, and in 1854 the court's judgment against him was set aside. He died the next year.[185]

Black Tariff: The Tariff of 1842, which was known as the Black Tariff, stipulated sweeping changes to the schedule and collection system, most of which were designed to augment its protective character. "The Black Tariff was signed into law somewhat reluctantly by President John Tyler, following a year of disputes with the Whig leaders in Congress over the restoration of national banking and the government's land disbursement policies. For the previous year, Whig leaders in Congress had sent bills to Tyler coupling the tariff hike with a public land disbursement package insisted upon by Henry Clay, prompting a presidential veto."[186] The resulting bill was acceptable to Tyler because it lacked the land disbursement provisions...."[187] "The main beneficiary industry to receive protection under the tariff was iron. Import taxes on iron goods, both raw and manufactured, amounted to almost two thirds of their price overall...."[188] "The impact of the Black Tariff was an almost immediate sharp decline in international trade.... The Tariff of 1842 was repealed in 1846."[189]

Transportation, Communication and Education: During Tyler's only term as president incredible changes were taking place in the nation's infrastructure. "For example, there were dramatic improvements in transportation, particularly in the development of turnpikes (toll roads) and canals, which allowed for easier travel and transport of goods and services. By the end of Tyler's term, the first telegraph line, between Washington and Baltimore, had been constructed. On May 24, 1844, Samuel Morse sent the following message from Baltimore to Washington: 'What hath God wrought?' What Morse had wrought was an invention that would make it possible within a few years to communicate instantaneously across the length and breadth of the continent.[190]

By the mid–1840s, "free primary education was available for all white children" in most of the northern states. "Public high schools began to supplant the private academies," and by the end of Tyler's term of office, there were "over 150 private denominational colleges" across the nation.[191]

Annexation of Texas: In his third State of the Union address, the President spoke of how much Texas seemed to be like a part of the United States:

> Considering that Texas is separated from the United States by a mere geographical line; that her territory, in the opinion of many, down to a later period formed a portion of the territory of the United States; that [it] is homogeneous in the population and pursuits with adjoining States, makes contributions to the commerce of the world in the same articles with them, and that most of the inhabitants have been citizens of the United States, speak the same language, and live under similar political institutions with ourselves, this Government is bound by every consideration of interest as well as sympathy to see that she shall be left free to act, especially in regard to her domestic affairs, unawed by force and unrestrained by the policy or views of other countries.[192]

Tyler saw the annexation as a chance to bring most of the world's cotton production under the American flag and to expand American trade into the Southwest. "Contemporaries characterized John Tyler as a man with talents not above mediocrity while historians rate him a weak president. Yet, he came up with a tactic for placing more power in the hands of the executive at the expense of Congress that later presidents would adopt. He wanted to acquire Texas but could not obtain a two-thirds majority in the Senate for a treaty of annexation. So, he asked the whole Congress to approve annexation with joint resolution that required only a mere majority. It agreed. Opponents, who called this action an abuse of power that evaded constitutional restraint, urged impeachment. Tyler prevailed, he

The Annexation of Texas to the Union, painting by Donald M. Yena (courtesy Texas State Library and Archives Commission).

explained later, because in handling foreign affairs he had been 'freer of the furies of factional politics than he had been in domestic affairs.'"[193] The plan was a success, and three days later, Tyler's term of office expired. "It was well understood that to annex Texas, with her boundaries thus in dispute, was to adopt, on the part of the United States, her territorial claims, and that to establish them, war with Mexico was inevitable. No secret was made of the fact that the whole project was in the interest of slavery."[194] Tyler considered the annexation of Texas as the crowning achievement of his presidency.

Later in life, he complained in letters to friends and relatives that he was not given sufficient credit for his role in annexation. In a letter to General Thomas Green, Tyler made his case for recognition:

> It would be indeed strange if my enemies could deprive me of credit of having annexed Texas to the Union. I presented the question — urged it first in the form of a treaty to the Senate — met the rejection of that treaty [the spring of 1844], by a prompt and immediate appeal to the H. of R.— fought the battle before the people and conquered its formidable adversaries with their trained bands, and two days before my term expired adopted and enforced the alternate resolution under which Texas took her place amid the fraternity of States. My successor did nothing but confirm what I had done.[195]

In letters to his son Robert, the ex-president explained: "When the Mexican Gulf shall be crowded with innumerable ships freighted with the rich productions of Texas ... then it will be seen that my labors were not in vain to advance the highest destinies of the country....

[The annexation of Texas] was not narrow, local or bigoted. It embraced the whole country and all its interests."[196]

Foreign Affairs — Major Events

In his first State of the Union message, Tyler described how the U.S. would deal with the rest of the world: "In regard to foreign nations, the groundwork of my policy will be justice in our part to all, submitting to injustice from none. While I shall sedulously cultivate the relations of peace and amity with one and all, it will be my most imperative duty to see that the honor of the country shall sustain no blemish. With a view to this, the condition of our military defenses will become a matter of anxious solicitude."[197]

Webster-Ashburton Treaty: A turning "point in U.S.-British relations came with the signing on August 9, 1842, of the Webster-Ashburton Treaty."[198] Negotiated by Alexander Baring, First Lord Ashburton, for Britain and U.S. secretary of state Daniel Webster, the treaty settled several serious matters between the two nations. "It adjusted the Maine–New Brunswick boundary,"[199] which had been unclear. The United States received most of the disputed territory in as well as navigational rights on the St. John River. The treaty settled the boundary between Lake Superior and Lake of the Woods. However, "the dispute over the Oregon border was left to a later date."[200]

Treaty of Wanghia: In 1844, the Treaty of Wanghia (Wang Hya) opened trade between the United States and China at five ports and granted "most favored nation" status to the United States. "The treaty is named after a village in northern Macau where the temple is located, called Mongha or Wangxia (simplified Chinese)."[201] It was modeled after the Treaty of Nanking between the United Kingdom and China, introducing the "principle of extraterritoriality" in the relations between China and the west.[202] "Extraterritorial status allowed certain foreign nationals to remain under the legal control of their home governments. This rendered them exempt from local arrest, lawsuits and taxation. The undercurrent of this idea was that the native population was less civilized than the foreign visitors and could not be trusted to mete out proper justice."[203] "The United States was represented by Caleb Cushing, a Massachusetts lawyer dispatched by President John Tyler under the pressures of American merchants concerned about the British dominance in Chinese trade. A physician and missionary, Peter Parker, served as Cushing's Chinese interpreter. The Qing Empire was represented by Qiying, the governor-general of Guangdong and Guangxi."[204] "Americans could buy land and build churches, hospitals, and burial grounds in the five treaty ports. They would pay a fixed tariff, in no case being 'subject to other or higher duties than are or shall be required of the people of any other nation whatever.' And there was the more comprehensive most-favored-nation clause: 'if additional advantages or privileges, of whatever description, be conceded hereafter by China to any other nation, the United States, and the citizens thereof, shall be entitled thereupon, to a complete, equal, and impartial participation in the same.'"[205] Provisions were made that "citizens of the United States accused of committing any crime in China were to be tried only by their own consul under American law and that disputes between American citizens in China should be regulated by their own government."[206] As a concession to China, "opium trade was explicitly declared illegal, and the U.S. agreed to hand over any offenders to Chinese officials."[207] The treaty gave missionaries the right to "build hospitals, churches, and cemeteries and allowed U.S. citizens "the right to learn Chinese by abolishing a law which hitherto forbade foreigners to do so."[208]

AFTER THE PRESIDENCY

Tyler made a doomed attempt at winning the Democratic nomination for president in 1844, creating a small party with the slogan "Tyler and Texas."[209] Realizing he could not be reelected, he used the threat of running independently to get wavering Democrats to support annexation of Texas. When the deal was struck, Tyler quit the campaign and threw his support to the Democrat candidate, James Knox Polk.[210] In his August 22, 1844, letter of withdrawal from the canvas, he reflected: "If the annexation of Texas shall crown off my public life, I shall neither retire ignominiously nor be soon forgotten."[211]

In essence, his fourth State of the Union address was his farewell speech:

> I shall carry with me into retirement the gratifying reflection that as my sole object throughout has been to advance the public good I may not entirely have failed in accomplishing it; and this gratification is heightened in no small degree by the fact that when under a deep and abiding sense of duty I have found myself constrained to resort to the qualified veto it has neither been followed by disapproval on the part of the people nor weakened in any degree their attachment to that great conservative feature of our Government.[212]

John Tyler was the only U.S. president to join the Confederacy. Some consider his action treasonable and Tyler a traitor. Others argue that many Americans believed a state had a "legal right to withdraw from the Union," pointing out that during the War of 1812, the "New England states considered secession" because of their opposition to what they labeled "President Madison's War."[213] Had Tyler survived to the end of the Civil War, no one can say what fate the Radical Republicans would have had in mind for him, considering the treatment of Jefferson Davis, president of the Confederacy. In his letters to Robert Tyler, Tyler proclaimed, "History will not do me justice."[214]

Washington Peace Convention: Tyler retired to his plantation in Virginia and remained out of active politics until the eve of the Civil War. However, in a letter to Colonel David L. Gardiner on December 7, 1849, Tyler addressed the ever-growing conflict over slavery: "I fear that we are destined to great trouble upon the slavery question and the end is not yet. I am a silent but not indifferent spectator of what is passing, and I confess ... that I am not without my fears and apprehension and yet I have much confidence in the good sense of the American people."[215]

Tyler emerged in 1860 as a strong voice for moderation and deliberation in the South. In February 1861, he sponsored and served as chair of the Washington Peace Convention, which sought a compromise to avoid civil war after South Carolina seceded from the Union. At the same time, the Confederate constitution was being drawn up at the Montgomery Convention. Tyler made a rousing speech, in the course of which he said:

> Our fathers created — we have to preserve. They built up through their wisdom and patriotism monuments which have eternalized their causes. You have before you, gentlemen, a task especially grand, equally sublime, quite as full of glory and immortality. You have to snatch from ruin a great and glorious Confederation; to preserve the Government and to invigorate the Constitution. I confess myself ambitious of sharing the glory of accomplishing this grand and magnificent result. To have our names enrolled in the Capital, to be repeated by future generations with grateful applause — this is an honor higher than the mountains, more enduring than monumental alabaster.[216]

When the U.S. Senate rejected Tyler's compromise plan, he urged Virginia to secede from the Union.[217]

Confederate States Congress: In 1861, the people of Virginia elected Tyler to the provisional Confederate Congress and then to the permanent Congress, but he died before he could take his seat.[218]

UNCLE SAM AND HIS SERVANTS.

"Uncle Sam and His Servants," lithograph published by James Baillie, 1844. An anti–Tyler cartoon lampooning the incumbent's efforts to secure a second term. With his shoulder to the door Tyler bars the entry of John C. Calhoun, Clay, Polk, and Andrew Jackson (Library of Congress).

His Papers: Papers of John Tyler are available from the Library of Congress, archival manuscript on microfilm: *The Letters and Times of the Tylers*, 3 volumes, Lyon Gardiner Tyler, 1884–1896, reprint: De Capo Press, 1970; *William Henry Harrison, 1773–1841: John Tyler, 1790–1862: Chronology, Documents, Bibliographical Aids*, David A. Durfee, ed., Oceana, 1970.

Health: Throughout his life Tyler suffered from poor health. When an influenza epidemic swept the country during his presidency, it was called the "Tyler grippe."[219] Having little faith in physicians, he regularly took the waters at various Virginia spas.[220] He was a believer in sulfur hydrotherapy and took massive doses of calomel regularly.[221] At age 30, he was forced to resign from the House of Representatives as the result of the effects of an illness which now would be described as a symmetric generalized subacute paralysis.[222] He regularly suffered from dysentery and respiratory infections. In the last years of his life, he was prone to colds, arthritis, and kidney problems. He wrote: "I have many aches and pains. They will attend on a sexogenarian, however, so be it, for I am convinced that it is all wisely ordained by providence."[223]

Death: On January 10, 1862, Mrs. Tyler joined her husband in Richmond a week earlier than planned because she had a dream in which she saw her husband's life was in danger. She was relieved to find him in good health but disconsolate about the outbreak of the Civil War.[224] The next morning, Tyler became dizzy and vomited bile, which had occurred on numerous other occasions. This time he "slumped unconscious to the floor but was revived."[225] His physicians did not consider the incident serious and allowed him to be up and about. A few days later, he "complained of headaches and a suffocating feeling. Ordered to bed, Tyler was treated with mustard plasters, brandy, and a morphine-containing cough medicine, but he died soon afterwards" at 12:15 A.M. on January 18, 1862.[226]

Place of Death: Tyler died in his Exchange Hotel room in Richmond, Virginia.[227]

Cause of Death: Tyler most likely died of a stroke brought on by bilious fever [a broad diagnosis which from ancient times had covered a variety of symptoms] and respiratory failure.[228] Modern physicians believed that he obviously had a vascular accident affecting the frontal part of his brain. His previous dizzy spells probably had been "little strokes."[229]

Final Words: Tyler was aroused from his sleep late on January 17 by feelings of suffocation. He felt he was dying and announced, "Doctor, I am going." The doctor replied, "I hope not, Sir." Tyler responded, "Perhaps, it is best."[230]

Place of Burial: There was no White House funeral for John Tyler. The federal government pointedly ignored his passing, considering him an enemy of the Union. There were few obituaries for him. The *New York Times* wrote: "He ended his life suddenly, last Friday, in Richmond — going down to death amid the ruins of his native State. He himself was one of the architects of its ruin; and beneath that melancholy wreck his name will be buried, instead of being inscribed on the Capitol's monumental marble, as a year ago he so much desired."[231] Tyler's body lay in state in the Confederate congress draped with a Confederate flag. His funeral was held at St. Paul's Episcopal Church. Around 150 carriages, including one carrying President Jefferson Davis, escorted him to Hollywood Cemetery at Richmond, named for its multitude of holly trees. Besides Tyler, President Monroe — whose grave is a mere 6 feet from that of Tyler — Jefferson Davis, General J.E.B. Stuart, General George Pickett, and 18,000 Confederate soldiers are buried in the cemetery.[232] For years the public lost track of Tyler's burial spot. It was marked only by a magnolia tree. It wasn't until the 20th century that an official marker was placed on his grave by Congress. Tyler's burial marker is a tall obelisk with some general information engraved. It features a likeness of the president's face looming over and staring down at passersby.[233]

Miscellanea

Presidential Trivia and Firsts: Tyler was the first vice president elevated to the presidency upon the death of the president. He was the second president to have been born after the signing of the Declaration of Independence.[234] Tyler was the first president whose wife died while he was in office and also the first president to marry while in office.[235] The tradition of playing "Hail to the Chief" whenever a president appears at state functions was started by Tyler's second wife, Julia.[236] Tyler was the first president to have a veto overridden.[237] He made the most cabinet changes of any single-term president.[238] Five years after leaving office he was so cash poor that he was unable to pay a bill for a paltry $1.25 until he sold his corn crop.[239] Tyler was born during George Washington's term in office; the youngest of his children lived to see the Truman administration.[240] Harry Truman claimed that Tyler was his great-great-great uncle, but this has not been established.[241] Tyler regularly held parties for his children and their friends at the White House.[242]

The Ghost of Sherwood Forest: "The real spirit of Sherwood Forest is the 'Gray Lady.' You can hear her rocking in her chair in the Grey Room holding a child. For over 100 years, almost every person who has lived at Sherwood has had an encounter with the 'Gray Lady.'"[243] It is believed that she has been in residence in the house since late in the 18th century, long before the Tylers occupied it.[244] She is called the Gray Lady because she apparently wore gray. It is believed that "she was a governess who had charge of a small child of the house at one time. It is speculated that she rocked the child to calm him because he was ill, but eventually he died."[245] The ghost can still be heard going up or down a hidden stairway from the second floor nursery to the Grey Room. Tyler's descendants have had psychic experts go through the house to give their impressions and one reported seeing a real woman at the top of the hidden stairway. She was wearing an off-colored dress with an apron and black shoes, and she disappeared as the psychic climbed the stairs.[246]

Tyler Family Garden: The Tyler Family Garden was dedicated at the College of William and Mary on April 30, 2004. It contains bronze busts of three members of the Tyler family: Lyon Gardiner Tyler, the 17th president of the college (1888–1919); his father, John Tyler, the 10th president of the United States; and John Tyler's father, who served as the 18th governor of the Commonwealth of Virginia.

The garden is the final element of a $5 million endowment gift from Mr. and Mrs. Harrison Ruffin Tyler. Mr. Tyler is the son of Gardiner Tyler. The garden is located outside the building housing the history department, which is now known as the Lyon Gardiner Tyler Department of History.[247]

A Man in His Prime: When John Tyler told friends about his decision to marry Julia Gardiner, a woman thirty years younger than himself; he was told that the move was imprudent. Tyler asked "How imprudent?" He was reminded of the age discrepancy, which he dismissed by announcing he was in the prime of his life. A friend asked if he had not heard the story of a no longer young Virginian who told his African waiter Toney that he was considering marrying a young woman in her teens. Toney shook his head and said, "Massa, you think you can stand that?" The gentleman echoed Tyler by announcing he was in his prime and could make the young lady happy. Toney responded: "Yes, but Massa, you is now in your prime, that's true; but when she is in her prime, then Massa, where will your prime be?" Tyler roared with laughter, but married Julia anyway.[248]

Evaluations of Tyler's Presidency

Mr. Tyler ... styles himself President of the United States, and not Vice President acting as President, which would be the correct style. It is a construction in direct violation of the grammar and context of the constitution, which confers upon the Vice President, on the decease of the President, not the office, but the duties of the said office.[249] — John Quincy Adams

Tyler is a political sectarian of the slave-drawing Virginian Jefferson school, principled against all improvement, with all the interests and passions and vices of slavery rooted in his moral and political constitution — he is a slave-monger whose talents are not above mediocrity, and with a spirit incapable of expansion to the dimensions of the station upon which he had been cast by the hand of Providence.[250] — John Quincy Adams

If a God-directed thunderbolt were to strike and annihilate the traitor, all would say that Heaven is just.[251] — Henry Clay

Tyler was a key participant in the leadership of an antebellum generation that grappled for at least four decades with the issues of sectionalism and the preservation of the Union.[252]— Edward P. Crapol

A kind and overruling providence has interfered to prolong our glorious Union ... for surely Tyler ... [will] stay the corruption of this clique who has got into power by deluding the people by the grossest of slanders.[253]— Andrew Jackson

[Tyler deserves] the lasting gratitude of his country [for] arresting the dominant majority in Congress in their mad career, and saving his country from the domination and political incubus of the money-power in the form of a National Bank.[254]— James K. Polk

He has been called a mediocre man; but this is unwarranted flattery. He was a politician of monumental littleness.[255]— Theodore Roosevelt

[He] lived in a time in which many brilliant and forceful men strode the American stage ... and he was overshadowed by all of them, as was the office of the President itself.... Had he surrendered his states' rights and anti–Bank principles he might have salvaged it. He chose not to surrender and the powerful Henry Clay crushed him.[256]— Robert Seager

One of the presidents we could have done without.... There are some things I admire about Tyler, but there are also plenty of things that weren't so admirable.... The reason I have a certain amount of grudging respect for John Tyler is that he knew his own mind and stuck to his decisions.[257]— Harry S Truman

Tyler did well with the short rope given him. But his shortcomings were exaggerated into damning faults, and his weaknesses into imbecilities, while his virtues were depicted as vices. Unlike other presidents, he did not rail against the injustices and sink into malice or bitterness. He was able to forgive his enemies most of the time, and that was his salvation.[258]— John Tebbel and Sarah Miles Watts

Chapter Notes

Preface

1. Arthur M. Schlesinger, Jr., "The Ultimate Approval Rating," New York Times Magazine, December 17, 1996.

2. "Man, Mood, and the Presidency," in *The Presidency Reappraised*, ed. Rexford G. Tugwell and Thomas E. Cronin (New York: Praeger, 1974).

3. Canadian born U.S. novelist, unsourced.

4. *The Cynic's Word Book* (New York: Doubleday, 1906).

5. *A Journey: My Political Life* (New York: Knopf, 2010).

6. *A Presidential Nation* (New York: W.W. Norton, 1975), 9.

7. Emmet John Hughes, "The Presidency as I Have Seen It," in *The Living Presidency: The Resources and Dilemmas of the American Presidential Office* (New York: Coward, McCann & Geohegan, 1972).

8. *Talk About America* (Penguin, 1981), chapter 6.

9. *The State of the Presidency*, 2nd. ed. (Boston: Little, Brown, 1960), 4.

10. Chinese Politician and communist leader who was the most powerful figure in the People's Republic of China from the late 1970s until his death in 1997.

11. Announcing his candidacy, April 4, 1900.

12. "The Character of Presidents," in *Jack London, Hemingway, and the Constitution* (New York: Random House, 1993).

13. *Compensation*, Essays, First Series (Penguin Putnam, 1841). Elizabeth Kortright Monroe has been quoted regarding President James Monroe: "My husband pays dear for his White House. It has cost him all his peace and the best of his manly attributes." Emerson's "Compensation" was published with his first series of essays in 1841. Since Mrs. Monroe's statement sounds contemporaneous with her husband's terms in the presidency, which ended in 1825, it is likely that Emerson heard the First Lady's complaint, and years later remembered and reused the lines when he wrote his classic essay.

14. *The Rise and Growth of American Politics* (New York: Macmillan, 1898), 22.

15. *New York Times*, October 13, 1985.

16. *The Power of the Modern Presidency* (Philadelphia: Temple University Press, 1974), 1.

17. *The Unfinished Country: A Book of American Symbols* (New York: Simon & Schuster, 1960), part 4.

18. South Carolina congressman after his state legislature nominated him for the presidency, December 1821.

19. Terrence O'Flaherty, "A Southern Newsman on a 'Creetivity' Kick," *San Francisco Chronicle*, January 10, 1982.

20. "The President," in *Parliament of Whores: A Lone Humorist Attempts to Explain the Entire U.S. Government* (New York: Vintage, 1991).

21. Samuel W. McCall, *The Life and Times of Thomas Brackett Reed* (Kessenger, 1914), 246.

22. *The Twilight of the Presidency* (New York: Dutton, 1970), 2.

23. The Loneliest Place in the World," *American Heritage*, August 1964.

24. *Decision-Making in the White House: The Olive Branch or the Arrows* (New York: Columbia University Press, 1963), 3.

25. *America and Americans* (New York: Bantam, 1966), 46.

26. *The President as World Leader* (Philadelphia: Lippincott, 1964), 23.

27. *In Search of History: A Personal Adventure* (New York: HarperCollins, 1978).

28. "A Song for Occupations," in *Leaves of Grass* (1855), 4.

Introduction

1. The response is attributed to Benjamin Franklin at the close of the Constitutional Convention of 1787, when he was queried as he left Independence Hall on the final day of deliberation. The incident was taken from the notes of Dr. James McHenry, one of Maryland's delegates to the convention. McHenry's notes were first published in The American Historical Review, vol. 11 (American Historical Association, University of Chicago Press, 1906).

2. United States Constitution, Article II, The Executive Branch, Section 1, The President.

3. Ibid.

4. U.S. Constitution, Section 3,

State of the Union, Convening Congress.

5. Ibid., Section 4, Disqualification.

6. Ibid., Article III, The Judicial Branch, Section 1, Judicial Powers.

7. Ibid., Article I, The Legislative Branch, Section 3, The Senate.

8. Ibid., Section 2, The House.

9. *United States Statutes at Large*, vol. 1, United States Congress Public Acts of the First Congress, 2nd Session, Chapter 3, March 26, 1790.

10. "Business Cycle Expansions and Contractions." National Bureau of Economic Research, November 19, 2008.

One. Washington

1. Donald, David Herbert, Lincoln (New York: Touchstone / Simon & Schuster, 1996), 38–39. Shortly after the Black Hawk war, Captain Abraham Lincoln returned to New Salem, where he met Abner Y. Ellis. In the summer and fall of 1833, the two young men boarded at the same log Tavern kept by Henry Onstott. Ellis heard Lincoln tell this anecdote about Colonel Ethan Allen of Revolutionary War fame.

2. Walther Reinhardt, *George Washington, die Geschichte einer Staatengründung* (Frankfurt, Germany: Societäts-Verlag, 1965), 5.

3. Mark J. Rozell, William D. Pederson, and Frank J. Williams, *George Washington and the Origins of the American Presidency* (Westport, CT: Greenwood, 2000), 188.

4. Ibid.

5. Washington Irving, *Life of George Washington* (New York: Putnam, 1857), 5: 433.

6. Jared Sparks, *The Life of George Washington* (Boston: F. Andrews, 1839), Appendix 1: 507.

7. Ibid.

8. Clifton D. Bryant, *Handbook of Death & Dying* (Thousand Oaks, CA: Sage, 2003), 1: 189–194.

9. Ethan M. Fishman. *George Washington: Foundation of Presidential Leadership and Character* (Westport, CT: Greenwood, 2001), 166.

10. The quote first appeared in the 1930s, "The Por-traits of Mary, the Mother of Washington," by Estelle Harris, *Daughters of the American Revolution Magazine* vol. 65 (1931).

11. Ron Chernow, *Washington: A Life* (New York: Penguin, 2010), chapter one.

12. Ibid.

13. Letter to Mary Ball Washington, February 15, 1787, *The Papers of George Washington, Confederation Series*, 6 vols., W.W. Abbot and Dorothy Twohig eds. (Charlottesville, Virginia: University Press of Virginia, 1992–1997), 5: 35 (Hereafter, PGW).

14. Robert F. Dalzell and Lee Baldwin Dalzell, *George Washington's Mount Vernon: At Home in Revolutionary America* (New York: Oxford University Press, 2000), 22.

15. Frank E. Grizzard, *George Washington: A Biographical Companion* (Santa Barbara, CA: ABC-CLIO, 2002), 331–332 (Hereafter, GWBC). Washington's trip to Bermuda was his only excursion outside what would become the United States of America.

16. Irving, 9.

17. Willard Sterne Randall, *George Washington: A Life* (New York: Macmillan, 1998), 9.

18. "Virginia Environment, Part I," *http://www.clements.umich.edu/exhibits/past/g.washington/case.02/case02.html*.

19. John William Tebbel, *George Washington's America* (New York: Dutton, 1954), 100.

20. George Washington, Letter to Robert Cary & Co., Nov. 30, 1759. *The Papers of George Washington: Colonial Series* 10 vols., W. Abbot et al., eds. (Charlottesville: University Press of Virginia 1983–95), 6: 375 (Hereafter, COL).

21. Richard Brookhiser, *Founding Father: Rediscovering George Washington* (New York: Free Press, 1997), 107.

22. William Guthrie Sayen, "George Washington's 'Unmannerly' Behavior: The Clash Between Civility and Honor," *Virginia Magazine of History and Biography* vol. 107, no. 1 (1999); Letter to [the London tailor] Charles Lawrence, Apr. 26, 1763, COL, 7: 201.

23. Ibid.

24. James Thomas Flexner, *George Washington*, 4 vols. (Boston: Little, Brown and Company, 1965–72), 3: 6.

25. Gordon S. Wood, *Empire of Liberty: A History of the Early Republic, 1789–1815* (New York: Oxford University Press, 2009), 73.

26. Nancy Churnin, "Fit Minds, Fit Bodies Helped Launch America," *Dallas Morning News*, July 2, 2008.

27. "Colonial Williamsburg," *The Journal of the Colonial Williamsburg Foundation*, vols. 26–27 (Williamsburg, VA: Colonial Williamsburg Foundation, 2004), 74.

28. Carla Killough McClafferty, *The Many Faces of George Washington: Remaking a Presidential Icon* (Minneapolis: Carolrhoda Books, 2011), 16.

29. Ibid., 78.

30. Ibid., 44.

31. Ibid., 44, 52–54, 131.

32. *The World Book Encyclopedia* (Glendale, CA: World Book, Inc., 2000), 21: 92.

33. Ibid., 91.

34. Henry Cabot Lodge, *George Washington* (Boston: Houghton Mifflin Company, 1889), 2: 348.

35. Sayen.

36. Charles Moore, ed., *Rules of Civility and Decent Behavior in Company and Conversation* (Boston: Hough-ton Mifflin, 1926), Introduction.

37. "Review of George Washington's Rules of Civility," *http://brothersjudd.com/index.cfm/fuseaction/reviews.detail/book_id/739*.

38. Chernow, *Washington: A Life*, Prelude.

39. Ibid.

40. Ibid.

41. William B. Allen, ed., *Works of Fisher Ames* (Indianapolis: Liberty Classics, 1983), 1: 519–538.

42. Marquis de Chastellux, *Travels in North America in the Years 1780, 1781, and 1782*, Howard C. Rice, Jr., translator (Williamsburg, VA: Williamsburg Institute of Early American History and Culture, 1963), 1: 113.

43. Letter to William Branch Giles, December 31, 1795; Thomas Jefferson, *The Writings of Thomas Jefferson: 1795–1801*, Andrew A. Lipscomb and Albert E Bergh, eds. (Washington, DC: Thomas Jefferson Memorial Association, 1903–1904), 41.

44. Joseph J. Ellis, *His Excellency: George Washington* (New York: Random House, 2005), Preface.

45. Kenneth W. Leish, *The American Heritage Pictorial History of the Presidents of the United States* (New York: Simon & Schuster, 1968), 1: 16.

46. "Timeline: Guide to all the Presidents," *http://www.scholastic.com/teachers/article/timeline-guide-all-presidents*.

47. Patricia Brady, *Martha Washington: An American Life* (New York: Penguin, 2006), 63.

48. Brady, 19.

49. Brady, 24–25, 50–51, 53.

50. Brady, 54.

51. Biography of Martha Washington — Welcome to the White House. *www.georgewbush-whitehouse.archives.gov/history/firstladies/*.

52. Brady, 65.

53. Letter to Mercy Otis Warren, quoted by Brady, 175–176.

54. Bruce Chadwick, *The General and Mrs. Washington* (Naperville, IL: Sourcebooks, 2007), 204.

55. Brady, Prologue.

56. Edward Everett Hale, *The Life of George Washington: Studied Anew* (New York: G.P. Putnam's Sons, 1887), 106.

57. Paul Leicester Ford, *The True George Washington* (Philadelphia: Lippincott, 1898), 92.

58. Chernow, chapter seven.

59. *The Writings of George Washington*, XI: 232.

60. *Appleton's Dictionary of New York and Its Vicinity* (New York: Appleton, 1898), 127.

61. Marvin Kitman, *The Making of the President 1789: The Unauthorized Campaign Biography* (New York: Harper & Row, 1989), 255.

62. Ibid., 261–262.

63. Carl Keith Greene, "Mrs. Kitty and Mr. Washington," *Times-Tribune*, July 9, 2009, *www.thetimestribune.com*.

64. Letter to Burwell Bassett, May 3, 1785, PGW.

65. Letter to Eleanor Parke Custis, Jan. 16, 1795, PGW.

66. Letter to Burwell Bassett, May 23, 1785, PGW.

67. Flexner, *Indispensable Man*, 42–43.

68. "George Washington," *www.crystalinks.com/geowashington.html*.

69. Frank E. Grizzard, Jr., *The Ways of Providence, Religion and George Washington* (Buena Vista, VA: Mariner Companies, 2006), 26.

70. Ibid., 39.

71. Ibid., 80.

72. Ibid.

73. Paul F. Boller, *George Washington & Religion* (Dallas, TX: Southern Methodist University Press, 1963), 16.

74. James Thomas Flexner, *George Washington, the Forge of Experience, 1732–1775* (Boston: Little, Brown, 1965), 216.

75. Barry Schwartz, *George Washington: The Making of an American Symbol* (Ithaca: Cornell University Press, 1900), 170.

76. Boller, 92.

77. George Washington, *The Writings of George Washington*, Jared Sparks, ed. (Boston: Ferdinand Andrews, Publisher, 1838), XII: 399–411 (Hereafter WGW).

78. George Washington, Circular to the States, Newburgh, New York, June 8, 1783. *The Writings of George Washington*, John C. Fitzpatrick, ed., 39 vols. (Washington DC: Government Printing Office, 1931–44), 26: 496.

79. William Sprague, *Annals of the American Pulpit* (New York: Robert Carter & Bros., 1857), 5: 394.

80. George Washington, "On the Puritan Celebration of Guy Fawkes Day," Orderly Book, November 5, 1775, WGW, 3: 144.

81. "George Washington and Religion," *http://www.virginiaplaces.org/religion/religiongw.html*.

82. Letter to Marquis de Lafayette, May 10, 1786, PGW.

83. Letter to the Roman Catholics of the United States, March 15, 1790, PGW.

84. Letter to the Hebrew Congregation, Newport, Rhode Island, August 17, 1790, PGW.

85. Letter to the Annual meeting of Quakers, September 28, 1789, PGW.

86. Letter to the General Committee of the United Baptist Churches of Virginia, May 10, 1789, PGW.

87. Randall, 27.

88. Edmund Ingalls: "George Washington and Mathematics Education," *The Mathematics Teacher* vol. 47 (1954), 409.

89. Rozell, 85.

90. Letter to Jonathan Boucher, July 9, 1771, PGW.

91. Peter A. Lillback, *George Wash-*

ington's Sacred Fire (West Conshohocken, PA: Providence Forum Press,
2006).

92. Randall, 28.

93. Robert F. Dalzell and Lee Baldwin Dalzell, *George Washington's Mount
Vernon: At Home in Revolutionary America* (New York: Oxford University Press,
2000), Preface.

94. Ibid., 58.

95. Albert Welles, *The Pedigree and
History of the Washington Family* (New
York: Society Library, 1879), 57.

96. Mo Rocca, *All the Presidents'
Pets* (New York: Random House, 2005),
224.

97. United States Cavalry Association, *Journal of the United States Cavalry Association* (Fort Leavenworth, KS:
Ketcheson & Reeves, 1920), 28: 510–
511.

98. Robert Leckie, *George Washington's War: The Saga of the American
Revolution* (New York: HarperCollins,
1993), 443.

99. Diane Lindsey Reeves, *Firefighter*
(New York: Ferguson, 2008), 27.

100. Shannon Jackson Arnold, *Everybody Loves Ice Cream: The Whole Scoop
on America's Favorite Treat* (Cincinnati,
OH: Emmis Books, 2004), 15.

101. Plutarch, "Cato the Younger,"
Plutarch's Lives (London: G.G. and J.
Robinson, 1801), 5: 117.

102. "George Washington, Surveyor
and Mapmaker," *http://memory.loc.gov/
ammem/gmdhtml/gwmaps.html*.

103. Paul K. Longmore, *The Invention of George Washington* (Charlottesville, VA: University of Virginia Press,
1999), 13.

104. "George Washington, Surveyor
and Mapmaker," *http://memory.loc.gov/
ammem/gmdhtml/gwmaps.html*.

105. Albert Henry Heusser, *George
Washington's Map Maker: A Biography
of Robert Erskine* (New Brunswick, NJ:
Rutgers University Press, 1928), 173.

106. "Making of America Project,"
The Atlantic Monthly vol. 31 (Boston:
MA: Atlantic Monthly Co., 1873), 402.

107. Letter to William Pearce, Oct.
6, 1793, PGW.

108. Letter to John Sinclair, July 20,
1794, PGW.

109. George Washington, *The Diaries of George Washington*, 6 vols.
Donald Jackson and Dorothy Twohig,
eds. (Charlottesville: University Press
of Virginia, 1976–79), Introduction to
vol. 1: xxvii.

110. Ibid., xxx.

111. Ibid.

112. Melvin Bradley, *The Missouri
Mule: His Origin and Times*, vols. 1–2,
Columbia, MO: Extension Division,
University of Missouri-Columbia,
1993), 39–40.

113. Ibid., 41.

114. Ibid.

115. Ibid., 19.

116. Paul Leland Haworth, *George
Washington: Farmer: Being an Account
of His Home Life and Agricultural Activities* (Indianapolis, IN: Bobbs-Merrill, 1915), 62, 124–125. GW wrote about

the life of a husbandman: "it is honorable. It is amusing, and, with judicious
management, it is profitable."

117. Ibid., 182.

118. Rees, 158.

119. Ibid., 118–120.

120. George Washington, *The Diaries of George Washington*, 128.

121. David McCullough, *1776* (New
York: Simon & Schuster, 2005), 45.

122. Grizzard, GWBC, 250.

123. William Gardner Bell, *Commanding Generals and Chiefs of Staff,
1775–2005: Portraits & Biographical
Sketches of the United States Army's Senior Officer* (Washington DC: Government Printing Office, 2006), 66.

124. Grizzard, GWBC, 143.

125. Ibid., 117.

126. Robert C. Alberts, *A Charming
Field for an Encounter* (Washington
DC: Office of Publications, National
Park Service, U.S. Dept. of the Interior,
1975), 20.

127. Grizzard, GWBC, 117–118.

128. Ibid., 118.

129. Ibid., 43.

130. Ibid., 34–35.

131. George Washington, *The Writings of George Washington: Official Letters Relating to the French War, and
Private Letters Before the American Revolution, 1754–May, 1775*, Jared Sparks,
ed. (Boston: American Stationers' Company, John B. Russell, 1834), 40.

132. Ibid.

133. Grizzard, GWBC, 86.

134. "George Washington: The Soldier Through the French and Indian
War," *http://www.ushistory.org/valleyfo
rge/washington/george1.html*.

135. Grizzard, GWBC, 115.

136. "George Washington," *http://
www.sc94.ameslab.gov/Tour/gwash.html*.

137. Longmore, 123–124.

138. George Mason, *The Papers of
George Mason, 1725–1792 1. 1749–1778*
(Chapel Hill: University of North Car-
olina Press, 1970, 168.

139. Ibid., 208.

140. Ibid., 214.

141. *Academic American Encyclopedia* (New York: Grolier, 1989), 20: 43.

142. "Charge to the Northern Expeditionary Force," Sept. 14, 1775, WGW,
3: 90.

143. Ron Fridell, *Prisoners of War*
(Singapore: Marshall Cavendish, 2007),
20: 19.

144. Edward G. Lengel, *General
George Washington: A Military Life*
(New York: Random House, 2007), 91.

145. Ibid., 117.

146. Ibid., 149.

147. "George Washington," *http://
www.sc94.ameslab.gov/Tour/gwash.html*.

148. Lengel, 152.

149. Ibid., 149.

150. Letter to John Armstrong, January 10, 1783, PGW.

151. Frank Freidel, *Presidents of the
United States of America* (Darby, PA:
Diane Publishing, 1994), 9.

152. Chernow, 83.

153. "George Washington: The Commander In Chief," *http://www.ushisto

ry.org/valleyforge/washington/george2.ht
ml*.

154. Rasmussen, 131.

155. Ibid., 134.

156. Paul Johnson, *George Washington: The Founding Father* (New York:
HarperCollins, 2009), 64.

157. Address to the Continental
Army before the Before the Battle of
Long Island, August 27, 1776, PGW.

158. Letter to Benjamin Rush, April
4, 1790, John Adams, *Papers of John
Adams*. Robert J. Taylor et. al, eds.
(Cambridge: Belknap Press of Harvard
University Press, 1977–).

159. Thomas B. Allen and Cheryl
Harness, *George Washington, Spymas-
ter: How the Americans Outspied the
British and Won the Revolutionary War*
(Margate, FL: National Geographic,
2007), 39–40.

160. Letter to John Hancock, June
28, 1776, PGW.

161. Irving, 441–443.

162. Ibid.

163. Ibid.

164. Ibid., 463.

165. Ibid.

166. "Conway Cabal," *www.en.wiki
pedia.org/wiki/Conway_Cabal*.

167. Letter to John Banister, April
21, 1778, PGW.

168. Letter to George Clinton, February 16, 1778, PGW.

169. Bruce Chadwick, *George Washington's War: The Forging of a Revolutionary Leader and the American Presidency* (Naperville, IL: Sourcebooks,
2005), 294–295.

170. Paul S. Boyer and Melvyn
Dubofsky, *The Oxford Companion to
United States History* (New York: Ox-
ford University Press, 2001), 816.

171. Ibid., 683.

172. Ibid., 857.

173. "American Revolutionary War,
the Siege of Yorktown," *http://www.
xtimeline.com/evt/view.aspx?id=15248*.
Cornwallis had been the field commander in New Jersey in December
1776 and January 1777, when Washington made his famous Delaware Crossing.

174. Ibid.

175. Ibid.

176. Ibid.

177. General Orders, April 18, 1783,
PGW.

178. Grizzard, 236–237.

179. Ibid.

180. Ibid.

181. John Ferling, *The Ascent of
George Washington: The Hidden Political Genius of an American Icon* (London: Bloomsbury, 2010), Preface.

182. Ibid.

183. Ibid., 232.

184. John H. Rhodehamel, *The Great
Experiment: George Washington and the
American Republic* (New Haven, CT:
Yale University Press, 1998), Foreword
by Gordon S. Wood.

185. Ibid; Letter to his former personal secretary, Tobias Lear, July 1799,
PGW.

186. Remarks at the first Continen-

tal Congress, Phila-delphia, Pennsylvania, May 14, 1787, Max Farrand, *The Framing of the Constitution of the United States* (New Haven, Yale University Press, September 10, 1962), 66.

187. Letter to Patrick Henry, September 24, 1787, PGW.

188. Richard Brookhiser, "George Washington," *Presidential Leadership*, James Taranto and Leonard Leo, eds. (New York: Free Press, 2004), 16.

189. Stephen Ambrose, *To America: Personal Reflec-tions of an Historian* (New York: Simon & Schuster, 2002), 10.

190. Letter to Alexander Hamilton, October 3, 1788, PGW.

191. Ibid.

192. "Major Events with George Washington," *http://library.thinkquest. org/11492/cgi-bin/pres.cgi/washington_george?events.*

193. Brookhiser, 16.

194. Letter to James Madison, May 15, 1789, PGW.

195. Letter to Bushrod Washington, July 27, 1789, PGW.

196. Richard Norton Smith, *Patriarch: George Washington and the New American Nation* (Boston: Houghton Mifflin, 1993), 360.

197. "Appointment and Nomination of Supreme Court Justices," *www. grin.com/en/e-book/37916.*

198. PGW, 476.

199. James MacGregor Burns and Susan Dunn, *George Washington* (New York: Macmillan, 2004), 107.

200. Letter to George Washington, April 16, 1874, Thomas Jefferson, *The Jeffersonian Cyclopedia: a Comprehensive Collection of the Views of Thomas Jefferson Classified and Arranged In Alphabetical Order Under Nine Thousand Titles Relating to Government, Politics, Law, Education, Political Economy, Finance, Science, Art, Literature, Religious Freedom, Morals, etc.,* James Foley, ed. (New York: Funk & Wagnalls Company, 1900), 1: 502 (Hereafter JC).

201. Paul Johnson, *George Washington: The Founding Father* (New York: HarperCollins, 2009), 94.

202. Ibid.

203. Benjamin Vaughan Abbott, *A Digest of the Reports of the United States Courts: From the Organization of the Government to the Year 1884. Comprising the Decisions of the United States Supreme Court, Those of the Circuit and District Courts, of the Court of Claims, and of the Courts of the District of Columbia; Together with Leading Provisions of the Statutes, and Important Auxiliary Information upon the National Jurisprudence* (New York: George S. Diossy, 1884), 1: 122.

204. Ibid.

205. The United States Constitution, Article I — The Legislative Branch, Section 3 — The Senate.

206. Letter to Attorney General Edmund Randolph, September 28, 1789, PGW.

207. Rozell, 139.

208. Jeanne Fogle and Elan Penn, *Washington, D.C.: A Pictorial Celebration, Part 3* (New York: Sterling Publishing Company, 2005), 6.

209. Ferling, *Ascent*, 415.

210. Brookhiser, 17.

211. Ferling, *Ascent*, 296–298.

212. *The Oxford Hand Book of American Political Parties and Interest Groups* (New York: Oxford University Press, 2007), iii.

213. Ferling, *Ascent*, 300.

214. Letter to Robert Morris, April 30, 1781, in Alexander Hamilton, *The Papers of Alexander Hamilton*, 27 vols., Harold C Syrett, Jacob E. Cooke, and Barbara, Chernow, eds. (New York: Columbia University Press, 1961–87), 462.

215. Brookhiser, 17.

216. *Encyclopedia of African American History*, Leslie M. Alexander, Walter C. Rucker, eds. (Santa Barbara, CA: ABC-CLIO, 2010), 1: 415.

217. "These Notes List the First 11 Presidents with Brief Reviews," *http:// www.writework.com/essay/these-notes-list-first-11-presidents-brief-reviews-their-p.*

218. S. E. Morison, *The Oxford History of the United States 1783–1917* (London: Oxford University Press, 1927), 182.

219. Brookhiser, 17.

220. Ibid.

221. Elliott Robert Barkan, *U.S. Immigration and Naturalization Laws and Issues* (Westport, CT: Greenwood, 1999), 11.

222. Letter to Francis Van der Kamp, May 28, 1788, PGW.

223. Fred L. Israel and Jim F. Watts, *Presidential Documents: The Speeches, Proclamations, and Policies That Have Shaped the Nation from Washington to Clinton* (New York: Psychology Press, 2000), 11–12.

224. Cynthia Clark Northrup and Elaine C. Prange Turney, *Encyclopedia of Tariffs and Trade in U.S. History: The Encyclopedia* (Westport, CT: Greenwood, 2003), 356–357.

225. Brookhiser, 18.

226. Alan Axelrod and Charles Phillips, *What Every American Should Know About American History: 225 Events that Shaped the Nation* (Avon, MA: Adams Media, 2008), 62.

227. Ibid.

228. Todd Estes, *The Jay Treaty Debate, Public Opinion, and the Evolution of Early American Political Culture* (Andover: University of Massachusetts Press, 2006), 91.

229. Ibid.

230. Ferling, *Ascent*, 346.

231. Letter to the public (Farewell Address), September 17, 1796, PGW.

232. Ibid.

233. Ibid.

234. Ferling, *Ascent*, 355.

235. Harry Truman, *Wit and Wisdom of Harry S Truman*, Alex Ayers, ed. (New York: Meridian Books, 1998).

236. "George Washington Papers: Essay: Creating the American Nation," *http://memory.loc.gov/ammem/gwhtml/gwletter.html.*

237. Letter to Henry Knox, January 5, 1785, PGW.

238. Ford, 78.

239. "Jared Sparks — Harvard Square Library | Unitarian," ww.harvardsquare library.org/HVDpresidents/sparks.php.

240. George Washington, *The Diaries of George Washington*, 6 vols. John C. Fitzpatrick, Donald Jackson and Dorothy Twohig, eds. (Charlottesville, Virginia: University Press of Virginia, 1976–1979), vol.1: "Washington as a Diarist," Introduction.

241. Terry M. May, *Historical Dictionary of the American Revolution* (Lanham, MD: Scarecrow, 2009), 414.

242. "The Health and Medical History of President George Washington," *www.doctorzebra.com/prez/g01.htm.*

243. Ibid.

244. George Washington, *The Life of General Washington: First President of the United States*, Charles Wentworth Upham, ed. (London: Office of the National Illustrated Library, 1852), 2: 293–294.

245. Ibid. 274.

246. Ibid.

247. "The Health and Medical History of President George Washington," *www.doctorzebra.com/prez/g01.htm.*

248. William J. Federer, *American Minute: Notable Events of American Significance Remembered on the Date They Occurred* (St. Louis, MO: Amerisearch, 2003), 357.

249. George Washington, *Last Words of General Washington: A Circumstantial Account of the Last Illness and Death of George Washington* (1892) (Whitefish, MT: Kessinger Publishing, LLC, 2010). Washington's last words, as recorded by his secretary Tobias Lear, at about eleven o'clock in the evening, December 14, 1799.

250. Ibid.

251. Ibid.

252. Ibid.

253. Ibid.

254. Irving, 452.

255. George Cochrane Hazelton, *The National Capitol: Its Architecture, Art, and History* (New York: J.F. Taylor, 1902), 292.

256. *American History*, vol. 34 (Harrisburg, PA: Cowles History Group, 1999), 144.

257. St Augustine, St. *Augustin on Homilies on the Gospel of John, Homilies on the First Epistle of John and Soliloquies: Nicene and Post-Nicene Fathers of the Christian* (Whitefish, MT: Kessinger Publishing, 2004), 275.

258. Resolution proposed to Congress on the death of Washington, December 28, 1799, from Lee's eulogy.

259. Clint Johnson, *Touring Virginia's and West Virginia's Civil War Sites* (Winston Salem, NC: John F. Blair, 1999), 120.

260. "Case 14: The Man, Part V," *George Washington: Getting to Know the Man Behind the Image*, William L. Clements Library, *www.clements.umi ch.edu/exhibits/past/g.washington/case.*

261. Ford, 20.

262. Clifton Fadiman and André Bernard, eds., *Bartlett's Book of Anecdotes* (Boston: Little, Brown, 2000), 561.

263. Henry Wiencek, *An Imperfect God: George Washington, His Slaves, and the Creation of America* (New York: Farrar, Straus and Giroux, 2003), address at the Virginia Foundation for the Humanities, December 2000.

264. Ibid.

265. Sidney Kaplan and Emma Nogrady Kaplan. *The Black Presence in the Era of the American Revolution* (Amherst, MA: University of Massachusetts Press, 1989), 64–69.

266. Quoted by Ann Rinaldi, C. Michael Dudash in their novel *Taking Liberty: The Story of Oney Judge, George Washington's Runaway Slave* (New York: Simon & Schuster, 2004).

267. Letter to Robert Morris, April 12, 1786, PGW.

268. Letter to John Francis Mercer, September 9, 1786, PGW.

269. Nancy Hurrelbrinck, "Freeing His Slaves Is One of Washington's Greatest Legacies," *Inside UVA* 31 2 (January 19, 2001), 8.

270. Wiencek, 355.

271. "Gilbert Stuart Painting of George Washington," http://www.piersonphoto.com/Pierson2.htm.

272. Ibid.

273. "George Washington (Vaughan Portrait) — National Gallery of Art," http://www.nga.gov/collection/gallery/gg60a/gg60a-1121.html.

274. "Gilbert Stuart Painting of George Washington," http://www.piersonphoto.com/Pierson2.htm.

275. "Gilbert Stuart — Washington," http://www.americanrevolution.org/washstu.html.

276. Ibid.

277. Samuel Putnam Avery, *Some Account of the "Gibbs-Channing" Portrait of George Washington. Painted by Gilbert Stuart* (New York: Private printer, 1900), 11–12.

278. "Gilbert Stuart," http://www.factbites.com/topics/Gilbert-Stuart.

279. "Gilbert Stuart — Washington," http://www.americanrevolution.org/washstu.html.

280. "Gilbert Stuart and the Woman Behind George Washington -Stuart's 'Unfinished' Washington Portrait," www.earlyamerica.com/.../gilbert-stuart.htm.

281. James Thomas Flexner, *George Washington in the American Revolution* (Boston: Little, Brown, 1968), 12–13.

282. "Washington Monument: District of Columbia, National Park Service," www.nps.gov/history/history/online_books/presidents/site.

283. Ibid.

284. Laural A. Bidwell, *Mount Rushmore & the Black Hills: Including the Badlands* (Berkeley, CA: Moon Handbooks, 2010), 26–27.

285. Patricia K. Kummer, *South Dakota* (Mankato, MN: Capstone Press, 2002), 7.

286. "George Washington," http://www.nndb.com/people/107/0000024035/.

287. George Washington, Addressing the Continental Congress, June 16, 1775, *A Century of Lawmaking for a New Nation: U.S. Congressional Documents and Debates, 1774–1875* (Library of Congress).

288. Marvin Kitman and George Washington, *George Washington's Expense Account* (New York: Simon & Schuster, 1970), 143.

289. Ibid., 31.

290. Ibid., 285.

291. Grizzard, GWBC, 222.

292. General Orders on Profanity, Headquarters, Newburg, New York, August 3, 1776, PGW.

293. "Why Was George Washington so Important to the United States," http://answers.yahoo.com/question/index?qid=20080125215333AAsCOut.

294. Response to a letter from Colonel Lewis Nicola, May 23, 1782, PGW.

295. Kenneth Dautrich, David A. Yalof, *American Government: Historical, Popular, and Global Perspectives* (Boston: Cengage Learning, 2011), 225.

296. Ibid., 223.

297. List of American Medals," http://www.ehow.com/list_7497099_list-american-medals.html.

298. War Department, General Order Number 3, February 22, 1932.

299. Ibid.

300. Ibid.

301. Marcus Cunliffe, *George Washington, Man and Monument* (Boston: Little, Brown, 1958), 22–24.

302. Ibid.

303. Farewell Address, September 17, 1796, PGW.

304. Gordon S. Wood, "The Greatness of George Washington," *The Virginia Quarterly Review*, www.vqronline.org/.../wood-greatness-george-washington.

305. Mason Locke Weems, *The Life and Memorable Actions of George Washington* (Philadelphia, J.B. Lippincott Co., [1800] 1918), chapter one; Attributed by Weems to "...an aged lady, who was a distant relative, and, when a girl, spent much of her time in the family...," who referred to young George as "cousin."

306. William Hardcastle Browne, *Odd Derivations of Words, Phrases, Slang, Synonyms and Proverbs* (Philadelphia: Arnold & Co., 1900), 163.

307. Henry Woodman and Mary Smith Woodman, *History of Valley Forge* (Oaks, PA: J.U. Francis, Sr., 1921), 65.

308. "History Is Elementary: George, We Hardly Knew Ye!" www.historyiselementary.blogspot.com/2006/03/george-we.

309. Ibid.

310. Quoted by Ina Jaffe, Present at the Creation (National Public Radio), George Washington Crossing the Delaware, February 18, 2002.

311. Ibid.

312. David Hackett Fischer, *Washington's Crossing* (New York: Oxford University Press, 2004), 4–5.

313. "The Quakers And The American Revolution : US American History," www.123helpme.com/preview.asp?id=157972.

314. The conversation is cited in an article on Warner's cousin Thomas Mifflin (*Appleton's Cyclopedia of American Biography*), James Grant Wilson, ed., John Fiske and Stanley L. Klos. 6 vols. (New York: D. Appleton and Company, 1887–1889, 1999).

315. Ibid.

316. Letter to the Annual Meeting of the Quakers, October 1789, PGW.

317. Harry Emerson Wildes, *Valley Forge* (New York: Macmillan, 1938), 174–5.

318. "The Valley Forge Fish Story," *The Shad Journal*, 2000, www.gwpapers.virginia.edu/articles/boyle.html.

319. J. Langguth, *Patriots* (New York: Simon & Schuster, 1989), 376.

320. Caroline Tiger, *General Howe's Dog: George Washington, the Battle of Germantown, and the Dog Who Crossed Enemy Lines* (New York: Chamberlain Bros., 2005), 95.

321. John R. Vile, *The Constitutional Convention of 1787* (Santa Barbara, CA: ABC-CLIO, 2005), 30.

322. "Partial List of Portrayals: General George Washington — Father of Our Country," www.historicportrayals.com.

323. "How George Washington Racked Up a $300,000 Fine for Overdue Library Books," *Christian Science Monitor*, April 19, 1010.

324. All these letters of George Washington can be found in PGW and COL.

325. Abraham Lincoln, "Temperance Address Delivered Before the Springfield Washington Temperance Society, February 22, 1842," Roy Prentice Basler, ed., *Abraham Lincoln: His Speeches and Writings* (Cleveland: World Publishing Co., 1946), 141.

326. James Garfield, *Maxims of James Abram Garfield, General, Patriotic, Political*, William Ralston Balch, compiler (Philadelphia, 1880), Pamphlet Collection, Library of Congress, 10.

327. David McCullough, *John Adams* (New York: Simon & Schuster, 2001), 414.

328. Robert Haven Schauffler, *Washington's Birthday: Its History, Observance, Spirit, and Significance as Related in Prose and Verse* (New York: Dodd, Mead, 1918), 143.

329. "Quotes about George Washington," Personal papers of Randolph G. Adams, historian, biographer, first director of the William L. Clements Library, www.lcweb2.loc.gov/ammem/dli2/techsumm/gwsamp/gw01.sgm.

330. Stephen Ambrose, 10.

331. Eulogy of Washington, February 8, 1800, *Works of Fisher Ames*, William B. Allen, ed. (Indianapolis: Liberty Classics, 1983), 1: 519–538.

332. Anonymous, sometimes attributed to Hubert Humphrey, in who may only have been repeating it his statement: "The Senate is a place filled with

goodwill and good intentions, and if the road to hell is paved with them, then it's a pretty good detour." The Washington quote appears in a joke book by comedian Joey Adams, *Encyclopedia of Humor* (New York: Bonanza Books, 1968), 395.

333. Anonymous, *The Philadelphia Aurora*, 1796. The paper was edited by Benjamin Franklin Bache, a grandson of Benjamin Franklin, who probably is responsible for the attack at the time of Washington's Farewell Address. The next day, an editorial in the paper carried on the attack against the nation's retiring first president, asserting: "The man who is the source of all the misfortune of our country is this day reduced to a level with his fellow citizens, and is no longer possessed of power to multiply evils upon the United States ... this day ought to be a jubilee in the United States."

334. Robert Bridges (1858–1941) American journalist and poet, who wrote under the pen name "Droch," Washington.

335. *Our Sacred Honor* (New York: Simon & Schuster, 1997).

336. *George Washington, Man and Monument* (Boston: Little, Brown, 1958).

337. Lafayette, in *The Home Book of Quotations, Selected and Arranged by Burton Stevenson* (New York: Dodd, Mead & Company, 1967), 2121.

338. Chauncey Mitchell Depew, *Orations, Addresses and Speeches of Chauncey M. Depew* (Private Printing, 1910), 21.

339. Ralph Waldo Emerson, *The Complete Works of Ralph Waldo Emerson* (Boston: Houghton, Mifflin, 1903), 27.

340. James Morton Smith, ed., "Cincinnatus Assayed: Washington in the Revolution," *George Washington: A Profile* (New York: Hill and Wang, 1969).

341. "A Toast at a Dinner at Versailles, 1778," Paul Dickson, *Toasts: Over 1500 of the Best Toasts, Sentiments, Blessings, and Graces* (New York: Crown, 1991).

342. Dorothy Twohig, Peter Henriques, and Don Higginbotham, "George Washington and the Legacy of Character," (Columbia University, Session 4, The Trustees of Columbia University in the City of New York).

343. David M. Kennedy and Thomas A. Bailey, *The American Spirit: United States History as Seen by Contemporaries* (Boston: Cengage, 209), 1: 211.

344. "Motley and Monarch," *The North American Review* (1885): 1.

345. James R. Gaines, *For Liberty and Glory: Washington, Lafayette and Their Revolutions* (New York: W.W. Norton, 2007), 116.

346. Henry Cabot Lodge, *George Washington*, 2 vols. (Boston: Houghton Mifflin, 1889); William Safire, *Lend Me Your Ears: Great Speeches in History* (New York: W.W. Norton, 2004), 316.

347. James Russell Lowell, *Under the Old Elm* ... (Boston: 1886), pt. iii, section 1.

348. An oration, delivered at Wethersfield, Connecticut, February 22, 1800, on the death of George Washington.

349. Washington Irving, *The Life and Times of Washington* (New York: G.P. Putnam & Sons, 1876), 783.

350. *Tributes to Washington*, Pamphlet No. 3, Albert Bushnell Hart, ed. (Washington, DC: George Washington Bicentennial Commission, 1931), 7–8.

351. Speaking to some young Americans to whom he granted an audience and inquired about the health of "the great Washington" and was told he was very well, Mason Weems, *A History of the Life and Death, Virtues and Exploits of General George Washington* (New York: Macy-Massius, 1927), chapter 1, 1.

352. Open letter to George Washington, July 30, 1796; David M. Kennedy, Lizabeth Cohen, and Thomas A. Bailey, *The American Pageant*, Vol. 1: A History of the American People to 1877 (Boston: Wadsworth, 2010), 212.

353. Glenn A. Phelps, *George Washington & American Constitutionalism* (Lawrence: University Press of Kansas, 2007).

354. "George Washington, Genius in Leadership," A presentation made at a meeting on February 22, 2000, of The George Washington Club, Ltd. (Wilmington, Delaware).

355. Mark Twain (Samuel Clemens), "Brief Biographical Sketch of George Washington," *The Celebrated Jumping Frog of Calaveras County, and Other Sketches* John Paul, ed. (New York: C.H. Webb, 1867).

356. Don Higginbotham, ed., *George Washington Reconsidered* (Charlottesville: University Press of Virginia, 2001) 116.

357. Speech at the completion of the Bunker Hill monument, June 17, 1843.

358. "The Decay of Lying: An Observation" (This essay was originally published in *Intentions*, 1891).

Two. John Adams

1. Thomas Oliphant, "Hold the Marble," Boston Globe, June 26, 2001.

2. John Adams, letter to Benjamin Rush, March 23, 1809, *The Spur of Fame: Dialogues of John Adams and Benjamin Rush, 1805–1813*, John Schutz and Douglass Adair, eds. (San Marino, CA: The Huntington Library, 1966), 139.

3. John Adams, *The Works of John Adams* (Boston: Little, Brown, 1856), 4 (Hereafter Works).

4. Benjamin Rush quoted in Joseph J. Ellis, *The Passionate Sage: The Character and Legacy of John Adams* (New York: W.W. Norton, 1994), 29.

5. Rebecca Stefoff, *John Adams: 2nd President of the United States* (Ada, OK: Garrett Educational Corp., 1988), 79.

6. Paul F. Boller, *Presidential Campaigns: From George Washington to George W. Bush* (New York: Oxford University Press, 2004), 4.

7. Thomas Jefferson, *Works*, 56.

8. Letter to Benjamin Rush, July 19, 1812, in Schutz and Adair, eds.; David McCullough, *John Adams* (New York: Simon & Schuster, 2001), 30.

9. McCullough, *John Adams*, 33.

10. "Downtown Boston — A Site on a Revolutionary War Road Trip," *www.revolutionaryday.com/usroute20/boston/default.htm*.

11. "Boston Brahmin," *www.en.wikipedia.org/wiki/Boston_Brahmin*.

12. "Zabdiel Boylston Biography," *http://biography.yourdictionary.com/zabdiel-boylston*.

13. Ibid.

14. "Boylston & Adams — Boylston — Family History & Genealogy," *www.boards.ancestry.com/surnames.boylston/1.16.1.1.100.1/mb.ashx*.

15. "Susanna Boylston," *www.en.wikipedia.org/wiki/Susanna_Boylston*.

16. Susan Page, "John Adams Gets His Turn, Finally," USA Today, July 5, 2001, 3.

17. McCullough, *John Adams*, 30.

18. John P. Diggins, *John Adams* (New York: Macmillan, 2003), 17.

19. "MHS Boylston Family Papers, 1688–1979," *www.masshist.org/findingaids/doc.cfm?fa=fa0238*.

20. John R. Bumgarner, *The Health of the Presidents: The 41 United States Presidents Through 1993 from a Physician's Point of View* (Jefferson, NC: McFarland, 1994), 9.

21. McCullough, *John Adams*, 18.

22. Simon Russell Beale portrayed John Adams in the film *John & Abigail Adams* (WGBH Boston in association with Green Umbrella, Ltd. for American Experience, 2005).

23. Victor A. McKusick, *Mendelian Inheritance in Man*, 9th ed. (Baltimore: Johns Hopkins University Press, 1990), MIM#109200.

24. A. Blinderman, "John Adams: Fears, Depressions, and Ailments," *NY State J Med.* 1977, 77: 273.

25. McCullough, *John Adams*, 470.

26. "Columns: John Adams: A Portrait of Our Second President," *http://www.sptimes.com/News/070101/Columns/John_Adams__A_portrai.shtml*.

27. Ibid.

28. McCullough, *John Adams*, 2–3.

29. C. Bradley Thompson, *The Revolutionary Writings of John Adams* (Indianapolis, IN: Liberty Fund, 2001), foreword.

30. "John Adams, 2d President of the United States: Early Career," *http://www.infoplease.com/ce6/people/A0856476.html*.

31. Joseph J. Ellis, *Passionate Sage: the Character and Legacy of John Adams* (New York: W.W. Norton & Company, 2001), 175.

32. Ibid.

33. Ibid.

34. F. Forrester Church, *So Help Me God: The Founding Fathers and the First Great Battle Over the Church* (Orlando, FL: Harcourt, 2007), 215.

35. Paul Johnson, *A History of the American People* (New York: HarperCollins, 2009) 227–231.

36. *Appleton's Cyclopædia of American Biography*, James Grant Wilson and John Fiske, eds. (New York: D. Appleton and Company, 1887), 1: 23.

37. Susan Page, 3.

38. McCullough, *John Adams*, 2.

39. Anne Husted Burleigh, *John Adams* (New Rochelle, NY: Arlington House), 173.

40. Epitaph for John Adams (1829), inscribed on one of the portals of the United First Parish Church Unitarian (Church of the Presidents), Quincy, MA.

41. Tom Paine, "Open Letter to the Citizens of the United States," November 22, 1802, *The Quotable Founding Fathers*, Buckner F. Melton, Jr. ed. (Washington DC: Potomac Books, Inc., 2004), 2; Chuck Raasch, "John Adams Would Be Surprised by Today's Politics," *USA Today*, July 19, 2004.

42. Manus Hand, "Dead Presidents on Dead Presidents," *www.diplom.org/manus*.

43. Alan Taylor, "John Adams," *The Reader's Companion to the American Presidency*, Alan Brinkley and Davis Dyer, eds. (Boston: Houghton Mifflin, 2004), 22.

44. "Diary, February 9, 1779," *Diary and Autobiog-raphy of John Adams*, 4 vols. L.H. Butterfield et. al. eds. (Cambridge: Belknap Press of Harvard University Press, 1961) (Hereafter JA Diary).

45. Letter to James Madison, January 30, 1787, *The Complete Thomas Jefferson Papers* (Manuscript Division at the Library of Congress).

46. "The Most Bizarre Presidential Scandals—John Adams' Ladies," *http://www.esquire.com/the-side/feature/bizarre-scandals-0808#ixzz1n22yqPVY*.

47. Ellen Carolina De Quincy Woodbury, *Dorothy Quincy, Wife of John Hancock: With Events of Her Time* (Suwanne, GA: The Neale Publishing Company, 1901), 19.

48. Draft of a letter to Richard Cranch, October 10, 1758, JA Diary.

49. Catherine Drinker Bowen, *John Adams and the American Revolution* (Boston: Little, Brown, 1950).

50. Joseph Cowley, *John Adams: Architect of Freedom (1735–1826)* (New York: IUniverse, 2009), 159.

51. "John Adams Marries Abigail Smith," *http://www.history.com/this-day-in-history/john-adams-marries-abigail-smith*.

52. Mildred Lewis Rutherford, *American Authors: A Hand-Book of American Literature from Early Colonial to Living Writers* (Atlanta, GA: The Franklin Printing and Publishing Co., 1894), 55.

53. February 1, 1763, JA Diary.

54. Natalie S. Bober, *Abigail Adams: Witness to a Revolution* (New York: Simon & Schuster, 1998), 7.

55. "Dear John, Dear Abigail: A Love Story Through Letters," *NPR*, www.npr.org/templates/story/story.php? storyId=130862704.

56. *Academic American Encyclopedia* (Danbury, CT: Grolier Inc., 1998), 1: 94.

57. "Abigail Adams," *www.aboutfamouspeople.com/article1049.html*.

58. Edith B. Gelles, *Portia: The World of Abigail Adams* (Bloomington: Indiana University Press, 1995), 47.

59. Abigail Adams, letter to John Adams, March 31, 1776, *The Letters of John and Abigail Adams*, Frank Shuffleton, ed. (New York: Penguin Classics, 2003) (Hereafter LJA).

60. Edith Belle Gelles, *Abigail Adams: A Writing Life* (New York: Routledge, 2002), 5.

61. Lynne Withey, *Dearest Friend: A Life of Abigail Adams* (New York: Simon & Schuster, 2002), 15.

62. Ibid., 62–63.

63. March 31, 1776, LJA.

64. April 14, 1776, LJA.

65. "The Retreat from War—John Adams," *www.presidentprofiles.com/Washington-Johnson/John-Adams*.

66. Gelles, *Portia*, 170.

67. May 12, 1780, LJA.

68. Jacqueline Ching, *Abigail Adams: A Revolutionary Woman* (Buffalo, NY: Rosen Publishing Group, 2002), 97.

69. "American Experience: John & Abigail Adams," *www.pbs.org/wgbh/amex/adams/peopleevents/p_adamskids.html*.

70. Ching, 97.

71. Sandra L. Quinn-Musgrove and Sanford Kanter, *America's Royalty: All the Presidents' Children* (Westport, CT: Greenwood, 1995), 15.

72. Ibid., 16.

73. Laurie Carter Noble, "Abigail Adams," *The Dictionary of Unitarian and Universalist Biography*, http://www25.uua.org/uuhs/duub/articles/abigailadams.html.

74. July 26, 1796, JA Diary.

75. Letter to Dr. Benjamin Rush, August 28, 1811, Works.

76. February 22, 1756, JA Diary.

77. Frederick J. Azbell, *Organized Religion Is..: Blind, Leading the Blind* (Bloomington, IN: AuthorHouse, 2010), 177.

78. Letter to Thomas Jefferson, April 19, 1817, *Correspondence of John Adams and Thomas Jefferson, 1812–1826*, Paul Wilstach, ed. (New York: Kraus Reprint, 1972) (Hereafter Correspondence); "Religion and the Federal Government," *Religion and the Founding of the American Republic* (Library of Congress), 157.

79. Letter to Benjamin Rush, June 12, 1812, Works.

80. June 28, 1813, Correspondence.

81. December 3, 1813, Correspondence.

82. February 16, 1756, JA Diary.

83. December 25, 1813, Correspondence.

84. Joseph C. Sommer, "Presidents Adams and the Religious Right," *http://www.humanismbyjoe.com/Adams_Family_Religion.htm*.

85. February 13, 1756, JA Diary.

86. September 3, 1816, Correspondence.

87. Letter to F.A. Van der Kamp, December 27, 1816, Works.

88. Ibid., February 16, 1809.

89. Letter to Benjamin Rush, August 28, 1811, Works.

90. McCullough, *John Adams*, 33.

91. Ibid., 35.

92. John Ferling, *John Adams: A Life* (Knoxville: University of Tennessee Press, 1992), 15.

93. Bumgarner, 9.

94. Ferling, 15.

95. "Classical Education of the Founding Fathers," *www.memoriapress.com/articles/founding-fathers.html*.

96. McCullough, *John Adams*, 35.

97. Ibid.

98. Ibid., 16.

99. Carl J. Richard, *Why We're All Romans: The Roman Contribution to the Western World* (Lanham, MD: Rowman & Littlefield, 2010), 122.

100. LJA, October 29, 1775, 117.

101. John Adams, "A Dissertation the Canon and Feudal Law," 1765, John P. Diggins, *The Portable John Adams* (New York: Penguin, 2004), 2.

102. McCullough, *John Adams*, 391.

103. Natalie S. Bober, *Abigail Adams: Witness to a Revolution* (New York: Simon & Schuster, 1998), 155.

104. "John Adams Unbound, Exhibition Content, September 22, 2006–April 29, 2007, Boston Public Library, Copley Square," *http://www.docstoc.com/docs/51655859*.

105. Letter to Elbridge Gerry, December 6, 1777, Works.

106. McCullough, *John Adams*, 18.

107. John Adams, *Legal Papers of John Adams* (Cambridge, MA: Harvard University Press, 1965), I: xix.

108. McCullough, *John Adams*, 18.

109. John Adams and Paul M. Zall, *Adams on Adams* (Lexington: University Press of Kentucky, 2004), 9.

110. Works, I: 28.

111. Letter to Richard Cranch, October 18, 1756, Works.

112. Works, 2: 103.

113. Tuesday, January 3, 1759, JA Diary.

114. Ibid.

115. "Adams, John," *http://www.autocww.colorado.edu/~blackmon/E64ContentFiles*.

116. "The American Revolution," *http://www.nps.gov/revwar/about_the_revolution/john_adams.html*.

117. "Adams, John," *http://www.autocww.colorado.edu/~blackmon/E64ContentFiles*.

118. 118. Ferling, 41.

119. "AmericanRevolution — The Braintree Instructions," *www.americanrevolution6c.wikispaces.com*.

120. Cowley, 22–29.

121. Ibid.

122. Ibid.

123. Ibid.

124. Ibid.

125. Ibid., 31–32.

126. "The Boston Massacre," *www.ushistory.org/declaration/related/massacre.htm*.

127. Frederic Kidder and John Adams, *History of the Boston Massacre, March 5, 1770: Consisting of the Narrative of the Town, the Trial of the Soldiers:*

and a Historical Introduction, Containing Unpublished Documents of John Adams, and Explanatory Notes (Albany, NY: J. Munsell, 1870), 29–31.

128. J. Jackson Owensby, The United States Declaration of Independence (Revisited) (Kernserville, NC: A-Argus Books, 2010), 267.

129. Ferling, 66–69.

130. John Adams, "Argument in Defense of the British Soldiers in the Boston Massacre Trials," Dec. 4, 1770, Works, 1: 114.

131. Ferling, 69.

132. March 5, 1773, JA Diary.

133. Appleton's Cyclopædia, 1: 16.

134. "John Adams UUA: Unitarian Universalist Association, Universalist History and Heritage Society," http://www25-temp.uua.org/uuhs/duub/articles/johnadams.html.

135. "John Adams: Clouds of Revolution," http://www.sparknotes.com/biography/johnadams/section3.rhtml.

136. "Dissertation on the Canon and Feudal Law," Boston Gazette, 1765.

137. Ibid.

138. Thomas Hutchinson and Andrew Oliver, The Letters of Governor Hutchinson, and Lieutenant Governor Oliver (Boston: W. Gilbert, 1774), 44.

139. Winton U. Solberg, The Constitutional Convention and the Formation of the Union (Champaign: University of Illinois Press, 1990), lxiv.

140. Novanglus, Boston Gazette, 1774–75.

141. Ibid.

142. Ibid.

143. Letter to Dr. Richard Price, April 19, 1790, Works.

144. Ibid.

145. "John Adams and the Massachusetts Constitution," http://www.mass.gov/courts/sjc/john-adams-b.html.

146. Works, 6: 63.

147. John Adams and John P. Diggins, 233.

148. "Neuman-Smith-Goodale Family," http://wc.rootsweb.ancestry.com/cgi-bin/igm.cgi?op=GET&db=michaelrneuman&id=I76973.

149. Daniel S. Burt, The Chronology of American Literature: America's Literary Achievements from the Colonial Era to Modern Times (Boston: Houghton Mifflin Harcourt, 2004), 77.

150. "Thoughts on Government," April, 1776, chapter 4, document 5, Papers 4: 86–93.

151. Ibid.

152. Ibid.

153. Ibid.

154. John Adams, "Discourses on Davila, I," Boston Gazette, March, 1805, Section V.

155. "Historic Roots of the Legislative Branch, Congress in the Constitutional Convention. Checks and Balances," http://www.enotes.com/government-checks-balances/historic-roots.

156. Ferling, 155.

157. Richard Brookhiser, "George Washington," Presidential Leadership, James Taranto and Leonard Leo, eds. (New York: Free Press, 2004), 19.

158. Mathew Spalding, "John Adams," Presidential Leadership, James Taranto and Leonard Leo, eds. (New York: Free Press, 2004), 22.

159. John Lord, Beacon Lights of History: American Statesmen (New York: Fords, Howard, and Hurlburt, 1894), 202.

160. Ibid., 200.

161. C. Bradley Thompson, John Adams and the Spirit of Liberty (Lawrence: University Press of Kansas, 2002), Introduction.

162. Ibid., 249.

163. Crowley, 37.

164. June 20, 1774, JA Diary.

165. Letter to Dr. Price, April 18, 1785, Works.

166. Works, 290.

167. October 9, 1774, LJA.

168. O. John Rogge, "The Rule of Law," ABA Journal (September 1960, Vol. 16), 982.

169. McCullough, John Adams, 222.

170. McCullough, quoted in "Plain Speaking," a review of John Adams, New York Times, May 27, 2001.

171. John Hannibal Sheppard, The Life of Samuel Tucker, Commodore in the American Revolution (Boston: A. Mudge and Son, 1868), 102–103.

172. Ibid.

173. Ibid.

174. McCullough, John Adams, 202.

175. Ferling, 219.

176. Appletons' Cyclopaedia, 409.

177. Burleigh, 195.

178. Ibid., 200.

179. McCullough, John Adams, 284.

180. McCullough, John Adams, 487.

181. McCullough, John Adams, 519–20.

182. McCullough, John Adams, 520.

183. James Grant, John Adams: Party of One (New York: Macmillan, 2006), 311.

184. McCullough, John Adams, 285.

185. Cheryl Harness, The Revolutionary John Adams (Washington, DC: National Geographic, 2008), 27.

186. "The Electoral College — Controversial Elections," www.archive.fairvote.org/e_college/controversial.htm.

187. Edward Channing, A Students' History of the United States (New York: Macmillan Co., 1912), 258–259.

188. Abigail Adams and John P. Kaminski, The Quotable Abigail Adams (Cambridge, MA: Harvard University Press, 2009), Introduction.

189. Spalding, 23.

190. William A. DeGregorio, The Complete Book of U.S. Presidents (New York: Barricade, 2001), 26.

191. Letter to Abigail Adams, November 2, 1800, McCullough, John Adams, 551.

192. Appleton's Cyclopædia, 1: 21.

193. Edward L. Ayers, Lewis L. Gould, David M. Oshinsky, and Jean R. Soderlund, American Passages: A History of the United (Stamford, CT: Cengage Learning, 2011), 1: 161.

194. Works, 9: 107.

195. McCullough, John Adams, 467.

196. McCullough, John Adams, 551.

197. "A.P.E.— John Adams's Domestic Policy," http://www.library.thinkquest.org/11492/cgi-bin/pres.cgi/adams_john.

198. "Oliver Wolcott, Jr.," www.en.wikipedia.org/wiki/Oliver_Wolcott_Jr.

199. Adams, Diggins, 148.

200. J. Thomas Scharf, History of Maryland: From the Earliest Period to the Present Day (Baltimore: John B. Piet, 1879), II: 437.

201. John Chester Miller, Crisis in Freedom: The Alien and Sedition Acts (Boston: Little, Brown, 1951), 20.

202. Ibid., 56.

203. Ibid., 141.

204. Ibid., 63–66.

205. Ibid., 59.

206. Ibid., 47.

207. Ibid., 165.

208. Select Documents Illustrative of the History of the United States, 1776–1861, William MacDonald, ed. (New York: Macmillan, 1898), 144.

209. Ibid., 147–148.

210. Ibid.

211. Ibid.

212. Ibid.

213. Paige Smith, John Adams: 1784–1826 (Westport, CT: Greenwood, 1969), 961.

214. Ibid.

215. Phillip I. Blumberg, Repressive Jurisprudence in the Early American Republic: The First Amendment and the Legacy of English Law (Cambridge: Cambridge University Press, 2010), 77–80.

216. Ibid., 116.

217. Ibid., 102–103. House of Representatives, January 20, 1789. Lyon spoke out against "the malign influence of Connecticut politicians." He charged that Adams and the Federalists only served the interests of the rich.

218. Ibid.

219. Ibid., 103.

220. Ibid., 103–105.

221. Ibid., 88.

222. Ibid., 130.

223. JC, 980.

224. William W. Davis, The Fries Rebellion, Seventeen Ninety Eight to Seventeen Ninety Nine (New York: Ayer Publishing, 1977), 33.

225. Ibid., 129–135.

226. Ferling, 339.

227. Zoltán Haraszti, John Adams & the Prophets of Progress (New York: Grosset & Dunlap, 1964), 221.

228. Alexander DeConde, The Quasi-War: The Politics and Diplomacy of the Undeclared War with France 1797–1801 (New York: Scribner, 1966), 116.

229. Ibid., 74.

230. Ibid., 93. The phrase originated with Rep. Robert Goodloe Harper, Chairman of the Committee on Ways and Means in Congress, on June 18, 1798.

231. Ibid., 104.

232. Message to the Senate and House of June 21, 1798, James D. Richardson, ed. A Compilation of the Messages and Papers of the Presidents, Prepared Under the Joint Committee on

Printing of the House and Senate, Pursuant to an Act of the Fifty-Second Congress of the United States (Washington, DC: Bureau of National Literature, 1897), 256.

233. Ibid., 121.

234. John Fenno, founder and editor, *Gazette of the United States*, a quasi-official Federalist publication, September 9, 1789. It was backing the government of the first president, George Washington. The Gazette proclaimed that its mission was to oppose the "raging madness" of those who criticized administration policies, including "politicians" such as Thomas Jefferson. The newspaper was financed by Alexander Hamilton, who used it to attack Jefferson.

235. McCullough, *John Adams*, 523.

236. Works, 9: 162.

237. DeConde, 250.

238. *Appleton's Cyclopædia*, 1: 23.

239. John Lamberton Harper, *American Machiavelli: Alexander Hamilton and the Origins of U.S. Foreign Policy* (Cambridge: Cambridge University Press, 2004), 253.

240. Ibid., 254–257.

241. McCullough, *John Adams*, 564.

242. Ibid.

243. McCullough, *John Adams*, 116.

244. Brian MacQuarrie, "Vast Library, Thoughts of John Adams Displayed," *The Boston Globe*, September 22, 2006.

245. Works, 2: 521.

246. Hugh Chisholm, *The Encyclopaedia Britannica: A Dictionary of Arts, Sciences, Literature and General Information* (New York: Encyclopaedia Britannica, 1910), 1: 176.

247. McCullough quoted in an interview with the *Boston Globe*, September 22, 2006.

248. Mary Wollstonecraft, *Historical and Moral View of the French Revolution* (London: J. Johnson, 1794), 404.

249. Written in the margins of his copy of Mary Wollstonecraft's '*Historical and Moral View of the French Revolution*,' 1812.

250. "American Experience: John & Abigail Adams," *www.pbs.org/wgbh/amex/adams/timeline/index.html*.

251. Letter to Jefferson, July 13, 1813, *Adams-Jefferson Letters*, 358.

252. Microfilms of the Adams Papers, Adams family, John Adams, Charles Francis Adams (Adams Manuscript Trust, Boston, Massachusetts Historical Society).

253. Correa Moylan Walsh, *The Political Science of John Adams: A Study in the Theory of Mixed Government and the Bicameral System* (New York: G.P. Putnam's Sons, 1915), 295.

254. John Adams, Discourses on Davila, "A Balanced Government," No. 13, 1790–1791, *Works*, VI: 280.

255. John Adams, as quoted by Robert F. Kennedy in his campaign treatise, "To Seek a Newer World" (Garden City, NY: Doubleday, 1975).

256. McCullough, *John Adams*, chapter eight: "Heir Apparent," a reference to his being the heir apparent to the presidency after Washington.

257. "The Health and Medical History of President John Adams," *http://www.doctorzebra.com/prez/g02.htm*.

258. Ibid.

259. Ibid.

260. Blinderman, 270.

261. Bumgarner, 11.

262. Ibid., 13.

263. "The Health and Medical History of President John Adams," *http://www.doctorzebra.com/prez/g02.htm*.

264. Ferling, 444.

265. *Appleton's Cyclopædia*, 381.

266. Blinderman, 270.

267. Ferling, 85.

268. Blinderman, 274.

269. McCullough, *John Adams*, 648.

270. Cowley, 158.

271. McCullough, *John Adams*, 648.

272. Laura Carter Holloway, *The Ladies of the White House: Or, in the Home of the Presidents: Being a Complete History of the Social and Domestic Lives of the Presidents From Washington to Hayes — 1789–1880* (Martin, TN: Bradley & Co., 1881), 124–125.

273. Ibid.

274. Ibid.

275. Ferling, 201.

276. Smith, 1043.

277. *Harper's Magazine* vol. 43 (New York: Harper's Magazine Co., 1871), 255.

278. Alexandra Mayes Birnbaum, *Birnbaum's United States 1993* (New York: HarperCollins Publishers, 1992), 1076.

279. Bruce Felton, *What Were They Thinking: Really Bad Ideas Throughout History* (Guildford, CT: Globe Pequot, 2007), 17.

280. Michael A. Genovese, *Encyclopedia of the American Presidency* (New York: Facts on File, 2009), 476.

281. Henry Mayer, *A Son of Thunder: Patrick Henry and the American Republic* (New York: Grove Press, 2001), 305.

282. Paul F. Boller, *Presidential Anecdotes* (New York: Oxford University Press, 1996), 27.

283. Ibid.

284. Ibid., 31.

285. Ibid.

286. Ibid.

287. Ibid., 33.

288. Grant, 354.

289. Lisa Fabrizio, "Report on the John Adams Symposium," *http://www.freerepublic.com/focus/f-news/780508/posts*.

290. Ellis, 227.

291. Lisa Fabrizio, "Report on the John Adams Symposium," *http://www.freerepublic.com/focus/f-news/780508/posts*.

292. Public Broadcasting Service, 13 episodes. Air date of first episode: January 20, 1976; Air date of final episode: April 13, 1976.

293. *1776* (1969), a musical play by Peter Stone (book), Sherman Edwards (music, lyrics) (46th Street Theatre, 1,217 performances; Tony, NYDCC Awards).

294. McCullough, *John Adams*, 75.

295. "David McCullough Interview," *www.neh.gov/whoweare/mccullough/interview.html*.

296. Various dates, JA Diary.

297. Ellis, 151.

298. Michael Foster, "A Reflection on the Legacy of John Adams: Lawyer, Patriot, Statesman," *http://www.innsofcourt.org/Content/Default.aspx?Id=5787*.

299. Hamilton drafted a statement expressing his views on the "great and intrinsic defects in [Adams's] character which unfit him for the office of chief magistrate." It was published at the end of October, 1800, as "Letter from Alexander Hamilton, Concerning the Public Conduct and Character of John Adams." Quoted by Page Smith, John Adams, 1784–1826 (Garden City, NY: Doubleday & Co., 1962).

300. McCullough, *John Adams*, 18.

301. Parrington, 211.

302. John Sanderson, *Biography of the Signers of the Declaration of Independence*, vol. III (Philadelphia: R.W. Pomeroy, 1823).

303. C. Bradley Thompson and Bernard Cohen *Science and the Founding Fathers* (New York: W.W. Norton & Co., 1995), 228–29.

Three. Jefferson

1. Jefferson's grave marker at the Monticello Graveyard.

2. Joseph J. Ellis, *American Sphinx: The Character of Thomas Jefferson* (New York: Knopf, 1997), 4.

3. "List of Nicknames of United States Presidents," *www.american-history-fun-facts.com/list-of-us-presidents*.

4. Thomas Jefferson, *Autobiography* (New York: G.P. Putnam's Sons, 1914 [1997]), 4 (Hereafter Autobiography).

5. Ibid.

6. Ibid.

7. James Horn, "Beyond the Falls: The Peopling of Jefferson's Virginia," Monticello Keepsake, November 5, 1999.

8. Autobiography, 22.

9. "Peter Jefferson," *www.en.wikipedia.org/wiki/Peter_Jefferson*.

10. "Shadwell," *www.monticello.org/site/research-and-collections/shadwell*.

11. Fawn McKay Brodie, *Thomas Jefferson: an Intimate History* (New York: W.W. Norton & Company, 1974).

12. Ibid., 34.

13. Ibid., 33.

14. "Peter Jefferson," *www.surveyhistory.org/peter_jefferson1.htm*.

15. Brodie, 42.

16. Ibid., 69–70.

17. Autobiography, 3.

18. Jefferson Randolph and Sarah Nicholas Randolph, *The Domestic Life of Thomas Jefferson* (New York: Harper & Brothers, 1871; New York: Ungar, 1958), 337.

19. Henry Adams, *History of the United States of America During the Administrations of Thomas Jefferson* (New York: Library of America, 1986), 126.

20. George Flower and Elihu Benjamin Washburne, *History of the English Settlement in Edwards County, Illinois: Founded in 1817 and 1818* (Chicago: Fergus Print. Co., 1882), 43.

21. Physical Descriptions of Thomas Jefferson, Monticello Report, Zanne Macdonald, Monticello Research Department, July 1992.

22. Ibid.

23. Ibid.

24. Ibid.

25. 1857 Letter to Henry S. Randall, *The Life of Thomas Jefferson*, 3 vols. (New York: Derby & Jackson, 1858.); Randolph, 392.

26. Thomas Jefferson and Merrill D. Peterson, *The Portable Thomas Jefferson* (New York: Penguin, 1977), 112.

27. Letter to Gideon Granger, 1814, *The Writings of Thomas Jefferson*, Memorial Edition, 20 vols. Andrew A. Lipscomb and Albert E. Bergh, eds. (Washington, DC: Thomas Jefferson Memorial Association, 1903–04), 14: 118 (Hereafter ME).

28. Duc de La Rochefoucauld-Liancourt, *Travels Through the United States* (London: R. Phillips, 1799), 28.

29. *Thomas Jefferson: A Brief Biography* (Chapel Hill: University of North Carolina Press, 2002), 212.

30. *Life of Jefferson* (Boston: Houghton Mifflin, 1883) quoted by President John F. Kennedy in a ceremony at which he was awarded an honorary degree from the University of North Carolina in Chapel Hill, October 12, 1961. Robert. Dallek, *An Unfinished Life: John F. Kennedy 1917–1963* (Boston: Little, Brown, 2003), 327.

31. W. S. Randall, *Thomas Jefferson: A Life* (New York: Holt, 1993); *Papers of Thomas Jefferson*, 60 Vols. Julian P. Boyd, ed. (Princeton, NJ: Princeton University Press, 1950–), 7: 585 (Hereafter PTJ).

32. John R. Bumgarner, *The Health of the Presidents: The 41 United States Presidents Through 1993 from a Physician's Point of View* (Jefferson, NC: McFarland, 1994), 16–23.

33. "Thomas Jefferson, A Memorandum, Services to My Country," *The Jefferson Cyclopedia: A Comprehensive Collection of the Views of Thomas Jefferson*, John Foley, ed. (New York: Funk & Wagnalls, 1900), 442 (Hereafter JC); *The Writings of Thomas Jefferson*, Federal Edition, 10 vols. Paul Leicester Ford, ed. (New York: G.P. Putnam's Sons, 1892–99), VII: 475 (Hereafter FE). Jefferson proceeded to list those things that may have made things a "little better," concluding with what he considered his major achievement, the founding of the University of Virginia.

34. *Letters of Benjamin Rush*, L.H. Butterfield, ed. (Philadelphia: American Philosophical Society, 1951), 2: 779.

35. Letter to Samuel Harrison Smith, November 1826, Jack N. Rakove ed., *James Madison, Writings* (New York: Library of America, 1999).

36. January 11, 1831, *The Diaries of John Quincy Adams*, 51 Vols. (Massachusetts Historical Society, a Digital Collection).

37. Abraham Lincoln, letter to H.L. Pierce, April 6, 1859, *Lincoln Letters* (The Bibliophile Society).

38. Theodore Roosevelt, *Theodore Roosevelt Cyclopedia*, Albert Bushnell Hart and Herbert Ronald Ferleger, eds. (Oyster Bay, NY: Theodore Roosevelt Association, 1882; Westport, CT: Meckler Corporation, 1989), Nat. Ed. VI, 373, 15.

39. Woodrow Wilson, "A Jefferson Day Address," April 13, 1916. *Papers of Woodrow Wilson*, Arthur S. Link, ed. (Princeton NJ: Princeton University Press), 36: 472–473, 476.

40. Manus Hand, "Dead Presidents on Dead Presidents," *www.diplom.org/manus*.

41. John F. Kennedy quoted by Helen Thomas, *Front Row at the White House: My Life and Times* (New York: Simon & Schuster, 1999), 59. Welcome toast at a White House dinner for Nobel Prize winners, April 29, 1962.

42. *The Memoirs of Richard Nixon* (New York: Simon & Schuster, 1990).

43. Willard Sterne Randall, *Thomas Jefferson: A Life* (New York: HarperCollins, 1994), 62–64.

44. Ibid., 65.

45. Ibid., 116.

46. Ibid.

47. Ibid., 115–117.

48. Wesley Hagood, *Presidential Sex: From the Founding Fathers to Bill Clinton* (Secaucus, NJ: Carol, 1998), 13.

49. Ibid.

50. Letter to Robert Smith, July 5, 1805, quoted by John Kukla, *Mr. Jefferson and His Women* (New York: Random House, 2008), chapter three, 41.

51. W.S. Randall, 156.

52. Ibid.

53. H.S. Randall, 63.

54. Brodie, 87.

55. "Martha Wayles Skelton Jefferson," *The Jefferson Encyclopedia*, cited by Henry S. Randall, *The Life of Thomas Jefferson*, 3 vols. (New York: Derby & Jackson, 1858), I: 63–4.

56. Andrew Burstein, *The Inner Jefferson: Portrait of a Grieving Optimist* (Charlottesville, VA: University Press of Virginia, 1997), 30.

57. W.S. Randall, 156.

58. Ibid., 157.

59. Ibid., 159.

60. H.S. Randall, I: 64–65.

61. Paul F. Boller, Jr., *Presidential Wives* (New York: Oxford University Press, 1998), 32–33.

62. Boller, 32.

63. Laurence Sterne, *The Life and Opinions of Tristram Shandy, Gentleman*, 9 vols. (London: Ann Ward [vol. 1–2], Dodsley [vol. 3–4], Becket & DeHondt [vol. 5–9] Vol. 9), chapter VIII, 204.

64. Quoted in Harpers' *New Monthly Magazine* (New York: Harper & Brothers, Publishers, 1871), 43: 370.

65. JC, I: 439.

66. Brodie, 169.

67. E.M. Halliday, *Understanding Thomas Jefferson* (New York: Perennial Harper Collins, 2001), 48–52.

68. Margaret Byrd Bassett, *Profiles and Portraits of American Presidents and Their Wives* (Freeport, ME: B. Wheelwright Co., 1969), 29.

69. Richard B. Bernstein, *Thomas Jefferson: The Revolu-tion of Ideas* (New York: Oxford University Press, 2004), 69.

70. W.S. Randall, 435.

71. Ibid.

72. Jefferson to Maria Cosway, Paris, October 12, 1786, PTJ, 10: 446.

73. Daphne Foskett, *Dictionary of British Miniature Painters* (New York: Praeger Publishers, 1972), 1: 220; Stephen Lloyd, "Richard Cosway, R.A.: The Artist as Collector, Connoisseur and Virtuoso," *Apollo* 133 (June 1991): 398–405.

74. W.S. Randall, 518.

75. Thomas Jefferson Encyclopedia, Maria Cosway article, *www.monticello.org/site/research-and-collections/tje*.

76. Michael Kilian, "The Hidden Side of Monticello," February 10, 2002, www.JesseJacksonJr.org.

77. Jan Lewis and Peter S. Onuf, *Sally Hemings & Thomas Jefferson: History, Memory, and Civic Culture* (Charlottesville, VA: University Press of Virginia, 1999), 88–89.

78. W.S. Randall, 556.

79. W.S. Randall, 180.

80. Lewis, 100.

81. W.S. Randall, 180.

82. JC, 621.

83. Annette Gordon-Reed, *The Hemingses of Monticello: An American Family* (New York: W.W. Norton, 2008), 115.

84. "Bringing Children out of Egypt," Plantation and Slavery, Monticello, *www.monticello.org:8081/site/plantation-and-slavery/*.

85. "Memoirs of Madison Hemings," *www.pbs.org/wgbh/pages/frontline/shows/jefferson/cron/*.

86. "Thomas Jefferson and Sally Hemings: A Brief Account," *www.monticello.org/site/plantation-and-slavery/thomas*. "Ten years later [referring to its 2000 report], TJF [Thomas Jefferson Foundation] and most historians now believe that, years after his wife's death, Thomas Jefferson was the father of the six children of Sally Hemings mentioned in Jefferson's records, including Beverly, Harriet, Madison and Eston Hemings."

87. Robert F. Turner, *The Jefferson-Hemings Controversy: Report of the Scholars Commission* (Durham: Carolina Academic Press, 2011), 55.

88. "Thomas Jefferson and Sally Hemings: A Brief Account," *www.monticello.org/site/plantation-and-slavery/thomas*.

89. "Martha Wayles Skelton Jefferson," *www.whitehouse.gov/about/first-ladies/marthajefferson*.

90. Randolph, 429.

91. Ibid., 301.

92. McCullough, *John Adams*, 582.

93. Charles B. Sanford, *The Religious Life of Thomas Jefferson* (Charlottes-

ville, VA: University Press of Virginia, 1987), 2.

94. Avery Cardinal Dulles, "The Deist Minimum," *First Things: A Monthly Journal of Religion and Public Life* 149 (January 2005): 25, passim.

95. Sanford, 12.

96. Letter to Francis Hopkinson, March 13, 1789, FE, V: 75.

97. Letter to Ezra Stiles Ely, June 25, 1819, ME, VII: 127.

98. Letter to William Short, Oct. 31, 1819, FE, X: 143.

99. Letter to Benjamin Rush, April 21, 1803.ME, X: 379.

100. Letter to William Short, April 13, 1820, ME, XI: 243.

101. Letter to Benjamin Waterhouse, June 26, 1822; ME, XV: 385.

102. Letter to William Short, April 13, 1820, George Sildes, *The Great Thoughts* (New York: Ballantine, 1985), 208.

103. Letter to Dr. Thomas Cooper, February 10, 1814, ME, 13–14: 91.

104. James H. Hutson, *Religion and the New Republic: Faith in the Founding of America* (Lanham, MD: Rowman & Littlefield. 2000), 22.

105. Ann W. Duncan and Steven L. Jones, *Church-State Issues in America Today: Religion and Government* (Westport, CT: Greenwood, 2008), 15.

106. "The Virginia Act for Establishing Religious Freedom, 1786," *Lawyers' Reports Annotated*, Book 42 (Rochester, NY: Lawyers' Co-operative Pub. Co., 1913), 341.

107. JC, 142.

108. Letter to Miles King, September 26, 1814, H.S. Randall, III: 451.

109. Letter to Thomas Law, June 13, 1814, ME, VI: 348.

110. David Barton, *The Myth of Separation* (Aledo, TX: WallBuilder Press, 1992). Barton's work has been well received by many fundamentalist Christians and political conservatives, but he has received harsh criticism from secular groups and professional historians. The quotation has been described as spurious because Burton conceded that he has not located primary sources for this and ten other alleged quotes from founding fathers and U.S. Supreme Court decisions. However, Barton maintained that the quotes were "completely consistent" with the views of the Founders.

111. Thomas Jefferson, *Notes on the State of Virginia*, Frank Shuffelton, ed. (First Published in France in 1785, New York: Penguin Books, 1999), 166.

112. Ibid. "Notes on Religion" FE, II: 102.

113. Letter to Mrs. Samuel H. Smith, August 6, 1816, Norman Cousins, *In God We Trust: The Religious Beliefs and Ideas of the American Founding Fathers* (New York: Harper Bros. 1958), 147.

114. JC, 744.

115. Letter to John Adams, August 22, 1813, FE, IX: 410.

116. Said to Quaker Minister William Canby, Autobiography, 210.

117. Letter to Horatio G. Spafford, March 17, 1814, JC, 559.

118. "John Quincy Adams, Diary, January 27, 1831, Manus Hand, Dead Presidents," *www.diplom.org/manus.*

119. Jennings L. Wagoner, *Jefferson and Education* (Chapel Hill: University of North Carolina Press, 2004), 20.

120. Randolph, 25.

121. Ibid., 351.

122. JC, 525.

123. Peterson, 11.

124. John B. Severance, *Thomas Jefferson: Architect of Democracy* (Boston: Houghton Mifflin Harcourt, 1998), 19–20.

125. Letter to George Wythe, August 13, 1786, FE, IV: 268.

126. James Parton, *Life of Thomas Jefferson: Third President of the United States* (Boston: J.R. Osgood and Company, 1874), 704.

127. Letter to James Madison, on December 20, 1787, FE, IV: 480.

128. "Aristotle's Ideas About Learning, Knowledge and Education," *www.brainmass.com/philosophy/great-philosophers/10919.*

129. "Thomas Jefferson and Education," *http://www.en.wikipedia.org/wiki/User:TrustTruth/Thomas_Jefferson_Education_Plan.*

130. Alf J. Mapp, *Thomas Jefferson: Passionate Pilgrim, The Presidency, The Founding of the University, and the Private Battle* (Lanham, MD: Rowman & Littlefield, 2009), 259.

131. Letter to P.S. DuPont de Nemours, April 24, 1816: FE, X: 25.

132. Thomas Jefferson, *Memoirs, Correspondence, and Private Papers of Thomas Jefferson*, vol. 1, Thomas Jefferson Randolph, ed. (Charlottesville, VA: F. Carr and Co., 1829, pp. 345–347.

133. Letter to John Adams, July 5, 1814 FE, IX: 464.

134. Letter to John Adams, August 1, 1816 ME, VII: 27.

135. Letter to George Ticknor on November 25, 1817 FE, X: 81.

136. Letter to John Adams, August 15, 1820. *Thomas Jefferson: Writings*, Merrill D. Peterson, ed. (New York: Library of America, 1994), 1440–1445.

137. Letter to Roger C. Weightman, June 24, 1826, ME, VII: 475.

138. Letter to George Washington, January 4, 1786, ME, XIX: 24.

139. Letter to James Madison, December 20, 1787, ME, 6: 392.

140. Letter to M.A. Jullien, 1818, ME, 15: 172.

141. Advice to Thomas Jefferson Smith, JC, 20.

142. "Presidents' Occupations," *www.infoplease.com/ipa/A0768854.htm.*

143. JC, 963.

144. Ibid.

145. W.S. Randall, 212.

146. Works, II: 111.

147. Joan R. Callahan. *50 Health Scares That Fizzled* (Santa Barbara, CA: ABC-CLIO, 2011), 99.

148. "Thomas Jefferson, Friends of the American Revolution," *http://21stcenturycicero.wordpress.com/faith/the-faith-of-our-fathers/thomas-jefferson/.*

149. Merrill D. Peterson, *Thomas Jefferson and the New Nation: A Biography* (New York: Oxford University Press, 1970), 589.

150. JC, 947.

151. Works, 253.

152. Thomas Jefferson, *Thomas Jefferson's Farm Book* (Chapel Hill: University of North Carolina Press, 2002), vii.

153. Ibid., xxi.

154. *Notes on the State of Virginia*, 170.

155. Letter to John Jay, 1785, JC, 322.

156. Letter to Thomas Knox, June 1, 1795, .Thomas Jefferson, Jerry Holmes, *Thomas Jefferson: A Chronology of His Thoughts* (Lanham, MD: Rowman & Littlefield, 2002), 146.

157. "Jefferson and the Patent System," *http://www.cti.itc.virginia.edu/~meg3c/classes/tcc313/200Rprojs/jefferson_invent/invent.html.*

158. Ibid.

159. Talbot Hamlin, *Benjamin Henry Latrobe* (New York: Oxford University Press, 1969), 270.

160. Silvio A. Bedini, *Jefferson and Science* (Chapel Hill: University of North Carolina Press, 2002), 76–77.

161. Ibid., 72, 89–90.

162. Trudi Strain Trueit, *Thomas Jefferson* (Tarrytown, NY: Marshall Cavendish, 2009), 54.

163. Jack McLaughlin, *Jefferson and Monticello: The Biography of a Builder* (New York: Macmillan, 1990), 324.

164. Charles Santore, *The Windsor Style in America: A Pictorial Study of the History and Regional Characteristics of the Most Popular Furniture Form of 18th-Century America, 1730–1830* (Philadelphia: Running Press, 1981), 199.

165. Bedini, 245.

166. Thomas Jefferson Foundation, *Thomas Jefferson's Monticello* (Chapel Hill: University of North Carolina Press, 2002), 1.

167. Letter to Dr. Gilmer, August 11, 1887, *Memoirs*, 220.

168. Letter to C.W. Peale, JC, 411.

169. Thomas Jefferson, Edwin Morris Betts, *Thomas Jefferson's Garden Book* (Charlottesville: University Press of Virginia, 1999), 324.

170. W.S. Randall, 192.

171. JC, 45.

172. "Traveling Hints," JC, 46.

173. S. Allen Chambers, *Poplar Forest and Thomas Jefferson* (Published for the Corporation for Jefferson's Poplar Forest in commemoration of the 250th anniversary of the birth of Thomas Jefferson, 1993), 56.

174. Ibid.

175. Melvin I. Urofsky, *The Levy Family and Monticello, 1834–1923: Saving Thomas Jefferson's House* (Charlottesville, VA: Thomas Jefferson Foundation, 2001), 75.

176. Daniel W Hamilton, *The Limits of Sovereignty: Property Confiscation in the Union and the Confederacy During the Civil War* (Chicago: University of Chicago Press, 2007), 118–119.

177. Thomas Jefferson Foundation

Thomas Jefferson's Monticello, by (Charlottesville, VA: Thomas Jefferson Foundation, 2002), 74.

178. Susan Stein, *Monticello: A Guidebook* (Charlottesville, VA: Thomas Jefferson Memorial Foundation, 1993), 110.

179. *Thomas Jefferson's Monticello*, 36.

180. JC, 471.

181. Margaret Truman, *The President's House, 1800 to the Present: The Secrets and History of the World's Most Famous Home* (New York: Random House, 1989), II.

182. Peterson, 400.

183. JC, 471; Joseph Wheelan, *Jefferson's Vendetta: The Pursuit of Aaron Burr and the Judiciary* (New York: Carroll & Graf, 2006), 65.

184. Natalie S. Bober, *Thomas Jefferson: Draftsman of a Nation* (Charlottesville: University Press of Virginia, 2008), 51.

185. Thomas Jefferson, *The Jefferson Bible, or The Life and Morals of Jesus of Nazareth* (Boston: Mobile Reference, 2010), 93.

186. Francis P. McManamon, Linda S. Cordell, Kent G. Lightfoot, George R. Milner, *Archaeology in America: Northeast and Southeast* (Santa Barbara, CA: ABC-CLIO, 2009), 112.

187. Letter to Peter Carr, 1785, JC, 318.

188. *Thomas Jefferson's Monticello*, 128.

189. New York Botanical Garden, *Addisonia: Colored Illustrations and Popular Descriptions of Plants* Volume 5 (New York: New York Botanical Garden, 1920), 31–32.

190. JC, 738.

191. Helge Lundholm, *The Psychology of Belief* (Durham: Duke University Press, 1936), 145.

192. Letter to John Adams, June 10, 1815, ME, VI:460.

193. Hannah Spahn, "Thomas Jefferson, Cosmopolitism, and the Enlightment," *A Companion to Thomas Jefferson*, Francis D. Cogliano, ed. (Maiden, MA: Wiley-Blackwell, 2012), 364–366.

194. Letter to Destutt Tracy, 1820, JC, 904.

195. *The Jefferson Bible*, 94.

196. Letter to Dr. Price, 1789, JC, 194.

197. Robert M.S. McDonald, "The (Federalist?) Presidency of Thomas Jefferson," *Companion to Thomas Jefferson*, chapter eleven.

198. Letter to A. Penna, 1809, JC, 891.

199. McDonald, "The (Federalist?) Presidency of Thomas Jefferson," *Companion to Thomas Jefferson*, chapter eleven.

200. James M. McPherson, *Battle Cry of Freedom: The Civil War Era* (New York: Oxford University Press, 2003), 23–24.

201. Ibid., 11.

202. JC, 832–835.

203. Dumas Malone, *Jefferson and His Times* (Boston: Little, Brown, 1968–75), 47.

204. *Signers of the Declaration of Independence* (1848) (Aledo, TX: Wall-Builder Press, 1995), 48.

205. Michael MacWhite, Address at the University of Virginia, April 13, 1931.

206. Merrill D. Peterson, *The Jefferson Image in the American Mind* (New York: Oxford University Press, 1960), 457.

207. Quoted in L.A. Harris, *The Fine Art of Political Wit* (New York: Dutton, 1964).

208. Thomas A. Saunders III, "'Jefferson Lives,' A Campaign for Monticello in the Twenty-First Century," *Monticello Newsletter* Vol. 11, No. 2 (Winter 2000).

209. Gordon S. Wood, "The Trials and Tribulations of Thomas Jefferson," *Jefferson Legacies*, Peter S. Onuf, ed. (Charlottesville: University Press of Virginia, 1993), 395.

210. Mapp, 101.

211. JC, 963–968.

212. JC, 307.

213. JC, 142.

214. JC, 241.

215. W.W. Hening, ed., *Statutes at Large of Virginia* vol. 12 (1823): 84–86.

216. JC, 131.

217. JC, 220.

218. Andrew J. Milson, *American Educational Thought: Essays from 1640–1940* (Charlotte, NC: IAP, 2009), 41–43.

219. *The Jefferson Bible*, 82.

220. Bober, 159.

221. JC, 950.

222. Jeremy D. Bailey, *Thomas Jefferson and Executive Power* (New York: Cambridge University Press, 2007), 29.

223. *The Jefferson Bible*, 82.

224. Francis D. Cogliano, *Thomas Jefferson: Reputation and Legacy* (Charlottesville, VA: University Press of Virginia, 2008), 159–160.

225. *Notes on the State of Virginia*, 136.

226. Letter to Baron De Moll, 1814, ME, VI: 363.

227. Note on the State of Virginia, ME, VIII: 361.

228. Parton, 268.

229. Cogliano, 225.

230. W.S. Randall, 273.

231. Declaration of Independence, 1776 as drawn by Jefferson.

232. Francis Newton Thorpe, *The Constitutional History of the United States* (Chicago: Callaghan & Co., 1901), 159.

233. Carl Lotus Becker, *The Declaration of Independence: A Study in the History of Political Ideas* (New York: Harcourt, Brace & Co., 1922), chapter V, "The Literary Qualities of the Declaration."

234. Carole Marsh, *Quit Bossing Us Around!: The Declaration of Independence* (Peachtree City, GA: Gallopade International, 2004), 14.

235. Thomas Jefferson to Isaac H. Tiffany, 1819; David Friedman, "A Positive Account of Property Rights," Originally published in *Social Philosophy & Policy* vol. 11, no. 2 (Summer 1994).

236. JC, 499–500.

237. Letter to Roger C. Weightman, June 24, 1826, ME, VII: 450.

238. Benjamin Franklin, *Benjamin Franklin: Autobiography & Selected Writings* (Milwaukee: American Liberty Press, 2010), 80.

239. *The Life and Writings of Thomas Jefferson: Including All of His Important Utterances on Public Questions* (Indianapolis: Bowen-Merrill Company, 1900), 266.

240. Letter to James Madison, December 20, 1787, ME, II: 330.

241. Letter to David Humphreys, March 18, 1789, ME, VII: 322.

242. United States. Congress, Joseph Gales and William Winston Seaton, *Register of Din Congress* (Gales & Seaton, 1830), 232.

243. "United States Secretary of State," *www.simple.wikipedia.org/wiki/United_States_Secretary_of_State*.

244. Robert J. Miller, *Native America, Discovered and Conquered: Thomas Jefferson, Lewis & Clark, and Manifest Destiny* (Lincoln: University of Nebraska Press. 2008), 57.

245. Letter to Dr. Walter Jones, JC, 117.

246. "Federalists vs. Democratic Republicans," *www.wowessays.com/dbase/ad1/avw114.shtml*.

247. Letter to President Washington, JC, 397.

248. Letter to John Taylor on May 28, 1816, ME, VI: 608.

249. National Bank Opinion, February 1791, JC, 68.

250. Phillip I. Blumberg, *Repressive Jurisprudence in the Early American Republic: The First Amendment and the Legacy of English Law* (New York: Cambridge University Press, 2010), 25.

251. Malone, 28.

252. John E. Ferling, *Adams Versus Jefferson* (New York: Oxford University Press, 2004), 51.

253. JC, 437.

254. JC, 242.

255. Letter to Elbridge Gerry, May 13, 1797, ME, IV: 171.

256. Kentucky and Virginia Resolutions., 1798–99, ME, IX: 464.

257. Ibid.

258. "Founding Fathers' Dirty Campaign," *www.articles.cnn.com/2008-08-22/living/mf.campaign.slurs*.

259. Paul F. Boller, *Presidential Campaigns: From George Washington to George W. Bush* (New York: Oxford University Press, 2004), 12.

260. "Founding Fathers' Dirty Campaign," *www.articles.cnn.com/2008-08-22/living/mf.campaign.slurs*.

261. Donald Richard Deskins, Hanes Walton, and Sherman C. Puckett, *Presidential Elections, 1789–2008* (Ann Arbor: University of Michigan Press, 2010), 38–39.

262. Letter to Levi Lincoln, 1807, JC, 111.

263. John Chaneski, *Presidential Word Search Puzzles: From George Washington to Barack Obama* (New York: Sterling Publishing Company, Inc., 2009), 10.

264. "Slavery in the United States," www.enotes.com/topic/Slavery_in_the_United_States.

265. Jacqueline Vaughn and Eric Edwin Otenyo, *Managerial Discretion in Government Decision Making* (Ontario: Jones & Bartlett Learning, 2007), 101.

266. First Inaugural Address, March 4, 1801, ME, VIII: 1.

267. Deskins, 41.

268. Irving C. Gaylord, *Burr-Hamilton Duel* (New York: Hamilton Bank of New York City, 1889), 6.

269. Buckner F. Melton, *Aaron Burr: Conspiracy to Treason* (New York: Wiley, 2002), 55.

270. Ibid., 217.

271. "Thomas Jefferson: The Patriot Files," www.patriotfiles.com/index.php?name=Sections&req=view.

272. "American President: Biography of Thomas Jefferson," www.millercenter.org/president/jefferson/essays/biography/print.

273. "American President: Thomas Jefferson — Domestic Affairs," www.millercenter.org/president/jefferson/essays/biography/4.

274. Thomas Jefferson, *A Manual of Parliamentary Practice: Composed Originally for the Use of the Senate of the United States* (Philadelphia: Hogan and Thompson, 1840).

275. Cogliano, 189.

276. David N. Mayer, *The Constitutional Thought of Thomas Jefferson* (Charlottesville: University Press of Virginia, 1994), 295–296.

277. Art Higginbotham, "Military Education Before West Point," *Thomas Jefferson's Military Academy: Founding West Point*, Robert M. S. McDonald, ed. (Charlottesville: University Press of Virginia, 2004), 23.

278. Randall M. Miller, *The Greenwood Encyclopedia of Daily Life in America: The War of Independence and Antebellum Expansion and Reform, 1763–1861* (Westport, CT: Greenwood, 2009), 200.

279. Cogliano, 55.

280. Mayer, 272–273.

281. Evan Haynes, *The Selection and Tenure of Judges* (Clark, NJ: The Lawbook Exchange, Ltd., 2005), 93.

282. McDonald, 112.

283. Rayner, 320.

284. Ibid.

285. Rayner, 322.

286. Amy Kukla and Jon Kukla, *Thomas Jefferson: Life, Liberty, and the Pursuit of Happiness* (New York: Rosen Publishing Group, 2005), 89.

287. Ibid.

288. "The Thomas Jefferson Papers — America and the Barbary Pirates," www.memory.loc.gov/ammem/collections/jefferson_papers/.

289. James N. Levitt, *Conservation in the Internet Age: Threats and Opportunities* (Washington, DC: Island Press, 2002), 22.

290. "Thomas Jefferson," www.knowsouthernhistory.net/Biographies/.

291. "Lewis & Clark: An Epic Journey." www.lewisclark.cet.edu/student/corps/clark2.html.

292. Congressional Record, V. 152, Pt. 17, November 9, 2006 to December 6, 2006 (Washington, DC: Government Printing Office, 2010), 21983.

293. Stephenie Ambrose Tubbs and Clay Jenkinson, *The Lewis and Clark Companion: An Encyclopedic Guide to the Voyage of Discovery* (New York: Macmillan, 2003), 62–68, 79–80.

294. Ibid.

295. Ibid., 240.

296. Ibid., 93.

297. Ibid., 44–45.

298. Ella E. Clark and Margot Edmonds, *Sacagawea of the Lewis and Clark Expedition* (Berkeley: University of California Press, 1983), 14–19.

299. Meriwether Lewis, William Clark and Elliott Coues, *The History of the Lewis and Clark Expedition*, Volume 2 (New York: Courier Dover Publications, 1979), 359.

300. Ibid., 576.

301. Ibid., 509.

302. John D. W Guice, Jay H Buckley, and James J. Holmberg, *By His Own Hand? The Mysterious Death of Meriwether Lewis* (Norman: University of Oklahoma Press, 2006), 159.

303. Clark and Edmonds, xxxv.

304. Letter to Arthur Campbell, September 1, 1797, ME, IV: 198.

305. Letter to Andrew Jackson, December 3, 1806, ME, XIX: 156.

306. Letter to Thomas Leiper, 1815, ME, .VI: 465.

307. JC, 286–287.

308. Trueit, 82.

309. Gregory Fremont-Barnes, *The Wars of the Barbary Pirates: To the Shores of Tripoli: The Rise of the US Navy And Marines* (Oxford: Osprey Publishing, 2006), 32.

310. Ibid.

311. "The Thomas Jefferson Papers — America and the Barbary Pirates," www.memory.loc.gov/ammem/collections/jefferson_papers/.

312. Letter to James Monroe, August 18, 1786, ME, I: 606.

313. "Barbary Pirates Shook America Out of Isolationism," www.libertytoday.com/?p=305.

314. Gregory Fremont-Barnes, 37.

315. "The Constitutional War Powers of the President," www.newman.baruch.cuny.edu/digital/2000/honors/bundy_1995.htm.

316. "Treaty of Tripoli, Article 11— Christian Nation Phrase," www.tektonics.org/qt/tripoli.html.

317. Charles Ingersoll, *History of the Second War* (Carlisle, MA: Applewood Books, 2009), 372.

318. Susan Tyler Hitchcock, *The University of Virginia: A Pictorial History* (Charlottesville: University Press of Virginia, 1999), 29.

319. Letter to George Ticknor on November 25, 1817, FE, X: 81.

320. *Jefferson Bible*, 88.

321. Letter to Dr. John P. Emmett, 1826, JC, 903.

322. Letter to Thomas Cooper on October 7, 1814, ME, VI: 389.

323. JC, 900.

324. "Thomas Jefferson," Library of Congress. Manuscript Division, 1974.

325. Letter to S.H. Smith, September 1814, JC, 502.

326. Letter to Vine Utley, March 31, 1819, ME, VII: 116.

327. Letter to N. Burwell, 1818, ME, VII: 102.

328. JC, 51, 697.

329. Letter to Nathaniel Macon, January 12, 1819, ME, VII: 111.

330. Letter to John Norvell, June 11, 1807, ME, V: 93.

331. Bumgarner, 16–23.

332. James M. Gabler, *Passions: The Wines and Travels of Thomas Jefferson* (Baltimore: Bacchus Press, 1995), 129–137.

333. Ibid., 205.

334. Ibid., 226.

335. Letter to M. De Neuville, 1818, JC, 948.

336. W.S. Randall, 443.

337. Bumgarner, 20–21.

338. Letter to Thomas Mann Jefferson, August 27, 1786, FE, IV: 293.

339. Letter to B.H. Latrobe, 1818, ME, VI: 74.

340. Letter to Vine Utley, March 31, 1819, ME, VII: 116.

341. Norm Lddgin, *Diagnosing Jefferson: Evidence of a Condition that Guided his Beliefs, Behavior, and Personal Associations* (Arlington, TX: Future Horizons, 2000).

342. H.S. Randall, 3: 245.

343. W.S. Randall, 542.

344. Urofsky, 40.

345. "Jefferson's Cause of Death," http://www.monticello.org/site/research-and-collections/jeffersons-cause-death.

346. B.L. Rayner, *Life of Thomas Jefferson* (Boston: Lilly, Wait, Colman, & Holden, 1834).

347. *Notes on the State of Virginia*, 66.

348. *Monuments and Historic Places of America* (New York: Macmillan Library Reference USA, 2000), 212.

349. "The History of Executive Privilege," www.ehow.com/about_65169 92_history-executive-privilege.htm.

350. Scott Patrick Johnson, *Trials of the Century: An Encyclopedia of Popular Culture and the Law* (Santa Barbara, CA: ABC-CLIO, 2010), 26.

351. "Thomas Jefferson's Personal Scrapbook Is Discovered," www.myspace.com/video/inaugural-speeches/thomas.

352. Mapp, 194.

353. James W. Loewen, *Lies My Teacher Told Me* (New York: Touchstone, 2007), 147.

354. Ibid., 148.

355. *Notes on the State of Virginia*, 168.

356. Stephen E. Adams, *To America: Personal Reflections of an Historian* (New York: Simon & Schuster, 2002), 4.

357. *Notes on the State of Virginia*, 169.

358. First draft of the Declaration of Independence, 1776 as drawn by Jefferson.

359. *Autobiography*, 1821, JC, 812.

360. Letter to James Heaton, May 20, 1826, Manuscript Division, Library of Congress.

361. W.S. Randall, 644.

362. *Notes on the State of Virginia*, 147.

363. Letter to Edward Coles, August 25, 1814, FE, IX: 478.

364. "Robert A. Nowlan, *A Chronicle of Mathematical People*," www.robertnowlan.com/pdfs/.

365. Ibid.

366. Ibid.

367. Ibid; Benjamin Banneker, Letter to Thomas Jefferson, Maryland, Baltimore Colony, August 19, 1791; "Excerpts from a Letter from Benjamin Banneker to Thomas Jefferson" www.eduplace.com/ss/hmss/5/unit/act5.1blm1.htm.

368. Ibid.

369. Ibid.

370. JC, 422.

371. Report of President Jefferson's meeting with a delegation of Native Americans, September 1808, as recorded in a letter to a Captain Hendrick, December 1808 (National Archives, Record Group).

372. Letter to Edward Carrington, January 16, 1787, ME, II: 100.

373. Tom Jewett, "Thomas Jefferson's Views Concerning Native Americans," *Early American Review* (summer/fall, 2002).

374. Opinion of Georgia Land Grants, May 1790, JC, 468.

375. "Thomas Jefferson — Know Southern History," http://www.knowsouthernhistory.net/Biographies/Thomas_Jefferson/.

376. Ibid.

377. Thomas Edward Watson, *The Life and Times of Thomas Jefferson* (New York: D. Appleton and Company, 1903), 400.

378. "Jefferson's Lump of Coal," www.nytimes.com/2006/12/24/books/review/Collins.html.

379. Ibid.

380. Letter to Mr. Bellini, 1785, JC, 372; John Aylmer, *The Un-Demanding Cook Book* (Bloomington, IN: AuthorHouse, 2008), 36.

381. *The Jefferson Bible*.

382. Letter to John Adams, January 24, 1814, ME 13–14: 72.

383. Letter to Charles Thomson, January 9, 1816, H.S. Randall, 451.

384. *"Jefferson in Paris,"* http://www.imdb.com/title/tt0113463/.

385. All of these maxims, aphorisms, and proverbs are found in Jefferson's Writings, either the Memorial Edition or the Federal Edition or both. More Information about them can be found by referring to *The Jefferson Cyclopedia*, edited by John P. Foley (New York: Funk & Wagnalls, 1900).

386. James Truslow Adams, ed. *Jeffersonian Principles and Hamiltonian Principles* (Boston: Little, Brown, and Co., 1932), xvii.

387. Charles A. Beard, *The Economic Origins of Jefferson Democracy* (New York: Macmillan, 1915).

388. Stephen Vincent Benét's poem "Thomas Jefferson," Merrill D. Peterson, *The Jefferson Image in the American Mind* (New York: Oxford University Press, 1960), xi.

389. John Dewey quoted by Adrienne Koch, *Thomas Jefferson, Great Lives Observed* (New York: Prentice-Hall, 1971).

390. Chief Justice Oliver Ellsworth speaking of Jefferson and his followers, 1800, H.J. Ford, *The Rise and Growth of American Politics* (New York: 1898), 113.

391. Annette Gordon-Reed, *Thomas Jefferson and Sally Hemings* (Charlottesville: University Press of Virginia, 1998).

392. George F. Hoar, "Special Introduction," *The Writings of Thomas Jefferson*, Lipscomb and Bergh, eds. (Washington, DC: The Thomas Jefferson Memorial Association, 1903–04).

393. Marquis de Lafayette quoted in Merrill D. Peterson, *Thomas Jefferson and the New Nation* (New York: Oxford University Press, 1970).

394. Dumas Malone, *Jefferson and His Times*.

395. Thomas Moore quoted in Fawn M. Brodie, *Thomas Jefferson, An Intimate History* (New York: W.W. Norton & Company, 1974).

396. Conor Cruise O'Brien, *The Long Affair: Thomas Jefferson and the French Revolution, 1785–1900* (Chicago: University of Chicago Press, 1998).

Four. Madison

1. Constantinos E. Scaros, Understanding the Constitution (Sudbury, MA: Jones & Bartlett Learning, 2011), 41.

2. John R. Vile, *Encyclopedia of Constitutional Amendments, Proposed Amendments, and Amending Issues, 1789–2002* (Santa Barbara, CA: ABC-CLIO, 2003), xxviii.

3. "James Madison — American History and World History," www.historycentral.com/presidents/madison.html.

4. Gary W. Ferris, *Presidential Places* (John F. Blair, Publisher, 1999), 37.

5. "Who Was the First President to Wear Long Pants?" www.wiki.answers.com/Q/...the_first_president_to_wear_long_pants.

6. March 10, 1834, quoted in The Constitutional Convention — Creating the Constitution (Washington DC: National Archives and Records Administration).

7. Richard Brookhiser, *James Madison* (New York: Basic Books, 2011), 16.

8. Garry Wills, *James Madison* (New York: Macmillan, 2002), 12.

9. Doug Wead, *The Raising of a President: The Mothers and Fathers of Our Nation's Leaders* (New York: Simon & Schuster, 2005), 326.

10. Barbara Mitchell, *Father of the Constitution: A Story about James Madison* (Minneapolis, MN: Millbrook Press, 2004), 20.

11. "John Madison — Lewis Bratti Genealogy," www.genealogy.lewisfamily.us/getperson.php?personID=I4314&.

12. Ibid.

13. "The Madisons,"www.montpelier.org/explore/community/madisons.php.

14. Douglas B. Chambers, *Murder at Montpelier: Igbo Africans in Virginia* (Oxford: University Press of Mississippi, 2009), 5–6.

15. "Mr. President — Your Health: James Madison (1751–1836)," *Minnesota Medicine* 50.10 (October, 1967): 1500.

16. Margaret Byrd Bassett, *Profiles & Portraits of American Presidents* (Freeport, ME: B. Wheelwright Co., 1964), 11.

17. Paul F. Boller Jr., *Presidential Anecdotes* (New York: Oxford University Press, 1981), 47.

18. James M. McPherson, *"To the Best of My Ability": The American Presidents* (New York: Dorling Kindersley, 2000), 36.

19. Ralph Louis Ketcham, *James Madison: A Biography* (Charlottesville: University Press of Virginia, 1971), 107.

20. Ibid., 620.

21. Henry Adams and Earl N Harbert, *History of the United States of America During the Administrations of Thomas Jefferson* (New York: Library of America, 1986), 128.

22. Ibid.

23. William A. DeGregorio, *Complete Book of U.S. Presidents* (New York: Barricade, 2001), 55.

24. Peter McNamara, *The Noblest Minds: Fame, Honor, and the American Founding* (Landham, MD: Rowman & Littlefield, 1999), 137.

25. Ibid.

26. Ibid.

27. Ibid.

28. "The Founders' Almanac — James Madison," www.site.heritage.org/research/features/almanac/madison.html.

29. Wills, ii.

30. Ketcham, 471.

31. Ron Chernow, *Alexander Hamilton* (New York: Penguin, 2005), 174.

32. Bassett, 33.

33. Stanley M. Elkin and Eric McKitrick, *The Age of Federalism* (New York: Oxford University Press, 1995), 79.

34. Letter to Thomas C. Flourney, October 1, 1812, Thomas Jefferson and Henry Augustine Washington, *The Writings of Thomas Jefferson: Correspondence* (Derbyshire, UK: H. W. Derby, 1859), 82.

35. Brookhiser, 30.

36. Ibid.

37. E. H. Gwynne-Thomas, *The Presidential Families* (New York: Hippocrene Books, 1989), 61.

38. Thomas Jefferson letter to Madison, summer 1783, *The Papers of James Madison: Presidential Series*, Robert A. Rutland, et al, eds. (Charlottesville: University Press of Virginia, 1984–) (Hereafter JMPS).

39. Brookhiser, 30.

40. Irving Brant, *James Madison* vol. II (Indianapolis: Bobbs-Merrill 1948), 37.

41. "Madison, Dolley Biography," http://www.s9.com/Biography/Madison-Dolley.

42. "Dolley Madison — NNDB: Tracking the entire world," http://www.nndb.com/people/644/000126266/.

43. Boller, 36–37.

44. Ibid., 37.

45. Zachary Kent, Dolley Madison: The Enemy Cannot Frighten a Free People (Berkeley Heights, NJ: Enslow Publishers, 2010), 28.

46. Ibid., 30.

47. Ibid.

48. Ibid., 33.

49. Ibid., 33.

50. "Dolley Madison's Life and Times," http://rotunda.upress.virginia.edu:8080/dmde/bio-intro.xqy.

51. Boller, Presidential Wives, 38–41.

52. Boller, 38–39.

53. Kent, 32.

54. Ibid., 33.

55. Boller, 38.

56. Kent, 66.

57. Lewis L. Gould, American First Ladies: Their Lives and Their Legacy (New York: Garland, 1996), 27.

58. Boller, 41.

59. Margaret Bayard Smith, The First Forty Years of Washington Society: Portrayed by the Family Letters of Mrs. Samuel Harrison Smith (Margaret Bayard) from the Collection of Her Grandson, J. Henley Smith (New York: Scribner, 1906), 62.

60. Maurine Hoffman Beasley, First Ladies and the Press: The Unfinished Partnership of the Media Age (Evanston, IL: Northwestern University Press, 2005), 34.

61. Maud Wilder Goodwin, Dolly Madison (New York: Scribner, 1896), 165.

62. Catherine Allgor, A Perfect Union: Dolley Madison and the Creation of the American Nation (New York: Macmillan, 2007), 153.

63. Ibid., 142.

64. "Dolley Madison," http://www.nndb.com/people/644/000126266/.

65. "British Troops Set Fire to the White House," www.history.com/this-day-in-history/british-troops-set.

66. Holly Cowan Shulman and David B. Mattern, Dolley Madison: Her Life, Letters, and Legacy (New York: Rosen Publishing Group, 2003), 63.

67. Ibid., 64.

68. Richard N. Côté, Strength and Honor: The Life of Dolley Madison (Mt. Pleasant, SC: Corinthian Books, 2005), 363.

69. The American Historical Magazine volume 4, issues 1–3 (New York: Publishing Society of New York, American Historical Society, National Americana Society, 1909), 654.

70. Ibid.

71. Kent, 84.

72. Ibid., 87.

73. "Dolley Madison," http://www.nndb.com/people/644/000126266/.

74. "Dolley Madison's Life and Times," http://rotunda.upress.virginia.edu:8080/dmde/bio-intro.xqy.

75. Patricia L. Dooley, The Early Republic: Primary Documents on Events from 1799 to 1820 (Westport, CT: Greenwood, 2004), 325.

76. Gould, 34.

77. Margaret Brown Klapthor and Allida M. Black, The First Ladies (Washington, DC: Government Printing Office, 2002), 14.

78. Kent, 109.

79. Ketcham, 6.

80. "John Payne Todd," http://www.montpelier.org/explore/community/madisons_johnpaynetodd.php.

81. Ketcham, 616.

82. Wead, 334.

83. "Whatever Happened to ... the Possible Relative of James Madison," www.washingtonpost.com/lifestyle/magazine/whatever.

84. "African American Seeks to Prove Genetic Link to James Madison," www.seattletimes.nwsource.com/.../2003743991_madison12.html.

85. "Link Sought to a Founding Father," The Boston Globe, www.boston.com/news/local/articles/2007/07/22/link.

86. "Using DNA to Examine James Madison," http://www.thegeneticgenealogist.com/2008/08/27/using-dna-to-examine-james-madisons-family-tree/.

87. Ibid.

88. Scott J. Kester, The Haunted Philosopher: James Madison, Republicanism, and Slavery (Landham, MD: Lexington Books, 2008), 99.

89. David Lynn Holmes, The Faiths of the Founding Fathers (New York: Oxford University Press, 2006, 92.

90. Ibid., 66.

91. Kester, 24.

92. Ketcham, 165.

93. Ketcham, 57.

94. John Witherspoon and Thomas P. Miller, The Selected Writings of John Witherspoon (Carbondale: Southern Illinois University Press, 1990), 212.

95. Philip Hamburger, Separation of Church and State (Cambridge, MA: Harvard University Press, 2004), 183.

96. Letter to William Bradford, January 24, 1774, JMPS.

97. "Memorial and Remonstrance against Religious Assessments," www.teachingamericanhistory.org/library/index.asp?document=309.

98. Ibid.

99. Letter from James Madison to Frederick Beasley, November 20, 1825, JMPS.

100. "The Thought of James Madison," http://www.thelockeinstitute.org/journals/luminary_v2_n1_p4.html.

101. Monty Rainey, "Founder of the Month — James Madison," http://juntosociety.com/founders/madison.htm. The Donald Robertson Scholarship is offered annually by the Madison Center in honor of James Madison's first teacher. Robertson's influence on the young Madison was enormous and it was said that this talented teacher "nurtured greatness and laid the foundation for some of the most fruitful careers in American history."

102. Ketcham, 21–22.

103. Ketcham, 23.

104. Rodney K. Smith, "James Madison, John Witherspoon, and Oliver Cowdery: The First Amendment and the 134th section of the Doctrine and Covenants," Brigham Young University Law Review (September 2003): 891–940.

105. Ketcham, 34.

106. Brant, 102.

107. Ketcham, 39.

108. "Madison, James. Presidents: A Reference History," www.encyclopedia.com/topic/James_Madison.aspx.

109. Susan P. Castillo, Colonial Encounters in New World Writing, 1500–1786: Performing America (Hoboken, NJ: Taylor & Francis, 2005), 223.

110. Ketcham, 38.

111. Ketcham, 32.

112. Second Annual Message to Congress, December 5, 1810, JMPS.

113. Letter to Albert Picket, September 1821, JMPS.

114. Letter to W.T. Barry, August 4, 1822, JMPS.

115. Ketcham, 145.

116. Ketcham, 104.

117. Ketcham, 145.

118. Ketcham, 64.

119. Edward A. Chappell, "The Restoration of James Madison's Montpelier," http://www.history.org/Foundation/journal/Spring05/montpelier.cfm.

120. Ibid.

121. Ibid.

122. Côté, 183.

123. Edward A. Chappell, "The Restoration of James Madison's Montpelier," http://www.history.org/Foundation/journal/Spring05/montpelier.cfm.

124. Ibid.

125. Ibid.

126. Ibid.

127. "Origins of the Name Montpelier," www.montpelier.org/explore/estate/montpelier_etymology.php.

128. "James Madison's Montpelier," www.montpelier.org/visit/index.php.

129. "Did James and Dolley Madison Have Any Pets?" http://www.experts123.com/q/did-james-and-dolley-madison-have-any-pets.htm.

130. Garrett Ward Sheldon, The Political Philosophy of James Madison (Baltimore: Johns Hopkins University Press, 2003), 3.

131. "James Madison (JamesMadisonLibrary)," www.librarything.com/profile/JamesMadisonLibrary.

132. "Federalist Papers," www.en.wikipedia.org/wiki/Federalist_Papers.

133. Ibid.

134. The Federalist; Or, The New Constitution, two volumes (New York: J. and A. McLean, 1788), 46. The series' correct title is The Federalist; the title The Federalist Papers did not emerge until the twentieth century.

135. Ibid., 43.

136. Ibid., 174.

137. Ibid., 239.

138. Ketcham, 50.

139. William Lee Miller, The Business of May Next: James Madison and the Founding (Charlottesville: University Press of Virginia, 1994), 17.

140. www.thelockeinstitute.org/jour nals/luminary_v2_n1_p4.html.

141. "The Virginia Plan — May 29, 1787 by James Madison," www.revolutio nary-war-and-beyond.com/virginia-plan.

142. Robert Alan Dahl, "Madisonian Democracy," in Dahl, et al., eds. The Democracy Sourcebook (Cambridge, MA: MIT Press, 2003), 207–16.

143. "Federalist vs. Antifederalist," www.fredericksburg.com/News/FLS/201 2/012012/01152012/672134.

144. "Famous Quotes by James Madison," www.quotesdaddy.com/auth or/James+Madison.

145. Lance Banning, "James Madison: Federalist," www.loc.gov/loc/madis on/banning-paper.html.

146. Ibid.

147. Ibid.

148. "Democratic-Republican Party," www.en.wikipedia.org/wiki/Democra tic-Republican_Party.

149. Robert A. Goldwin, From Parchment to Power: How James Madison Used the Bill of Rights to Save the Constitution (Washington, DC: American Enterprise Institute, 1997), 9.

150. Ketcham, 471.

151. John R. Vile, William D. Pederson, and Frank J. Williams, James Madison: Philosopher, Founder, and Statesman (Athens: Ohio University Press, 2008), 245.

152. Clay Gaynor, "How Well Do You Know James Madison: Meet the Man Behind the Name," www.thebree ze.org/archives/10.14.04/focus/focus1.sht ml.

153. Drew R. McCoy, The Last of the Fathers: James Madison and the Republican Legacy (New York: Cambridge University Press, 1991), 34.

154. Martin Diamond, "Democracy and the Federalist: A Reconsideration of the Framer's Intent," The American Political Science Review vol. 53, issue 1 (March 1959): 66.

155. 1981 Washington Post column. Quoted by Bruce Kaufmann, "James Madison: Godfather of the Constitution," Early American Review (Summer, 1997).

156. Wills, 164.

157. David B. Mattern, James Madison: Patriot, Politician, and President (New York: Rosen Publishing Group, 2005), 47.

158. James Grant Wilson and John Fiske, Appleton's Cyclopædia of American Biography volume 4 (New York: D. Appleton and Company, 1888), 165.

159. Wills, 36.

160. James Madison and Erastus Howard Scott, Journal of the Federal Convention (Chicago: Scott, Foresman and Co., 1898).

161. Garrett Ward Sheldon, The Political Philosophy of James Madison (Baltimore: Johns Hopkins University Press, 2003), 45.

162. James Madison, The Constitution a Pro-Slavery Compact: or, Extracts from the Madison Papers, etc. (New York: American Anti-Slavery Society, 1856), 111.

163. Lance Banning, "James Madison, the Statute for Religious Freedom, and the Crisis of Republican Convictions," The Virginia Statute for Religious Freedom: Its Evolution and Consequences in American History Merrill D. Peterson and Robert C. Vaughan, eds. (New York: Cambridge University Press, 2003), 110.

164. Ibid.

165. Rutland, 65.

166. Tim McNeese, U.S. Constitution (Dayton, OH: Lorenz Educational Press, 2001), 19.

167. "James Madison," www.jack millercenter.org/tag/james-madison.

168. Rutland, 63.

169. Speech at the Constitutional Convention, Philadelphia, June 6, 1788, The Debates in the Several State Conventions on the Adoption of the Federal Constitution, 5 Vols. Jonathan Elliott, ed. (Philadelphia: J. B. Lippincott Company, 1901) 3: 536–37 30.

170. Goldwin, 8.

171. Jerry W. Markham, A Financial History of the United States vols. 1–2 (Armonk, NY: M.E. Sharpe, 2002), 89.

172. Ketcham, 337.

173. Ketcham, 322.

174. "James Madison, Constitution of United States," www.futurecasts.com/ Rakove,%20James%20Madison.htm.

175. "Early Animosities," http://ww w.archives.gov/exhibits/treasures_of_con gress/text/page4_text.html.

176. James Madison, Thomas Jefferson, and Virginia. General Assembly. House of Delegates, Resolutions of Virginia and Kentucky (Richmond, VA: R.I. Smith, 1826).

177. Ibid., 19.

178. Ibid., 51.

179. McCoy, 89.

180. William W. Van Alstyne, Interpretations of the First Amendment (Durham: Duke University Press, 1984), 4.

181. "A More Perfect Union: The Creation of the U.S. Constitution," http://www.archives.gov/exhibits/char ters/constitution_history.html. "The anti-Federalists, demanding a more concise, unequivocal Constitution, one that laid out for all to see the right of the people and limitations of the power of government, claimed that the brevity of the document only revealed its inferior nature."

182. Ibid., Richard Henry Lee argued that trading the old government for the new without a bill of rights, would be trading Scylla for Charybdis.

183. Richard E. Labunski, James Madison and the Struggle for the Bill of Rights (New York: Oxford University Press, 2006), 104.

184. The Annals of Congress, House of Representatives, First Congress, 1st Session, 448–460.

185. "History of the United States Constitution," http://www.en.wikiped ia.org/wiki/...of_the_United_States_Co nstitution.

186. "United States Bill of Rights," http://www.en.wikipedia.org/wiki/Unite d_States_Bill_of_Rights.

187. Charles Hobson, The Great Chief Justice: John Marshall and the Rule of Law (Lawrence: University Press of Kansas, 2000), 90.

188. "A Closer Look into the Life of James Madison," http://www.slideshare. net/mrbeerbaitnammo/gvpt444-multi media-project-a-closer-look-into-the-life-of-james-madison-by-timothy-c-irwin.

189. Richard Heath Dabney, John Randolph: A Character Sketch vol. 555, issue 4 (Chicago: The University Association, 1898), 72.

190. World Almanac and Book of Facts (New York: Facts on File; Newspaper Enterprise Association, 1938), 907.

191. Vile, 252.

192. Wills, 12.

193. Francis Curtis, The Republican Party: A History of Its Fifty Years' Existence and a record of Its Measures and Leaders, 1854–1904 (New York: G.P. Putnam's Sons, 1904).

194. "U.S. Senate: George Clinton, 4th Vice President (1805–1812)," http:// www.senate.gov/artandhistory/history/co mmon/generic/VP_George_Clinton.htm.

195. LIFE Magazine vol. 39, no. 1 (July 4, 1955): 62.

196. Boston Gazette, March 26, 1812.

197. Edward S. Kaplan, The Bank of the United States and the American Economy (Westport, CT: Greenwood, 1999), 23, 55–56.

198. Mary Beth Norton, Carol Sheriff, David M. Katzman, David W. Katzman, David W. Blight, Howard P. Chudacoff, and Fredrik Logevall, A People and a Nation: A History of the United States to 1877, Vols. 1–2 (Stamford, CT: Cengage Learning, 2007), 239.

199. "Nullification," www.en.wikipe dia.org/wiki/Nullification.

200. Virginia Resolutions, Amendment I (Speech and Press), December 21, 1798 Document 19, 1.

201. Ibid., 78.

202. McCoy. 136.

203. Robert Allen Rutland, James Madison: The Founding Father (Columbia: University of Missouri Press, 1997), 182–183.

204. Ketcham, 323.

205. Brant, 453.

206. Journal of the House of Representatives of the United States, Monday, June 1, 1812, http://memory.loc. gov/cgi-bin/query/r?ammem/hlaw: @field%20(DOCID+@lit(hj008201)).

207. David Stephen Heidler and Jeanne T. Heidler, Encyclopedia of the War of 1812 (Annapolis, MD: Naval Institute Press, 2004), 153.

208. Mattern, 78.

209. Ibid.

210. David Fitz Enz, Old Ironsides: Eagle of the Sea: The Story of the USS Constitution (Lanham, MD: Taylor Trade Publications, 2009).

211. Rutland, 229.

212. Rutland, 215.

213. Rutland, 229.

214. Kevin Ambrose, Dan Henry and Andy Weiss, Washington Weather

(Gallatin, TN: Historical Enterprises, 2002), 31–32.

215. Sabrina Crewe and Scott Ingram, *The Writing of "The Star-Spangled Banner"* (Milwaukee, WI: Garteth Stevens, 2004).

216. Rutland, 231.

217. Ibid.

218. Wills, 149.

219. Dan Elish, *James Madison* (Tarrytown, NY: Marshall Cavendish, 2007), 81.

220. McNeese, 58.

221. "The Hartford Convention — The War For State's Rights," *http://civil war.bluegrass.net/secessioncrisis/hart fordconvention.htm.*

222. Ibid.

223. Rutland, 248.

224. JMPS, 63.

225. "James Madison," *www.encyclo pedia.com/topic/James_Madison.aspx.*

226. Mattern, 91.

227. Gould, 33.

228. Wills, 162.

229. Ibid., 162–163.

230. James Madison, *The Papers of James Madison* (Georgetown, DC: Langtree & O'Sullivan, 1840).

231. "Mr. President — Your Health: James Madison (1751–1836)," *Minnesota Medicine* 50.10 (October, 1967): 1500.

232. Letter to William Bradford, November 9, 1772, JMPS: 1.

233. Wills, 114.

234. "Mr. President — Your Health: James Madison (1751–1836)," *Minnesota Medicine* 50.10 (October, 1967): 1500.

235. Ibid.

236. Ibid.

237. Letter to James Monroe, April 21, 1831, JMPS; Quoted in Paul M. Zall, *Dolley Madison*, 69.

238. Letter to Jared Sparks, June 1, 1831, JMPS. Quoted in Drew R. McCoy, *The Last of the Fathers: James Madison & the Republican Legacy* (New York: Cambridge University Press), xi.

239. "Mr. President — Your Health: James Madison (1751–1836)," *Minnesota Medicine* 50.10 (October, 1967): 1500.

240. "James Madison's Obituary: From the *Connecticut Observer*, Saturday, July 9, 1836," *www.diplom.org/ma nus/Presidents/jmj/jmjobit.html.*

241. Paul Jennings, *A Colored Man's Reminiscences of James Madison* (Ithaca, NY: Cornell University Library, 1865), Preface.

242. Ibid.

243. "Advice to My Country," December 1834, JMPS.

244. "James Madison (1751–1836)," *www.findagrave.com/cgi-bin/fg.cgi?page =gr&GRid=661.*

245. Côté, 360.

246. "A History of the City of Madison," *http://www.cityofmadison.com/ visitors/visitormadisonhistory.cfm.*

247. Ketcham, 475.

248. "History of James Madison University," *http://universitydir.com/ james-madison-university/.*

249. JMPS, 239.

250. Letter to Frances Wright, September 1, 1825, JMPS. "James Madi-

son's Attitude Toward the Negro," *The Journal of Negro History* vol. 6, no. 1 (January 1921): 74–102. Regrettably Madison had no remedy for it.

251. Speech in the House of Representatives May 13, 1789, *The Founders' Constitution* volume 3, Article 1, Section 9, Clause 1, Document 16.

252. Letter to Marquis de Lafayette, February 1, 1830, JMPS; John D. Salliant, "The American Enlightenment in Africa: Jefferson's Colonizationism and Black Virginians' Migration to Liberia, 1776–1840," *Eighteenth-Century Studies* vol. 31, no. 3 (Spring 1998): 261–282.

253. JMPS, 134.

254. Early Lee Fox, *The American Colonization Society* (Baltimore: Johns Hopkins University Press, 1919), 62.

255. "Madison and Slavery," *www. montpelier.org/explore/community/slav ery_and_madison.php.*

256. Before departing for Philadelphia in November 1790, Ketcham, 374, 703.

257. Elizabeth Dowling Taylor, *A Slave in the White House: Paul Jennings and the Madisons* (New York: Macmillan, 2012), 21.

258. "James Madison and Executive Power," *http://www.new.civiced.org/res ources/curriculum/madison.*

259. Ruby Hawk, "Paul Jennings: White House Slave," *http://ruby-hawk. quazen.com/reference/biography/paul-jennings-white-house-slave/#ixzz1ng ZDCbSE.*

260. Jennings. 15.

261. Edward Hartnett, " A 'Uniform And Entire' Constitution; Or, What if Madison Had Won?" *https://litigation-essentials.lexisnexis.com/webcd/app?acti on=DocumentDisplay&crawlid=1&doct ype=cite&docid=15+Const.+Comment ary+251&srctype=smi&srcid=3B15&key =0ef08199755759d66a4b600d4a96b04f.*

262. Debates in Congress, Amendments to the Constitution; Monday, August 17, 1789, *1 Annals of Congress*, 757 *et seq.* (Washington, DC: Gales and Seaton, 1834).

263. "Amendment I (Speech and Press)," *http://press-pubs.uchicago.edu/ founders/documents/amendI_speechs14. html.*

264. "Fourteenth Amendment to the United States Constitution," *www. en.wikipedia.org/wiki/...Amendment_to _the_United_States.*

265. "U.S. Constitution: Bill of Rights," *www.thomaslegion.net/consti tutionoftheunitedstatesbillof.*

266. House of Representatives, Amendments, Aug. 24, 1789, Dumbauld 213–16, Article 1.

267. "Bill of Rights?" *www.answers. yahoo.com/question/index?qid=2006112 0093530AAjEfaz.*

268. James Madison and Henry Dilworth Gilpin, *The Papers of James Madison* (New York: J. & H. G. Langley, 1841), 269.

269. "An Attempt to Establish a Library of Congress," January 23, 1783 (Madison's notes of debate in Congress, 1782–3, JMPS).

270. "The James Madison Research Library and Information Center," *www. madisonbrigade.com/library_jm_docu ments.htm.*

271. Elizabeth Fleet, "Madison's Detached Memoranda," *William & Mary Quarterly*, 3d ser. (October 1946) 3: 554–62.

272. "*Magnificent Doll* (1946)," *www. imdb.com/title/tt0038715.*

273. Unless otherwise specified, each of the remarks in this section has JMPS as its source.

274. Brant, 226.

275. Letter to an unidentified correspondent, April 1812.

276. Letter to Cesar Rodney, December 29, 1812.

277. Clement Eaton, *Henry Clay and the Art of American Politics* (Boston: Little, Brown and Company, 1957), 90.

278. Brant, 399.

279. Ibid.

280. McCoy, 17.

281. Pierce's sketch of fellow delegates of the Constitutional Convention; Max Farrand, *Records of the Federal Convention of 1787* (New Haven: Yale University Press, 1966), 94 (Oddly, Pierce misspelled Madison's surname, giving it as Maddison).

282. Jack N. Rakove, *James Madison and the Creation of the American Republic* (London: Longman, [1990] 2002).

283. Letter to Benjamin Rush, June 20, 1812.

284. Harold Seessel Schultz, *James Madison* (New York: Twayne, 1970), 10.

285. Robert Vincent Remini, *Daniel Webster: The Man and His Time* (New York: W.W. Norton & Company, 1997), 107.

286. Schultz, 5.

287. Wills, 163.

Five. Monroe

1. The Boston Columbian Centinel, Harry Ammon, James Monroe: The Quest for National Identity (Charlottesville: University Press of Virginia, 1990), 366.

2. George Morgan, *The Life of James Monroe* (Boston: Small, Maynard and Company, 1921), 411.

3. "Monroe, James," *www.funtriv ia.com/en/world/monroe-james-1373 3.html.*

4. "James Monroe Museum and Memorial Library," *www.jamesmonroe museum.umw.edu/about-james-monr oe/research/.*

5. Ammon, 2.

6. Ammon, 3.

7. Ammon, 1–2.

8. "James Madison Democratic," *www.staff.gps.edu/mines/APUSH%20- %20Monroe's%20early%20years.htm.*

9. John R. Bumgarner, *The Health of the Presidents: The 41 United States Presidents Through 1993 from a Physician's Point of View* (Jefferson, NC: McFarland, 1994), 32; "James Monroe," *www.nndb.com/people/026/000043894.*

10. Ammon, 368.

11. Harlow Giles Unger, *The Last Founding Father: James Monroe and a Nation's Call to Greatness* (Cambridge, MA: Da Capo Press, 2010).

12. *The Encyclopedia Americana* (Albertson, NY: Americana Corp., 1977), 19: 379.

13. Ammon, 4.

14. Larry Schweikart and Michael Allen, *A Patriot's History of the United States: From Columbus's Great Discovery to the War on Terror* (New York: Penguin, 2007), 184.

15. Ammon, xvi.

16. Ammon, 61.

17. "Elizabeth Monroe," *http://www.firstladies.org/biographies/firstladies.aspx?biography=5*.

18. Ammon, 61–62.

19. "Early Political and Diplomatic Career — James Monroe," *www.presidentprofiles.com/Washington-Johnson/James-Monroe*.

20. Ammon, 137–138.

21. Margaret Brown Klapthor and Allida M. Black, *The First Ladies* (Washington DC: Government Printing Office, 2002), 17.

22. "Elizabeth Monroe," *www.womenhistoryblog.com/.../elizabeth-kortright-monroe.html*.

23. Cass R. Sandak, *The Monroes* (New York: Crestwood House, 1993), 41.

24. "Elizabeth Monroe," *http://www.womenhistoryblog.com/2011/03/elizabeth-kortright-monroe.html*.

25. Robert P. Watson, *The Presidents' Wives: Reassess-ing the Office of First Lady* (Boulder, CO: Lynne Rienner Publishers, 2000), 76.

26. Patrick L. O'Neill, *Virginia's Presidential Homes* (Mount Pleasant, SC: Arcadia Publishing, 2010), 71.

27. Ibid.

28. Klapthor, 17.

29. William A. DeGregorio, *The Complete Book of U.S. Presidents* (New York: Barricade, 2001), 74.

30. "Presidential Children: The Monroe Daughters," *http://www.suite101.com/article.cfm/presidents_and_first_ladies/47423*.

31. Ibid.

32. Doug Wead, *All the Presidents' Children: Triumph and Tragedy in the Lives of America's First Families* (New York: Simon & Schuster, 2004), 223–224.

33. David L. Holmes, "The Religion of James Mon-roe," *http://www.vqronline.org/articles/2003/autumn/holmes-religion-james-monroe/*.

34. Ibid.

35. Bliss Isley, *The Presidents: Men of Faith* (Boston: W.A. Wilde Co., 1953).

36. Quoted by Franklin Steiner, *The Religious Beliefs of Our Presidents* (Amherst, NY: Prometheus Books, 1995), 94.

37. "James Monroe, First Inaugural Address, Tuesday, March 4, 1817," *www.bartleby.com/124/pres20.html*.

38. David L. Holmes, "The Religion of James Monroe," *http://www.vqronline.org/articles/2003/autumn/holmes-religion-james-monroe/*.

39. David L. Holmes, "Religion of James Monroe," *http://www.vqronline.org/articles/2003/autumn/holmes-religion-james-monroe/*; David L. Holmes, *The Faiths of the Founding Fathers* (New York: Oxford University Press, 2006).

40. Bishop William Meade, *Old Churches, Ministers, and Families of Virginia* (Philadelphia: Lippincott, 1857), 292.

41. Holmes, 107.

42. Ibid., 105.

43. "James Monroe, First Inaugural Address, Tuesday, March 4, 1817," *www.bartleby.com/124/pres20.html*.

44. Ibid.

45. "Eighth State of the Union Message to Congress, December 7, 1824," *www.jamesmonroe.org/message8.html*.

46. Holmes, 103.

47. William Penn Cresson, *James Monroe* (Chapel Hill: University of North Carolina Press, 1946), 8.

48. "China Hall, Westmoreland County, Virginia," *www.kirnanfarmsoutfitters.com/kirnanhistory.htm*.

49. "James Monroe," *www.ourgeorgiahistory.com/ogh/james_monroe*.

50. Holmes, 107.

51. Gary Hart, *James Monroe*, American Presidents Series (New York: Henry Holt & Co., 2005), 14.

52. Ammon, 14.

53. "What's Wrong with This Painting?" *www.ushistory.org/washingtoncrossing/history/whatswrong.htm*.

54. Calista McCabe Courtenay, *George Washington* (New York: Samuel Gabriel Sons & Company, 1917), Cover.

55. David Hackett Fischer, *Washington Crossing* (New York: Oxford University Press, 2004), 231.

56. Ibid., 247.

57. Bumgarner, 32–33.

58. "James Monroe — Historic Clothing," *www.histclo.com/pres/Ind19/monroe.html*.

59. Hart, 3.

60. James Monroe, Daniel Preston, and Marlena C. DeLong, *The Papers of James Monroe: Selected Correspondence and Papers, 1776–1794* (Westport, CT: Greenwood Press), 30 (Hereafter Papers).

61. Calder Loth, *The Virginia Landmarks Register* (Charlottesville: University Press of Virginia, 2000), 184.

62. "James Monroe Museum and Memorial Library," *www.jamesmonroemuseum.umw.edu*.

63. Papers, 10.

64. John T. Marck, "James Monroe and Ash Lawn-Highland," *www.aboutfamouspeople.com/article5005.html*.

65. David Edwin Lillard, *Journey Through Hallowed Ground: The Official Guide to Where America Happened from Gettysburg to Monticello* (Herndon, VA: Capital Books, 2006), 145–146.

66. "Highland," *www.cr.nps.gov/nr/travel/journey/hig.htm*.

67. Lillard, 147.

68. "Elizabeth Kortright Monroe," *www.factbites.com/topics/Elizabeth-Kortright-Monroe*.

69. "Highland," *www.cr.nps.gov/nr/travel/journey/hig.htm*.

70. Ibid.

71. "Presidential Pastimes, Part I," *www.archive.suite101.com/article.cfm/presidents*.

72. Henry Franklin Graff, *The Presidents: A Reference History* (New York: Simon & Schuster, 2002), 72.

73. "James Monroe," *www.usa-presidents.info/monroe.htm*.

74. "The Hartford Convention — The War for State's Rights," *www.civilwar.bluegrass.net/.../hartfordconvention.html*.

75. Ammon is quoted by T. J. Graczewski in a review of *James Monroe: The Quest for National Identity*, *http://www.amazon.com/review/R2L9WFWJ5BAOVD/ref=cm_cr_pr_viewpnt#R2L9WFWJ5BAOVD*.

76. *The Encyclopedia Americana* (New York: Americana Corp., 1977), 19: 370.

77. "Ash Lawn-Highland," *www.ashlawnhighland.org/jamesmonroe.htm*.

78. First Inaugural Address, March 4, 1817.

79. "James Monroe," *www.ourgeorgiahistory.com/ogh/james_monroe*.

80. "James Monroe," *http://www.knowsouthernhistory.net/Biographies/James_Monroe*.

81. Monroe's proposal was finally approved in the July 7, 1786 Congressional resolution, Jorge M. Robert, "James Monroe and the Three-to-Five Clause of the Northwest Ordinance," *www.earlyamerica.com/review/2001_summer_fall/monroe.html*.

82. Ibid.

83. Ammon, 53.

84. Ammon, 71–73.

85. "James Monroe," *www.ourgeorgiahistory.com/ogh/james_monroe*.

86. Arthur Scherr, "The Limits of Republican Ideology: James Monroe in Themidorian Paris, 1794–1796," *Mid-America: An Historical Review* 79, no. 1 (Winter 1997): 35.

87. "James Monroe,"*http://www.encyclopedia.com/topic/James_Monroe.aspx*.

88. "James Monroe," *www.mapsofworld.com/usa/presidents/james-monroe.html*.

89. "The Spanish Cession," *http://www.mrvanduyne.com/youngnation/monroe/florida.html*.

90. "The War of 1812," *www.shmoop.com/war-1812/timeline.html*.

91. "The Jefferson Presidency," *www.shmoop.com/jefferson-presidency/timeline.html*.

92. Ammon, 186.

93. Ibid., 185.

94. Ibid., 277.

95. Ibid., 174.

96. Ibid., 255.

97. Ibid., 273.

98. Ibid.

99. Ibid., 273–274.

100. Ibid., 335–342.

101. Ibid.

102. Letter to Henry Fox, July 5, 1815; *Letters to Henry Fox*, Lord Holland, Earl

of Ilchester, ed. (Privately printed at the Chiswick Press, for the Roxburghe Club in London, 1915).

103. Letter to Joseph Alston, November 15, 1815; David O. Stewart, "Burr on Monroe," December 19, 2009.

104. Larry Sabato and Howard R. Ernst, *Encyclopedia of American Political Parties and Elections* (New York: Facts on File, 2007), 304.

105. Ammon, 474.

106. "First Inaugural Address," *www.bartleby.com/124/pres20.html*.

107. "Second Inaugural Address, March 5, 1821," *www.bartleby.com/124/pres21.html*.

108. "Arts Club of Washington," *www.artsclubofwashington.org/history*.

109. "BW Calendar," *www.bunniewise.com/BW-Calendar.html*.

110. "White House History: Decorative Arts," *www.whitehousehistory.org/whha_timelines/images/*.

111. "United States Presidents—History and Trivia," *www.francesfarmersrevenge.com/stuff/archive/oldnews2/*.

112. Peleg Dennis Harrison, *The Stars and Stripes and Other American Flags* (Boston: Little, Brown, and Company, 1908), 76–78.

113. Elizabeth Jewell, *U.S. Presidents Factbook* (New York: Random House, 2005), 44.

114. Letter to John Adams, 1820, Quoted in Hart, 78.

115. L. Edward Purcell, *Vice Presidents: A Biographical Dictionary* (New York: Infobase Publishing, 2010), 55–63.

116. "Miracle on 34th Street — The Film Guide," *www.filmguide.wikia.com/wiki/Miracle_on_34th_Street*.

117. Hart, 71.

118. Ammon, 4.

119. "The James Monroe Administration: Las of the 'Virginia Dynasty,'" *www.academicamerican.com/jeffersonjackson/topics/monroe*.

120. Larry Sabato and Howard R. Ernst, *Encyclopedia of American Political Parties and Elections* (New York: Infobase Publishing, 2006), 306.

121. "The James Monroe Administration: Las of the 'Virginia Dynasty,'" *www.academicamerican.com/jeffersonjackson/topics/monroe*.

122. Samuel Willard Crompton, *McCulloch v. Maryland: Implied Powers of the Federal Government* (New York: Infobase Publishing, 2007), 50.

123. Ibid.

124. Murray N. Rothbard, *The Panic of 1819: Reactions and Policies* (Auburn, AL: Ludwig von Mises Institute, 2007), 1–2.

125. Ibid., 31.

126. Ibid., 31–32.

127. "Third Annual Address to Congress, December 7, 1819," *www.swetspeeches.com/s/98-james-monroe-third-annual-message*.

128. Rothbard, 30–32.

129. Ibid.

130. "James Monroe Summary," *http://www.bookrags.com/history/president-james-monroe/12.html*.

131. Ibid.

132. "American History: Monroe Doctrine Warns Europe Not to Interfere in the Americas," *www.manythings.org/voa/history/51.html*.

133. Ibid.

134. Ibid.

135. "Missouri Compromise: Primary Documents of American History," *http://www.loc.gov/rr/program/bib/ourdocs/Missouri.html*.

136. Benson John Lossing, "History of the Civil War Illustrated 1912," *www.scribd.com/doc/43462628/History-of-the-Civil-War*.

137. Letter to William Short from April 13, 1820, *The Thomas Jefferson Papers* at the Library of Congress.

138. "Missouri Compromise," *http://www.loc.gov/rr/program/bib/ourdocs/Missouri.html*.

139. "American History: Monroe Doctrine Warns Europe Not to Interfere in the Americas," *www.manythings.org/voa/history/51.html*.

140. "Dred Scott Case: the Supreme Court Decision," *www.pbs.org/wgbh/aia/part4/4h2933.html*.

141. Ibid.

142. Ibid.

143. Frederick Jackson Turner, *Rise of the New West, 1819–1829* (New York: Harper & Bros., 1906), 236–242.

144. Ibid.

145. Ibid.

146. Ibid.

147. Ibid.

148. "Treaty of 1818," *http://en.wikipedia.org/wiki/Treaty_of_1818*.

149. "Strange Maps: Border between Canada and USA," *http://blog.proud-geek.com/2007/07/06/strange-maps-border-between-canada-and-usa*.

150. William M. Davidson, *A History of the United States* (Glenville, IL: Scott, Foresman and Company, 1902), 288–289.

151. Adam Wasserman, *A People's History of Florida, 1513–1876: How Africans, Seminoles, Women, and Lower Class Whites Shaped the Sunshine State* (Sarasota, FL: Adam Wasserman, 2009), 183–184.

152. Ibid.

153. Ibid.

154. "President James Monroe Summary," *http://www.bookrags.com/history/president-james-monroe/03.html*.

155. William Fiddian Reddaway, *The Monroe Doctrine* (Cambridge: Cambridge University Press, 1898), 80.

156. "Major Events with James Monroe," *http://library.thinkquest.org/11492/cgi-bin/pres.cgi/monroe_james?event*.

157. "United States of America," *http://www.cartage.org.lb/en/themes/geoghist/histories/history/hiscountries/u/unitedstates.html*.

158. Charles Grenfill Washburn, *Theodore Roosevelt: The Logic of His Career* (Boston Houghton Mifflin, 1916), 89–92.

159. Seventh annual message to Congress, December 2, 1823, *www.free*

republic.com/focus/f-news/1036329/posts.

160. The White House Historical Association, "White House Tours: The Blue Room," *http://www.whitehousehistory.org/whha_tours/whitehouse_tour/05.html*.

161. "President James Monroe," *http://www.stuffaboutstates.com/presidents/james_monroe.htm*.

162. Letter to General Roger Jones in 1826; Daniel Preston, ed. *A Comprehensive Catalogue of the Correspondence and Papers of James Monroe*, 2 vols. (Westport, CT: Greenwood, 2000).

163. Dorothy Schneider and Carl J. Schneider, *First Ladies: A Biographical Dictionary* (New York: Infobase Publishing, 2010), 40.

164. Wead, 226.

165. Letter to Charles Fenton Mercer, March 24, 1808; Preston.

166. "James Monroe," *www.encyclopedia.com/topic/James_Monroe.aspx*.

167. Ibid.

168. Henry A. Graff, "The Wealth of Presidents," *American Heritage Magazine* vol. 17, issue 6 (October, 1966).

169. "James Monroe," *www.encyclopedia.com/topic/James_Monroe.aspx*.

170. "James Monroe," *www.absoluteastronomy.com/topics/James_Monroe*.

171. Ammon, xix.

172. Bumgarner, 33.

173. Ibid., 34.

174. Ibid., 35.

175. Ibid.

176. "James Monroe (1758–1831)," *http://www.findagrave.com/cgibin/fg.cgi?page*.

177. "How Did Each President Die?" *www.diplom.org/manus/Presidents/faq/causes.html*.

178. "James Monroe's Obituary from *Niles' Weekly Register* (Baltimore), July 23, 1831," *http://www.diplom.org/manus/Presidents/jm/jmobit.html*.

179. "James Monroe (1758–1831)," *www.findagrave.com/cgi-bin/fg.cgi?page=gr&GRid=724*.

180. John A. Bremer, *Constitution Making in Indiana: A Source Book of Constitutional Documents, with Historical Introduction and Critical Notes* (Indianapolis: Indiana Historical Commission, 1916), 130.

181. "Monroe's Tour of New England Summary," *www.bookrags.com/research/monroes-tour-of-new-england-aaw-01*.

182. Speech to Massachusetts Society of the Cincinnati, Boston, Massachusetts, July 4, 1817; Francis Samuel Drake, *Memorials of the Society of the Cincinnati of Massachusetts* (Boston: Printed for the Society, 1873), 70.

183. "Ash Lawn-Highland," *www.ashlawnhighland.org/jm — slavery.htm*.

184. Letter to Thomas Jefferson, September 15, 1800, Preston, ibid.

185. James Monroe, *The Writings of James Monroe: Including a Collection of His Public and Private Papers and Correspondence Now for the First Time Printed*, S.M. Hamilton, ed. (New York: G.P. Putnam's Sons, 1900), 3: 247.

186. Ibid., 3: 208.
187. Ibid., 3: 292–294.
188. Ibid., 6: 196.
189. Ibid., 7: 26.
190. Ron Chernow, *Alexander Hamilton* (New York: Penguin, 2005), 415–416.
191. Chernow, 416.
192. Ibid.
193. Ibid., 364.
194. Ibid.
195. Ibid., 365.
196. Ibid., 365–366.
197. Ibid., 416.
198. Ibid.
199. Ibid., 417.
200. Ibid.
201. *"Alexander Hamilton* (1931), www.imdb.com/title/tt0021595.
202. Chernow, 530.
203. Ibid., 529.
204. Ibid., 538.
205. Ibid., 538–540.
206. Broadus Mitchell, *Alexander Hamilton: The National Adventure* (New York: Macmillan, 1962), 409.
207. Ibid., 410–413.
208. "The Reynolds Pamphlet," http://oll.libertyfund.org/?option=com_s taticxt&staticfile=show.php%3Ftitle=13 84&chapter=107490&layout=html&Ite mid=27.
209. Ibid.
210. Mitchell, 418.
211. "Thomas Paine," http://www.ushistory.org/PAINE.
212. Ibid.
213. Letter to Thomas Paine, remarking on the American public's indifference to Paine's accomplishments during the Revolution because Paine had published "The Age of Reason," an anti–Bible tract, quoted from Robert Green Ingersoll, *Vindication of Thomas Paine* (Boston: J. P. Mendum, 1877).
214. Ingersoll.
215. "Thomas Paine," http://www.ushistory.org/PAINE.
216. Thomas Jefferson, "Like a fire bell in the night" Letter to John Holmes, April 22, 1820, Library of Congress.
217. Alusine Jalloh and Toyin Falola, *The United States and West Africa: Interactions and Relations* (Rochester, NY: University Rochester Press, 2008), 20.
218. Ibid.
219. "Office of Institutional Diversity," http://www.bridgew.edu/HOBA/Cuffee.cfm.
220. "American Colonization Society," www.slavenorth.com/colonize.htm.
221. Ibid.
222. Ibid.
223. Ibid.
224. "Liberian Declaration of Independence," www.onliberia.org/con_decl aration.htm.
225. "Liberia," www.sio.midco.net/dansmapstamps/liberia.htm.
226. John V. Quarstein, Julie Steere Clevenger, and Molly Joseph Ward, *Old Point Comfort Resort: Hospitality, Health and History on Virginia's Chesapeake Bay* (Charleston, SC: The History Press, 2009), 19–20.
227. Dolores Riccio and Joan Bingham, *Haunted Houses U.S.A.* (New York: Simon & Schuster, 1989), 157–160.
228. "2008 Andrew Jackson Presidential Coin," http://www.amazon.co m/2008-Andrew-Jackson-Presidential-Coin/dp/B00140SD6S.
229. "James Monroe Dollar," http://jamesmonroedollar.com/.
230. Ammon, 169.
231. Daniel C. Gillman, *James Monroe* (New York: Chelsea House, [1898] 1983).
232. Alfred Steinberg, *The First Ten: The Founding Presidents and Their Administrations* (New York: Doubleday, 1967).
233. Manus Hand, "Dead Presidents on Dead Presidents, Quotations by One Dead President about Another." www.diplom.org/manus/Presidents/ratings/pr ez.htm.
234. *National Intelligencer*, October 17, 1820.
235. Letter to S.L. Gouverneur, August 8, 1818; *Correspondence of John C. Calhoun*, J. Franklin Jameson, ed., from the Annual Report of the American Historical Association for 1899 (Washington, DC: Government Printing Office, 1900).
236. George Dangerfield, *The Era of Good Feelings* (Lanham, MD: Ivan R. Dee, [1952] 1989).
237. Hart.
238. Maryland House of Delegates in honor of retiring President James Monroe, 1825.
239. Hezekiah Niles, editor of the *Baltimore Weekly Register* objecting to the fanfare Monroe received as he traveled up the eastern seaboard.
240. Carl Schurz, *Life of Henry Clay*, 2 vols. (Boston: Houghton Mifflin, 1899).
241. W.P. Cresson, *James Monroe* (Chapel Hill: University of North Carolina Press, 1946).

Six. J. Q. Adams

1. "The Diaries of John Quincy Adams: A Digital Collection," www.masshist.org/jqadiaries/, June 4, 1819 (Hereafter JQA Diary).
2. June 4, 1819, JQA Diary.
3. Edward Everett Hale, *Old and New* (Boston: H.O. Houghton and Co., 1875), 10: 508.
4. Paul C. Nagel, *John Quincy Adams: A Public Life, a Private Life* (Cambridge, MA: Harvard University Press, 1999), 10.
5. Letter from John Adams to JQA when the latter was 10; Sean Wilentz, *The Rise of American Democracy: Jefferson to Lincoln* (New York: W.W. Norton, 2005), 257.
6. Nagel, 9.
7. Hugh Montgomery-Massingberd, ed, *Burke's Presidential Families of the United States of America*, 2d ed. (London: Burke's Peerage Limited, 1981), 57, 69.
8. Nagel, 4.
9. Ibid., 5.
10. William A. DeGregorio, *The Complete Book of U.S. Presidents* (New York: Barricade, 2001), 89.
11. Nagel, 72.
12. Joseph Nathan Kane, *Presidential Fact Book* (New York: Random House, 1998), 43.
13. Ibid.
14. Joseph Wheelan, *Mr. Adams's Last Crusade: John Quincy Adams's Extraordinary Post-Presidential Life in Congress* (New York: PublicAffairs, 2009), 236.
15. Henry Franklin Graff, *The Presidents: A Reference History* (New York: Simon & Schuster, 2002), 87.
16. Candace Scott, Amazon.com review of Paul C. Nagel, *John Quincy Adams: A Public Life, a Private Life*, January 2, 2001, http://www.amazon.com/John-Quincy-Adams-Public-Private/product-reviews/0674479408.
17. John Fiske, quoted by Beckles Willson, *America's Ambassadors to England, 1785–1928: A Narrative of Anglo-American Diplomatic Relations* (New York: Ayer Publishing, 1968), 116.
18. Ibid.
19. "John Quincy Adams," http://www25.uua.org/uuhs/duub/articles/joh nquincyadams.html.
20. Senator Rufus Choate quoted by William Safire, *Safire's Political Dictionary* (New York: Oxford University Press, 2009), 349.
21. Marie B. Hecht, *John Quincy Adams, A Personal History of an Independent Man* (New York: Macmillan, 1972), 276.
22. Alfred Steinberg, *The First Ten: The Founding Presidents and Their Administrations* (Garden City, NY: Doubleday, 1967), 254.
23. "John Quincy Adams," http://www.nndb.com/people/370/000026292/.
24. Nagel, 22.
25. Ibid. He said he had left Passy carrying dreams of her that lasted long after he returned to America.
26. Ibid., 21.
27. Ibid.
28. Ibid., 16.
29. Ibid., Nagel wrote "Johnny tried in many ways by letter to reassure his mother. He was well aware of the 'vice and folly' on all sides in Europe, he wrote, and 'I hope I shall never be tempted by them.' Likewise, John Adams did his share to calm Abigail's fears. 'My little son gives me great pleasure." He spoke of Johnny's "assiduity to his books and his discreet behavior.' With generosity and tact, John added that this was because 'The lessons of his Mamma are a constant law to him.'"
30. Ibid., 63–66.
31. Paul F. Boller Jr., *Presidential Wives* (New York: Oxford University Press, 1998), 53 55.
32. Ibid.
33. Nagel, 41.
34. Ibid., 93.
35. Boller, 53.
36. "American President: John Quincy Adams: A Life in Brief," www.millercenter.org/president/jqadams/es says/biography/.

37. Boller, 55.
38. Nagel, 108.
39. Boller, 56.
40. Paul C. Nagel, *The Adams Women: Abigail and Louisa Adams, Their Sisters and Daughters* (Cambridge, MA: Harvard University Press, 1999), 175 (Hereafter, Nagel: AW).
41. Ibid., 41, 150, 209.
42. Ibid., 143.
43. Ibid., 187.
44. Ibid., 190.
45. Ibid., 221.
46. Margaret Brown Klapthor and Allida M. Black, *The First Ladies* (Washington DC: Government Printing Office, 2002), 18.
47. Nagel, 246.
48. Robert Vincent Remini, *John Quincy Adams* (New York: Macmillan, 2002), 40.
49. Margaret Bassett, *Profiles & Portraits of American Presidents & Their Wives* (Freeport, ME: The Bond Wheelwright Company, 1969), 67.
50. Klapthor, 18.
51. Lewis L. Gould, *American First Ladies: Their Lives and Their Legacy* (New York: Routledge, 2001), 51.
52. "Louisa Adams Biography: National First Ladies' Library," *www.first ladies.org/biographies/firstladies.aspx?bi ography=6.*
53. Gore Vidal, *United States: Essays: 1952–1992* (New York: Broadway Books, 2001), 654.
54. Nagel: AW, 217.
55. Gould, 55.
56. Michael O'Brien, *Henry Adams and the Southern Question* (Athens: University of Georgia Press, 2005), 24.
57. Gould, 50.
58. Garry Wills, *Henry Adams and the Making of America* (Boston: Houghton Mifflin Harcourt, 2007), 16.
59. Philip Secor, *Presidential Profiles: From George Washington to G. W. Bush* (Bloomington, IN: iUniverse, 2008), 77.
60. Nagel, 317.
61. "Adams, Charles Francis— Biographical Information," *www.bioguide. congress.gov/scripts/biodisplay.pl?index= A000032.*
62. "American President: A Reference Resource, John Quincy Adams Front Page," *www.millercenter.org/presi dent/jqadams/essays/biography/.*
63. "History of the Congregational Church," *www.gene.kellerhouse-webst er.com/church.html.*
64. "John Quincy Adams," *www.uu a.org/uuhs/duub/articles/johnquincyad ams.html.*
65. Ibid.
66. Nagel, 202.
67. Letter to Richard Anderson, May 25, 1823, Papers, Library of Congress Manuscript Division.
68. Nagel, 189.
69. "John Quincy Adams," *www.u ua.org/uuhs/duub/articles/johnquinc yadams.html.*
70. Ibid.
71. Ibid.
72. Ibid.
73. Nagel, 124.

74. David Scott Domke and Kevin M. Coe, *The God Strategy: How Religion Became a Political Weapon in America* (New York: Oxford University Press, 2008), 215.
75. *Bible Society Record*, Vols. 1–2 (New York: American Bible Society, 1856), 202.
76. William Federer, *America's God and Country, Encyclopedia of Quotations* (St. Louis, MO: Amerisearch, Inc. 1995), 19–20.
77. John Quincy Adams, *Letters of John Quincy Adams, to His Son, on the Bible and Its Teachings* (Auburn: James M. Alden, 1850), 61.
78. Remini, 73.
79. John Quincy Adams, *The Diary of John Quincy Adams*, Allan Nevins, ed. (New York: F. Ungar, 1969).
80. Samuel Hanson Cox, Thomas Chalmers, Nathanael Emmons, and John Quincy Adams, *Interviews: Memorable and Useful* (New York: Harper & Brothers, 1853), 272.
81. John Quincy Adams, *The Diary of John Quincy Adams*, Allan Nevins, ed. (New York: F. Ungar, 1969).
82. Ibid.
83. Ibid.
84. Ibid.
85. *Adams on Jesus Christ and Christianity, Relative to Muhammad and Islam* (series of essays [1830]), from Andrew G. Bostom, "John Quincy Adams Knew Jihad," *Front Page Magazine*, September 29, 2004, *http://archive.frontpagemag. com/readArticle.aspx?ARTID=11283* (Hereafter Christ/Islam).
86. Remini, 4.
87. Ibid., 6.
88. Nagel, 15.
89. Ibid., 20.
90. Ibid., 22.
91. "John Quincy Adams— Battles for the American System," *http://www. alternate-healing-science-christian.ca/ lovescapenovels/love_history_4.htm.*
92. Christ/Islam.
93. Nagel, 72.
94. Letter to Abigail Adams, September 27, 1778; Massachusetts Historical Society, *MHS Miscellany* No. 90 (Spring 2006): 4. Written while JQA was traveling with his father John Commissioner to France.
95. "John Quincy Adams," *http:// www.biography.com/people/john-quin cy-adams-9175983.*
96. John Adams, *The Bible Lessons of John Quincy Adams for His Son* (San Antonio, TX: Vision Forum, 2002), 27.
97. Nagel, 73.
98. Ibid., 73–74.
99. Ibid., 75.
100. "Marcellus," *Columbian Centinel*, February 17, 1793; Worthington Chauncy Ford, ed., *Writings of John Quincy Adams*, Vol. I: 1779–1796 (New York: Greenwood Press, 1968). On April 24, 1793, JQA began "Marcellus" articles that called for the neutrality of the United States in the British-French War. He argued that the change in the French Government pardoned the United States of the treaty obligations.

101. Nagel, 76.
102. Ibid., 81.
103. Gary W. Ferris, *Presidential Places: A Guide to the Historic Sites of U.S. Presidents* (Winston Salem, NC: John F. Blair, Publisher, 1999), 46.
104. Nagel, 6.
105. Thomas Morton, *The New England Canaan, 1637*, Jack Dempsey, ed., *'New English Canaan' by Thomas Morton of Merrymount: Text & Notes* (Scituate, MA: Digital Scanning, 2000).
106. "The Settlement of Braintree," *http://www.brownellfamily.rootsweb.an cestry.com/Braintree.html.*
107. Amy Schrager Lang, Prophetic Woman: *Anne Hutchinson and the Problem of Dissent in the Literature of New England* (Berkeley: University of California Press, 1987), 65.
108. "The Settlement of Braintree," *http://www.brownellfamily.rootsweb.an cestry.com/Braintree.html.*
109. Hecht, 454.
110. Schneider, 48.
111. John Quincy Adams and Jean de La Fontaine, *Fables Choisies: Mises en Vers* (Charleston, SC: BiblioLife, 2009).
112. Lynn H. Parsons, *John Quincy Adams* (Lanham, MD: Rowman & Littlefield, 1999), 235.
113. JQA Diary, 41.
114. Paul E. Teed, *John Quincy Adams: Yankee Nationalist* (New York: Nova Science Publishers, 2006), 16–18, 26–31, 8, 124.
115. "John Quincy Adams: First Annual Message to Congress," *www. milestonedocuments.com/documents/vie w/john-quincy-adams.*
116. Richards, Leonard L. *The Life and Times of Congressman John Quincy Adams* (New York: Oxford University Press, 1996), 248.
117. Howard Fast, *War and Peace: Observations on Our Times* (Armonk, NY: M.E. Sharpe, Inc., 1993), 243.
118. Teed, 13–14.
119. *Encyclopædia Britannica* (Chicago: Encyclopædia Britannica, 1968), 1: 126.
120. Parsons, 47.
121. Teed, 38.
122. Nagel, 119.
123. Ibid., 184–186.
124. James Alton James and Albert Hart Sanford, *American History* (New York: Scribner, 1909), 255.
125. Adams Family Correspondence. Six of a projected 14 volumes from the Adams Family Correspondence series have been published. The published volumes cover the years 1761–1785. These volumes include family correspondence from the entire Adams family. A comprehensive published collection of John Quincy Adams papers does not yet exist. John Quincy Adams's papers are part of the Adams Papers project at the Massachusetts Historical Society. The project, through Harvard University Press, plans to publish the papers of the Adams family from 1753 to 1889.
126. Nagel, 123.

127. Ibid., 205.
128. Teed, 54–55.
129. *Writings*, 5: 372.
130. Teed, 64.
131. Remini, 34–35.
132. JQA Diary, 1804, a few months after becoming a Senator. Denise Henderson, "John Quincy Adams Battles for the American System," *The New Federalist*, September 8, 1989 (Reprinted in *The American Patriot*, November 16, 2007), 58.
133. Ralph Ketcham, *Presidents Above Party: The First American Presidency, 1789–1829* (Chapel Hill: University of North Carolina Press, 1987.
134. Remini, 36–39.
135. Ibid.
136. Ibid.
137. Mara Louise Pratt, *Chadwick, American History Stories* (Boston: Educational Pub. Co., 1890), 46–47.
138. John Fiske, *The Presidents of the United States, 1789–1914* (New York: Scribner's Sons, 1914), 4: 274.
139. Nagel, 172.
140. Teed, 47.
141. Remini, 39.
142. Inaugural Oration, Harvard College, June 12, 1806; Henderson, 58–59.
143. *Writings*, 7: 344–335.
144. Henderson, 58–59.
145. Ibid.
146. "John Quincy Adams as Secretary of State," *www.americaslibrary.gov/aa/jqadams/aa_jqadams_secretary*.
147. Remini, 153.
148. John Quincy Adams's Account of the Cabinet Meeting of November 7, 1823; Samuel Flagg Bemis, *John Quincy Adams and the Foundations of American Foreign Policy* (Westport, CT: Greenwood Press, 1981), 385.
149. "John Quincy Adams," *http://www.johnqadams.org/*.
150. "John Quincy Adams — Early Life," *www.experiencefestival.com/a/John_Quincy_Adams_-_Early*.
151. James Grant Wilson and John Fiske, *Appleton's Cyclopædia of American Biography* (New York: D. Appleton and Company, 1887), 1: 26.
152. Ibid.
153. Ibid.
154. Ibid., 27.
155. Ibid.
156. Joseph Wheelan, *Mr. Adams's Last Crusade: John Quincy Adams's Extraordinary Post-Presidential Life in Congress* (New York: PublicAffairs, 2008), 48.
157. Ibid., 44.
158. JQA Diary, 1828.
159. "John Quincy Adams," *www.novelguide.com/a/discover/prh_01/prh_01_00017.html*.
160. Edward Pessen, "John Quincy Adams," *http://www.presidentprofiles.com/Washington-Johnson/Adams-John-Quincy.html*.
161. Wilson, 27.
162. Parsons, 193.
163. Martha S. Hewson, *John Quincy Adams* (New York: Infobase Publishing, 2003), 67.

164. James West Davidson and Mark H. Lytle, *The United States: A History of the Republic* (Upper Saddle River, NJ: Prentice Hall, 1990), 255.
165. Remini, 78–80.
166. Bemis, 69.
167. Teed, 102.
168. "National Park Service — The Presidents (John Quincy Adams)," *www.nps.gov/history/history/online_books/presidents/bio6.htm*.
169. "American President: Biography of John Quincy Adams," *www.millercenter.org/president/jqadams/essays/biography/print*.
170. William Earl Weeks, *John Quincy Adams and American Global Empire* (Lexington: University Press of Kentucky, 2002), 13.
171. Nagel, 170.
172. "The Presidency of John Quincy Adams," *www.digitalhistory.uh.edu/database/article_display.cfm?*.
173. Edward Everett, *A Eulogy on the Life and Character of John Quincy Adams: Delivered at the Request of the Legislature of Massachusetts, in Faneuil Hall, April 15, 1848* (Boston: Dutton and Wentworth, state printers, 1848), 35–37.
174. "John Quincy Adams on Government Responsibility for Internal Improvements, Letter to John McLean, May 6, 1824," *www.icue.nbcunifiles.com/icue/files/icue/site/pdf/32993.pdf*.
175. Parsons, 214.
176. Junius P. Rodriguez, *Slavery in the United States: A Social, Political, and Historical Encyclopedia* (Santa Barbara, CA: ABC-CLIO, 2007), 2: 426.
177. Henry Adams, *The Degradation of the Democratic Dogma* (New York: Macmillan, 1919), 25.
178. JQA Diary, 1837; Samuel Bemis, *John Quincy Adams and the Union* (New York: Knopf, 1956).
179. JQA Diary, November 29, 1820.
180. Wilbur Fisk Gordy, *History of United States* (New York: C. Scribner's Sons, 1911), 245–246.
181. F.W., Taussig, *The Tariff History of the United States*, Part I, 5th Ed. (New York: G.P. Putnam's Sons, 1910), 88–89.
182. "Tariff of 1828 — United States History," *www.u-s-history.com/pages/h268.html*.
183. Remini, 116.
184. David A. Midgley and Phillip Lefton, *Barron's How to Prepare for SAT II: American History and Social Studies* (Hauppauge, NY: Barron's Educational Series, 1988), 110.
185. Elizabeth Jewell, *U.S. Presidents Factbook* (Boston: Random House Reference, 2005), 50.
186. James E. Lewis, *John Quincy Adams: Policymaker for the Union* (Lanham, MD: Rowman & Littlefield, 2001), 142.
187. JQA Diary, January 1, 1829.
188. Ibid.
189. JQA Diary, December 11, 1828.
190. JQA Diary, January 18, 1829.
191. Christ/Islam.
192. Ibid.

193. Ibid.
194. JQA Diary, November 6, 1830.
195. Frank Freidel, *Presidents of the United States of America* (Darby, PA: Diane Publishing, 1994), 18.
196. Lewis, 130.
197. JQA Diary, 1843.
198. Speech in the House of Representatives May 18, 1836; Parsons, 231.
199. Timothy Sandefur, "Liberal Originalism: A Past for the Future," *Harvard Journal of Law and Public Policy* 27 (Spring 2004): 515–6.
200. Parsons, 234–235.
201. Walter Buell, *Joshua Giddings* (Cleveland: W.W. Williams, 1882), 79.
202. Parsons, 160.
203. JQA Diary, September 2, 1837.
204. "The 'Gag' Rule," *www.archives.gov/exhibits/treasures_of_congress/text/*.
205. William Lee Miller, *Arguing About Slavery: John Quincy Adams and the Great Battle in the United States Congress* (New York: Vintage Books, 1998), 580.
206. David C. Frederick, "John Quincy Adams, Slavery, and the Disappearance of the Right of Petition," *Law and History Review*, vol. 9 issue 1 (Spring 1991): 113–155.
207. Bennett Champ Clark, *John Quincy Adams: Old Man Eloquent* (Boston: Little, Brown & Co., 1933), 360.
208. Parsons, 231–233.
209. JQA Diary, March 11, 1845.
210. JQA Diary, February 6, 1842.
211. JQA Diary; *Memoirs of John Quincy Adams, taken from his diaries, 1794–1848*, Charles Francis Adams, ed. (Philadelphia: J.B. Lippincott, 1875), II: 159.
212. Teed, xvi.
213. JQA Diary, March 3, 1820.
214. Letter to Richard C. Anderson, August 29, 1820, *Memoirs of John Quincy Adams*, V: 5–11, 13.
215. G. J. Barker-Benfield, *Abigail and John Adams: The Americanization of Sensibility* (Chicago: University of Chicago Press, 2010); See also William Jerry MacLean, "Othello Scorned: The Racial Thought of John Quincy Adams." *Journal of the Early Republic* 4 (Summer 1984): 143–60.
216. Nina Burleigh, *The Stranger and the Statesman: James Smithson, John Quincy Adams, and the Making of America's Greatest Museum: The Smithsonian* (New York: HarperCollins, 2004), 2, 16–17, 140–143.
217. Ibid., 9.
218. Ibid., 232.
219. House Report 181, January 19, 1835.
220. Report on the establishment of the Smithsonian Institution, 1846, Josiah Quincy. *Memoir of the life of John Quincy Adams* (Boston: Crosby, Nicholls, and Lee Co., 1860), 265. John Quincy Adams chaired a House of Representative Committee to consider the bequest of James Smithson. He reported the committee's findings to the entire House in January 1836.

221. Heather P. Ewing, *The Lost World of James Smithson: Science, Revolution, and the Birth of the Smithsonian* (Bloomsbury, NJ: Bloomsbury, 2007), 250–256.

222. Russell Kirk, *The Conservative Mind: From Burke to Eliot*, 7th ed. (Washington, DC: Regnery Press, 2001), 231.

223. Nagel, 366.

224. Paul F. Boller Jr., *Presidential Anecdotes* (New York: Oxford University Press, 1981), 61.

225. February 13, 1847, Josiah Quincy, 425; Henderson, 67.

226. JQA Diary, 1839; Nevins.

227. Ralph Waldo Emerson, *Selected Journals: 1841–1877* (New York: Library of America, 2010).

228. JQA Diary, 1840.

229. R.V. Remini, *Martin Van Buren and the Making of the Democratic Party* (New York: Columbia University Press, [1959] 1970).

230. "How Did Each President Die?" *www.python.net/crew/manus/Presidents/faq/causes.html*.

231. William Henry Seward and John Mather Austin, *Life and Public Services of John Quincy Adams, Sixth President of the United States; With the Eulogy Delivered Before the Legislature of New York* (Auburn, NY: Derby, Miller and Co., 1849), *http://www.archive.org/stream/lifepublicservic00sewa/lifepublicservic00sewa_djvu.txt*.

232. "John Quincy Adams," *www.uua.org/uuhs/duub/articles/johnquincyadams.html*.

233. Bemis, 538.

234. Nagel, 416.

235. Parsons, 260.

236. Hecht, 311.

237. Bemis 106.

238. John Quincy Adams, *Dermot MacMorrogh, or, the Conquest of Ireland. An Historical Tale of the Twelfth Century in Four Cantos* (Boston: Carter, Hendee and Co., 1832).

239. Shannon Robinson, "The Legacy of John Quincy Adams," *www.helium.com/items/645228-Colonial-Early-American?page=2*.

240. "John Quincy Adams," *http://www.en.metapedia.org/wiki/John_Quincy_Adams*.

241. Ralph Keyes, *Euphemania: Our Love Affair with Euphemisms* (New York: Hachette Digital, Inc, 2010), 117.

242. Nagel, 309.

243. Caroline Sutton, *How Did They Do That* (New York: HarperCollins, 1985), "How Did John Quincy Adams Meet the Press?"

244. Published in *The Quincy Patriot*, September 25, 1841.

245. "L'Amistad Case (1839–1840)" by the Reverend Joshua Leavitt, *American History Told by Contemporaries ... National Expansion, 1783–1845*, Albert Bushnell Hart, ed. (New York: Macmillian, 1910), 626–629.

246. Ibid.

247. Ibid.

248. Ibid.

249. This is a quote from the movie

Amistad (1997) and certainly sounds like Adams, who was portrayed by Anthony Hopkins in the award-winning film.

250. Clifton Johnson, "The Amistad Case and Its Consequences in U.S. History" *Journal of the New Haven Colony Historical Society* vol. 36, no. 2 (Spring 1990). New Haven Colony Historical Society.

251. JQA Diary, Spring 1841.

252. *The Amistad Case — The Arguments of John Quincy Adams*, February 24, 1841 and March 1, 1841 (Originally published in 1841 by S.W. Benedict).

253. "The Amistad Case," *http://www.npg.si.edu/col/amistad/*.

254. John Quincy Adams, *Amistad Argument* (White-fish, MT: Kessinger Publishing, 2004), 34.

255. Supreme Court of the United States, 40 U.S. 518, January 1841 Term.

256. Leavitt, 629.

257. Paul M. Bessel, "Presidents Article," *http://www.bessel.org/presmas.htm*.

258. John Quincy Adams and Freemasonry — Power of Prophecy: The..., *http://www.texemarrs.com/072001/john_quincy.htm*.

259. Ibid.

260. Each of these diary entries is included in Allan Nevins, ed., *The Diary of John Quincy Adams* or *Memoirs of John Quincy Adams, Taken from His diaries, 1794–1848*, Charles Francis Adams, ed., or both.

261. Letter from John Adams to his son, September 19, 1795, relating Washington's observation.

262. Letter to Martin Van Buren, January 23, 1838.

263. "Dead Presidents on Dead Presidents," *http://www.diplom.org/manus/Presidents/ratings/prez.html*.

264. Ibid.

265. Ibid.

266. Ibid.

267. Hecht, 490.

268. *The New York Times*, quoted in Leonard Falkner's *The President Who Wouldn't Retire: John Quincy Adams* (New York: Coward-McCann, 1967).

269. Bemis, 55.

270. "John Quincy Adams Knew Jihad," *FrontPage* Magazine, *http://archive.frontpagemag.com/readArticle.aspx?ARTID=11283*.

271. James Schouler, *Eighty Years of Union* (New York: Dodd, Mead & Company, 1903), 225.

272. "John Quincy Adams," *Encyclopedia Britannica* (1911).

273. *The New Federalist Newspaper*, Sept. 8, 1989, Oct. 13, 1989, May 15, 1995, and Aug. 24, 1998.

274. "John Quincy Adams Battles for the American System," *www.schillerinstitute.org/educ/hist/american_patriot_jqa.pdf*.

275. Bemis' *John Quincy Adams and the Foundation of American Foreign Policy* (Westport, CT: Greenwood-Heinemann Publishing, 1981), 123.

276. Philip Hone, *The Diary of Philip Hone, 1828–1851*, Bayard Tuckerman,

ed. (New York: Dodd, Mead & Co., 1889), *http://www.archive.org/stream/diaryofphiliphon02honeuoft/diaryofphiliphon02honeuoft_djvu.txt*.

277. Letter to Charles Bagot, January 22, 1827, *www.trivia-library.com/a/6th-us-president-john-quincy-adams*.

278. "Trivia on 6th U.S. President: John Quincy Adams," *http://www.trivia-library.com/a/6th-us-president-john-quincy-adams.htm*.

279. Bemis, *Adams and the Union*, 438.

280. Theodore Parker, *Historic Americans* (Boston: H.P. Fuller, 1870), *http://www.archive.org/stream/historicamerica00parkgoog/historicamerica00parkgoog_djvu.txt*.

281. Hecht, 430.

282. Alfred Steinberg, *The First Ten: The Founding Presidents and Their Administrations* (Garden City, NY: Doubleday, 1967), 246.

Seven. Jackson

1. Quoted by Kevin Baker, "The Temper Thing: How Bad Is It When Presidents Get Really Sore?" American Heritage Magazine vol. 51, no. 3 (May/June 2000).

2. Statement of Senator John F. Kennedy, Chairman, Special Committee on the Senate Reception Room, on the Senate Floor May 1, 1957.

3. Robert V. Remini, *Andrew Jackson and the Course of American Empire, 1767–1821* (New York: Harper & Row, 1977), 378 (Hereafter, *Empire*).

4. Augustus C. Buell, *History of Andrew Jackson: Pioneer, Patriot, Soldier, Politician, President*, Vol. 2 (New York: C. Scribner's Sons, 1904), 363.

5. "U.S. Presidents," *www.classroomhelp.com/Presidentsjackson.html*.

6. Marker L-11, NC 75 (South Main Street) at Rehobeth Road in Waxhaw, North Carolina.

7. "U.S. Presidents," *www.classroomhelp.com/Presidentsjackson.html*.

8. William Shepard Walsh, *Handy-Book of Literary Curiosities* (Philadelphia: J.B. Lippincott Co., 1892), 459.

9. "Jackson, Andrew," *http://ncpedia.org/biography/jackson-andrew*.

10. "Andrew Jackson," *http://americanhistory.si.edu/presidency/home.html*.

11. George Earlie Shankle, *American Nicknames; Their Origin and Significance* (New York: Wilson, 1955), 589.

12. "Sharp Knife and the Cherokee Nation," *www.everything2.com/title/Sharp+Knife+and+The+Cherokee+Nation*.

13. "Andrew Jackson," *www.gardenofpraise.com/ibdjack.htm*.

14. Harold I. Gullan, *First Fathers: the Men Who Inspired Our Presidents* (Hoboken, NJ: J: John Wiley & Sons. 2004) xii.

15. "Jackson's Military Career," *www.oppapers.com/essays/Jacksons-Military-Career*.

16. Ibid.

17. Ibid.

18. Ibid.

19. Thomas E. Watson, *The Life and Times of Andrew Jackson* (Thompson, GA: Jefferson Pub. 1912), 17.

20. Ibid.

21. Ibid.

22. Ibid.

23. Ibid., 18.

24. "Jackson, Andrew," *http://ncpedia.org/biography/jackson-andrew.*

25. "Andrew Jackson Biography," *www.focusdep.com/biographies/Andrew/Jackson.*

26. "Andrew Jackson," *www.virtualology.com/uspresidents/andrewjackson.org.*

27. "Andrew Jackson," *www.jpopwallpaper.info/622-andrew-jackson.html.*

28. "Stonewall Jackson Related to Andrew Jackson?" *http://www.genealogymagazine.com/stonjac.html.*

29. Ibid.

30. Cyrus Townsend Brady, *The True Andrew Jackson* (Philadelphia: Lippincott & Co., 1906), 136.

31. Marquis. James, *The Life of Andrew Jackson* (Indianapolis: Bobbs-Merrill, 1938), 17.

32. Remini, *Empire,* 32.

33. James Parton, *Life of Andrew Jackson,* Vol. I (New York: Mason Bros., 1860), 112. 14.

34. Parton, Vol. III, 598.

35. Matthew Warshauer, *Andrew Jackson and the Politics of Martial Law: Nationalism, Civil Liberties, and Partisanship* (Knoxville: University of Tennessee Press, 2007), 60.

36. Frederick Austin Ogg, *The Reign of Andrew Jackson: A Chronicle of the Frontier in Politics* (New Haven, CT: Yale University Press, 1919), 21, *http://www.gutenberg.org/ebooks/13009.*

37. "American President: Andrew Jackson — Family Life," *www.millercenter.org/president/jackson/essays/biography/7.*

38. "Inauguration of President Andrew Jackson, 1829," *www.inaugural.senate.gov/history/chronology/ajackson1829.cfm.*

39. "Andrew Jackson," *www.uthealthleader.org/.../2008/andrewjackson-1105.htm.*

40. "Division of Military History and Diplomacy, National Museum of American History" *www.americanhistory.si.edu/militaryhistory/collection/object.asp?ID=766.*

41. Andrew Burstein, *The Passions of Andrew Jackson* (New York: Knopf, 2003), 230.

42. Ibid.

43. "Andrew Jackson: Good, Evil and the Presidency," *www.pbs.org/kcet/andrewjackson/alife/wild_young_man.html.*

44. Ibid.

45. "Some Say 'Old Hickory' Deserves More Recognition in Salisbury," *http://www.salisburypost.com/News/031410-wineka-column-Andrew-Jackson.*

46. Hendrik Booraem, *Young Hickory: The Making of Andrew Jackson* (London: Taylor Trade Publishing, 2001).

47. Barney Sneiderman, *Warriors*

Seven: *Seven American Commanders, Seven Wars, and the Irony of Battle* (New York: Savas Beatie, 2006), 47.

48. Edward Eggleston, "Andrew Jackson," from *A First Book in American History* (New York: American Book Co., 1889), *http://www.mainlesson.com/display.php?author=eggleston&book=first&story=jackson&PHPSESSID=4c463e017ada34bae481444632719202.*

49. William L. O'Neill, "Old Slickery," *New York Times,* November 20, 2005, *http://www.nytimes.com/2005/11/20/books/review/20oneill.html?_r=2.*

50. "Trivia on U.S. President Andrew Jackson — Early Life," *www.trivia-library.com/b/u-s-president-andrew-jackson.*

51. Eulogy on the life and character of Gen. Andrew Jackson pronounced by the Hon. Levi Woodbury, in the Universalist church, Portsmouth, NH, July 2, 1845.

52. H.W. Brands, "People's Choice," *Smithsonian Magazine* (October, 2005): *http://www.smithsonianmag.com/history-archaeology/Peoples_Choice.html.*

53. "Jacksonian Democracy," *http://www.academicamerican.com/jeffersonjackson/topics/jacksoniandemocracy.html.*

54. Ibid.

55. Margaret Bassett, *Profiles & Portraits of American Presidents & Their Wives* (Freeport, ME: The Bond Wheelwright Company, 1969), 70.

56. H.W. Brands, *Andrew Jackson, His Life and Times* (Garden City, NY: Doubleday, 2005).

57. William Garrott Brown, *Andrew Jackson* (Boston: Houghton-Mifflin, 1900), chapter 1, 1.

58. William Cullen Bryant, *New York Evening Post,* March 1, 1837; William Cullen Bryant II, ed., *Power for Sanity: Selected Editorials of William Cullen Bryant, 1829–1861* (New York: Fordham University Press, 1994), 64.

59. David and Jeanne Heidler, *Jackson and the Quest for Empire* (Mechanicsburg, PA: Stackpole Books, 2003).

60. Ibid.

61. Brands, *Andrew Jackson, His Life and Times,* 72.

62. Albert Marrin, *Old Hickory: Andrew Jackson and the American People* (New York: Penguin, 2004), 40.

63. Gloria J. Browne-Marshall, "The Realities of Enslaved Female Africans in America" extracted from *Failing Our Black Children: Statutory Rape Laws, Moral Reform and the Hypocrisy of Denial,* 2002, *www.en.wikipedia.org/wiki/Female_slavery.*

64. Marrin, 40–41.

65. Browne-Marshall.

66. Patricia Brady, *A Being So Gentle: The Frontier Love Story of Rachel and Andrew Jackson* (New York: Palgrave Macmillan, 2011), 19.

67. Ibid., 24–26.

68. Ibid., 33.

69. Ibid., 34.

70. Ibid., 34–35.

71. Ibid.

72. Ibid.

73. James Parton quoted by Harriet

Taylor Upton, *Our Early Presidents, Their Wives and Children: From Washington to Jackson* (Boston: D. Lothrop, 1890), 347.

74. John Spencer Bassett, *The Life of Andrew Jackson* (Whitefish, MT: Kessinger Publishing, [1916] 2006), 16.

75. Paul F. Boller Jr., *Presidential Wives* (New York: Oxford University Press, 1998), 66.

76. Ibid., 67.

77. P. Brady, 36.

78. Boller, 67.

79. Ibid.

80. P. Brady, 47.

81. Ibid., 48–49.

82. P. Brady, 52–53.

83. P. Brady, 47.

84. P. Brady, 47.

85. Boller, 67–68.

86. Boller, 68.

87. Boller, 68.

88. "History and Genealogy of the Robards Family (1910)," *www.worldvitalrecords.com/...ix=ia_historygenealogy00roba.*

89. " Rachel and Andrew Jackson: A Love Story," *www.wnpt.org/productions/rachel/rachel_mardiv/index.html.*

90. Boller, 68.

91. "American Presidents Blog: The Jackson Marriage," *www.american-presidents.org/2007/01/jackson-marriage.html.*

92. Boller, 69.

93. Cyrus Townsend Brady, 174–176.

94. Charles Hammond, *Cincinnati Gazette,* 1828.

95. "American History: Tragedy Hits as Jackson Prepares for His Inauguration," *www.manythings.org/voa/history/56.html.*

96. Boller, 65.

97. Robert P. Watson, *American First Ladies* Vol. 1 (Pasadena, CA: Salem Press, 2006), 57.

98. Rae Lindsay, *The Presidents' First Ladies* (Englewood Cliffs, NJ: R & R Writers/Agents, Inc., 2001), 137.

99. Samuel Gordon Heiskell, *Andrew Jackson and Early Tennessee History* (Nashville, TN: Ambrose Print Co., 1918).

100. Brands, *Andrew Jackson, His Life and Times,* 43.

101. Ibid., 148.

102. Marrin, 58.

103. Cyrus Townsend Brady, 366.

104. Letter to Ellen Hanson, March 25, 1835, from Peter Roberts, "Andrew Jackson" page in "God and Country" section of "Science Resources on the Net," November 2005, *http://www.geocities.com/peterroberts.geo/Relig-Politics/AJackson.html.*

105. Andrew Jackson, *Correspondence of Andrew Jackson,* John Spencer Bassett, ed. (Washington, DC: Carnegie Institution of Washington, 1926–35), 5: 194.

106. *Protestants and Other Americans United for Separation of Church and State* Vols. 27–29 (Washington, DC: Americans United for Separation of Church and State, 1974), 151.

107. "The Religion of Andrew Jackson, 7th U.S. President," *www.adherents.com/people/pj/Andrew_Jackson.html.*

108. *Correspondence of Andrew Jackson* vol. 5, issue 371 (Washington, DC: Carnegie Institution of Washington, 1931), 333.

109. Remini, *Course of American Democracy,* 356.

110. "Harvard and Andrew Jackson, Almost Chosen People," *http://almostchosenpeople.wordpress.com/2012/02/24/harvard-and-andrew-jackson/.*

111. Ibid.

112. Parton, I: 61.

113. William O. Foss, *Childhoods of the American Presidents* (Jefferson NC: McFarland, 2005), 39.

114. Meacham, 15.

115. Ibid.

116. Ibid., 20.

117. Andrew Jackson Fought at Least 13 Duels," *www.buzzfeed.com/stuartb2/andrew-jackson-fought-at-least.*

118. "The Jackson/Dickinson Duel," *http://www.visitlogancounty.net/default.aspx?cityID=2&subsection=false&itemid=39.* A poltroon is an abject or contemptible coward.

119. Ibid.

120. "Andrew Jackson Kills Charles Dickinson in Duel" *http://www.history.com/this-day-in-history/andrew-jackson-kills-charles-dickinson-in-duel.*

121. "The Jackson/Dickinson Duel," *http://www.visitlogancounty.net/default.aspx?cityID=2&subsection=false&itemid=39.*

122. Ibid.

123. Ibid.

124. Ibid.

125. Meacham, 26.

126. Ibid.

127. Ibid.

128. "The History of Caroline County, Maryland, from Its Beginning," *www.mdgenweb.org/caroline/Duel.htm.*

129. Today ... on This Date," *Martinsville Daily,* December 10, 2010, *www.martinsvilledaily.com/archive/index.php/t-1254-p-2.html.*

130. Sneiderman, 51.

131. Ibid.

132. Ibid., 52.

133. Ibid.

134. Ibid.

135. "Slavery," *www.thehermitage.com/mansion-grounds/farm/slavery.*

136. "Gardens and Grounds," *www.thehermitage.com/mansion-grounds/gardens-grounds/places.*

137. Ibid.

138. Ibid.

139. "Archaeology at the Hermitage," *www.thehermitage.com/visit/school-programs/sm_files/.*

140. "Gardens and Grounds," *www.thehermitage.com/mansion-grounds/gardens-grounds/places.*

141. "The Hermitage," *www.wordiq.com/definition/The_Hermitage.*

142. Ibid.

143. "Travel Images from Nostalgiaville," *www.travel.nostalgiaville.com/Tennessee/Davidson/37076.*

144. "Gardens and Grounds," *www.thehermitage.com/mansion-grounds/gardens-grounds/places.*

145. Ibid.

146. "The Hermitage — Home of President Andrew Jackson," *www.nashville.about.com/od/nashvillesfamous/a/hermitage.htm.*

147. Ibid.

148. "Jumping into Jacksonian Democracy — Sam Patch," *www.very-clever.com/information/xbddkxjxtxhxuxie.*

149. "A Green Horse Is a Natural, Economical and Eco-Friendly Way," *www.agreenhorse.blogspot.com/2009/12/horses-of-military-war.html.*

150. Ibid.

151. Ibid.

152. Michael A. Genovese, *Encyclopedia of the American Presidency* (New York: Infobase Publishing, 2010), 390.

153. "Andrew Jackson and Horse Racing in Early America," *http://william-1-wunder.suite101.com/andrew-jackson-and-horse-racing-in-early-america-a402970#ixzz1pUJKXajI.*

154. Marquis James, 98.

155. Buell, Vol. II, 65–66.

156. Ibid.

157. Ibid., 66.

158. Ibid., 96.

159. Ibid., 155–157.

160. Ibid.

161. Ibid.

162. Ibid.

163. Ibid.

164. Benton Rain Patterson, *The Generals: Andrew Jackson, Sir Edward Pakenham, and the Road to the Battle of New Orleans* (New York: New York University Press, 2005), 41–42.

165. Ibid.

166. Christopher G. Marquis, "Andrew Jackson: Lawyer, Judge and Legislator," *American Heritage Magazine* (April, 2006).

167. "Andrew Jackson," *www.virtualology.com/andrewjackson.*

168. Ibid.

169. Brands, *Andrew Jackson, His Life and Times,* 104–105.

170. Ibid.

171. Ibid.

172. Ibid., 106–109.

173. Ibid.

174. Ibid.

175. "Battle of Horseshoe Bend — Jackson DefeatsRed Stick Creeks," *http://www.burnpit.us/2010/03/battle-horseshoe-bend-%E2%80%93-jackson-defeats-red-stick-creeks.*

176. Ibid.

177. "Fort Mims," *www.creekwarandwarof1812.com/FortMims.html.*

178. "LongleyPix — Our Texas Family, Doris Ross Brock Johnston's," *www.ourtexasfamily.com/Longley-Patterson-Campbell/Longley.*

179. Ibid.

180. Thomas Edward Watson, *The Life and Times of Andrew Jackson* (Thomson, GA: Press of the Jeffersonian Pub. Co., 1912), 184–185.

181. "Horseshoe Bend, Battle of (1814)," *www.what-when-how.com/the-american-economy/horseshoe-bend.*

182. Sam Houston, *The Autobiography of Sam Houston,* Donald Day and Harry Herbert Ullom, eds. (Norman: University of Oklahoma Press, 1954), 12.

183. "Horseshoe Bend, Battle of (1814)," *www.what-when-how.com/the-american-economy/horseshoe-bend.*

184. "Cherokee, North Carolina," *http://www.cherokee-nc.com/;* The White House, Eastern Band of Cherokee Nation, Library of Congress, National Archives and Records Administration.

185. Ibid.

186. "The December Defense: Andrew Jackson Arrives at New Orleans," *www.galafilm.com/1812/e/events/orl_amer_dec.html.*

187. "Governor William Charles Cole Claiborne of Louisiana, 1812," *www.la-cemeteries.com/Governors/Claiborne/Claiborne,Willliam.*

188. Remini, *The Battle of New Orleans* (New York: Penguin, 1999), chapter two.

189. Ibid.

190. Zachariah Frederick Smith, *The Battle of New Orleans* (Louisville, KY: J.P. Morton, 1904), 26.

191. Ibid.

192. Ibid., 70.

193. Ibid., 77–78.

194. Ibid., 78.

195. Ibid., 80.

196. Ibid., 81.

197. Ibid., 81.

198. Letter to Robert Hays, January 8, 1815, Burke Davis, *Old Hickory: A Life of Andrew Jackson* (New York: Dial Press, 1977), 150.

199. Burke Davis, *Old Hickory: A Life of Andrew Jack-son* (New York: Dial Press, 1977), 150.

200. "The Unerring Hand of Providence, *www.americanclarion.com/2012/01/08/the-unerring-hand.* Andrew Jackson commented to Major Dravezac on his confidence before the Battle.

201. Smith, 125–126.

202. " Battle of New Orleans," *www.absoluteastronomy.com/topics/Battle_of_New_Orleans.*

203. "Louisiana Museum, The Battle of New Orleans: A Sergeant's Account," *www.corvalliscommunitypages.com/.../neworleansbattleall.htm.*

204. Ibid.

205. "Martial Law in New Orleans," *www.scribd.com/doc/29421399/4/Martial-Law-in-New-Orleans.*

206. "Proclamation to the People of Louisiana," from Mobile, September 21, 1814, *The East Tennessee Historical Society's Publications,* vols. 22–24 (Knoxville: East Tennessee Historical Society, 1950), 41.

207. Caleb Crain, "Bad Precedent: Andrew Jackson's Attack on Habeas Corpus," *The New Yorker,* January 29, 2007, 3.

208. January 8, 1815 address to his officers, Charles Gayarré, *History of Louisiana* (New York: William J. Widdleton, 1867), 614–615.

209. "Seminole Wars," *New Georgia Encyclopedia, www.georgiaencyclopedia.org/nge/Article.jsp?id=h-842.*

210. Brent Richards Weisman, *Unconquered People* (Gainesville, FL: University Press of Florida, 1999), 22–24.

211. "Florida History," *www.flheritage.com/kids/history.cfm.*

212. "First Seminole War," *www.us-history.com/pages/h1129.html.*

213. "The Seminole Wars," *www.flheritage.com/facts/history/seminole/wars.cfm.*

214. Ibid.

215. Ibid.

216. John Missall and Mary Lou Missall, *The Seminole Wars: America's Longest Indian Conflict* (Gainesville: University Press of Florida. 2004), 16–20.

217. Ibid., 20.

218. Ibid., 24–27.

219. Ibid.

220. "The Negro Fort, Story Panel 1 of 8 — Part One, Early Years — Rebellion," *www.johnhorse.com/trail/01/b/12.htm.*

221. Adam Wasserman, "The Negro Fort Massacre," *A People's History of Florida 1513–1876: How Africans, Seminoles, Women, and Lower Class Whites Shaped the Sunshine State,* 4th ed. (CreateSpace, 2009), 168.

222. Ibid.

223. Ibid.

224. Missall, 28–32.

225. "Seminole Wars," *www.absoluteastronomy.com/topics/Seminole_Wars.*

226. Missall, 36–37.

227. United States. Congress, *Documents, legislative and executive of the Congress of the United States,* Part 5, Volume 1 (New York: Gales and Seaton, 1832), 704–705.

228. Missall, 39–40.

229. James Parton, "The First Seminole War," *www.historycentral.com/documents/FSeminole.html.*

230. Missall, 33.

231. Ibid., 40–41.

232. Ibid., 41–42.

233. Ibid., 42.

234. "Not the Same Old Hickory: The Contested Legacy of Andrew Jackson," *www.findarticles.com/p/articles/mi_m1568/is_1_36/ai_n6006332.*

235. Missall, 46–47.

236. Ibid., 45.

237. Ibid., 44, 47–50.

238. Sean Wilentz, *The Rise of American Democracy: Jefferson to Lincoln* (New York: Norton, 2005); "History of the United States Democratic Party," *www.xtimeline.com/evt/view.aspx?id=187598.*

239. "History of the United States Democratic Party," *en.wikipedia.org/wiki/History_of_the_United_States_Democratic_Party#cite_note-4.*

240. John Ashworth, "Agrarians" & "Aristocrats": Party Political Ideology in the United States, 1837–1846* (Cambridge: Swift, 1983), *www.conservapedia.com/Democrat.*

241. William MacDonald, *Jacksonian Democracy, 1829–1837* (New York: Harper & Bros., 1906), 42.

242. Alexander Keyssar, *The Right to Vote: The Contested History of Democracy in the United States,* 2d. ed. (New York: Basic Books, 2009), 29.

243. David S. Heidler and Jeanne T. Heidler, *Manifest Destiny* (Westport, CT: Greenwood Press, 2003).

244. Moisei Ostrogorski, *Democracy and the Party System in the United States* (Charleston, SC: Nabu Press, [1910] 2010).

245. Forrest McDonald, *States' Rights and the Union: Imperium in Imperio, 1776–1876* (Lawrence: University of Kansas Press, 2002) 97–120.

246. Louis Hartz, *Economic Policy and Democratic Thought: Pennsylvania, 1776–1860* (Chcago: Quadrangle Paperbacks, 1968).

247. Bray Hammond, *Banks and Politics in America: From the Revolution to the Civil War* (Princeton, NJ: Princeton University Press, 1957).

248. Brands, *Andrew Jackson, His Life and Times,* 478.

249. "Henry Clay," *www.juntosociety.com/othercandidates/henryclay.html.*

250. Hal Morris, "The American Whig Party (1834–1856)," *www.odur.let.rug.nl/~usa/E/uswhig/whigsxx.htm.*

251. William Kloss and Diane K. Skvarla, *United States Senate Catalogue of Fine Art* (Washington, DC: Government Printing Office), 196.

252. Ibid.

253. Letter to John Coffee, October 25, 1823; Remini, *Life of Andrew Jackson,* 144 [in the Senate it is not on record that he ever spoke at all].

254. "Andrew Jackson," *www.xtimeline.com/evt/view.aspx?id=236644.*

255. Parton, *Jackson,* II: 339–41.

256. Letter to John Coffee, October 25, 1823, Parton, *Jackson,* I: 227.

257. Hal Morris, "A Brief Biography of Andrew Jackson 1767–1845," *www.jmisc.net/jksn-bio.htm.*

258. "Rachel and Andrew Jackson: A Love Story," *www.wnpt.org/productions/rachel/timeline/1791_1811.html.*

259. Parton, I: xviii.

260. Paul F. Boller Jr., *Presidential Campaigns: From George Washington to George W. Bush* (New York: Oxford University Press, 2004), chapter ten, 33.

261. Ibid., 33–35.

262. "Literature," *http://xroads.virginia.edu/~ma97/price/lit.htm.*

263. Boller, *Presidential Campaigns,* 36–37.

264. "Presidential Elections 1824," *www.historycentral.com/elections/1824.html.*

265. Remini, *Empire,* 30.

266. Ilona Nickels, "Party Animals: The Donkey and the Elephant," *http://www.ilonanickels.com/CC_partyanimals.html.*

267. Thomas Jefferson, *The Writings of Thomas Jefferson,* 10 vols. Paul Leicester Ford, ed (New York: G.P. Putnam's Sons, 1892–99), 10: 331, Federal Edition (Hereafter, FE).

268. "Presidential Campaigns: A Cartoon History, 1789–1976," *www.indiana.edu/~libsalc/cartoons/1828.html.*

269. Ibid.

270. Political Extracts from the Leading Adams Papers, *The Massachusetts Journal* (Boston: 1828) as quoted in Norma Basch, "Marriage, Morals, and Politics in the 1828 Election," *The Journal of American History* vol. 80, no. 3 (December, 1993): 905.

271. Remini, *The Election of Andrew Jackson* (Philadelphia: Lippincott, 1963), 153.

272. Isaac Hill, "John Quincy Adams, Pimp!" *www.elektratig.blogspot.com/2009/09/john-quincy-adams-pimp.*

273. "The 1828 Presidential Election Had Plenty of Mudslinging," *www.tricities.com/news/2008/mar/02/-tri_2008_03_02_0057.*

274. "Andrew Jackson Biography," *www.profiles.incredible-people.com/andrew-jackson.*

275. Boller, *Presidential Campaigns,* chapter eleven.

276. Richard Kenin and Justin Wintle, *The Dictionary of Biographical Quotations of British and American Subjects* (New York: Walter de Gruyter, 1978).

277. "The Jackson Years," *www.onlineartdirector.com/kbsamples2/polihist/jackson.htm.*

278. "Andrew Jackson, Our First Independent Populist President," *www.independentpopulist.blogspot.com/2007/11/franklin-d.html.*

279. Brands, *Andrew Jackson, His Life and Times,* 534.

280. "Andrew Jackson Biography," *www.thomaslegion.net/president_andrew_jackson.html.*

281. State of the Union Address, December 8, 1829; J.D. Richardson, ed. *Compilation of the Messages and Papers of the Presidents,* vol. II (Washington, DC: Government Printing Office, 1908) (Hereafter, *Compilation*).

282. "United States Presidential Elections: 1832," *www.unitedstatespresidentialelection.blogspot.com/.../1832.html.*

283. "U.S. Senate: Martin Van Buren, 8th Vice President," *www.senate.gov/.../common/generic/VP_Martin_VanBuren.htm.*

284. "The Inauguration of President Andrew Jackson, 1829," *www.eyewitnesstohistory.com/jacksoninauguration.htm.*

285. Margaret Bayard Smith, *The First Forty Years of Washington Society* (New York: Scribner, 1906), 290–291.

286. "Andrew Jackson — Policy, War, Election," *www.presidentprofiles.com/Washington-Johnson/Jackson-Andrew.html.*

287. "Andrew Jackson's The Hermitage," *www.cr.nps.gov/nr/travel/presidents/jackson_hermitage.html.*

288. Daniel Feller, "King Andrew and the Bank," *Humanities* vol. 29, no. 1 (January/ February, 2008).

289. Cyrus Townsend Brady, 315.

290. "Andrew Jackson," *www.whitehouse.gov/about/presidents/andrewjackson.*

291. John Spencer Bassett, 437.

292. "Andrew Jackson: 7th President, 1829–1837," *The Independent,* Jan. 17, 2009, www.independent.co.uk/news/presidents/andrew-jackson-1391112.html.

293. "Andrew Jackson Biography," www.profiles.incredible-people.com/andrew-jackson.

294. Harold C. Syrett, *Andrew Jackson: His Contri-bution to the American Tradition* (Indianapolis: Bobbs-Merrill, 1953), 28.

295. "Andrew Jackson : Good, Evil and the Presidency," www.pbs.org/kcet/andrewjackson/glossary.

296. Remini, *The Life of Andrew Jackson*, 207–208.

297. "The Story of Peggy Eaton," www.foundersofamerica.org/making.html.

298. Ibid.

299. "Andrew Jackson: The Petticoat Affair," www.historynet.com/andrew-jackson-the-petticoat-affair.

300. Richard B. Latner, "Andrew Jackson," *The Presidents: A Reference History*, Henry Graff, ed. (New York: Scribner's, 1996).

301. "Andrew Jackson: Part One — Peggy Eaton," http://www.buyandhold.com/bh/en/education/history/2002/a_jackson_pt_1.html.

302. Ibid.

303. "The Petticoat Affair — The Scandalous Story of Margaret Eaton," www.scandalouswoman.blogspot.com/2009/01/petticoat-affair.

304. "Andrew Jackson: Peggy Eaton Affair," www.fns.d211.org/.../Andrew%20Jackson%20Peggy%20Eaton%20...; Ameican President — Andrew Jackson," http://www.americanpresident.org/KoTrain/Courses/AJA/AJA_Presidential_Moments.htm.

305. "Margaret Eaton," www.tennesseeencyclopedia.net/entry.php?rec=423.

306. "The Petticoat Affair — The Scandalous Story of Margaret Eaton," www.scandalouswoman.blogspot.com/2009/01/petticoat-affair.

307. Ibid.

308. Benjamin Perley Poore, *Perley's Reminiscences of Sixty Years in the National Metropolis*, 2 vols. (New York: A.W. Stolp, 1886), I: 120–125.

309. Ibid.

310. Ibid.

311. Kirsten E. Wood, "'One Woman So Dangerous to Public Morals': Gender and Power in the Eaton Affair," *Journal of the Early Republic* vol. 17, no. 2 (Summer, 1997): 237–275.

312. "The Peggy Eaton Affair," www.academicamerican.com/jeffersonjackson/topics/eaton.htm.

313. "Jacksonian Democracy," www.academicamerican.com/jeffersonjackson/topics/eaton.htm.

314. "Indian Removal," www.pbs.org/wgbh/aia/part4/4p2959.html.

315. "Society in Abolitionists," www.shmoop.com/abolition/society.html.

316. "Indian Removal Act of 1830," www.studyworld.com/indian_removal_act_of_1830.htm.

317. James Atkins Shackford, *David Crockett: The Man and the Legend* (Chapel Hill: University of North Carolina Press, 1994), 133.

318. "Indian Removal," www.pbs.org/wgbh/aia/part4/4p2959.html.

319. Ibid.

320. "Indian Removal Act of 1830," www.studyworld.com/indian_removal_act_of_1830.htm.

321. August 30, 1830, Choctaw Chiefs, Record Group 46, E 326, National Archives.

322. State of the Union Message to Congress, December 8, 1830, J.D. Richardson, *Compilation*.

323. March 28, 1835, Marquis James, *The Life of Andrew Jackson* (Indianapolis: Bobbs-Merrill, 1938), 539–540.

324. Ibid.

325. President Andrew Jackson's Case for the Removal Act, First Annual Message to Congress, December 8, 1829, J.D. Richardson, *Compilation*.

326. "Samuel Austin Worcester — About North Georgia," www.ngeorgia.com/ang/Samuel_Austin_Worcester.

327. "New Georgia Encyclopedia: Worcester v. Georgia (1832)" www.georgiaencyclopedia.org/nge/Article.jsp?id=h-2720.

328. "Treaty of New Echota, 1835 Treaty of New Echota History," www.thomaslegion.net/treatyofnewechota.html.

329. State of the Union Message to Congress, December 1833, J.D. Richardson, *Compilation*.

330. "The Trail of Tears — Cherokee Indians Forcibly Removed," www.ngeorgia.com/history/nghisttt.html.

331. Ibid.

332. "Martin Van Buren — National Museum of American History," www.americanhistory.si.edu/presidency/timeline/pres_era/.

333. "Black Hawk War," www.u-s-history.com/pages/h336.html.

334. Ibid.

335. "Black Hawk War of 1832," www.lincoln.lib.niu.edu/blackhawk.

336. Ibid.

337. State of the Union Address, December 8, 1829, J.D. Richardson, *Compilation*.

338. "Election of 1832," www.u-s-history.com/pages/h332.html.

339. "Presidential Elections 1832," www.historycentral.com/elections/1832.html.

340. "The Political Graveyard: Election of 1832," http://politicalgraveyard.com/offices/pres-vp-1832.html.

341. "Second Bank of the United States," www.u-s-history.com/pages/h256.html.

342. Bray Hammond, 84–85.

343. Christopher Westley, "The Debate Over Money Manipulations: A Short History," *Intercollegiate Review* 45, 1–2 (Fall 2010): 3–11.

344. Bray Hammond, 96–97.

345. "Second Bank of the United States," www.u-s-history.com/pages/h256.html.

346. Andrew Jackson and David Maydole Matteson, *Correspondence of Andrew Jackson*, Vol. 4 (Washington, DC: Carnegie institution of Washington, 1935), 446.

347. "Andrew Jackson and the Central Bank," www.democraticunderground.com/discuss/duboard.php?az.

348. Nicholas Biddle, *The Correspondence of Nicholas Biddle*, ed. Reginald C. McGrane (New York: Houghton Mifflin, 1919) p. 222.

349. Robert Firth, *The Enemy Within* (eBookIt.com, 2011), 68. Said at a meeting where the president was discussing the Bank Renewal Bill with a delegation of wildcat bankers in 1832.

350. Second State of the Union Message, December 8, 1830, J.D. Richardson, *Compilation*.

351. Martin Van Buren, *The Autobiography of Martin Van Buren*, John Clement Fitzpatrick, ed., published in *Annual Report of the American Historical Association for the Year 1918* vol. II (Washington, DC: Smithsonian Institute, 1920), chapter XLIII: 625.

352. "Andrew Jackson," www.truthcontrol.com/node/andrew-jackson.

353. United States Congress, *Register of Debates in Congress* (Washington, DC: Gales & Seaton, 1837), 2176. Response to Biddle's threat, 1832.

354. Veto message, July 10, 1832, Richardson, *Compilation*, 1139–1154.

355. First Session of the 22nd Congress, July 11, 1832, Richard N. Current, *Daniel Webster and the Rise of National Conservatism* (Boston: Little, Brown and Company, 1955), 77.

356. Letter to Martin Van Buren, January 3, 1834, Remini, *The Life of Andrew Jackson*, 272.

357. Misunderstood Precedent: Andrew Jackson and the Real Case," www.thefreelibrary.com/Misunderstood+precedent%3a+Andrew.

358. Protest message, April 15, 1834, Richardson, *Compilation*, III: 3.

359. "U.S. Senate: Art & History Home, Historical Minutes, 1801," www.senate.gov/.../minute/Senate_Censures_President.htm.

360. "Andrew Jackson Biography," www.profiles.incredible-people.com/andrew-jackson.

361. "South Carolina Exposition and Protest of 1832. Supreme Court of the United States: Andrew Jackson." www.public-domain-content.com/encyclopedia/US_Supreme.

362. Glyndon G. Van Deusen, *The Jacksonian Era, 1828–1848* (New York: Waveland Press, 1959), 44.

363. Parton, *Jackson*, III: 283.

364. Letter to Joel Poinsett, December 2, 1832, Andrew Jackson, *The Statesmanship of Andrew Jackson as Told in His Writings and Speeches*, Francis Newton Thorpe, ed. (New York: Tandy-Thomas Co., 1909), 19.

365. Proclamation attacks the South Carolina Convention that passed the nullification ordinance, December 10, 1832, Richardson, *Compilation*, II: 640–656.

366. Proclamation, December 19, 1832, Jackson warns the people of South Carolina to obey the laws, Syrett, 36.

367. Buell, *History of Jackson*, II: 243.

368. Ibid.

369. "An Ordinance to Dissolve the Union between the State of South Car-

olina," *www.teachingushistory.org/lessons/Ordinance.htm*.

370. Special message to Congress, January 16, 1833, Richardson, *Compilation*, V: 626–653.

371. Letter to James Hamilton, son of Alexander Hamilton, February 23, 1833. Jackson offers his view of the underlying political motives behind the nullification controversy, Gilder Lehrman, document number: GLC 5176.

372. Letter to Andrew I, Crawford, May 1, 1833, Marion Mills Miller, *Great Debates in American History: State Rights (1798–1861); Slavery (1858–1861)* (New York: Current Literature Pub. Co., 1913), 5: 333.

373. James W. Clarke *American Assassins: The Darker Side of Politics* (Princeton, NJ: Princeton University Press, 1982).

374. Ibid.

375. Ibid.

376. Ibid.

377. Meacham, 298–299.

378. Ibid.

379. Ibid., 254.

380. Letter to Captain John Donelson III, September 3, 1821, Burke Davis, 177.

381. David M Kennedy and Bailey Cohen. *The American Pageant*, 13th ed. (Boston: Houghton Mifflin Company, 2006), 256–265.

382. "Andrew Jackson," *www.scribd.com/doc/48431079/ANDREW-JACKSON*.

383. Ibid.

384. "Andrew Jackson: Good, Evil & The Presidency," *www.pbs.org/kcet/andrewjackson/edu/foreignaffairs.html*.

385. Sixth annual message to Congress, December 1, 1834, J.D. Richardson, *Compilation*.

386. "A Life in Brief — Andrew Jackson," *www.scribd.com/doc/14245074*.

387. Farewell Address, March 4, 1837, J.D. Richardson, *Compilation*.

388. Ibid.

389. "The Health of the President: Andrew Jackson," *http://www.healthguidance.org/entry/8908/1/The-Health-Of-The-President-Andrew-Jackson.html*.

390. Thomas Hart Benton, *Thirty Years View*, 2 vols. (Westport, CT: Greenwood, [1866] 1968), I: 735.

391. "The Health of the President: Andrew Jackson," *http://www.healthguidance.org/entry/8908/1/The-Health-Of-The-President-Andrew-Jackson.html*

392. "Preservation," *www.thehermitage.com/mansion-grounds/mansion/preservation*.

393. "Andrew Jackson," *www.u-s-history.com/pages/h154.html*.

394. "American President: Andrew," *www.millercenter.org/president/jackson*.

395. Remini, *Life of Jackson*, 9.

396. "The Health of the President: Andrew Jackson," *http://www.healthguidance.org/entry/8908/1/The-Health-Of-The-President-Andrew-Jackson.html*.

397. Parton, *Jackson*, I, 667.

398. "The Health of the President: Andrew Jackson," *http://www.healthguidance.org/entry/8908/1/The-Health-Of-The-President-Andrew-Jackson.html*.

399. Lu Ann Paletta and Fred L Worth, *The World Almanac of Presidential Facts* (New York: World Almanac Books, 1988).

400. "America's Least Healthy Presidents: 6. Andrew Jackson," *www.fitnessmagazine.com/workout/real-plans/stay-fit/*.

401. Letter to Amos Kendall, April 26, 1844, *www.gilderlehrman.org/.../el8749dd-210f-4fc5-943a-50711911420*.

402. "America's Least Healthy Presidents: 6. Andrew Jackson," *www.fitnessmagazine.com/workout/real-plans/stay-fit/*.

403. Statement made during his final illness, June 1, 1845, *The Life of Andrew Jackson*, 356.

404. Comment on his deathbed, Henry Thomas and Dana Lee Thomas, *50 Great Americans: Their Inspiring Lives and Achievements* (New York: Doubleday, 1948), 114.

405. Remini, *Jackson*, 355.

406. Ibid.

407. Ibid., 356.

408. Ibid., 523.

409. Ibid., 84.

410. "Andrew Jackson (1767 — 1845)," *www.findagrave.com/cgi-bin/fg.cgi?GRid=534&page=gr*.

411. Ibid.

412. Letter to James Duncan Elliott, March 27, 1845, Parton, *The Life of Andrew Jackson*, III: 666.

413. "Andrew Jackson's Firsts and Related Media," *www.history.com/videos/andrew-jacksons-firsts*; Richard Lederer, *Presidential Trivia: The Feats, Fates, Families, Foibles, and Firsts of Our American Presidents* (Layton, UT: Gibbs Smith, 2007).

414. Refers to an 1845 photograph by Matthew Brady, *The Gallery of Illustrious Americans* (1850).

415. "Andrew Jackson," *www.multilingualarchive.com/ma/enwiki/en/Andrew_Jackson*.

416. Ibid.

417. "Andrew Jackson Filmography," *www.imdb.com/title/tt0046204*.

418. "Andrew Jackson's Firsts and Related Media," *www.history.com/videos/andrew-jacksons-firsts*.

419. "What Were Andrew Jackson's Views on Slavery?" *www.answers.yahoo.com/question/index?qid=20080718125535AAMS9HQ*.

420. "Slavery," *www.thehermitage.com/mansion-grounds/farm/slavery*.

421. "Review of Brady, A Being So Gentle," *http://jacksonianamerica.com/2011/08/29/review-of-brady-a-being-so-gentle-the-frontier-love-story-of-rachel-and-andrew-jackson/*.

422. "Abolition," *www.countriesquest.com/.../jacksonian.../abolition.htm*.

423. "Andrew Jackson and the Indian Removal Act," *http://www.historynet.com/andrew-jackson-and-the-indian-removal-act.htm*.

424. Ibid.

425. Christina Berry, "Andrew Jackson — The Worst President the Cherokee Ever Met," *http://www.allthingscherokee.com/articles_culture_events_020201*.

426. Cherokee Indian Removal, 1838–39, Letter to his children, December 11, 1890, John Ehle, *Trail of Tears: The Rise and Fall of the Cherokee Nation* (New York: Random House Digital, 2011), 393–394.

427. Robert V. Remini in *The Legacy of Andrew Jackson: Essays on Democracy, Indian Removal and Slavery* (Baton Rouge: Louisiana State University Press, 1990).

428. Ibid.

429. Carl Byker, "The Two Andrew Jacksons," *Los Angeles Times*, December 12, 2007.

430. Meade Minnigerode, *Presidential Years, 1787–1860* (New York: G.P Putnam's Sons, 1928).

431. J.C. Fitzpatrick, ed., *Autobiography of Martin Van Buren* (Washington, DC: American Historical Society, 1920), 312.

432. Jackson Day Address, January 8, 1936, Franklin D. Roosevelt, *The Public Papers and Addresses of Franklin D. Roosevelt* (New York: Random House, 1938), 40.

433. Hand, "Dead Presidents on Dead Presidents," *www.python.net/crew/manus/Presidents/ratings/prez.html*.

434. Arthur M. Schlesinger Jr., *The Age of Jackson* (Boston: Little, Brown, 1945).

435. Editorial writer, *Portland Daily Advertiser*, August 9, 1832.

436. United States Congress, Thomas Hart Benton, *Abridgment of the Debates of Congress, from 1789 to 1856: Dec. 7, 1835-March 3, 1839* (New York: D. Appleton, 1860), 101.

437. Matthew L. Davis, *Memoirs of Aaron Burr, Complete* (Middlesex, England: Echo Library, 2007), 573.

438. Burstein, *The Passions of Andrew Jackson*.

439. Ibid.

440. John Caldwell Calhoun, *Speeches of John C. Calhoun: Delivered in the Congress of the United States from 1811 to the Present Time* (New York: Harper & Bros., 1843), 136.

441. Alfred Steinberg, *The First Ten*. 265.

442. Davy Crockett, *A Narrative of the Life of David Crockett, of the State of Tennessee, Written by Himself* (Philadelphia: Cary and Hart, 1834), 159–160.

443. Eulogy delivered at Philadelphia, June 26, 1845. James Washington Sheahan, *The Life of Stephen A. Douglas* (New York: Harper, 1860), 69.

444. January 1, 1844, Robert W. Johannsen, *Stephen A. Douglas* (New York: Oxford University Press, 1973).

445. A political enemy of Jackson and a vice presidential candidate in 1824. Henry Adams, ed. *The Writings of Albert Gallatin*, 3 vols. (New York: Peter Smith, [1879] 1943).

446. Richard Hofstadter, *The American Political Tradition and the Men Who Made It* (New York: Knopf, 1948).

447. First president of Texas, Quotation comes from the "Life of Sam Houston" at Sam Houston Memorial Museum. He served under Andrew Jackson in the campaign against the Creek Indians, allies of the British. After the war, Jackson was instrumental in securing Houston a position as an Indian agent to the Cherokee. Houston named one of his sons after Jackson.

448. Vachel Lindsay, "The Statue of Old Andrew Jackson." Written while America was in the midst of the war with Germany, August, 1918.

449. Chief Justice of the Supreme Court commenting on Jackson's inaugural party, Parton, *Jackson*, 169–170.

450. "Eulogy — on the Death of Andrew Jackson," John William Ward, *Andrew Jackson: A Symbol for an Age* (New York: Oxford University Press, 1962), 28.

451. Marquis James, *Andrew Jackson — Portrait of a President* (Indianapolis: Bobbs-Merrill Co., 1937).

452. Vernon Parrington, *Main Currents in American Thought* (Norman: University of Oklahoma Press, 1987).

453. J.R. Poinsett, "Oration on the Life and Character of Andrew Jackson," July 4, 1845, Alexander Rayden, "Setting The Record Straight: Remini, Jackson and the Spoils System," March 13, 2006, "Amazon.com: Customer Reviews: *Andrew Jackson: The Course of American Democracy, 1833–1845*," *www.amazon.com/Andrew-Jackson-American.../0801859131*

454. G.V. Deusen, *William Henry Seward* (Boston: Little, Brown, 1967).

455. Peter Temin, *The Jacksonian Economy* (New York: W.W. Norton, 1969), 16–17.

456. Alexis de Tocqueville, *Democracy in America* (New York: Penguin Books, 2003).

Eight. Van Buren

1. Davy Crockett, The Life of Martin Van Buren (New York: Nafis and Cornish, [1835] 1845), preface, v.

2. Ibid., iv.

3. "NYC Marks 400th Anniversary of Dutch Arrival," *www.msnbc.msn.com/id/30310941/ns/travel-destination*.

4. "Martin Van Buren," *http://www.americanpresidents.org/presidents/president.asp?PresidentNumber=8*.

5. Edward L. Widmer, *Martin Van Buren* (New York: Macmillan, 2005), 4.

6. "Abraham Van Buren (1737–1817)," *www.findagrave.com/cgi-bin/fg.cgi?page=gr&GRid=6659682*.

7. "Martin Van Buren: Life Before the Presidency," *www.millercenter.org/president/vanburen/essays/biography/2*.

8. William Lyon Mackenzie, *The Life and Times of Martin Van Buren: The Correspondence of His Friends, Family and Pupils* (Boston: Cooke, 1846), 18–19.

9. Ibid., 19.

10. Ibid.

11. "Reading 1: The Life of Martin Van Buren," *www.nps.gov/nr/twhp/wwwlps/lessons/39vanburen/39facts1.htm*.

12. "Walter Gilbert Genealogy: Cornelis Maessen Van Buren," *www.otal.umd.edu/~walt/gen/htmfile/1922.htm*; Harriett C. Waite Van Buren Peckman, *Van Buren Family; History of Cornelis Maessen Van Buren* (Brooklyn, NY: Higginson Book Co., 1913).

13. Peckman, 32.

14. The select surnames website. *www.selectsurnames2.com/vanburen.html*.

15. Widmer, 19.

16. Rosemarie Ostler, *Slinging Mud: Rude Nicknames, Scurrilous Slogans, and Insulting Slang from Two Centuries of American Politics* (New York: Penguin, 2011).

17. Ibid.

18. " Martin Van Buren with Ham," *www.presidentialham.com/u-s-presidents/martin-van-buren-with-ham*.

19. Lewis W. Koenig, "The Rise of the Little Magician," *American Heritage Magazine* vol. 13, issue 4 (1962), *http://www.americanheritage.com/content/rise-little-magician*.

20. "Political Parties," *www.testas.cas.okstate.edu/cas2/Politicalscience/templates*.

21. Denis Tilden Lynch, *An Epoch and a Man: Martin Van Buren and His Times* (New York: H. Liveright, 1929), 454.

22. "Brief Biographies of Jackson Era Characters (V)," *http://www.jmisc.net/BIOG-V.htm*.

23. "U.S. Senate: Martin Van Buren, 8th Vice President," *www.senate.gov/artandhistory/history/common/generic/VP_Martin_VanBuren*.

24. James A. Hamilton, *Reminiscences of James A. Hamilton; or, Men and Events, at Home and Abroad, During Three Quarters of a Century* (New York: C. Scribner & Co., 1869), 42.

25. Jeffrey Rogers Hummel, "Martin Van Buren: The American Gladstone" *Mises Daily*, June 24, 2006, *www.mises.org/daily/2201/Martin-Van-Buren-The-American-Gladstone*.

26. Rosemarie Ostler, *Slinging Mud: Rude Nicknames, Scurrilous Slogans, and Insulting Slang from Two Centuries of American Politics* (New York: Penguin, 2011). "Martin Van Buren (Democrat) vs. Four Whig Candidates."

27. Ibid.

28. Hummel.

29. "Official Announcement of the Death of Martin Van Buren," Mayor's Office New York, July 26, 1862, *New York Times* on July 28, 1862.

30. Glyndon G. Van Deusen, *The Jacksonian Era* (New York: Waveland Press, 1959), 114.

31. "Reading 1: The Life of Martin Van Buren," *www.nps.gov/nr/twhp/wwwlps/lessons/39vanburen/39facts1.htm*.

32. Ibid.

33. "Hannah Van Buren," *www.womenhistoryblog.com*.

34. "Hannah Van Buren Biography," *www.firstladies.org/biographies/firstladies.aspx?biography=8*.

35. Ibid.

36. "Hannah Van Buren," *www.leben.us/volume-05-volume-5-issue-3/289-hannah-van-buren*.

37. Lynch, 170.

38. "Angelica Singleton Van Buren," *www.southcarolinastatemuseum.org/women/VanBuren.html*.

39. Betty Boyd Caroli, *First Ladies* (New York: Oxford University Press, 2003), 41.

40. Major L. Wilson, *Presidency of Martin Van Buren* (Lawrence: University Press of Kansas, 1984), 59.

41. Margaret Byrd Bassett, *Profiles & Portraits of American Presidents & Their Wives* (Freeport, ME: B. Wheelwright Co.; distributed by Grosset & Dunlap, New York, 1969), 86.

42. Caroline Evensen Lazo, *Martin Van Buren* (Minneapolis: Lerner, 2005), 56.

43. "The Religion of Martin Van Buren, 8th U.S. President," *www.adherents.com/people/pv/Martin_Van_Buren.html*.

44. Inaugural Address, March 4, 1837, J.D. Richardson, *Compilation*, vol. III: 401ff.

45. "The Religion of Martin Van Buren, 8th U.S. President," *www.adherents.com/people/pv/Martin_Van_Buren.html*.

46. Mark O. Hatfield, with the Senate Historical Office, *Vice Presidents of the United States, 1789–1993* (Washington, DC: U.S. Government Printing Office, 1997), 105–106.

47. Ibid.

48. William M. Holland, *The Life and Political Opinions of Martin Van Buren, Vice President of the United States* (Hartford: Belknap & Hamersley, 1836), 15–16, 26.

49. J.C. Fitzpatrick, ed., *Autobiography of Martin Van Buren* (Washington, DC: American Historical Society, 1920), 11.

50. Ibid., 11–12.

51. "Martin Van Buren (1782–1862), Eighth President," *www.blog.royaltrigger.com/2010/12/martin-van-buren-1782–1862*.

52. "Portrait and Biographical Album," *www.usgennet.org/usa/ne/topic/resources/.../pbal/.../balc0009.htm*.

53. "Martin Van Buren: Life Before the Presidency," *www.millercenter.org/president/vanburen/essays/biography/2*.

54. "Martin Van Buren (1782–1862), Eighth President," *www.blog.royaltrigger.com/2010/12/martin-van-buren-1782–1862*.

55. " Martin Van Buren — Hall of North and South Americans," *www.famousamericans.net/martinvanburen*.

56. Mackenzie, 23.

57. Ibid., 21.

58. Irvin Haas, *Historic Homes of the American Presidents* (Mineola, NY: Courier Dover Publications, 1991), 39–46.

59. Ibid.

60. Ibid.

61. Ibid.

62. Ibid.

63. National Park Service, "Historic Furnishings Report for 'Lindenwald' Martin Van Buren National Historic Site," http://www.nps.gov/mava/historyculture/upload/Historic-Furnshings-Plan.PDF.

64. "Martin Van Buren National Historic Site," www.usa-c2c.com/mvbreview.html.

65. Brian Jay Jones, Washington Irving: An American Original (New York: Arcade Publishing, 2008), 311.

66. "Kinderhook Connection History," www.kinderhookconnection.com/history.htm.

67. "White House Pets— The Early Years: New York Cats," www.examiner.com/article/white-house-pets-the-early-years.

68. "Favorite Foods of the U.S. Presidents," www.makeandtakes.com/favorite-foods-of-the-u-s-presidents.

69. 8 Martin Van Buren — US Presidents Challenge," www.librarything.com/topic/51486.

70. "Martin Van Buren — His Early Years," http://www.home.earthlink.net/~gjhweb3/mvb-earl.htm.

71. "Martin Van Buren — Presidential Years," www.home.earthlink.net/~gjhweb2/mvb-pres.htm.

72. Hummel, www.mises.org/daily/2201.

73. Ibid.

74. Ibid.

75. Ibid.

76. "Martin Van Buren, by Ted Widmer," http://www.bomcclub.com/biography-books/leaders-&-royalty-books/martin-van-buren-by-ted-widmer-1002995580.html.

77. Ibid.

78. "Martin Van Buren Facts," http://www.encyclopedia.com/topic/Martin_Van_Buren.aspx.

79. Autobiography, 101.

80. Gerald Leonard, "Review of Albrecht Koschnik, "Let A Common Interest Bind Us Together": Associations, Partisanship, and Culture in Philadelphia, 1775–1840, Journal of the Early Republic vol. 28, no. 3 (Fall 2008): 494–497.

81. Ibid.

82. Ibid.

83. Messages and Papers of the Presidents: Andrew Jackson and Martin Van Buren (Rockville, MD: Wildside Press LLC, 2009), 1528.

84. "Reading 1: The Life of Martin Van Buren," www.nps.gov/nr/twhp/wwwlps/lessons/39vanburen/39facts1.htm.

85. "The Presidents of the United States, 1789–1914," http://en.wikisource.org/wiki/The_Presidents_of_the_United_States,_1789-1914/Martin_Van_Buren.

86. "Reading 1: The Life of Martin Van Buren," www.nps.gov/nr/twhp/wwwlps/lessons/39vanburen/39facts1.htm.

87. "Martin Van Buren — His Early Years," www.home.earthlink.net/~gjhweb3/mvb-earl.htm.

88. Lazo, 26–27, 30.

89. "U.S. Senate: Martin Van Buren, 8th Vice President," www.senate.gov/artandhistory/history/common/generic/VP_Martin_VanBuren.

90. James C. Welling, "Martin Van Buren," The Presidents of the Untied States, 1789–1914, James Grant Wilson and John Fiske, eds. (New York: C. Scribner's Sons, 1914), http://www.virtualology.com/.../usvicepresidents/MARTINVANBUREN.ORG/.

91. Holland, 127–129.

92. Ibid., 171.

93. "Albany Regency," www.u-s-history.com/pages/h224.html.

94. Thurlow Weed Barnes, Life of Thurlow Weed vol. II (Boston: Houghton, Mifflin, and Co., 1884), 36.

95. "Albany Regency," http://www.econlib.org/library/YPDBooks/Lalor/llCy32.html.

96. "U.S. Senate: Martin Van Buren, 8th Vice President," www.senate.gov/artandhistory/history/common/generic/VP_Martin_VanBuren.

97. Ibid.

98. Ibid.

99. "Martin Van Buren," www.tutorgig.info/ed/Martin_Van_Buren.

100. "Van Buren and the Erie Canal," www.americantalleyrand.com/?p=60.

101. "1825 Erie Canal Opened," www.historycentral.com/Ant/Eirie.html.

102. "U.S. Senate: Martin Van Buren, 8th Vice President," www.senate.gov/artandhistory/history/common/generic/VP_Martin_VanBuren.

103. Ibid.

104. Ibid.

105. Ibid.

106. "Martin Van Buren — His Early Years," http://www.home.earthlink.net/~gjhweb3/mvb-earl.htm.

107. Koenig.

108. BreAnn Rumsch, Martin Van Buren (Edina, MN: ABDO, 2009), 18.

109. Robin Santos Doak, Martin Van Buren (Minneapolis: Compass Point Books, 2003), 28.

110. "Martin Van Buren (1782–1862), Eighth President," www.blog.royaltrigger.com/2010/12/martin-van-buren-1782-1862.

111. Koenig.

112. "Andrew Jackson," www.virtualology.com/andrewjackson.

113. Ibid.

114. John W. Burgess, The Middle Period, 1817–1858 (New York: Scribner's' Sons, 1910), chapter II.

115. "U.S. Senate: John C. Calhoun," http://www.senate.gov/artandhistory/art/artifact/Painting_32_00009.htm#bio.

116. Ibid.

117. Ibid.

118. Ibid.

119. Ibid.

120. "Martin Van Buren," www.u-s-history.com/pages/h156.html.

121. Ibid.

122. "Martin Van Buren," www.en.wikipedia.org/wiki/Martin_van_buren.

123. "Martin Van Buren," www.u-s-history.com/pages/h156.html.

124. "U.S. Senate: John C. Calhoun," http://www.senate.gov/artandhistory/art/artifact/Painting_32_00009.htm#bio.

125. "U.S. Senate: Martin Van Buren, 8th Vice President," www.senate.gov/artandhistory/history/common/generic/VP_Martin_VanBuren.

126. Ibid.

127. "Martin Van Buren — His Early Years," www.home.earthlink.net/~gjhweb3/mvb-earl.htm.

128. "U.S. Senate: Martin Van Buren, 8th Vice President," www.senate.gov/artandhistory/history/common/generic/VP_Martin_VanBuren.

129. "Hail to the Chief: United States Presidents— History and Trivia," http://www.francesfarmersrevenge.com/stuff/archive/oldnews2/prez.htm.

130. "U.S. Senate: Martin Van Buren, 8th Vice President," www.senate.gov/artandhistory/history/common/generic/VP_Martin_VanBuren.

131. "Election of 1836," www.u-s-history.com/pages/h350.html.

132. Richardson, Compilations, 25.

133. "Election of 1836," www.u-s-history.com/pages/h350.html.

134. Inaugural address, March 4, 1837, Richardson, Compilation.

135. "Martin Van Buren," www.library.kiwix.org:4202/A/Martin_Van_Buren.html.

136. "Martin Van Buren," www.kinderhookconnection.com/history4.htm.

137. "Martin Van Buren," www.encyclopedia.com/topic/Martin_Van_Buren.aspx.

138. "The Presidency of Andrew Jackson," http://www.digitalhistory.uh.edu/database/article_display.cfm?HHID=637.

139. "The 1828 Campaign of Andrew Jackson," www.ed2.neh.gov/curriculum-unit/1828-campaign-andrew-jackson.

140. John V. Denson, Reassessing the Presidency: The Rise of the Executive State and the Decline of Freedom (Auburn, AL: Ludwig von Mises Institute, 2001), 170.

141. "Presidential Review: Andrew Jackson, Martin Van Buren," www.thestudentreview.co.uk/2011/08/presidential-review.

142. "U.S. Senate: Martin Van Buren, 8th Vice President," www.senate.gov/artandhistory/history/common/generic/VP_Martin_VanBuren.

143. Ibid.

144. Widmer, ii.

145. Autobiography, 106.

146. Ibid.

147. Ibid.

148. Robert Bolt, "Richard M. Johnson," Louisville Journal, July 17, 1840.

149. Jessica M. Lepler, "1837: Anatomy of a Panic," Brandeis University, 2008, 284–285.

150. Ibid.

151. Robert V. Remini and Wesley K. Clark, Andrew Jackson (New York: Macmillan, 2009), 180.

152. "Andrew Jackson," www.knowsouthernhistory.net/Biographies/Andrew_Jackson.

153. Ibid.

154. "Panic of 1837: Van Buren's First Challenge," www.u-s-history.com/pages/h967.html.

155. William Osborn Stoddard, *Andrew Jackson and Martin Van Buren* (New York: F.A. Stokes, 1887), 300.

156. "President Jackson's Effect on Capitalism," *http://www.ehow.com/info_8572846_president-jacksons-effect-capitalism.html.*

157. "Panic of 1837," *www.encyclopedia.com/doc/1G2-3406400695.html.*

158. Widmer, 101.

159. Edward M Shephard, *Life of Martin Van Buren* (Boston: Houghton, Mifflin Company. 1888), 389.

160. "Martin Van Ruin: Specie Circular," *www.presidentsbythebook.blogspot.com/2009/09/martin-van-ruin.*

161. "Martin Van Buren," *http://www.vanburen-mi.org/History/Martin_Van_Buren.html.*

162. Shephard, 310.

163. "Maritn Van Buren," *http://www.vanburen-mi.org/History/Martin_Van_Buren.html.*

164. "Panic of 1837," *http://www.presidentprofiles.com/Washington-Johnson/Martin-Van-Buren-Panic-of-1837.html#ixzz1q2VxhytX.*

165. Lepler, 287.

166. Lepler, 290.

167. Ibid.

168. Ibid.

169. Ibid.

170. Lepler, 291.

171. "Martin Van Buren — Setting the Stage," *www.nps.gov/nr/twhp/wwwlps/lessons/39vanburen/39setting.htm.*

172. Special session of Congress, September 4, 1837, Richardson, *Compilations*, III: 324–346.

173. "Panic of 1837," *http://www.presidentprofiles.com/Washington-Johnson/Martin-Van-Buren-Panic-of-1837.html#ixzz1q2VxhytX.*

174. Special Session of the Senate and House of Representatives, September 4, 1837, Richardson, *Compilations*, Vol. III, Part II, "Martin Van Buren," 338–339.

175. Third State of the Union Message to Congress, January 1, 1840, Richardson, *Compilations*, "Martin Van Buren," 342; John T. Woolley and Gerhard Peters, *The American Presidency Project*, http://www.presidency.ucsb.edu/.

176. Major L. Wilson, *The Presidency of Martin Van Buren* (Lawrence: University Press of Kansas, 1984), 100, 145.

177. Hummel.

178. Shephard, 346.

179. "Martin Van Buren and the Panic of 1837," *www.another-opinion.blogspot.com/2009/03/martin-van-buren.*

180. William Seale, "About the Gold Spoon Oration," *http://www.whitehousehistory.org/whha_publications/publications_documents/whitehousehistory_10.pdf.*

181. Ibid.

182. Ibid.

183. Ibid.

184. Ibid.

185. Doak, 23.

186. Ron Field, *The Seminole Wars, 1818–58* (New York: Osprey, 2009), 8.

187. "Martin Van Buren," *www.nnp.org/nni/Publications/Dutch-American/buren.html.*

188. Field, 12–13.

189. "Martin Van Buren — His Presidential Years," *www.home.earthlink.net/~gjhweb2/mvb-pres.htm.*

190. "Martin Van Buren," .

191. Amy H. Sturgis, *The Trail of Tears and Indian Removal* (Westport, CT: Greenwood, 2007), 39–40.

192. First State of the Union Message, December 5, 1837, Richardson, *Compilations*.

193. Second State of the Union Message, December 3, 1838, Richardson, *Compilations*, "Martin Van Buren," 275.

194. "Story of President Martin Van Buren," *www.surftofind.com/8.*

195. "Martin Van Buren — His Presidential Years," *www.home.earthlink.net/~gjhweb2/mvb-pres.htm.*

196. Ibid.

197. "The Amistad Case," *http://www.archives.gov/education/lessons/amistad/.*

198. *New York Morning Herald*, a strongly anti-abolitionist newspaper, September 2, 1837, "Lewis Tappan and the Amistad Case," *www.law.umkc.edu/faculty/projects/ftrials/trialheroes/Tappan.*

199. "Martin Van Buren — His Presidential Years," *http://home.earthlink.net/~gjhweb2/mvb-pres.htm.*

200. "Lewis Tappan and the Amistad Case," *http://law.umkc.edu/faculty/projects/ftrials/trialheroes/Tappanessay.html.*

201. Ibid.

202. January 2, 1840, *Argument of John Quincy Adams Before the Supreme Court of the United States in the Case of the United States, Appellants, vs. Cinque, and Other Africans* (New York: S.W. Benedict, 1841), 77.

203. "Martin Van Buren," *http://www.infoplease.com/ipa/A0760593.html#ixzz1q7kJcVJy.*

204. "Martin Van Buren — Presidential Years," *http://home.earthlink.net/~gjhweb2/mvb-pres.htm.*

205. Ibid.

206. "Foreign affairs— Martin Van Buren," *http://www.presidentprofiles.com/Washington-Johnson/Martin-Van-Buren-Foreign-affairs.html.*

207. Inaugural Address, Richardson, *Compilations*, "Martin Van Buren," 11.

208. State of the Union Message to Congress, December 5, 1840, Richardson, *Compilations*, "Martin Van Buren," 120.

209. "The Caroline Affair," *http://www.u-s-history.com/pages/h296.html.*

210. Ibid.

211. Ibid.

212. Message to Congress on January 8, 1838, Richardson, *Compilations*, "Martin Van Buren," 120.

213. "Foreign affairs— Martin Van Buren," *http://www.presidentprofiles.com/Washington-Johnson/Martin-Van-Buren-Foreign-affairs.html.*

214. "The Border Dispute and the 'Aroostook War,'" *www.upperstjohn.com/history/northeastborder.htm.*

215. "Foreign affairs— Martin Van Buren," *http://www.presidentprofiles.com/Washington-Johnson/Martin-Van-Buren-Foreign-affairs.html.*

216. Ibid.

217. Ibid.

218. "Webster-Ashburton Treaty," *www.people.maine.com/publius/almanac/encycweb/htm/websashb.htm.*

219. "Campaign of 1840," *http://www.presidentprofiles.com/Washington-Johnson/Martin-Van-Buren-Campaign-of-1840.html#ixzz1q82up6wz.*

220. Ibid.

221. Gleaves Whitney, ed., *American Presidents: Fare-well Messages to the Nation, 1796–2001* (Lanham, MD: Lexington Books, 2003), 99.

222. "James Knox Polk," *www.millercenter.org/president/polk/essays/biography/print.*

223. O.C. Gardiner, *The Great Issue; Or, The Three Presidential Candidates, Being a Brief Historical Sketch of the Free Soil Question in the United States, from the Congresses of 1774 and '87 to the Present Time* (New York: W.C. Bryant, 1848), *http://www.archive.org/stream/greatissueorthr00gardgoog/greatissueorthr00gardgoog_djvu.txt.*

224. Widmer, 154.

225. Ibid.

226. "Portrait and Biographical Album of Isabella County, Michigan," *www.quod.lib.umich.edu/cgi/t/text/text-idx?c=micounty;cc=mi.*

227. "Lindenwald," *www.factbites.com/topics/Lindenwald.*

228. "Martin Van Buren: Life After the Presidency," *www.millercenter.org/president/vanburen/essays/biography/6.*

229. Manus Hand, Dead Presidents on Dead Presidents, www.diplom.org/manus/Presidents/ratings/prez.htm.

230. Bumgarner, John R. *The Health of the Presidents: The 41 United States Presidents through 1993 from a Physician's Point of View* (Jefferson, NC: McFarland, 1994), 57.

231. Ibid.

232. Ibid.

233. Acknowledgment made during his last illness, Stephen Abbott Northrup, *A Cloud of Wisdom* (Portland, OR: American Heritage Ministries, 1987), 228.

234. Bumgarner, 57.

235. John Niven, *Martin Van Buren: The Romantic Age of American Politics* (New York: Oxford University Press, 1983), 611.

236. Bumgarner, 57.

237. Edward Augustus Collier, *A History of Old Kinderhook from Aboriginal Days to the Present Time* (New York: G. Putnam's, 1914), 424.

238. Ibid., 426.

239. Ibid., 424.

240. Ibid., 425.

241. Grolier Educational Staff, *New Book of Knowledge 1992* (Danbury, CT: Grolier Inc., 1992), 452.

242. "Witchcraft & the Suspicion of Witchery," *http://www.scribd.com/doc/49520877/Witchcraft-the-Suspicion-of-Witchery.*

243. Ibid.

244. *The American Presidents* (Danbury, CT: Grolier Inc., 1992), 56.

245. Widmer, 140.

246. Gore Vidal, *Burr: A Novel* (New York: Random House Digital, 2011), chapter three.

247. Lyndon Orr, "Famous Affinities of History," *www.authorama.com/famous-affinities-of-history-ii-3.html*.

248. Fitzwilliam Byrdsall, *The History of the Loco-Foco, or Equal Rights Party: Its Movements, Conventions and Proceedings* (New York: Clement & Packard, 1842), I: 13–16.

249. Ibid., 21–23.

250. Boller, *Presidential Anecdotes* (New York: Oxford University Press, 1996), 89.

251. Lynch, 299.

252. Ibid.

253. Joseph Fielding Smith, *Church History and Modern Revelation* (Salt Lake City: Deseret, 1946–49), 167–173.

254. "United States vs. Mormon Church," *www.biblebelievers.net/Cults/Mormonism/FortyYears/kjcfor*.

255. Edgar Allan Poe, *Complete Works of Edgar Allen Poe: Tales* (New York: Fred De Fau & Co., 1902), 256–269.

256. Comment on England under her new queen, 18-year-old Victoria, December 1837. He is quoting a line from poet Thomas Gray's poem "The Bard." Elizabeth Frost-Knappman, *The World Almanac of Presidential Quotations:Quotations from America's Presidents* (Pharos Books, 1993), "Youth" entry; Thomas Gray, Robert Carruthers, *Select Poems of Thomas Gray* (New York: Harper & Brothers, 1876), 61.

257. *The Autobiography of Martin Van Buren* (Washington, DC: Government Printing Office, 1920).

258. Comment 1803, quoted in Bob Dole, *Great Presidential Wit* (New York: Scribner, 2001), 214.

259. Ted Goodman, ed., *The Forbes Book of Business Quotes* (New York: Black Dog & Leventhal, 2006), 597.

260. Martin Van Buren, *Inquiry into the Origin and Course of Political Parties in the United States* (New York: Hurd & Houghton, 1867), 290.

261. November 1824. Comment to Roger Skinner, who led the Bucktails while Van Buren was in Washington, after the Regency suffered a crushing defeat by DeWitt Clinton, Denis Tilden Lynch, 271.

262. Niven, 367.

263. Niven, 293.

264. Shepard, 284.

265. Edward M. Shepard, "Martin Van Buren," *American Statesmen*, 32 vols. John K. Mokse Jr., ed. (Boston: Houghton Mifflin, 1899), vol. XVIII: 449.

266. John Quincy Adams, *Memoirs of John Quincy Adams*, Volume 9 (Philadelphia: J.B. Lippincott, 1876).

267. Elizabeth Jewell, "Martin Van Buren," *U.S. Presidents Factbook* (Boston: Random House Reference, 2005), 2.

268. Jon Meacham, *American Lion: Andrew Jackson in the White House* (New York: Random House, 2008), 308.

269. 1847, Hand, "Dead Presidents," *www.diplom.org/manus/Presidents/ratings/prez.htm*.

270. July 24, 1862, Meacham, 348.

271. Tribute to Van Buren's ability to bring together disparate political groups, 1827, Richard Kenin and Justin Wintle, *The Dictionary of Biographical Quotations of British and American Subjects* (New York: Walter de Gruyter, 1978), Van Buren, Martin entry.

272. A close acquaintance quoted by Jabez D. Hammond, *The History of Political Parties of New York, 1842* (Buffalo: Phinney & Co., 1850).

273. *New York Courier* and *Enquirer*, quoted in Holmes Alexander, *The American Talleyrand: The Career and Contemporaries of Martin Van Buren, Eight President* (Kent: Russell & Russell, 1968).

274. Kenin and Wintle, "Martin Van Buren," *United States Magazine & Democratic Review* (July 1844).

275. *Twenty Years of Congress from Lincoln to Garfield*, 2 vols. (Norwich, CT: Henry Bill Publishing Co., 1884–1886).

276. Davy Crockett, *Life of Martin Van Buren*, 29.

277. Philip Hone, *The Diary of Philip Hone, 1828–1851* (New York: Dodd, Mead, and company, 1889), I: 163.

278. Hummel.

279. Pierre Munro Irving, *The Life and Letters of Washington Irving* (New York: Putnam, 1862), vol. 2: 482.

280. Koenig.

281. Jerome Mushkat and Joseph G. Rayback, *Martin Van Buren: Law, Politics, and the Shaping of Republican Ideology* (DeKalb: Northern Illinois University Press, 1997), 143.

282. Schlesinger, 263.

Nine. W. H. Harrison

1. Paul F. Boller Jr., Presidential Campaigns from George Washington to George W. Bush (New York: Oxford University Press, 2004), 73.

2. Robert Vincent Remini, *Henry Clay: Statesman for the Union* (New York: W.W. Norton & Company, 1993), 562.

3. "Berkeley Plantation," *www.berkeleyplantation.com/*.

4. Irvin Haas, *Historic Homes of the American Presidents* (Mineola, NY: Courier Dover Publications, 1991), 47–50.

5. Graham Woodlief, "History of the First Thanksgiving," *www.berkeleyplantation.com/history_new_world.html*.

6. Ibid.

7. Ibid.

8. Ibid.

9. Ibid.

10. "James River Plantations: Berkeley," *www.jamesriverplantations.org/Berkeley.html*.

11. "Berkeley Plantation," *www.rkeleyplantation.com/*.

12. Jari Villanueva, "The Story of Taps," *www.berkeleyplantation.com/history_taps.html*.

13. "The Drummer Boy Returns," *www.berkeleyplantation.com/history_drummer_boy.htm*.

14. "William Harrison Biography," *www.zacharytaylorbiography.com/william-harrison-presidency.php*.

15. "William Henry Harrison: Life Before the Presidency," *www.millercenter.org/president/harrison/essays/biography/2*.

16. National Park Service, "Signers of the Declaration (Benjamin Harrison)," *http://www.nps.gov/history/history/online_books/declaration/bio.htm*.

17. Declaration of Independence, U.S. Constitution, *http://www.constitutionfacts.com/?section=aboutUs&page=siteMap.cfm&404=true*.

18. Charles William Calhoun, *Benjamin Harrison* (New York: Macmillan, 2005), 7.

19. William Judson Hampton, *Our Presidents and Their Mothers* (New York: Cornhill Publishing Company, 1922), 74.

20. Ibid.

21. Ibid.

22. Bruce Roberts and Elizabeth Kedash, Plantation Homes of the James River (Chapel Hill: University of North Carolina Press, 1990), 32.

23. "Benjamin Harrison," *www.dsdi1776.com/Signers/Benjamin%20Harrison.html*.

24. "Biography of William Henry Harrison," *www.millercenter.org/president/harrison/essays/biography/print*.

25. Roberts and Kedash, 32.

26. "William Henry Harrison—Historic Clothing," *http://histclo.com/pres/Ind19/harrisonw.html*.

27. "William Henry Harrison with Ham," *www.presidentialham.com/.../william-henry-harrison-with-ham*; William A. DeGregorio, *The Complete Book of U.S. Presidents*, 7th ed. (Fort Lee, NJ: Barricade Books, 2009).

28. Isaac Rand Jackson, *The Life of William Henry Harrison: The People's Candidate for the Presidency* (Philadelphia: C. Sherman & Co., Printers, 1840), 56.

29. Freeman Cleaves, *Old Tippecanoe: William Henry Harrison and His Times* (New York: Scribner's Sons, 1939), 257.

30. Jackson, 56.

31. Letter to James Heaton, November 27, 1830, *William Henry Harrison Papers and Documents, 1791–1864* (Manuscript and Visual Collections Department, William Henry Smith Memorial Library, Indiana Historical Society, Indianapolis) (Hereafter, *Papers*).

32. Cleaves, 22.

33. Ibid.

34. Ibid.

35. Nancy Beck Young, "Anna Tuthill Symmes Harrison," *American First Ladies: Their Lives and Their Legacies* Lewis L. Gould, ed. (New York: Routledge, 2001), 61.

36. Ibid., 58.

37. Ibid., 59.

38. Bob Dole, *Great Presidential Wit: I Wish I Was in This Book* (New York: Scribner, 2001), 222.

39. Young, 59.

40. Ibid.

41. "William Henry Harrison: Life Before the Presidency," *www.millercenter.org/president/harrison/essays/biography/2.*

42. Paul F. Boller Jr., *Presidential Wives: An Anecdotal History* (New York: Oxford University Press, 1998), 77.

43. "Anna Symmes Harrison," *www.northbendohio.org/AnnaSymmesHarrison.html.*

44. "Anna Harrison Biography," *www.firstladies.org/biographies/firstladies.aspx?biography=9.*

45. Boller, *Presidential Wives*, 75.

46. "Anna Symmes Harrison," *www.northbendohio.org/AnnaSymmesHarrison.html.*

47. "Anna Harrison Biography," *www.firstladies.org/biographies/firstladies.aspx?biography=9.*

48. "Anna Symmes Harrison," *www.northbendohio.org/AnnaSymmesHarrison.html.*

49. Ibid.

50. Boller, *Presidential Wives*, 77.

51. "Anna Harrison Biography," *www.firstladies.org/biographies/firstladies.aspx?biography=9.*

52. William DeGregorio, *The Complete Book of Presidents* (New York: Grammercy Books, 2001), 138–139.

53. Ibid.

54. Ibid.

55. Ibid.

56. Ibid.

57. Ibid.

58. Ibid.

59. "William Henry Harrison: Life Before the Presidency," *www.millercenter.org/president/harrison/essays/biography/2.*

60. Franklin Steiner, *The Religious Beliefs of Our Presidents: From Washington to F.D.R.* (Amherst, NY: Prometheus Books, 1936).

61. Edmund Fuller and David E. Green, *God in the White House: The Faiths of American Presidents* (New York: Crown, 1968), 236. Fuller pronounced Harrison "one of the least religious presidents."

62. Franklin Morris, *The Christian Life & Character of the Civil Institution of the United States* (Philadelphia: George W. Childs, 1864), 605–606.

63. Inaugural Address, March 4, 1841, Davis Newton Lott, ed., *The Inaugural Addresses of American Presidents* (New York: Holt, Rinehart & Winston, 1961), 86.

64. Ibid.

65. Jackson, 3.

66. Ibid; Jackson attributed Harrison's abandoning the study of medicine was decided by his patriotic wish to defend his country from the "barbarous hostilities of the Indians on our northwest frontier."

67. "Grouseland," *www.grouselandfoundation.org/.*

68. Ibid.

69. Robert Martin Owens, *Mr. Jefferson's Hammer: William Henry Harrison and the Origins of American Indian Policy* (Norman: University of Oklahoma Press, 2007), 56–57.

70. Ibid., 57–58.

71. Samuel Jones Burr, *The Life and Times of William Henry Harrison* (New York: R.W. Pomeroy, 1840), 257.

72. Ibid., 258.

73. Ibid.

74. "John Scott Harrison (1804–1878)," *www.findagrave.com/...GRid=8624&pt=John%20Scott%20Harrison.*

75. Jackson, 12.

76. Elizabeth Jewell, *U.S. Presidents Factbook* (New York: Random House, 2006), 76.

77. Gail Collins, *William Henry Harrison: The American Presidents Series: The 9th President, 1841* (New York: Macmillan, 2012), 45–46.

78. Ibid.

79. Richard Day and William Hopper, *Vincennes* (Charleston, SC: Arcadia Publishing, 1998), 21.

80. Samuel P. Huntington, *The Soldier and the State: The Theory and Politics of Civil-Military Relations* (Cambridge, MA: Harvard University Press, 1981), 158.

81. Jackson, 46.

82. William Harrison Mace, *A Primary History: Stories of Heroism* (Chicago: Rand, McNally & Company, 1900), 284–288.

83. Cleaves, 120.

84. "Henry Clay's Remarks in House and Senate," *www.docstoc.com/docs/10268068.*

85. Mace, 283.

86. William Henry Harrison, *A Discourse on the Aborigines of the Ohio Valley* (Chicago: Fergus Printing Company, 1883), 27, 57.

87. John Sugden, *Tecumseh: A Life* (New York: Macmillian, 1999), 79–81.

88. Edward Eggleston and L. E. Seelye, *Tecumseh and the Shawnee Prophet* (New York: Dodd, Mead and Co., 1878), 182–186.

89. Robin Santos Doak, *William Henry Harrison* (Minneapolis: Compass Point Books, 2003), 23.

90. Burr, 222–226.

91. Ibid., 226–230.

92. Benjamin Drake, *Life of Tecumseh and of His Brother the Prophet* (Cincinnati: BiblioBazaar, 1841), 133.

93. William Henry Harrison, Inaugural Address, Thursday, March 4, 1841, *Inaugural Addresses of the Presidents of the United States* (Washington, DC: Government Printing Office, 1989), *www.bartleby.com/124/pres26.html.*

94. Ibid.

95. Letter to John Brown Dillon, October 12, 1838, *Papers.*

96. Norma Lois Peterson, *The Presidencies of William Henry Harrison & John Tyler* (Lawrence: University Press of Kansas, 1989), 138.

97. "The Story of President William Henry Harrison," *http://surftofind.com/9.*

98. Ralph Waldo Emerson, A. W. Plumstead, and Harrison Hayford, *The Journals and Miscellaneous Notebooks of Ralph Waldo Emerson* (Cambridge, MA: Harvard University Printing Office, 1969), 448.

99. Doak, 15.

100. Ralph D. Gray, *Indiana History: A Book of Read-ings* (Indianapolis: Indiana University Press, 1994), 59.

101. Ibid.

102. Ibid., 59–60.

103. "William H. Harrison," *http://www.ohiohistorycentral.org/entry.php?rec=190.*

104. Ibid.

105. Ibid.

106. Ibid.

107. Ibid.

108. Ibid.

109. "William Henry Harrison," *http://www.wordiq.com/definition/William_Henry_Harrison.*

110. "Indiana Territory," *http://www.ohiohistorycentral.org/entry.php?rec=733.*

111. Ibid.

112. "Harris, Benjamin," *Appletons' Cyclopædia of American Biography*, James Grant Wilson and John Fiske, eds. (New York: D. Appleton, 1887–1889), *http://en.wikisource.org/wiki/Appletons%27_Cyclop%C3%A6dia_of_American_Biography/Harrison,_Benjamin.*

113. Ibid.

114. John Van Ness Yates, *History of the State of New York* (New York: A.T. Goodrich, 1824–26), *http://olivercowdery.com/texts/1824Yate.htm.*

115. "American Indian Quotes," *http://www.stevenredhead.com/Native/profile.html.*

116. "Harris, Benjamin," *Appletons' Cyclopædia of American Biography.*

117. Reed Beard, *The Battle of Tippecanoe, Historical Sketches of the Famous Field upon which General William Henry Harrison Won Renown that aided Him in Reaching the Presidency — Lives of the Prophet and Tecumseh, with Many Interesting Incidents of Their Rise and Overthrow* (Chicago: Tippecanoe Pub. Co., 1911), *http://www.archive.org/stream/battleoftippecan00bearuoft/battleoftippecan00bearuoft_djvu.txt.*

118. William Osborn Stoddard, *William Henry Harrison, John Tyler and James Knox Polk* vol. 5 (New York: F.A. Stokes & Company, 1888), 104.

119. "Biography of William Henry Harrison," *http://millercenter.org/president/harrison/essays/biography/print.*

120. "William Henry Harrison," *http://www.nndb.com/people/886/000031793/.*

121. Burr, 252–253.

122. "William Henry Harrison: Life Before the Presidency," *www.millercenter.org/president/harrison/essays/biography/2.*

123. Aileen Weintraub, *How to Draw Ohio's Sights and Symbols* (New York: Rosen Publishing Group, 2002), 6.

124. Robert P. Wettemann, *Privilege*

Versus Equality (Santa Barbara, CA: ABC-CLIO, 2009), 23.

125. Dorothy Burne Goebel, *William Henry Harrison, A Political Biography* vol. 14 (Indianapolis: Historical Bureau of the Indiana Library and Historical Department, 1926), 164.

126. Fred J. Milligan, *Ohio's Founding Fathers* (Lincoln, NE: iUniverse, 2003), 109.

127. "William Henry Harrison," *http://www.nndb.com/people/886/000031793/*.

128. "William Henry Harrison," *http://www.knowsouthernhistory.net/Biographies/William_Harrison/*.

129. "Theodore Dwight Weld, 1803–1895," *http://docsouth.unc.edu/neh/weld/weld.html*.

130. Jewel, 72.

131. Ibid.

132. Ibid.

133. Ibid.

134. Letter to Stephen Van Rennesselar in 1836, Collins, 75.

135. "William Henry Harrison 'Tippecanoe and Tyler Too' 1840," *www.retrocampaigns.com/William_Henry_Harrison_Tippecanoe*.

136. "Election of 1840 — Campaign Used Songs and Slogans," *www.history1800s.about.com/od/leaders/a/1840campaign.htm*.

137. Edward Morse Shepard, *Martin Van Buren* (Bos-ton: Houghton Mifflin, 1899), 378.

138. "William Henry Harrison: Campaigns," *www.millercenter.org/president/harrison/essays/biography/3*.

139. Shepard, 378.

140. Shepard, 379.

141. "The Campaign of 1840: The Candidates," *www.edsitement.neh.gov/lesson-plan/campaign-1840-candidates*.

142. "Election of 1840 — Campaign Used Songs and Slogans," *www.history1800s.about.com/od/leaders/a/1840campaign.htm*.

143. "The Campaign of 1840: The Campaign," *http://edsitement.neh.gov/lesson-plan/campaign-1840-campaign*.

144. "U.S. Presidential Elections Facts & Chronologies," *www.giltroy.com/US_Presidential_Elections_Facts_Chronologies.doc*.

145. "The Western Hero," *www.xroads.virginia.edu/~UG02/reno/harrison.html*.

146. "U.S. Presidential Elections Facts & Chronologies," *www.giltroy.com/US_Presidential_Elections_Facts_Chronologies.doc*.

147. Whig Convention, Dayton, Ohio, September 18, 1840, Hermann Von Holst, John Joseph Lalor, Paul Shorey, and Ira Hutchinson Brainerd, *The Constitutional and Political History of the United States, 1828–1846* (Chicago: Callaghan and Company, 1879), 378.

148. William G. Shade, Ballard C. Campbell and Craig R. Coenen, *American Presidential Campaigns and Elections* vol. I (Armonk, NY: Sharpe Reference, 2003), 306.

149. Joslyn Pine, *American Presidents' Wit and Wisdom: A Book of Quotations* (Mineola, NY: Courier Dover Publications, 2002), 32.

150. *Baltimore Republican*, December 11, 1839, cited by Robert Gray Gunderson, *The Log-Cabin Campaign* (Lexington: University of Kentucky Press, 1957), 74.

151. "Election of 1840 — Campaign Used Songs and Slogans," *www.history1800s.about.com/od/leaders/a/1840campaign.htm*.

152. "William Henry Harrison," *www.absoluteastronomy.com/topics/William_Henry_Harrison*.

153. "Election of 1840 — Campaign Used Songs and Slogans," *www.history1800s.about.com/od/leaders/a/1840campaign.htm*.

154. "1840 U.S. Presidential Campaign," *www.historynet.com/...1840-us-presidential-campaign.htm*.

155. "Election of 1840 — Campaign Used Songs and Slogans," *www.history1800s.about.com/od/leaders/a/1840campaign.htm*.

156. Kenneth R. Stevens, *William Henry Harrison: A Bibliography* (Westport, CT: Greenwood, 1998), 152.

157. "How Do You Feel About Jackson?" *www.iws.collin.edu/sbostelmann/History%201301/Lecture%20*.

158. "White House History," *www.whitehousehistory.org/whha_timelines/*.

159. "William Henry Harrison: Life Before the Presidency," *www.millercenter.org/president/harrison/essays/biography/2*.

160. "William Henry Harrison," *www.library.kiwix.org:4201/A/William_Henry_Harrison.html*.

161. "United States Presidential Election, 1840," *www.english.turkcebilgi.com/United+States+presidential*.

162. "1840 U.S. Presidential Campaign," *http://www.historynet.com/american-history-1840-us-presidential-campaign.htm*.

163. "U.S. Presidential Elections Facts & Chronologies," *www.giltroy.com/US_Presidential_Elections_Facts_Chronologies.doc*.

164. Ibid.

165. Ibid.

166. "1840 U.S. Presidential Campaign," *http://www.historynet.com/american-history-1840-us-presidential-campaign.htm*.

167. Ibid.

168. "U.S. Presidential Elections Facts & Chronologies," *www.giltroy.com/US_Presidential_Elections_Facts_Chronologies.doc*.

169. George W. Julian, *Political Recollections 1840 to 1872* (Chicago: McClurg & Co., 1883), chapter one, *www.gutenberg.org/files/22959/22959.txt*.

170. "You're An Atheist, Madam!" *www.alternet.org/election2012/154346/you%27re_an_atheist*.

171. "William Henry Harrison," *www.millercenter.org/president/harrison/essays/biography/3*.

172. List of nicknames of United States presidents. *www.en.wikipedia.org/wiki/List_of_Presidents_of_the_United*.

173. "U.S. Presidential Elections Facts & Chronologies," *www.giltroy.com/US_Presidential_Elections_Facts_Chronologies.doc*.

174. "oter Participation 1824–1968," *www.title24uscode.org/vote.htm*.

175. Stevens, 161.

176. "William Henry Harrison 'Tippecanoe and Tyler Too' 1840," *www.retrocampaigns.com/William_Henry_Harrison_Tippecanoe*.

177. George W. Julian, *Political Recollections 1840 to 1872* (Chicago: McClurg & Co., 1883), chapter one, *www.gutenberg.org/files/22959/22959.txt*.

178. Sean Wilentz, *The Rise of American Democracy: Jefferson to Lincoln* (New York: W.W. Norton, 2005), 503.

179. William J. Federer, *Treasury of Presidential Quotations* (St. Louis, MO: Amerisearch, Inc., 2004), 73.

180. "Anna Harrison," *http://en.wikipedia.org/wiki/Anna_Harrison*.

181. Paul F. Boller Jr., *Presidential Anecdotes* (New York: Oxford University Press, 1996), 92.

182. Committee on inaugural address, *Inaugural Addresses of the Presidents of the United States: From George Washington, 1789 to George H.W. Bush, 1989* (New York: Cosimo, Inc., 2008), 79.

183. Daniel Webster, *Reminiscences and Anecdotes of Daniel Webster*, Peter Harvey, ed. (Boston: Little, Brown and Company, 1878), 160–163.

184. *Inaugural Addresses*, March 4, 1841, *www.bartleby.com/124/pres26.html*.

185. William Wesley Woollen, *Biographical and Historical Sketches of Early Indiana* (Manchester, NH: Ayer Publishing, 1975), 50.

186. Cleaves, 136.

187. Edward B. MacMahon, and Leonard Curry, *Medical Cover-Ups in the White House* (Washington, DC: Farragut, 1987), 18.

188. "U.S. Senate: Art & History Home, John Tyler, Tenth Vice President," *www.senate.gov/artandhistory/history/.../VP_John_Tyler.htm*.

189. "Twenty-fifth Amendment to the United States Constitution," *www.doctorzebra.com/prez/a_amendment25.htm*.

190. "Political Review: William Henry Harrison," *www.apexamreview.com/index.php?option=com_content&view*.

191. Alan Brinkley and Davis Dyer, "Harrison's Proclamation for Special Session of Congress," *The American Presidency* (Boston: MA: Houghton Mifflin, 2004).

192. Indiana Historical Bureau, Indiana Historical Commission, *Indiana Historical Collections* (Indianapolis, IN: Indiana Historical Bureau, 1922), 7: 471.

193. "William Henry Harrison and the West," *www.du.edu/~jcalvert/hist/harrison.htm*.

194. Marquis James, *The Life of Andrew Jackson* (Indianapolis: Bobbs-Merrill, 1938), 456.

195. MacMahon, 13.

196. MacMahon 18.
197. Ibid.
198. "William Henry Harrison Is Born," http://www.history.com/this-day-in-history/william-henry-harrison-is-born.
199. Benjamin Parsons, "Eulogy on the Private and Public Character, and Public Services of the Late President Harrison" (Pensacola, 1841).
200. Cleaves, 160.
201. "William Henry Harrison," http://allthingswilliam.com/presidents/harrison.html.
202. Charles S. Todd and Benjamin Drake, Sketches of the Civil and Military Services of William Henry Harrison (Cincinnati: BiblioBazaar, 1841), 208.
203. Ibid.
204. "State Funerals Bound by Rules, History, Judgment," www.msnbc.msn.com/id/5151474/ns/us_news-the_legacy.
205. "Dead Presidents, April 4, 1841," www.deadpresidents.tumblr.com/post/30832889/april-4-1841.
206. Ohio Historical Society, "Harrison Tomb," http://ohsweb.ohiohistory.org/places/sw11/.
207. "Harrison's Tomb — North Bend, Ohio History and Government," www.northbendohio.org/HarrisonsTomb.html.
208. "William Henry Harrison and the West," http://www.du.edu/%7Ejcalvert/hist/harrison.htm.
209. Ibid.
210. Ibid.
211. Ibid.
212. "Tecumseh's Curse," www.deadpresidents.tumblr.com/post/337969483/tecumsehs-curse.
213. Ibid.
214. "Biography of William Henry Harrison," http://millercenter.org/president/harrison/essays/biography/print.
215. "James G. Birney," www.nndb.com/people/258/000050108/.
216. Ibid.
217. Ibid.
218. Ibid.
219. Ibid.
220. Samuel Flagg Bemis, John Quincy Adams and the Union (New York: Knopf, 1956), 419.
221. Ibid.
222. John Quincy Adams, Memoirs of John Quincy Adams, Charles Francis Adams, ed. (Philadelphia: J.B. Lippincott, 1875), vol 10: 366.
223. Marquis James, The Life of Andrew Jackson (Indianapolis: Bobbs-Merrill, 1938), 745.
224. John G. Nicolay and John Hay, eds, Complete Works of Abraham Lincoln (New York: F.D. Tandy Company, 1894), 257.
225. Manus Hand, "Dead Presidents on Dead Presidents," www.diplom.org/manus/Presidents/ratings/prez.htm.
226. Washington Globe, June 11, 1840, Alan Brinkley, Davis Dyer, The American Presidency (Boston: Houghton Mifflin Harcourt, 2004), 118.
227. M.J. Heale, The Making of American Politics, 1750–1850 (London: Longman Group, 1977).

228. Wilcomb E. Washburn, "Campaign Banners," American Heritage Magazine vol. 23, issue 6 (October 1972, volume 23).
229. 1814, Cleaves, 223.
230. Isaac Rand Jackson, 10.

Ten. Tyler

1. "Tyler, John," Appletons' Cyclopædia of American Biography, James Grant Wilson and John Fiske, eds. (New York: D. Appleton, 1887–1889), http://en.wikisource.org/wiki/The_Presidents_of_the_United_States,_1789–1914/John_Tyler.
2. Ibid.
3. Lyle Emerson Nelson, John Tyler: A Rare Career (New York: Nova Publishers, 2008), 2.
4. Robin Santos Doak, John Tyler (Minneapolis: Compass Point Books, 2003), 52.
5. Elizabeth Jewell, U.S. Presidents Factbook (New York: Random House, 2005), 1831.
6. Nelson, 2.
7. Ibid.
8. "Biographical Directory of Federal Judges, John Tyler," http://www.uscourts.gov/JudgesAndJudgeships/BiographicalDirectoryOfJudges.aspx.
9. "Biography of John Tyler," www.millercenter.org/president/tyler/essays/biography/print.
10. "Biographical Directory of Federal Judges, John Tyler," http://www.uscourts.gov/JudgesAndJudgeships/BiographicalDirectoryOfJudges.aspx.
11. Jeff C. Young, The Fathers of American Presidents: From Augustine Washington to William Blythe and Roger Clinton (Jefferson, NC: McFarland, 1997), 45.
12. Robert Seager II, And Tyler Too, A Biography of John and Julia Gardiner Tyler (New York: McGraw-Hill, 1963), 50.
13. Nelson, 2.
14. Doug Wead, The Raising of a President: The Mothers and Fathers of Our Nation's Leaders (New York: Atria Books, 2005), 335.
15. Jewell, 1844.
16. Lyon Gardiner Tyler, The Letters and Times of the Tylers vol. 1 (Richmond, VA: Whittet & Shepperson, 1884), 42.
17. "John Tyler's Obituary," The New York Times, http://starship.python.net/crew/manus/Presidents/jt/jtobit.html.
18. Wat Tyler, Life and Adventures of Wat Tyler, the Good and the Brave (London: H.G. Collins, 1851), 159–160.
19. Ibid., 156.
20. "Wat Tyler's Rebellion," www.home.earthlink.net/~dlaw70/wat.htm.
21. Ibid.
22. "The Peasants Are Revolting," www.historyonyx.blogspot.com/2011/05/peasants-are-revolting.html.
23. Wat Tyler, 171–172.
24. "Wat Tyler's Rebellion," www.home.earthlink.net/~dlaw70/wat.htm.
25. "The Peasants Are Revolting,"

www.historyonyx.blogspot.com/2011/05/peasants-are-revolting.html.
26. L.G. Tyler, 546.
27. Ibid.
28. Ibid., 546–547.
29. Oliver Perry Chitwood, John Tyler, Champion of the Old South (New York: Appleton-Century Co., 1939; Newtown, CT: American Political Biography Press, 1971), 12.
30. Ibid., 13.
31. Ibid., 151.
32. Ibid.
33. Ibid.
34. Ibid., 152.
35. Steven O'Brien, Paula McGuire, and James M. McPherson, American Political Leaders: From Colonial Times to Present (Santa Barbara, CA: ABC-CLIO, 1991), 405.
36. Seager, 372.
37. Chitwood, 22.
38. Ibid., 23.
39. Ibid., 24.
40. Ibid., 24–25.
41. Ibid., 25.
42. Laura Carter Holloway, Ladies of the White House (New York: U.S. Publication Company, 1870), 384.
43. Ibid.
44. Paul F. Boller Jr., Presidential Wives: An Anecdotal History (New York: Oxford University Press, 1998), 80.
45. "Letitia Tyler Biography," http://www.firstladies.org/biographies/firstladies.aspx?biography=10.
46. Ibid.
47. Boller, Presidential Wives, 78.
48. "Letitia Tyler Biography," http://www.firstladies.org/biographies/firstladies.aspx?biography=10.
49. Holloway, 341–342.
50. Ibid., 431–432.
51. Melba Porter Hay, "Letitia Christian Tyler," American First Ladies: Their Lives and Their Legacy, Lewis L. Gould, ed. (New York: Routledge, 2001), 67–68.
52. "Letitia Tyler Biography," http://www.firstladies.org/biographies/firstladies.aspx?biography=10.
53. Ibid.
54. Ibid.
55. Ibid.
56. Boller, 81.
57. "Our Campaigns: Candidate — Julia Gardiner Tyler," www.ourcampaigns.com/CandidateDetail.html?CandidateID=34117.
58. "Letitia Tyler Biography," http://www.firstladies.org/biographies/firstladies.aspx?biography=10.
59. Ibid.
60. Ibid.
61. Ibid.
62. "Our Campaigns: Candidate — Julia Gardiner Tyler," www.ourcampaigns.com/CandidateDetail.html?CandidateID=34117.
63. Ibid.
64. Ibid.
65. Mary Ormsbee Whitton, First First Ladies, 1789–1865 (New York: Kessenger Publishing, [1948] 2008), 188.
66. Seager, 196.
67. Ibid., 200.

68. "Our Campaigns: Candidate — Julia Gardiner Tyler," *www.ourcampaigns.com/CandidateDetail.html?CandidateID=34117*.

69. Seager, 207.

70. Boller, 82.

71. Seager, 257.

72. Ibid.

73. "Our Campaigns: Candidate — Julia Gardiner Tyler," *www.ourcampaigns.com/CandidateDetail.html?CandidateID=34117*.

74. Carl Sferrazza Anthony, *First Ladies: The Saga of the Presidents' Wives and Their Power, 1789–1961* (New York: William Morrow, 1990), 126.

75. "Our Campaigns: Candidate — Julia Gardiner Tyler," *www.ourcampaigns.com/CandidateDetail.html?CandidateID=34117*.

76. Ibid.

77. Ibid.

78. Ibid.

79. "Letitia Tyler Biography," *http://www.firstladies.org/biographies/firstladies.aspx?biography=10*.

80. "Our Campaigns: Candidate — Julia Gardiner Tyler," *www.ourcampaigns.com/CandidateDetail.html?CandidateID=34117*.

81. Letter to the Duchess of Sutherland and Ladies of England, January 24, 1853, *Southern Literary Messenger*, Vol. 19 (Richmond, VA: MacFarlane, Fergusson & Co., 1853), 122.

82. Ibid.

83. Ibid.

84. Crapol, *Pursuit of Destiny*, 242.

85. Ibid.

86. Ibid., 272.

87. Lewis L. Gould, *American First Ladies: Their Lives and Their Legacy* (London: Taylor & Francis, 2001), 77.

88. Ibid., 78.

89. Ibid.

90. Ibid.

91. "John Tyler — Our White House; Looking In, Looking Out," *http://ourwhitehouse.org/prespgs/jtyler.html*.

92. Doug Wead, *All the Presidents' Children: Triumph and Tragedy in the Lives of America's First Families* (New York: Simon & Schuster, 2004), 43.

93. Doug Phillips, "The Grand Family of America's Birthday," *WorldNet Daily*, March 30, 2007, *http://www.wnd.com/2007/03/40856/*.

94. "John Dunjee," *www.freebase.com/view/en/john_dunjee*.

95. Seager, 109.

96. "God in America: God in the White House," *www.pbs.org/godinamerica/god-in-the-white-house*.

97. Letter of July 10, 1843 to Joseph Simpson, cited by Bernard Lewis, *From Babel to Dragomans* (New York: Oxford University Press, 2004), 331.

98. Letter to Robert Tyler, May 19, 1856, Franklin Steiner, *The Religious Beliefs Of Our Presidents* (Amherst, NY: Prometheus Books, 1995); See also John Tyler Papers, Library of Congress Manuscript Division.

99. "John Tyler — Tenth President of the United States," *http://www.all-biographies.com/presidents/john_tyler.htm*.

100. Chitwood, 16–18.

101. "John Tyler — Special Collections Research Center," *www.scrc.swem.wm.edu/wiki/index.php/John_Tyler*.

102. "Chancellor — Special Collections Research Center," *www.scrc.swem.wm.edu/wiki/index.php/Chancellor*.

103. Ibid.

104. Ibid.

105. "The College of William and Mary During the Civil War," *www.guides.swem.wm.edu/content.php?pid=6662&sid=41792*.

106. Ibid.

107. Ibid.

108. "United States Presidents," *http://www.francesfarmersrevenge.com/stuff/archive/oldnews2/prez.htm*.

109. Lu Ann Paletta and Fred L. Worth, *The World Almanac of Presidential Facts* (New York: World Almanac Education, 1993).

110. "Sherwood Forest Plantation — Home of President John Tyler," *www.sherwoodforest.org/*.

111. Ibid.

112. Ibid.

113. Ibid.

114. Crapol, 249.

115. Dorothy Schneider and Carl J. Schneider, *First Ladies: A Biographical Dictionary* (New York: Infobase Publishing, 2010), 66.

116. Kate Havelin, *John Tyler* (Minneapolis: Twenty-First Century Books, 2005), 83.

117. Megan M. Gunderson, *John Tyler* (Edina, MN: ABDO, 2009), 10.

118. Seager, 15.

119. "Presidents as Poets: John Tyler," *www.loc.gov/rr/program/bib/prespoetry/jt.html*.

120. Ibid.

121. Ibid.

122. Gary May, *John Tyler* (New York: Time Books/Henry Holt and Co., 2004), 14.

123. Ibid., 17.

124. Crapol, 12–13.

125. "Tippecanoe and Tyler, Too!— HiddenMysteries Conspiracy Archive," *http://www.hiddenmysteries.org/conspiracy/reststory/tyler.html*.

126. Crapol, 11.

127. Edward P. Crapol, "John Tyler and the Pursuit of National Destiny," *Journal of the Early American Republic* vol. 17, no.3 (October 1997).

128. "John Tyler," *www.home.nas.com/lopresti/ps10.htm*.

129. L.G. Tyler, *Letters*, vol. 1.

130. May, 24.

131. Ibid.

132. John Garland Pollard, *Virginia Born Presidents: Addresses Delivered on the Occasions of Unveiling the Busts of Virginia Born Presidents at Old Hall of the House of Delegates, Richmond, Virginia* (New York: American Book Company, 1932), 161.

133. Crapol, 35–36.

134. Doak, 14.

135. Crapol, 39

136. Nelson, 16.

137. Crapol, 39.

138. Jane C. Walker, *John Tyler: A President of Many Firsts* (Blacksburg, VA: McDonald & Woodward, 2001), 12.

139. L.G. Tyler, *Letters*, 2: 447.

140. L.G. Tyler, *Letters*, 2: 499.

141. L.G. Tyler, *Letters*, 2: 435.

142. Speech in Congress, February 24, 1834, against the policies of Andrew Jackson, Seager, 94.

143. Seager, 99.

144. William Ogden Niles, "Mr. Tyler's Letter, February 29, 1836," *Niles' Weekly Register* vol. 50, March 12, 1856, 26.

145. Gales and Seaton, *Register of Debates, Senate, Twenty-fourth Congress, 1st Session*, 636.

146. Oliver Perry Chitwood, *John Tyler, Champion of the Old South* (New York: Appleton-Century, 1939), 39–40.

147. Nelson, 25.

148. Michael F. Holt, *The Rise and Fall of the American Whig Party: Jacksonian Politics and the Onset of the Civil War* (New York: Oxford University Press, 2003), 128.

149. April 9, 1841, Chitwood, 173.

150. May, 3.

151. Nelson, 32.

152. John T. Woolley and Gerhard Peters, *Messages and Papers of the Presidents* (The American Presidency Project [*http://www.presidency.ucsb.edu/*]. Santa Barbara, CA); See also: U.S. Presidents' Lives, "John Tyler," *The Independent*, January 17, 2009.

153. Havelin, 61.

154. Chitwood, 202–203.

155. Chitwood, 270.

156. John Fiske, "The Presidents of the United States, 1789–1914: John Tyler," *Encyclopædia Britannica*, James Grant Wilson ed. (New York: Cambridge University Press, 1910–1911).

157. Ibid.

158. Ibid.

159. Ibid.

160. Chitwood, 217–251.

161. Letter to Virginia Governor L.W. Tazewell, November 2, 1841, L.G. Tyler, *Letters*, 131.

162. Seager, 147.

163. Wilson and Fiske, *Appletons' Cyclopaedia of American Biography*, VI: 198.

164. Ibid.

165. Letter to Robert McCandlish, July 10, 1842, Sean Wilentz, *The Rise of American Democracy: Jefferson to Lincoln* (New York: W.W. Norton, 2005), 80.

166. Chitwood, 330.

167. Chitwood, 326–330.

168. Seager, 210–211

169. Crapol, 194–197.

170. Eugene H. Roseboom, *A History of Presidential Elections* (New York: Macmillan, 1970), 124.

171. "Origins & Development of the United States Senate — Powers and Procedures: Nominations," *http://www.senate.gov/artandhistory/history/common/briefing/Nominations.htm*.

172. U.S. Constitution, article II, section 1.

173. "John Tyler: Impact and Legacy," *http://millercenter.org/president/tyler/essays/biography/9*.

174. Crapol, 10.
175. Veto message, August 16, 1841. Richardson, *Compilations*, 1917.
176. "John Tyler (1841–1845)," *www.kipnotes.com/John%20Tyler.htm*.
177. "How Did the Preemption Act and the Homestead Act Shape the Nation," *http://answers.yahoo.com/question/index?qid=20100308074231AAiS6Gr*.
178. Ibid.
179. "Dorr Rebellion," *http://www.knowledgerush.com/kr/encyclopedia/Dorr_Rebellion/*.
180. Ibid.
181. Ibid.
182. Ibid.
183. Letter to Governor Samuel Ward King, April 11, 1842, Woolley and Peters.
184. Ibid.
185. "Presidential Democracy," *http://www.knowledgerush.com/kr/encyclopedia/Presidential_democracy/*.
186. "Tariff of 1842," *www.artandpopularculture.com/Tariff_of_1842*.
187. Fiske, *The Presidents of the United States, 1789–1914*, 92.
188. "Tariff of 1842," *www.artandpopularculture.com/Tariff_of_1842*.
189. Ibid.
190. "American President: Biography of John Tyler," *http://millercenter.org/president/tyler/essays/biography/print*.
191. Ibid.
192. Third State of the Union Message, December 1843, Richardson, *Compilations*.
193. "The Quasi-war and After — Presidential Power," *www.americanforeignrelations.com/O-W/Presidential-Power…*.
194. "Missouri Compromise of 1820, Legends of Kansas," *www.legendsofkansas.com/missouricompromise2.html*.
195. Feb. 29, 1856, Edward. P. Crapol, "John Tyler and the Pursuit of National Destiny," *Journal of the Early American Republic* vol. 17, no.3 October 1997); Hunt-ington Letters, Tyler Collection.
196. Seager, 324.
197. Address Accepting Office; First State of the Union Message to Congress, April 6, 1841, Richardson, *Compilations*, 1230.
198. "Webster-Ashburton Treaty," *http://www.u-s-history.com/pages/h357.htm*.
199. Ibid.
200. Ibid.
201. "Treaty of Wanghia — A Diplomatic Agreement between the Qing," *www.history.cultural-china.com/en/34History6512.html*.
202. Treaty of Peace, Amity, and Commerce, with tariff of duties, signed at Wang Hiya (in the outskirts of Macao) July 3, 1844, "Treaty of Wanghia," *http://en.wikipedia.org/wiki/Treaty_of_Wanghia*.
203. "Trade Treaty with China," *www.u-s-history.com/pages/h358.html*.
204. "Treaty of Wanghia — A Diplomatic Agreement between the Qing," *www.history.cultural-china.com/en/34History6512.html*.
205. "The Treaty of Wanghia (1845)," *http://riceonhistory.wordpress.com/2012/01/11/the-treaty-of-wanghia-1845/*.
206. "Treaty of Wanghia — A Diplomatic Agreement between the Qing," *www.history.cultural-china.com/en/34History6512.html*.
207. Ibid.
208. Ibid.
209. "John Tyler," *www.kerkchart.com/2011/10/27/john-tyler*.
210. Havelin, 90.
211. May, document transcript.
212. Fourth State of the Union Message, December 3, 1844, Thomas Hart Benton, ed., *Abridgment of the Debates of Congress, from 1789 to 1856* (New York: Appleton and Company, 1856), 164.
213. President John Tyler Is Not a Traitor to His Country," *http://www.emorywheel.com/detail.php?n=25146*.
214. Letters to Robert Tyler, March 18, 1847, and April 16, 1850, L.G. Tyler, *Letters*, 3: 468, 3: 483.
215. Letter to Colonel David L. Gardiner, December 7, 1849, Crapol.
216. Cited in his obituary, *The New York Times*, January 19, 1862.
217. "Tyler, John, "*Encyclopaedia Britannica* (Chicago: Encyclopaedia Britannica, 1973), I: 422–433.
218. "John Tyler," *http://www.encyclopedia.com/topic/John_Tyler.aspx*.
219. Paul F. Boller Jr., *Presidential Anecdotes* (New York: Oxford University Press, 1981), 97.
220. John R. Bumgarner, *The Health of the Presidents: The 41 United States Presidents Through 1993 from a Physician's Point of View* (Jefferson, NC: McFarland, 1994), 65.
221. Ibid.
222. Bumgarner, 64–65.
223. Ibid., 65–66.
224. May, 144.
225. Bumgarner, 65.
226. Ibid.
227. May, 145.
228. May, 144.
229. Bumgarner, 66.
230. May, 144–145.
231. "Death of Ex-President Tyler," *The New York Times*, *www.python.net/crew/manus/Presidents/jt/jtobit.html*.
232. May, 145–146.
233. "Presidential Graves," *www.travelin-tigers.com/ztravel/prez9107.htm*.
234. "Presidents of the United States," *http://www.ipl.org/div/potus/jtyler.htm*.
235. Ibid.
236. Ibid.
237. Ibid.
238. Ibid.
239. Ibid.
240. Ibid.
241. Ibid.
242. Ibid.
243. "Ghosts at Sherwood Forest Plantation," *www.sherwoodforest.org/Ghosts.html*.
244. Ibid.
245. Ibid.
246. Ibid.
247. "W&M Dedicates Garden in Honor of Tyler Family Legacy," *http://www.wm.edu/as/history/news/wm-dedicates-garden-in-honor-of-tyler-family-legacy.php*.
248. Henry A. Wise, *Seven Decades of the Union: The Humanities and Materialism* (Philadelphia: J.B. Lippincott & Co., 1872), 233.
249. Leonard. Falkner, *The President Who Wouldn't Retire* (New York: Coward-McCann, 1967).
250. Morgan, 11.
251. White House Christmas Cards and Messages from John Tyler," *www.whitehousechristmascards.com/category/john-tyler*.
252. Crapol.
253. Marquis James.
254. Charles Grier Sellers, *James K. Polk, Jacksonian* (Princeton, NJ: Princeton University Press, 1957), 449.
255. Theodore Roosevelt, *Thomas H. Benton* (Boston, Houghton, Mifflin, 1899), 212.
256. Seager, xvi.
257. Manus Hand, "Dead Presidents on Dead Presidents," *www.diplom.org/manus/Presidents/ratings/prez.htm*.
258. *The Press and the Presidency: From George Washington to Ronald Reagan* (New York: Oxford University Press, 1985).

References and Further Readings

Introduction

Abbott, Philip. *The Challenge of the American Presidency.* Long Grove, IL: Waveland, 2004.

Angle, Paul M., ed. *By These Words: Great Documents of American Liberty.* Chicago: Rand McNally, 1954.

Antieau, Chester James. *Our Two Centuries of Law and Life, 1775–1975: The Work of the Supreme Court and the Impact of Both Congress and Presidents.* Littleton, CO: Fred B. Rothman, 2001.

Bailey, Harry A., and Jay M. Shafritz. *The American Presidency: Historical and Contemporary Perspectives.* Chicago: Dorsey, 1988.

Barber, James David. *Politics by Humans: Research on American Leadership.* Durham: Duke University Press, 1988.

_____. *Presidential Character: Predicting Performance in the White House.* Upper Saddle River, NJ: Prentice-Hall, 1992.

Bassett, Margaret. *Profiles and Portraits of American Presidents & Their Wives.* New York: Grosset & Dunlap, 1969.

Bausum, Ann. *Our Country's Presidents: All You Need to Know about the Presidents, from George Washington to Barack Obama.* Washington, DC: National Geographic Books, 2009.

Beard, Charles A. *An Economic Interpretation of the Constitution of the United States.* New York: Macmillan, 1961.

Berkey, William Augustus. *The Money Question: The Legal Tender Paper Monetary System of the United States. An Analysis of the Specie Basis or Bank Currency System, and of the Legal Tender Paper Money System.* New York: W.W. Hart, 1876.

Bernstein, Richard B. *Are We a Nation? The Making of the Constitution.* Cambridge, MA: Harvard University Press, 1987.

Boller, Paul F., Jr. *Presidential Anecdotes.* New York: Oxford University Press, 1996.

_____. *Presidential Campaigns.* New York: Oxford University Press, 2004.

Brinkley, Alan, and Davis Dyer, eds. *The American Presidency.* Boston: Houghton Mifflin, 2004.

Brown, H. Lowell *High Crimes and Misdemeanors in Presidential Impeachment.* New York: Macmillan, 2010.

Bumgarner, John R. (M.D.). *The Health of Presidents.* Jefferson, NC: McFarland, 1994.

Campbell, Karlyn Kohrs, and Kathleen Hall Jamieson. *Deeds Done in Words: Presidential Rhetoric and the Genres of Governance.* Chicago: University of Chicago Press, 1990.

Chambers, William Nisbet, and Walter Dean Burnham. *American Party Systems: Stages of Political Development.* New York: Oxford University Press, 1972.

Countryman, Edward, ed. *What Did the Constitution Mean to Early Americans?* New York: St. Martin's, 1999.

Crockett, David A. *The Opposition Presidency: Leadership and the Constraints of History.* College Station: Texas A&M University Press, 2002.

Cronin, Thomas E. *Inventing the American Presidency.* Lawrence: University Press of Kansas, 1989.

Dallek, Robert. *Hail to the Chief: The Making and Unmaking of American Presidents.* New York: Hyperion, 1996.

DeConde, Alexander, Richard Dean Burns, and Fredrik Logevall. *Encyclopedia of American Foreign Policy.* New York: Simon & Schuster, 2001.

DeGregorio, William A. *The Complete Book of U.S. Presidents.* New York: Barricade, 2005.

Edling, Max M. *A Revolution in Favor of Government: Origins of the U.S. Constitution and the Making of the American State.* New York: Oxford University Press, 2003.

Edwards, George C. *The Strategic President: Persuasion and Opportunity in Presidential Leadership.* Princeton, NJ: Princeton University Press, 2009.

Ellis, Richard J. *Founding the American Presidency.* Landham, MD: Rowman & Littlefield, 1999.

_____, ed. *Speaking to the People: The Rhetorical Presidency in Historical Perspective.* Amherst: University of Massachusetts Press, 1998.

Faber, Charles, and Richard B. Faber. *The American Presidents Ranked by Performance.* Jefferson, NC: McFarland, 2000.

Fields, Wayne. *Union of Words: A History of Presidential Eloquence.* Mankato, MN: Free Press, 1996.

Fisher, Louis. *Constitutional Conflicts Between Congress and the President.* Lawrence: University Press of Kansas, 2007.

Ford, Henry Jones. *The Rise and Growth of American Politics.* New York: Macmillan, 1898.

Gelderman, Carol. *All the President's Words: The Bully Pulpit and the Creation of the Virtual Presidency.* New York: Walker, 1997.

Genovese, Michael A. *The Power of the American Presidency: 1789–2000.* New York: Oxford University Press, 2001.

George, Alexander L., and Juliette L. George. *Presidential Personality and Performance.* Boulder, CO: Westview, 1998.

Gilbert, Robert E. *The Mortal Presidency: Illness and Anguish in the White House.* New York: Fordham University Press, 1998.

Gillon, Steven M., Cathy D. Matson. *The American Experiment: A History of the United States.* Stamford CT: Cengage Learning, 2008.

Graff, Henry Franklin. *The Presidents: A Reference History.* New York: Simon & Schuster, 2002.

Hall, Kermit, James W. Ely, and Joel

B. Grossman. *The Oxford Companion to the Supreme Court of the United States*. New York: Oxford University Press, 2005.

Hargrove, Erwin C. *The President as Leader: Appealing to the Better Angels of Our Nature*. Lawrence: University Press of Kansas, 1998.

Hess, Debra. *The White House*. Tarrytown, NY: Marshall Cavendish, 2003.

Jackson, Andrew. *The Statesmanship of Andrew Jackson as Told in His Writings and Speeches*. New York: The Tandy-Thomas Company, 1909.

Jensen, Merrill. *The Articles of Confederation: An Interpretation of the Social-Constitutional History of the American Revolution, 1774–1781*. Madison: University of Wisconsin Press, 1959.

Kammen, Michael. *A Machine That Would Go on Itself: The Constitution in American Culture*. New York: Alfred A. Knopf, 1986.

Langston, Thomas S. *With Reverence and Contempt: How Americans Think About Their President*. Baltimore: Johns Hopkins University Press, 1995.

Lawson, Don. *Famous Presidential Scandals*. Berkeley Heights, NJ: Enslow, 1990.

LeLoup, Lance, and Stephen A. Shull. *Congress and the President: The Policy Connection*. New York: Longman, 2002.

Lorant, Stefan. *The Glorious Burden: The American Presidency*. Lenox, MA: Authors Edition, 1976.

McDonald, Forrest. *The American Presidency: An Intellectual History*. Lawrence: University Press of Kansas, 1994.

McPherson. James M. *To the Best of My Ability: The American Presidents*. New York: DK, 2000.

Medvic, Stephen K. *Campaigns and Elections: Players and Processes*. Stamford, CT: Cengage Learning, 2009.

Michaelsen, William B. *Creating the American Presidency, 1775–1789*. Lanham, MD: University Press of America, 1987.

Piffner, James, and Roger H. Davidson. *Understanding the Presidency*. New York: Longman, 2003.

Powell, H. Jefferson. *A Community Built on Words: The Constitution in American Political Culture*. Chicago: University of Chicago Press, 2002.

Reedy, George E. *The Twilight of the Presidency*. New York: Dutton, 1970.

Rozell, Mark J., and Gleaves Whitney. *Religion and the American Presidency*. New York: Palgrave Macmillan, 2007.

Shogan, Colleen J. *The Moral Rhetoric of American Presidents*. College Station: Texas A&M University Press, 2006.

Stuckey, Mary E. *Defining Americans: The Presidency and National Identity*. Lawrence: University Press of Kansas, 2004.

_____. *The President as Interpreter-in-Chief*. New York: Chatham House, 1991.

Taussig, Frank William. *The Tariff History of the United States: A Series of Essays by F.W. Taussig*. New York: G.P. Putnam's Sons, 1888.

Tucker, Spencer C. *U.S. Leadership in Wartime: Clashes, Controversy, and Compromise*. Santa Barbara, CA: ABC-CLIO, 2009.

Vought, Hans P. *The Bully Pulpit and the Melting Pot: American Presidents and the Immigrant, 1897–1933*. Macon, GA: Mercer University Press, 2004.

Washington, George. *The Writings of George Washington*, Vol. 13. New York: G.P. Putnam's Sons, 1892.

Watson, Robert P., ed. *Life in the White House: A Social History of the First Family and the President's House*. Albany: State University of New York.

Wolfe, Christopher. *How to Read the Constitution: Originalism, Constitutional Interpretation, and Judicial Power*. Landham, MD: Rowman & Littlefield, 1996.

One. Washington

Alden, John R. *George Washington: A Biography*. Baton Rouge: Louisiana State University Press, 1984.

Ammon, Harry. *The Génet Mission*. New York: W.W. Norton, 1973.

Axelrod, Alan. *Blooding at Great Meadows: Young George Washington and the Battle That Shaped the Man*. Philadelphia: Running Press, 2007.

Barkan, Elliott Robert. *U.S. Immigration and Naturalization Laws and Issues*. Westport, CT: Greenwood, 1999.

Bell, William Gardner. *Commanding Generals and Chiefs of Staff, 1775–2005: Portraits and Biographical Sketches of the United States Army's Senior Officer*. Washington, DC: U.S. Government Printing Office, 2006.

Bemis, Samuel Flagg. *Jay's Treaty: A Study in Commerce and Diplomacy*. New Haven: Yale University Press, 1962.

_____. *Pinckney's Treaty: America's Advantage from Europe's Distress, 1783–1800*. New Haven: Yale University Press, 1960.

Bennett, William J., ed. *Our Sacred Honor: Words of Advice from the Founders in Stories, Letters, Poems, and Speeches*. New York: Simon & Schuster, 1997.

Boller, Paul F., Jr. *George Washington and Religion*. Dallas: Southern Methodist University Press, 1963.

Bowman, Albert. *The Struggle for Neutrality: Franco-American Diplomacy During the Federalist Era*. Knoxville: University of Tennessee Press, 1974.

Boyer Paul S., and Melvyn Dubofsky. *The Oxford Companion to United States History*. New York: Oxford University Press, 2001.

Bridges, Robert. "Washington," in *Hoyt's New Cyclopedia of Practical Quotations*. New York: Funk & Wagnalls Co., 1922.

Brookhiser, Richard. *Founding Father: Rediscovering George Washington*. New York: Free Press, 1996.

Bryan, Helen. *Martha Washington: First Lady of Liberty*. Los Angeles: Wiley, 2002.

Bumgarner, John R. *The Health of the Presidents*. Jefferson, NC: McFarland, 2004.

Burns, James MacGregor, and Susan Dunn. *George Washington*. New York: Times Books, 2004.

Busch, Noel F. *Winter Quarters: George Washington and the Continental Army at Valley Forge*. New York: Liveright, 1974.

Chadwick, Bruce. *The General and Mrs. Washington*. Naperville, IL: Sourcebooks, 2007.

_____. *George Washington's War: The Forging of a Revolutionary Leader and the American Presidency*. Naperville, IL: Sourcebooks, Inc., 2005.

Chambers, William Nisbet. *Political Parties in a New Nation: The American Experience, 1776–1809*. New York: Oxford University Press, 1963.

Chernow, Ron. *Washington: A Life*. New York: Penguin Group, 2010.

Clary, David A. *Adopted Son: Washington, Lafayette, and the Friendship That Saved the Revolution*. New York: Bantam, 2007.

Crutchfield, James A. *George Washington: First in War, First in Peace*. New York: Forge, 2005.

Cunliffe, Marcus. *George Washington, Man and Monument*. Boston: Little, Brown, 1958.

Dalzell, Robert F., Jr., and Lee Brown Dalzell. *George Washington's Mount Vernon: At Home in Revolutionary*

America. New York: Oxford University Press, 1998.

Dautrich, Kenneth, and David A. Yalof, *American Government: Historical, Popular, and Global Perspectives.* Boston: Cengage Learning, 2011.

DeConde, Alexander. *Entangling Alliances: Policies and Diplomacy Under George Washington.* Durham: Duke University Press, 1958.

Deforest, Elizabeth Kellam. *The Gardens and Grounds of Mount Vernon: How George Washington Planned and Planted Them.* Mount Vernon, VA: Mount Vernon Ladies' Association of the Union, 1982.

Edgar, Gregory T. *Campaign of 1776: The Road to Trenton.* Westminster, MD: Heritage, 1995.

Elkin, Stanley M., and Eric McKitrick. *The Age of Federalism.* New York: Oxford University Press, 1993.

Ellis, Joseph J. *His Excellency: George Washington.* New York: Alfred A. Knopf, 2004.

Estes, Todd. *The Jay Treaty Debate, Public Opinion, and the Evolution of Early American Political Culture.* Andover, MA: University of Massachusetts Press, 2006.

Ferling, John. *The Ascent of George Washington: The Hidden Political Genius of an American Icon.* New York: Bloomsbury Press, 2009.

_____. *The First of Men: A Life of George Washington,* NY: Oxford University Press, 2010.

Fields, Joseph E., comp. *Worthy Partner: The Papers of Martha Washington.* Westport, CT: Greenwood, 1994.

Fischer, David Hackett. *Washington's Crossing.* New York: Oxford University Press, 2004.

Fishman, Ethan M. *George Washington: Foundation of Presidential Leadership and Character.* Westport, CT: Greenwood, 2001.

Flexner, James Thomas. *George Washington: A Biography.* 4 vols. Boston: Little, Brown, 1965–1972.

_____. *George Washington: The Forge of Experience, 1732–1775.* Boston: Little, Brown, 1965.

_____. *George Washington in the American Revolution.* Boston: Little, Brown, 1968.

_____. *On Desperate Seas: A Biography of Gilbert Stuart.* New York: Fordham University Press, 1995.

_____. *Washington: The Indispensable Man.* New York: Back Bay Books, Little Brown and Company, 1974.

Freeman, Douglas S. *George Washington: A Biography.* 7 vols. New York: Scribner's Sons, 1948–1957.

Gaines, James R. *For Liberty and Glory: Washington, Lafayette and Their Revolutions.* New York: W.W. Norton, 2007.

Grizzard, Frank E. *George Washington: A Biographical Companion,* Santa Barbara, CA: ABC-CLIO, 2002.

_____. *The Ways of Providence, Religion and George Washington,* Buena Vista, VA: Mariner Companies, 2006.

Hale, Edward Everett. *The Life of George Washington: Studied Anew.* New York: G.P. Putnam's Sons, 1887.

Haworth, Paul Leland. *George Washington: Farmer: Being an Account of His Home Life and Agricultural Activities.* Indianapolis, IN: Bobbs-Merrill, 1915.

Hazelton, George Cochrane. *The National Capitol: Its Architecture, Art, and History.* New York: J.F. Taylor, 1902.

Henriques, Peter R. *Realistic Visionary: A Portrait of George Washington.* Charlottesville: University of Virginia Press, 2006.

Herbert. Donald David. *Lincoln.* New York: Touchstone/Simon & Schuster, 1996.

Hirschfeld, Fritz. *George Washington and Slavery: A Documentary Portrayal.* Kansas City: University of Missouri Press, 1997.

Israel, Fred L., and Jim F. Watts. *Presidential Documents: The Speeches, Proclamations, and Policies That Have Shaped the Nation from Washington to Clinton.* New York: Psychology Press, 2000.

Irving, Washington. *Life of George Washington.* New York: Putnam, 1857.

Johnson, Paul. *George Washington: The Founding Father.* New York: HarperCollins, 2009.

Jones, Robert F. *George Washington: Ordinary Man, Extraordinary Leader.* New York: Fordham University Press, 2002.

Kaplan, Sidney, and Emma Nogrady Kaplan. *The Black Presence in the Era of the American Revolution.* Amherst, MA: The University of Massachusetts Press, 1989.

Kitman, Marvin. *George Washington's Expense Account.* New York: Grove, 2000.

_____. *The Making of the President 1789: The Unauthorized Campaign Biography.* New York: Harper & Row, 1989.

Krensky, Stephen. *George Washington: The Man Who Would Not Be King.* New York: Scholastic, 1991.

Leckie, Robert. *George Washington's War: The Saga of the American Revolution.* New York: HarperCollins, 1993.

Lengel, Edward G. *General George Washington: A Military Life.* New York: Random House, 2007.

_____. *This Glorious Struggle: George Washington's Revolutionary War Letters.* New York: HarperCollins, 2008.

Lillback, Peter A. *George Washington's Sacred Fire.* West Conshohocken, PA: Providence Forum Press, 2006.

Lodge, Henry Cabot. *George Washington.* 2 vols. New York: Houghton Mifflin, 1889 and 1917; Nashville: Cumberland House, 2004.

Longmore, Paul K. *The Invention of George Washington.* Charlottesville: University of Virginia Press, 1999.

Marshall, John. *Life of George Washington.* 5 vols. 1805; special ed; Reprint, Indianapolis: Liberty Fund, 2000.

Mason, George. *The Papers of George Mason, 1725–1792: 1749–1778.* Chapel Hill: University of North Carolina Press, 1970.

May, Terry M. *Historical Dictionary of the American Revolution.* Lanham, MD: Scarecrow, 2009.

McClafferty, Carla Killough. *The Many Faces of George Washington: Remaking a Presidential Icon.* Minneapolis: Carolrhoda Books, 2011.

McCullough, David. *John Adams.* New York: Simon & Schuster, 2001.

_____. *1776.* New York: Simon & Schuster, 2005.

Morison, S. E. *The Oxford History of the United States 1783–1917.* London: Oxford University Press, 1927.

Phelps, Glenn. *George Washington and American Constitutionalism.* Lawrence: University Press of Kansas, 1993.

Randall, Willard Sterne. *George Washington: A Life.* New York: Macmillan, 1998.

Rees, James, and Stephen Spignani. *George Washington's Leadership Lessons.* Los Angeles: Wiley, 2007.

Rhodehamel, John H. *The Great Experiment: George Washington and the American Republic.* New Haven, CT: Yale University Press, 1998.

Rozell, Mark J., William D. Pederson, and Frank J. Williams, *George Washington and the Origins of the American Presidency.* Westport, CT: Greenwood, 2000.

Sayen, William Guthrie. "George Washington's 'Unmannerly' Behavior: The Clash between Civility and Honor." Mount Vernon: George Washington Symposium, November 15, 1997.

Smith, Richard Norton. *Patriarch:*

George Washington and the New American Nation. Boston: Houghton Mifflin, 1993.

Sparks, Jared. *The Life of George Washington.* Boston: F. Andrews, 1839.

Tebbel, John William. *George Washington's America.* New York: Dutton, 1954.

Truman, Harry. *Wit and Wisdom of Harry S. Truman,* Alex Ayers, ed. New York: Plume Publishers, Penguin Group. 1998.

Vile, John R. *The Constitutional Convention of 1787.* Santa Barbara, CA: ABC-CLIO, 2005.

Washington, George. *George Washington: The Diaries of George Washington,* 6 vols. Donald Jackson and Dorothy Twohig, eds. Charlottesville: University of Virginia Press, 1976–79.

_____. *The Writings of George Washington,* Jared Sparks, ed. Boston: Ferdinand Andrews, Publisher, 1838.

_____. *The Writings of George Washington: Official Letters Relating to the French War, and Private Letters Before the American Revolution, 1754–May, 1775,* Jared Sparks, ed. Boston: American Stationers' Company, John B. Russell, 1834.

Weems, Mason Locke. *A History of the Life and Death, Virtues and Exploits of General George Washington.* 1800; reprint, Philadelphia: J.B. Lippincott, 1918.

Wiencek, Henry. *An Imperfect God: George Washington, His Slaves, and the Creation of America.* New York: Farrar, Strauss and Giroux, 2003.

Wildes, Harry Emerson. *Valley Forge.* New York: Macmillan, 1938.

Wills, Garry. *Cincinnatus: George Washington and the Enlightenment.* New York: Doubleday, 1984.

Wilson, Woodrow. *George Washington.* 1896; reprint, NY: Cosimo Classics, 2004.

Wister, Owen. *The Seven Ages of Washington: A Biography.* 1907; reprint, NY: Macmillan, 1917.

Wood, Gordon S. *Empire of Liberty: a History of the Early Republic, 1789–1815.* New York: Oxford University Press, 2009.

Woodman, Henry, and Mary Smith Woodman, *History of Valley Forge.* Oaks, PA: J.U. Francis, sr., 1921.

Two. John Adams

Adams, Abigail, John P. Kaminski. *The Quotable Abigail Adams.* Cambridge, MA: Harvard University Press, 2009.

Adams, Charles Francis, ed. *The Works of John Adams, Second President of the United States.* 10 vols. Boston: Little, Brown, 1850–1856.

Adams, James Thurlow. *The Adams Family.* Boston: Little, Brown, 1930; reprint, Westport, CT: Greenwood, 1974.

Adams, John. *Legal Papers of John Adams.* Cambridge, MA: Harvard University Press, 1965.

_____. *The Revolutionary Writings of John Adams.* C. Bradley Thompson, comp. Indianapolis: Liberty Fund, 2000.

_____. *The Works of John Adams, Second President of the United States: With a Life of the Author.* 10 vols. Charles Francis Adams, ed. Boston: Little, Brown, 1850–1856.

_____, and John P. Diggins. *The Portable John Adams.* New York: Penguin, 2004.

_____, and Paul M. Zall. *Adams on Adams.* Lexington: University Press of Kentucky, 2004.

_____, and Thomas Jefferson. *The Adams-Jefferson Letters.* Lester J. Coppen, ed. Chapel Hill: University of North Carolina Press, 1959.

Akers, Charles W. *Abigail Adams: An American Woman.* Boston: Little, Brown, 1980.

Azbell, Frederick J. *Organized Religion Is … Blind, Leading the Blind.* Bloomington, IN: AuthorHouse, 2010.

Blumberg, Phillip I. *Repressive Jurisprudence in the Early American Republic: The First Amendment and the Legacy of English Law.* Cambridge: Cambridge University Press, 2010.

Bober, Natalie S. *Abigail Adams: Witness to a Revolution.* New York: Simon & Schuster, 1998.

Boller, Paul F., Jr. *Presidential Anecdotes.* New York: Oxford University Press, 1996.

_____. *Presidential Campaigns: From George Washington to George W. Bush.* New York: Oxford University Press, 2004.

Bowen, Catherine Drinker. *John Adams and the American Revolution.* Boston: Little, Brown, 1950.

Breamer, Howard F. *John Adams, 1735–1826.* New York: Oceana, 1967.

Brookhiser, Richard. *America's First Dynasty: The Adamses, 1735–1918.* Mankato, MN: Free Press, 2002.

Brown, Ralph. *The Presidency of John Adams.* Lawrence: University Press of Kansas, 1975.

Bumgarner, John R. (M.D.). *The Health of the Presidents.* Jefferson, NC: McFarland, 2004.

Burleigh, Anne Husted. *John Adams.* New Rochelle, NY: Arlington House, 1969.

Butterfield, L.H. *The Book of Abigail and John: Selected Letters of the Adams Family, 1762–1784.* Cambridge, MA: Harvard University Press, 1975.

_____. *The Earliest Diary of John Adams.* Cambridge, MA: Harvard University Press, 1966.

Cappon, Lester J., ed. *The Adams-Jefferson Letters: The Complete Correspondence Between Thomas Jefferson and Abigail and John Adams.* Chapel Hill: University of North Carolina Press, 1988.

Ching, Jacqueline. *Abigail Adams: A Revolutionary Woman.* Buffalo, NY: Rosen, 2002.

Church, F. Forrester. *So Help Me God: The Founding Fathers and the First Great Battle Over the Church.* Orlando, FL: Harcourt, Inc. 2007.

Cowley, Joseph. *John Adams: Architect of Freedom (1735–1826).* New York: IUniverse, 2009.

Dauer, Manning J. *The Adams Federalists.* Baltimore: Johns Hopkins University Press, 1953.

Davis, William W. *The Fries Rebellion, Seventeen Ninety Eight to Seventeen Ninety Nine.* New York: Ayer Publishing, 1977.

DeConde, Alexander. *The Quasi-War: The Politics and Diplomacy of the Undeclared War with France, 1797–1801.* New York: Scribner's, 1966.

DeGregorio, William A. *The Complete Book of U.S. Presidents.* New York: Barricade, 2005.

Diggins, John P. *John Adams.* Austin: Holt, Rinehart & Winston, 2003.

Elkin, Stanley, and Eric McKitrick. *The Age of Federalism.* New York: Oxford University Press, 1993.

Ellis, Joseph J. *Passionate Sage: The Character and Legacy of John Adams.* New York: W.W. Norton, 1993.

Ferling, John. *John Adams: A Life.* Knoxville: University of Tennessee Press, 1992.

_____. *Setting the World Ablaze: Washington, Adams and Jefferson and the American Revolution.* New York: Oxford University Press, 2000.

Gelles, Edith B. *Abigail Adams: A Writing Life.* New York: Routledge, 2002.

_____. *Portia: The World of Abigail Adams.* Bloomington: Indiana University Press, 1995.

Grant, James. *John Adams: Party of One.* New York: Farrar, Straus, and Giroux, 2005.

Hand, Manus. "Dead Presidents on

Dead Presidents: Quotations by One Dead President by Others." manus@diplom.org.

Handler, Edward. *America and Europe in the Political Thought of John Adams*. Cambridge, MA: Harvard University Press, 1964.

Haraszti, Zoltan. *John Adams and the Prophets of Progress*. Cambridge, MA: Harvard University Press, 1952.

Harper, John Lamberton. *American Machiavelli: Alexander Hamilton and the Origins of U.S. Foreign Policy*. Cambridge: Cambridge University Press, 2004.

Holloway, Laura Carter. *The Ladies of the White House: Or, in the Home of the Presidents: Being a Complete History of the Social and Domestic Lives of the Presidents from Washington to Hayes — 1789– 1880*. Martin, TN: Bradley & Co., 1881.

Howe, John R. *The Changing Political Thought of John Adams*. Princeton, NJ: Princeton University Press, 1966.

Hutson, James H. *John Adams and the Diplomacy of the American Revolution*. Lexington: University Press of Kentucky, 1980.

Johnson, Paul. *A History of the American People*. New York: HarperCollins e-books, Kindle ed., 2009.

Kidder, Frederic, and John Adams. *History of the Boston Massacre, March 5, 1770: Consisting of the Narrative of the Town, the Trial of the Soldiers: and a Historical Introduction, Containing Unpublished Documents of John Adams, and Explanatory Notes*. Albany, NY: J. Munsell's Sons, 1870.

Kurtz, Stephen G. *The Presidency of John Adams: The Collapse of Federalism*. Philadelphia: University of Pennsylvania Press, 1957.

Levin, Phyllis Lee. *Abigail Adams: A Biography*. New York: St. Martin's, 1987.

Lord, John. *Beacon Lights of History: American Statesmen*. New York: Fords, Howard, and Hurlburt, 1894.

Mayer, Henry. *A Son of Thunder: Patrick Henry and the American Republic*. New York: Grove Press, 2001.

McCullough, David. *John Adams*. New York: Simon & Schuster, 2001.

Miller, John Chester. *Crisis in Freedom: The Alien and Sedition Acts*. Boston: Little, Brown, 1951.

Owensby, Jackson. *The United States Declaration of Independence* (Revisited). Kernserville, NC: A-Argus Books, 2010.

Quinn-Musgrove, Sandra L., and Sanford Kanter. *America's Royalty: All the Presidents' Children*. Westport, CT: Greenwood, 1995.

Ryerson, Richard Alan, ed. *John Adams and the Founding of the Republic*. Boston: Massachusetts Historical Society, 2001.

Sanderson, John. *Biography of the Signers of the Declaration of Independence*, Vol. III. Philadelphia: R.W. Pomeroy, 1823.

Shaw, Peter. *The Character of John Adams*. Chapel Hill: University of North Carolina Press, 1976.

Shepherd, Jack. *The Adams Chronicles: Four Generations of Greatness*. Boston: Little, Brown, 1975.

Sheppard, John Hannibal. *The Life of Samuel Tucker, Commodore in the American Revolution*. Boston: A. Mudge and Son, 1868.

Smith, James Morton. *Freedom's Fetters: The Alien and Sedition Laws and American Civil Liberties*. Ithaca, NY: Cornell University Press, 1956.

Smith, Paige. *John Adams: 1784– 1826*. Westport, CT: Greenwood, 1969.

Solberg, Winton U. *The Constitutional Convention and the Formation of the Union*. Champaign, IL: University of Illinois Press, 1990.

Stefoff, Rebecca. *John Adams: 2nd President of the United States*. Ada, OK: Garrett Educational Corp., 1988.

Stinchcombe, William C. *The XYZ Affair*. Westport, CT: Greenwood, 1981.

Thompson, C. Bradley. *John Adams and the Spirit of Liberty*. Lawrence: University Press of Kansas, 1998.

_____, and Bernard Cohen. *Science and the Founding Fathers*. New York: W.W. Norton & Co., 1995.

Walsh, Correa Moylan. *The Political Science of John Adams: A Study in the Theory of Mixed Government and the Bicameral System*. New York: G.P. Putnam's Sons, 1915.

Weisberger, Bernard A. *America Afire: Jefferson, Adams, and the Revolutionary Election of 1800*. New York: Morrow, 2000.

White, Leonard D. *The Federalists: A Study in Administrative History*. New York: Macmillan, 1948.

Wilstach, Paul. *Correspondence of John Adams and Thomas Jefferson, 1812–1826*. New York: Kraus Reprint, 1972.

Withey, Lynne. *Dearest Friend: A Life of Abigail Adams*. New York: Free Press, 1981.

Zall, Paul M. *Adams on Adams*. Lexington: University Press of Kentucky, 2004.

Three. Jefferson

Ackerman, Bruce. *The Failure of the Founding Fathers: Jefferson, Marshall, and the Rise of Presidential Democracy*. Cambridge, MA: Harvard University Press, 2005.

Adams, Henry. *History of the United States of America During the Administrations of Thomas Jefferson*. New York: Library of America, 1986.

Adams, William Howard. *The Paris Years of Thomas Jefferson*. New Haven: Yale University Press, 2000.

Ambrose, Stephen E. *Undaunted Courage: Meriwether Lewis, Thomas Jefferson, and the Opening of the American West*. New York: Simon & Schuster, 1996.

Bailey, Jeremy D. *Thomas Jefferson and Executive Power*. Cambridge, NY: Cambridge University Press, 2007.

Banning, Lance. *The Jeffersonian Persuasion: Evolution of a Party Ideology*. Ithaca, NY: Cornell University Press, 1978.

Bassett, Margaret Byrd. *Profiles & Portraits of American Presidents & Their Wives*. Freeport, ME: B. Wheelwright Co.; distributed by Grosset & Dunlap, New York, 1969.

Beard, Charles A. *The Economic Origins of Jefferson Democracy*. New York: Macmillan, 1915.

Becker, Carl Lotus. *The Declaration of Independence: A Study in the History of Political Ideas*. New York: Harcourt, Brace, 1922.

Bedini, Silvio A. *Jefferson and Science*. Chapel Hill: University of North Carolina Press, 2002.

Beran, Michael Knox. *Jefferson's Demons: A Portrait of a Restless Mind*. Washington, DC: Free Press, 2003.

Bernstein, R.B. *Thomas Jefferson*. New York: Oxford University Press, 2003.

_____. *Thomas Jefferson: The Revolution of Ideas*. New York: Oxford University Press, 2004.

Bober, Natalie S. *Thomas Jefferson: Draftsman of a Nation*. Charlottesville: University of Virginia Press, 2007.

Boller, Paul F., Jr., *Presidential Campaigns: From George Washington to George W. Bush*. New York: Oxford University Press, 2004.

_____. *Presidential Wives*. New York: Oxford University Press, 1998.

Boorstin, Daniel J. *The Lost World of Thomas Jefferson*. Chicago: University of Chicago Press, 1993.

Boyd, Julian, et al., eds. *Papers of Thomas Jefferson*. Princeton, NJ: Princeton University Press, 1950–.

Brodie, Fawn M. *Thomas Jefferson: An Intimate History*. New York: W.W. Norton, 1974.

Bumgarner, John R. *The Health of the Presidents*. Jefferson, NC: McFarland, 2004.

Burstein, Andrew. *The Inner Jefferson: Portrait of a Grieving Optimist*. Charlottesville: University of Virginia Press, 1995.

_____. *Jefferson's Secrets: Death and Desire at Monticello*. New York: Basic, 2005.

Cappon, Lester J., ed. *The Adams-Jefferson Letters*. Chapel Hill: University of North Carolina Press, 1959.

Cerami, Charles, and Robert M. Silverstein. *Jefferson's Great Gamble: The Remarkable Story of Jefferson, Napoleon and the Men Behind the Louisiana Purchase*. Naperville, IL: Sourcebooks, 2003.

Clark, Ella E., Margot Edmonds. *Sacagawea of the Lewis and Clark Expedition*. Berkeley: University of California Press, 1983.

Cogliano, Frances D. *Thomas Jefferson: Reputation and Legacy*. Charlottesville: University of Virginia Press, 2006.

Crawford, Allan Pall. *Twilight at Monticello: The Final Years of Thomas Jefferson*. New York: Random House, 2008.

DeGregorio, William A. *The Complete Book of U.S. Presidents*. New York: Barricade, 2005.

Dewey, Donald. *Marshall versus Jefferson: The Political Background of Marbury vs. Madison*. New York: Knopf, 1970.

Dreisbach, Daniel. *Thomas Jefferson and the Wall of Separation Between Church and State*. New York: New York University Press, 2003.

Duncan, Ann W., Steven L. Jones. *Church-State Issues in America Today: Religion and Government*. Westport, CT: Praeger, 2008.

Dunn, Susan. *Jefferson's Second Revolution: The Election of 1800 and the Triumph of Republicanism*. New York: Vintage, 1998.

Ellis, Joseph J. *American Sphinx: The Character of Thomas Jefferson*. New York: Knopf, 1996.

Ferling, John. *Adams vs. Jefferson: The Tumultuous Election of 1800*. New York: Oxford University Press, 2004.

Ford, Paul Leicester, ed. *The Writings of Thomas Jefferson*. 10 vols. New York: G.P. Putnam's Sons, 1893–1899.

Frary, I.T. *Jefferson: Architect and Builder*. Richmond, VA: Garrett & Massie, 1950.

Fremont-Barnes, Gregory. *The Wars of the Barbary Pirates: To the Shores of Tripoli: The Rise of the U.S. Navy and Marines*. Oxford: Osprey Publishing, 2006.

Gabler, James M. *Passions: The Wines and Travels of Thomas Jefferson*. Baltimore: Bacchus Press Ltd., 1995.

Gordon-Reed, Annette. *Thomas Jefferson and Sally Hemings: An American Controversy*. Charlottesville: University of Virginia Press, 1997.

Hailman, John R. *Thomas Jefferson on Wine*. Jackson: University Press of Mississippi, 2006.

Halliday, E.M. *Understanding Thomas Jefferson*. New York: Harper Perennial, 2002.

Hayes, Kevin J. *The Road to Monticello: The Life and Mind of Thomas Jefferson*. New York: Oxford University Press, 2008.

Hellenbrand, Harold. *The Unfinished Revolution: Education and Politics in the Thought of Thomas Jefferson*. Newark: University of Delaware Press, 1990.

Hitchens, Christopher. *Thomas Jefferson: Author of America*. New York: Atlas/HarperCollins, 2005.

Hoar, George F. "Special Introduction," in *The Writings of Thomas Jefferson*. Lipscomb and Bergh, eds. Washington, DC: Thomas Jefferson Memorial Association of the United States, 1903.

Hutson, James H. *Religion and the New Republic: Faith in the Founding of America*. Lanham, MD: Rowman & Littlefield. 2000.

Jackson, Donald, ed. *Letters of the Lewis and Clark Expedition with Related Documents, 1783–1854*. 2 vols. Champaign: University of Illinois Press, 1978.

Jefferson, Thomas. *Autobiography*. New York: G.P. Putnam's Sons, 1914.

_____. *The Autobiography of Thomas Jefferson, 1743–1790*. Paul Leicester Ford, ed. Philadelphia: University of Pennsylvania Press, 2005.

_____. *The Jefferson Cyclopedia: A Comprehensive Collection of the Views of Thomas Jefferson*. John Foley, ed. New York: Funk & Wagnalls, 1900.

_____. *The Papers of Thomas Jefferson*. Julian P. Boyd, et al., eds. 30 volumes to date, 60 planned. Princeton, NJ: Princeton University Press, 1950–.

Johnstone, Robert J. *Jefferson and the Presidency: Leadership in the Young Republic*. Ithaca, NY: Cornell University Press, 1978.

_____, and Merrill D. Peterson. *The Portable Thomas Jefferson*. New York: Penguin, 1977.

Kukla, Amy, and Jon Kukla. *Thomas Jefferson: Life, Liberty, and the Pursuit of Happiness*. New York: Rosen, 2005.

Kukla, Jon. *A Wilderness So Immense: The Louisiana Purchase and the Destiny of America*. New York: Knopf, 2003.

Ledgin, Norm. *Diagnosing Jefferson: Evidence of a Condition that Guided His Beliefs, Behavior, and Personal Associations*. Arlington, TX: Future Horizons, 2000.

Lerner, Max. *Thomas Jefferson: America's Philosopher-King*. Piscataway, NJ: Transaction, 1996.

Lewis, Jan, Peter S. Onuf. *Sally Hemings & Thomas Jefferson: History, Memory, and Civic Culture*. Charlottesville: University of Virginia Press, 1999.

Lewis, Meriwether, William Clark, and Elliott Coues. *The History of the Lewis and Clark Expedition*. New York: Courier Dover Publications, 1979.

Lipscomb, Andrew A., and Albert Ellery Bergh, eds. *The Writings of Thomas Jefferson*. 20 vols. Washington, DC: Thomas Jefferson Memorial Association, 1903–04.

Malone, Dumas. *Jefferson and His Times*. 6 vols. Charlottesville: University of Virginia Press, 1948–1981.

Mapp, Alf J., Jr. *Thomas Jefferson: A Strange Case of Mistaken Identity*. Lanham, MD: Madison, 1987.

_____. *Thomas Jefferson: America's Paradoxical Patriot*. Lanham, MD: Rowman & Littlefield, 2007.

_____. *Thomas Jefferson: Passionate Pilgrim, the Presidency, the Founding of the University, and the Private Battle*. Lanham, MD: Rowman & Littlefield, 2009.

Mayer, David N. *The Constitutional Thought of Thomas Jefferson*. Charlottesville: University of Virginia Press, 1994.

McColley, Robert. *Slavery and Jeffersonian Virginia*. Champaign: University of Illinois Press, 1964.

McCoy, Drew R. *The Elusive Republic: Political Economy in Jeffersonian America*. New York: Norton, 1982.

McDonald, Forrest. *The Presidency of Thomas Jefferson*. Lawrence: University Press of Kansas, 1976.

McLaughlin, Jack. *Jefferson and Monticello: The Biography of a Builder*. New York: Macmillan, 1990.

McPherson, James M. *Battle Cry of Freedom: The Civil War Era*. New York: Oxford University Press, 2003.

Melton, Buckner F. *Aaron Burr: Conspiracy to Treason*. New York: Wiley, 2002.

Miller, Robert J. *Native America,*

Discovered and Conquered: Thomas Jefferson, Lewis & Clark, and Manifest Destiny. Lincoln: University of Nebraska Press. 2008.

Moulton, Gary E. *The Journals of the Lewis and Clark Expedition.* 13 vols. Lincoln: University of Nebraska Press, 1983–2001.

O'Brien, Conor Cruise. *The Long Affair: Thomas Jefferson and the French Revolution, 1785–1900.* Chicago: University of Chicago Press, 1998.

Onuf, Peter S. *Jefferson's Empire: The Language of American Nationhood.* Charlottesville: University of Virginia Press, 2000.

_____. *The Mind of Thomas Jefferson.* Charlottesville: University of Virginia Press, 2007.

Parton, James. *Life of Thomas Jefferson: Third President of the United States.* Boston: J.R. Osgood and Company, 1874.

Peterson, Merrill D. *Adams and Jefferson: A Revolutionary Dialogue.* New York: Oxford University Press, 1978.

_____. *The Jefferson Image in the American Mind.* Charlottesville: University of Virginia Press, 1998.

_____. *Thomas Jefferson and the New Nation: A Biography.* Norwalk, CT: Easton, 1987.

_____, ed. *Thomas Jefferson Writings.* Des Moines, IA: Library of America, 1995–2007.

Randall, W.S. *Thomas Jefferson: A Life.* New York: Holt, 1993.

Randolph, Thomas Jefferson, ed. *The Memoirs, Correspondence and Private Papers of Thomas Jefferson.* 4 vols. London: H. Colburn and R. Bentley, 1829.

_____, and Sarah Nicholas Randolph. *The Domestic Life of Thomas Jefferson.* New York: Harper & Brothers, 1871; Charleston, SC: Forgotten Books, 1947.

Rayner, B.L. *Life of Thomas Jefferson.* Boston: Lilly, Wait, Colman, & Holden, 1834.

Roche, O.I.A., ed. *The Jefferson Bible: With the Annotated Commentaries on Religion of Thomas Jefferson.* New York: Clarkson N. Potter, 1964.

Sanford, Charles B. *Religious Life of Thomas Jefferson.* Charlottesville: University of Virginia Press, 1984.

Severance, John B. *Thomas Jefferson: Architect of Democracy.* Boston: Houghton Mifflin Harcourt, 1998.

Sheldon, Garrett Ward. *The Political Philosophy of Thomas Jefferson.* Baltimore: Johns Hopkins University Press, 1993.

Shuffleton, Frank. *Thomas Jefferson: A Comprehensive, Annotated Biography.* New York: Garland, 1992.

Simon, James F. *What Kind of Nation: Thomas Jefferson, John Marshall, and the Epic Struggle to Create a United States.* New York: Simon & Schuster, 2002.

Sloan, Herbert E. *Principle and Interest: Thomas Jefferson and the Politics of Debt.* Charlottesville: University of Virginia Press, 2001.

Spivak, Burton I. *Jefferson's English Crisis: Commerce, Embargo, and the Republican Revolution.* Charlottesville: University of Virginia Press, 1979.

Thorpe, Francis Newton. *The Constitutional History of the United States.* Chicago: Callaghan & Co., 1901.

Trueit, Trudi Strain. *Thomas Jefferson.* Tarrytown, NY: Marshall Cavendish, 2009.

Tubbs, Stephanie Ambrose, and Clay Jenkinson. *The Lewis and Clark Companion: An Encyclopedic Guide to the Voyage of Discovery.* New York: Macmillan, 2003.

Turner, Robert F. *The Jefferson-Hemings Controversy: Report of the Scholars Commission.* Durham: Carolina Academic Press, 2011.

Urofsky, Melvin I. *The Levy Family and Monticello, 1834–1923: Saving Thomas Jefferson's House.* Charlottesville: University of Virginia Press, 2001.

Wagoner, Jennings L. *Jefferson and Education.* Chapel Hill: University of North Carolina Press, 2004.

Wallace, Anthony F.C. *Jefferson and the Indians: The Tragic Fate of the First Americans.* Cambridge, MA: Harvard University Press, 1999.

Watson, Thomas Edward. *The Life and Times of Thomas Jefferson.* New York: D. Appleton and Company, 1903.

Wheelan, Joseph. *Jefferson's Vendetta: The Pursuit of Aaron Burr and the Judiciary.* New York: Carroll & Graf, 2006.

_____. *Jefferson's War: America's First War on Terror, 1801–1805.* New York: Carroll & Graf, 2003.

Wills, Garry. *Inventing America: Jefferson's Declaration of Independence.* New York: Doubleday, 1978.

_____. *Negro President: Jefferson and the Slave Power.* Boston: Houghton Mifflin, 2003.

Zack, Richard. *The Pirate Coast: Thomas Jefferson, the First Marines, and the Secret Mission of 1805.* New York: Hyperion, 2005.

Four. Madison

Adams, Henry, and Earl N. Harbert. *History of the United States of America During the Administrations of Thomas Jefferson.* New York: Library of America, 1986.

Allgor, Catherine. *A Perfect Union: Dolley Madison and the Creation of the American Nation.* New York: Macmillan, 2007.

Ambrose, Kevin, Dan Henry, and Andy Wiess. *Washington Weather: The Weather Sourcebook for the D.C. Area.* Fairfax, VA: Historical Enterprises, 2002.

Arnett, Ethel Stephens. *Mrs. James Madison: The Incomparable Dolley.* Warrenton, VA: Piedmont, 1972.

Banning, Lance. *Jefferson and Madison: Three Conversations from the Founding.* Boulder, CO: Madison House, 1995.

_____. *The Sacred Fire of Liberty: James Madison and the Founding of the Federal Republic.* Ithaca, NY: Cornell University Press, 1995.

Bassett, Margaret Byrd. *Profiles & Portraits of American Presidents.* Freeport, ME: B. Wheelwright Co., 1964.

Beasley, Maurine Hoffman. *First Ladies and the Press: The Unfinished Partnership of the Media Age.* Evanston, IL: Northwestern University Press, 2005.

Boller, Paul F., Jr. *Presidential Anecdotes.* New York: Oxford University Press, 1981.

_____. *Presidential Wives: An Anecdotal History.* New York: Oxford University Press, 1998.

Brandt, Irving. *James Madison.* 6 vols. Indianapolis: Bobbs-Merrill, 1941–1961.

Brookhiser, Richard. *James Madison.* New York: Basic Books, 2011.

Brown, Roger H. *The Republic in Peril: 1812.* New York: Columbia University Press, 1964.

Bumgarner, John R. (M.D.). *The Health of the Presidents.* Jefferson, NC: McFarland, 2004.

Burns, Edward McNall. *James Madison: Philosopher of the Constitution.* Piscataway, NJ: Rutgers University Press, 1938.

Chambers, Douglas B. *Murder at Montpelier: Igbo Africans in Virginia.* Jackson: University Press of Mississippi, 2009.

Chernow, Ron. *Alexander Hamilton.* New York: Penguin, 2005.

Côté, Richard N. *Strength and Honor: The Life of Dolley Madison.* Mt. Pleasant, SC: Corinthian Books, 2005.

Curtis, Francis *The Republican Party: A History of Its Fifty Years' Existence and a record of Its Measures and Leaders, 1854–1904.* New York: G.P. Putnam's Sons, 1904.

DeGregorio, William A. *Complete Book of U.S. Presidents*. New York: Barricade, 2001.

Dooley, Patricia L. *The Early Republic: Primary Documents on Events from 1799 to 1820*. Westport, CT: Greenwood, 2004.

Elish, Dan. *James Madison*. Tarrytown, NY: Marshall Cavendish, 2007.

Elkin, Stanley M., and Eric McKitrick. *The Age of Federalism*. New York: Oxford University Press, 1995.

Enz, David Fitz. *Old Ironsides: Eagle of the Sea: The Story of the USS Constitution*. Lanham, MD: Taylor Trade Publications, 2009.

Fox, Early Lee. *The American Colonization Society*. Baltimore: Johns Hopkins University Press, 1919.

Goldwin, Robert A. *From Parchment to Power: How James Madison Used the Bill of Rights to Save the Constitution*. American Enterprise Institute, 1997.

Goodwin, Maud Wilder. *Dolly Madison*. New York: Scribner, 1896.

Gould, Lewis L. *American First Ladies: Their Lives and Their Legacy*. London: Taylor & Francis, 2001.

Gwynne-Thomas, E.H. *The Presidential Families*. New York: Hippocrene Books, 1989.

Hobson, Charles. *The Great Chief Justice: John Marshall and the Rule of Law* (American Political Thought), Lawrence: University Press of Kansas, 2000.

Holmes, David Lynn. *The Faiths of the Founding Fathers*. New York: Oxford University Press, 2006.

Hunt, Galliard, ed. *The Writings of James Madison*. 9 vols. New York: G.P. Putnam's Sons, 1900–1910.

Hutchinson, William T., et al., eds. *The Papers of James Madison*. Charlottesville: University of Virginia Press, 1962–.

Jennings, Paul. *A Colored Man's Reminiscences of James Madison*. Ithaca, NY: Cornell University Library, 1865.

Kaplan, Edward S. *The Bank of the United States and the American Economy*. Westport, CT: Greenwood, 1999.

Kent, Zachary. *Dolley Madison: The Enemy Cannot Frighten a Free People*. Berkeley Heights, NJ: Enslow Publishers, 2010.

Kester, Scott J. *The Haunted Philosopher: James Madison, Republicanism, and Slavery*. Landham, MD: Lexington Books, 2008.

Ketcham, Ralph. *James Madison: A Biography*. 1971; reprint, Charlottesville: University of Virginia Press, 1990.

Klapthor, Margaret Brown, and All-ida M. Black. *The First Ladies*. Washington, DC: Government Printing Office, 2002.

Koch, Adrienne. *Jefferson and Madison*. 1950; reprint, Birmingham, AL: Palladium, 2000.

Labunski, Richard E. *James Madison and the Struggle for the Bill of Rights*. New York: Oxford University Press, 2006.

Leibiger, Stuart. *Founding Friendship: George Washington, James Madison and the Creation of the American Republic*. Charlottesville: University of Virginia Press, 1999.

Leiner, Frederick C. *The End of Barbary Terror: America's 1815 War against the Pirates of North Africa*. New York: Oxford University Press, 2006.

Madison, James. *The Constitution a Pro-Slavery Compact: or, Extracts from the Madison Papers, etc.* New York: American Anti-Slavery Society, 1845.

_____. *The Federalist; Or, The New Constitution*, two volumes. New York: J. and A. McLean, 1788.

_____. *The Papers of James Madison*. Georgetown, DC: Langtree & O'Sullivan, 1840.

_____, and Erastus Howard Scott. *Journal of the Federal Convention*. Chicago: Scott, Foresman and Co., 1898.

_____, and Henry Dilworth Gilpin. *The Papers of James Madison, Purchased by Order of Congress; Being His Correspondence and Reports of Debates During the Congress of the Confederation and His Reports of Debates in the Federal Convention; Now Published from the Original Manuscripts*. New York: J. & H.G. Langley, 1841.

Mahon, John. *The War of 1812*. Gainesville: University of Florida Press, 1972.

Malone, Mary. *James Madison*. Berkeley Heights, NJ: Enslow, 1997.

Markham, Jerry W. *A Financial History of the United States*. Armonk, NY: M.E. Sharpe, 2002.

Mattern, David B. *James Madison: Patriot, Politician, and President*. New York: Rosen, 2005.

_____, and Holly Shulman. *The Selected Letters of Dolley Payne Madison*. Charlottesville: University of Virginia Press, 2003.

Matthews, Richard K. *If Men Were Angels: James Madison and the Heartless Empire of Reason*. Lawrence: University Press of Kansas, 1995.

McCoy, Drew R. *The Last of the Fathers: James Madison and the Republican Legacy*. Cambridge, NY: Cambridge University Press, 1989.

McNamara, Peter. *The Noblest Minds: Fame, Honor, and the American Founding*. Lanham MD: Rowman & Littlefield, 1999.

McPherson, James M. *"To the Best of My Ability": The American Presidents*. New York: Dorling Kindersley, 2000.

Meyers, Marvin, ed. *The Mind of the Founder: Sources of the Political Thought of James Madison*. Rev. ed. Waltham, MA: Brandeis University Press, 1981.

Miller, William Lee. *The Business of May Next: James Madison and the Founding*. Charlottesville: University of Virginia Press, 1992.

Mitchell, Barbara. *Father of the Constitution: A Story About James Madison*. Minneapolis: Millbrook Press, 2004.

Rakove, Jack N. *James Madison and the Creation of the American Republic*. 1990; reprint, London: Longman, 2002.

Read, James H. *Power Versus Liberty: Madison, Hamilton, Wilson, Jay, and Jefferson*. Charlottesville: University of Virginia Press, 2000.

Rives, William Cabell. *History of the Life and Times of James Madison*. 3 vols. Boston: Little, Brown, 1859–1868.

Rosen, Gary. *American Compact: James Madison and the Problem of Founding*. Lawrence: University Press of Kansas, 1999.

Rutland, Robert A. *James Madison: The Founding Father*. 1987; reprint, Columbia: University of Missouri Press, 1997.

_____. *James Madison and the American Nation, 1751–1836: An Encyclopedia*. New York: Simon & Schuster, 1994.

_____. *Madison's Alternatives: The Jeffersonian Republicans and the Coming of War, 1805–1812*. Philadelphia: J.B. Lippincott, 1973.

_____. *The Presidency of James Madison*. Lawrence: University Press of Kansas, 1990.

Scaros, Constantinos E. *Understanding the Constitution*. Sudbury, MA: Jones & Bartlett Learning, 2011.

Sheldon, Garrett W. *The Political Philosophy of James Madison*. Baltimore: Johns Hopkins University Press, 2001.

Shulman, Holly Cowan, David B. Mattern. *Dolley Madison: Her Life, Letters, and Legacy*. New York: Rosen, 2003.

Shultz, Harold Seessel. *James Madison*. New York: Twayne, 1970.

Smith, James M., ed. *The Republic of Letters: the Correspondence between Thomas Jefferson and James*

Madison, 1776–1826. 3 vols. New York: Norton, 1995.

Smith, Margaret Bayard. *The First Forty Years of Washington Society: Portrayed by the Family Letters of Mrs. Samuel Harrison Smith (Margaret Bayard) from the Collection of Her Grandson, J. Henley Smith.* New York: Scribner, 1906.

Stagg, John C.A. *Mr. Madison's War: Politics, Diplomacy, and Warfare in the Early American Republic.* Princeton, NJ: Princeton University Press, 1983.

Van Alstyne, William W. *Interpretations of the First Amendment.* Durham: Duke University Press, 1984.

Vile, John R., William D. Pederson, and Frank J. Williams. *James Madison: Philosopher, Founder, and Statesman.* Athens: Ohio University Press, 2008.

Wead, Doug. *The Raising of a President: The Mothers and Fathers of Our Nation's Leaders.* New York: Simon & Schuster, 2005.

Wills, Garry. *James Madison.* New York: Times Books, 2002.

Wilson, James Grant, and John Fiske, eds. *Appleton's Cyclopædia of American Biography.* New York: D. Apple-ton and Company, 1888.

Zall, Paul M. *Dolley Madison.* Huntington, NY: Nova History Publications, 2001.

Five. Monroe

Adams, John Quincy. *The Lives of James Madison and James Monroe.* Boston: Phillips, Sampson, 1850.

Ammon, Harry. *James Monroe: The Quest for National Identity.* Charlottesville: University of Virginia Press, 1990.

Bemis, Samuel Flagg. *John Quincy Adams and the Foundations of American Foreign Policy.* New York: Norton, 1973.

Bumgarner, John R. (M.D.). *The Health of the Presidents.* Jefferson, NC: McFarland, 2004.

Chernow, Ron. *Alexander Hamilton.* New York: Penguin, 2005.

Cresson, W.P. *James Monroe.* 1946; Reprint, Norwalk, CT: Easton Press, 1986.

Crompton, Samuel Willard. *McCulloch v. MD: Implied Powers of the Federal Government.* New York: Infobase Publishing, 2007.

Cunningham, Noble E., Jr. *Jefferson and Monroe: Constant Friendship and Respect.* Charlottesville, VA: Thomas Jefferson Foundation, 2003.

_____. *The Presidency of James Monroe.* Lawrence: University Press of Kansas, 1996.

Dangerfield, George. *Defiance to the Old World: The Story Behind the Monroe Doctrine.* New York: Putnam, 1970.

_____. *The Era of Good Feelings.* 1952; reprint, Lanham, MD: Ivan R. Dee, 1989.

DeGregorio, William A. *The Complete Book of U.S. Presidents.* New York: Barricade, 2005.

DeRose, Chris. *Founding Rivals: Madison vs. Monroe, The Bill of Rights, and The Election that Saved a Nation.* Washington, DC: Regnery, 2011.

Fischer, David Hackett. *Washington Crossing.* New York: Oxford University Press, 2004.

Gilman, Daniel Coit. *James Monroe.* 1898; reprint, Broomall, PA: Chelsea House, 1983.

Hart, Gary. *James Monroe.* New York: Times Books, 2005.

Jalloh, Alusine, and Toyin Falola. *The United States and West Africa: Interactions and Relations.* Rochester, NY: University Rochester Press, 2008.

Jewell, Elizabeth. *U.S. Presidents Factbook.* New York: Random House, 2005.

Klapthor, Margaret Brown, and Allida M. Black. *The First Ladies.* Washington, DC: Government Printing Office, 2002.

Langston-Harrison, Lee. *Images of a President: Portraits of James Monroe.* Fredericksburg, VA: James Monroe Museum, 1992.

_____. *A Presidential Legacy: The Monroe Collection.* Fredericksburg, VA: James Monroe Museum, 1997.

Levy, Debbie. *James Monroe.* Minneapolis: Lerner, 2004.

May, Ernest R. *The Making of the Monroe Doctrine.* Cambridge: Belknap Press of Harvard University, 1992.

Meade, William. *Old Churches, Ministers, and Families of Virginia.* Philadelphia: J.B. Lippincott, 1857.

Mitchell, Broadus. *Alexander Hamilton: The National Adventure.* New York: Macmillan, 1962.

Monroe, James. *The Autobiography of James Monroe.* Stuart Gerry Brown, ed. Syracuse, NY: Syracuse University Press, 1992.

_____. *James Monroe, 1758–1831; Chronology, Documents, Bibliographical Aids.* Ian Elliot, ed. Dobbs Ferry, NY: Oceana Publications, 1969.

_____. *James Monroe Papers in Virginia Repositories.* Curtis Wiswell Garrison and David Lawrence Thomas, eds. University of Virginia Library, Charlottesville, 1969.

_____. *The People, the Sovereigns.* Richmond, VA: James River, 1987.

_____. *The Writings of James Monroe: Including a Collection of His Public and Private Papers and Correspondence Now for the First Time Printed,* Vol. 3. S.M. Hamilton, ed. New York: G.P. Putnam's sons, 1900.

_____, Daniel Preston, and Marlena C. DeLong. *The Papers of James Monroe: Selected Correspondence and Papers, 1776–1794.* Westport, CT: Greenwood, 2003.

Moore, Glover. *The Missouri Compromise, 1819–1821.* Gloucester, MA: Peter Smith, 1967.

Morgan, George. *The Life of James Monroe.* Boston: Small, Maynard and Company, 1921.

Perkins, Dexter. *The Monroe Doctrine, 1823–1826.* Gloucester, MA: P. Smith, 1965.

Reddaway, William Fiddian. *The Monroe Doctrine.* Cambridge: Cambridge University Press, 1898.

Rothbard, Murray N. *The Panic of 1819: Reactions and Policies.* Auburn, AL: Ludwig von Mises Institute, 2007.

Sandak, Cass R. *The Monroes.* New York: Crestwood House, 1993.

Schneider, Dorothy, and Carl J. Schneider. *First Ladies: A Biographical Dictionary.* New York: Infobase Publishing, 2010.

Soulsby, Hugh R. *The Right of Search and the Slave Trade in Anglo-American Relations, 1814–1862.* Baltimore: Johns Hopkins Press, 1933.

Steinberg, Alfred. *The First Ten: The Founding Presidents and Their Administrations.* New York: Doubleday, 1967.

Steiner, Franklin. *The Religious Beliefs of our Presidents.* Amherst, NY: Prometheus, 1995.

Styron, Arthur. *The Last of the Cocked Hats: James Monroe and the Virginia Dynasty.* Norman: University of Oklahoma Press, 1945.

Unger, Harlow Giles *The Last Founding Father: James Monroe and a Nation's Call to Greatness.* New York: Da Capo Press, 2010.

Waldo, Samuel Putnam. *The Tour of James Monroe, President of the United States, in the Year 1817.* Hartford, CT: F.D. Bolles & Co., 1818.

Wasserman, Adam. *A People's History of Florida 1513–1876: How Africans, Seminoles, Women, and Lower Class Whites Shaped the Sunshine State.* Sarasota, FL: Adam Wasserman, 2009.

Watson, Robert P. *The Presidents' Wives: Reassessing the Office of*

First Lady. Boulder, CO: Lynne Rienner Publishers, 2000.

Wead, Doug. *All the Presidents' Children: Triumph and Tragedy in the Lives of America's First Families.* New York: Simon & Schuster, 2004.

Wilmerding, Lucius, Jr., *James Monroe, Public Claimant.* New Brunswick, NJ: Rutgers University Press, 1960.

Wilson, Charles Morrow. *The Monroe Doctrine: An American Frame of Mind.* Princeton, NJ: Auerbach, 1971.

Wootton, James. *Elizabeth Kortright Monroe.* Williamsburg, VA: College of William and Mary, 1987.

Six. J. Q. Adams

Adams, Henry. *The Education of Henry Adams.* Boston: Massachusetts Historical Society, 1919.

Adams, James Truslow. *The Adams Family.* Akron, OH: Literary Guild, 1930.

Adams, John Quincy. *Dermot MacMorrogh, or The Conquest of Ireland.* Boston: Carter, Hendee Co., 1832.

_____. *Diary of John Quincy Adams.* Cambridge, MA: Harvard University Press, 1981.

_____. *Lectures on Rhetoric and Oratory.* 2 vols. 1810; Reprint, New York: Russell & Russell, 1962.

_____. *Letters of John Quincy Adams to His Son on the Bible and Its Teachings.* Charles Francis Adams, ed. Philadelphia: J.B. Lippincott 1848.

_____. *Memoirs of John Quincy Adams, Taken from His Diaries, 1794–1848.* Charles Francis Adams, ed. Philadelphia: J.B. Lippincott, 1874–1877.

_____. *Poems of Religion and Society, by John Quincy Adams, Sixth President of the United States ... with Notices of His Life and Character,* John Davis and T.H. Benton, eds. Auburn, NY: Miller, Orton Mulligan, 1854.

Allen, David Grayson, et al., eds. *Diary of John Quincy Adams.* Cambridge, MA: Belknap Press of Harvard University Press, 1981.

Bassett, Margaret. *Profiles & Portraits of American Presidents & Their Wives.* Freeport, ME: The Bond Wheelwright Company, 1969.

Bemis, Samuel Flagg. *John Quincy Adams and the Foundations of American Foreign Policy.* New York: Knopf, 1949.

_____. *John Quincy Adams and the Union.* New York: Knopf, 1956.

Bobbé. Dorothie. *Mr. & Mrs. John Quincy Adams: An Adventure in Patriotism.* New York: Minton, Balch & Company, 1930.

Boller, Paul F., Jr. *Presidential Anecdotes.* New York: Oxford University Press, 1981.

_____. *Presidential Wives.* New York: Oxford University Press, 1988.

Brookhiser, Richard. *America's First Dynasty: The Adamses, 1735–1918.* New York: Free Press, 2002.

Bumgarner, John R. (M.D.). *The Health of the Presidents.* Jefferson, NC: McFarland, 2004.

Burleigh, Nina. *The Stranger and the Statesman: James Smithson, John Quincy Adams, and the Making of America's Greatest Museum, the Smithsonian.* New York: HarperCollins, 2003.

Butterfield, Lyman H., et al., eds. *The Adams Family Correspondence.* Cambridge, MA: Belknap Press of Harvard University Press, 1963–.

Clark, Bennett Champ. *John Quincy Adams, "Old Man Eloquent."* Boston: Little, Brown, Co., 1932.

Cox, Samuel Hanson, Thomas Chalmers, Nathanael Emmons, and John Quincy Adams. *Interviews: Memorable and Useful.* New York: Harper & Brothers, 1853.

DeGregorio, William A. *The Complete Book of U.S. Presidents.* New York: Barricade, 2005.

East, Robert Abraham. *John Quincy Adams: The Critical Years: 1785–1794.* New York: Bookman Associates, 1962.

Ewing, Heather P. *The Lost World of James Smithson: Science, Revolution, and the Birth of the Smithsonian.* New York: Bloomsbury, 2007.

Falkner, Leonard. *The President Who Wouldn't Retire: John Quincy Adams.* New York: Coward-McCann, 1967.

Ford, Worthington Chauncey, ed. *Writings of John Quincy Adams.* 1913; Reprint, New York: Greenwood, 1968.

Gould, Lewis L., ed. *American First Ladies: Their Lives and Their Legacy.* New York: Routledge, 2001.

Graff, Henry Franklin. *The Presidents: A Reference History.* New York: Simon & Schuster, 2002.

Hargreaves, Mary. *The Presidency of John Quincy Adams.* Lawrence: University Press of Kansas, 1985.

Hecht, Marie B. *John Quincy Adams: A Personal History of an Independent Man.* New York: Macmillan, 1972.

Hewson, Martha S. *John Quincy Adams.* New York: Infobase Publishing, 2003.

Ketcham, Ralph. *Presidents Above Party: The First American Presidency, 1789–1829.* Chapel Hill: University of North Carolina Press, 1987.

Klapthor, Margaret Brown, and Allida M. Black. *The First Ladies.* Washington, DC: Government Printing Office, 2002.

LaFeber, Walter, ed. *John Quincy Adams and American Continental Empire: Letters, Papers and Speeches.* Chicago: Quadrangle Books, 1965.

Lewis, James E., Jr. *John Quincy Adams: Policymaker for the Union.* Wilmington, DE: Scholarly Resources, 2001.

Lipsky, George A. *John Quincy Adams, His Theory and Ideas.* New York: Crowell, 1950.

Lomask. Milton. *John Quincy Adams: Son of the American Revolution.* Ariel Books. 1965.

Miller, William Lee. *Arguing About Slavery: The Great Battle in the United States Congress.* New York: Vintage, 1996.

Morse, John Torrey, Jr. *John Quincy Adams.* 1898; Reprint, with new introduction by Lynn H. Parsons, New York: Chelsea House, 1980.

Morton, Thomas. *The New England Canaan, 1637.* Jack Dempsey, ed. Scituate, MA: Digital Scanning 2000.

Myers, Walter Dean. *Amistad: A Long Road to Freedom.* London: Puffin, 2001.

Nagel, Paul C. *The Adams Women: Abigail and Louisa Adams; Their Sisters and Daughters.* New York: Oxford University Press, 1987.

_____. *John Quincy Adams: A Public Life, a Private Life.* Cambridge, MA: Harvard University Press, 1999.

Nevins, Allan, ed. *The Diary of John Quincy Adams, 1794–1845: American Diplomacy, and Political, Social, and Intellectual Life, from Washington to Polk.* 1951; Reprint, New York: F. Ungar, 1969.

O'Brien, Michael. *Henry Adams and the Southern Question.* Athens: University of Georgia Press, 2005.

Parsons, Lynn H. *John Quincy Adams.* Madison, WI: Madison House, 1998.

Quincy, Josiah. *Memoir of the Life of John Quincy Adams.* Boston: Phillips, Sampson Co., 1858.

Remini, Robert V. *John Quincy Adams.* New York: Times Books, 2002.

Richards, Leonard. *The Life and Times of Congressman John Quincy Adams.* New York: Oxford University Press, 1986.

Rodriguez, Junius P. *Slavery in the United States: A Social, Political,* and Historical Encyclopedia. Santa Barbara, CA: ABC-CLIO, 2007.

Russell, Greg. John Quincy Adams and the Public Virtues of Diplomacy. Columbia: University Press of Missouri, 1995.

Seward, William H. Life and Public Service of John Quincy Adams. Charleston, SC: BiblioBazaar, 2006.

Shepherd, Jack. The Adams Chronicles: Four Generations of Greatness. Boston: Little, Brown, 1975.

_____. Cannibals of the Heart: A Personal Biography of Louisa Catherine and John Quincy Adams. New York: McGraw-Hill, 1980.

Steinberg, Alfred. The First Ten. Garden City, NY: Doubleday, 1967.

Taussig, F.W. The Tariff History of the United States. 8th ed., rev. New York: Capricorn Books, 1964.

Teed, Paul E. John Quincy Adams: Yankee Nationalist. New York: Nova Publishers, 2006.

U.S. Congress. Token of a Nation's Sorrow: Addresses in the Congress of the United States, and Funeral Solemnities on the Death of John Quincy Adams. 30th Cong., 1st sess., 1847–1848. Washington, DC: J.G.S. Gideon, 1848.

Weeks, William Earl. John Quincy Adams and the American Global Empire. Lexington: University Press of Kentucky, 1992.

Wheelan, Joseph. Mr. Adams's Last Crusade: John Quincy Adams's Extraordinary Post-Presidential Life in Congress. New York: PublicAffairs, 2008.

Wills, Garry. Henry Adams and the Making of America. Boston: Houghton Mifflin Harcourt, 2007.

Wood. Gary V. Heir to the Fathers: John Quincy Adams and the Spirit of Constitutional Government. Lanham, MD: Lexington Books. 2004.

Seven. Jackson

Anderson, William, ed. Cherokee Removal: Before and After. Athens: University of Georgia Press, 1991.

Aronson, Sidney. Status and Kinship in the Higher Civil Service: Standards of Selection in the Administrations of John Adams, Thomas Jefferson and Andrew Jackson. Cambridge, MA: Harvard University Press, 1964.

Bassett, John Spencer. The Life of Andrew Jackson. 1911; Reprint of 1931 ed. (2 vols. in 1), Hamden, CT: Archon Books, 1967.

_____, and Daniel M. Matteson, eds. Correspondence of Andrew Jackson. 7 vols. 1926–1935; Reprint (7 vols. in 6), New York: Kraus Reprint, 1969.

Bassett, Margaret. Profiles & Portraits of American Presidents & Their Wives. Freeport, ME: Bond Wheelwright Company, 1969.

Biddle, Nicholas. The Correspondence of Nicholas Biddle Dealing with National Affairs, 1807–1844. Reginald C. McGrane, ed. 1919; Reprint, Boston: J.S. Canner, 1966.

Belohlavek, John M. Let the Eagle Soar: The Foreign Policy of Andrew Jackson. Lincoln: University of Nebraska Press, 1985.

Boller, Paul F., Jr. Presidential Campaigns: From George Washington to George W. Bush. New York: Oxford University Press, 2004.

_____. Presidential Wives. New York: Oxford University Press, 1998.

Booraem, Hendrik. Young Hickory: The Making of Andrew Jackson. Lanham, MD: Taylor Trade, 2001.

Brady, Cyrus Townsend. The True Andrew Jackson. Philadelphia: J.B. Lippincott Co., 1906.

Brady, Patricia. A Being So Gentle: The Frontier Love Story of Rachel and Andrew Jackson. New York: Palgrave Macmillan, 2011.

Brands, H.W. Andrew Jackson: His Life and Times. Garden City, NY: Doubleday, 2005.

Brown, William Garrott. Andrew Jackson. New York: Houghton, Mifflin & Co., 1900.

Buchanan, John. Jackson's Way: Andrew Jackson and the People of the Western Waters. New York: J. Wiley, 2001.

Buell, August C. The History of Andrew Jackson. 2 vols. 1904; Reprint, New York: Forgotten Books, 2010.

Bumgarner, John R. (M.D.). The Health of the Presidents. Jefferson, NC: McFarland, 2004.

Burstein, Andrew. The Passions of Andrew Jackson. New York: Knopf, 2003.

Catterall, Ralph C.H. The Second Bank of the United States. Chicago: University of Chicago Press, 1903.

Chidsey, Donald Barr. Andrew Jackson: Hero. Nashville, TN: Nelson, 1976.

Coit, Margaret L. Andrew Jackson. Boston: Houghton Mifflin & Co., 1965.

Cole, Donald B. The Presidency of Andrew Jackson. Lawrence: University Press of Kansas, 1993.

Cooper, William J. The South and the Politics of Slavery, 1828–1856. Baton Rouge: Louisiana State University Press, 1987.

Crenson, Mathew A. The Federal Machine: Beginnings of Bureaucracy in Jacksonian America. Baltimore: Johns Hopkins University Press, 1975.

Curtis, James C. Andrew Jackson and the Search for Vindication. Boston: Little, Brown & Co., 1976.

Davis, Burke. Old Hickory: A Life of Andrew Jackson. New York: Dial Press, 1977.

DeGregorio, William A. The Complete Book of U.S. Presidents. New York: Barricade, 2005.

Duane, William J. Narrative and Correspondence Concerning the Removal of the Deposits. 1838; Reprint, New York: Burt Franklin, 1965.

Eaton, John Henry, and John Reid. The Life of Andrew Jackson. Frank L. Owsley, Jr., ed. 1817; Reprint, University: University of Alabama Press, 1974.

Ehle, John. Trail of Tears: The Rise and Fall of the Cherokee Nation. New York: Doubleday, 1988.

Ellis, Richard E. The Union at Risk: Jacksonian Democracy, States' Rights and the Nullification Crisis. New York: Oxford University Press, 1987.

Ely, James W., Jr., and Theodore Brown, Jr., eds. Legal Papers of Andrew Jackson. Knoxville: University of Tennessee Press, 1987.

Feller, Daniel. The Jacksonian Promise, America, 1815–1840. Baltimore: Johns Hopkins University Press, 1995.

_____. The Public Lands in Jacksonian Politics. Madison: University of Wisconsin Press, 1984.

Foss, William O. Childhoods of the American Presidents. Jefferson NC: McFarland, 2005.

Freehling, William W. Prelude to Civil War: The Nullification Controversy in South Carolina, 1816–1836. New York: Harper & Row, 1966.

_____. The Road to Disunion: Secessionists at Bay, 1776–1854. New York: Oxford University Press, 1990.

Gammon, Samuel Rhea. The Presidential Campaign of 1832. Baltimore: Johns Hopkins University Press, 1922.

Goodpasture, Albert Virgil. Andrew Jackson, Tennessee and the Union. Nashville: Brandon Printing Co., 1895.

Govan, Thomas P. Nelson Biddle: Nationalist and Public Banker, 1786–1844. Chicago: University of Chicago Press, 1959.

Groom, Winston. Patriotic Fire: Andrew Jackson and Jean Lafitte at the Battle of New Orleans. New York: Knopf, 2006.

Gullan, Harold I. First Fathers: The Men Who Inspired Our Presidents.

Hoboken, NJ: John Wiley & Sons. 2004.

Heidler, David, and Jeannie Heidler. *Old Hickory's War: Andrew Jackson and the Quest for Empire.* Mechanicsburg, PA: Stackpole, 1996.

Heiskell, Samuel Gordon. *Andrew Jackson and Early Tennessee History.* Nashville: Ambrose Printing Co., 1918.

Holt, Michael F. *The Rise and Fall of the American Whig Party: Jacksonian Politics and the Onset of the Civil War.* New York: Oxford University Press, 1999.

James, Marquis. *The Life of Andrew Jackson, Complete in One Volume.* 1933–1937; New ed. Indianapolis: Bobbs-Merrill Co., 1938. Originally published in 2 vols. *Andrew Jackson, the Border Captain* (1933), and *Andrew Jackson, Portrait of a President* (1937).

Johnson, Gerald White. *Andrew Jackson, an Epic in Homespun.* New York: Minton, Balch & Co., 1927.

Kendall, Amos. *Life of Andrew Jackson, Private, Military, and Civil.* 6 vols. New York: n.p., 1843–1844.

Kohl, Lawrence Frederick. *The Politics of Individualism: Parties and the American Character in the Jacksonian Era.* New York: Oxford University Press, 1989.

Latner, Richard B. *The Presidency of Andrew Jackson: White House Politics, 1829–1837.* Athens: University of Georgia Press, 1979.

Lindsay, Rae. *The Presidents' First Ladies.* Englewood Cliffs, NJ: R & R Writers/Agents, Inc., 2001.

Lindsay, David. *Andrew Jackson and John C. Calhoun.* Hauppauge, NY: Barron's Educational Series, 1973.

Marrin, Albert. *Old Hickory: Andrew Jackson and the American People.* New York: Penguin, 2004.

Marszalek, John F. *The Petticoat Affair: Manners, Mutiny, and Sex in Andrew Jackson's White House.* Mankato, MN: Free Press, 1997.

McCormick, Richard P. *The Second American Party System: Party Formation in the Jacksonian Era.* Chapel Hill: University of North Carolina Press, 1966.

MacDonald, William. *Jacksonian Democracy, 1829–1837.* New York: Harper & Bros., 1906.

McFaul, John M. *The Politics of Jacksonian Finance.* Ithaca, NY: Cornell University Press, 1972.

McLoughlin, William. *Cherokee Renascence in the New Republic.* Princeton, NJ: Princeton University Press, 1986.

Meacham, Jon. *American Lion: Andrew Jackson in the White House.* New York: Random House, 2008.

Miller, William Lee. *Arguing About Slavery: The Great Battle in the United States Congress.* New York: Knopf, 1993.

Missall, John, and Mary Lou Missall. *The Seminole Wars: America's Longest Indian Conflict.* Gainesville: University of Florida Press. 2004.

Moser, Harold D., Sharon Macpherson, John Reinbold, and Daniel Feller, eds. *The Papers of Andrew Jackson 1770–1845.* Wilmington, DE: Scholarly Resources, 1987.

Nichols, Roger. *Black Hawk and the Warrior's Path.* Arlington Heights, IL: Harlan Davidson, 1992.

_____. *Black Hawk's Autobiography.* Ames: Iowa State University Press, 1999.

Nye, Russel B. *Fettered Freedom: Civil Liberties and the Slavery Controversy, 1830–1860.* East Lansing: Michigan State University Press, 1949.

Ogg, Frederick Austin. *The Reign of Andrew Jackson: A Chronicle of the Frontier in Politics.* New Haven, CT: Yale University Press, 1919.

Parton, James. *A Life of Andrew Jackson.* 3 vols. Boston: Houghton-Mifflin, 1859–1860.

Patterson, Benton Rain. *The Generals: Andrew Jackson, Sir Edward Pakenham, and the Road to the Battle of New Orleans.* New York: New York University Press, 2005.

Poore, Benjamin Perley. *Perley's Reminiscences of Sixty Years in the National Metropolis.* 2 vols. New York: A.W. Stolp, 1886.

Prucha, Francis Paul. *The Great Father: The United States and the American Indians.* 2 vols. Lincoln: University of Nebraska Press, 1984.

_____, ed. *Documents of United States Indian Policy.* Lincoln: University of Nebraska Press, 1975.

Remini, Robert V. *Andrew Jackson and His Indian Wars.* New York: Viking, 2001.

_____. *Andrew Jackson and the Bank War: A Study in the Growth of Presidential Power.* New York: Norton, 1967.

_____. *Andrew Jackson and the Course of American Empire, 1767–1821.* New York: Harper & Row, 1977.

_____. *Andrew Jackson and the Course of American Empire, 1822–1832.* New York: Harper & Row, 1981.

_____. *Andrew Jackson and the Course of American Empire, 1833–1845.* New York: Harper & Row, 1984.

_____. *Henry Clay: Statesman for the Union.* New York: Norton, 1991.

_____. *The Legacy of Andrew Jackson: Essays on Democracy, Indian Removal and Slavery.* Baton Rouge:

Louisiana State University Press, 1988.

Robards, James Harvey. *History and Genealogy of the Robards Family.* Whiteland, IN: n.p., 1910.

Rogin, Michael Paul, and Mary Elizabeth Young. *Fathers and Children: Andrew Jackson and the Subjugation of the American Indian.* New York: Knopf, 1975.

Satz, Ronald N. *American Indian Policy in the Jacksonian Era.* Lincoln: University of Nebraska Press, 1975.

Schlesinger, Arthur M., Jr. *The Age of Jackson.* Boston: Little, Brown, 1945.

Sharp, James Roger. *The Jacksonians Versus the Banks: Politics in the States after the Panic of 1837.* New York: Columbia University Press, 1970.

Smith, Margaret Bayard. *The First Forty Years of Washington Society.* New York: Scribner, 1906.

Smith, Zachariah Frederick. *The Battle of New Orleans.* Louisville, KY: J.P. Morton, 1904.

Sumner, William Graham. *Andrew Jackson.* 1882; Reprint of 1899 ed., with new introduction by Robert V. Remini, New York: Chelsea House, 1980.

Syrett, Harold C. *Andrew Jackson: His Contribution to the American Tradition.* 1953; Reprint, Westport, CT: Greenwood, 1971.

Taylor, George Rogers. *Jackson vs. Biddle's Bank: The Struggle Over the Second Bank of the United States.* 2d ed. Lexington, MA: Heath, 1972.

Temin, Peter. *The Jacksonian Economy.* New York: Norton, 1969.

United States Congress. *Speeches on the Passage of the Bill for Removal of the Indians.* 21st Congress, 1st Session. 1830; Reprint, Millwood, NY: Kraus, 1973.

Van Deusen, Glyndon G. *The Jacksonian Era, 1828–1848.* New York: Waveland, 1959.

_____. *The Life of Henry Clay.* Boston: Little, Brown, 1973.

Wallace, Anthony F. C. *The Long, Bitter Trail: Andrew Jackson and the Indians.* New York: Hill and Wang, 1993.

Warshauer, Matthew. *Andrew Jackson and the Politics of Martial Law: Nationalism, Civil Liberties, and Partisanship.* Knoxville: University of Tennessee Press, 2007.

Watson, Harry L. *Andrew Jackson vs. Henry Clay: Democracy and Development in Antebellum America.* Boston: Beford/St. Martins, 1998.

_____. *Liberty and Power: The Politics of Jacksonian America.* New York: Hill and Wang, 1990.

Wiltse, Charles M. *John C. Calhoun,*

Nationalist, 1782–1828. Indianapolis: Bobbs-Merrill, 1944.

_____. *John C. Calhoun, Nullifier, 1829–1839*. Indianapolis: Bobbs-Merrill, 1949.

_____. *John C. Calhoun, Sectionalist, 1840–1850*. Indianapolis: Bobbs-Merrill, 1951.

Watson, Harry L. *Liberty and Power: The Politics of Jacksonian America*. New York: Hill and Wang, 2006.

White, Leonard D. *The Jacksonians: A Study in Administrative History 1829–1861*. New York: Macmillan, 1954.

Whitney, Ellen. ed. *The Black Hawk War, 1831–1832*. 2 vols. in 4. Springfield: Illinois State Historical Library, 1970.

Wilburn, Jean Alexander. *Biddle's Bank: The Crucial Years*. New York: Columbia University Press, 1967.

Wilentz, Sean. *Andrew Jackson*. New York: Times Books, 2005.

Eight. Van Buren

Alexander, Holmes. *The American Talleyrand: The Career and Contemporaries of Martin Van Buren, Eighth President*. New York: Harper & Bros., 1935.

Bancroft, George. *Martin Van Buren to the End of His Public Career*. New York: Harper & Brothers, 1889.

Bassett, Margaret Byrd. *Profiles & Portraits of American Presidents & Their Wives*. Freeport, ME: B. Wheelwright Co.; distributed by Grosset & Dunlap, New York, 1969.

Boller, Paul, F., Jr. *Presidential Anecdotes*. New York: Oxford University Press, 1996.

Bumgarner, John R. (M.D.). *The Health of the Presidents*. Jefferson, NC: McFarland, 2004.

Butler, William Allen. *Martin Van Buren: Lawyer, Statesman and Man*. New York: D. Appleton & Co., 1862.

Byrdsall, Fitzwilliam. *The History of the Loco-Foco, or Equal Rights Party: Its Movements, Conventions and Proceedings*. New York: Clement & Packard, 1842.

Cable, Mary. *Black Odyssey: The Case of the Slave Ship Amistad*. New York: Viking Press, 1971.

Caroli, Betty Boyd. *First Ladies*. New York: Oxford University Press, 2003.

Cole, Donald B. *Martin Van Buren and the American Politics System*. Princeton, NJ: Princeton University Press, 1984.

Collier, Edward Augustus. *A History of Old Kinderhook from Aboriginal Days to the Present Time*. New York: G. Putnam's, 1914.

Cooper, William J. *The South and the Politics of Slavery, 1828–1856*. Baton Rouge: Louisiana State University Press, 1987.

Corey, Albert B. *The Crisis of 1830–1842 in Canadian-American Relations*. New Haven, CT: Yale University Press, 1941.

Curtis, James C. *The Fox at Bay: Martin Van Buren and the Presidency, 1837–1841*. Lexington: University Press of Kentucky, 1970.

DeGregorio, William A. *The Complete Book of U.S. Presidents*. New York: Barricade, 2005.

Field, Ron. *The Seminole Wars 1818–58*. Oxford: Osprey Publishing, 2009.

Fitzpatrick, John C., ed. *The Autobiography of Martin Van Buren*. 2 vols. 1920; Reprint, New York: Da Capo Press, 1973. Originally published as *American Historical Association Annual Report for the Year 1918*.

Fitzpatrick, John, ed. *The Autobiography of Martin Van Buren*. Washington, DC: Government Printing Office, 1920.

Foreman, Grant. *Indian Removal: The Emigration of the Five Civilized Tribes of Indians*. Norman: University of Oklahoma Press, 1957.

Hargrove, Jim. *Martin Van Buren: Eighth President of the United States*. Danbury, CT: Grolier, 1987.

Hofstadter, Richard. *The Idea of a Party System; the Rise of Legitimate Opposition in the United States, 1780–1840*. Berkeley: University of California Press, 1969.

Holland, William M. *The Life and Political Opinions of Martin Van Buren, Vice President of the United States*. Hartford: Belknap & Hamersley, 1836.

Holt, Michael F. *The Rise and Fall of the American Whig Party: Jacksonian Politics and the Onset of the Civil War*. New York: Oxford University Press, 1999.

Irelan, John R. *History of the Life, Administration, and Times of Martin Van Buren, Eighth President of the United States*. Chicago: Fairbank & Palmer, 1887.

Jewell, Elizabeth. *U.S. Presidents Factbook*. New York: Random House, 2005.

Lazo, Caroline Evensen. *Martin Van Buren*. Minneapolis: Twenty-First Century Books, 2005.

Lepler, Jessica M. "1837: Anatomy of a Panic." ProQuest, 2007.

Lynch, Denis Tilden. *An Epoch and a Man: Martin Van Buren and His Times*. Port Washington, NY: Kennikat, 1971.

Mackenzie, William Lyon. *The Life and Times of Martin Van Buren: The Correspondence of His Friends, Family and Pupils*. Boston: Cooke & Co., 1846.

Mahon, John. *History of the Second Seminole War, 1835–1842*. Gainesville: University of Florida Press, 1967.

McGrane, Reginald Charles. *The Panic of 1837: Some Financial Problems of the Jacksonian Era*. Chicago: University of Chicago Press, 1924.

Mushkat, Jerome, and Joseph G. Rayback. *Martin Van Buren: Law, Politics, and the Shaping of Republican Ideology*. De Kalb: Northern Illinois University Press, 1997.

Niven, John. *Martin Van Buren: The Romantic Age of American Politics*. New York: Oxford University Press, 1958.

Ostler, Rosemarie. *Slinging Mud: Rude Nicknames, Scurrilous Slogans, and Insulting Slang from Two Centuries of American Politics* New York: Penguin, 2011.

Pletcher, David M. *The Diplomacy of Annexation: Texas, Oregon and the Mexican War*. Columbia: University of Missouri Press, 1973.

Remini, Robert V. *Martin Van Buren and the Making of the Democratic Party*. New York: Columbia University Press, 1959.

Rozema, Vicki. *Voices from the Trail of Tears*. Las Vegas: Blair, 2003.

Rumsch, BreAnn. *Martin Van Buren*. Edina, MN: ABDO, 2009.

Shepard, Edward Morse. *Martin Van Buren*. 1892; reprint, New York: Chelsea House, 1980.

Silbey, Joel. *Martin Van Buren and the Emergence of American Popular Politics*. Boca Raton, FL: American Profile Series, 2002.

Sloan, Irving J., ed. *Martin Van Buren: Chronology, Documents, Biographical Aids*. Dobbs Ferry, NY: Oceans, 1969.

Stoddard, William Osborn. *Andrew Jackson and Martin Van Buren*. New York: F.A. Stokes, 1887.

Sturgis, Amy H. *The Trail of Tears and Indian Removal*. Westport, CT: Greenwood, 2007.

Van Buren, Martin. *Inquiry into the Origin and Course of Political Parties in the United States*. Abraham Van Buren and John Van Buren, eds. New York: Hurd & Houghton, 1867.

West, Elisabeth H., ed. *The Calendar of the Papers of Martin Van Buren*. Washington, DC: Library of Congress, 1910.

Widmer, Ted. *Martin Van Buren.* New York: Holt, 2005.

Wilson, Major. *The Presidency of Martin Van Buren.* Lawrence: University Press of Kansas, 1984.

Nine. W. H. Harrison

Bird, H. *War for the West, 1790–1813.* New York: Oxford University Press, 1971.

Boller, Paul F., Jr. *Presidential Campaigns from George Washington to George W. Bush.* New York: Oxford University Press, 2004.

_____. *Presidential Wives: An Anecdotal History.* New York: Oxford University Press, 1998.

Brock, William R. *Parties and Political Conscience: American Dilemmas, 1840–1850.* Millwood, NY: KTO, 1979.

Bumgarner, John R. (M.D.) *The Health of the Presidents.* Jefferson, NC: McFarland, 2004.

Burr, Samuel Jones. *The Life and Times of William Henry Harrison.* New York, NY: R.W. Pomeroy, 1840.

Calhoun, Charles William. *Benjamin Harrison.* New York: Macmillan, 2005.

Clanin, Douglas E., ed. *The Papers of William Henry Harrison, 1800–1815.* Indianapolis: Indiana Historical Society, 1994.

Cleaves, Freeman. *Old Tippecanoe: William Henry Harrison and His Times.* New York: Scribner's, 1939.

Collins, Gail. *William Henry Harrison: The American Presidents Series: The 9th President, 1841.* New York: Macmillan, 2012.

Cronin, John William, and W. Harvey Wise, Jr., comps. *A Bibliography of William Henry Harrison, John Tyler, James Knox Polk.* Washington, DC: Riverford Publishing Co., 1935.

DeGregorio, William A. *The Complete Book of U.S. Presidents.* New York: Barricade, 2005.

Doak, Robin Santos. *William Henry Harrison.* Minneapolis: Compass Point Books, 2003.

Drake, Benjamin. *The Life of Tecumseh, and of His Brother the Prophet.* Cincinnati: E. Morgan, 1841.

Durfee, David A., comp. *William Henry Harrison, 1773–1841: John Tyler, 1790–1862: Chronology, Documents, Bibliographical Aids.* Dobbs Ferry, NY: Oceana Publications, 1970.

Eggleston, Edward, and L.E. Seelye. *Tecumseh and the Shawnee Prophet.* New York: Dodd, Mead and Co., 1878.

Esarey, Logan, ed. *Messages and Letters of William Henry Harrison.* 2 vols. 1922; Reprint, New York: Arno, 1975.

Fuller, Edmund, David E. Green. *God in the White House: The Faiths of American Presidents.* New York: Crown, 1968.

Goebel, Dorothy Burne. *William Henry Harrison: A Political Biography.* Indianapolis: Indiana Library and Historical Society, 1926.

Gould, Lewis L. *American First Ladies: Their Lives and Their Legacies.* New York: Routledge, 2001.

Green, James A. *William Henry Harrison: His Life and Times.* Richmond, VA: Garrett and Massie, 1941.

Gunderson, Robert G. *The Log-Cabin Campaign.* Lexington: Kentucky University Press, 1957.

Harrison, William Henry. *A Discourse on the Aborigines of the Ohio Valley.* Chicago: Fergus Printing Company, 1883.

_____. *The Messages and Letters of William Henry Harrison.* 2 vols. Logan Esarey, ed. 1922; Reprint, New York: Arno Press, 1975.

Heale, M.J. *The Making of American Politics, 1750–1850.* London: Longman, 1977.

Houston, James A. *Counterpoint: Tecumseh vs. William Henry Harrison.* New York: Anchor House, 2004.

Jackson, Isaac. *The Life of William Henry Harrison of Ohio.* Whitefish, MT: Kessenger, 2007.

Montgomery, Henry. *The Life of Major-General William H. Harrison, Ninth President of the United States.* Philadelphia: Porter & Coates, 1852.

Norton, Anthony Banning, ed. *The Great Revolution of 1840: Reminiscences of the Log Cabin and Hard Cider Campaign.* New York: Norton, 1888.

Owens, Robert M. *Mr. Jefferson's Hammer: William Henry Harrison and the Origins of the American Indian Policy.* Norman: University of Oklahoma Press, 2007.

Peterson, Merrill D. *The Great Triumvirate: Webster, Clay and Calhoun.* New York: Oxford University Press, 1987.

Peterson, Norma L. *The Presidencies of William Henry Harrison and John Tyler.* Lawrence: University Press of Kansas, 1989.

Remini, Robert Vincent. *Henry Clay: Statesman for the Union.* New York: W.W. Norton & Company, 1993.

Shepard, Edward Morse. *Martin Van Buren.* Boston: Houghton Mifflin, 1899.

Sugden, John. *Tecumseh: A Life.* New York: Macmillan, 1999.

Todd, Charles S., and Benjamin Drake. *Sketches of the Civil and Military Services of William Henry Harrison.* Cincinnati: BiblioBazaar, 1841; Reprint, Whitefish, MT: Kessenger, 2007.

Wilentz, Sean. *The Rise of American Democracy: Jefferson to Lincoln.* New York, W.W. Norton, 2005.

Ten. Tyler

Anthony, Carl Sferrazza. *First Ladies: The Saga of the Presidents' Wives and Their Power, 1789–1961.* New York: William Morrow, 1990.

Bayh, Birch. *One Heartbeat Away: Presidential Disability and Succession.* Indianapolis: Bobbs-Merrill, 1968.

Boller, Paul F., Jr. *Presidential Anecdotes.* New York: Oxford University Press, 1981.

_____. *Presidential Wives: An Anecdotal History.* New York: Oxford University Press, 1998.

Bumgarner, John R. (M.D.). *The Health of the Presidents.* Jefferson, NC: McFarland, 2004.

Chidsey, Donald Barr. *And Tyler, Too.* Nashville, TN: Thomas Nelson, 1978.

Chitwood, Oliver Perry. *John Tyler: Champion of the Old South.* New York: Appleton-Century, 1939.

Collins, H.G. *Life and Adventures of Wat Tyler, the Good and the Brave.* London: H.G. Collins, 1851.

Cooper, William, Jr. *The South and the Politics of Slavery, 1828–1856.* Baton Rouge: Louisiana State University Press, 1970.

Crapol, Edward P. *John Tyler: The Accidental President.* Chapel Hill: University of North Carolina Press, 2006.

DeGregorio, William A. *The Complete Book of U.S. Presidents.* New York: Barricade, 2005.

Dennison, George M. *The Door War: Republicanism on Trial, 1831–1861.* Lexington: University Press of Kentucky, 1976.

Doak, Robin Santos. *John Tyler.* Minneapolis: Compass Point Books, 2003.

Gettleman, Marvin E. *The Dorr Rebellion: A Study in American Radicalism, 1833–1849.* New York: Random House, 1973.

Gould, Lewis L. *American First Ladies: Their Lives and Their Legacy.* London: Taylor & Francis, 2001.

Holloway, Laura Carter. *Ladies of the White House.* New York: U.S. Publication Company, 1870.

Jones, Howard. *To the Webster-Ashburton Treaty: A Study in Anglo-American Relations, 1783–1843.* Chapel Hill: University of North Carolina Press, 1977.

Mann, Nancy Wilson. *Tylers and Gardiners on the Village Green: Williamsburg, Virginia, and East Hampton, Long Island.* New York: Vantage, 1983.

May, Gary. *John Tyler.* The American Presidents Series: The 10th President, 1841–1845. New York: Times Books/Henry Holt and Co., 2008.

Merk, Frederick. *Fruits of Propaganda in the Tyler Administration.* Cambridge, MA: Harvard University Press, 1971.

_____. *Slavery and the Annexation of Texas.* New York: Knopf, 1972.

Monroe, Dan. *The Republican Vision of John Tyler.* College Station: Texas A&M Press, 2003.

Morgan, Robert J. *A Whig Embattled: The Presidency Under John Tyler.* Lincoln: University of Nebraska Press, 1954.

Nelson, Lyle Emerson. *John Tyler: A Rare Career.* New York: Nova Publishers, 2008.

Jewell, Elizabeth. *U.S. Presidents Factbook.* New York: Random House, 2005.

Peterson, Norma Lois. *The Presidencies of William Henry Harrison and John Tyler.* Lawrence: University Press of Kansas, 1989.

Reeves, Jesse Siddall. *American Diplomacy under Tyler and Polk.* Baltimore: Johns Hopkins Press, 1907; Reprint, Gloucester, MA: P. Smith, 1967.

Schneider, Dorothy, Carl J. Schneider. *First Ladies: A Biographical Dictionary.* New York: Infobase Publishing, 2010.

Seager, Robert, II. *And Tyler, Too: A Biography of John and Julia Gardiner Tyler.* New York: McGraw-Hill, 1963.

Sewell, Richard H. *Ballots for Freedom: Antislavery Politics in the United States, 1837–1860.* New York: Oxford University Press, 1976.

Tyler, Lyon Gardiner. *The Letters and Times of the Tylers.* Richmond, VA: Whittet & Shepperson, 1884.

Walker, Jane C. *John Tyler: A President of Many Firsts.* Granville, OH: McDonald & Woodward, 2001.

Wead, Doug. *The Raising of a President: The Mothers and Fathers of Our Nation's Leaders.* New York: Atria Books, 2005.

Whitton, Mary Ormsbee. *First First Ladies, 1789–1865,* New York, 1948; Reprint, Whitefish, MT: Kessenger Publishing, 2008.

Wise, Henry A. *Seven Decades of the Union. The Humanities and Materialism.* Philadelphia: J.B. Lippincott & Co., 1872.

Young, Jeff C. *The Fathers of American Presidents: From Augustine Washington to William Blythe and Roger Clinton.* Jefferson, NC: McFarland & Co., 1997.

Index

Abolition movement 60, 129, 213, 217, 239–241, 247, 301, 326, 330, 359–360, 373; *see also* African Americans; slavery

Adams, Abigail Amelia, "Nabby" 79

Adams, Abigail Smith 70, 77–79, 83, 90, 92–96, 105–107, 118, 219, 224, 229, 245

Adams, Charles 79, 219

Adams, Charles Francis 224, 225

Adams, Deacon John 74, 105

Adams, George Washington 225

Adams, Henry 224

Adams, John 1, 4, 5, 14–16, 29, 44, 47, 49–51, 63, 73–108, 122, 128, 130, 131, 133, 134, 136, 141, 143–145, 152, 160, 170, 171, 181, 189, 196, 208, 219, 221, 227, 245, 346; after his presidency 101; Alien and Sedition Acts 96–98; ancestors 75; appearance 75; birth 73; Boston Massacre 85–87; "Braintree Instructions" 85; cabinet 95; children 79; the Continental Congress 91–92; death and burial 104–105; diary entries 107; diplomatic roles 92–93; "A Dissertation on the Canon and Feudal Law" 89; domestic affairs 96; education 82–83; evaluations of 107–108; family 73–75; foreign affairs 98; Fries Rebellion of 1799, 98; health 104; home, "Peacefield" 83; marriage and romances 77–79; miscellanea 105–106; mistresses 106; motto 83–84; nicknames and titles 73; "Novanglus Letters" 89; occupation 84; papers and books 101, 103; personality and character 75–77; political philosophy and party affiliation 89–91; political writings 89; presidency 94–95; presidential election of 1796 94; presidential election of 1800 100–101; recreational pastimes and interests 84; religion and religious beliefs 80–82; reputation 106; Supreme Court appointments 96; vice-presidency 93–94; Vice President Thomas Jefferson 95; XYZ Affair 99–100

Adams, John Quincy 1, 5, 14–16, 19, 76, 79, 92, 101, 144, 193, 199, 200, 205–207, 219–253, 264, 266, 277–280, 303, 316, 317, 327, 330, 335, 349, 354, 360, 374, 376, 386; after the presidency 238–239; ancestors 221; appearance 221; birth 219; Boylston professor of rhetoric and oratory 233; cabinet 235; cabinet position 233–234; children 225; death and burial 245; diary entries 250–251; diplomatic roles 230; domestic affairs 235; education 227–228; Erie Canal 237; evaluations of 251–253; family 219–220; foreign affairs 237–238; and freemasonry 249; Gag Rule 240–242; health 244; home, "Old House" 228–229; House of Representatives 239; internal improvements 235–237; marriage and romances 221–224; minister to Great Britain 231–232; minister to Prussia 230; minister to Russia 230–231; minister to The Netherlands 230; miscellanea 245–246; motto 229; nicknames and titles 219; occupation 228; papers and diaries 243; personality and character 221; pets and animals 229; political offices 232–233; political philosophy and party affiliation 230; presidency 234–235; recreational pastimes and interests 229–230; religion and religious beliefs 225–227; Smithsonian Institute 243; Supreme Court appointments 235; Tariff of 1828 237; Treaty of Ghent 231; Vice President John C. Calhoun 235

Adams, Louisa Catherine Johnson 222–225, 229

Adams, Samuel 84, 94, 105

Adams, Susanna Boylston 74

Adams, Thomas Boylston 219

Adams, William 231

Adams National Historical Park 73, 219

Adams-Onís Treaty 233

Addison, Joseph 38, 165

Advertisements 144, 356

African Americans 5, 54, 147–149, 163, 216, 217, 267, 268, 301

Agriculture 38, 52, 79, 123, 124, 130, 135, 175, 178, 194, 198, 201

Albany Regency ("Bucktails") 314–316; *see also* Van Buren, Martin

Alden, John and Priscilla 75

Alexander I, Czar 231, 280

Algeria 140, 141, 143

Alien and Sedition Acts 73, 96–98, 133, 136, 171, 174, 175

Alien Enemies Act 96

Allen, Ethan 23

Allen, Captain William 254

Ambrister, Robert 76, 277; *see also* Jackson, Andrew

Amendments to the U.S. Constitution 4, 9, 13–15, 49, 52, 55, 68, 120, 133, 136, 137, 171, 172, 174, 178, 183, 202–204, 282, 348, 356, 378; *see also* Bill of Rights

American Bible Association 226

"The American Cincinnatus" 23

American Colonization Society 182, 216, 217, 286, 359; *see also* Liberia; Monroe, James

"American Fabius" 23

American Indians 3, 6, 18, 26, 40, 41–43, 72, 74, 79, 83, 85, 113, 127, 134, 137, 138, 140, 151, 174, 175, 190, 193, 205, 216, 229, 239, 240, 254, 257, 259, 261, 262, 265, 270–272, 274–276, 278, 281, 286–290, 292, 302–304, 325, 343–348, 350, 351, 353, 357, 359

American Philosophical Society 133

American Revolution 23, 76, 87, 89, 131, 179, 222, 246, 257, 275, 277

American system 167, 204, 295, 317, 348; *see also* Adams, John Quincy; Clay, Henry

Amistad ("Friendship") Affair 1, 247, 248, 326–327; *see also* Adams, John Quincy; Cinque (Senge Pieh); *habeus corpus*; slavery; Story, Joseph; Supreme Court; Van Buren, Martin

Anglicans 34, 59, 120, 129, 155, 163, 164, 192

Anglophobia 258

Annexation of Texas 3, 6, 239, 271, 291, 297, 327, 330, 342, 377, 380–383; *see also* Adams, John Quincy; Tyler, John

Anti-Federalists Party 14, 94, 195

Anti-Jacksonian Party 15

Anti-Mason Party 15, 249, 291, 350

Anti-slavery petitions 5, 239–241, 301; *see also* Adams, John Quincy; Gag Rule

Arbuthnot, Alexander James 276, 277; *see also* Jackson, Andrew

Architecture, architects 79, 91, 108, 121, 126, 143, 154, 184, 248

Aristocracy, aristocrats 15, 19, 103, 154, 169, 258, 277, 278, 280, 314, 362, 365, 373

Aristotle 83, 122, 144, 183
Arminius, Jacobus 80
Aroostook War 329; *see also* Van Buren, Martin
Articles of Confederation and Perpetual Union 9, 14, 48, 91, 168, 196
Asia, Asians 54, 306
Asperger syndrome 145; *see also* Jefferson, Thomas
Assassination attempts 44, 240, 259, 296, 305, 359; *see also* Adams, John Quincy; Jackson, Andrew; Washington, George
Astronomy, astronomers 112, 149, 150, 227, 243
Atheism, atheists 82, 89, 112, 118, 120, 121, 134, 154, 225, 238, 354
Atkinson, Brigadier General Henry 290; *see also* Black Hawk War
"Atlas of Independence" 73; *see also* Adams, John
Attorney General 17, 50, 51, 69, 84, 95, 135, 165, 173, 200, 206, 235, 247, 282, 287, 314, 321, 356, 372, 378
Attucks, Crispus 85, 88; *see also* Boston Massacre
Avery, Waigthstill 270

Bache, Benjamin Franklin 96, 97; *see also* Adams, John
Bacon, Edmund 111
Bacon, Francis 29, 121, 183, 192, 251
Bainbridge, Captain William 141, 142; *see also* Barbary pirates
Bank Act of 1791 52
Bank of the United States 6, 18, 19, 52, 133, 171, 173, 207, 277, 291–294, 318, 319, 378
Banks, Sir Joseph 243; *see also* Smithsonian Institution
Banks and banking 18, 52, 91, 201, 202, 275, 277, 291–293, 297, 310, 322–324, 333, 371
Banneker, Benjamin 149, 150; *see also* Jefferson, Thomas
Baptists 36, 120, 164, 265, 266, 369
Barbary pirates 140, 141, 143; *see also* Bainbridge, William; Eaton, Captain William; Jefferson, Thomas; *Philadelphia* (frigate); Rodgers, Commodore John
Battle of Bad Axe River 290
Battle of Brandywine 44
Battle of Bunker Hill 219, 395
Battle of Fallen Timbers 344
Battle of Hanging Rock 257
Battle of Horseshoe Bend 271, 272
Battle of Lake Champlain 314
Battle of Lake Erie 175, 176, 344, 345
Battle of Long Island 44
Battle of New Orleans 1, 177, 178, 180, 231, 234, 256, 259, 272–274, 301
Battle of Saratoga 44, 46
Battle of Stone Ferry 257, 298
Battle of Thames 175, 345
Battle of Tippecanoe 345–348, 350, 355, 360
Battle of Trenton 43, 65, 193–194
Battle (Siege) of Yorktown 33, 45, 46, 60, 340
Battles 1, 6, 41, 43, 44, 46, 67, 175,

176, 180, 194, 219, 231, 234, 256, 257–259, 271–274, 298, 301, 302, 314, 342–345, 347, 348, 350, 353, 360, 364, 371, 381
Bayard James A., Sr. 231
Benton, Jesse 267
Benton, Thomas Hart 169, 245, 267, 293, 295, 298, 303
Berkeley Plantation 337–340; *see also* Harrison, William Henry
Bible 80–82, 120, 147, 149, 152, 192, 225, 226, 228, 230, 266, 342
Biddle, Nicholas 292, 293; *see also* Bank of the United States; Jackson, Andrew
Bigamy 235, 264, 279; *see also* Jackson, Andrew
Bill of Rights 1, 9, 52, 132, 155, 171–172, 183, 196, 339
Bipolar disorder 112
Black Hawk War 217, 289, 290; *see also* Atkinson, Brigadier General Henry; Chief Black Hawk
Black Hills 62
Boggs, Governor Lilburn 334
Bohun, Henry de 111
Bolívar, Simón 6, 63, 206, 349
Books 36, 68, 83, 84, 103, 110, 121, 123, 125, 126, 128, 144, 149, 152, 165, 183, 222, 243, 252, 311, 312, 330, 369, 370
"Booze" 359
Borglum, Gutzon 62
Boston 42, 61, 73, 74, 76, 84–86, 88, 89, 91, 92, 104, 106, 107, 173, 187, 210, 221, 223–225, 227–229, 232, 245
Boston (frigate) 92
Boston Massacre 85, 87, 88, 107
Boston Tea Party 42, 91
Boylston, Zabdiel 74
Boylston professor of rhetoric and oratory 233; *see also* Adams, John Quincy
Brackenridge, Hugh Henry 165
Braddock, General Edward 41
Bradford, William, Jr. 51, 164, 165
Braintree, Massachusetts 74, 75, 81, 85, 93, 219, 223, 228, 229
"Braintree Instructions" 93
A Brief System of Logick 165; *see also* Madison, James
British Parliament 10, 15, 42, 85, 89, 91, 129
Bruce, King Robert 111
The Buccaneer (movie) 273
Budget-balancing authority 16
"Bully Pulpit" 12, 282
Burk, John Daly 97
Burning: of the Executive Mansion 162, 175–177, 198; *see also* Jennings, Paul; Madison, Dolley; Madison, James
Burr, Aaron 14, 43, 94, 100, 134, 135, 147, 160, 184, 198, 214, 304, 307, 314, 333
Burr-Hamilton Duel 135, 184, 312
Burwell, Rebecca 113
Bush, George W. 13, 217, 359
Business 78, 84, 91, 101, 103, 128, 153, 159, 160, 202, 210, 231, 291, 298, 314, 320, 322, 346, 350

"By the Eternal" 260, 292; *see also* Jackson, Andrew

Cabinet 4, 10, 12–13, 50, 54, 95, 99, 132, 135, 141, 162, 172, 173, 175, 185, 191, 198, 200, 205, 206, 233–235, 260, 277, 282, 284–287, 316–318, 320, 321, 326, 335, 356, 357, 367, 376, 378, 385
Caesar, Julius 38, 303
Calhoun, John C. 6, 185, 200, 205, 206, 218, 234, 235, 237, 243, 254, 256, 278, 282, 291, 205, 295, 301, 304, 316–318, 348, 355, 377, 378, 384
Callender, James Thomas 116, 134, 214
Calvinism 80, 81, 181
Campaign slogans 4, 173, 330, 351, 353, 359, 382
Canada 137, 175, 204, 232, 290, 328, 329, 344
Capitalism 369
Caroline Affair 328, 329
Carter, Jimmy 33
Cass, Lewis 330, 332, 367
Catholicism 35, 80, 118, 120, 191, 192, 225, 265, 266, 276, 277, 265, 367, 369, 370
Cato the Younger 38
Censure 240, 252, 293, 294, 348, 374, 375
Census 18, 59
Central government 9, 14, 15, 18, 19, 48, 52, 53, 90, 155, 167, 170, 195, 288, 294, 372; limited 9, 15, 195, 312, 313; strong 14, 18, 19, 90, 155, 195
Chalmette Plantation 273
Charbonneau, Toussaint 138
Charles City Rifles 372; *see also* Tyler, John
Chase, Supreme Court Justice Samuel 51, 147
Chastellux, Marquis de 29, 115
Checks and balances 9, 90, 168, 378
Cherokee Indians 154, 171, 272, 287–289, 302, 325; *see also* Burnett, Private John G.; Jackson, Andrew; Ross, John; Scott, Winfield; Trail of Tears; Van Buren, Martin; *Worcester v. Georgia*
Cherry tree myth 64, 65
Chesapeake (ship) 92
Chesapeake and Ohio Canal 236
Chesapeake Bay 23, 337
Chickasaw Indians 287
Chief Black Hawk 217, 290
Chief Justice of the Supreme Court 17, 43, 51, 52, 59, 74, 95, 96, 98, 113, 118–120, 147, 152, 154, 171, 189, 193, 201, 204, 282, 283
Chinese immigrants 18
Choctaw Indians 287
Christian education 164
Christian nation 230
Christianity 34, 35, 80, 82, 119, 120, 152, 164, 192, 225–227, 230, 238, 242, 251, 262, 264–266, 288, 309, 310, 330, 332, 342, 365, 366, 370
Christmas 43, 45, 151, 152, 193, 231, 367
Church of England 34, 119, 164, 191
Cicero 83, 84, 228, 353, 364

Cincinnatus, Lucius Quinctius 23, 353
Cinque (Sengbe Pieh) 247–249; *see also* Adams, John Quincy; *Amistad*; Van Buren, Martin
Citizen Genêt Affair 54, 55, 228
Civil liberties 15, 239, 313
Civil War 5, 25, 59, 62, 127, 134, 177, 209, 217, 235, 279, 295, 319, 320, 327, 354, 355, 371, 373, 383, 385
Clark, George Rogers 137
Clark, William 127, 137–140; *see also* Jefferson, Thomas; Lewis, Meriwether; Lewis and Clark Expedition; Louisiana Purchase
Clay, Henry 6, 7, 14, 15, 18, 185, 200, 203, 204, 217, 231, 234, 235, 252, 254, 256, 277–279, 291, 292, 294, 295, 304, 319, 334, 343, 350–352, 356, 371, 374, 376–378, 380, 384, 386, 387; *see also* Bank of the United States; Missouri Compromise
Clergy 34, 80, 83, 120, 121, 164, 167, 208, 217, 251, 289, 339, 342
Cleveland, Grover 13, 14, 16, 311)
Clinton, Bill 16
Clinton, DeWitt 173, 237, 252, 314, 315; *see also* "Clinton's Ditch"; Erie Canal; Van Buren, Martin
Clinton, George 46, 135, 173
"Clinton's Ditch" 237
Cock fighting 269
Coercive Acts 42
Coffin handbill 281
Coinage Act of 1791 53
Coinage Act of 1836 297
Cold War 19
College of New Jersey (now Princeton University) 165, 168
College of William and Mary 121, 128, 165, 187, 192–194, 362, 365, 370, 371, 386
Colonialism, colonies 25, 38, 42, 84, 111, 148, 156, 216, 229, 230, 243, 247, 337, 339
Columbia River 140
Commander-in-Chief 2, 19, 38, 40, 41, 44–46, 60, 62, 67, 99, 186
Commissioner to France 92, 115
Compromise Bill of 1820 203
Compromise Tariff of 1833 319, 374
The Confederacy 127, 217, 369, 383
Congregationalism 77, 225, 245
Congress 1, 3, 5, 9, 11, 12, 15–18, 21, 33, 42–44, 47, 49–54, 56–59, 62, 63, 65, 67, 70, 93–98, 100, 106, 111, 112, 132, 133, 136, 137, 140, 141, 143, 146, 156, 160, 165, 166, 171, 172, 174, 175, 178, 179, 183, 184, 190, 193, 196, 199–205, 207–209, 216–217, 224, 230, 233–241, 243–244, 245, 250, 251, 271, 277, 278, 282, 284, 286–289, 292, 293, 25, 297, 298, 301, 303, 311, 320–324, 326, 327, 329, 330, 339, 341, 342, 345, 346, 348, 355–357, 365, 366, 371, 374, 376–380, 383, 385, 387; *see also* Constitution
Constitution 4, 9–12, 14–18, 42, 48, 49, 51, 52, 55, 68, 73, 77, 82, 89–91, 93, 101, 103, 112, 120, 128, 130, 132, 133, 136, 137, 153, 155, 163, 164, 167–172, 174, 175, 181–184, 186, 195, 196,

201–204, 209, 210, 215, 221, 226, 240, 241, 249, 252, 265, 282, 288, 293–295, 305, 313–315, 320, 324, 326, 332, 339, 355, 356, 360, 362, 365, 370, 372–379, 383, 386
Constitution ("Old Ironsides") 175, 177
Constitutional Convention 5, 9, 48, 67, 91, 132, 170, 172, 173, 178, 179, 200, 295, 304, 315
Constitutionality 5, 17, 42, 48, 49, 54, 55, 68, 72, 98, 130, 133, 137, 155, 162, 169, 170, 174, 178, 183, 201, 203, 204, 233, 237, 239, 265, 277, 292, 293, 317, 323, 325, 356, 374, 380
Continental Congress 1, 9, 42, 62, 63, 78, 91, 106, 123, 129, 131, 132, 134, 136, 166, 170, 195, 208, 339
Conway Cabal 44, 45; *see also* Gates, Brigadier General Horation; Lafayette, Marquis de
Coolidge, Calvin 14, 62
Córdoba, General José Maria 349; *see also* Bolívar, Simón; Harrison, William Henry
Cornwallis, General Lord 46, 112
"The Corps of Volunteers for North West Discovery" 138; *see also* Lewis and Clark Expedition
"Corrupt Bargain" 234, 280; *see also* Adams, John Quincy; Clay, Henry; Jackson, Andrew
Cosway, Maria Hadfield 115, 116, 152, 165
Cosway, Richard 115
Cotton 162, 252, 268, 269, 273, 274, 301, 320–322, 380
Court of St. James 93
Covey, Thomas 247; *see also Amistad*
Crawford, William H. 234, 275, 278, 279, 316–318
Crazy Horse Memorial 62
Creek Indians 254, 257, 265, 271, 275, 276, 281, 287, 302
Cricket 37
Crockett, David "Davy" A. 184, 286, 296, 304, 306, 309, 336
Crop rotation 123
Cross 82
Crossing the Delaware 43, 54, 65, 67, 193
Cuba 247, 326
Cuffee, Paul 216
Custis, Eleanor Parke "Nelly" 33
Custis, George Washington Parke "Wash" 33, 65
Custis, John Parke "Jackie" 33
Custis, Martha Parke "Patsy" 33
Custis, Parker 33

Dade Code 164
Dame and Latin School 82
Dana, Francis 227, 230, 245
Dancing 33, 76, 112, 172, 227, 259, 286, 351, 368, 371
Davis, Jefferson 217, 383, 385
Debt 52–54, 135m 163, 182, 207, 265, 291, 297, 322, 324
Declaration of Independence 1, 9, 91, 104, 106, 109, 112, 123, 130, 131, 145, 147, 149, 173, 198, 217, 333, 339, 342, 362, 385

Declaration of War 5, 175
Defense Department see War Department
Deism, deist 34, 118, 119, 164, 192, 370
Delambre, Jean Baptiste Joseph 242, 243
Democracy 7, 21, 71, 103, 128, 129, 154, 167, 168, 190, 230, 240, 260, 277, 279, 280, 282, 284, 303, 309, 313–315, 323, 335
Democratic government 90, 91
Democratic Party 15, 133, 252, 277, 279, 285, 297, 314, 327, 333; *see also* Democrats
Democratic Republican Party 15, 48, 96, 128, 169, 195, 307, 314; Anti-Federalists 14, 55, 94, 96, 97, 99, 128, 133, 169, 173, 195, 198, 230, 232, 234, 279, 307, 312, 314
Democrats 15, 133, 252, 277–280, 282, 285, 291, 293, 297, 314, 319, 321, 323, 327, 333, 334, 337, 339, 350, 352–354, 373, 383
Depression (economic) 6, 19, 114, 127, 175, 201, 202, 297, 309, 320–324, 329, 353; *see also* Panics
Depression (mental condition) 57, 104, 114, 221, 222, 224, 238, 243, 298
Despotism, despots 103, 120, 121, 130, 147, 153, 171, 178, 233, 256, 294, 303, 374
"Detached Memorandum" 184
Diaries of presidents 34, 39, 40, 56, 77, 80, 84, 91, 99, 101, 103, 107, 144, 208, 219, 225, 227, 228, 232, 234, 237, 238–241, 243, 244, 247–251, 354
Dickinson, Charles 266, 267, 269; *see also* Jackson, Andrew
Diplomacy, diplomats 5, 6, 54, 76, 79, 83, 92, 99, 123, 131, 132, 137, 151, 160, 161, 163, 190, 191, 194–196, 205, 207, 221–223, 227, 228, 230, 231, 239, 246, 251, 297, 326, 349
"A Dissertation on the Canon and Feudal Law" 89; *see also* Adams, John
District of Columbia 9, 13, 52, 326, 378
Divorce 79, 263; *see also* Jackson, Andrew
DNA analysis 117, 163
Donelson, Emily 264
Dorr, Thomas William 379–380; *see also* King, Samuel Ward
"Dove parties" 161
Dred Scott Decision 204; *see also* Supreme Court
Duane, William 97
Dumas, Mathieu, aide-de-camp 46
Dunjee, John William 369; *see also* Tyler, John
DuPont, Annie Rogers, and William 167; *see also* Montpelier
DuPont de Nemours, P.S. 122
Dutch Reform Church 311
Dwight, Timothy 134

Eaton, John 282, 285, 286, 300
Eaton, Peggy O'Neal 285, 286, 318
Eaton, Captain William 141; *see also* Barbary pirates

"Eaton Malaria" 286; *see also* Jackson, Andrew; Van Buren, Martin
E.C. Booz distillery 359
Education 4, 24, 36, 69, 74, 78, 82, 83, 90, 91, 109, 113, 121–123, 129, 130, 141, 144, 164–166, 182, 185, 187, 193, 217, 224, 227, 228, 236, 266, 287, 292, 311, 312, 340, 342, 348, 370, 371, 380
Eisenhower, Dwight David 14, 17
"Elastic clause" 201; *see also* Congress; Supreme Court
Elections and campaigns 7, 13–15, 48, 81, 94–96, 98, 100, 134–136, 183, 196, 198, 199, 209, 218, 230, 234, 235, 239, 245, 257, 264, 74, 278–280, 282, 315, 316, 318, 319, 321, 327, 329, 330, 334, 339, 341, 345, 350, 351, 354, 355, 358–360, 375; 1788 presidential 49–50; 1792 presidential 49; 1796 presidential 94; 1800 presidential 14, 95, 100, 118, 134; 1804 presidential 134, 135; 1808 presidential 173; 1812 presidential 173; 1816 presidential 198; 1820 presidential 199, 200; 1824 presidential 234, 278, 279; 1828 presidential 235, 279, 281, 326; 1832 presidential 291; 1836 presidential 319, 320, 333, 350; 1840 presidential 308, 309, 329, 337, 339, 340, 342, 348, 350, 351–355, 383; 2000 presidential 13; *see also* Electoral College
Electoral College 13–15, 50; 93, 94, 134, 135, 136, 173, 198, 199, 209, 210, 234, 235, 279, 280, 282, 291, 319–321, 329, 330, 350, 354, 375, 379; *see also* Elections
Ellsworth, Oliver 17, 51, 52, 96, 99, 154
Emancipation 148, 202, 216, 248, 250, 295, 346, 359–360, 373, 374
Embargo Act of 1807 19, 140, 172, 173, 213
Emerson, Ralph Waldo 7, 71, 244, 346
English Law 85
Enlightment 89, 168
Entangling Alliances 55, 327; *see also* Washington, George; Farewell addresses
Epilepsy 33, 180, 191
Episcopalians 120, 164, 192, 265, 266, 342, 369
Equality 191, 196, 217, 292, 342
Equestrian Statues 261, 300
"Era of Good Feeling" 5, 201; *see also* Monroe, James
Erie Canal 237, 315, 316; *see also* Clinton, DeWitt
Erskine, Robert, Geographer of the Continental Army 38
Esselman, John N. 299
Europe 1, 5, 18, 46, 53–55, 76, 79, 89, 90, 100, 117, 122, 123, 127, 128, 132, 133, 140, 141, 151, 158, 161, 163, 164, 173, 194, 196–198, 201, 204–206, 211, 222, 224, 227, 230, 231, 243, 269, 272, 273, 297, 306, 311, 318, 330, 367
Evans, Rudolph 146
Executions 44, 164, 215, 277, 281, 295; *see also* assassination attempts
Executive Branch, executive powers

1–5, 7, 9–12, 16, 20, 49, 57, 60, 63, 68, 83, 90, 94, 103, 112, 130, 132, 147, 158, 161, 167–169, 235, 252, 278, 280, 293, 297, 302, 322, 330, 334, 355, 362, 372, 379, 380; *see also* Constitution; Separation of Powers
Executive Mansion 1, 5, 95, 105, 113, 116, 161, 162, 175, 191, 194, 199, 206, 207, 224, 229, 245, 259–261, 265, 279, 282, 287, 298, 301, 309, 310, 318, 324, 325, 330, 334, 341, 343, 350, 354, 355, 357, 358, 365–368, 371, 372, 379, 385; *see also* White House
Exitus acta probat ("The end justifies the means") 37; *see also* Washington, George

Fairfax, George William 32, 33, 38
Fairfax, Sarah Cary "Sally" 32, 33, 37; *see also* Washington, George
Fairfax, Thomas Lord 38
Fairfax, William 25, 32, 33
Fairfax Resolves 42, 43
Fall of Washington, D.C. 161, 162, 175–178, 198, 274; *see also* War of 1812
Faneuil Hall 104, 225
Farewell addresses: Andrew Jackson 297, 298; George Washington 14, 55, 56, 59, 64; Martin Van Buren 329, 330
Farmer's Almanac 23, 149; *see also* Banneker, Benjamin
Farming see Agriculture
"Father of American Exceptionalism" 128; *see also* Jefferson, Thomas
"Father of Archeology" 127; *see also* Jefferson, Thomas
"Father of His Country" 23, 34, 68, 94; *see also* Washington, George
"Father of the Bill of Rights" 155; *see also* Madison, James
"Father of the Constitution" 155; *see also* Madison, James
"Father of the Declaration of Independence" 127; *see also* Jefferson, Thomas
Fauntleroy, Betsey 33; *see also* Washington, George
Federal Government 1, 9, 12, 17, 18, 49, 52, 54, 62, 128, 154, 169, 174, 175, 183, 185, 201, 217, 235, 236, 241, 277, 278, 291, 295, 312, 322, 323, 348, 373, 374, 379, 385
"Federal sovereignty" 89, 201
Federalist Papers 5, 165, 167, 168; *see also* Hamilton, Alexander; Jay, John; Madison, James
Federalist Party 5, 14, 15, 17, 18, 47, 48, 55, 90, 94–100, 128, 133–137, 151, 160, 161, 165, 167, 169, 171–173, 177, 187, 195–198, 230–232, 278, 312, 314, 315, 350
Federation of Central America 237, 238
"Ferry Farm" 24, 25; *see also* Washington, Mary Ball
Fifth Amendment of the Constitution 204
Filibuster 325; *see also* Congress
Final words (of presidents) 58, 104, 146, 181, 208, 245, 299, 332, 358, 385

"first lady" 4, 61, 151, 161, 162, 191, 207, 223, 265, 279, 340, 341, 368; *see also* Madison, Dolley
First Seminole War 205; *see also* Jackson, Andrew; Seminoles
Fiscal Bank Bill 378–379
"Five Civilized Tribes" (Cherokee, Seminole, Choctaw, Creek, Chickasaw) 154, 205, 254, 257, 265, 271, 272, 274–276, 281, 282, 287–289, 299, 302, 317, 325, 377; *see also* Indian Removal; Trail of Tears
Flag (U.S.) 66, 137, 193, 199, 380; *see also* "Stars and Stripes"
Floyd, Catherine "Kitty" 159; *see also* Madison, James
Floyd, John 291
Floyd, Sergeant Charles 138
Fontaine, Jean de La 229; *see also* Adams, John Quincy
Ford, Gerald 14, 40, 249
Fort Duquesne (Renamed Fort Pitt) 40–42
Fort Laramie 62
Fort McHenry 177
Fort Mims 271
Fort Monroe 217
Fort Necessity 40, 41
Fort Prospect Bluff ("Negro Fort") 275, 276
Fort St. Philip 273
Fort Stanwys 113
Fort Washington 343, 344
The 49th Parallel 204, 205, 233; *see also* Gallatin, Albert; Goulburn, Henry; Robinson, Frederick John; Rush, Richard
Founding fathers 1, 3, 4, 12, 26, 30, 52, 72, 82, 101, 104, 106, 158, 192, 198, 228
Fox hunting 37
Fox Indians 289, 290
France 15, 18, 19, 30, 40, 46, 50, 54, 55, 63, 92, 93, 96, 98, 99, 103, 115–118, 123, 127, 131–133, 135, 137, 140, 144, 152, 154, 158, 167, 171–173, 191–192, 194, 196–199, 202, 204, 206, 207, 209, 215, 222, 227, 228, 230, 232, 233, 237, 243, 297, 330, 363, 367
Francis, Josiah 276
Franklin, Benjamin 9, 11, 29, 30, 34, 44, 47, 71, 73, 83, 91–93, 96, 105–107, 130, 131
Frazier, Mary 222, 224; *see also* Adams, John Quincy
Free Soil Party 225, 327, 330, 331; *see also* Van Buren, Martin
Free speech 96, 98, 175, 240, 241, 330, 360
Freedom of the Press 52, 87, 93, 95, 98, 113, 134, 144, 153, 155, 172, 183, 196, 308, 318, 325, 360
Freemasons 192, 249, 278; *see also* Anti-Mason Party
Free-Soil Party 15, 225, 237, 330, 331
French and Indian War, The Seven Years' War 40–43, 72, 83, 85, 113, 190; *see also* Braddock, General Edward; Fort Duquesne; Fort Necessity; Pitt, William; Walpole, Henry; Washington, George

French Chamber of Deputies 297
French Revolution 54, 89, 99, 101, 111, 133, 152, 190, 196, 215, 216
Freneau, Phillip 165
Fries, John 98
Fries Rebellion 98
Fugitive Slave Act of 1793 53, 54

Gabriel's Insurrection 210; see also Slavery
Gag Rule, gag rule cane 240–242; see also Adams, John Quincy
Gallatin, Albert 136, 173, 185, 186, 204, 231, 304
Gambier, James Lord 231
Gardens 26, 36, 337
Gates, General Horatio 44–47
Gelston, David 215
"The General" 371; see also Tyler, John
General of the Armies of the United States 40
Genêt, Edmond-Charles 54, 55, 228; see also Citizen Genêt Affair
Genn, James 38
George III, King 123
Gerry, Elbridge 83, 99, 173
Gerrymandering 83, 99, 173
Ghost of Sherwood Forest 386
Gibbs, J. Willard 247; see also Amistad
Gilpin, Henry D. 247; see also Amistad
"Give Me Liberty or Give Me Death Speech" 124; see also Henry, Patrick
God 34–36, 44, 48, 58, 78, 80, 89, 103–105, 118–120, 122, 124, 127, 134, 146–148, 164, 192, 218, 225, 226, 230, 237–239, 246, 248, 250, 254, 264–267, 270, 273, 292, 298, 299, 304, 310, 329, 339, 342, 360, 369, 370, 376, 380, 386
Gore, Al 13
Goulburn, Henry 204, 231
Government of the United States 9–18
"Granary to the World" 40; see also Washington, George
"Granny Harrison, the petticoat general" 339; see also Harrison, William Henry
Grant, Ulysses S. 62, 217
Great Britain 14, 15, 18, 19, 23, 40, 42, 46, 47, 50, 54, 55, 68, 84, 85, 89, 91–93, 98, 99, 105, 106, 110, 115, 128, 140, 171, 173, 175, 191, 196–198, 204, 206, 211, 217, 225, 231, 232, 235, 237, 238, 241, 242, 250, 271, 273, 275, 277, 278, 314, 317, 318, 329, 344, 382
Great Lakes 195, 201, 237, 314, 316
Greene, Kitty 33; see also Washington, George
Greene, Nathaniel 33, 46
Gregorian calendar 23, 73, 109
Gridley, Jeremy 84, 89
Grist mill 140, 182
Griswold, Roger 97
"Grouseland" 342, 343; see also Harrison, William Henry
Guerrilla warfare 43; see also Washington, George
Guy Fawkes Day 35; see also Washington, George

Habeas corpus 134, 196, 249, 274
The Hague 93, 230
"Hail to the Chief" 385
Hamilton, Alexander 12, 14, 18, 29, 43, 47, 49, 50, 52–55, 71, 79, 94, 95, 99, 105, 108, 128, 132–135, 154, 158, 167, 171, 184, 196, 232, 291, 307, 312; "Concerning the Public Conduct and Character of John Adams" 100; Hamilton-Reynolds Scandal 211–215
Harrison, Anna Tuthill Symmes 340, 341, 355
Harrison, Benjamin (president) 13
Harrison, Benjamin V. 50, 68, 339, 340
Harrison, Jane Irwin 341
Harrison, William Henry 1, 5, 16, 17, 252, 295, 308, 319, 329, 337–361, 369, 375, 384; ancestors 339–340; appearance 340; birth 337–339; Cabinet 356; children 341–342; death and burial 357–359; education 342; family 339; governor of Indian Territory 346–348; health 357; home, "Grouseland" 342–343; Indian Wars 343–344; marriage and romances 340–341; military service 343; miscellanea 359–360; motto 343; nicknames and titles 339; observations about 360–361; occupation 343; Ohio state senator 348–349; only official act as president 356–357; papers 357; personality and character 340; political offices 345; political philosophy and party affiliation 345–346; presidency 355–356; presidential campaign of 1836 350; presidential campaign of 1840 351–355; recreational pastimes and interests 343; religion and religious beliefs 342; Tecumseh's curse 359; U.S. minister to Columbia 349–350; U.S. Representative 348; U.S Senate 349; Vice President John Tyler 356; War of 1812 344–345
Harrison Land Act of 1800 346
The Hartford Convention 177–178, 195; see also Madison, James
Harvard College 56, 74, 82–84, 103, 225–227, 233, 243, 266
Haunting of Fort Monroe 217; see also Monroe, James
Hawkins, John 125
Hawthorne, Nathaniel 229
Headright System 156
"Hellhound of Slavery" 219; see also Adams, John Quincy
Hemings, Betty 117
Hemings, Eston 117
Hemings, Madison 117
Hemings, Sally 116–118, 134, 148, 152; see also Jefferson, Thomas
Henry, Patrick 42, 49, 68, 129, 158, 172, 362; "Give me liberty or give me death" speech 124
"The Hermitage" 259, 264, 267–269; see also Jackson, Andrew
"Hero of New Orleans" 256; see also Jackson, Andrew
Hessian mercenaries 43, 65; see also Revolutionary War

Hewlett, Richard 44
Hickey, Private Thomas 44; see also Washington, George
Highland Plantation 194, 195; see also Monroe, James
Hitler, Adolf 303
Hoban, James 19
Hollywood Cemetery, Richmond, Virginia 208, 209, 369, 385; see also Monroe, James; Tyler, John; Tyler, Julia
Homathlemico 276; see also Jackson, Andrew
Homer 121
Horses: "General" 371; "His Whiskers" 343; "Liberty" 167; 176, 259, 260; "Nelson" and "Blueskin" 39; 59, 75, 111, 112, 115, 127; "Sam Patch" 269; "Truxton" 266, 269
Horticulturalist 123
Houdon, Jean-Antoine 26, 27; see also Washington, George
House of Representatives 5, 9, 12, 13–19, 91, 97, 119, 134, 147, 171–173, 182, 184, 200, 203, 204, 214, 225, 232, 234, 235, 239–245, 272, 279, 282, 311, 316, 319, 324, 346, 349, 350, 374, 375, 384
Howard, John E. 199
Howe, Sir William 42, 67
Hudson River 195, 237
Hume, David 83, 165, 183
Hunter, Alexander 358; see also Harrison, William Henry
Hutchinson, Anne 229
Hutchinson, Governor Thomas 89
Hutchinson, William 180

Ice cream 38, 152; see also Jefferson, Thomas; Washington, George
Immigration, immigrants 18, 54, 96, 136, 156, 306, 307, 334, 379
Impeachment 10, 16, 17, 377, 380
Impressments 196; see also War of 1812
Inaugural Ball 182; see also Madison, Dolley
Indentured servants 54, 156
Independent Democrats 291
Independent Treasure Bill of 1840 323–324
Independent Treasury 320–324; see also Van Buren, Martin
Indian removal 3; Andrew Jackson 286–290, 302, 303; 325
Indian Removal Act of 1830 286–290
Indian Territory (now Oklahoma) 6, 286, 289, 302, 325
Indiana Territory 342, 346
Indians see American Indians
Industrial Revolution 18, 128, 379
Industries 52, 128, 200, 202, 239, 277, 380
Inflation 305, 322, 323, 350, 354
Infrastructure 274, 380
Ingersoll, Jared 174, 185, 186
Inquiry into the Origin and Course of Political Parties in the United States 330; see also Van Buren, Martin
Interior Department 235
Internal improvements 202, 234–239, 317, 349; see also Adams, John Quincy

Inventions, inventors 38, 123–125, 127, 149–150
Irish immigrants 18, 96, 277, 334, 379
Irving, Washington 156; "The Legend of Sleepy Hollow" 313; 336; see also Van Buren, Martin
Islam 238; see also Adams, John Quincy

Jackson, Andrew 1, 5, 6, 14–16, 18, 19, 177, 180, 205, 206, 234–236, 243, 245, 249, 251, 254–305, 306, 313, 316–325, 329, 333, 335, 343, 348, 349, 353, 357, 360, 373–375, 384, 387; after the presidency 298; ancestors 258; appearance 258–259; assassination attempt 295–297; Battle of New Orleans 272–274; birth 254; Black Hawk War 289, 290; Cabinet 282; children 265–266; coffin handbill 280; death and burial 299–300; domestic affairs 291–294; dueling 266–267; education 266; evaluations of 303–305; Executions 274–277; family 257–258; farewell address 297–298; first term 284; foreign affairs 290; foreign affairs 297; governor of Florida Territory 278; health 298–299; home, "The Hermitage" 267–269; Indian removal 286–290; inscription on Rachel's tomb 265; invasion of Florida 274–277; Jackson Square 300–301; Jacksonian democracy 2772; justice of the Tennessee Supreme Court 278; Kitchen Cabinet 284–285; "Manifest Destiny" 277; marriage and romances 261–265; motto 280; nicknames and titles 254–257; Nullification Crisis 294–295; occupation 269–270; papers 298; Peggy Eaton affair 285–286; people's inauguration 282–284; personality and character 259–261; pets and animals 269; political offices 277; political philosophy and party affiliation 277–278; presidency 280–282; presidential campaign of 1824 278–279; presidential campaign of 1828 279–281; presidential campaign of 1832 291; recreational pastimes and interests 269; religion and religious beliefs 265–266; second bank of the united states 291–294; second term 291–294; Seminole War 274–277; and slavery 301; soldier 270–272; Specie Circular of 1836 297; spoils system 284; states admitted to the union 282; Supreme Court appointments 282; vice presidents John C. Calhoun, Martin Van Buren 282; worst president ever? 301–303
Jackson, Andrew, Jr., 265, 298
Jackson, Bruce 163
Jackson, Elizabeth "Betty" Hutchinson 257, 258, 280
Jackson, Rachel Donelson Robards 235, 258, 259, 261–269; inscription on her tomb 265; 279–280; 299–301
Jackson, Sarah Yorke 265
Jackson, Thomas "Stonewall" 258

Jacksonian Democracy 277, 309
Jacksonian Democrat Party 373
James Monroe Museum and Memorial Library 208
Jay, John 17, 47, 51, 52, 55, 61, 93, 98, 133, 167, 171, 195, 196, 278
Jay-Gardoqui Treaty 195
Jay Treaty of 1794 55, 98, 133, 171, 196, 278
Jefferson, Isaac 117
Jefferson, Jane 110
Jefferson, Martha Washington, "Patsy" 118, 152
Jefferson, Martha Wayles Skelton 112–114; inscription on her gravestone 115, 117
Jefferson, Mary (later Maria, "Polly") 112, 117, 118, 152
Jefferson, Peter 109, 110, 121
Jefferson, Thomas 15, 12–16, 19, 20, 29, 34, 48–50, 54, 55, 62, 77, 80–82, 91, 92, 94–100, 103, 104, 109–154, 158–160, 164, 166, 16–174, 178, 181, 185, 189, 190, 192, 194, 196, 197, 200, 203, 205, 208, 210, 214, 216, 228, 230, 232, 279, 284, 291, 303, 311, 355, 362, 370; after the presidency 141–143; and American Indians 149, 151; ancestors 110, 111; appearance 111; Barbary pirates 140, 141; and Benjamin Banneker 149, 150; birth 109; Cabinet 135, 136; children (legitimate) 118; Clement Clark Moore lambastes Jefferson 151–152; constitutional amendments 136; death and burial 145–146; Declaration of Independence 130, 135; diplomatic roles 131, 132; domestic affairs 136; education 121–123; embargo act 140; family 109, 110; foreign affairs 133; governor 129, 130; health 144–145; home, "Monticello" 125–127; inventor 124–125; Jefferson Bible 152; Jefferson in Paris 152; Jefferson Memorial monument 146; Jefferson recipes 152; Lewis and Clark Expedition 137–140; Louisiana Purchase 137; Marbury v. Madison 136–137; Maria Hadfield Cosway 115–116; marriage and romances 113; Martha Skelton Jefferson 113–115; maxims, aphorisms and proverbs 152–154; motto 127; nicknames and titles 109; observations about 154; occupation 123; papers 143, 144; personality and character 111–113; political offices 128; political philosophy and party affiliations 128, 129; presidency 134, 135; recreational pastimes and interests 127, 128; religion and religious beliefs 118–121; Sally Hemings 116–118; and slavery 147–148; states admitted to the union 136; Supreme Court appointments 136; ten golden rules 122–123; vice-presidency 133, 134; vice presidents Aaron Burr, George Clinton 135
Jefferson Day Dinner 294, 318; see also Jackson, Andrew
Jefferson in Paris (the movie) 152
Jeffersonian Democracy 154, 277

Jeffersonian Republicans 48, 94
Jennings, Paul 181; "A Colored Man's Reminiscences of James Madison" 182
Jesus Christ 34, 80, 81, 119, 121, 152, 192, 226, 230, 238, 266, 330
Jocelyn, Simeon S. 247; see also Amistad
John, King 111
Johnson, Lyndon B. 14, 16
Johnson, Richard M. 321, 343, 345
"Join or Die" 11; see also Franklin, Benjamin
Judaism 35, 80, 82, 120, 250, 303, 370
Judicial Branch 9–12, 17, 42, 51, 69, 83, 90, 136, 168, 249, 313; see also Constitution; Separation of Powers
Judiciary 12, 17, 51, 90, 132, 135, 136, 294
Judiciary Act of 1789 17, 51, 136
Julian calendar 23, 73
July 4, 1776 131
Junaluska, Chief 272; see also Jackson, Andrew

Kant, Immanuel 227
Kearse, Bettye 163
"Keep the Ball Rolling" 359; see also Harrison, William Henry
Key, Francis Scott 116, 177, 217, 296
King, Rufus 173, 198, 199, 315
King, Samuel Ward 379
"King Andrew the First" 256, 278, 284, 294
"King of the Wild Frontier" 287; see also Crockett, David "Davy" A.
Kitchen Cabinet 284, 285, 317; see also Jackson, Andrew
Korean War 40, 60

"Lady Presidentress" 368; see also Tyler, Julia
Lafayette, Adrienne de Noailles 33, 190
Lafayette, Marquis de 33, 35, 45, 68, 69–71, 154, 182, 229, 340
Lafitte, Jean 273, 301
Laissez-faire economics 202, 277, 323
Lakota 62; see also Crazy Horse Monument; Mount Rushmore
"The Last Cocked Hat" 187; see also Monroe, James
Latin and Greek 36, 77, 80, 82–84, 101, 105, 113, 121, 123, 144, 152, 160, 165, 167, 191, 193, 194, 198, 225, 227, 228, 231, 250, 266, 270
Latrobe, Benjamin H. 20, 125
Laurens, Henry 44, 70
Lawrence, Richard 296; see also Jackson, Andrew
Lawyers 5, 52, 83, 84, 87, 92, 247, 249, 266, 270, 289, 308, 311, 312, 333, 341, 342, 364, 382
League of Nations 15
Lear, Tobias 58; see also Washington, George
Leavitt, the Rev. Joshua 247; see also Amistad
Ledgin, Norm 145; see also Asperger Syndrom
Lee, Henry 291, 343
Lee, Light Horse Harry 37, 59, 113; see also Washington, George

Lee, Richard Henry 161
Legislative Branch 9–12, 15, 16, 18, 60, 83, 85, 90, 103, 108, 120, 132, 136, 164, 168, 169, 216; *see also* Constitution; Separation of Powers
Leinster House 19, 20; *see also* White House
L'Enfant, Pierre 53, 149
Leonard, Daniel 89
Leopard (British ship) 232; *see also* War of 1812
Leutze, Emanuel Gottlieb 65, 66, 193; *see also* Washington, George
Levy, Jefferson Monroe 126, 127
Levy, Commodore Uriah 126, 127; *see also* Jefferson, Thomas
Lewis, Meriwether 127, 137–140
Lewis and Clark Expedition 127, 137–140
Liberia 216, 217
Liberty 9, 36, 38, 49, 50, 56, 60, 64, 70, 79, 82, 83, 85, 89, 98, 107, 112, 121, 122, 124, 129–133, 147, 149, 151, 153, 154, 163–168, 170, 172, 185, 196, 206, 210, 216, 218, 223, 225, 230, 233, 236, 239, 250, 279, 284, 294, 298, 304, 335, 360, 374
Libraries 7, 36, 56, 57, 68, 84, 103, 112, 128, 141, 143, 144, 170, 175, 179, 183, 184, 208, 245, 298, 330, 357, 369, 383; *see also* Library of Congress
Library of Congress 56, 57, 143, 144, 175, 179, 183, 184, 296, 330, 357, 383
Libya 140, 141, 143
"Lighthouses of the Skies" 235; *see also* Adams, John Quincy
Lincoln, Abraham 16, 23, 62, 70, 217, 335, 360
Lincoln, General Benjamin 46; *see also* Washington, George; Yorktown
"Lindenwald" 311–313, 332; *see also* Van Buren, Martin
"Little Magician" 306, 308, 315, 316, 336; *see also* Van Buren, Martin
Livingston, Robert R. 91, 92, 130, 131, 137, 153, 196; *see also* Declaration of Independence
Locke, John 29, 89, 121, 165, 183, 192
Log cabin 254, 332, 352–354, 359–360
"Log Cabin and Hard Cider" 352, 353; *see also* Harrison, William Henry
Louisiana Purchase 5, 127, 137, 151, 172, 196, 197, 202, 204, 272, 275; *see also* Jefferson, Thomas; Lewis and Clark Expedition
Louisiana Territory 135, 137, 140, 202–204, 232, 248
Louisiana Treaty 197
Loyalists 44, 93, 257, 328
Lyon, Matthew 97, 98; *see also* Adams, John; Alien and Sedition Acts

Mackenzie, William Lyon 328
Macon Bill 173
Madison, Dolley 1, 5, 151, 159–163, 166, 167, 179, 181–184, 191, 223, 310, 367–368
Madison, James 1, 5, 12, 14, 16–19, 29, 49, 55, 77, 115, 122, 132, 133, 135, 136, 146, 155–186, 198, 192, 195–198, 205, 223, 230, 232, 272, 291,

308, 344, 355, 363; after the presidency 178–179; ancestors 156; appearance 156; attempt to establish a Library of Congress 183–184; Bill of Rights 172, 183; birth 155; Cabinet 173; Cabinet position 172; children 162–163; *A Colored Man's Reminiscences of James Madison* 182–183; comments on Madison's gifts 169–170; Constitutional Convention 170–171; Continental Congress 170; death and burial 180–181; detached memorandum 184; domestic affairs 174; education 165–166; family 155–156; Federalist Papers 167–168; first retirement 171–172; foreign affairs 175–177; further remarks By 184–185; Hartford convention 177–178; health 180–181; Hollywood's Dolley 184; home, "Montpelier"166–167; House of Representatives 171; marriage and romances 159–162; military service 166; nicknames and titles 155; Nullification Acts 175–175; occupation 166; papers 179–180; personality and character 156–158; pets and animals 167; political offices 168; political philosophy and party affiliation 168–169; presidency 173; recreational pastimes and interests 167; religion and religious beliefs 163–165; and slavery 182; speaking of 185–186; states admitted to the union 173; Supreme Court appointments 173; vice presidents George Clinton, Elbridge Gerry 173; Virginia legislature 170
"Madman of Massachusetts" 219
Magna Carta 111
"Make Us Free" 248; *see also Amistad*
"Manifest Destiny" 3, 277, 346
Manure 40; *see also* Washington, George
Marbles ("Little Bowls") 37, 84, 259, 357
Marbury v. Madison 17, 136; *see also* Supreme Court
Marcy, William L. 284; *see also* Jackson, Andrew
Marshall, John 17, 43, 71, 95, 96, 99, 113, 136, 147, 193, 201, 283, 289, 304
Martial law 274, 379
Mason, George 42, 68, 171
Mason and Dixon Line 233
Mathematics 36, 79, 121, 137, 141, 144, 165, 193, 227
Mather, Cotton 74; *see also* Adams, John
Matthews, Mayor David 44
"Maypole of Merrymount" 228, 229; *see also* Adams, John Quincy
Maysville Road Bill 317; *see also* Van Buren, Martin
McCullough v. Maryland 201; *see also* Supreme Court
Media, newspapers 85, 96, 97, 100, 134, 144, 147, 235, 246, 250, 266, 271, 279, 280, 288, 303, 334, 350
"Memorial and Remonstrance" 164, 185
Mendi Tribe 247, 249; *see also Amistad*

Merrymount (Mare Mount) 228, 229; *see also* Adams, John Quincy
Messiah 7, 119
"Midnight judges" 136; *see also* Adams, John; Jefferson, Thomas
Militia 54, 74, 109, 137, 166, 187, 193, 210, 219, 257, 262, 266, 270, 271, 273, 274, 276, 280, 281, 290, 307, 329, 347, 348, 372, 379
"Millions for defense, but not a penny for tribute" 99; *see also* XYZ Affair
Miracle on 34th Street 200
Mississippi River 55, 138, 195, 203, 208, 270, 275, 290
The Missouri Compromise 201–204, 233, 241, 373, 374
Missouri Enabling Bill 202
Missouri Territory 140, 202
Moldboard 123, 124; *see also* Jefferson, Thomas
Money 21, 36, 47, 53, 62, 89, 99, 119, 123, 127 129, 133, 153, 184, 201, 207, 243, 253, 280, 291–293, 297, 304, 315, 319, 322–324, 329, 333, 342, 387
Monroe, Elizabeth Kortright, "La belle Américane" 190, 191, 193, 194, 199, 207, 214
Monroe, James 1, 5, 15, 19, 43, 66, 137, 141, 173, 178, 181, 187–218, 233, 234, 243, 249, 273, 278, 317, 318, 343, 348, 362, 385; after the presidency 206–208; ancestors 189; appearance 189; birth 187; Cabinet 200; Cabinet positions 198; children 191; and the Continental Congress 195–196; death and burial 208–209; domestic affairs 200–201; education 193; family 187–188; First Seminole War and the purchase of Florida 205; foreign affairs 204–205; 49th parallel 204–205; governor of Virginia 197; Hamilton-Reynolds scandal 211–215; haunting of Fort Monroe 217; health 208; home, "Highland" 194–195; lawyer 194; Liberia 216–217; marriage and romances 189–191; *McCullough v. Maryland* 201; military service 193–194; minster to France 196–197; Missouri Compromise 202–204; Monroe Doctrine 205–206; Monroe Dollar 217–218; nicknames and titles 187; observations about 218; occupation 193; Old Glory 199; Panic of 1819 201–202; papers 208; personality and character 189; political offices 195; political philosophy and party affiliation 195; presidency 198–199; presidential election of 1820, 199–200; president's home 199; recreational pastimes 195; religion and religious beliefs 191–193; and slavery 210–211; speech to the Massachusetts Society of the Cincinnatus 210; states admitted to the union 200; Supreme Court appointments 200; tariff of 1824 204; Tom Paine 215–216; United States Senate 196; Vice President Daniel D. Tompkins 200

Monroe Doctrine 5, 19, 205, 206, 218
Monroe Dollar 217
Monrovia 189, 217
Montez, Pedro 247; see also Amistad
Monticello 104, 109–111, 114–118, 121, 123, 125–127, 129, 141, 144, 145, 152, 166, 194; see also Jefferson, Thomas
Montpelier 155, 156, 160, 163, 166, 167, 169, 171, 178, 181; see also Madison, James
Montpelier Foundation 167
Moore, Clement Clark 151
Moral law 118
"More General Diffusion of Knowledge" 129
Morgan, General Daniel 46
Morgan, Captain William 249
Mormons (Church of Latter Day Saints) 334
Morocco 140, 141, 143
Morton, Thomas 228
Mount Rushmore 62, 147
Mount Vernon 1, 25, 26, 27, 30, 32, 34, 36, 37–39, 42, 56, 59–61
Mount Wollaston 73, 75, 228, 229
Mrs. Madison's Crush 161
Mudslinging 235, 353, 354
Muhammad 238
Muhlenberg, Frederick 211–215
Mules 39; see also Washington, George
Music 1, 66, 79, 106, 110, 112, 114, 116, 121, 154, 217, 223, 224, 227, 337, 349, 352, 354, 372
Myths: Cherry tree myth 64, 65; Washington throwing a silver dollar across the Potomac 65

Napoleon Bonaparte 63, 71, 99, 137, 140, 173, 194, 198, 201, 209, 231, 245, 297
National debt 53, 54, 135, 265, 291, 297, 322; see also Hamilton, Alexander; Jackson, Andrew
National Republican Party 15
Natural law 121
Naturalization Act of 1790 18, 54, 96, 136
Negro Fort 275
Nelson, Admiral Horatio 99
Nemours, P.S. DuPont de 122
The Netherlands 93, 230, 308
Neutrality 50, 54, 55, 172, 173, 276, 327, 329
Neutrality Proclamation of 1793 54
The New England Canaan 228
New Orleans 1, 137, 177–180, 197, 231, 234, 256, 259, 272–274, 300, 301
New York City 17, 38, 42, 44, 46–48, 52, 59, 67, 79, 94, 151, 190, 191, 200, 208, 216, 247, 278, 307, 309, 312, 322, 323, 330, 333, 334, 339, 340, 366, 367, 369
New York Library 68
New York Stock Exchange 53
Newburgh Conspiracy 47
Newton, Sir Isaac 29, 108, 121, 165, 192
Niagara Falls 328
"No-Heirs Madison" 162
Non-Intercourse Act 173; see also Jefferson, Thomas
Northwest Ordinance of 1787 196

Northwest Territory 6, 129, 132, 133, 195, 196, 343–346
"Notes on the State of Virginia" 123–124, 140–141; see also Jefferson, Thomas
"Novanglus Letters" 89; see also Adams, John
Nullification 6, 134, 174, 237, 294, 295, 318, 319, 321, 373
Nullification Acts 134, 174; see also Jefferson, Thomas
Nullification Crisis of 1832 6, 294, 295, 318, 319, 321, 373; see also Jackson, Andrew

"O.K." 333; see also Van Buren, Martin
Oath of Office 11
"Old Hickory" 15, 254, 256, 279, 283, 298, 300, 316, 320; see also Jackson, Andrew
"Old Ironsides" 175–177; see also Constitution
"Old Kinderhook" 306, 333; see also Van Buren, Martin
"Old Man Eloquent" 219; see also Adams, John Quincy
"Old Tippecanoe" 308, 339, 356; see also Harrison, William Henry
Old Toby 140; see also Lewis and Clark Expedition
Oliphant, Thomas 73
Olive tree 123; see also Jefferson, Thomas
110 Rules of Civility & Decent Behavior in Company and Conversation 36–37; see also Washington, George
"Opinion on the Constitutionality of the Bill for Establishing a National Bank" 133; see also Jefferson, Thomas
Oregon Territory 204, 238, 382
Otis, James 101
Oval office 20, 21, 292
Overton, Judge John 264; see also Jackson, Andrew

Paine, Thomas 72, 77, 80, 90, 105, 215, 216, 228; The Age of Reason 80, 215; Common Sense 90, 105, 215; The Rights of Man 215, 228
Pakenham, General Edward 180, 272, 274
Panama Congress of 1826 238
Panics (Recessions and Depressions): Panic of 1797 19; Panic of 1819 19, 201, 202; Panic of 1837 6, 19, 297, 320–323
Parliamentary System, Prime Minister 10, 42, 46, 93, 129
Party boss 313; see also Van Buren, Martin
Patriots and patriotism 15, 35, 56, 66, 76, 83, 91, 95, 105, 112, 177, 199, 210, 253, 275, 298, 305, 309, 335, 375, 383
Patronage 135, 194, 234, 253, 277, 284, 313, 315, 346, 374; see also Spoils System
Peace of Paris 230
"Peacefield" ("The Old House") 83, 104
Peale, Charles Wilson 123, 125, 138, 159

"Pearl Harbor of the Slavery Controversy" 240; see also Adams, John Quincy
Pennies for Monticello 123
People's Inauguration 282–284; see also Jackson, Andrew
Philadelphia 9, 20, 35, 43, 45, 48, 54, 59–61, 66, 75, 79, 94, 96, 106, 137, 141, 159, 160, 190, 232, 268, 294, 339, 340, 342, 366
Philadelphia (frigate) 141, 143; see also War of 1812
Philipse, Mary 33; see also Washington, George
Pickering, Timothy 50, 95, 232
Pike, General Zebulon 341
Pilgrims 75, 228
Pinckney, Charles Cotesworth 99, 100, 102, 106, 135, 173
Pinckney, Henry C. 240
Pinckney, Thomas 94
Pinckney, William 173, 196
Pinckney Treaty of 1795 55
Pitt, William 42
Plantation, planters 25, 30, 36, 38, 40, 56, 60, 62, 109, 110, 115, 123, 126, 162, 163, 166, 171, 179, 182, 189, 194, 195, 202, 247, 254, 262, 263, 266–269, 273–275, 278, 284, 298, 301, 337–339, 342, 362, 365, 368–371, 383
Plato 83, 119, 144, 183
Plummer, Governor George 199
Pocket veto 16
Poe, Edgar Allan 217, 334
Poems, poetry 77, 79, 127, 147, 148, 151, 165, 213, 227, 230, 243, 245, 246, 372
"Poet of the Revolution" 165; see also Freneau, Philip
Poindexter, George 297
Political factions 47, 55, 133, 136, 158, 168, 171, 234, 270, 272, 313–315, 333
Political machine 313–315; see also Van Buren, Martin
Political parties 12–15, 47, 94, 133, 136, 178, 230, 251, 313, 314, 330; symbols: donkey 279
Politics, politicians 3, 48, 55, 72, 77, 79, 85, 89, 106, 109, 126, 128, 130, 147, 161, 169, 171, 185, 191, 192, 217, 224, 226, 236, 252, 270, 277, 279, 282, 284, 285, 298, 303, 307, 309, 312–315, 320, 326, 333–336, 349, 365, 366, 369, 375, 381, 383
Polk, James K. 16, 240, 298, 330, 335, 371, 383, 384, 387
Polygraph 125; see also Jefferson, Thomas
Poplar Forest 126, 145; see also Jefferson, Thomas
Popular Democracy 277
Popular vote 13, 14, 235, 245, 279, 280, 291, 319, 329, 354
Population 3, 59, 85, 134, 160, 162, 182, 196, 201, 203, 216, 270, 272, 288, 302, 324, 373, 379, 380, 382
Populist 280
Post Office 12, 53
Postmaster General 12, 50

Potato famine 18

Potomac River 23, 36, 38, 40, 52, 59, 65, 176, 187, 189, 246, 367

Prayer 34, 35, 64, 65, 82, 120, 148, 167, 192, 208, 226, 245, 265, 335, 337, 339, 375

Preemption Act of 1841 379

Prejudice 4, 112, 121, 122, 217, 260, 266, 282, 286, 293, 303, 314

Presbyterians 59, 120, 164, 208, 265, 266, 269, 340

Presidential election rules 136

Presidential health 24, 25, 30, 57, 103, 104, 111, 118, 120, 122, 144, 145, 165–167, 180, 207, 208, 243, 244, 246, 267, 272, 298, 299, 330, 351, 357, 364, 374, 384, 385

Presidential monuments 126, 61, 66, 73, 115, 181, 208, 383, 385; Jefferson Monument 146; Mount Rushmore 62, 147; Washington Monument 61, 62, 71

Presidential oath of office 12

Presidential papers: Andrew Jackson 298; George Washington 56, 57; James Madison 178–180; James Monroe 208; John Adams 101, 103; John Quincy Adams 243; John Tyler 383; Martin Van Buren 330; Thomas Jefferson 143; William Henry Harrison 357

Presidential qualifications 11

Presidential salary 21, 62, 63, 333

Presidential system 10

The President's Lady 301; see also Jackson, Andrew

Presiding officer of the U.S. Senate 94

Preston, Captain Thomas 85–87; see also Boston Massacre

Princeton (frigate) 367, 368

Profanity 63, 353

Prussia 223, 230

Public education 129

"Publius" 167; see also Madison, James

Purchase of Florida 205

Puritans 75, 82, 229, 339

Purple Heart medal 63, 64; see also Washington, George

Putnam, Rufus 84

Quakers (Society of Friends) 36, 66–68, 120, 159, 160, 216, 226, 239

Qualifications to be president 11–12

Quasi War 99; see also Adams, John

Quincy, Hannah 77

Quincy, Josiah 77, 87

Quincy, Josiah III 244

Quincy, Massachusetts 73, 79, 81, 245

Racism, racists 3, 147, 151, 210, 242, 286, 303

Randolph, Edmund 50, 51, 110, 115, 372

Randolph, Ellen 311; see also Van Buren, Martin

Randolph, Jane 109, 110

Randolph, Jefferson 111

Randolph, John 129, 173, 197, 204, 221, 253, 334

Randolph, Martha 114

Randolph, Robert B. 118, 297

Randolph, Sarah 113

Randolph, Thomas Mann 110

Randolph, Thomas Mann, Jr. 118

Randolph, William 109, 110

Rappahannock River 23, 25, 65; see also Washington, George

"Red Fox of Kinderhook" 306; see also Van Buren, Martin

Religion 4, 34–36, 52, 56, 80–82, 107, 118–121, 129, 134, 153, 159, 163–165, 170, 184, 185, 191–193, 225–227, 230, 236, 238, 239, 242, 246, 251, 253, 265–266, 299, 311, 342, 360, 369–370; see also Bible; Christianity; Clergy; God; Islam; Jesus Christ; Judaism; Religious freedom; Religious tolerance; Separation of Church and State

Religious freedom: bills and calls for 109, 119, 120, 129, 164, 170, 184, 192, 225, 229, 342, 370

Religious tolerance 35, 266, 370

Republic 9, 29, 47, 49, 62, 71, 72, 89, 90, 99, 132, 133, 137, 167, 168, 169, 171, 194, 205, 208, 215, 217, 230, 233, 235, 271, 279, 292, 304, 349, 351, 360

Republican Party 15

Republicanism 90, 158, 168, 169, 195, 336

Revolutionary War 1, 15, 24, 26, 30, 33, 35, 38, 42, 44, 46, 54, 55, 59, 60, 63, 64, 93, 98, 99, 106, 119, 137, 159, 166, 168, 170, 187, 189, 193, 194, 198, 230, 266, 269, 270, 275, 298, 300, 371

Reynolds, James, and Maria see Hamilton-Reynolds Scandal

Right of succession 378

Right to petition 240; see also Adams, John Quincy

Robards, Lewis 264–265; see also Jackson, Andrew; Jackson, Rachel

Robards family, history and genealogy of 26, 264; see also Jackson, Andrew

Robertson, Donald 165

Robinson, John 274

Rochambeau, General Comte de 46; see also Yorktown

Rocky Mountains 137–139, 201, 233

Rodgers, Commodore John 141

Roelof, Lord Beusichen 308; see also Van Buren, Martin

Roosevelt, Franklin D. 14, 16, 63, 146, 249, 303, 359

Roosevelt, Theodore 12, 14, 62, 112, 205, 249, 387

Roots Project 163

Rose Garden 20

Ross, John 289

Royall, Anne Newport 246

Ruiz, José 247; see also Amistad

Runnymede 111

Rush, Benjamin 73, 76, 153, 185, 342

Rush, Richard 173, 185, 186, 200, 204, 235

Rush-Bagot Convention 232

Russell, Benjamin 173

Russell, Jonathon 231

Russia 163, 205, 206, 224, 225, 227, 228, 230, 231, 233, 245, 250, 280

Russo-Turkish War 238

Rutledge, John 17, 51, 52

"Sable Genius" see Banneker, Benjamin

Sacagawea 138–140; see also Lewis and Clark Expedition

"Sage of Monticello" 109; see also Jefferson, Thomas

St. Louis 137, 138, 140

Sauk Indians 289, 290

Schuller, Friedrich 230

Science 26, 27, 79, 108, 112, 121–123, 137, 138, 145, 149, 154, 166, 221, 233, 236, 239, 243, 311, 357

Scott, Dred 204; see also Dred Scott Decision; Supreme Court

Scott, Marion DuPont, and Randolph 167; see also Jefferson, Thomas

Scott, Winfield General 217, 289, 311, 325, 329

Seal of the President of the United States 10

Second Bank of the United States 173, 291, 293, 378

Sedition Act 73, 96–98, 133, 136, 171, 174, 175; see also Adams, John

Seider, Christopher 85

Self-government 55, 89, 131

Seminole Wars, Seminole 205, 274–276, 288, 299, 317, 325, 377; see also Battle of Horseshoe Bend; Cherokees; Junaluska, Chief; Negro Fort

Senate, Senators 9, 12, 13, 17, 18, 51, 52, 59, 73, 91, 94, 99, 112, 147, 169, 171, 172, 184, 190, 194–196, 203, 204, 209, 211, 230–237, 243, 278, 279, 282, 284, 285, 289, 293, 294, 295, 297, 298, 301, 306, 307, 313–316, 318, 319, 321, 324, 341, 343, 349, 351, 352, 365–367–381, 383

Separation of Church and State 36, 80, 119, 120, 129, 164, 184, 265, 370

Separation of Powers 90, 167

Sergeant, John 291

1776 1, 106

Sevier, John 270, 271

Sewell, Jonathan 76

Shad at Valley Forge 67; see also Washington, George

"Shadwell" 109, 110, 113, 121, 144

"Sharp Knife" 256; see also Jackson, Andrew

Shawnee Indians 343, 344, 350, 359

Sherman, Roger 91, 92, 130, 131

Sierra Leone 216, 326

Silkworms 229; see also Monroe, Elizabeth

Single crop farming 39

Slave trade 18, 211, 242, 346, 359–360

Slavery 1–3, 5, 18, 26, 44, 53, 54, 58–61, 90, 101, 107, 110, 114, 116, 117, 123, 130, 134, 136, 144, 145, 147–149, 152, 154, 156, 159, 163, 165–167, 170, 179, 182, 201–204, 210–212, 216, 217, 219, 233, 234, 236, 237, 239–242, 245, 247, 249–251, 261, 262, 266, 274–276, 286, 297, 300, 301, 303, 307, 320, 325–327, 330, 339, 346–348, 350, 359–360, 362, 369–371, 373, 383, 386

Smallpox outbreak of 1721 74

Smith, Captain John 217

Smith, Joseph 334; *see also* Van Buren, Martin
Smith, the Rev. William 77, 80, 105, 229
Smith, William Stephens 321
Smithsonian Institution, James Smithson 240, 243, 353
"South Carolina Exposition and Protest" 237; *see also* Calhoun, John C.
Spain 39, 54, 55, 93, 135, 144, 195, 196, 202, 205, 233, 275–278, 327
Sparks, Jared 34, 56, 181
Specie, The Specie Circular of 1836 19, 40, 125, 201, 202, 292, 293, 297, 322, 323; *see also* Jackson, Andrew; Panics, Panic of 1837
Speleologist 127; *see also* Jefferson, Thomas
Spoils System 1, 234, 284, 317; *see also* Jackson, Andrew
Stamp Act 85, 89
Standish, Miles 229
"Star Spangled Banner" 177; *see also* Key, Francis Scott
State Department 59, 95, 198, 207
State funeral 358–359; *see also* Harrison, William Henry
States admitted to the Union: Alabama 1819 200; Arkansas 1836 282; Florida 1845 378; Illinois 1818 200; Indiana 1816 173; Kentucky 1792 52; Louisiana 1812 173; Maine 1820 200; Michigan 1837 282; Mississippi 1817 200; Missouri 1821 200; North Carolina 1789 52; Ohio 1803 136; Rhode Island 1790 52; Tennessee 1796 52; Vermont 1791 52
States' Rights 52, 98, 128, 134, 137, 177, 178, 235, 277, 288, 291, 316, 346, 350, 362, 372, 374–376, 387
"Statute for Virginia for Religious Freedom" 109, 119, 120, 129, 164, 170; *see also* Jefferson, Thomas
Sterne, Laurence 114; *see also* Jefferson, Thomas
Steuben, Baron Nicholas von 46; *see also* Revolutionary War
Stoddert, Benjamin 95, 96, 136
Story, Joseph 172, 189, 218, 249; *see also* Amistad
Stuart, Gilbert 26, 61, 74, 78, 159, 161, 162
Sultan of Oman 313; *see also* Van Buren, Martin
"A Summary View of the Rights of British America" 123; *see also* Jefferson, Thomas
Sundial 125; *see also* Jefferson, Thomas
Superintendent of Indian Affairs 347; *see also* Harrison, William Henry
Supreme Court 4, 9, 12, 17, 33, 51, 52, 59, 95, 96, 98, 113, 136, 147, 173, 174, 183, 200, 201, 204, 231, 235, 247–249, 282, 289, 303, 313, 321, 325, 327, 367, 378; *see also* Dred Scott Decision; *Marbury v. Madison*; *McCulloch v. Maryland*; *Worcester v. Georgia*
Surveying, surveyors 38, 110, 137
Sylvester, Francis 308; *see also* Van Buren, Martin

Sylvester, Margaret 311; *see also* Van Buren, Martin

Tacitus 83, 121, 352
Taft, William Howard 20
Talleyrand, Charles 99, 137; *see also* Louisiana Purchase; XYZ Affair
Taney, Roger B. 204, 284, 285
Tappan, Lewis 247, 249; *see also* Amistad
"Taps" 339
Tariffs 3, 6, 19, 91, 173, 201, 204, 234–237, 282, 294, 318, 319, 322, 333, 350, 373, 376, 382; Tariff of 1789 54; Tariff of 1816 19; Tariff of 1824 201; Tariff of 1828 (Tariff of Abominations) 237, 294; Tariff of 1832 294; Tariff of 1833 (Compromise tariff) 319, 374; Tariff of 1842 (Black tariff) 380
Tarring and feathering 86
Taxes, taxation 9, 18, 19, 21, 42, 54, 85, 87, 91, 98, 99, 101, 119, 121, 129, 135, 164, 170, 184, 201, 203, 204, 293, 315, 363, 364, 380, 382
Taylor, Zachary 15, 162, 330, 332
Tecumseh 343–345, 347, 349, 359
Tecumseh's Curse 359
Ten Commandments 226
Ten Golden Rules 122, 123
Tenskwatawa (The Prophet) 344, 347, 359
Territorial Governor of Indiana 341; *see also* Harrison, William Henry
Texas 3, 6, 239, 271, 291, 297, 327, 330, 342, 377, 380, 381–383; *see also* Annexation of Texas
36°30' parallel 204
Thomas, Senator Jesse B. 203
Thomas Jefferson Foundation 117, 123
"Thoughts on Government" 90; *see also* Adams, John
Tiger cubs 313; *see also* Van Buren, Martin
Tillotson, John 226
Timberlake, Lt. John "Bow" 285
"Tippecanoe and Tyler too" 353; *see also* Harrison, William Henry
"To Ellen" 127; *see also* Jefferson, Thomas
Tobacco 26, 39, 84, 104, 110, 144, 152, 162, 179, 187, 194, 260, 299, 359, 362
Todd, John, Jr. 160, 184
Todd, John Payne 160; *see also* Madison, Dolley
Toilets (outhouse) 23, 245, 312
Tompkins, Daniel D. 200, 314
Tories (Loyalists) 15, 277, 278, 314
Townshend Acts 85
Trail of Tears 151, 289, 325
Transportation 202, 235, 380
Treason, traitors 17, 44, 96, 98, 135, 147, 240, 295, 333, 379, 383
Treasury Department 59
Treaties 15, 46, 47, 93, 99, 141, 196, 204, 211, 230, 271, 290, 297, 317, 326, 380, 381; Treaty of Alliance of 1778 98; Treaty of Fort Laramie 68; Treaty of Ghent 177, 178, 231, 274; Treaty of Greenville 344, 347; Treaty of Grouseland 343, 347;

Treaty of New Echota 289; Treaty of Paris 93, 105, 132, 133, 195, 275, 329; Treaty of Wanghia 382
Triangular Trade 211; *see also* Monroe, James; Slavery
"Tribune of the People" 16; *see also* Jackson, Andrew
Tribute 99, 140, 141
Trinitarians 226
Truman, Harry S 218, 249, 252, 303, 330, 360, 385, 387
Tuckahoe 110; *see also* Jefferson, Thomas
Tunisia 140, 141, 143
Tyler, John 1, 6, 14, 209, 325, 350, 352, 353, 356, 362–387; after the presidency 383; ancestors 363–364; Annexation of Texas 380–382; appearance 364; birth 362; Black tariff 380; Cabinet 378; children 369; Confederate States Congress 383; death and burial 385; domestic affairs 378; Dorr Rebellion 379–380; education 370–371; estimates of Tyler's presidency 386–387; family 36–363; Fiscal Bank Bill 378–379; foreign affairs 382; the Ghost of Sherwood Forest 386; governor of Virginia 374; health 384; home, "Sherwood Forest" 371; marriage and romances 365–369; military service 372; nickname and titles 362; occupation 372; papers 384; personality and character 364–365; pets and animals 371; political offices 372; political philosophy and party affiliation 372–373; Preemption Act 379; presidency 375–379; recreational pastimes and interests 371–372; religion and religious beliefs 369–370; states admitted to the union 378; Supreme Court appointments 378; transportation, communication and education 380; Treaty of Wanghia 382; Tyler family garden 386; U.S. House of Representatives 374; U.S. Senate 374–375; vice president 375; Washington Peace Conference 383; Webster-Ashburton Treaty 382

Uncle Sam 177, 384
Unconstitutional see Constitutionality
Unemployment 19, 322, 323, 350
Union 4, 9, 16, 18, 49, 52, 64, 66, 68, 69, 91, 111, 128, 134, 169, 174, 177, 178, 181, 186, 195, 198, 199, 202–204, 209, 218, 221, 236–238, 242, 245, 248, 250, 277, 294, 295, 297, 298, 326, 327, 332, 335, 339, 348, 355, 360, 369, 371, 373, 374, 379, 381, 383, 385, 386, 387
Unitarianism 80, 104, 225, 226
United First Parish Church, "Old Stone Temple" 80, 81, 104
United States Capitol 20, 54, 58, 62, 100, 131, 149, 175, 176, 179, 245, 282, 283, 301, 355, 376, 385
United States Marine Band 198

United States Marine Corps 95
United States Military Academy at West Point, New York 136
United States Navy 275, 337
University of Virginia 57, 109, 122, 129, 130, 141, 158, 178, 180, 189, 208

Valley Forge 37, 45, 46, 64, 67, 193
Van Buren, Angelica Singleton 210
Van Buren, Hannah Hoes 309
Van Buren, Martin 1, 6, 225, 247, 252, 254, 282, 285–287, 289, 291–293, 297–298, 303, 306–336, 350, 351, 353–355, 375; after the presidency 329; the *Amistad* Affair 326–327; ancestors 307; appearance 308–309; Aroostook War 329; birth 306; books and papers 330; Cabinet role 316; Campaign of 1836 319–320; Campaign of 1840 329–330; Caroline Affair 328–329; children 311; death and burial 330, 332–333; domestic affairs 321–325; education 311–312; family 306–307; foreign affairs 327–328; the fox at work 317–318; governor of New York 316; health 330; home, "Lindenwald" 312–313; marriage and romances 309–311; Maysville Veto 317; Minister to England 318; miscellanea 333–334; New York State Senator 314; nicknames and titles 306; observations about 335–336; occupation 312; personality and character 309; pets and animals 313; pithy comments by 334–335; political offices 313; political philosophy and party affiliation 313–314; presidency 320–321; recreational pastimes and interests 313; religion and religious beliefs 311; Second Seminole War 325; slavery 326; Supreme Court appointments 321; Texas 327; Trail of Tears 325–326; United States Senator 314–316; vice-presidency 318–319; Vice President Richard M. Johnson 321
Van Ness, Peter 312
Venable, Abraham 211, 215
Vergennes, Count 93, 98
Veto, veto messages 10, 16, 18, 19, 134, 174, 237, 282, 291–294, 317, 345, 356, 376, 378–380, 383, 385; *see also* Pocket veto
"Virginia and Kentucky Resolutions" 133, 171, 174; *see also* Jefferson, Thomas; Madison, James
Virginia Constitutional Convention 170, 178
Virginia House of Burgesses 109, 125, 362
Virginia Reel 371; *see also* Tyler, John
"A Visit from St. Nicholas" 151; *see also* Moore, Clement
Voltaire 89, 165, 183, 227

Walker Betsey Moore 113
Walker, General John 113
Walpole, Horace 41
"The Wants of Man" 246; *see also* Adams, John Quincy

War Department 59, 63
"War Hawks" 235
War of 1812 1, 18, 39, 144, 161–163, 175, 177, 178, 187, 199–201, 231, 238, 254, 256, 271, 275, 290, 298, 300, 313, 314, 317, 339, 341, 343, 344, 383
Warren, Earl 17
Washington, Augustine 23–25, 36
Washington, Bushrod 33, 49, 68, 69, 96
Washington, George 1, 4, 9, 12, 14, 19–21, 23–72, 91, 94, 95, 99, 124, 129, 133, 140, 160–162, 169, 182, 187, 192, 193, 196, 199, 202, 228, 230, 235, 249, 278, 339, 340, 343, 355, 371; after the presidency 56; amendments to the constitution 52; ancestors 25–26; appearance 26–27; army strength 67–68; assassination plot 44; Bank Act of 1791 52–53; birth 23; Cabinet 50–51; Cherry tree myth 64; children 33; Citizen Genêt Affair 54–55; Conway Cabal 44–45; crossing the Delaware 65–66; death and burial 57–59; domestic affairs 52; education 36; estimates of 70–72; expense account 63; Fairfax Resolves 42; family 23–25; family motto 37; farewell address 55–56; first presidential election 48–50; fish story 67; foreign affairs 54; French and Indian War 40–42; Fugitive Slave Act 53–54; health 57; hero worship 64; home, "Mount Vernon" 36–37; Howe's dog 67; Jay Treaty 55; letters of 66–68–70; marriage and romances 30–33; military service 40; Mount Rushmore 62; movie portrayals of 68; Naturalization Act 54; Neutrality Proclamation 54; Newburgh Conspiracy 47; nicknames and titles 23; occupations 38–40; overdue books 68; paintings of 61; papers 56–57; personality and character 27–30; pets and animals 37; Pinckney Treaty 55; political philosophy and party affiliation 47–48; post office and other creations 53; profanity 63; Purple Heart medal 63–64; and the Quakers 66–67; recreational pastimes and interests 37, 38; religion and religious beliefs 34–36; Revolutionary War 42–44; salutation 67; silver dollar myth 65; and slavery 60–61; states added to the union 52; Supreme Court appointments 51–52; surrender at Yorktown 46–47; Tariff of 1789 54; Valley Forge 45–46; Vice President John Adams 50; Washington Monument 62; Whiskey Rebellion 54
Washington, Lawrence 24, 25, 36, 59
Washington, Martha Dandridge Custis 30–33, 36, 56, 59, 61, 68
Washington, Mary Ball 24, 25, 59
Washington, D.C. 13, 19, 20, 23, 62, 95, 125, 134, 146, 149, 162, 182, 223, 242, 243, 245, 282, 285, 301, 320, 357, 367

Washington Crossing the Delaware 43, 46, 54, 65, 66, 193
Washington Monument 61, 71
"Washington of the West" 339; *see also* Harrison, William Henry
Washington Old Hall 25
Washington Peace Conference 383; *see also* Tyler, John
Wayne, General "Mad Anthony" 33, 344
Weather Bureau 377
Webster, Daniel 15, 18, 72, 104, 111, 182, 186, 204, 217, 286, 292, 293, 319, 329, 350, 352, 355, 356, 358, 374, 377, 382
Webster-Ashburton Treaty 329, 382
Weems, Parson Mason Locke 64, 65
Wheat 39, 110, 162, 313, 371
Wheel cipher 124; *see also* Jefferson, Thomas
Whig Party 15, 18, 241, 253, 277, 278, 295, 297, 308, 314, 319–325, 329–332, 334, 337, 346, 350–355, 359, 374–380
Whiskey 40, 54, 135, 144, 170, 182, 270, 306, 339, 343, 357, 359
Whiskey Rebellion 54, 137
White, Hugh Lawson 319, 350
White House 1, 4, 5, 8, 12, 13, 19, 20, 21, 52, 59, 61, 66, 95, 105, 113, 116, 161, 175, 186, 190, 191, 192, 194, 199, 206, 207, 209, 224, 229, 245, 259–261, 265, 279, 282, 287, 298, 301, 309–311, 313, 318, 324, 325, 330, 334, 341, 343, 350, 354, 355, 357, 358, 365, 367–369, 371, 372, 379, 385
White House Easter Egg Roll 161; *see also* Madison, Dolley
Wieland, Christoph Martin 230
Wilson, Woodrow 15, 111, 112, 200
Wine 35, 63, 75, 114, 123, 144, 145, 154, 194, 229, 230, 299, 313, 330, 337, 339
Wirt, William 200, 206, 235, 291
Wise, General Henry A. 351, 365
Witherspoon, John 164, 165; *see also* Madison, James
Wolcott, Oliver 50, 77, 95, 212, 214
Wollaston, Captain 73, 228; *see also* Adams, John Quincy
Wollstonecraft, Mary 103
Women's causes 78
Women's education 166
Women's Rights 3, 239
Worcester v. Georgia 289
"The World Turned Upside Down" 46; *see also* Yorktown
Writ of Assistance 101
Wythe, George 121, 123, 130

XYZ Affair 99–100; *see also* Adams, John

"Yankee Doodle Dandy" 198
York (Toronto), burning of 175
Yorktown 33, 45, 46, 60, 340
Youth 27, 61, 64, 69, 72, 73, 103, 112, 122, 185, 258, 259, 306, 311, 334, 339, 375